The Principles of Psychology

By William James

(Volume 1 of 2)

Complete with Illustrations and Tables

Published by Pantianos Classics

ISBN-13: 978-1545519929

First published in 1890

This version derives from a revised text, first published in 1918

William James, photographed in maturity

Contents

Introduction v

Volume I 7

Chapter I - The Scope of Psychology 7
Chapter II - The Functions of the Brain 11
Chapter III - On Some General Conditions of Brain-Activity 41
Chapter IV - Habit 51
Chapter V - The Automaton-Theory 61
Chapter VI - The Mind-Stuff Theory 68
Chapter VII - The Methods and Snares of Psychology 84
Chapter VIII - The Relations of Minds to Other Things 90
Chapter IX - The Stream of Thought 100
Chapter X - The Consciousness of Self 126
Chapter XI – Attention 171
Chapter XII – Conception - The Sense Of Sameness 196
Chapter XIII - Discrimination and Comparison 206
Chapter XIV - Association 234
Chapter XV - The Perception of Time 257
Chapter XVI - Memory 274

Introduction

The treatise which follows has in the main grown up in connection with the author's class-room instruction in Psychology, although if is true that some of the chapters are more 'metaphysical,' and others fuller of detail, than is suitable for students who are going over the subject for the first time. The consequence of this is that, in spite of the exclusion of the important subjects of pleasure and pain, and moral and aesthetic feelings and judgments, the work has grown to a length which no one can regret more than the writer himself. The man must indeed be sanguine who, in this crowded age, can hope to have many readers for fourteen hundred continuous pages from his pen. But wer Vieles bringt wird Manchem etwas bringen; and, by judiciously skipping according to their several needs, I am sure that many sorts of readers, even those who are just beginning the study of the subject, will find my book of use. Since the beginners are most in need of guidance, I suggest for their behoof that they omit altogether on a first reading chapters 6, 7, 8, 10, 12, 13, 15, 17, 20, 21, and 28. The better to awaken the neophyte's interest, it is possible that the wise order would be to pass directly from chapter 4 to chapters 23, 24, 25, and 26, and thence to return to the first volume again. Chapter 20, on Space-perception, is a terrible thing, which, unless written with all that detail, could not be fairly treated at all. An abridgment of it, called "The Spatial Quale,' which appeared in the Journal of Speculative Philosophy, vol. XIII. p. 64, may be found by some persons a useful substitute for the entire chapter.

I have kept close to the point of view of natural science throughout the book. Every natural science assumes certain data uncritically, and declines to challenge the elements between which its own 'laws' obtain, and from which its own deductions are carried on. Psychology, the science of finite individual minds, assumes as its data (1) thoughts and feelings, and (2) a physical world in time and space with which they coexist and which (3) they know. Of course these data themselves are discussable; but the discussion of them (as of other elements) is called metaphysics and falls outside the province of this book. This book, assuming that thoughts and feelings exist and are vehicles of knowledge, thereupon contends that psychology when she has ascertained the empirical correlation of the various sorts of thought or feeling with definite conditions of the brain, can go no farther—can go no farther, that is, as a, natural science. If she goes farther she becomes metaphysical. All attempts to explain our phenomenally given thoughts as products of deeper-lying entities (whether the latter be named 'Soul,' 'Transcendental Ego,' 'Ideas,' or 'Elementary Units of Consciousness') are metaphysical. This book consequently rejects both the associationist and the spiritualist theories; and in this strictly positivistic point of view consists the only feature of it for which I feel tempted to claim originality. Of course this point of view is anything but ultimate. Men must keep thinking; and the data assumed by psychology, just like those assumed by physics and the other natural sciences, must some time be overhauled. The effort to overhaul them clearly and thoroughly is metaphysics; but metaphysics can only perform her task well when distinctly conscious of its great extent. Metaphysics fragmentary, irresponsible, and half-awake, and unconscious that she is metaphysical, spoils two good things when she injects herself into a natural science. And it seems to me that the theories both of a spiritual agent and of associated 'ideas' are, as they figure in the psychology-books, just such metaphysics as this. Even if their results be true, it would be as well to keep them, as thus presented, out of psychology as it is to keep the results of idealism out of physics.

I have therefore treated our passing thoughts as integers, and regarded the mere laws of their coexistence with brain-states as the ultimate laws for our science. The reader will in vain seek for any closed system in the book. It is mainly a mess of descriptive details, running out into queries which only a metaphysics alive to the weight of her task can hope successfully to deal with. That will perhaps be centuries hence; and meanwhile the best mark of health that a science can show is this unfinished-seeming front.

The completion of the book has been so slow that several chapters have been published successively in Mind, the Journal of Speculative Philosophy, the Popular Science Monthly, and Scribner's Magazine. Acknowledgment is made in the proper places.

The bibliography, I regret to say, is quite unsystematic. I have habitually given my authority for special experimental facts; but beyond that I have aimed mainly to cite books that would probably be actually used by the ordinary American college-student in his collateral reading. The bibliography in W. Volkmann von Volkmar's Lehrbuch der Psychologie (1875) is so complete, up to its date, that there is no need of an inferior duplicate. And for more recent references, Sully's Outlines, Dewey's Psychology, and Baldwin's Handbook of Psychology may be advantageously used.

Finally, where one owes to so many, it seems absurd to single out particular creditors; yet I cannot resist the temptation at the end of my first literary venture to record my gratitude for the inspiration I have got from the writings of J. S. Mill, Lotze, Renouvier, Hodgson, and Wundt, and from the intellectual companionship (to name only five names) of Chauncey Wright and Charles Peirce in old times, and more recently of Stanley Hall, James Putnam, and Josiah Royce.

Harvard University,

August 1890

Volume I

Chapter I - The Scope of Psychology

Psychology is the Science of Mental Life, both of its phenomena and of their conditions. The phenomena are such things as we call feelings, desires, cognitions, reasonings, decisions, and the like; and, superficially considered, their variety and complexity is such as to leave a chaotic impression on the observer. The most natural and consequently the earliest way of unifying the material was, first, to classify it as well as might be, and, secondly, to affiliate the diverse mental modes thus found, upon a simple entity, the personal Soul, of which they are taken to be so many facultative manifestations. Now, for instance, the Soul manifests its faculty of Memory, now of Reasoning, now of Volition, or again its Imagination or its Appetite. This is the orthodox 'spiritualistic' theory of scholasticism and of common-sense. Another and a less obvious way of unifying the chaos is to seek common elements in the divers mental facts rather than a common agent behind them, and to explain them constructively by the various forms of arrangement of these elements, as one explains houses by stones and bricks. The 'associationist' schools of Herbart in Germany, and of Hume, the Mills and Bain in Britain, have thus constructed a psychology without a soul by taking discrete 'ideas,' faint or vivid, and showing how, by their cohesions, repulsions, and forms of succession, such things as reminiscences, perceptions, emotions, volitions, passions, theories, and all the other furnishings of an individual's mind may be engendered. The very Self or ego of the individual comes in this way to be viewed no longer as the pre-existing source of the representations, but rather as their last and most complicated fruit.

Now, if we strive rigorously to simplify the phenomena in either of these ways, we soon become aware of inadequacies in our method. Any particular cognition, for example, or recollection, is accounted for on the soul-theory by being referred to the spiritual faculties of Cognition or of Memory. These faculties themselves are thought of as absolute properties of the soul; that is, to take the case of memory, no reason is given why we should remember a fact as it happened, except that so to remember it constitutes the essence of our Recollective Power. We may, as spiritualists, try to explain our memory's failures and blunders by secondary causes. But its successes can invoke no factors save the existence of certain objective things to be remembered on the one hand, and of our faculty of memory on the other. When, for instance, I recall my graduation-day, and drag all its incidents and emotions up from death's dateless night, no mechanical cause can explain this process, nor can any analysis reduce it to lower terms or make its nature seem other than an ultimate datum, which, whether we rebel or not at its mysteriousness, must simply be taken for granted if we are to psychologize at all. However the associationist may represent the present ideas as thronging and arranging themselves, still, the spiritualist insists, he has in the end to admit that something, be it brain, be it 'ideas,' be it 'association,' knows past time as past, and fills it out with this or that event. And when the spiritualist calls memory an 'irreducible faculty,' he says no more than this admission of the associationist already grants.

And yet the admission is far from being a satisfactory simplification of the concrete facts. For why should this absolute god-given Faculty retain so much better the events of yesterday than those of last year, and, best of all, those of an hour ago? Why, again, in old age should its grasp of childhood's events seem firmest? Why should illness and exhaustion enfeeble it? Why should repeating an experience strengthen our recollection of it? Why should drugs, fevers, asphyxia, and excitement resuscitate things long since forgotten? If we content ourselves with merely affirming that the faculty of memory is so peculiarly constituted by nature as to exhibit just these oddities, we seem little the better for having invoked it, for our explanation becomes as complicated as that of the crude facts with which we started. Moreover there is something grotesque and irrational in the supposition that the soul is equipped with elementary powers of such an ingeniously intricate sort. Why should our memory cling more easily to the near than the remote? Why should it lose its grasp of proper sooner than of abstract names? Such peculiarities seem quite fantastic; and might, for aught we can see a priori, be the precise opposites of what they are. Evidently, then, the faculty does not exist absolutely, but works under conditions; and the quest of the conditions becomes the psychologist's most interesting task.

However firmly he may hold to the soul and her remembering faculty, he must acknowledge that she never exerts the latter without a cue, and that something must always precede and remind us of whatever we are to recollect. "An idea!" says the associationist, "an idea associated with the remembered thing; and this explains also why things repeatedly met with are more easily recollected, for their associates on the various occasions furnish so many distinct avenues of recall." But this does not explain the effects of fever, exhaustion, hypnotism, old age, and the like. And in general, the pure associationist's account of our mental life is almost as bewildering as that of the pure spiritualist. This multitude of ideas, existing absolutely, yet clinging together, and weaving an endless carpet of themselves, like dominoes in ceaseless change, or the bits of glass in a kaleidoscope,-whence do they get their fantastic laws of clinging, and why do they cling in just the shapes they do?

For this the associationist must introduce the order of experience in the outer world. The dance of the ideas is a copy, somewhat mutilated and altered, of the order of phenomena. But the slightest reflection shows that phenomena have absolutely no power to influence our ideas until they have first impressed our senses and our brain. The bare existence of a past fact is no ground for our remembering it. Unless we have seen it, or somehow undergone it, we shall never know of its having been. The experiences of the body are thus one of the conditions of the faculty of memory being what it is. And a very small amount of reflection on facts shows that one part of the body, namely, the brain, is the part whose experiences are directly concerned. If the nervous communication be cut off between the brain and other parts, the experiences of those other parts are non-existent for the mind. The eye is blind, the ear deaf, the hand insensible and motionless. And conversely, if the brain be injured, consciousness is abolished or altered, even although every other organ in the body be ready to play its normal part. A blow on the head, a sudden subtraction of blood, the pressure of an apoplectic hemorrhage, may have the first effect; whilst a very few ounces of alcohol or grains of opium or hasheesh, or a whiff of chloroform or nitrous oxide gas, are sure to have the second. The delirium of fever, the altered self of insanity, are all due to foreign matters circulating through the brain, or to pathological changes in that organ's substance. The fact that the brain is the one immediate bodily condition of the mental operations is indeed so universally admitted nowadays that I need spend no more time in illustrating it, but will simply postulate it and pass on. The whole remainder of the book will be more or less of a proof that the postulate was correct.

Bodily experiences, therefore, and more particularly brain-experiences, must take a place amongst those conditions of the mental life of which Psychology need take account. The spiritualist and the associationist must both be 'cerebralists,' to the extent at least of admitting that certain peculiarities in the way of working of their own favorite principles are explicable only by the fact that the brain laws are a codeterminant of the result.

Our first conclusion, then, is that a certain amount of brain-physiology must be presupposed or included in Psychology[1].

In still another way the psychologist is forced to be something of a nerve-physiologist. Mental phenomena are not only conditioned a parte ante by bodily processes; but they lead to them a parte post. That they lead to acts is of course the most familiar of truths, but I do not merely mean acts in the sense of voluntary and deliberate muscular performances. Mental states occasion also changes in the calibre of blood-vessels, or alteration in the heartbeats, or processes more subtle still, in glands and viscera. If these are taken into account, as well as acts which follow at some remote period because the mental state was once there, it will be safe to lay down the general law that no mental modification ever occurs which is not accompanied or followed by a bodily change. The ideas and feelings, e.g., which these present printed characters excite in the reader's mind not only occasion movements of his eyes and nascent movements of articulation in him, but will some day make him speak, or take sides in a discussion, or give advice, or choose a book to read, differently from what would have been the case had they never impressed his retina. Our psychology must therefore take account not only of the conditions antecedent to mental states, but of their resultant consequences as well.

But actions originally prompted by conscious intelligence may grow so automatic by dint of habit as to be apparently unconsciously performed. Standing, walking, buttoning and unbuttoning, piano-playing, talking, even saying one's prayers, may be done when the mind is absorbed in other things. The performances of animal instinct seem semi-automatic, and the reflex acts of self-preservation certainly are so. Yet they resemble intelligent acts in bringing about the same ends at which the animals' consciousness, on other occasions, deliberately aims. Shall the study of such machine-like yet purposive acts as these be included in Psychology?

The boundary-line of the mental is certainly vague. It is better not to be pedantic, but to let the science be as vague as its subject, and include such phenomena as these if by so doing we can throw any light on the main business in hand. It will ere long be seen, I trust, that we can; and that we gain much more by a broad than by a narrow conception of our subject. At a certain stage in the development of every science a degree of vagueness is what best consists with fertility. On the whole, few recent formulas have done more real service of a rough sort in psychology than the

Spencerian one that the essence of mental life and of bodily life are one, namely, 'the adjustment of inner to outer relations.' Such a formula is vagueness incarnate; but because it takes into account the fact that minds inhabit environments which act on them and on which they in turn react; because, in short, it takes mind in the midst of all its concrete relations, it is immensely more fertile than the old-fashioned 'rational psychology,' which treated the soul as a detached existent, sufficient unto itself, and assumed to consider only its nature and properties. I shall therefore feel free to make any sallies into zoology or into pure nerve-physiology which may seem instructive for our purposes, but otherwise shall leave those sciences to the physiologists.

Can we state more distinctly still the manner in which the mental life seems to intervene between impressions made from without upon the body, and reactions of the body upon the outer world again? Let us look at a few facts.

If some iron filings be sprinkled on a table and a magnet brought near them, they will fly through the air for a certain distance and stick to its surface. A savage seeing the phenomenon explains it as the result of an attraction or love between the magnet and the filings. But let a card cover the poles of the magnet, and the filings will press forever against its surface without its ever occurring to them to pass around its sides and thus come into more direct contact with the object of their love. Blow bubbles through a tube into the bottom of a pail of water, they will rise to the surface and mingle with the air. Their action may again be poetically interpreted as due to a longing to recombine with the mother-atmosphere above the surface. But if you invert a jar full of water over the pail, they will rise and remain lodged beneath its bottom, shut in from the outer air, although a slight deflection from their course at the outset, or a re-descent towards the rim of the jar, when they found their upward course impeded, could easily have set them free.

If now we pass from such actions as these to those of living things, we notice a striking difference. Romeo wants Juliet as the filings want the magnet; and if no obstacles intervene he moves towards her by as straight a line as they. But Romeo and Juliet, if a wall be built between them, do not remain idiotically pressing their faces against its opposite sides like the magnet and the filings with the card. Romeo soon finds a circuitous way, by scaling the wall or otherwise, of touching Juliet's lips directly. With the filings the path is fixed; whether it reaches the end depends on accidents. With the lover it is the end which is fixed, the path may be modified indefinitely.

Suppose a living frog in the position in which we placed our bubbles of air, namely, at the bottom of a jar of water. The want of breath will soon make him also long to rejoin the mother-atmosphere, and he will take the shortest path to his end by swimming straight upwards. But if a jar full of water be inverted over him, he will not, like the bubbles, perpetually press his nose against its unyielding roof, but will restlessly explore the neighborhood until by re-descending again he has discovered a path around its brim to the goal of his desires. Again the fixed end, the varying means!

Such contrasts between living and inanimate performances end by leading men to deny that in the physical world final purposes exist at all. Loves and desires are to-day no longer imputed to particles of iron or of air. No one supposes now that the end of any activity which they may display is an ideal purpose presiding over the activity from its outset and soliciting or drawing it into being by a sort of vis a fronte. The end, on the contrary, is deemed a mere passive result, pushed into being a tergo, having had, so to speak, no voice in its own production. Alter, the pre-existing conditions, and with inorganic materials you bring forth each time a different apparent end. But with intelligent agents, altering the conditions changes the activity displayed, but not the end reached; for here the idea of the yet unrealized end co-operates with the conditions to determine what the activities shall be.

The Pursuance of future ends and the choice of means for their attainment, are thus the mark and criterion of the presence of mentality in a phenomenon. We all use this test to discriminate between an intelligent and a mechanical performance. We impute no mentality to sticks and stones, because they never seem to move for the sake of anything, but always when pushed, and then indifferently and with no sign of choice. So we unhesitatingly call them senseless.

Just so we form our decision upon the deepest of all philosophic problems: Is the Kosmos an expression of intelligence rational in its inward nature, or a brute external fact pure and simple? If we find ourselves, in contemplating it, unable to banish the impression that it is a realm of final purposes, that it exists for the sake of something, we place intelligence at tile heart of it and have a religion. If, on the contrary, in surveying its irremediable flux, we can think of the present only as so much mere mechanical sprouting from the past, occurring with no reference to the future, we are atheists and materialists.

In the lengthy discussions which psychologists have carried on about the amount of intelligence displayed by lower mammals, or the amount of consciousness involved in the functions of the nerve-centres of reptiles, the same test has always been applied: Is the character of the actions such that we must believe them to be performed for the sake of their result? The result in question, as we shall hereafter abundantly see, is as a rule a useful one,-the animal is, on the whole, safer under the circumstances for bringing it forth. So far the action has a teleological character; but such mere outward teleology as this might still be the blind result of vis a tergo. The growth and movements of plants, the processes of development, digestion, secretion, etc., in animals, supply innumerable instances of performances useful to the individual which may nevertheless be, and by most of us are supposed to be, produced by automatic mechanism. The physiologist does not confidently assert conscious intelligence in the frog's spinal cord until he has shown that the useful result which the nervous machinery brings forth under a given irritation remains the same when the machinery is altered. If, to take the stock-instance, the right knee of a headless frog be irritated with acid, the right foot will wipe it off. When, however, this foot is amputated, the animal will often raise the left foot to the spot and wipe the offending material away.

Pfluger and Lewes reason from such facts in the following way: If the first reaction were the result of mere machinery, they say; if that irritated portion of the skin discharged the right leg as a trigger discharges its own barrel of a shotgun; then amputating the right foot would indeed frustrate the wiping, but would not make the left leg move. It would simply result in the right stump moving through the empty air (which is in fact the phenomenon sometimes observed). The right trigger makes no effort to discharge the left barrel if the right one be unloaded; nor does an electrical machine ever get restless because it can only emit sparks, and not hem pillow-cases like a sewing-machine.

If, on the contrary, the right leg originally moved for the purpose of wiping the acid, then nothing is more natural than that, when the easiest means of effecting that purpose prove fruitless, other means should be tried. Every failure must keep the animal in a state of disappointment which will lead to all sorts of new trials and devices; and tranquillity will not ensue till one of these, by a happy stroke, achieves the wished-for end.

In a similar way Goltz ascribes intelligence to the frog's optic lobes and cerebellum. We alluded above to the manner in which a sound frog imprisoned in water will discover an outlet to the atmosphere. Goltz found that frogs deprived of their cerebral hemispheres would often exhibit a like ingenuity. Such a frog, after rising from the bottom and finding his farther upward progress checked by the glass bell which has been inverted over him, will not persist in butting his nose against the obstacle until dead of suffocation, but will often re-descend and emerge from under its rim as if, not a definite mechanical propulsion upwards, but rather a conscious desire to reach the air by hook or crook were the main-spring of his activity. Goltz concluded from this that the hemispheres are not the seat of intellectual power in frogs. He made the same inference from observing that a brainless frog will turn over from his back to his belly when one of his legs is sewed up, although the movements required are then very different from those excited under normal circumstances by the same annoying position. They seem determined, consequently, not merely by the antecedent irritant, but by the final end,-though the irritant of course is what makes the end desired. Another brilliant German author, Liebmann[2], argues against the brain's mechanism accounting for mental action, by very similar considerations. A machine as such, he says, will bring forth right results when it is in good order, and wrong results if out of repair. But both kinds of result flow with equally fatal necessity from their conditions. We cannot suppose the clock-work whose structure fatally determines it to a certain rate of speed, noticing that this speed is too slow or too fast and vainly trying to correct it. Its conscience, if it have any, should be as good as that of the best chronometer, for both alike obey equally well the same eternal mechanical laws-laws from behind. But if the brain be out of order and the man says "Twice four are two," instead of "Twice four are eight," or else "I must go to the coal to buy the wharf," instead of "I must go to the wharf to buy the coal," instantly there arises a consciousness of error. The wrong performance, though it obey the same mechanical law as the right, is nevertheless condemned,-condemned as contradicting the inner law-the law from in front, the purpose or ideal for which the brain should act, whether it do so or not.

We need not discuss here whether these writers in drawing their conclusion have done justice to all the premises involved in the cases they treat of. We quote their arguments only to show how they appeal to the principle that no actions but such as are done for an end, and show a choice of means, can be called indubitable expressions of Mind. I shall then adopt this as the criterion by which to circumscribe the subject-matter of this work so far as action enters into it. Many nervous performances will therefore be unmentioned, as being purely physiological. Nor will the anatomy of the nervous system and organs of sense be described anew. The reader will find in H.N. Martin's Human Body, in G.T. Ladd's Physiological Psychology, and in all the other standard Anatomies and Physiologies, a mass of information which we must regard as preliminary and take for granted in the present work[3]. Of the functions of the cerebral hemispheres, however, since they directly subserve consciousness, it will be well to give some little account.

Notes

[1] Cf. George T.Ladd: Elements of Physiological Psychology (1887), pt. III, chap. III, 9, 12
[2] Zur Analysis der Wirklichkeit, p. 489
[3] Nothing is easier than to familiarize one's self with the mammalian brain. Get a sheep's head, a small saw, chisel, scalpel and forceps (all three can best be had from a surgical-instrument maker), and unravel its parts either by the aid of a human dissecting book, such as Holden's Manual of Anatomy, or by the specific directions ad hoc given in such books as Foster and Langley's Practical Physiology (Macmillan) or Morrell's Comparative Anatomy, and Guide to Dissection (Longman & Co.).

Chapter II - The Functions of the Brain

If I begin chopping the foot of a tree, its branches are unmoved by my act, and its leaves murmur as peacefully as ever in the wind. If, on the contrary, I do violence to the foot of a fellow-man, the rest of his body instantly responds to the aggression by movements of alarm or defence. The reason of this difference is that the man has a nervous system whilst the tree has none; and the function of the nervous system is to bring each part into harmonious co-operation with every other. The afferent nerves, when excited by some physical irritant, be this as gross in its mode of operation as a chopping axe or as subtle as the waves of light, conveys the excitement to the nervous centres. The commotion set up in the centres does not stop there, but discharges itself, if at all strong, through the efferent nerves into muscles and glands, exciting movements of the limbs and viscera, or acts of secretion, which vary with the animal, and with the irritant applied. These acts of response have usually the common character of being of service. They ward off the noxious stimulus and support the beneficial one; whilst if, in itself indifferent, the stimulus be a sign of some distant circumstance of practical importance, the animal's acts are addressed to this circumstance so as to avoid its perils or secure its benefits, as the case may be. To take a common example, if I hear the conductor calling ' All aboard!' as I enter the depot, my heart first stops, then palpitates, and my legs respond to the air-waves falling on my tympanum by quickening their movements. If I stumble as I run, the sensation of falling provokes a movement of the hands towards the direction of the fall, the effect of which is to shield the body from too sudden a shock. If a cinder enter my eye, its lids close forcibly and a copious flow of tears tends to wash it out.

These three responses to a sensational stimulus differ, however, in many respects. The closure of the eye and the lachrymation are quite involuntary, and so is the disturbance of the heart. Such involuntary responses we know as 'reflex' acts. The motion of the arms to break the shock of falling may also be called reflex, since it occurs too quickly to be deliberately intended. Whether it be instinctive or whether it result from the pedestrian education of childhood may be doubtful; it is, at any rate, less automatic than the previous acts, for a man might by conscious effort learn to perform it more skilfully, or even to suppress it altogether. Actions of this kind, into which instinct and volition enter upon equal terms, have been called 'semi-reflex.' The act of running towards the train, on the other hand, has no instinctive element about it. It is purely the result of education, and is preceded by a consciousness of the purpose to be attained and a distinct mandate of the will. It is a 'voluntary act.' Thus the animal's reflex and voluntary performances shade into each other gradually, being connected by acts which may often occur automatically, but may also be modified by conscious intelligence.

An outside observer, unable to perceive the accompanying consciousness, might be wholly at a loss to discriminate between the automatic acts and those which volition escorted. But if the criterion of mind's existence be the choice of the proper means for the attainment of a supposed end, all the acts seem to be inspired by intelligence, for appropriateness characterizes them all alike. This fact, now, has led to two quite opposite theories about the relation to consciousness of the nervous functions. Some authors, finding that the higher voluntary ones seem to require the guidance of feeling, conclude that over the lowest reflexes some such feeling also presides, though it may be a feeling of which we remain unconscious. Others, finding that reflex and semi-automatic acts may, notwithstanding their appropriateness, take place with an unconsciousness apparently complete, fly to the opposite extreme and maintain that the appropriateness even of voluntary actions owes nothing to the fact that consciousness attends them. They are, according to these writers, results of physiological mechanism pure and simple. In a near chapter we shall return to this controversy again. Let us now look a little more closely at the brain and at the ways in which its states may be supposed to condition those of the mind.

The Frog's Nerve-Centres

Both the minute anatomy and the detailed physiology of the brain are achievements of the present generation, or rather we may say (beginning with Meynert) of the past twenty years. Many points are still obscure and subject to controversy; but a general way of conceiving the organ has been reached on all hands which in its main feature seems not unlikely to stand, and which even gives a most plausible scheme of the way in which cerebral and mental operations go hand in hand.

The best way to enter the subject will be to take a lower creature, like a frog, and study by the vivisectional method the functions of his different nerve-centres. The frog's nerve-centres are figured in the accompanying diagram, which needs no further explanation. I will first proceed to state what happens when various amounts of the anterior parts are removed, in different frogs, in the way in which an ordinary student removes them; that is, with no

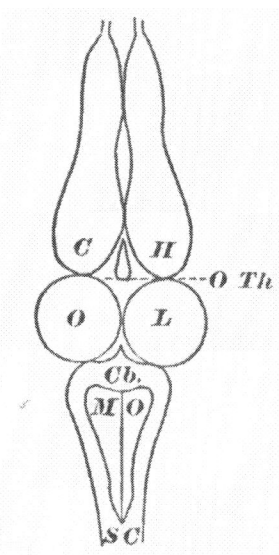

FIG. 1.—C H, Cerebral Hemispheres; O Th, Optic Thalami; O L, Optic Lobes; Cb, Cerebellum; M O, Medulla Oblongata; S C, Spinal Cord.

extreme precautions as to the purity of the operation. We shall in this way reach a very simple conception of the functions of the various centres, involving the strongest possible contrast between the cerebral hemispheres and the lower lobes. This sharp conception will have didactic advantages, for it is often very instructive to start with too simple a formula and correct it later on. Our first formula, as we shall later see, will have to be softened down somewhat by the results of more careful experimentation both on frogs and birds, and by those of the most recent observations on dogs, monkeys, and man. But it will put us, from the outset, in clear possession of some fundamental notions and distinctions which we could otherwise not gain so well, and none of which the later more completed view will overturn.

If, then, we reduce the frog's nervous system to the spinal cord alone, by making a section behind the base of the skull, between the spinal cord and the medulla oblongata, thereby cutting off the brain from all connection with the rest of the body, the frog will still continue to live, but with a very peculiarly modified activity. It ceases to breathe or swallow; it lies flat on its belly, and does not, like a normal frog, sit up on its fore paws, though its hind legs are kept, as usual, folded against its body and immediately resume this position if drawn out. If thrown on its back, it lies there quietly, without turning over like a normal frog. Locomotion and voice seem entirely abolished. If we suspend it by the nose, and irritate different portions of its skin by acid, it performs a set of remarkable 'defensive' movements calculated to wipe away the irritant. Thus, if the breast be touched, both fore paws will rub it vigorously; if we touch the outer side of the elbow, the hind foot of the same side will rise directly to the spot and wipe it. The back of the foot will rub the knee if that be attacked, whilst if the foot be cut away, the stump will make ineffectual movements, and then, in many frogs, a pause will come, as if for deliberation, succeeded by a rapid passage of the opposite unmutilated foot to the acidulated spot.

The most striking character of all these movements, after their teleological appropriateness, is their precision. They vary, in sensitive frogs and with a proper amount of irritation, so little as almost to resemble in their machine-like regularity the performances of a jumping-jack, whose legs must twitch whenever you pull the string. The spinal cord of the frog thus contains arrangements of cells and fibres fitted to convert skin irritations into movements of defence. We may call it the centre for defensive movements in this animal. We may indeed go farther than this, and by cutting the spinal cord in various places find that its separate segments are independent mechanisms, for appropriate activities of the head and of the arms and legs respectively. The segment governing the arms is especially active, in male frogs, in the breeding season; and these members alone with the breast and back appertaining to them, everything else being cut away, will then actively grasp a finger placed between them and remain hanging to it for a considerable time.

The spinal cord in other animals has analogous powers. Even in man it makes movements of defence. Paraplegics draw up their legs when tickled; and Robin, on tickling the breast of a criminal an hour after decapitation, saw the arm and hand move towards the spot. Of the lower functions of the mammalian cord, studied so ably by Goltz and others, this is not the place to speak.

If, in a second animal, the cut be made just behind the optic lobes so that the cerebellum and medulla oblongata remain attached to the cord, then swallowing, breathing, crawling, and a rather enfeebled jumping and swimming are added to the movements previously observed.[1] There are other reflexes too. The animal, thrown on his back, immediately turns over to his belly. Placed in a shallow bowl, which is floated on water and made to rotate, he responds to the rotation by first turning his head and then waltzing around with his entire body, in the opposite direction to the whirling of the bowl. If his support be tilted so that his head points downwards, he points it up; he points it down if it be pointed upwards, to the right if it be pointed to the left, etc. But his reactions do not go farther than these movements of the head.; He will not, like frogs whose thalami are preserved, climb up a board if the latter be tilted, but will slide off it to the ground.

If the cut be made on another frog between the thalami and the optic lobes, the locomotion both on land and water becomes quite normal, and, in addition to the reflexes already shown by the lower centres, he croaks regularly whenever he is pinched under the arms. He compensates rotations, etc., by movements of the head, and turns over from his back; but still drops off his tilted board. As his optic nerves are destroyed by the usual operation, it is impossible to say whether he will avoid obstacles placed in his path.

When, finally, a frog's cerebral hemispheres alone are cut off by a section between them and the thalami which preserves the latter, an unpractised observer would not at first suspect anything abnormal about the animal. Not only is he capable, on proper instigation, of all the acts already described, but he guides himself by sight, so that if an obstacle be set up between him and the light, and he be forced to move forward, he either jumps over it or swerves to one side. He manifests sexual passion at the proper season, and, unlike an altogether brainless frog, which embraces anything placed between his arms, postpones this reflex act until a female of his own species is provided. Thus far, as aforesaid, a person unfamiliar with frogs might not suspect a mutilation; but even such a person would soon remark the almost entire absence of spontaneous motion-that is, motion unprovoked by any present incitation of sense. The continued movements of swimming, performed by the creature in the water, seem to be the fatal result of the contact of that fluid with its skin. They cease when a stick, for example, touches his hands. This is a sensible irritant towards which the feet are automatically drawn by reflex action, and on which the animal remains sitting. He manifests no hunger, and will suffer a fly to crawl over his nose unsnapped at. Fear, too, seems to have deserted him. In a word, he is an extremely complex machine whose actions, so far as they go, tend to self-preservation; but still a machine, in this sense-that it seems to contain no incalculable element. By applying the right sensory stimulus to him we are almost as certain of getting a fixed response as an organist is of hearing a certain tone when he pulls out a certain stop.

But now if to the lower centres we add the cerebral hemispheres, or if, in other words, we make an intact animal the subject of our observations, all this is changed. In addition to the previous responses to present incitements of sense, our frog now goes through long and complex acts of locomotion spontaneously, or as if moved by what in ourselves we should call an idea. His reactions to outward stimuli vary their form, too. Instead of making simple defensive movements with his hind legs like a headless frog if touched, or of giving one or two leaps and then sitting still like a hemisphereless one, he makes persistent and varied efforts at escape, as if, not the mere contact of the physiologist's hand, but the notion of danger suggested by it were now his spur. Led by the feeling of hunger, too, he goes in search of insects, fish, or smaller frogs, and varies his procedure with each species of victim. The physiologist cannot by manipulating him elicit croaking, crawling up a board, swimming or stopping, at will. His conduct has become incalculable. We can no longer foretell it exactly. Effort to escape is his dominant reaction, but he may do anything else, even swell up and become perfectly passive in our hands.

Such are the phenomena commonly observed, and such the impressions which one naturally receives. Certain general conclusions follow irresistibly. First of all the following:

The acts of all the centres involve the use of the same muscles. When a headless frog's hind leg wipes the acid, he calls into play all the leg-muscles which a frog with his full medulla oblongata and cerebellum uses when he turns from his back to his belly. Their contractions are, however, combined differently in the two cases, so that the results vary widely. We must consequently conclude that specific arrangements of cells and fibres exist in the cord for wiping, in the medulla for turning over, etc. Similarly they exist in the thalami for jumping over seen obstacles and for balancing the moved body; in the optic lobes for creeping backwards, or what not. But in the hemispheres, since the presence of these organs brings no new elementary form of movement with it, but only determines differently the occasions on which the movements shall occur, making the usual stimuli less fatal and machine-like; we need suppose no such machinery directly co-ordinative of muscular contractions to exist. We may rather assume, when the mandate for a wiping-movement is sent forth by the hemispheres, that a current goes straight to the wiping-arrangement in the spinal cord, exciting this arrangement as a whole. Similarly, if an intact frog wishes to jump over a stone which he sees, all he need do is to excite from the hemispheres the jumping-centre in the thalami or wherever it may be, and the latter will provide for the details of the execution. It is like a general ordering a colonel to make a certain movement, but not telling him how it shall be done.[2]

The same muscle, then, repeatedly represented at different heights; and at each it enters into a different combination with other muscles to co-operate in some special form of concerted movement. At each height the movement is discharged by some particular form of sensorial stimulus. Thus in the cord, the skin alone occasions movements; in the upper part of the optic lobes, the eyes are added; in the thalami, the semi-circular canals would seem to play a part; whilst the stimuli which discharge the hemispheres would seem not so much to be elementary sorts of sensation, as groups of sensations forming determinate objects or things. Prey is not pursued nor are enemies shunned by ordinary hemisphereless frogs. Those reactions upon complex circumstances which we call instinctive rather than reflex, are already in this animal dependent on the brain's highest lobes, and still more is this the case with animals higher in the zoological scale.

The results are just the same if, instead of a frog, we take a pigeon, and cut out his hemispheres as they are ordinarily cut out for a lecture-room demonstration. There is not a movement natural to him which this brainless bird cannot perform if expressly excited thereto; only the inner promptings seem deficient, and when left to himself he spends most of his time crouched on the ground with his head sunk between his shoulders as if asleep.

General Notion of Hemispheres

All these facts lead us, when we think about them, to some such explanatory conception as this: The lower centres act from present sensational stimuli alone; the hemispheres act from perceptions and considerations, the sensations which they may receive, serving only as suggesters of these. But what are perceptions but sensations grouped together? and what are considerations but expectations, in the fancy, of sensations which will be felt one way or another according as action takes this course or that? If I step aside on seeing a rattlesnake, from considering how dangerous an animal he is, the mental materials which constitute my prudential reflection are images more or less vivid of the movement of his head, of a sudden pain in my leg, of a state of terror, a swelling of the limb, a chill, delirium, unconsciousness, etc., etc., and the ruin of my hopes. But all these images are constructed out of my past experiences. They are reproductions of what I have felt or witnessed. They are, in short, remote sensations; and the difference between the hemisphereless animal and the whole one may be concisely expressed by saying that the one obeys absent, the other only present, objects.

The hemispheres would then seem to be the seat of memory. Vestiges of past experience must in some way be stored up in them, and must, when aroused by present stimuli, first appear as representations of distant goods and evils; and then must discharge into the appropriate motor channels for warding off the evil and securing the benefits of the good. If we liken the nervous currents to electric currents, we can compare the nervous system, C, below the hemispheres to a direct circuit from sense-organ to muscle along the line S...C...M of Fig. 2. The hemisphere, H, adds the long circuit or loop-line through which the current may pass when for any reason the direct line is not used.

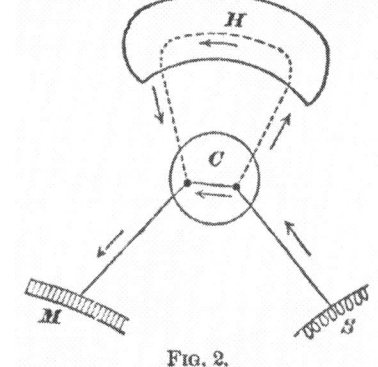

Fig. 2.

Thus, a tired wayfarer on a hot day throws himself on the damp earth beneath a maple-tree. The sensations of delicious rest and coolness pouring themselves through the direct line would naturally discharge into the muscles of complete extension: he would abandon himself to the dangerous repose. But the loop-line being open, part of the current is drafted along it, and awakens rheumatic or catarral reminiscences, which prevail over the instigations of sense, and make the man arise and pursue his way to where he may enjoy his rest more safely. Presently we shall examine the manner in which the hemispheric loop-line may be supposed to serve as a reservoir for such reminiscences as these. Meanwhile I will ask the reader to notice some corollaries of its being such a reservoir.

First, no animal without it can deliberate, pause, postpone, nicely weigh one motive against another, or compare. Prudence, in a word, is for such a creature an impossible virtue. Accordingly we see that nature removes those functions in the exercise of which prudence is a virtue from the lower centres and hands them over to the cerebrum. Wherever a creature has to deal with complex features of the environment, prudence is a virtue. The higher animals have so to deal; and the more complex the features, the higher we call the animals. The fewer of his acts, then, can such an animal perform without the help of the organs in question. In the frog many acts devolve wholly on the lower centres; in the bird fewer; in the rodent fewer still; in the dog very few indeed; and in apes and men hardly any at all.

The advantages of this are obvious. Take the prehension of food as an example and suppose it to be a reflex performance of the lower centres. The animal will be condemned fatally and irresistibly to snap at it whenever presented, no matter what the circumstances may be; he can no more disobey this prompting than water can refuse to boil when a fire is kindled under the pot. His life will again and again pay the forfeit of his gluttony.

Exposure to retaliation, to other enemies, to traps, to poisons, to the dangers of repletion, must be regular parts of his existence. His lack of all thought by which to weigh the danger against the attractiveness of the bait, and of all volition to remain hungry a little while longer, is the direct measure of his lowness in the mental scale. And those fishes which, like our cunners and sculpins, are no sooner thrown back from the hook into the water, than they automatically seize the hook again, would soon expiate the degradation of their intelligence by the extinction of their type, did not their exaggerated fecundity atone for their imprudence. Appetite and the acts it prompts have consequently become in all higher vertebrates functions of the cerebrum. They disappear when the physiologist's knife has left the subordinate centres alone in place. The brainless pigeon will starve though left on a corn-heap. Take again the sexual function. In birds this devolves exclusively upon the hemispheres. When these are shorn away the pigeon pays no attention to the billings and cooings of its mate. And Goltz found that a bitch in heat would excite no emotion in male dogs who had suffered large loss of cerebral tissue. Those who have read Darwin's 'Descent of Man' know what immense importance in the amelioration of the breed in birds this author ascribes to the mere fact of sexual selection. The sexual act is not performed until every condition of circumstance and sentiment is fulfilled, until time, place, and partner all are fit. But in frogs and toads this passion devolves on the lower centres. They show consequently a machine-like obedience to the present incitement of sense, and an almost total exclusion of the power of choice. Copulation occurs per fas aut nefas, occasionally between males, often with dead females, in puddles exposed on the highway, and the male may be cut in two without letting go his hold. Every spring an immense sacrifice of batrachian life takes place from these causes alone.

No one need be told how dependent all human social elevation is upon the prevalence of chastity. Hardly any factor measures more than this the difference between civilization and barbarism. Physiologically interpreted, chastity means nothing more than the fact that present solicitations of sense are overpowered by suggestions of aesthetic and moral fitness which the circumstances awaken in the cerebrum ; and that upon the inhibitory or permissive influence of these alone action directly depends.

Within the psychic life due to the cerebrum itself the same general distinction obtains, between considerations of the more immediate and considerations of the more remote. In all ages the man whose determinations are swayed by reference to the most distant ends has been held to possess the highest intelligence. The tramp who lives from hour to hour; the bohemian whose engagements are from day to day; the bachelor who builds but for a single life; the father who acts for another generation ; the patriot who thinks of a whole community and many generations; and finally, the philosopher and saint whose cares are for humanity and for eternity,-these range themselves in an unbroken hierarchy, wherein each successive grade results from an increased manifestation of the special form of action by which the cerebral centres are distinguished from all below them.

In the 'loop-line' along which the memories and ideas of the distant are supposed to lie, the action, so far as it is a physical process, must be interpreted after the type of the action in the lower centres. If regarded here as a reflex process, it must be reflex there as well. The current in both places runs out into the muscles only after it has first run in; but whilst the path by which it runs out is determined in the lower centres by reflections few and fixed amongst the cell-arrangements, in the hemispheres the reflections are many and instable. This, it will be seen, is only a difference of degree and not of kind, and does not change the reflex type. The conception of all action as conforming to this type is the fundamental conception of modern nerve-physiology. So much for our general preliminary conception of the nerve-centres! Let us define it more distinctly before we see how well physiological observation will bear it out in detail.

The Education of the Hemispheres

Nerve-currents run in through sense-organs, and whilst provoking reflex acts in the lower centres, they arouse ideas in the hemispheres, which either permit the reflexes in question, check them, or substitute others for them. All ideas being in the last resort reminiscences, the question to answer is: How can processes become organized in the hemispheres which correspond to reminiscences in the mind ?[3]

Nothing is easier than to conceive a possible way in which this might be done, provided four assumptions be granted. These assumptions (which after all are inevitable in any event) are:

1) The same cerebral process which, when aroused from without by a sense-organ, gives the perception of an object, will give an idea of the same object when aroused by other cerebral processes from within.
2) If processes 1, 2, 3, 4 have once been aroused together or in immediate succession, any subsequent arousal of any one of them (whether from without or within) will tend to arouse the others in the original order.[This is the so-called law of association.]
3) Every sensorial excitement propagated to a lower centre tends to spread upwards and arouse an idea.
4) Every idea tends ultimately either to produce a movement or to check one which otherwise would be produced.

Suppose now (these assumptions being granted) that we have a baby before us who sees a candle-flame for the first time, and, by virtue of a reflex tendency common in babies of a certain age, extends his hand to grasp it, so that his fingers get burned. So far we have two reflex currents in play: first, from the eye to the extension movement, along the line 1-1-1-1 of Fig. 3; and second, from the finger to the movement of drawing back the hand, along the line 2-2-2-2.

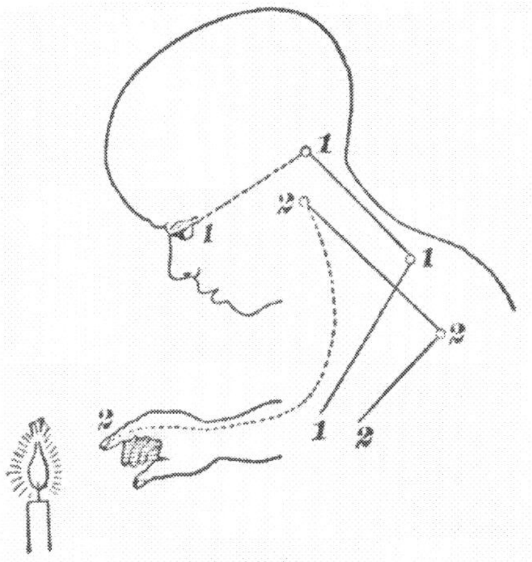

If this were the baby's whole nervous system, and if the reflexes were once for all organic, we should have no alteration in his behavior, no matter how often the experience recurred. The retinal image of the flame would always make the arm shoot forward, the burning of the finger would always send it back. But we know that 'the burnt child dreads the fire,' and that one experience usually protects the fingers forever. The point is to see how the hemispheres may bring this result to pass.

We must complicate our diagram (see Fig. 4). Let the current 1-1, from the eye, discharge upward as well as downward when it reaches the lower centre for vision, and arouse the perceptional

FIG. 3.

process s1 in the hemispheres; let the feeling of the arm's extension also send up a current which leaves a trace of itself, m1; let the burnt finger leave an analogous trace, s2; and let the movement of retraction leave m2. These four processes will now, by virtue of assumption 2), be associated together by the path s1-m1-s2-m2 running from the first to the last, so that if anything touches off s1, ideas of the extension, of the burnt finger, and of the retraction will pass in rapid succession through the mind. The effect on the child's conduct when the candle-flame is next presented is easy to imagine. Of course the sight of it arouses the grasping reflex; but it arouses simultaneously the idea thereof, together with that of the consequent pain, and of the final retraction of the hand; and if these cerebral processes prevail in strength over the immediate sensation in the centres below, the last idea will be the cue by which the final action is discharged. The grasping will be arrested in mid-career, the hand drawn back, and the child's fingers saved.

In all this we assume that the hemispheres do not natively couple any particular sense-impression with any special motor discharge. They only register, and preserve traces of, such couplings as are already organized in the reflex centres below. But this brings it inevitably about that, when a chain of experiences has been already registered and the first link is impressed once again from without, the last link will often be awakened in idea long before it can exist in fact. And if this last link were previously coupled with a motion, that motion may now come from the mere ideal suggestion without waiting for the actual impression to arise. Thus an animal with hemispheres acts in anticipation of future things; or, to use our previous formula, he acts from considerations of distant good and ill. If we give the name of partners to the original couplings of impressions with motions in a reflex way, then we may say that the function of the hemispheres is simply to bring about exchanges among the partners. Movement mn, which natively is sensation sn's partner, becomes through the hemispheres the partner of sensation s1, s2 or s3. It is like the great commutating switch-board at a central telephone station. No new elementary process is involved; no impression nor any motion peculiar to the hemispheres; but any number of combinations impossible to the lower machinery taken alone, and an endless consequent increase in the possibilities of behavior on the creature's part.

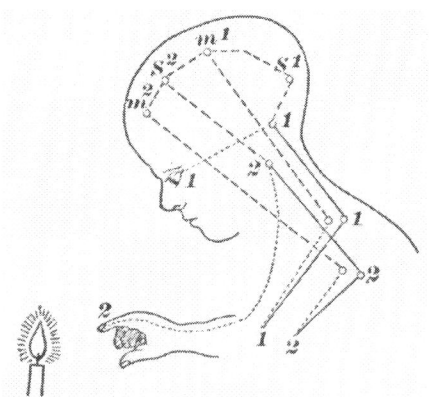

FIG. 4.—The dotted lines stand for afferent paths, the broken lines for paths between the centres; the entire lines for efferent paths.

All this, as a mere scheme,[4] is so clear and so concordant with the general look of the facts as almost to impose itself on our belief; but it is anything but clear in detail. The brain-physiology of late years has with great effort sought to work out the paths by which these couplings of sensations with movements take place, both in the hemispheres and in the centres below.

So we must next test our scheme by the facts discovered in this direction. We shall conclude, I think, after taking them all into account, that the scheme probably makes the lower centres too machine-like and the hemispheres not quite machine-like enough, and must consequently be softened down a little. So much I may say in advance. Meanwhile, before plunging into the details which await us, it will somewhat clear our ideas if we contrast the modern way of looking at the matter with the phrenological conception which but lately preceded it.

The Phrenological Conception

In a certain sense Gall was the first to seek to explain in detail how the brain could subserve our mental operations. His way of proceeding was only too simple. He took the faculty-psychology as his ultimatum on the mental side, and he made no farther psychological analysis. Wherever he found an individual with some strongly-marked trait of character he examined his head; and if he found the latter prominent in a certain region, he said without more ado that that region was the 'organ' of the trait or faculty in question. The traits were of very diverse constitution, some being simple sensibilities like 'weight' or 'color'; some being instinctive tendencies like 'alimentiveness' or 'amativeness;' and others, again, being complex resultants like 'conscientiousness,' 'individuality.' Phrenology fell promptly into disrepute among scientific men because observation seemed to show that large faculties and large 'bumps' might fail to coexist; because the scheme of Gall was so vast as hardly to admit of accurate determination at all-who of us can say even of his own brothers whether their perceptions of weight and of time are well developed or not?-because the followers of Gall and Spurzheim were unable to reform these errors in any appreciable degree; and, finally, because the whole analysis of faculties was vague and erroneous from a psychologic point of view. Popular professors of the lore have nevertheless continued to command the admiration of popular audiences; and there seems no doubt that Phrenology, however little it satisfy our scientific curiosity about the functions of different portions of the brain, may still be, in the hands of intelligent practitioners, a useful help in the art of reading character. A hooked nose and a firm jaw are usually signs of practical energy; soft, delicate hands are signs of refined sensibility. Even so may a prominent eye be a sign of power over language, and a bull-neck a sign of sensuality. But the brain behind the eye and neck need no more be the organ of the signified faculty than the jaw is the organ of the will or the hand the organ of refinement. These correlations between mind and body are, however, so frequent that the 'characters' given by phrenologists are often remarkable for knowingness and insight.

Phrenology hardly does more than restate the problem. To answer the question, "Why do I like children?" by saying, "Because you have a large organ of philoprogenitiveness," but renames the phenomenon to be explained. What is my philoprogenitiveness? Of what mental elements does it consist? And how can a part of the brain be its organ? A science of the mind must reduce such complex manifestations as 'philoprogenitiveness' to their elements. A science of the brain must point out the functions of its elements. A science of the relations of mind and brain must show how the elementary ingredients of the former correspond to the elementary functions of the latter. But phrenology, except by occasional coincidence, takes no account of elements at all. Its 'faculties,' as a rule, are fully equipped persons in a particular mental attitude. Take, for example, the 'faculty' of language. It involves in reality a host of distinct powers. We must first have images of concrete things and ideas of abstract qualities and relations; we must next have the memory of words and then the capacity so to associate each idea or image with a particular word that, when the word is heard, the idea shall forthwith enter our mind. We must conversely, as soon as the idea arises in our mind, associate with it a mental image of the word, and by means of this image we must innervate our articulatory apparatus so as to reproduce the word as physical sound. To read or to write a language other elements still must be introduced. But it is plain that the faculty of spoken language alone is so complicated as to call into play almost all the elementary powers which the mind possesses, memory, imagination, association, judgment, and volition. A portion of the brain competent to be the adequate seat of such a faculty would needs be an entire brain in miniature,-just as the faculty itself is really a specification of the entire man, a sort of homunculus. Yet just such homunculi are for the most part the phrenological organs. As Lange says:

"We have a parliament of little men together, each of whom, as happens also in a real parliament, possesses but a single idea which he ceaselessly strives to make prevail"-benevolence, firmness, hope, and the rest. "Instead of one soul, phrenology gives us forty, each alone as enigmatic as the full aggregate psychic life can be. Instead of dividing the latter into effective elements, she divides it into personal beings of peculiar character ..'Herr Pastor, sure there be a horse inside,' called out the peasants to X after their spiritual shepherd had spent hours in explaining to them the construction of the locomotive. With a horse inside truly everything becomes clear, even though it be a queer enough sort of horse-the horse itself calls for no explanation! Phrenology takes a start to get beyond the point of view of the ghost-like soul entity, but she ends by populating the whole skull with ghosts of the same order."[5]

Modern Science conceives of the matter in a very different way. Brain and mind alike consist of simple elements, sensory and motor. "All nervous centres," says Dr. Hughlings Jackson,[6] "from the lowest to the very highest (the) substrata of consciousness), are made up of nothing else than nervous arrangements, representing impressions and movements. . . I do not see of what other materials the brain can be made." Meynert represents the matter similarly when he calls the cortex of the hemispheres the surface of projection for every muscle and every sensitive point of the body. The muscles and the sensitive points are represented each by a cortical point, and the brain is nothing but the sum of all these cortical points, to which, on the mental side, as many ideas correspond. Ideas of sensation, ideas of motion are, on the other hand, the elementary factors out of which the mind is built up by the associationists in psychology. There is a complete parallelism between the two analyses, the same diagram of little dots, circles, or triangles joined by lines symbolizes equally well the cerebral and mental processes : the dots stand for cells or ideas, the lines for fibres or associations. We shall have later to criticise this analysis so far as it relates to the mind; but there is no doubt that it is a most convenient, and has been a most useful, hypothesis, formulating the facts in an extremely natural way.

If, then, we grant that motor and sensory ideas variously associated are the materials of the mind, all we need do to get a complete diagram of the mind's and the brain's relations should be to ascertain which sensory idea corresponds to which sensational surface of projection, and which motor idea to which muscular surface of projection. The associations would then correspond to the fibrous connections between the various surfaces. This distinct cerebral localization of the various elementary sorts of idea has been treated as a 'postulate' by many physiologists (e.g. Munk); and the most stirring controversy in nerve-physiology which the present generation has seen has been the localization-question.

The Localization of Functions in the Hemispheres.

Up to 1870, the opinion which prevailed was that which the experiments of Flourens on pigeons' brains had made plausible, namely, that the different functions of the hemispheres were not locally separated, but carried on each by the aid of the whole organ. Hitzig in 1870 showed, however, that in a dog's brain highly specialized movements could be produced by electric irritation of determinate regions of the cortex; and Ferrier and Munk, half a dozen years later, seemed to prove, either by irritations or excisions or both, that there were equally determinate regions connected with the senses of sight, touch, hearing, and smell. Munk's special sensorial localizations, however, disagreed with Ferrier's; and Goltz, from his extirpation-experiments, came to a conclusion adverse to strict localization of any kind. The controversy is not yet over. I will not pretend to say anything more of it historically, but give a brief account of the condition in which matters at present stand.

The one thing which is perfectly well established is this, that the 'central' convolutions, on either side of the fissure of Rolando, and (at least in the monkey) the calloso-marginal convolution (which is continuous with them on the mesial surface where one hemisphere is applied against the other), form the region by which all the motor incitations which leave the cortex pass out, on their way to those executive centres in the region of the pons, medulla, and spinal cord from which the muscular contractions are discharged in the last resort. The existence of this so-called 'motor zone' is established by the lines of evidence successively given below:

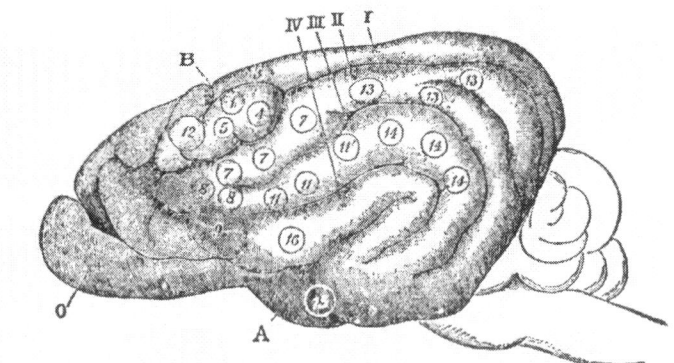

FIG. 5.—Left Hemisphere of Dog's Brain, after Ferrier. A, the fissure of Sylvius. B, the crucial sulcus. O, the olfactory bulb. I, II, III, IV, indicate the first, second, third, and fourth external convolutions respectively. (1), (4), and (5) are on the sigmoid gyrus.

(1) Cortical Irritations. Electrical currents of small intensity applied to the surface of the said convolutions in dogs, monkeys, and other animals, produce well-defined movements in face, fore-limb, hind-limb, tail, or trunk, according as one point or another of the surface is irritated. These movements affect almost invariably the side opposite to the brain irritations : If the left hemisphere be excited, the movement is of the right leg, side of face, etc. All the objections at first raised against the validity of these experiments have been overcome. The movements are certainly not due to irritations of the base of the brain by the downward spread of the current, for: a) mechanical irritations will produce them, though less easily than electrical; b) shifting the electrodes to a point close by on the surface changes the movement in ways quite inexplicable by changed physical conduction of the current; c) if the cortical 'centre' for a certain movement be cut under with a sharp knife but left in situ, although the electric conductivity is physically unaltered by the operation, the physiological conductivity is gone and currents of the same strength no longer produce the movements which they did; d) the time-interval between the application of the electric stimulus to the cortex and the resultant movement is what it would be if the cortex acted physiologically and not merely physically in transmitting the irritation. It is namely a well-known fact that when a nerve-current has to pass through the spinal cord to excite a muscle by reflex action, the time is longer than if it passes directly down the motor nerve: the cells of the cord take a certain time to discharge. Similarly, when a stimulus is applied directly to the cortex the muscle contracts two or three hundredths of a second later than it does when the place on the cortex is cut away and the electrodes are applied to the white fibres below.[7]

(2) Cortical Ablations. When the cortical spot which is found to produce a movement of the fore-leg, in a dog, is excised (see spot 5 in Fig. 5), the leg in question becomes peculiarly affected. At first it seems paralyzed. Soon, however, it is used with the other legs, but badly. The animal does not bear his weight on it, allows it to rest on its dorsal surface, stands with it crossing the other leg, does not remove it if it hangs over the edge of a table, can no longer 'give the paw' at word of command if able to do so before the operation, does not use it for scratching the ground, or holding a bone as formerly, lets it slip out when running on a smooth surface or when shaking himself, etc., etc. Sensibility of all kinds seems diminished as well as motility, but of this I shall speak later on. Moreover the dog tends in voluntary movements to swerve towards the side of the brain-lesion instead of going straight forward. All these symptoms gradually decrease, so that even with a very severe brain-lesion the dog may be outwardly indistinguishable from a well dog after eight or ten weeks. Still, a slight chloroformization will reproduce the disturbances, even then. There is a certain appearance of ataxic in-coördination in the movements -the dog lifts his

fore-feet high and brings them down with more strength than usual, and yet the trouble is not ordinary lack of co-ordination.
Neither is there paralysis. The strength of whatever movements are made is as great as ever-dogs with extensive destruction of the motor zone can jump as high and bite as hard as ever they did, but they seem less easily moved to do anything with the affected parts. Dr. Loeb, who has studied the motor disturbances of dogs more carefully than any one, conceives of them en masse as effects of an increased inertia in all the processes of innervation towards the side opposed to the lesion. All such movements require an unwonted effort for their execution; and when only the normally usual effort is made they fall behind in effectiveness.[8]

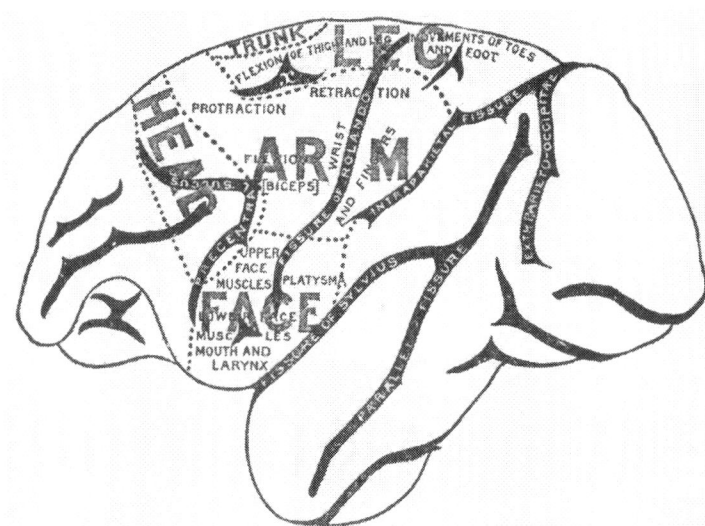

FIG. 6.—Left Hemisphere of Monkey's Brain. Outer Surface.

Even when the entire motor zone of a dog is removed, there is no permanent paralysis of any part, but only this curious sort of relative inertia when the two sides of the body are compared; and this itself becomes hardly noticeable after a number of weeks have elapsed. Prof Goltz has described a dog whose entire left hemisphere was destroyed, and who retained only a slight motor inertia on the right half of the body. In particular he could use his right paw for holding a bone whilst gnawing it, or for reaching after a piece of meat.
Had he been taught to give his paw before the operations, it would have been curious to see whether that faculty also came back. His tactile sensibility was permanently diminished on the right side.[9] In monkeys a genuine paralysis follows upon ablations of the cortex in the motor region. This paralysis affects parts of the body which vary with the brain-parts removed. The monkey's opposite arm or leg hangs flaccid, or at most takes a small part in associated movements. When the entire region is removed there is a genuine and permanent hemiplegia in which the arm is more affected than the leg; and this is followed months later by contracture of the muscles, as in man after inveterate hemiplegia.[10] According to Schaefer and Horsley, the trunk-muscles also become paralyzed after destruction of the marginal convolution on both sides (see Fig. 7). These differences between dogs and monkeys show the danger of drawing general conclusions from experiments done on any one sort of animal. I subjoin the figures given by the last-named authors of the motor regions in the monkey's brain.[11]

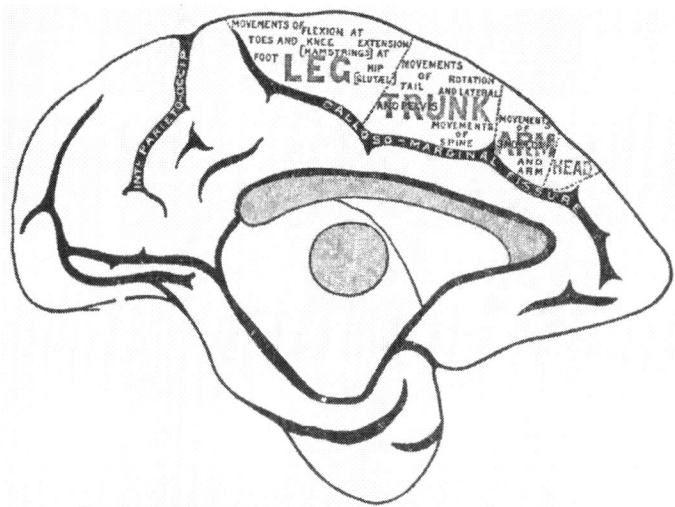

Fig. 7.—Left Hemisphere of Monkey's Brain. Mesial Surface.

In man we are necessarily reduced to the observation post-mortem of cortical ablations produced by accident or disease (tumor, hemorrhage, softening, etc.). What results during life from such conditions is either localized spasm, or palsy of certain muscles of the opposite side. The cortical regions which invariably produce these results are homologous with those which we have just been studying in the dog, cat, ape, etc. Figs. 8 and 9 show the result of 169 cases carefully studied by Exner. The parts shaded are regions where lesions produced no motor disturbance. Those left white were, on the contrary, never injured without motor disturbances of some sort.

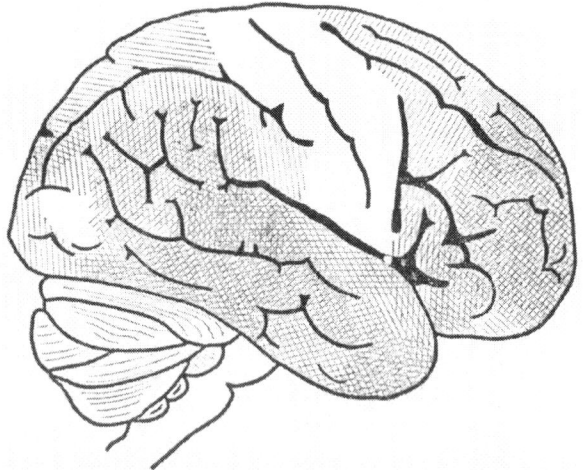

Fig. 8.—Right Hemisphere of Human Brain. Lateral Surface.

Where the injury to the cortical substance is profound in man, the paralysis is permanent and is succeeded by muscular rigidity in the paralyzed parts, just as it may be in the monkey.

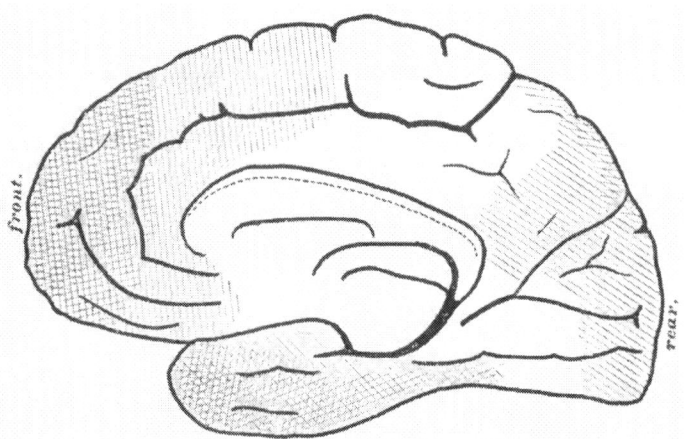

Fig. 9.—Right Hemisphere of Human Brain. Mesial Surface.

(3)   Descending degenerations show the intimate connection of the rolandic regions of the cortex with the motor tracts of the cord. When, either in man or in the lower animals, these regions are destroyed, a peculiar degenerative change known as secondary sclerosis is found to extend downwards through the white fibrous substance of the brain in a perfectly definite manner, affecting certain distinct strands which pass through the inner capsule, crura, and pons, into the anterior pyramids of the medulla oblongata, and from thence (partly crossing to the other side) downwards into the anterior (direct) and lateral (crossed) columns of the spinal cord.

(4)   Anatomical proof of the continuity of the rolandic regions with these motor columns of the cord is also clearly given. Flechsig's 'Pyramidenbahn' forms an uninterrupted strand (distinctly traceable in human embryos, before its fibres have acquired their white 'medullary sheath') passing upwards from the pyramids of the medulla, and traversing the internal capsule and corona radiata to the convolutions in question (Fig. 10). None of the inferior gray matter of the brain seems to have any connection with this important fibrous strand. It passes directly from the cortex to the motor arrangements in the cord, depending for its proper nutrition (as the facts of degeneration show) on the influence of the cortical cells, just as motor nerves depend for their nutrition on that of the cells of the spinal cord. Electrical stimulation of this motor strand in any accessible part of its course has been shown in dogs to produce movements analogous to those which excitement of the cortical surface calls forth.

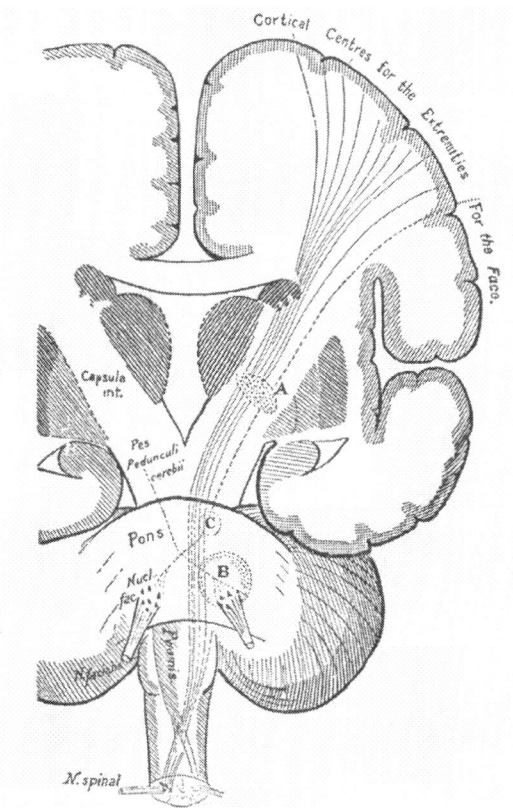

Fig. 10.—Schematic Transverse Section of Brain showing Motor Strand.—After Edinger.

One of the most instructive proofs of motor localization in the cortex is that furnished by the disease now called aphemia, or motor Aphasia. Motor aphasia is neither loss of voice nor paralysis of the tongue or lips. The patient's voice is as strong as ever, and all the innervations of his hypoglossal and facial nerves, except those necessary for speaking, may go on perfectly well. He can laugh and cry, and even sing; but he either is unable to utter any words at all; or a few meaningless stock phrases form his only speech ; or else he speaks incoherently and confusedly, mispronouncing, misplacing, and misusing his words in various degrees. Sometimes his speech is a mere broth of unintelligible syllables. In cases of pure motor aphasia the patient recognizes his mistakes and suffers acutely from them.

Now whenever a patient dies in such a condition as this, and an examination of his brain is permitted, it is found that the lowest frontal gyrus (see Fig. 11) is the seat of injury. Broca first noticed this fact in 1861, and since then the gyrus has gone by the name of Broca's convolution.

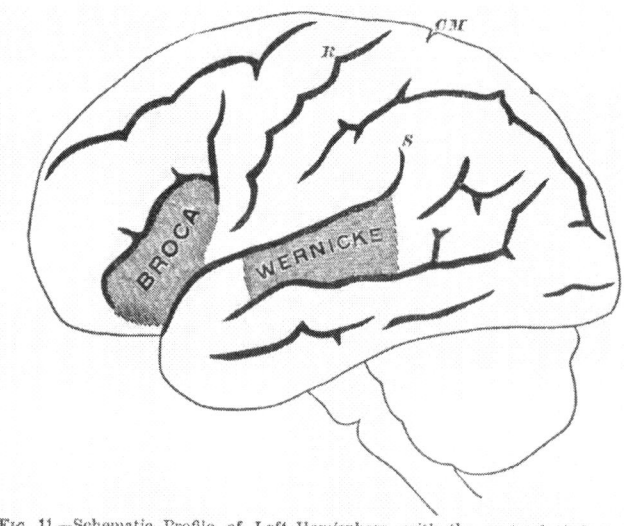

Fig. 11.—Schematic Profile of Left Hemisphere, with the parts shaded whose destruction causes motor ('Broca') and sensory ('Wernicke') Aphasia.

The injury in right-handed people is found on the left hemisphere, and in left-handed people on the right hemisphere. Most people, in fact, are left-brained, that is, all their delicate and specialized movements are handed over to the charge of the left hemisphere. The ordinary right-handedness for such movements is only a consequence of that fact, a consequence which shows outwardly on account of that extensive decussation of the fibres whereby most of those from the left hemisphere pass to the right half of the body only. But the left-brainedness might exist in equal measure and not show outwardly. This would happen wherever organs on both sides of the body could be governed by the left hemisphere; and just such a case seems offered by the vocal organs, in that highly delicate and special motor service which we call speech. Either hemisphere can innervate them bilaterally, just as either seems able to innervate bilaterally the muscles of the trunk, ribs, and diaphragm. Of the special movements of speech, however, it would appear (from the facts of aphasia) that the left hemisphere in most persons habitually takes exclusive charge. With that hemisphere thrown out of gear, speech is undone; even though the opposite hemisphere still be there for the performance of less specialized acts, such as the various movements required in eating.

It will be noticed that Broca's region is homologous with the parts ascertained to produce movements of the lips, tongue, and larynx when excited by electric currents in apes (cf. Fig. 6). The evidence is therefore as complete as it well can be that the motor incitations to these organs leave the brain by the lower frontal region.

Victims of motor aphasia generally have other disorders. One which interests us in this connection has been called agraphia: they have lost the power to write. They can read writing and understand it; but either cannot use the pen at all or make egregious mistakes with it. The seat of the lesion here is less well determined, owing to an insufficient number of good cases to conclude from.[12] There is no doubt, however, that it is (in right-handed people) on the left side, and little doubt that it consists of elements of the hand-and-arm region specialized for that service. The symptom may exist when there is little or no disability in the hand for other uses. If it does not get well, the patient usually educates his right hemisphere, i.e. learns to write with his left hand. In other cases of which we shall say more a few pages later on, the patient can write both spontaneously and at dictation, but cannot read even what he has himself written! All these phenomena are now quite clearly explained by separate brain-centres for the various feelings and movements and tracts for associating these together. But their minute discussion belongs to medicine rather than to general psychology, and I can only use them here to illustrate the principles of motor localization.[13] Under the heads of sight and hearing I shall have a little more to say.

The different lines of proof which I have taken up establish conclusively the proposition that all the motor impulses which leave the cortex pass out, in healthy animals, from the convolutions about the fissure of Rolando.

When, however, it comes to defining precisely what is involved in a motor impulse leaving the cortex, things grow more obscure. Does the impulse start independently from the convolutions in question, or does it start elsewhere and merely flow through? And to what particular phase of psychic activity does the activity of these centres correspond? Opinions and authorities here divide; but it will be better, before entering into these deeper aspects of the problem, to cast a glance at the facts which have been made out concerning the relations of the cortex to sight, hearing, and smell.

Sight.

Ferrier was the first in the field here. He found, when the angular convolution (that lying between the 'intra parietal' and 'external occipital' fissures, and bending round the top of the fissure of Sylvius, in Fig. 6) was excited in the monkey, that movements of the eyes and head as if for vision occurred; and that when it was extirpated, what he supposed to be total and permanent blindness of the opposite eye followed. Munk almost immediately declared total and permanent blindness to follow from destruction of the occipital lobe in monkeys as well as dogs, and said that the angular gyrus had nothing to do with sight, but was only the centre for tactile sensibility of the eyeball. Munk's absolute tone about his observations and his theoretic arrogance have led to his ruin as an authority. But he did two things of permanent value. He was the first to distinguish in these vivisections between sensorial and psychic blindness, and to describe the phenomenon of restitution of the visual function after its first impairment by an operation; and the first to notice the hemiopic character of the visual disturbances which result when only one hemisphere is injured. Sensorial blindness is absolute insensibility to light; psychic blindness is inability to recognize the meaning of the optical impressions, as when we see a page of Chinese print but it suggests nothing to us. A hemiopic disturbance of vision is one in which neither retina is affected in its totality, but in which, for example, the left portion of each retina is blind, so that the animal sees nothing situated in space towards its right. Later observations have corroborated this hemiopic character of all the disturbances of sight from injury to a single hemisphere in the higher animals; and the question whether an animal's apparent blindness is sensorial or only psychic has, since Munk's first publications, been the most urgent one to answer, in all observations relative to the function of sight.

Goltz almost simultaneously with Ferrier and Munk reported experiments which led him to deny that the visual function was essentially bound up with any one localized portion of the hemispheres. Other divergent results soon came in from many quarters, so that, without going into the history of the matter any more, I may report the existing state of the case as follows:[14]

In fishes, frogs, and lizards vision persists when the hemispheres are entirely removed. This is admitted for frogs and fishes even by Munk, who denies it for birds.

All of Munk's birds seemed totally blind (blind sensorially) after removal of the hemispheres by his operation. The following of a candle by the head and winking at a threatened blow, which are ordinarily held to prove the retention of crude optical sensations by the lower centres in supposed hemisphereless pigeons, are by Munk ascribed to vestiges of the visual sphere of the cortex left behind by the imperfection of the operation. But Schrader, who operated after Munk and with every apparent guarantee of completeness, found that all his pigeons saw after two or three weeks had elapsed, and the inhibitions resulting from the wound had passed away. They invariably avoided even the slightest obstacles, flew very regularly towards certain perches, etc., differing toto coelo in these respects with certain simply blinded pigeons who were kept with them for comparison. They did not pick up food strewn on the ground, however. Schrader found that they would do this if even a small part of the frontal region of the hemispheres was left, and ascribes their non-self-feeding when deprived of their occipital cerebrum not to a visual, but to a motor, defect, a sort of alimentary aphasia.[15]

In presence of such discord as that between Munk and his opponents one must carefully note how differently significant is loss, from preservation, of a function after an operation on the brain. The loss of the function does not necessarily show that it is dependent on the part cut out; but its preservation does show that it is not dependent: and this is true though the loss should be observed ninety-nine times and the preservation only once in a hundred similar excisions. That birds and mammals can be blinded by cortical ablation is undoubted; the only question is, must they be so? Only then can the cortex be certainly called the 'seat of sight.' The blindness may always be due to one of those remote effects of the wound on distant parts, inhibitions, extensions of inflammation,-interferences, in a word,- upon which Brown-Séquard and Goltz have rightly insisted, and the importance of which becomes more manifest every day. Such effects are transient; whereas the symptoms of deprivation (Ausfallserscheinungen, as Goltz calls them) which come from the actual loss of the cut-out region must from the nature of the case be permanent. Blindness in the pigeons, so far as it passes away, cannot possibly be charged to their seat of vision being lost, but only to some influence which temporarily depresses the activity of that seat. The same is true mutatis mutandis of all the other effects of operations, and as we pass to mammals we shall see still more the importance of the remark.

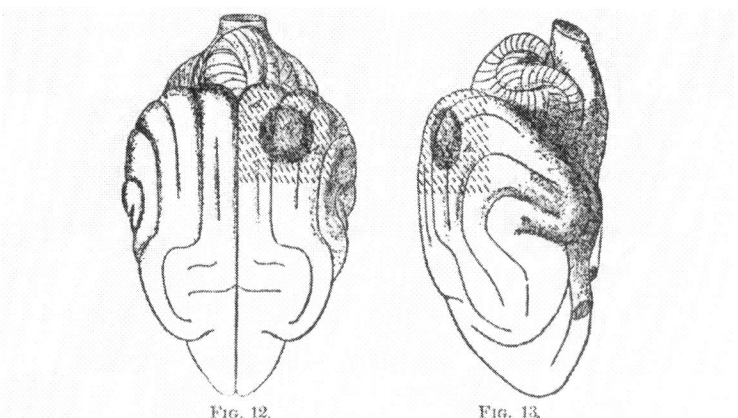

Fig. 12. Fig. 13.
The Dog's visual centre according to Munk, the entire striated region, A, A, being the exclusive seat of vision, and the dark central circle, A', being correlated with the retinal centre of the opposite eye.

In rabbits loss of the entire cortex seems compatible with the preservation of enough sight to guide the poor animals' movements, and enable them to avoid obstacles. Christiani's observations and discussions seem conclusively to have established this, although Munk found that all his animals were made totally blind.[16]

In dogs also Munk found absolute stone-blindness after ablation of the occipital lobes. He went farther and mapped out determinate portions of the cortex thereupon, which he considered correlated with definite segments of the two retinae, so that destruction of given portions of the cortex produces blindness of the retinal centre, top, bottom, or right or left side, of the same or opposite eye. There seems little doubt that this definite correlation is mythological. Other observers, Hitzig, Goltz, Luciani, Loeb, Exner, etc., find, whatever part of the cortex may be ablated on one side, that there usually results a hemiopic disturbance of both eyes, slight and transient when the anterior lobes are the parts attacked, grave when an occipital lobe is the seat of injury, and lasting in proportion to the latter's extent. According to Loeb, the defect is a dimness of vision ('hemiamblyopia') in which (however severe) the centres remain the best seeing portions of the retina, just as they are in normal dogs. The lateral or temporal part of each retina seems to be in exclusive connection with the cortex of its own side. The centre and nasal part of each seems, on the contrary, to be connected with the cortex of the opposite hemispheres. Loeb, who takes broader views than any one, conceives the hemiamblyopia as he conceives the motor disturbances, namely, as the expression of an increased inertia in the whole optical machinery, of which the result is to make the animal respond with greater effort to impressions coming from the half of space opposed to the side of the lesion. If a dog has right hemiamblyopia, say, and two pieces of meat are hung before him at once, he invariably turns first to the one on his left. But if the lesion be a slight one, shaking slightly the piece of meat on his right (this makes of it a stronger stimulus) makes him seize upon it first. If only one piece of meat be offered, he takes it, on whichever side it be.

When both occipital lobes are extensively destroyed total blindness may result. Munk maps out his 'Sehsphäre' definitely, and says that blindness must result when the entire shaded part, marked A, A, in Figs. 12 and 13, is involved in the lesion. Discrepant reports of other observations he explains as due to incomplete ablation. Luciani, Goltz, and Lannegrace, however, contend that they have made complete bilateral extirpations of Munk's Sehsphäre more than once, and found a sort of crude indiscriminating sight of objects to return in a few weeks.[17]

The question whether a dog is blind or not is harder to solve than would at first appear; for simply blinded dogs, in places to which they are accustomed, show little of their loss and avoid all obstacles; whilst dogs whose occipital lobes are gone may run against things frequently and yet see notwithstanding. The best proof that they may see is that which Goltz's dogs furnished: they carefully avoided, as it seemed, strips of sunshine or paper on the floor, as if they were solid obstacles. This no really blind dog would do. Luciani tested his dogs when hungry (a condition which sharpens their attention) by strewing pieces of meat and pieces of cork before them. If they went straight at them, they saw; and if they chose the meat and left the cork, they saw discriminatingly. The quarrel is very acrimonious; indeed the subject of localization of functions in the brain seems to have a peculiar effect on the temper of those who cultivate it experimentally. The amount of preserved vision which Goltz and Luciani report seems hardly to be worth considering, on the one hand; and on the other, Munk admits in his penultimate paper that out of 85 dogs he only 'succeeded' 4 times in his operation of producing complete blindness by complete extirpation of his 'Sehsphäre'.[18] The safe conclusion for us is that Luciani's diagram, Fig. 14, represents something like the truth.

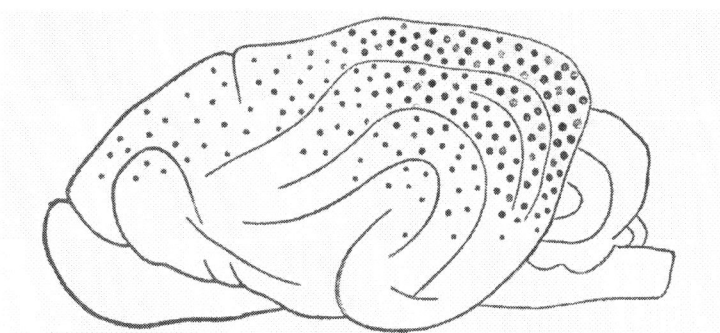
Fig. 14.—Distribution of the Visual Function in the Cortex, according to Luciani.

The occipital lobes are far more important for vision than any other part of the cortex, so that their complete destruction makes the animal almost blind. As for the crude sensibility to light which may then remain, nothing exact is known either about its nature or its seat.
In the monkey, doctors also disagree. The truth seems, however, to be that the occipital lobes in this animal also are the part connected most intimately with the visual function. The function would seem to go on when very small portions of them are left, for Ferrier found no 'appreciable impairment' of it after almost complete destruction of them on both sides. On the other hand, he found complete and permanent blindness to ensue when they and the angular gyri in addition were destroyed on both sides. Munk, as well as Brown and Schaefer, found no disturbance of sight from destroying the angular gyri alone, although Ferrier found blindness to ensue. This blindness was probably due to inhibitions exerted in distans, or to cutting of the white optical fibres passing under the angular gyri on their way to the occipital lobes. Brown and Schaefer got complete and permanent blindness in one monkey from total destruction of both occipital lobes. Luciani and Seppili, performing this operation on two monkeys, found that the animals were only mentally, not sensorially, blind. After some weeks they saw their food, but could not distinguish by sight between figs and pieces of cork. Luciani and Seppili seem, however, not to have extirpated the entire lobes. When one lobe only is injured the affection of sight is hemiopic in monkeys: in this all observers agree. On the whole, then, Munk's original location of vision in the occipital lobes is confirmed by the later evidence.[19]
In man we have more exact results, since we are not driven to interpret the vision from the outward conduct. On the other hand, however, we cannot vivisect, but must wait for pathological lesions to turn up. The pathologists who have discussed these (the literature is tedious ad libitum) conclude that the occipital lobes are the indispensable part for vision in man. Hemiopic disturbance in both eyes comes from lesion of either one of them, and total blindness, sensorial as well as psychic, from destruction of both.
Hemiopia may also result from lesion in other parts, especially the neighboring angular and supra-marginal gyri, and it may accompany extensive injury in the motor region of the cortex. In these cases it seems probable that it is due to an actio in distans, probably to the interruption of fibres proceeding from the occipital lobe. There seem to be a few cases on record where there was injury to the occipital lobes without visual defect. Ferrier has collected as many as possible to prove his localization in the angular gyrus.[20] A strict application of logical principles would make one of these cases outweigh one hundred contrary ones. And yet, remembering how imperfect observations may be, and how individual brains may vary, it would certainly be rash for their sake to throw away the enormous amount of positive evidence for the occipital lobes. Individual variability is always a possible explanation of an anomalous case. There is no more prominent anatomical fact than that of the 'decussation of the pyramids,' nor any more usual pathological fact than its consequence, that left-handed hemorrhages into the motor region produce right-handed paralyses. And yet the decussation is variable in amount, and seems sometimes to be absent altogether.[21] If, in such a case as this last, the left brain were to become the seat of apoplexy, the left and not the right half of the body would be the one to suffer paralysis.
The schema on the opposite page, copied from Dr.Seguin, expresses, on the whole, the probable truth about the regions concerned in vision. Not the entire occipital lobes, but the so-called cunei, and the first convolutions, are the cortical parts most intimately concerned. Nothnagel agrees with Seguin in this limitation of the essential tracts.[22]
A most interesting effect of cortical disorder is mental blindness. This consists not so much in insensibility to optical impressions, as in inability to understand them. Psychologically it is interpretable as loss of associations between optical sensations and what they signify; and any interruption of the paths between the optic centres and the centres for other ideas ought to bring it about. Thus,printed letters of the alphabet, or words, signify certain sounds and certain articulatory movements. If the connection between the articulating or auditory centres, on the one hand, and the visual centres on the other, be ruptured, we ought a priori to expect that the sight of words would fail to awaken the idea of their sound, or the movement for pronouncing them.

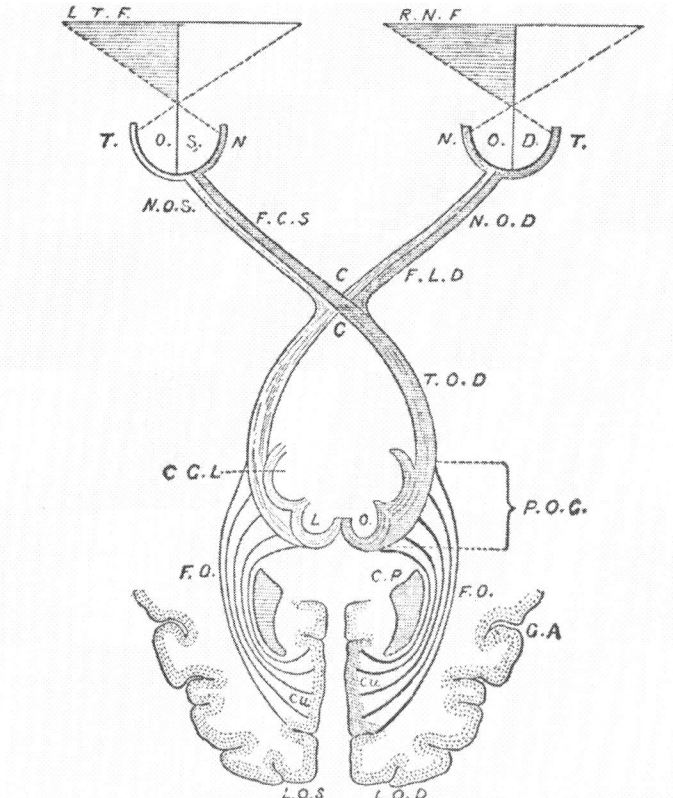

Fig. 15.—Scheme of the mechanism of vision, after Seguin. The *cuneus* convolution (Cu) of the right occipital lobe is supposed to be injured, and all the parts which lead to it are darkly shaded to show that they fail to exert their function. F. O. are the intra-hemispheric optical fibres. P. O. C. is the region of the lower optic centres (corpora geniculata and quadrigemina). T. O. D. is the right optic tract; C, the chiasma; F. L. D. are the fibres going to the lateral or temporal half T of the right retina; and F. C. S are those going to the central or nasal half of the left retina. O. D. is the right, and O S. the left eyeball. The rightward half of each is therefore blind: in other words, the right nasal field, R. N. F., and the left temporal field, L. T. F., have become invisible to the subject with the lesion at Cu.

We ought, in short, to have alexia, or inability to read: and this is just what we do have in many cases of extensive injury about the fronto-temporal regions, as a complication of aphasic disease. Nothnagel suggests that whilst the cuneus is the seat of optical sensations, the other parts of the occipital lobe may be the field of optical memories and ideas, from the loss of which mental blindness should ensue. In fact, all the medical authors speak of mental blindness as if it must consist in the loss of visual images from the memory. It seems to me, however, that this is a psychological misapprehension. A man whose power of visual imagination has decayed (no unusual phenomenon in its lighter grades) is not mentally blind in the least, for he recognizes perfectly all that he sees. On the other hand, he may be mentally blind, with his optical imagination well preserved; as in the interesting case publislied by Wilbrand in 1887.[23] In the still more interesting case of mental blindness recently published by Lissauer,[24] though the patient made the most ludicrous mistakes, calling for instance a clothes-brush a pair of spectacles, an umbrella a plant with flowers, an apple a portrait of a lady, etc. etc., he seemed, according to the reporter, to have his mental images fairly well preserved. It is in fact the momentary loss of our non-optical images which makes us mentally blind, just as it is that of our non-auditory images which makes us mentally deaf. I am mentally deaf if, hearing a bell, I can't recall how it looks; and mentally blind if, seeing it, I can't recall its sound or its name. As a matter of fact, I should have to be not merely mentally blind, but stone-blind, if all my visual images were lost. For although I am blind to the right half of the field of view if my left occipital region is injured, and to the left half if my right region is injured, such hemianopsia does not deprive me of visual images, experience seeming to show that the unaffected hemisphere is always sufficient for production of these. To abolish them entirely I should have to be deprived of both occipital lobes, and that would deprive me not only of my inward images of sight, but of my sight altogether.[25] Recent pathological annals seem to offer a few such cases.[26] Meanwhile there are a number of cases of mental blindness, especially for written language, coupled with hemianopsia, usually of the rightward field of view. These are all explicable by the breaking down, through disease, of the connecting tracts between the occipital lobes and other parts of the brain, especially those which go to the centres for speech in the frontal and temporal regions of the left hemisphere. They are to be classed among disturbances of conduction or of association; and nowhere can I find any fact which should force us to believe that optical images need[27] be lost in mental blindness, or that the cerebral centres for such images are locally distinct from those for direct sensations from the eyes.[28]

Where an object fails to be recognized by sight, it often happens that the patient will recognize and name it as soon as he touches it with his hand. This shows in an interesting way how numerous the associative paths are which all end by running out of the brain through the channel of speech. The hand-path is open, though the eye-path be closed. When mental blindness is most complete, neither sight, touch, nor sound avails to steer the patient, and a sort of dementia which has been called asymbolia or apraxia is the result. The commonest articles are not understood. The patient will put his breeches on one shoulder and his hat upon the other, will bite into the soap and lay his shoes on the table, or take his food into his hand and throw it down again, not knowing what to do with it, etc. Such disorder can only come from extensive brain-injury.[29]

The method of degeneration corroborates the other evidence localizing the tracts of vision. In young animals one gets secondary degeneration of the occipital regions from destroying an eyeball, and, vice versa, degeneration of the optic nerves from destroying the occipital regions. The corpora geniculata, thalami, and subcortical fibres leading to the occipital lobes are also found atrophied in these cases. The phenomena are not uniform, but are indisputable;[30] so that, taking all lines of evidence together, the special connection of vision with the occipital lobes is perfectly made out. It should be added that the occipital lobes have frequently been found shrunken in cases of inveterate blindness in man.

Hearing.

Hearing is hardly as definitely localized as sight. In the dog, Luciani's diagram will show the regions which directly or indirectly affect it for the worse when injured. As with sight, one-sided lesions produce symptoms on both sides. The mixture of black dots and gray dots in the diagram is meant to represent this mixture of 'crossed' and 'uncrossed' connections, though of course no topographical exactitude is aimed at. Of all the region, the temporal lobe is the most important part; yet permanent absolute deafness did not result in a dog of Luciani's, even from bilateral destruction of both temporal lobes in their entirety.[31]

In the monkey, Ferrier and Yeo once found permanent deafness to follow destruction of the upper temporal convolution (the one just below the fissure of Sylvius in Fig.6) on both sides. Brown and Schaefer found, on the contrary, that in several monkeys this operation failed to noticeably affect the hearing. In one animal, indeed, both entire temporal lobes were destroyed. After a week or two of depression of the mental faculties this beast recovered and became one of the brightest monkeys possible, domineering over all his mates, and admitted by all who saw him to have all his senses, including hearing, 'perfectly acute.'[32] Terrible recriminations have, as usual, ensued between the investigators, Ferrier denying that Brown and Schaefer's ablations were complete,[33] Schaefer that Ferrier's monkey was really deaf.[34] In this unsatisfactory condition the subject must be left, although there seems no reason to doubt that Brown and Schaefer's observation is the more important of the two.

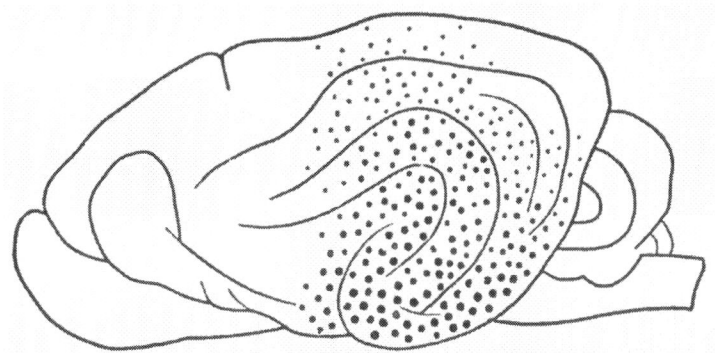

FIG. 16.—Luciani's Hearing Region.

In man the temporal lobe is unquestionably, the seat of the hearing function, and the superior convolution adjacent to the sylvian fissure is its most important part. The phenomena of aphasia show this. We studied motor aphasia a few pages back; we must now consider sensory aphasia.

Our knowledge of this disease has had three stages: we may talk of the period of Broca, the period of Wernicke, and the period of Charcot. What Broca's discovery was we have seen. Wernicke was the first to discriminate those cases in which the patient can not even understand speech from those in which he can understand, only not talk; and to ascribe the former condition to lesion of the temporal lobe.[35] The condition in question is word-deafness, and the disease is auditory aphasia. The latest statistical survey of the subject is that by Dr. Allen Starr.[36] In the seven cases of pure word-deafness which he has collected, cases in which the patient could read, talk, and write, but not understand what was said to him, the lesion was limited to the first and second temporal convolutions in their posterior two thirds. The lesion (in right-handed, i.e. left-brained, persons) is always on the left side, like the lesion in motor aphasia. Crude hearing would not be abolished, even were the left centre for it utterly destroyed; the right centre would still provide for that. But the linguistic use of hearing appears bound up with the integrity of the left centre more or less exclusively. Here it must be that words heard enter into association with the things which they represent, on the one hand, and with the movements necessary for pronouncing them, on the other. In a large majority of Dr. Starr's fifty cases, the power either to name objects or to talk coherently was impaired. This shows that in most of us (as Wernicke said) speech must go on from auditory cues; that is, it must be that our ideas do not innervate our motor centres directly, but only after first arousing the mental sound of the words. This is the immediate stimulus to articulation; and where the possibility of this is abolished by the destruction of its usual channel in the left temporal lobe, the articulation must suffer. In the few cases in which the channel is abolished with no bad effect on speech we must suppose an idiosyncrasy. The patient must innervate his speech-organs either from the corresponding portion of the other hemisphere or directly from the centres of ideation, those, namely, of vision, touch, etc., without leaning on the auditory region. It is the minuter analysis of the facts in the light of such individual differences as these which constitutes Charcot's contribution towards clearing up the subject.

Every namable thing, act, or relation has numerous properties, qualities, or aspects. In our minds the properties of each thing, together with its name, form an associated group. If different parts of the brain are severally concerned with the several properties, and a farther part with the hearing, and still another with the uttering, of the name, there must inevitably be brought about (through the law of association which we shall later study) such a dynamic connection amongst all these brain-parts that the activity of anyone of them will be likely to awaken the activity of all the rest. When we are talking as we think, the ultimate process is that of utterance. If the brain-part for that be injured, speech is impossible or disorderly, even though all the other brain-parts be intact: and this is just the condition of things which we found to be brought about by limited lesion of the left inferior frontal convolution. But back of that last act various orders of succession are possible in the associations of a talking man's ideas. The more usual order seems to be from the tactile, visual, or other properties of the things thought-about to the sound of their names, and then to the latter's utterance. But if in a certain individual the thought of the look of an object or of the look of its printed name be the process which habitually precedes articulation, then the loss of the hearing centre will pro tanto not affect that individual's speech. He will be mentally deaf, i.e. his understanding of speech will suffer, but he will not be aphasic. In this way it is possible to explain the seven cases of pure word-deafness which figure in Dr. Starr's table.

If this order of association be ingrained and habitual in that individual, injury to his visual centres will make him not only word-blind, but aphasic as well. His speech will become confused in consequence of an occipital lesion. Naunyn, consequently, plotting out on a diagram of the hemisphere the 71 irreproachably reported cases of aphasia which he was able to collect, finds that the lesions concentrate themselves in three places: first, on Broca's, centre; second, on Wernicke's; third, on the supra-marginal and angular gyri under which those fibres pass which connect the visual centres with the rest of the brain [37](see Fig. 17). With this result Dr. Starr's analysis of purely sensory cases agrees.

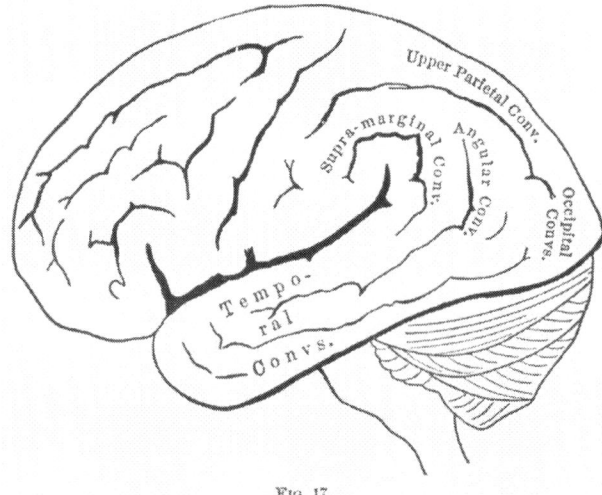

FIG. 17.

In a later chapter we shall again return to these differences in the effectiveness of the sensory spheres in different individuals. Meanwhile few things show more beautifully than the history of our knowledge of aphasia how the sagacity and patience of many banded workers are in time certain to analyze the darkest confusion into an orderly display.[38] There is no 'centre of Speech' in the brain any more than there is a faculty of Speech in the mind. The entire brain, more or less, is at work in a man who uses language. The subjoined diagram, from Ross, shows the four parts most critically concerned, and, in the light of our text, needs no farther explanation (see Fig. 18).

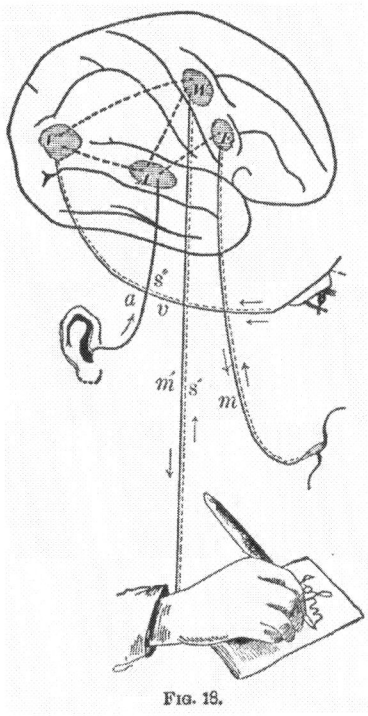
FIG. 18.

Smell.

Everything conspires to point to the median descending part of the temporal lobes as being the organs of smell. Even Ferrier and Munk agree on the hippocampal gyrus, though Ferrier restricts olfaction, as Munk does not to the lobule or uncinate process of the convolution, reserving the rest of it for touch.
Anatomy and pathology also point to the hippocampal gyrus; but as the matter is less interesting from the point of view of human psychology than were sight and hearing, I will say no more, but simply add Luciani and Seppili's diagram of the dog's smell-centre.[39]

Taste

Of we know little that is definite.[sic] What little there is points to the lower temporal regions again. Consult Ferrier as below.

Touch.

Interesting problems arise with regard to the seat of tactile and muscular sensibility. Hitzig, whose experiments on dogs' brains fifteen years ago opened the entire subject which we are discussing, ascribed the disorders of motility observed after ablations of the motor region to a loss of what he called muscular consciousness.

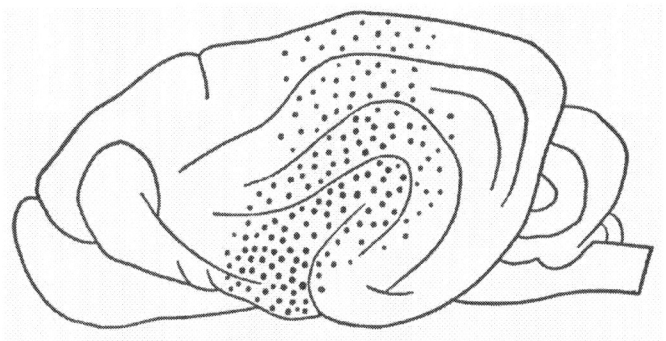
FIG. 19.—Luciani's Olfactory Region in the Dog.

The animals do not notice eccentric positions of their limbs, will stand with their legs crossed, with the affected paw resting on its back or hanging over a table's edge, etc.; and do not resist our bending and stretching of it as they resist with the unaffected paw. Goltz, Munk, Schiff, Herzen, and others promptly ascertained an equal defect of cutaneous sensibility to pain, touch, and cold. The paw is not withdrawn when pinched, remains standing in cold water, etc. Ferrier meanwhile denied that there was any true anaesthesia produced by ablations in the motor zone, and explains the appearance of it as an effect of the sluggish motor responses of the affected side.[40] Munk [41]and Schiff [42], on the contrary, conceive of the 'motor zone' as essentially sensory, and in different ways explain the motor disorders as secondary results of the anaesthesia which is always there. Munk calls the motor zone the Fühlsphäre of the animal's limbs, etc., and makes it coördinate with the Sehsphäre, the Hörsphäre, etc., the entire cortex being, according to him, nothing but a projection-surface for sensations, with no exclusively or essentially motor part. Such a view would be important if true, through its bearings on the psychology of volition. What is the truth? As regards the fact of cutaneous anaesthesia from motor-zone ablations, all other observers are against Ferrier, so that he is probably wrong in denying it. On the other hand, Munk and Schiff are wrong in making the motor symptoms depend on the anaesthesia, for in certain rare cases they have been observed to exist not only without insensibility, but with actual hyperaesthesia of the parts.[43] The motor and sensory symptoms seem, therefore, to be independent variables.

In monkeys the latest experiments are those of Horsley and Schaefer,[44] whose results Ferrier accepts. They find that excision of the hippocampal convolution produces transient insensibility of the opposite side of the body, and that permanent insensibility is produced by destruction of its continuation upwards above the corpus callosum, the so-called gyrus fornicatus (the part just below the 'calloso-marginal fissure' in Fig.7). The insensibility is at its maximum when the entire tract comprising both convolutions is destroyed. Ferrier says that the sensibility of monkeys is 'entirely unaffected' by ablations of the motor zone,[45] and Horsley and Schaefer consider it by no means necessarily abolished.[46] Luciani found it diminished in his three experiments on apes.[47] In man we have the fact that one-sided paralysis from disease of the opposite motor zone may or may not be accompanied with anaesthesia of the parts.

Luciani, who believes that the motor zone is also sensory, tries to minimize the value of this evidence by pointing to the insufficiency with which patients are examined. He himself believes that in dogs the tactile sphere extends backwards and forwards of the directly excitable region, into the frontal and parietal lobes (see Fig. 20). Nothnagel considers that pathological evidence points in the same direction;[48] and Dr. Mills, carefully reviewing the evidence, adds the gyri fornicatus and hippocampi to the cutaneo-muscular region in man.[49] If one compare Luciani's diagrams together (Figs. 14,16, 19, 20) one will see that the entire parietal region of the dog's skull is common to the four senses of sight, hearing, smell, and touch, including muscular feeling. The corresponding region in the human brain (upper parietal and supra-marginal gyri-see Fig. 17) seems to be a somewhat similar place of conflux. Optical aphasias and motor and tactile disturbances all result from its injury, especially when that is on the left side.[50] The lower we go in the animal scale the less differentiated the functions of the several brain-parts seem to be.[51] It may be that the region in question still represents in ourselves something like this primitive condition, and that the surrounding parts, in adapting themselves more and more to specialized and narrow functions, have left it as a sort of carrefour through which they send currents and converse. That it should be connected with musculo-cutaneous feeling is, however, no reason why the motor zone proper should not be so connected too. And the cases of paralysis from the motor zone with no accompanying anaesthesia may be explicable without denying all sensory function to that region. For, as my colleague Dr.James Putnam informs me, sensibility is always harder to kill than motility, even where we know for a certainty that the lesion affects tracts that are both sensory and motor. Persons whose hand is paralyzed in its movements from compression of arm-nerves during sleep, still feel with their fingers; and they may still feel in their feet when their legs are paralyzed by bruising of the spinal cord. In a similar way, the motor cortex might be sensitive as well as motor, and yet by this greater subtlety (or whatever the peculiarity may be) in the sensory currents, the sensibility might survive an amount of injury there by which the motility was destroyed. Nothnagel considers that there are grounds for supposing the muscular sense to be exclusively connected with the parietal lobe and not with the motor zone. "Disease of this lobe gives pure ataxy without palsy, and of the motor zone pure palsy without loss of muscular sense.[52]" He fails, however, to convince more competent critics than the present writer,[53] so I conclude with them that as yet we have no decisive grounds for locating muscular and cutaneous feeling apart. Much still remains to be learned about the relations between musculo-cutaneous sensibility and the cortex, but one thing is certain: that neither the occipital, the forward frontal, nor the temporal lobes seem to have anything essential to do with it in man. It is knit up with the performances of the motor zone and of the convolutions backwards and midwards of them. The reader must remember this conclusion when we come to the chapter on the Will.

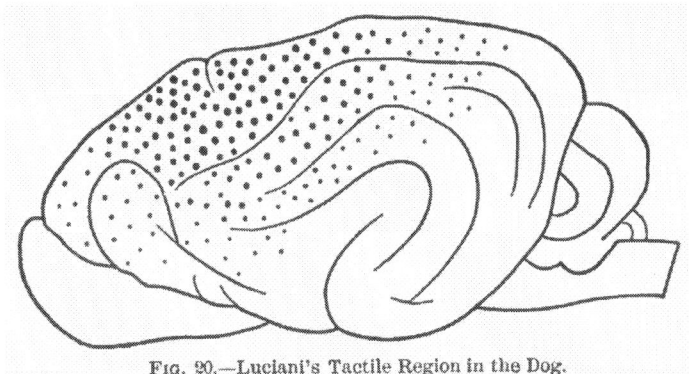
Fig. 90.—Luciani's Tactile Region in the Dog.

I must add a word about the connection of aphasia with the tactile sense. I spoke of those cases in which the patient can write but not read his own writing. He cannot read by his eyes ; but he can read by the feeling in his fingers, if he retrace the letters in the air. It is convenient for such a patient to have a pen in hand whilst reading in this way, in order to make the usual feeling of writing more complete.[54] In such a case we must suppose that the path between the optical and the graphic centres remains open, whilst that between the optical and the auditory and articulatory centres is closed. Only thus can we understand how the look of the writing should fail to suggest the sound of the words to the patient's mind, whilst it still suggests the proper movements of graphic imitation. These movements in their turn must of course be felt, and the feeling of them must be associated with the centres for hearing and pronouncing the words. The injury in cases like this where very special combinations fail, whilst others go on as usual, must always be supposed to be of the nature of increased resistance to the passage of certain currents of association. If any of the elements of mental function were destroyed the incapacity would necessarily be much more formidable. A patient who can both read and write with his fingers most likely uses an identical 'graphic' centre, at once sensory and motor, for both operations.

I have now given, as far as the nature of this book will allow, a complete account of the present state of the localization-question. In its main outlines it stands firm, though much has still to be discovered. The anterior frontal lobes, for example, so far as is yet known, have no definite functions. Goltz finds that dogs bereft of them both are incessantly in motion, and excitable by every small stimulus. They are irascible and amative in an extraordinary degree, and their sides grow bare with perpetual reflex scratching; but they show no local troubles of either motion or sensibility. In monkeys not even this lack of inhibitory ability is shown, and neither stimulation nor excision of the prefrontal lobes produces any symptoms whatever. One monkey of Horsley and Schaefer's was as tame, and did certain tricks as well, after as before the operation.[55] It is probable that we have about reached the limits of what can be learned about brain-functions from vivisecting inferior animals, and that we must hereafter look more exclusively to human pathology for light. The existence of separate speech and writing centres in the left hemisphere in man; the fact that palsy from cortical injury is so much more complete and enduring in man and the monkey than in dogs; and the farther fact that it seems more difficult to get complete sensorial blindness from cortical ablations in the lower animals than in man, all show that functions get more specially localized as evolution goes on. In birds localization seems hardly to exist, and in rodents it is much less conspicuous than in carnivora. Even for man, however, Munk's way of mapping out the cortex into absolute areas within which only one movement or sensation is represented is surely false. The truth seems to be rather that, although there is a correspondence of certain regions of the brain to certain regions of the body, yet the several parts within each bodily region are represented throughout the whole of the corresponding brain-region like pepper and salt sprinkled from the same caster. This, however, does not prevent each 'part' from having its focus at one spot within the brain-region. The various brain-regions merge into each other in the same mixed way. As Mr.Horsley says: "There are border centres, and the area of representation of the face merges into that for the representation of the upper limb. If there was a focal lesion at that point, you would have the movements of these two parts starting together."[56] The accompanying figure from Paneth shows just how the matter stands in the dog.[57]

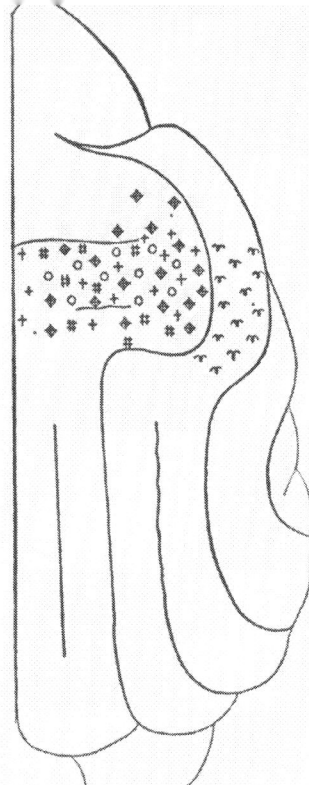

FIG. 21.—Dog's motor centres, right hemisphere, according to Paneth.—The points of the motor region are correlated as follows with muscles: the *loops* with the *orbicularis palpebrarum;* the *plain crosses* with the *flexor,* the *crosses inscribed in circles* with the *extensor, digitorum communis* of the fore-paw; the *plain circles* with the *abductor pollicis longus;* the *double crosses* with the *extensor communis* of the hind-limb.

I am speaking now of localizations breadthwise over the brain-surface. It is conceivable that there might be also localizations depthwise through the cortex. The more superficial cells are smaller, the deepest layer of them is large; and it has been suggested that the superficial cells are sensorial, the deeper ones motor;[58] or that the superficial ones in the motor region are correlated with the extremities of the organs to be moved(fingers, etc.), the deeper ones with the more central segments (wrist, elbow, etc.).[59] It need hardly be said that all such theories are as yet but guesses.

We thus see that the postulate of Meynert and Jackson which we started with on p.30 is on the whole most satisfactorily corroborated by subsequent objective research. The highest centres do probably contain nothing but arrangements for representing impressions and movements, and other arrangements for coupling the activity of these arrangements together.[60] Currents pouring in from the sense-organs first excite some arrangements, which in turn excite others, until at last a motor discharge downwards of some sort occurs.

When this is once clearly grasped there remains little ground for keeping up that old controversy about the motor zone, as to whether it is in reality motor or sensitive. The whole cortex, inasmuch as currents run through it, is both. All the currents probably have feelings going with them, and sooner or later bring movements about. In one aspect, then, every centre is afferent, in another efferent, even the motor cells of the spinal cord having these two aspects inseparably conjoined. Marique,[61] and Exner and Paneth[62] have shown that by cutting round a 'motor' centre and so separating it from the influence of the rest of the cortex, the same disorders are produced as by cutting it out, so that really it is only the mouth of the funnel, as it were, through which the stream of innervation, starting from elsewhere, pours;[63] consciousness accompanying the stream, and being mainly of things seen if the stream is strongest occipitally, of things heard if it is strongest temporally, of things felt, etc., if the stream occupies most intensely the 'motor zone.' It seems to me that some broad and vague formulation like this is as much as we can safely venture on in the present state of science; and in subsequent chapters I expect to give confirmatory reasons for my view.

Man's Consciousness Limited to the Hemispheres

But is the consciousness which accompanies the activity of the cortex the only consciousness that man has? or are his lower centres conscious as well?

This is a difficult question to decide, how difficult one only learns when one discovers that the cortex-consciousness itself of certain objects can be seemingly annihilated in any good hypnotic subject by a bare wave of his operator's hand, and yet be proved by circumstantial evidence to exist all the while in a split-off condition, quite as 'ejective'[64] to the rest of the subject's mind as that mind is to the mind of the bystanders.[65] The lower centres themselves may conceivably all the while have a split-off consciousness of their own, similarly ejective to the cortex-consciousness; but whether they have it or not can never be known from merely introspective evidence. Meanwhile the fact that occipital destruction in man may cause a blindness which is apparently absolute (no feeling remaining either of light or dark over one half of the field of view), would lead us to suppose that if our lower optical centres, the corpora quadrigemina, and thalami, do have any consciousness, it is at all events a consciousness which does not mix with that which accompanies the cortical activities, and which has nothing to do with our personal Self. In lower animals this may not be so much the case. The traces of sight found (supra, p. 46) in dogs and monkeys whose occipital lobes were entirely destroyed, may possibly have been due to the fact that the lower centres of these animals saw, and that what they saw was not ejective but objective to the remaining cortex, i.e. it formed part of one and the same inner world with the things which that cortex perceived. It may be, however, that the phenomena were due to the fact that in these animals the cortical 'centres' for vision reach outside of the occipital zone, and that destruction of the latter fails to remove them as completely as in man. This, as we know, is the opinion of the experimenters themselves. For practical purposes, nevertheless, and limiting the meaning of the word consciousness to the personal self of the individual, we can pretty confidently answer the question prefixed to this paragraph by saying that the cortex is the sole organ of consciousness in man.[66] If there be any consciousness pertaining to the lower centres, it is a consciousness of which the self knows nothing.

The Restitution of Function

Another problem, not so metaphysical, remains. The most general and striking fact connected with cortical injury is that of the restoration of function. Functions lost at first are after a few days or weeks restored. How are we to understand this restitution?
Two theories are in the field:

1) Restitution is due to the vicarious action either of the rest of the cortex or of centres lower down, acquiring functions which until then they had not performed;
2) It is due to the remaining centres (whether cortical or 'lower') resuming functions which they had always had, but of which the wound had temporarily inhibited the exercise. This is the view of which Goltz and Brown-Séquard are the most distinguished defenders.

Inhibition is a vera causa, of that there can be no doubt. The pneumogastric nerve inhibits the heart, the splanchnic inhibits the intestinal movements, and the superior laryngeal those of inspiration. The nerve-irritations which may inhibit the contraction of arterioles are innumerable, and reflex actions are often repressed by the simultaneous excitement of other sensory nerves. For all such facts the reader must consult the treatises on physiology. What concerns us here is the inhibition exerted by different parts of the nerve-centres, when irritated, on the activity of distant parts. The flaccidity of a frog from 'shock,' for a minute or so after his medulla oblongata is cut, is an inhibition from the seat of injury which quickly passes away.
What is known as 'surgical shock' (unconsciousness, pallor, dilatation of splanchnic blood-vessels, and general syncope and collapse) in the human subject is an inhibition which lasts a longer time. Goltz, Freusberg, and others, cutting the spinal cord in dogs, proved that there were functions inhibited still longer by the wound, but which reestablished themselves ultimately if the animal was kept alive. The lumbar region of the cord was thus found to contain independent vaso-motor centres, centres for erection, for control of the sphincters, etc., which could be excited to activity by tactile stimuli and as readily reinhibited by others simultaneously applied.[67] We may therefore plausibly suppose that the rapid reappearance of motility, vision, etc., after their first disappearance in consequence of a cortical mutilation, is due to the passing off of inhibitions exerted by the irritated surface of the wound. The only question is whether all restorations of function must be explained in this one simple way, or whether some part of them may not be owing to the formation of entirely new paths in the remaining centres, by which they become 'educated' to duties which they did not originally possess. In favor of an indefinite extension of the inhibition theory facts may be cited such as the following: In dogs whose disturbances due to cortical lesion have disappeared, they may in consequence of some inner or outer accident reappear in all their intensity for 24 hours or so and then disappear again.[68] In a dog made half blind by an operation, and then shut up in the dark, vision comes back just as quickly as in other similar dogs whose sight is exercised systematically every day.[69] A dog which has learned to beg before the operation recommences this practice quite spontaneously a week after a double-sided ablation of the motor zone.[70] Occasionally, in a pigeon (or even, it is said, in a dog) we see the disturbances less marked immediately after the operation than they are half an hour later.[71] This would be impossible were they due to the subtraction of the organs which normally carried them on. Moreover the entire drift of recent physiological and pathological speculation is towards enthroning inhibition as an ever-present and indispensable condition of orderly activity. We shall see how great is its importance, in the chapter on the Will. Mr. Charles Mercier considers that no muscular contraction, once begun, would ever stop without it, short of exhaustion of the system;[72] and Brown-Séquard has for years been accumulating examples to show how far its influence extends.[73] Under these circumstances it seems as if error might more probably lie in cutailing its sphere too much than in stretching it too far as an explanation of the phenomena following cortical lesion.[74]
On the other hand, if we admit no re-education of centres, we not only fly in the face of an a priori probability, but we find ourselves compelled by facts to suppose an almost incredible number of functions natively lodged in the centres below the thalami or even in those below the corpora quadrigemina. I will consider the a priori objection after first taking a look at the facts which I have in mind. They confront us the moment we ask ourselves just which are the parts which perform the functions abolished by an operation after sufficient time has elapsed for restoration to occur?.
The first observers thought that they must be the corresponding parts of the opposite or intact hemisphere. But as long ago as 1875 Carville and Duret tested this by cutting out the fore-leg-centre on one side, in a dog, and then, after waiting till restitution had occurred, cutting it out on the opposite side as well. Goltz and others have done the same thing.[75] If the opposite side were really the seat of the restored function, the original palsy should have appeared again and been permanent. But it did not appear at all; there appeared only a palsy of the hitherto unaffected side.

The next supposition is that the parts surrounding the cut-out region learn vicariously to perform its duties. But here, again, experiment seems to upset the hypothesis, so far as the motor zone goes at least; for we may wait till motility has returned in the affected limb, and then both irritate the cortex surrounding the wound without exciting the limb to movement, and ablate it, without bringing back the vanished palsy.[76] It would accordingly seem that the cerebral centres below the cortex must be the seat of the regained activities. But Goltz destroyed a dog's entire left hemisphere, together with the corpus striatum and the thalamus on that side, and kept him alive until a surprisingly small amount of motor and tactile disturbance remained.[77] These centres cannot here have accounted for the restitution. He has even, as it would appear,[78] ablated both the hemispheres of a dog, and kept him alive 51 days, able to walk and stand. The corpora striata and thalami in this dog were also practically gone. In view of such results we seem driven, with M.Francois-Franck,[79] to fall back on the ganglia lower still, or even on the spinal cord as the 'vicarious' organ of which we are in quest. If the abeyance of function between the operation and the restoration was due exclusively to inhiibition, then we must suppose these lowest centres to be in reality extremely accomplished organs. They must always have done what we now find them doing after function is restored, even when the hemispheres were intact. Of course this is conceivably the case; yet it does not seem very plausible. And the a priori considerations which a moment since I said I should urge, make it less plausible still. For, in the first place, the brain is essentially a place of currents, which run in organized paths. Loss of function can only mean one of two things, either that a current can no longer run in, or that if it runs in, it can no longer run out, by its old path. Either of these inabilities may come from a local ablation; and 'restitution' can then only mean that, in spite of a temporary block, an inrunning current has at last become enabled to flow out by its old path again-e.g., the sound of 'give your paw' discharges after some weeks into the same canine muscles into which it used to discharge before the operation. As far as the cortex itself goes, since one of the purposes for which it actually exists is the production of new paths,[80] the only question before us is: Is the formation of these particular 'vicarious' paths too much to expect of its plastic powers? It would certainly be too much to expect that a hemisphere should receive currents from optic fibres whose arriving-place within it is destroyed, or that it should discharge into fibres of the pyramidal strand if their place of exit is broken down. Such lesions as these must be irreparable within that hemisphere. Yet even then, through the other hemisphere, the corpus callosum, and the bilateral connections in the spinal cord, one can imagine some road by which the old muscles might eventually be innervated by the same incoming currents which innervated them before the block. And for all minor interruptions, not involving the arriving-place of the 'cortico-petal' or the place of exit of the 'cortico-fugal' fibres, roundabout paths of some sort through the affected hemisphere itself must exist, for every point of it is, remotely at least, in potential communication with every other point. The normal paths are only paths of least resistance. If they get blocked or cut, paths formerly more resistant become the least resistant paths under the changed conditions. It must never be forgotten that a current that runs in has got to run out somewhere; and if it only once succeeds by accident in striking into its old place of exit again, the thrill of satisfaction which the consciousness connected with the whole residual brain then receives will reinforce and fix the paths of that moment and make them more likely to be struck into again. The resultant feeling that the old habitual act is at last successfully back again, becomes itself a new stimulus which stamps all the existing currents in. It is matter of experience that such feelings of successful achievement do tend to fix in our memory whatever processes have led to them; and we shall have a good deal more to say upon the subject when we come to the Chapter on the Will.

My conclusion then is this: that some of the restitution of function (especially where the cortical lesion is not too great) is probably due to genuinely vicarious function on the part of the centres that remain; whilst some of it is due to the passing off of inhibitions. In other words, both the vicarious theory and the inhibition theory are true in their measure. But as for determining that measure, or saying which centres are vicarious, and to what extent they can learn new tricks, that is impossible at present.

Final Correction of the Meynert Scheme.

And now, after learning all these facts, what are we to think of the child and the candle-flame, and of that scheme which provisionally imposed itself on our acceptance after surveying the actions of the frog? (Cf. pp. 25-6, supra.) It will be remembered that we then considered the lower centres en masse as machines for responding to present sense-impressions exclusively, and the hemispheres as equally exclusive organs of action from inward considerations or ideas; and that, following Meynert, we supposed the hemispheres to have no native tendencies to determinate activity, but to be merely superadded organs for breaking up the various reflexes performed by the lower centres, and combining their motor and sensory elements in novel ways. It will also be remembered that I prophesied that we should be obliged to soften down the sharpness of this distinction after we had completed our survey of the farther facts. The time has now come for that correction to be made.

Wider and completer observations show us both that the lower centres are more spontaneous, and that the hemispheres are more automatic, than the Meynert scheme allows. Schrader's observations in Goltz's Laboratory on hemisphereless frogs[81] and pigeons[82] give an idea quite different from the picture of these creatures which is classically current. Steiner's[83] observations on frogs already went a good way in the same direction, showing, for example, that locomotion is a well-developed function of the medulla oblongata. But Schrader, by great care in the operation, and by keeping the frogs a long time alive, found that at least in some of them the spinal cord would produce movements of locomotion when the frog was smartly roused by a poke, and that swimming and croaking could sometimes be performed when nothing above the medulla oblongata remained.[84] Schrader's hemisphereless frogs moved spontaneously, ate flies, buried themselves in the ground, and in short did many things which before his observations were supposed to be impossible unless the hemispheres remained. Steinert[85] and Vulpian have remarked an even greater vivacity in fishes deprived of their hemispheres. Vulpian says of his brainless carps[86] that three days after the operation one of them darted at food and at a knot tied on the end of a string, holding the latter so tight between his jaws that his head was drawn out of water. Later, "they see morsels of white of egg; the moment these sink through the water in front of them, they follow and seize them, sometimes after they are on the bottom, sometimes before they have reached it. In capturing and swallowing this food they execute just the same movements as the intact carps which are in the same aquarium. The only difference is that they seem to see them at less distance, seek them with less impetuosity and less perseverance in all the points of the bottom of the aquarium, but they struggle (so to speak) sometimes with the sound carps to grasp the morsels. It is certain that they do not confound these bits of white of egg with other white bodies, small pebbles for example, which are at the bottom of the water. The same carp which, three days after operation, seized the knot on a piece of string, no longer snaps at it now, but if one brings it near her, she draws away from it by swimming backwards before it comes into contact with her mouth."[87] Already on pp.9-10,as the reader may remember, we instanced those adaptations of conduct to new conditions, on the part of the frog's spinal cord and thalami, which led Pfüger and Lewes on the one hand and Goltz on the other to locate in these organs an intelligence akin to that of which the hemispheres are the seat.

When it comes to birds deprived of their hemispheres, the evidence that some of their acts have conscious purpose behind them is quite as persuasive. In pigeons Schrader found that the state of somnolence lasted only three or four days, after which time the birds began indefatigably to walk about the room. They climbed out of boxes in which they were put, jumped over or flew up upon obstacles, and their sight was so perfect that neither in walking nor flying did they ever strike any object in the room. They had also definite ends or purposes, flying straight for more convenient perching places when made uncomfortable by movements imparted to those on which they stood; and of several possible perches they always chose the most convenient. "If we give the dove the choice of a horizontal bar (Reck) or an equally distant table to fly to, she always gives decided preference to the table. Indeed she chooses the table even if it is several meters farther off than the bar or the chair." Placed on the back of a chair, she flies first to the seat and then to the floor, and in general ,"will forsake a high position, although it give her sufficiently firm support, and in order to reach the ground will make use of the environing objects as intermediate goals of flight, showing a perfectly correct judgment of their distance. Although able to fly directly to the ground, she prefers to make the journey in successive stages. . . . Once on the ground, she hardly ever rises spontaneously into the air."[88] Young rabbits deprived of their hemispheres will stand, run, start at noises, avoid obstacles in their path, and give responsive cries of suffering when hurt. Rats will do the same, and throw themselves moreover into an attitude of defence. Dogs never survive such an operation if performed at once. But Goltz's latest dog, mentioned on p. 70, which is said to have been kept alive for fifty-one days after both hemispheres had been removed by a series of ablations and the corpora striata and thalami had softened away, shows how much the mid-brain centres and the cord can do even in the canine species. Taken together, the number of reactions shown to exist in the lower centres by these observations make out a pretty good case for the Meynert scheme, as applied to these lower animals. That scheme demands hemispheres which shall be mere supplements or organs of repetition, and in the light of these observations they obviously are so to a great extent. But the Meynert scheme also demands that the reactions of the lower centres shall all be native, and we are not absolutely sure that some of those which we have been considering may not have been acquired after the injury; and it furthermore demands that they should be machine-like, whereas the expression of some of them makes us doubt whether they may not be guided by an intelligence of low degree. Even in the lower animals, then, there is reason to soften down that opposition between the hemispheres and the lower centres which the scheme demands. The hemispheres may, it is true, only supplement the lower centres, but the latter resemble the former in nature and have some small amount at least of 'spontaneity' and choice.

But when we come to monkeys and man the scheme well-nigh breaks down altogether; for we find that the hemispheres do not simply repeat voluntarily actions which the lower centres perform as machines. There are many functions which the lower centres cannot by themselves perform at all. When the motor cortex is injured in a man or a monkey genuine paralysis ensues, which in man is incurable, and almost or quite equally so in the ape. Dr. Seguin knew a man with hemi-blindness, from cortical injury, which had persisted unaltered for twenty-three years. 'Traumatic inhibition' cannot possibly account for this. The blindness must have been an 'Ausfallserscheinung,' due to the loss of vision's essential organ. It would seem, then, that in these higher creatures the lower centres must be less adequate than they are farther down in the zoological scale; and that even for certain elementary combinations of movement and impression the co-operation of the hemispheres is necessary from the start. Even in birds and dogs the power of eating properly is lost when the frontal lobes are cut off.[89]

The plain truth is that neither in man nor beast are the hemispheres the virgin organs which our scheme called them. So far from being unorganized at birth, they must have native tendencies to reaction of a determinate sort.[90] These are the tendencies which we know as emotions and instincts, and which we must study with some detail in later chapters of this book. Both instincts and emotions are reactions upon special sorts of objects of perception; they depend on the hemispheres; and they are in the first instance reflex, that is, they take place the first time the exciting object is met, are accompanied by no forethought or deliberation, and are irresistible. But they are modifiable to a certain extent by experience, and on later occasions of meeting the exciting object, the instincts expecially have less of the blind impulsive character which they had at first. All this will be explained at some length in Chapter XXIV. Meanwhile we can say that the multiplicity of emotional and instincitive reactions in man, together with his extensive associative power, permit of extensive recouplings of the original sensory and motor partners. The consequences of one instinctive reaction often prove to be the inciters of an opposite reaction, and being suggested on later occasions by the original object, may then suppress the first reaction altogether, just as in the case of the child and the flame. For this education the hemispheres do not need to be tabuloe rasoe at first, as the Meynert scheme would have them; and so far from their being educated by the lower centres exclusively, they educate themselves.[91]

We have already noticed the absence of reactions from fear and hunger in the ordinary brainless frog. Schrader gives a striking account of the instinctless condition of his brainless pigeons, active as they were in the way of locomotion and voice. "The hemisphereless animal moves in a world of bodies which ... are all of equal value for him.... He is, to use Goltz's apt expression, impersonal.... Every object is for him only a space-occupying mass, he turns out of his path for an ordinary pigeon no otherwise than for a stone. He may try to climb over both. All authors agree that they never found any difference, whether it was an inanimate body, a cat, a dog, or a bird of prey which came in their pigeon's way. The creature knows neither friends nor enemies, in the thickest company it lives like a hermit. The languishing cooing of the male awakens no more impression than the rattling of the peas, or the call-whistle which in the days before the injury used to make the birds hasten to be fed. Quite as little as the earlier observers have I seen hemisphereless she-birds answer the courting of the male. A hemisphereless male will coo all day long and show distinct signs of sexual excitement, but his activity is without any object, it is entirely indifferent to him whether the she-bird be there or not. If one is placed near him, he leaves her unnoticed.... As the male pays no attention to the female, so she pays none to her young. The brood may follow the mother ceaselessly calling for food, but they might as well ask it from a stone.... The hemisphereless pigeon is in the highest degree tame, and fears man as little as cat or bird of prey."[92]

Putting together now all the facts and reflections which we have been through, it seems to me that we can no longer hold strictly to the Meynert scheme. If anywhere, it will apply to the lowest animals; but in them especially the lower centres seem to have a degree of spontaneity and choice. On the whole, I think that we are driven to substitute for it some such general conception as the following, which allows for zoological differences as we know them, and is vague and elastic enough to receive any number of future discoveries of detail.

Conclusion

All the centres, in all animals, whilst they are in one aspect mechanisms, probably are, or at least once were, organs of consciousness in another, although the consciousness is doubtless much more developed in the hemispheres than it is anywhere else. The consciousness must everywhere prefer some of the sensations which it gets to others; and if it can remember these in their absence, however dimly, they must be its ends of desire. If, moreover, it can identify in memory any motor discharges which may have led to such ends, and associate the latter with them, then these motor discharges themselves may in turn become desired as means. This is the development of will; and its realization must of course be proportional to the possible complication of the consciousness. Even the spinal cord may possibly have some little power of will in this sense, and of effort towards modified behavior in consequence of new experiences of sensibility.[93]

All nervous centres have then in the first instance one essential function, that of 'intelligent' action. They feel, prefer one thing to another, and have 'ends.' Like all other organs, however, they evolve from ancestor to descendant, and their evolution takes two directions the lower centres passing downwards into more unhesitating automatism, and the higher ones upwards into larger intellectuality.[94] Thus it may happen that those functions which can safely

grow uniform and fatal become least accompanied by mind, and that their organ, the spinal cord, becomes a more and more soulless machine; whilst on the contrary those functions which it benefits the animal to have adapted to delicate environing variations pass more and more to the hemispheres, whose anatomical structure and attendant consciousness grow more and more elaborate as zoological evolution proceeds. In this way it might come about that in man and the monkeys the basal ganglia should do fewer things by themselves than they can do in dogs, fewer in dogs than in rabbits, fewer in rabbits than in hawks,[95] fewer in hawks than in pigeons, fewer in pigeons than in frogs, fewer in frogs than in fishes, and that the hemispheres should correspondingly do more. This passage of functions forward to the ever-enlarging hemispheres would be itself one of the evolutive changes, to be explained like the development of the hemispheres themselves, either by fortunate variation or by inherited effects of use. The reflexes, on this view, upon which the education of our human hemispheres depends, would not be due to the basal ganglia alone. They would be tendencies in the hemispheres themselves, modifiable by education, unlike the reflexes of the medulla oblongata, pons, optic lobes and spinal cord. Such cerebral reflexes, if they exist, form a basis quite as good as that which the Meynert scheme offers, for the acquisition of memories and associations which may later result in all sorts of 'changes of partners' in the psychic world. The diagram of the baby and the candle can be re-edited, if need be, as an entirely cortical transaction. The original tendency to touch will be a cortical instinct; the burn will leave an image in another part of the cortex, which, being recalled by association, will inhibit the touching tendency the next time the candle is perceived, and excite the tendency to withdraw-so that the retinal picture will, upon that next time, be coupled with the original motor partner of the pain. We thus get whatever psychological truth the Meynert scheme possesses without entangling ourselves on a dubious anatomy and physiology.
Some such shadowy view of the evolution of the centres, of the relation of consciousness to them, and of the hemispheres to the, other lobes, is, it seems to me, that in which it is safest to indulge. If it has no other advantage, it at any rate makes us realize how enormous are the gaps in our knowledge, the moment we try to cover the facts by any one formula of a general kind.

Notes

[1] It should be said that this particular cut commonly proves fatal. The text refers to the rare cases which survive.
[2] I confine myself to the frog for simplicity's sake. In higher animals, especially the ape and man, it would seem as if not only determinate combinations of muscles, but limited groups or even single muscles could be innervated from the hemispheres.
[3] I hope that the reader will take no umbrage at my so mixing the physical and mental, and talking of reflex acts and hemispheres and reminiscences in the same breath, as if they were homogeneous quantities and factors of one causal chain. I have done so deliberately; for although I admit that from the radically physical point of view it is easy to conceive of the chain of events amongst the cells and fibres as complete in itself, and that whilst so conceiving it one need make no mention of ideas,' I yet suspect that point of view of being an unreal abstraction. Reflexes in centres may take place even where accompanying feelings or ideas guide them. In another chapter I shall try to show reasons for not abandoning this common-sense position; meanwhile language lends itself so much more easily to the mixed way of describing , that I will continue to employ the latter. The more radical-minded reader can alway read 'ideational process' for idea'.
[4] I shall call it hereafter for shortness 'the Meynert scheme;' for the child-and-flame example, as well as the whole general notion that the hemispheres are a supernumerary surface for the projection and association of sensations and movements natively coupled in the centres below, is due to Th. Meynert, the Austrian anatomist. For a popular account of his views, see his pamphlet 'Zur Mechanik des Gehirnbaues,' Vienna, 1874. His most recent development of them is embodied in his 'Psychiatry,' a clinical treatise on diseases of the forebrain, translated by B.Sachs, New York, 1885.
[5] Geschichte des Materialismus, 2d ed., II. p 345.
[6] West Riding Asylum Reports, 1876, p. 267.
[7] For a thorough discussion of the various objections, see Ferrier's 'Functions of the Brain,' 2d ed., pp. 227-234, and Franois-Franck's 'Leons sur les Fonctions Motrices du Cerveau'(1887), Leon 31. The most minutely accurate experiments on irritation of cortical points are those of Paneth, in Pflüger's Archiv, vol 37, p. 528.-Recently the skull has been fearlessly opened by surgeons, and operations upon the human brain performed, sometimes with the happiest results. In some of these operations the cortex has been electrically excited for the purpose of more exactly localizing the spot, and the movements first observed in dogs and monkeys have then been verified in men.
[8] J. Loeb: 'Beiträge zur Physiologie des Grosshirns;' Pflüger's Arciv, XXXIX. 293. I simplify the author's statement.
[9] Goltz: Pflüger's Archiv, XLII. 419.
[10] 'Hemiplegia' means one-sided palsy.
[11] Philosophical Transactions, vol. 179, pp. 6, 10(1888). In a later paper (ibid. p. 205) Messrs. Beevor and Horsley go into the localization still more minutely, showing spots from which single muscles or single digits can be made to contract.
[12] Nothnagel und Naunyn : Die Localization in den Gehirnkrankheiten (Wiesbaden, 1887), p.34
[13] An accessible account of the history of our knowledge of motor aphasia is in W.A. Hammond's 'Treatise on the Diseases of the Nervous System,' chapter VII.

[14] The history up to 1885 may be found in A.Christiani: Zur Physiologie des Gehirnes (Berlin, 1885)
[15] Pflüger's Archiv, vol.44, p.176. Munk (Berlin Academy Sitzsungsberichte, 1889, XXXI) returns to the charge, denying the extirpations of Schrader to be complete: "Microscopic portions of the Sehsphäre must remain."
[16] A.Christiani: Zur Physiol. D. Gehirnes (Berlin, 1885), chaps. II, III, IV. H. Munk: Berlin Akad. Stzgsb. 1884, XXIV.
[17] Luciani und Seppili: Die Functions-Localization auf der Grosshirnrinde (Deutsch von Fraenkel), Leipzig, 1886, Dogs M, N, and S. Goltz in Pflüger's Archiv, vol.34, pp. 490-6; vol. 42, p. 454. Cf. also Munk: Berlin Akad. Stzgsb. 1886, VII, VIII, pp. 113-121, and Loeb: Pflüger's Archiv, vol. 39, p. 337.
[18] Berlin Akad. Sitzungsberichte, 1886, VII, VIII, p. 124.
[19] H. Munk: Functionen der Grosshirnrinde (Berlin, 1881), pp. 36-40. Ferrier: Functions, etc., 2d ed., chap. IX, pt. I. Brown and Schaefer: Philos. Transactions, vol. 179, p. 321. Luciani u. Seppili, op. Cit. Pp. 131-138. Lannegrace found traces of sight with both occipital lobes destroyed, and in one monkey even when angular gyri and occipital lobes were destroyed altogether. His paper is in the Archives de Médecine Expérimentale for January and March, 1889. I only know it from the abstract in the Neurologisches Centralblatt, 1889, pp. 108-420. The reporter doubts the evidence of vision in the monkey. It appears to have consisted in avoiding obstacles and in emotional disturbance in the presence of men.
[20] Localization of Cerebral Disease (1878), pp. 117-8.
[21] For cases see Flechsig : Die Leitungsbahnen in Gehirn u. Rückenmark (Leipzig, 1876), pp. 112, 272; Exner's Untersuchungen, etc., p. 83; Ferrier's Localization, etc., p. 11; Francois-Franck's Cerveau Moteur, p. 63, note.
[22] E. C. Seguin: Hemianopsia of Cerebral Origin, in Journal of Nervous and Mental Disease, vol. XIII. P. 30. Nothnagel und Naunyn: Ueber die Localization der Gehirnkrankheiten (Wiesbaden, 1887), p. 10.
[23] Die Seelenblindheit, etc., p. 51 ff. The mental blindness was in this woman's case moderate in degree.
[24] Archiv f. Psychiatrie, vol. 21, p. 222.
[25] Nothnagel (loc. cit. p.22) says: "Dies trifft aber nicht zu." He gives, however, no case in support of his opinion that double-sided cortical lesion may make one stone-blind and yet not destroy one's visual images; so that I do not know whether it is an observation of fact or an a priori assumption.
[26] In a case published by C.S. Freund: Archiv f. Psychiatrie, vol. XX, the occipital lobes were injured, but their cortex was not destroyed, on both sides. There was still vision. Cf. pp. 291-5.
[27] I say 'need,' for I do not of course deny the possible coexistence of the two symptoms. Many a brain-lesion might block optical associations and at the same time impair optical imagination, without entirely stopping vision. Such a case seems to have been the remarkable on from Charcot which I shall give rather fully in the chapter on Imagination.
[28] Freund (in the article cited above "Ueber optisched Aphasie und Seelenblindheit') and Bruns ('Ein Fall von Alexie,' etc., in the Neurologisches Centralblatt for 1888, pp. 581, 509) explain their cases by brokendown conduction. Wilbrand, whose painstaking monograph on mental blindness was referred to a moment ago, gives none but a priori reasons for his belief that the optical 'Erinnerungsfeld' must be locally distinct from the Wahrnehmungsfeld (cf. pp. 84, 93). The a priori reasons are really the other way. Mauthner ('Gehirn u. Auge' (1881), p. 487 ff.) tries to show that the 'mental blindness' of Munk's dogs and apes after occipital mutilation was not such, but real dimness of sight. The best case of mental blindness yet reported is that by Lissauer, as below. The reader will also do well to read Bernard: De 1 Aphasie(1881) chap. V; Ballet: Le Langage Intérieur (1886), chap. VIII; and Jas. Ross's little book on Aphasia (1887), p. 74.
[29] For a case see Wernicke's Lehrb. D. Gehirnkrankheiten, vol. II. p. 554(1881).
[30] The latest account of them is the paper Über die optischen Centren u. Bahnen' by von Monakow in the Archiv für Psychiatrie, vol. XX. p. 714.
[31] Die Functions-Localization, etc., Dog X; see also p. 161.
[32] Philos. Trans., vol. 179, p. 312.
[33] Brain, vol. XI. p. 10.
[34] Ibid. p. 147.
[35] Der aphasische Symptomencomplex (1874). See in Fig. 11 the convolution marked WERNICKE.
[36] 'The Pathology of Sensory Aphasia,' 'Brain,' July, 1889.
[37] Nothnagel und Naunyn: op. cit., plates.
[38] Ballet's and Bernard's works cited on p. 51 are the most accessible documents of Charcot's school. Bastian's book on the Brain as an Organ of Mind(last three chapters) is also good.
[39] For details, see Ferrier's 'Functions,' chap, IX. Pt. III, and Chas. K. Mills: Transactions of Congress of American Physicians and Surgeons, 1888, vol. I. p. 278.
[40] Functions of the Brain, chap. X. 14.
[41] Uber die Functionen d. Grosshirnrinde (1881), p. 50.
[42] Lezioni di Fisiologia sperimentale sul sistema nervoso encefalico (1873), p. 527 ff. Also 'Brain,' vol. IX. p. 298.
[43] Bechterew (Pflüger's Archiv., vol. 35, p. 137) found no anaesthesia in a cat with motor symptoms from ablation of sigmoid gyrus. Luciani got hyperaesthesia coexistent with cortical motor defect in a dog, by simultaneously hemisecting the spinal cord (Luciani u. Seppili, op. cit. p. 234). Goltz frequently found hyperaesthesia of the whole body to accompany motor defect after ablation of both frontal lobes, and he once found it after ablating the motor zone (Pflüger's Archiv, vol. 34, p. 471).
[44] Philos. Transactions, vol. 179, p. 20 ff.
[45] Functions, p. 375.

[46] Pp. 15-17.
[47] Luciani u. Sepplili, op. cit. pp. 275-288.
[48] Op. cit. p. 18.
[49] Trans. Of Congress, etc., p. 272.
[50] See Exner's Unters. üb. Localization, plate XXV.
[51] Cf. Ferrier's Functions, etc., chap. IV and chap. X, 6 to 9.
[52] Op. cit. p.17.
[53] E.g. Starr, loc. cit. p. 272; Leyden, Beiträge zur Lehre v. d. Localization im Gehirn(1888), p. 72.
[54] Bernard, op. cit. p. 84.
[55] Philos. Trans., vol. 179, p. 3.
[56] Trans. Of Congress of Am. Phys. And Surg. 1888, vol. I.p. 343. Beevor and Horsley's paper on electric stimulation of the monkey's brain is the most beautiful work yet done for precision. See Phil. Trans., vol. 179, p. 205, especially the plates.
[57] Pflüger's Archiv, vol. 37, p. 523 (1885).
[58] By Luys in his generally preposterous book 'The Brain'; also by Horsley.
[59] C. Mercier: The Nervous System and the Mind, p. 124.
[60] The frontal lobes as yet remain a puzzle. Wundt tries to explain them as an organ of 'apperception' (Grundzüge d. Physiologischen Psychologie, 3d ed., vol. I. p. 233 ff.), but I confess myself unable to apprehend clearly the Wundtian philosophy so far as this word enters into it, so must be contented with this bare reference.- Until quite recently it was common to talk of an 'ideational centre' as of something distinct from the aggregate of other centres. Fortunately this custom is already on the wane.
[61] Rech.Exp. sur le Fonctionnement des Centres Psycho-moteurs(Burssels, 1885).
[62] Pflüger's Archiv, vol. 44, p. 544.
[63] I ought to add, however, that Franois-Franck(Fonctions Motrices, p. 370) got, in two dogs and a cat, a different result from this sort of 'circumvallation.'
[64] For this word, see T.K. Clifford's Lectures and Essays(1879), vol. II p. 72.
[65] See below, Chapter VIII.
[66] Cf. Ferrier's Functions, pp. 120, 147, 414. See also Vulpian: Leons sur la Physiol. Du Syst. Nerveux, p. 548; Luciani u. Seppili, op. cit. pp. 404-5; H. Maudsley: Physiology of Mind (1876), pp. 138 ff., 197 ff., and 241 ff. In G.H. Lewes's Physical Basis of Mind, Problem IV: 'The Reflex Theory,' a very full history of the question is given.
[67] Goltz: Pflüger's Archiv, vol. 8, p. 460; Freusberg: ibid. vol. 10, p. 174.
[68] Goltz: Verrichtungen des Grosshirns. p. 73.
[69] Loeb: Pflüger's Archiv, vol 39, p. 276.
[70] Ibid, p. 289.
[71] Schrader: ibid. vol. 44, p. 218.
[72] The Nervous System and the Mind (1888), chaps. III, VI; also in Brain, vol. XI. p. 361.
[73] Brown-Séquard has given a résumé of his opinions in the Archives de Physiologie for Oct. 1889, 5me, Série, vol. I. p 751.
[74] Goltz first applied the inhibition thoery to the brain in his 'Verrichtungen des Grosshirns,'p. 39 ff. On the general philosophy of Inhibition the reader may consult Brunton's ' Pharmakology and Therapeutics,' p. 154 ff., and also 'Nature,' vol. 27, p. 419 ff.
[75] E.g. Herzen, Herman u. Schwalbe's Jahres-bericht for 1886, Physiol. Abth. P. 38. (Experiments on new-born puppies.)
[76] Franois-Franck: op.cit. p. 382. Results are somewhat contradictory.
[77] Pflüger's Archiv, vol. 42, p. 419.
[78] Neurologisches Centralblatt, 1889, p. 372.
[79] Op. cit. p. 387. See pp. 378 to 388 for a discussion of the whole question. Compare also Wundt's Physiol. Psych., 3d ed., I. 225 ff., and Luciani u. Seppili, pp. 243, 293.
[80] The Chapters on Habit, Association, Memory, and Perception will change our present preliminary conjecture that that is one of its essential uses, into an unshakable conviction.
[81] Pflüger's Archiv, vol. 41, p. 75 (1887).
[82] Ibid., vol. 44, p. 175 (1889).
[83] Untersuchungen über die Physiologie des Froschirns, 1885.
[84] Loc. cit. pp. 80, 82-3. Schrader also found a biting-reflex developed when the medulla oblongata is cut through just behind the cerebellum.
[85] Berlin Akad. Sitzungsberichte for 1886.
[86] Comptes Rendus, vol. 102, p. 90.
[87] Comptes Rendus de l'Acad. D. Sciences, vol. 102, p. 1530
[88] Loc. cit. p. 216.
[89] Goltz: Pflüger's Archiv, vol. 42, p. 447; Schrader : ibid. vol. 44, p. 219 ff. It is possible that this symptom may be an effect of traumatic inihition however.
[90] A few years ago one of the strongest arguements for the theory that the hemispheres are purely supernumerary was Soltmann's often-quoted observation that in new-born puppies the motor zone of the cortex is not excitable by electricity and

only becomes so in the course of a fortnight, presumably after the experiences of the lower centres have educated it to motor duties. Paneth's later observations, however, seem to show that Soltmann may have been misled through overnarcotizing his victims (Pflüger's Archiv, vol. 37, p. 202). In the Neurologisches Centralblatt for 1889, p. 513, Bechterw returns to the subject on Soltmann's side without however, noticing Paneth's work.

[91] Münsterberg (Die Willenshandlung, 1888, p. 134) challenges Meynert's scheme in toto, saying that whilst we have in our personal experience plenty of examples of acts which were at first voluntary becoming secondarily automatic and reflex, we have no conscious record of a single originally reflex act growing voluntary. -As far as conscious record is concerned, we could not possibly have it even if the Meynert scheme were wholly true, for the education of the hemispheres which that scheme postulates must in the nature of things antedate recollection. But it seems to me that Münsterberg's rejection of the scheme may possibly be correct as regards reflexes from the lower centres. Everywhere in this department of psychogenesis we are made to feel how ignorant we really are.

[92] Pflüger's Archiv, vol. 44. p. 230-1.

[93] Naturally, as Schiff long ago pointed out (Lehrb. D. Muskel-u. Nervenphysiologie, 1859, p. 213 ff.), the 'Rückenmarksseele,' if it now exist, can have no higher sense-consciousness, for its incoming currents are solely from the skin. But it may, in its dim way, both feel, prefer, and desire. See, for the view favorable to the text: B.H. Lewes, The Physiology of Common Life(1860), chap. IX. Goltz (Nervencentren des Frosches, 1869, pp. 102-130) thinks that the frog's cord has no adaptive power. This may be the case in such experiments as his, because the beheaded frog's short span of life does not give it time to learn the new tricks asked for. But Rosenthal (Biologisches Centralblatt, vol. IV. p. 247) and Mendelssohn (Berlin Akad. Sitzungsberichte, 1885, p. 107) in their investigations on the simple reflexes of the frog's cord, show that there is some adaptation to new conditions, inasmuch as when usual paths of conduction are interrupted by a cut, new paths are taken. According to Rosenthal, these grow more pervious (i.e. require a smaller stimulus) in proportion as they are more often traversed.

[94] Whether this evolution takes place through the inheritance of habits acquired, or through the preservation of lucky variations, is an alternative which we need not discuss here. We shall consider it in the last chapter in the book. For our present purpose the modus operandi of the evolution makes no difference, provided it be admitted to occur.

[95] See Schrader's Observations, loc. cit.

Chapter III - On Some General Conditions of Brain-Activity

The elementary properties of nerve-tissue on which the brain-functions depend are far from being satisfactorily made out. The scheme that suggests itself in the first instance to the mind, because it is so obvious, is certainly false: I mean the notion that each cell stands for an idea or part of an idea, and that the ideas are associated or 'bound into bundles' (to use a phrase of Locke's) by the fibres. If we make a symbolic diagram on a blackboard, of the laws of association between ideas, we are inevitably led to draw circles, or closed figures of some kind, and to connect them by lines. When we hear that the nerve-centres contain cells which send off fibres, we say that Nature has realized our diagram for us, and that the mechanical substratum of thought is plain. In some way, it is true, our diagram must be realized in the brain; but surely in no such visible and palpable way as we at first suppose.[1] An enormous number of the cellular bodies in the hemispheres are fibreless. Where fibres are sent off they soon divide into untraceable ramifications; and nowhere do we see a simple coarse anatomical connection, like a line on the blackboard, between two cells. Too much anatomy has been found to order for theoretic purposes, even by the anatomists; and the popular-science notions of cells and fibres are almost wholly wide of the truth. Let us therefore relegate the subject of the intimate workings of the brain to the physiology of the future, save in respect to a few points of which a word must now be said. And first of [sic]

The Summation of Stimuli

[sic] in the same nerve-tract. This is a property extremely important for the understanding of a great many phenomena of the neural, and consequently of the mental, life; and it behooves us to gain a clear conception of what it means before we proceed any farther.

The law is this, that a stimulus which would be inadequate by itself to excite a nerve-centre to effective discharge may, by acting with one or more other stimuli (equally ineffectual by themselves alone) bring the discharge about. The natural way to consider this is as a summation of tensions which at last overcome a resistance. The first of them produce a 'latent excitement' or a 'heightened irritability'-the phrase is immaterial so far as practical consequences go; the last is the straw which breaks the camel's back. Where the neural process is one that has consciousness for its accompaniment, the final explosion would in all cases seem to involve a vivid state of feeling of a more or less substantive kind. But there is no ground for supposing that the tensions whilst yet submaximal or outwardly ineffective, may not also have a share in determining the total consciousness present in the individual at the time. In later chapters we shall see abundant reason to suppose that they do have such a share, and that without their contribution the fringe of relations which is at every moment a vital ingredient of the mind's object, would not come to consciousness at all.

The subject belongs too much to physiology for the evidence to be cited in detail in these pages. I will throw into a note a few references for such readers as may be interested in following it out,[2] and simply say that the direct electrical irritation of the cortical centres sufficiently proves the point. For it was found by the earliest experimenters here that whereas it takes an exceedingly strong current to produce any movement when a single induction-shock is used, a rapid succession of induction-shocks ('faradization') will produce movements when the current is comparatively weak. A single quotation from an excellent investigation will exhibit this law under further aspects:

"If we continue to stimulate the cortex at short intervals with the strength of current which produces the minimal muscular contraction [of the dog's digital extensor muscle], the amount of contraction gradually increases till it reaches the maximum. Each earlier stimulation leaves thus an effect behind it, which increases the efficacy of the following one. In this summation of the stimuli....the following points may be noted: 1) Single stimuli entirely inefficacious when alone may become efficacious by sufficiently rapid reiteration. If the current used is very much less than that which provokes the first beginning of contraction, a very large number of successive shocks may be needed before the movement appears-20, 50, once 106 shocks were needed. 2) The summation takes place easily in proportion to the shortness of the interval between the stimuli. A current too weak to give effective summation when its shocks are 3 seconds apart will be capable of so doing when the interval is shortened to 1 second. 3) Not only electrical irritation leaves a modification which goes to swell the following stimulus, but every sort of irritant which can produce a contraction does so. If in any way a reflex contraction of the muscle experimented on has been produced, or if it is contracted spontaneously by the animal (as not unfrequently happens 'by sympathy,' during a deep inspiration), it is found that an electrical stimulus, until then inoperative, operates energetically if immediately applied."[3]

Furthermore:

"In a certain stage of the morphia-narcosis an ineffectively weak shock will become powerfully effective, if, immediately before its application to the motor centre, the skin of certain parts of the body is exposed to gentle tactile stimulation....If, having ascertained the subminimal strength of current and convinced one's self repeatedly of its inefficacy, we draw our hand a single time lightly over the skin of the paw whose cortical centre is the object of stimulation, we find the current at once strongly effective. The increase of irritability lasts some seconds before it disappears. Sometimes the effect of a single light stroking of the paw is only sufficient to make the previously ineffectual current produce a very weak contraction. Repeating the tactile stimulation will then, as a rule, increase the contraction's extent."[4]

We constantly use the summation of stimuli in our practical appeals. If a car-horse balks, the final way of starting him is by applying a number of customary incitements at once. If the driver uses reins and voice, if one bystander pulls at his head, another lashes his hind quarters, and the conductor rings the bell, and the dismounted passengers shove the car, all at the same moment, his obstinacy generally yields, and he goes on his way rejoicing. If we are striving to remember a lost name or fact, we think of as many 'cues' as possible, so that by their joint action they may recall what no one of them can recall alone. The sight of a dead prey will often not stimulate a beast to pursuit, but if the sight of movement be added to that of form, pursuit occurs. "Brücke noted that his brainless hen, which made no attempt to peck at the grain under her very eyes, began pecking if the grain were thrown on the ground with force, so as to produce a rattling sound." [5] "Dr. Allen Thomson hatched out some chickens on a carpet, where he kept them for several days. They showed no inclination to scrape,...but when Dr. Thomson sprinkled a little gravel on the carpet,...the chickens immediately began their scraping movements."[6] A strange person, and darkness, are both of them stimuli to fear and mistrust in dogs (and for the matter of that, in men). Neither circumstance alone may awaken outward manifestations, but together, i.e. when the stange man is met in the dark, the dog will be excited to violent defiance.[7] Street-hawkers well know the efficacy of summation, for they arrange themselves in a line upon the sidewalk, and the passer often buys from the last one of them, through the effect of the reiterated solicitation, what he refused to buy from the first in the row. Aphasia shows many examples of summation. A patient who cannot name an object simply shown him, will name it if he touches as well as sees it, etc.

Instances of summation might be multiplied indefinitely, but it is hardly worth while to forestall subsequent chapters. Those on Instinct, the Stream of Thought, Attention, Discrimination, Association, Memory, Aesthetics, and Will, will contain numerous exemplifications of the reach of the principle in the purely psychological field.

Reaction-Time

One of the lines of experimental investigation most diligently followed of late years is that of the ascertainment of the time occupied by nervous events. Helmholtz led off by discovering the rapidity of the current in the sciatic nerve of the frog. But the methods he used were soon applied to the sensory nerves and the centres, and the results caused much popular scientific admiration when described as measurements of the 'velocity of thought.' The phrase 'quick as thought' had from time immemorial signified all that was wonderful and elusive of determination in the line of speed; and the way in which Science laid her doomful hand upon this mystery reminded people of the day when Franklin first 'eripuit coelo fulmen,' foreshadowing the region of a newer and colder race of gods. We shall take up the various operations measured, each in the chapter to which it more naturally pertains. I may say, however, immediately, that the phrase 'velocity of thought' is misleading, for it is by no means clear in any of the cases what particular act of thought occurs during the time which is measured. 'Velocity of nerve-action' is liable to the same criticism, for in most cases we do not know what particular nerve-processes occur. What the times in question really represent is the total duration of certain reactions upon stimuli.

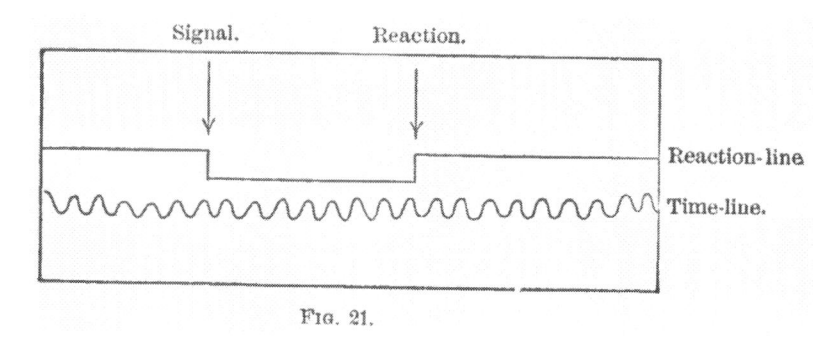

FIG. 21.

Certain of the conditions of the reaction are prepared beforehand; they consist in the assumption of those motor and sensory tensions which we name the expectant state. Just what happens during the actual time occupied by the reaction (in other words, just what is added to the pre-existent tensions to produce the actual discharge) is not made out at present, either from the neural or from the mental point of view.

The method is essentially the same is all these investigations. A signal of some sort is communicated to the subject, and at the same instant records itself on a time-registering apparatus. The subject then makes a muscular movement of some sort, which is the 'reaction,' and which also records itself automatically. The time found to have elapsed between the two records is the total time of that observation. The time-registering instruments are of various types. One type is that of the revolving drum covered with smoked paper, on which one electric pen traces a line which the signal breaks and the 'reaction' draws again; whilst another electric pen (connected with a pendulum or a rod of metal vibrating at a known rate) traces alongside of the former line a 'time-line' of which each undulation or link stands for a certain fraction of a second, and against which the break in the reaction-line can be measured. Compare Fig.21, where the line is broken by the signal at the first arrow, and continued again by the reaction at the second. Ludwig's Kymograph, Marey's Chronograph are good examples of this type of instrument.

Another type of instrument is represented by the stopwatch, of which the most perfect from is Hipp's Chronoscope. The hand on the dial measures intervals as short as 1/1000 of a second. The signal (by an appropriate electric connection) starts it; the reaction stops it; and by reading off its initial and terminal positions we have immediately and with no farther trouble the time we seek.

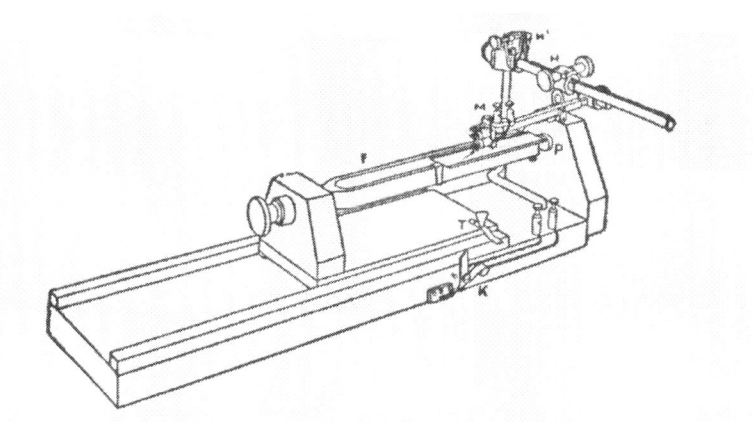

FIG. 22.—Bowditch's Reaction-timer. F, tuning-fork carrying a little plate which holds the paper on which the electric pen M makes the tracing, and sliding in grooves on the base-board. P, a plug which spreads the prongs of the fork apart when it is pushed forward to its extreme limit, and releases them when it is drawn back to a certain point. The fork then vibrates, and, its backward movement continuing, an undulating line is drawn on the smoked paper by the pen. At T is a tongue fixed to the carriage of the fork, and at K an electric key which the tongue opens and with which the electric pen is connected. At the instant of opening, the pen changes its place and the undulating line is drawn at a different level on the paper. The opening can be made to serve as a signal to the reacter in a variety of ways, and his reaction can be made to close the pen again, when the line returns to its first level. The reaction time = the number of undulations traced at the second level.

A still simpler instrument, though one not very satisfactory in its working, is the 'psychodometer' of Exner & Obersteiner, of which I picture a modification devised by my colleague Professor H.P. Bowditch, which works very well.

The manner in which the signal and reaction are connected with the chronographic apparatus varies indefinitely in different experiments. Every new problem requires some new electric or mechanical disposition of apparatus. [8]

The least complicated time-measurement is that known as simple reaction-time, in which there is but one possible signal and one possible movement, and both are known in advance. The movement is generally the closing of an electric key with the hand. The foot, the jaw, the lips, even the eyelid, have been in turn made organs of reaction, and the apparatus has been modified accordingly.[9] The time usually elapsing between stimulus and movement lies between one and three tenths of a second, varying according to circumstances which will be mentioned anon.

The subject of experiment, whenever the reactions are short and regular, is in a state of extreme tension, and feels, when the signal comes, as if it started the reaction, by a sort of fatality, and as if no psychic process of perception or volition had a chance to intervene. The whole succession is so rapid that perception seems to be retrospective, and the time-order of events to be read off in memory rather than known at the moment. This at least is my own personal experience in the matter, and with it I find others to agree. The question is, What happens inside of us, either in brain or mind? and to answer that we must analyze just what processes the reaction involves. It is evident that some time is lost in each of the following stages:

1. The stimulus excites the peripheral sense-organ adequately for a current to pass into the sensory nerve;
2. The sensory nerve is traversed;
3. The transformation (or reflection) of the sensory into a motor current occurs in the centres;
4. The spinal cord and motor nerve are traversed;
5. The motor current excites the muscle to the contracting point.

Time is also lost, of course, outside the muscle, in the joints, skin, etc., and between the parts of the apparatus; and when the stimulus which serves as signal is applied to the skin of the trunk or limbs, time is lost in the sensorial conduction through the spinal cord.

The stage marked 3 is the only one that interests us here. The other stages answer to purely physiological processes, but stage 3 is psycho-physical; that is, it is a higher-central process, and has probably some sort of consciousness accompanying it. What sort?

Wundt has little difficulty in deciding that it is consciousness of a quite elaborate kind. He distinguishes between two stages in the conscious reception of an impression, calling one perception, and the other apperception, and likening the one to the mere entrance of an object into the periphery of the field of vision, and the other to its coming to occupy the focus or point of view. Inattentive awareness of an object, and attention to it, are, it seems to me, equivalents for perception and apperception, as Wundt uses the words. To these two forms of awareness of the impression Wundt adds the conscious volition to react, gives to the trio the name of 'psycho-physical' processes, and assumes that they actually follow upon each other in the succession in which they have been named.[10] So at least I understand him. The simplest way to determine the time taken up by this psycho-physical stage No. 3 would be to determine separately the duration of the several purely physical processes, 1, 2, 4, and 5, and to subtract them from the total reaction-time. Such attempts have been made.[11] But the data for calculation are too inaccurate for use, and, as Wundt himself admits,[12] the precise duration of stage 3 must at present be left enveloped with that of the other processes, in the total reaction-time.

My own belief is that no such succession of conscious feelings as Wundt describes takes place during stage 3. It is a process of central excitement and discharge, with which doubtless some feeling coexists, but what feeling we cannot tell, because it is so fugitive and so immediately eclipsed by the more substantive and enduring memory of the impression as it came in, and of the executed movement of response. Feeling of the impression, attention to it, thought of the reaction, volition to react, would, undoubtedly, all be links of the process under other conditions,[13] and would lead to the same reaction-after an indefinitely longer time. But these other conditions are not those of the experiments we are discussing; and it is mythological psychology (of which we shall see many later examples) to conclude that because two mental processes lead to the same result they must be similar in their inward subjective constitution. The feeling of stage 3 is certainly no articulate perception. It can be nothing but the mere sense of a reflex discharge. The reaction whose time is measured is, in short, a reflex action pure and simple, and not a psychic act. A foregoing psychic condition is, it is true, a prerequisite for this reflex action. The preparation of the attention and volition; the expectation of the signal and the readiness of the hand to move, the instant it shall come; the nervous tension in which the subject waits, are all conditions of the formation in him for the time being of a new path or arc of reflex discharge. The tract from the sense-organ which receives the stimulus, into the motor centre which discharges the reaction, is already tingling with premonitory innervation, is raised to such a pitch of heightened irritability by the expectant attention, that the signal is instantaneously sufficient to cause the overflow.[14] No other tract of the nervous system is, at the moment, in this hair-trigger condition. The consequences is that one sometimes responds to a wrong signal, especially if it be an impression of the same kind with the signal we expect.[15] But if by chance we are tired, or the signal is unexpectedly weak, and we do not react instantly, but only after an express perception that the signal has come, and an express volition, the time becomes quite disproportionately long (a second or more, according to Exner[16]), and we feel that the process is in nature altogether different.

In fact, the reaction-time experiments are a case to which we can immediately apply what we have just learned about the summation of stimuli. 'Expectant attention' is but the subjective name for what objectively is a partial stimulation of a certain pathway, the pathway from the 'centre' for the signal to that for the discharge. In Chapter XI we shall see that all attention involves excitement from within of the tract concerned in feeling the objects to which attention is given. The tract here is the excito-motor arc about to be traversed. The signal is but the spark from without which touches off a train already laid. The performance, under these conditions, exactly resembles any reflex action. The only difference is that whilst, in the ordinarily so-called reflex acts, the reflex arc is a permanent result of organic growth, it is here a transient result of previous cerebral conditions.[17]

I am happy to say that since the preeceding paragraphs (and the notes thereto appertaining) were written, Wundt has himself become converted to the view which I defend. He now admits that in the shortest reactions "there is neither apperception nor will, but that they are merely brain-reflexes due to practice."[18] The means of his conversion are certain experiments performed in his laboratory by Herr L. Lange,[19] who was led to distinguish between two ways of setting the attention in reacting on a signal, and who found that they gave very different time-results. In the 'extreme sensorial' way, as Lange calls it, of reacting, one keeps one's mind as intent as possible upon the expected signal, and 'purposely avoids'[20] thinking of the movement to be executed; in the 'extreme muscular' way one 'does not think at all'[21] of the signal, but stands as ready as possible for the movement. The muscular reactions are much shorter than the sensorial ones, the average difference being in the neighborhood of a tenth of a second. Wundt accordingly calls them 'shortened reactions' and, with Lange, admits them to be mere reflexes; whilst the sensorial reactions he calls 'complete,' and holds to his original conception as far as they are concerned. The facts, however, do not seem to me to warrant even this amount of fidelity to the original Wundtian position. When we begin to react in the 'extreme sensorial' way, Lange says that we get times so very long that they must be rejected from the count as non-typical. "Only after the reacter has succeeded by repeated and conscientious practice in bringing about an extremely precise co-ordination of his voluntary impulse with his sense-impression do we get times which can be regarded as typical sensorial reaction-times."[22] Now it seems to me that these excessive and 'untypical' times are probably the real 'complete times,' the only ones in which distinct processes of actual perception and volition occur. The typical sensorial time which is attained by practice is probably another sort of reflex, less perfect than the reflexes prepared by straining one's attention towards the movement.[23] The times are much more variable in the sensorial way than in the muscular. The several muscular reactions differ little from each other. Only in them does the phenomenon occur of reacting on a false signal, or of reacting before the signal. Times intermediate between these two types occur according as the attention fails to turn itself exclusively to one of the extremes. It is obvious that Herr Lange's distinction between the two types of reaction is a highly important one, and that the 'extreme muscular method,' giving both the shortest times and the most constant ones, ought to be aimed at in all comparative investigations. Herr Lange's own muscular time averaged 0".123; his sensorial time, 0".230.

These reaction-time experiments are then in no sense measurements of the swiftness of thought. Only when we complicate them is there a chance for anything like an intellectual operation to occur. They may be complicated in various ways. The reaction may be withheld until the signal has consciously awakened a distinct idea (Wundt's discrimination-time, association-time) and then performed. Or there may be a variety of possible signals, each with a different reaction assigned to it, and the reacter may be uncertain which one he is about to receive. The reaction would then hardly seem to occur without a preliminary recognition and choice. We shall see, however, in the appropriate chapters, that the discrimination and choice involved in such a reaction are widely different from the intellectual operations of which we are ordinarily conscious under those names. Meanwhile the simple reaction-time remains as the starting point of all these superinduced complications. It is the fundamental physiological constant in all time-measurements. As such, its own variations have an interest, and must be briefly passed in review.[24]

The reaction-time varies with the individual and his age. An individual may have it particularly long in respect of signals of one sense (Buccola, p.147), but not of others. Old and uncultivated people have it long (nearly a second, in an old pauper observed by Exner, Pflüger's Archiv, VII. 612-4). Children have it long (half a second, Herzen in Buccola, p.152).

Practice shortens it to a quantity which is for each individual a minimum beyond which no farther reduction can be made. The aforesaid old pauper's time was, after much practice, reduced to 0.1866 sec. (loc. cit. p.626).

Fatigue lengthens it.

Concentration of attention shortens it. Details will be given in the chapter on Attention.

The nature of the signal makes it vary.[25] Wundt writes:

"I found that the reaction-time for impressions on the skin with electric stimulus is less than for true touch-sensations, as the following averages show:

	Average.	Average Variation.
Sound	0.167 sec.	0.0221 sec.
Light	0.222 "	0.0219 "
Electric skin-sensation	0.201 "	0.0115 "
Touch-sensations	0.213 "	0.0134 "

" I here bring together the averages which have been obtained by some other observers:

	Hirsch.	Hankel.	Exner.
Sound	0.149	0.1505	0.1360
Light	0.200	0.2246	0.1506
Skin-sensation	0.182	0.1546	0.1337"

[26]

Thermic reactions have been lately measured by A. Goldscheider and by Vintschgau (1887), who find them slower than reactions from touch. That from heat especially is very slow, more so than from cold, the differences (according to Goldscheider) depending on the nerve-terminations in the skin.

Gustatory reactions were measured by Vintschgau. They differed according to the substances used, running up to half a second as a maximum when identification took place. The mere perception of the presence of the substance on the tongue varied from 0".159 to 0".219 (Pflüger's Archiv, XIV.529).

Olfactory reactions have been studied by Vintschgau, Buccola, and Beaunis. They are slow, averaging about half a second (cf. Beaunis, Recherches exp. sur l'Activité Cérébrale, 1884, p.49 ff.)

It will be observed that sound is more promptly reacted on than either sight or touch. Taste and smell are slower than either. One individual, who reacted to touch upon the tip of the tongue in 0".125, took 0".993 to react upon the taste of quinine applied to the same spot. In another, upon the base of the tongue, the reaction to touch being 0".141, that to sugar was 0".552 (Vintschgau, quoted by Buccola, p.103). Buccola found the reaction to odors to vary from 0".334 to 0".681, according to the perfume used and the individual.

The intensity of the signal makes a difference. The intenser the stimulus the shorter the time. Herzen (Grundlinien einer allgem. Psychophysiologie, p.101) compared the reaction from a corn on the toe with that from the skin of the hand of the same subject. The two places were stimulated simultaneously, and the subject tried to react simultaneously with both hand and foot, but the foot always went quickest. When the sound skin of the foot was touched instead of the corn, it was the hand which always reacted first. Wundt tries to show that when the signal is made barely perceptible, the time is probably the same in all the senses, namely about 0.332" (Physiol. Psych., 2d ed., II. 224).

Where the signal is of touch, the place to which it is applied makes a difference in the resultant reaction-time. G.S. Hall and V. Kries found (Archiv f. Anat. u. Physiol., 1879) that when the finger-tip was the place the reaction was shorter than when the middle of the upper arm was used, in spite of the greater length of nerve-trunk to be traversed in the latter case. This discovery invalidates the measurements of the rapidity of transmission of the current in human nerves, for they are all based on the method of comparing reaction-times from places near the root and near the extremity of a limb. The same observers found that signals seen by the periphery of the retina gave longer times than the same signals seen by direct vision.

The season makes a difference, the time being some hundredths of a second shorter on cold winter days (Vintschgau apud Exner, Hermann's Hdbh., p.270).

Intoxicants alter the time. Coffee and tea appear to shorten it. Small doses of wine and alcohol first shorten and then lengthen it; but the shortening stage tends to disappear if a large dose be given immediately. This, at least, is the report of two German observers. Dr. J. W. Warren, whose observations are more thorough than any previous ones, could find no very decided effects from ordinary doses (Journal of Physiology, VIII. 311). Morphia lengthens the time. Amyl-nitrite lengthens it, but after the inhalation it may fall to less than the normal. Ether and chloroform lengthen it (for authorities, etc., see Buccola, p.189).

Certain diseased states naturally lengthen the time.

The hypnotic trance has no constant effect, sometimes shortening and sometimes lengthening it (Hall, Mind, VIII. 170; James, Proc. Am. Soc. for Psych. Research, 246).

The time taken to inhibit a movement (e.g. to cease contraction of jaw-muscles) seems to be about the same as to produce one (Gad, Archiv f.(Anat.u.) Physiol., 1887, 468; Orchansky, ibid., 1889, 1885).

An immense amount of work has been done on reaction-time, of which I have cited but a small part. It is a sort of work which appeals particularly to patient and exact minds, and they have not failed to profit by the opportunity.

FIG. 23.—Sphymographic pulse-tracing. *A*, during intellectual repose ; *B*, during intellectual activity. (Mosso.)

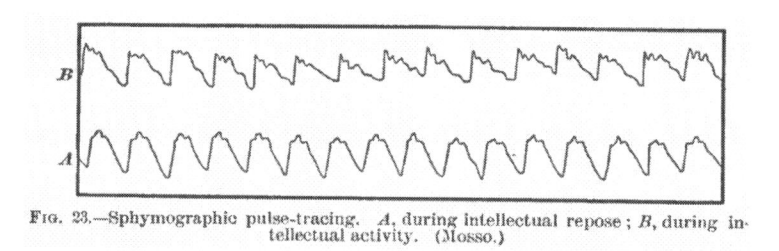

Cerebral Blood-Supply.

The next point to occupy our attention is the changes of circulation which accompany cerebral activity.

All parts of the cortex, when electrically excited, produce alterations both of respiration and circulation. The blood-pressure rises, as a rule, all over the body, no matter where the cortical irritation is applied, though the motor zone

is the most sensitive region for the purpose. Elsewhere the current must be strong enough for an epileptic attack to be produced.[27] Slowing and quickening of the heart are also observed, and are independent of the vaso-constrictive phenomenon. Mosso, using his ingenious 'plethysmograph' as an indicator, discovered that the blood-supply to the arms diminished during intellectual activity, and found furthermore that the arterial tension (as shown by the sphygmograph) was increased in these members (see Fig.23).
So slight an emotion as that produced by the entrance of Professor Ludwig into the laboratory was instantly followed by a shrinkage of the arms.[28] The brain itself is an excessively vascular organ, a sponge full of blood, in fact; and another of Mosso's inventions showed that when less blood went to the arms, more went to the head. The subject to be observed lay on a delicately balanced table which could tip downward either at the head or at the foot if the weight of either end were increased. The moment emotional or intellectual activity began in the subject, down went the balance at the head-end, in consequence of the redistribution of blood in his system. But the best proof of the immediate afflux of blood to the brain during mental activity is due to Mosso's observations on three persons whose brain had been laid bare by lesion of the skull. By means of apparatus described in his book,[29] this physiologist was enabled to let the brain-pulse record itself directly by a tracing. The intra-cranial blood-pressure rose immediately whenever the subject was spoken to, or when he began to think actively, as in solving a problem in mental arithmetic. Mosso gives in his work a large number of reproductions of tracings which show the instantaneity of the change of blood-supply, whenever the mental activity was quickened by any cause whatever, intellectual or emotional. He relates of his female subject that one day whilst tracing her brain-pulse he observed a sudden rise with no apparent outer or inner cause. She however confessed to him afterwards that at that moment she had caught sight of a skull on top of a piece of furniture in the room, and that this had given her a slight emotion. The fluctuations of the blood-supply to the brain were independent of respiratory changes,[30] and followed the quickening of mental activity almost immediately. We must suppose a very delicate adjustment whereby the circulation follows the needs of the cerebral activity. Blood very likely may rush to each region of the cortex according as it is most active, but of this we know nothing. I need hardly say that the activity of the nervous matter is the primary phenomenon, and the afflux of blood its secondary consequence. Many popular writers talk as if it were the other way about, and as if mental activity were due to the afflux of blood. But, as Professor H.N. Martin has well said, "that belief has no physiological foundation whatever; it is even directly opposed to all that we know of cell life."[31] A chronic pathological congestion may, it is true, have secondary consequences, but the primary congestions which we have been considering follow the activity of the brain-cells by an adaptive reflex vaso-motor mechanism doubtless as elaborate as that which harmonizes blood-supply with cell-action in any muscle or gland. Of the changes in the cerebral circulation during sleep, I will speak in the chapter which treats of that subject.

Cerebral Thermometry.

Brain-activity seems accompanied by a local disengagement of heat. The earliest careful work in this direction was by Dr. J.S. Lombard in 1867. Dr. Lombard's latest results include the records of over 60,000 observations.[32] He noted the changes in delicate thermometers and electric piles placed against the scalp in human beings, and found that any intellectual effort, such as computing, composing, reciting poetry silently or aloud, and especially that emotional excitement such as an anger fit, caused a general rise of temperature, which rarely exceeded a degree Fahrenheit. The rise was in most cases more marked in the middle region of the head than elsewhere. Strange to say, it was greater in reciting poetry silently than in reciting it aloud. Dr. Lombard's explanation is that "in internal recitation an additional portion of energy, which in recitation aloud, was converted into nervous and muscular force, now appears as heat."[33] I should suggest rather, if we must have a theory, that the surplus of heat in recitation to one's self is due to inhibitory processes which are absent when we recite aloud. In the chapter on the Will we shall see that the simple central process is to speak when we think; to think silently involves a check in addition. In 1870 the indefatigable Schiff took up the subject, experimenting on live dogs and chickens, plunging thermo-electric needles into the substance of their brain, to eliminate possible errors from vascular changes in the skin when the thermometers were placed upon the scalp. After habituation was established, he tested the animals with various sensations, tactile, optic, olfactory, and auditory. He found very regularly an immediate deflection of the galvanometer, indicating an abrupt alteration of the intra-cerebral temperature. When, for instance, he presented an empty roll of paper to the nose of his dog as it lay motionless, there was a small deflection, but when a piece of meat was in the paper the deflection was much greater. Schiff concluded from these and other experiments that sensorial activity heats the brain-tissue, but he did not try to localize the increment of heat beyond finding that it was in both hemispheres, whatever might be the sensation applied.[34] Dr. R.W. Amidon in 1880 made a farther step forward, in localizing the heat produced by voluntary muscular contractions. Applying a number of delicate surface-thermometers simultaneously against the scalp, he found that when different muscles of the body were made to contract vigorously for ten minutes or more, different regions of the scalp rose in temperature, that the regions were well focalized, and that the rise of temperature was often considerably over a Fahrenheit degree. As a result of his investigations he gives a diagram in which numbered regions represent the centres of highest temperature for the various special movements which were investigated. To a large extent they correspond to the centres for the same movements assigned by Ferrier and others on other grounds; only they cover more of the skull.[35]

Phosphorus and Thought

Chemical action must of course accompany brain-activity. But little definite is known of its exact nature. Cholesterin and creatin are both excrementitious products, and are both found in the brain. The subject belongs to chemistry rather than to psychology, and I only mention it here for the sake of saying a word about a wide-spread popular error about brain-activity and phosphorus. 'Ohne Phosphor, kein Gedanke,' was a noted war-cry of the 'materialists' during the excitement on that subject which filled Germany in the '60s. The brain, like every other organ of the body, contains phosphorus, and a score of other chemicals besides. Why the phosphorus should be picked out as its essence, no one knows. It would be equally true to say 'Ohne Wasser kein Gedanke,' or 'Ohne Kochsalz kein Gedanke'; for thought would stop as quickly if the brain should dry up or lose its NaCl as if it lost its phosphorus. In America the phosphorus-delusion has twined itself round a saying quoted (rightly or wrongly) from Professor L. Agassiz, to the effect that fishermen are more intelligent than farmers because they eat so much fish, which contains so much phosphorus. All the facts may be doubted.

The only straight way to ascertain the importance of phosphorus to thought would be to find whether more is excreted by the brain during mental activity than during rest. Unfortunately we cannot do this directly, but can only gauge the amount of PO_5 in the urine, which represents other organs as well as the brain, and this procedure, as Dr. Edes says, is like measuring the rise of water at the mouth of the Mississippi to tell where there has been a thunder-storm in Minnesota.[36] It has been adopted, however, by a variety of observers, some of whom found the phosphates in the urine diminished, whilst others found them increased, by intellectual work. On the whole, it is impossible to trace any constant relation. In maniacal excitement less phosphorus than usual seems to be excreted. More is excreted during sleep. There are differences between the alkaline and earthy phosphates into which I will not enter, as my only aim is to show that the popular way of looking at the matter has no exact foundation.[37] The fact that phosphorous-preparations may do good in nervous exhaustion proves nothing as to the part played by phosphorus in mental activity. Like iron, arsenic, and other remedies it is a stimulant or tonic, of whose intimate workings in the system we know absolutely nothing, and which moreover does good in an extremely small number of the cases in which it is prescribed.

The phosphorous-philosophers have often compared thought to a secretion. "The brain secretes thought, as the kidneys secrete urine, or as the liver secretes bile," are phrases which one sometimes hears. The lame analogy need hardly be pointed out. The materials which the brain pours into the blood (cholesterin, creatin, xanthin, or whatever they may be) are the analogues of the urine and the bile, being in fact real material excreta. As far as these matters go, the brain is a ductless gland. But we know of nothing connected with liver-and kidney-activity which can be in the remotest degree compared with the stream of thought that accompanies the brain's material secretions.

There remains another feature of general brain-physiology, and indeed for psychological purposes the most important feature of all. I refer to the aptitude of the brain for acquiring habits. But I will treat of that in a chapter by itself.

Notes

[1] I shall myself in later places indulge in much of this schematization. The reader will understand once for all that it is symbolic; and that the use of it is hardly more than to show what a deep congruity there is between mental processes and mechanical processes of some kind, not necessarily of the exact kind portrayed.

[2] Valentin: Archiv f. d. gesammt. Physiol., 1873, p.458. Stirling: Leipzig Acad. Berichte, 1875, p.372 (Journal of Physiol., 1875). J. Ward: Archiv f. (Anat. u.) Physiol., 1880, p.72. H. Sewall: Johns Hopkins Studies, 1880, p.30. Kronecker u. Nicolaides: Archiv f. (Anat.u.) Physiol., 1880, p.437. Exner: Archiv f. die ges. Physiol., Bd. 28, p.487 (1882). Eckhard: in Hermann's Hdbch. D. Physiol., Bd. I. Thl. II. p.31. François-Franck: Leçons sur les Fonctions motrices du Cerveau, p.51 ff., 339.-For the process of summation in nerves and muscles, cf. Hermann: ibid. Thl. I. p.109, and vol. I. p.40. Also Wundt: Physiol. Psych., I. 243 ff.; Richet: Travaux du Laboratoire de Marey, 1877, p.97; L'Homme et l'Intelligence, pp.24 ff., 468; Revue Philosophique, t.XXI. p. 564. Kronecker u. Hall: Archiv f. (Anat.u.) Physiol., 1879; Schönlein: ibid. 1882, p.357. Sertoli (Hofmann and Schwalbe's Jahresbericht, 1882. p.25. De Watteville: Neurologisches Centralblatt, 1883, No. 7. Grünhagen: Arch. f. d. ges. Physiol., Bd. 34, p.301(1884).

[3] Bubnoff und Heidenhain: Ueber Erregungs-und Hemmungsvorgänge innerhalb der motorischen Hirncentren. Archiv f. d. ges. Physiol., Bd.26, p.156(1881).

[4] Archiv f. d. ges. Physiol., Bd.26, p.176(1881). Exner thinks (ibid. Bd.28, p.497(1882) that the summation here occurs in the spinal cord. It makes no difference where this particular summation occurs, so far as the general philosophy of summation goes.

[5] G.H. Lewes: Physical Basis of Mind, p.479, where many similar examples are given, 487-9.

[6] Romanes: Mental Evolution in Animals, p.163.

[7] See a similar instance in Mach: Beiträge zur Analyse der Empfindungen, p.36, a sparrow being the animal. My young children are afraid of their own pug-dog, if he enters their room after they are in bed and the lights are out. Compare this statement also: "The first question to a peasant seldom proves more than a flapper to rouse the torpid adjustments of his ears. The invariable answer of a Scottish peasant is, 'What's your wull?'-that of the English, a vacant stare. A second and even a third question may be required to elicit an answer." (R.Fowler: Some Observations on the Mental State of the Blind, and Deaf, and Dumb (Salisbury, 1843), p.14.)

[8] The reader will find a great deal about chronographic apparatus in J. Marey: La Méthode Graphique, pt. II. chap. II. One can make pretty fair measurements with no other instrument than a watch, by making a large number of reactions, each serving as a signal for the following one, and dividing the total time they take by their number. Dr. O. W. Holmes first suggested this method., which has been ingeniously elaborated and applied by Professor Jastrow. See Science' for September 10, 1886.

[9] See, for a few modifications, Cattell, Mind, XI. 220 ff.

[10] Physiol. Psych., II. 221-2. Cf. also the first edition, 728-9. I must confess to finding all Wundt's utterances about 'apperception' both vacillating and obscure. I see no use whatever for the word, as he employs it, in Psychology. Attention, perception, conception, volition, are its ample equivalents. Why we should need a single word to denote all these things by turns, Wundt fails to make clear. Consult, however, his pupil Staude's article, 'Uber den Begriff der Apperception,' etc., in Wundt's periodical Psychologische Studien, I. 149, which may be supposed official. For minute criticism of Wundt's 'apperception,' see Marty: Vierteljahrschrift f. wiss. Philos., X. 346.

[11] By Exner, for example, Pflüger's Archiv, VII. 628 ff.

[12] P.222. Cf. also Richet, Rev. Philos., VI. 395-6.

[13] For instance, if, on the previous day, one had resolved to act on a signal when it should come, and it now came whilst we were engaged in other things, and reminded us of the resolve.

[14] "I need hardly mention that success in these experiments depends in a high degree on our concentration of attention. If inattentive, one gets very discrepant figures...This concentration of the attention is in the highest degree exhausting. After some experiments in which I was concerned to get results as uniform as possible, I was covered with perspiration and excessively fatigued although I had as quietly in my chair all the while." (Exner, loc. cit. VII. 618.)

[15] Wundt, Physiol. Psych., II.226.

[16] Pflüger's Archiv, VII.616.

[17] In short, what M. Delboeuf calls an 'organe adventice.' The reaction-time, moreover, is quite compatible with the reaction itself being of a reflex order. Some reflexes (sneezing, e.g.) are very slow. The only time-measurement of a reflex act in the human subject with which I am acquainted is Exner's measurement of winking (in Pflüger's Archiv f. d. gesammt. Physiol., Bd. VIII. P.526, 1874). He found that when the stimulus was a flash of light it took the wink 0.2168 sec. to occur. A strong electric shock to the cornea shortened the time ot 0.0578 sec. The ordinary 'reaction-time' is midway between these values. Exner 'reduces' his times by eliminating the physiological process of conduction. His 'reduced winking-time' is then 0.471 as a minimum (ibid. 531), whilst his reduced reaction-time is 0.0828 (ibid. VII. 637). These figures have really no scientific value beyond that of showing, according to Exner's own belief (VII. 531) that reaction-time and reflex-time measure processes of essentially the same order. His description, moreover, of the process is an excellent description of a reflex act. "Every one," says he, "who makes reaction-time experiments for the first time is surprised to dind how little he is master of his own movements, so soon as it becomes a question of executing them with a maximum of speed. Not only does their energy lie, as it were, outside the field of choice, but even the time in which the movement occurs depends only partly upon ourselves. We jerk our arm, and we can afterwards tell with astonishing precision whether we have jerked it quicker or slower than another time, although we have no power to jerk it exactly at the wished-for moment."-Wundt himself admits that when we await a strong signal with tense preparation there is no consciousness of any duality of 'apperception' and motor response; the two are continuous (Physiol. Psych., II. 226).-Mr. Cattell's view is identical with the one I defend. "I think," he says, "that if the processes of perception and willing are present at all they are very rudimentary....The subject, by a voluntary effort[before the signal comes], puts the lines of communication between the centre for "the stimulus " and the centre for the co-ordination of motions...in a state of unstable equilibrium. When, therefore, a nervous impulse reaches the "former centre," it causes brain-changes in two directions; an impulse moves along to the cortex and calls forth there a perception corresponding to the stimulus, while at the same time an impulse follows a line of small resistance to the centre for the co-ordination of motions, and the proper nervous impulse, already prepared and waiting for the signal, is sent from the centre to the muscle of the hand. When the reaction has often been made the entire cerebral process becomes automatic, the impulse of itself takes the well-travelled way to the motor centre and releases the motor impulse." (Mind, XI. 232-3.) - Finally, Prof. Lipps has, in his elaborate way (Grundtatsachen, 179-188), made mince-meat of the view that stage 3 involves either conscious perception or conscious will.

[18] Physiol. Psych. 3d. edition (1887), vol. II p.266.

[19] *Philosophische Studien, vol. IV. p.479 (1888).*
[20] *Loc. cit. p.488.*
[21] *Loc. cit. p.487.*
[22] *Loc. cit. p.489.*
[23] *Lange has an interesting hypothesis as to the brain-process concerned in the latter, for which I can only refer to his essay.*
[24] *The reader who wishes to know more about the matter will find a most faithful compilation of all that has been done, together with much original matter, in G. Buccola's 'Legge del Tempo.' etc. See also chapter XVI of Wundt's Physiol. Psychology; Exner in Hermann's Hdbch., Bd. 2, Thl. II. pp.252-280; also Ribot's Contemp. Germ. Psych., chap. VIII.*
[25] *The nature of the movement also seems to make it vary. Mr. B. I. Gilman and I reacted to the same signal by simply raising our hand, and again by carrying our hand towards our back. The moment registered was always that at which the hand broke and electric contact in starting to move. But it started one or two hundredths of a second later when the more extensive movement was the one to be made. Orchansky, on the other hand, experimenting on contractions of the masseter muscle, found (Archiv f. (Anat.u.) Physiol., 1889, p.187) that the greater the amplitude of contraction intended, the shorter grew the time of reaction. He explains this by the fact that a more ample contraction makes a greater appeal to the attention, and this shortens the times.*
[26] *Physiol. Psych., II. 223.*
[27] *François-Franck, Fonctions Motrices, Leçon XXII.*
[28] *La Paura (1884), p.117.*
[29] *Ueber den Kreislauf des Blutes im menschlichen Gehirn (1881), chap. II. The Introduction gives the history of our previous knowledge of the subject.*
[30] *In this conclusion M. Gley (Archives de Physiologie, 1881, p.742) agrees with Professor Mosso. Gley found his pulse rise 1-3 beats, his carotid dilate, and his radial artery contract during hard mental work.*
[31] *Address before Med. and Chirurg. Society of Maryland, 1879.*
[32] *See his book. "Experimental Researches on the Regional Temperature of the Head" (London, 1879).*
[33] *Loc. cit. p.195.*
[34] *The most convenient account of Schiff's experiments is by Prof. Herzen, in the Revue Philosophique, vol. III. p.36.*
[35] *A New Study of Cerebral Cortical Localization (N.Y., Putnam, 1880), pp.48-53.*
[36] *Archives of Medicine, vol. X, No. 1 (1883)*
[37] *Without multiplying references, I will simply cite Mendel (Archiv f. Psychiatrie, vol, III, 1871), Mairet (Archives de Neurologie, vol. IX, 1885), and Beaunis (Rech. Expérimentales sur l'Activité Cérébrale, 1887). Richet gives a partial bibliography in the Revue Scientifique, vol. 38, p.788 (1886).*

Chapter IV - Habit[1]

When we look at living creatures from an outward point of view, one of the first things that strike us is that they are bundles of habits. In wild animals, the usual round of daily behavior seems a necessity implanted at birth; in animals domesticated, and especially in man, it seems, to a great extent, to be the result of education. The habits to which there is an innate tendency are called instincts; some of those due to education would by most persons be called acts of reason. It thus appears that habit covers a very large part of life, and that one engaged in studying the objective manifestations of mind is bound at the very outset to define clearly just what its limits are.

The moment one tries to define what habit is, one is led to the fundamental properties of matter. The laws of Nature are nothing but the immutable habits which the different elementary sorts of matter follow in their actions and reactions upon each other. In the organic world, however, the habits are more variable than this. Even instincts vary from one individual to another of a kind; and are modified in the same individual, as we shall later see, to suit the exigencies of the case. The habits of an elementary particle of matter cannot change (on the principles of the atomistic philosophy), because the particle is itself an unchangeable thing; but those of a compound mass of matter can change, because they are in the last instance due to the structure of the compound, and either outward forces or inward tensions can, from one hour to another, turn that structure into something different from what it was. That is, they can do so if the body be plastic enough to maintain its integrity, and be not disrupted when its structure yields. The change of structure here spoken of need not involve the outward shape; it may be invisible and molecular, as when a bar of iron becomes magnetic or crystalline through the action of certain outward causes, or India-rubber becomes friable, or plaster 'sets.' All these changes are rather slow; the material in question opposes a certain resistance to the modifying cause, which it takes time to overcome, but the gradual yielding whereof often saves the material from being disintegrated altogether. When the structure has yielded, the same inertia becomes a condition of its comparative permanence in the new form, and of the new habits the body then manifests. Plasticity, then, in the wide sense of the word, means the possession of a structure weak enough to yield to an influence, but strong enough not to yield all at once. Each relatively stable phase of equilibrium in such a structure is marked by what we may call a new set of habits. Organic matter, especially nervous tissue, seems endowed with a very extraordinary degree of plasticity of this sort; so that we may without hesitation lay down as our first proposition the following, that the phenomena of habit in living beings are due to the plasticity [2] of the organic materials of which their bodies are composed.

But the philosophy of habit is thus, in the first instance, a chapter in physics rather than in physiology or psychology. That it is at bottom a physical principle is admitted by all good recent writers on the subject. They call attention to analogues of acquired habits exhibited by dead matter. Thus, M. Léon Dumont, whose essay on habit is perhaps the most philosophical account yet published, writes:

"Every one knows how a garment, after having been worn a certain time, clings to the shape of the body better than when it was new; there has been a change in the tissue, and this change is a new habit of cohesion. A lock works better after being used some time; at the outset more force was required to overcome certain roughnesses in the mechanism. The overcoming of their resistance is a phenomenon of habituation. It costs less trouble to fold a paper when it has been folded already. This saving of trouble is due to the essential nature of habit, which brings it about that, to reproduce the effect, a less amount of the outward cause is required. The sounds of a violin improve by use in the hands of an able artist, because the fibres of the wood at last contract habits of vibration conformed to harmonic relations. This is what gives such inestimable value to instruments that have belonged to great masters. Water, in flowing, hollows out for itself a channel, which grows broader and deeper; and, after having ceased to flow, it resumes, when it flows again, the path traced by itself before. Just so, the impressions of outer objects fashion for themselves in the nervous system more and more appropriate paths, and these vital phenomena recur under similar excitements from without, when they have been interrupted a certain time."[3]

Not in the nervous system alone. A scar anywhere is a locus minoris resistentioe, more liable to be abraded, inflamed, to suffer pain and cold, than are the neighboring parts. A sprained ankle, a dislocated arm, are in danger of being sprained or dislocated again; joints that have once been attacked by rheumatism or gout, mucous membranes that have been the seat of catarrh, are with each fresh recurrence more prone to a relapse, until often the morbid state chronically substitutes itself for the sound one. And if we ascend to the nervous system, we find how many so-called functional diseases seem to keep themselves going simply because they happen to have once begun; and how the forcible cutting short by medicine of a few attacks is often sufficient to enable the physiological forces to get possession of the field again, and to bring the organs back to functions of health. Epilepsies, neuralgias, convulsive affections of various sorts, insomnias, are so many cases in point. And, to take what are more obviously habits, the success with which a 'weaning' treatment can often be applied to the victims of unhealthy indulgence of passion, or of mere complaining or irascible disposition, shows us how much the morbid manifestations themselves were due to the mere inertia of the nervous organs, when once launched on a false career.

Can we now form a notion of what the inward physical changes may be like, in organs whose habits have thus struck into new paths? In other words, can we say just what mechanical facts the expression 'change of habit' covers when it is applied to a nervous system? Certainly we cannot in anything like a minute or definite way. But our usual scientific custom of interpreting hidden molecular events after the analogy of visible massive ones enables us to frame easily an abstract and general scheme of processes which the physical changes in question may be like. And when once the possibility of some kind of mechanical interpretation is established, Mechanical Science, in her present mood, will not hesitate to set her brand of ownership upon the matter, feeling sure that it is only a question of time when the exact mechanical explanation of the case shall be found out.

If habits are due to the plasticity of materials to outward agents, we can immediately see to what outward influences, if to any, the brain-matter is plastic. Not to mechanical pressures, not to thermal changes, not to any of the forces to which all the other organs of our body are exposed; for nature has carefully shut up our brain and spinal cord in bony boxes where no influences of this sort can get at them. She has floated them in fluid so that only the severest shocks can give them a concussion, and blanketed and wrapped them about in an altogether exceptional way. The only impressions that can be made upon them are through the blood, on the one hand, and through the sensory nerve-roots, on the other; and it is to the infinitely attenuated currents that pour in through these latter channels that the hemispherical cortex shows itself to be so peculiarly susceptible. The currents, once in, must find a way out. In getting out they leave their traces in the paths which they take. The only thing they can do, in short, is to deepen old paths or to make new ones; and the whole plasticity of the brain sums itself up in two words when we call it an organ in which currents pouring in from the sense-organs make with extreme facility paths which do not easily disappear. For, of course, a simple habit, like every other nervous event - the habit of snuffling, for example, or of putting one's hands into one's pockets, or of biting one's nails - is, mechanically, nothing but a reflex discharge; and its anatomical substratum must be a path in the system. The most complex habits, as we shall presently see more fully, are, from the same point of view, nothing but concatenated discharges in the nerve-centres, due to the presence there of systems of reflex paths, so organized as to wake each other up successively - the impression produced by one muscular contraction serving as a stimulus to provoke the next, until a final impression inhibits the process and closes the chain. The only difficult mechanical problem is to explain the formulation de novo of a simple reflex or path in a pre-existing nervous system. Here, as in so many other cases, it is only the premier pas qui coûte. For the entire nervous system is nothing but a system of paths between a sensory terminus a quo and a muscular, glandular, or other terminus ad quem. A path once traversed by a nerve-current might be expected to follow the law of most of the paths we know, and to be scooped out and made more permeable than before;[4] and this ought to be repeated with each new passage of the current. Whatever obstructions may have kept it at first from being a path should then, little by little, and more and more, be swept out of the way, until at last it might become a natural drainage-channel. This is what happens where either solids or liquids pass over a path; there seems no reason why is should not happen where the thing that passes is a mere wave of rearrangement in matter that does not displace itself, but merely changes chemically or turns itself round in place, or vibrates across the line. The most plausible views of the nerve-current make it out to be the passage of some such wave of rearrangement as this. If only a part of the matter of the path were to 'rearrange' itself, the neighboring parts remaining inert, it is easy to see how their inertness might oppose a friction which it would take many waves of rearrangement to break down and overcome. If we call the path itself the 'organ,' and the wave of rearrangement the 'function,' then it is obviously a case for repeating the celebrated French formula of 'La fonction fait l'organe.'

So nothing is easier than to imagine how, when a current once has traversed a path, it should traverse it more readily still a second time. But what made it ever traverse it the first time?[5] In answering this question we can only fall back on our general conception of a nervous system as a mass of matter whose parts, constantly kept in states of different tension, are as constantly tending to equalize their states. The equalization between any two points occurs through whatever path may at the moment be most pervious. But, as a given point of the system may belong, actually or potentially, to many different paths, and, as the play of nutrition is subject to accidental changes, blocks may from time to time occur, and make currents shoot through unwonted lines. Such an unwonted line would be a new-created path, which if traversed repeatedly, would become the beginning of a new reflex arc. All this is vague to the last degree, and amounts to little more than saying that a new path may be formed by the sort of chances that in nervous material are likely to occur. But, vague as it is, it is really the last word of our wisdom in the matter.[6]

It must be noticed that the growth of structural modification in living matter may be more rapid than in any lifeless mass, because the incessant nutritive renovation of which the living matter is the seat tends often to corroborate and fix the impressed modification, rather than to counteract it by renewing the original constitution of the tissue that has been impressed. Thus, we notice after exercising our muscles or our brain in a new way, that we can do so no longer at that time; but after a day or two of rest, when we resume the discipline, our increase in skill not seldom surprises us. I have often noticed this in learning a tune; and it has led a German author to say that we learn to swim during the winter and to skate during the summer.

Dr. Carpenter writes:[7]

"It is a matter of universal experience that every kind of training for special aptitudes is both far more effective, and leaves a more permanent impress, when exerted on the growing organism than when brought to bear on the adult. The effect of such training is shown in the tendency of the organ to 'grow to' the mode in which it is habitually exercised; as is evidenced by the increased size and power of particular sets of muscles, and the extraordinary flexibility of joints, which are acquired by such as have been early exercised in gymnastic performances...There is no part of the organism of man in which the reconstructive activity is so great, during the whole period of life, as it is in the ganglionic substance of the brain. This is indicated by the enormous supply of blood which it receives....It is, moreover, a fact of great significance that the nerve-substance is specially distinguished by its reparative power. For while injuries of other tissues (such as the muscular) which are distinguished by the speciality of their structure and endowments, are repaired by substance of a lower or less specialized type, those of nerve-substance are repaired by a complete reproduction of the normal tissue; as is evidenced in the sensibility of the newly forming skin which is closing over an open wound, or in the recovery of the sensibility of a piece of 'transplanted' skin, which has for a time been rendered insensible by the complete interruption of the continuity of its nerves. The most remarkable example of this reproduction, however, is afforded by the results of M. Brown-Séquard's[8] experiments upon the gradual restoration of the functional activity of the spinal cord after its complete division; which takes place in way that indicates rather a reproduction of the whole, or the lower part of the cord and of the nerves proceeding from it, than a mere reunion of divided surfaces. This reproduction is but a special manifestation of the reconstructive change which is always taking place in the nervous system; it being not less obvious to the eye of reason that the 'waste' occasioned by its functional activity must be constantly repaired by the production of new tissue, than it is to the eye of sense that such reparation supplies an actual loss of substance by disease or injury.

"Now, in this constant and active reconstruction of the nervous system, we recognize a most marked conformity to the general plan manifested in the nutrition of the organism as a whole. For, in the first place, it is obvious that there is a tendency to the production of a determinate type of structure; which type is often not merely that of the species, but some special modification of it which characterized one or both of the progenitors. But this type is peculiarly liable to modification during the early period of life; in which the functional activity of the nervous system (and particularly of the brain) is extraordinarily great, and the reconstructive process proportionally active. And this modifiability expresses itself in the formation of the mechanism by which those secondarily automatic modes of movement come to be established, which, in man, take the place of those that are congenital in most of the animals beneath him; and those modes of sense-perception come to be acquired, which are elsewhere clearly instinctive. For there can be no reasonable doubt that, in both cases, a nervous mechanism is developed in the course of this self-education, corresponding with that which the lower animals inherit from their parents. The plan of that rebuilding process, which is necessary to maintain the integrity of the organism generally, and which goes on with peculiar activity in this portion of it, is thus being incessantly modified; and in this manner all that portion of it which ministers to the external life of sense and motion that is shared by man with the animal kingdom at large, becomes at adult age the expression of the habits which the individual has acquired during the period of growth and development. Of these habits, some are common to the race generally, while others are peculiar to the individual; those of the former kind (such as walking erect) being universally acquired, save where physical inability prevents; while for the latter a special training is needed, which is usually the more effective the earlier it is begun - as is remarkably seen in the case of such feats of dexterity as require a conjoint education of the perspective and of the motor powers. And when thus developed during the period of growth, so as to have become a part of the constitution of the adult, the acquired mechanism is thenceforth maintained in the ordinary course of the nutritive operations, so as to be ready for use when called upon, even after long inaction.

"What is so clearly true of the nervous apparatus of animal life can scarcely be otherwise than true of that which ministers to the automatic activity of the mind. For, as already shown, the study of psychology has evolved no more certain result than that there are uniformities of mental action which are so entirely conformable to those of bodily action as to indicate their intimate relation to a 'mechanism of thought and feeling,' acting under the like conditions with that of sense and motion. The psychical principles of association, indeed, and the physiological principles of nutrition, simply express - the former in terms of mind, the latter in terms of brain - the universally admitted fact that any sequence of mental action which has been frequently repeated tends to perpetuate itself; so that we find ourselves automatically prompted to think, feel, or do what we have been before accustomed to think, feel, or do, under like circumstances, without any consciously formed purpose, or anticipation of results. For there is no reason to regard the cerebrum as an exception to the general principle that, while each part of the organism tends to form itself in accordance with the mode in which it is habitually exercised, this tendency will be especially strong in the nervous apparatus, in virtue of that incessant regeneration which is the very condition of its functional activity. It scarcely, indeed, admits of doubt that every state of ideational consciousness which is either very strong or is habitually repeated leaves an organic impression on the cerebrum; in virtue of which that same state may be reproduced at any future time, in respondence to a suggestion fitted to excite it. . . . . . The 'strength of early association' is a fact so universally recognized that the expression of it has become proverbial; and this precisely accords with the physiological principle that, during the period of growth and development, the formative activity of the brain will be most amenable to directing influences. It is in this way that what is early 'learned by heart' becomes branded in (as it were) upon the cerebrum; so that its 'traces' are never lost, even though the conscious memory of it may have completely faded out. For, when the organic modification has been once fixed in the growing brain, it becomes a part of the normal fabric, and is regularly maintained by nutritive substitution; so that it may endure to the end of life, like the scar of a wound."

Dr. Carpenter's phrase that our nervous system grows to the modes in which it has been exercised expresses the philosophy of habit in a nutshell. We may now trace some of the practical applications of the principle to human life. The first result of it is that habit simplifies the movements required to achieve a given result, makes them more accurate and diminishes fatigue.

"The beginner at the piano not only moves his finger up and down in order to depress the key, he moves the whole hand, the forearm and even the entire body, especially moving its least rigid part, the head, as if he would press down the key with that organ too. Often a contraction of the abdominal muscles occurs as well. Principally, however, the impulse is determined to the motion of the hand and of the single finger. This is, in the first place, because the movement of the finger is the movement thought of, and, in the second place, because its movement and that of the key are the movements we try to perceive, along with the results of the latter on the ear. The more often the process is repeated, the more easily the movement follows, on account of the increase in permeability of the nerves engaged.

"But the more easily the movement occurs, the slighter is the stimulus required to set it up; and the slighter the stimulus is, the more its effect is confined to the fingers alone.

"Thus, an impulse which originally spread its effects over the whole body, or at least over many of its movable parts, is gradually determined to a single definite organ, in which it effects the contraction of a few limited muscles. In this change the thoughts and perceptions which start the impulse acquire more and more intimate causal relations with a particular group of motor nerves.

"To recur to a simile, at least partially apt, imagine the nervous system to represent a drainage-system, inclining, on the whole, toward certain muscles, but with the escape thither somewhat clogged. Then streams of water will, on the whole, tend most to fill the drains that go towards these muscles and to wash out the escape. In case of a sudden 'flushing,' however, the whole system of channels will fill itself, and the water overflow everywhere before it escapes. But a moderate quantity of water invading the system will flow through the proper escape alone.

"Just so with the piano-player. As soon as his impulse, which has gradually learned to confine itself to single muscles, grows extreme, it overflows into larger muscular regions. He usually plays with his fingers, his body being at rest. But no sooner does he get excited than his whole body becomes 'animated,' and he moves his head and trunk, in particular, as if these also were organs with which he meant to belabor the keys."[9]

Man in born with a tendency to do more things than he has ready-made arrangements for in his nerve-centres. Most of the performances of other animals are automatic. But in him the number of them is so enormous, that most of them must be the fruit of painful study. If practice did not make perfect, nor habit economize the expense of nervous and muscular energy, he would therefore be in a sorry plight. As Dr. Maudsley says: [10]

:If an act became no easier after being done several times, if the careful direction of consciousness were necessary to its accomplishment on each occasion, it is evident that the whole activity of a lifetime might be confined to one or two deeds - that no progress could take place in development. A man might be occupied all day in dressing and un-dressing himself; the attitude of his body would absorb all his attention and energy; the washing of his hands or the fastening of a button would be as difficult to him on each occasion as to the child on its first trial; and he would, furthermore, be completely exhausted by his exertions. Think of the pains necessary to teach a child to stand, of the many efforts which it must make, and of the ease with which it at last stands, unconscious of any effort. For while secondarily automatic acts are accomplished with comparatively little weariness - in this regard approaching the organic movements, or the original reflex movements - the conscious effort of the will soon produces exhaustion. A spinal cord without . . . memory would simply be an idiotic spinal cord . . . It is impossible for an individual to realize how much he owes to its automatic agency until disease has impaired its functions."

The next result is that habit diminishes the conscious attention with which our acts are performed.

One may state this abstractly thus: If an act require for its execution a chain, A, B, C, D, E, F, G, etc., of successive nervous events, then in the first performances of the action the conscious will must choose each of these events from a number of wrong alternatives that tend to present themselves; but habit soon brings it about that each event calls up its own appropriate successor without any alternative offering itself, and without any reference to the conscious will, until at last the whole chain, A, B, C, D, E, F, G, rattles itself off as soon as A occurs, just as if A and the rest of the chain were fused into a continuous stream. When we are learning to walk, to ride, to swim, skate, fence, write, play, or sing, we interrupt ourselves at every step by unnecessary movements and false notes. When we are proficients, on the contrary, the results not only follow with the very minimum of muscular action requisite to bring them forth, they also follow from a single instantaneous 'cue.' The marksman sees the bird, and, before he knows it, he has aimed and shot. A gleam in his adversary's eye, a momentary pressure from his rapier, and the fencer finds that he has instantly made the right parry and return. A glance at the musical hieroglyphics, and the pianist's fingers have ripped through a cataract of notes. And not only is it the right thing at the right time that we thus involuntarily do, but the wrong thing also, if it be an habitual thing. Who is there that has never wound up his watch on taking off his waistcoat in the daytime, or taken his latchkey out on arriving at the door-step of a friend? Very absent-minded persons in going to their bedroom to dress for dinner have been known to take off one garment after another and finally to get into bed, merely because that was the habitual issue of the first few movements when performed at a later hour. The writer well remembers how, on revisiting Paris after ten years' absence, and, finding himself in the street in which for one winter he had attended school, he lost himself in a brown study, from which he was awakened by finding himself upon the stairs which led to the apartment in a house many streets away in which he had lived during that earlier time, and to which his steps from the school had then habitually led. We all of us have a definite routine manner of performing certain daily offices connected with the toilet, with the opening and shutting of familiar cupboards, and the like. Our lower centres know the order of these movements, and show their knowledge by their 'surprise' if the objects are altered so as to oblige the movement to be made in a different way. But our higher thought-centres know hardly anything about the matter. Few men can tell off-hand which sock, shoe, or trousers-leg they put on first. They must first mentally rehearse the act; and even that is often insufficient - the act must be performed. So of the questions, Which valve of my double door opens first? Which way does my door swing? etc. I cannot tell the answer; yet my hand never makes a mistake. No one can describe the order in which he brushes his hair or teeth; yet it is likely that the order is a pretty fixed one in all of us.

These results may be expressed as follows:

In action grown habitual, what instigates each new muscular contraction to take place in its appointed order is not a thought or a perception, but the sensation occasioned by the muscular contraction just finished. A strictly voluntary act has to be guided by idea, perception, and volition, throughout its whole course. In an habitual action, mere sensation is a sufficient guide, and the upper regions of brain and mind are set comparatively free. A diagram will make the matter clear:

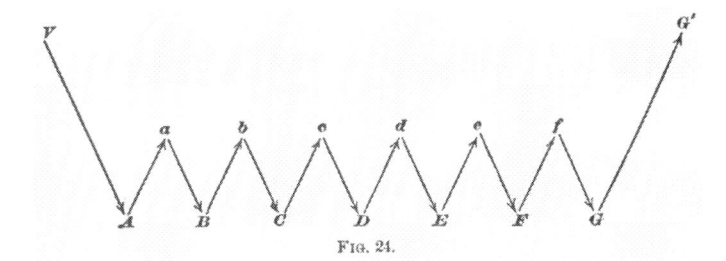

FIG. 24.

Let A, B, C, D, E, F, G represent an habitual chain of muscular contractions, and let a, b, c, d, e, f stand for the respective sensations which these contractions excite in us when they are successively performed. Such sensations will usually be of the muscles, skin, or joints of the parts moved, but they may also be effects of the movement upon the eye or the ear. Through them, and through them alone, we are made aware whether the contraction has or has not occurred. When the series, A, B, C, D, E, F, G, is being learned, each of these sensations becomes the object of a separate perception by the mind. By it we test each movement, to see if it be right before advancing to the next. We hesitate, compare, choose, revoke, reject, etc., by intellectual means; and the order by which the next movement is discharged is an express order from the ideational centres after this deliberation has been gone through.

In habitual action, on the contrary, the only impulse which the centres of idea or perception need send down is the initial impulse, the command to start. This is represented in the diagram by V; it may be a thought of the first movement or of the last result, or a mere perception of some of the habitual conditions of the chain, the presence, e.g., of the keyboard near the hand. In the present case, no sooner has the conscious thought or volition instigated movement A, than A, through the sensation a of its own occurrence, awakens B reflexly; B then excites C through b, and so on till the chain is ended when the intellect generally takes cognizance of the final result. The process, in fact, resembles the passage of a wave of 'peristaltic' motion down the bowels. The intellectual perception at the end is indicated in the diagram by the effect of G being represented, at G', in the ideational centres above the merely sensational line. The sensational impressions, a, b, c, d, e, f, are all supposed to have their seat below the ideational lines. That our ideational centres, if involved at all by a, b, c, d, e, f, are involved in a minimal degree, is shown by the fact that the attention may be wholly absorbed elsewhere. We may say our prayers, or repeat the alphabet, with our attention far away.

"A musical performer will play a piece which has become familiar by repetition while carrying on an animated conversation, or while continuously engrossed by some train of deeply interesting thought; the accustomed sequence of movements being directly prompted by the sight of the notes, or by the remembered succession of the sounds (if the piece is played from memory), aided in both cases by the guiding sensations derived from the muscles themselves. But, further, a higher degree of the same 'training' (acting on an organism specially fitted to profit by it) enables an accomplished pianist to play a difficult piece of music at sight; the movements of the hands and fingers following so immediately upon the sight of the notes that it seems impossible to believe that any but the very shortest and most direct track can be the channel of the nervous communication through which they are called forth. The following curious example of the same class of acquired aptitudes, which differ from instincts only in being prompted to action by the will, is furnished by Robert Houdin:

"'With a view of cultivating the rapidity of visual and tactile perception, and the precision of respondent movements, which are necessary for the success in every kind of prestidigitation, Houdin early practised the art of juggling with balls in the air; and having, after a month's practice, become thorough master of the art of keeping up four balls at once, he placed a book before him, and, while the balls were in the air, accustomed himself to read without hesitation. 'This,' he says, 'will probably seem to my readers very extraordinary; but I shall surprise them still more when I say that I have just amused myself with repeating this curious experiment. Though thirty years have elapsed since the time I was writing, and though I have scarcely once touched the balls during that period, I can still manage to read with ease while keeping three balls up.'" (Autobiography, p. 26.)[11]

We have called a, b, c, d, e, f, the antecedents of the successive muscular attractions, by the name of sensations. Some authors seem to deny that they are even this. If not even this, they can only be centripetal nerve-currents, not sufficient to arouse feeling, but sufficient to arouse motor response.[12] It may be at once admitted that they are not distinct volitions. The will, if any will be present, limits itself to a permission that they exert their motor effects, Dr. Carpenter writes:

"There may still be metaphysicians who maintain that actions which were originally prompted by the will with a distinct intention, and which are still entirely under its control, can never cease to be volitional; and that either an infinitesimally small amount of will is required to sustain them when they have been once set going, or that the will is in a sort of pendulum-like oscillation between the two actions - the maintenance of the train of thought, and the maintenance of the train of movement. But if only an infinitesimally small amount of will is necessary to sustain them, is not this tantamount to saying that they go on by a force of their own? And does not the experience of the perfect continuity of our train of thought during the performance of movements that have become habitual, entirely negative the hypothesis of oscillation? Besides, if such an oscillation existed, there must be intervals in which each action goes on of itself; so that its essentially automatic character is virtually admitted. The physiological explanation, that the mechanism of locomotion, as of other habitual movements, grows to the mode in which it is early exercised, and that it then works automatically under the general control and direction of the will, can scarcely be put down by any assumption of an hypothetical necessity, which rests only on the basis of ignorance of one side of our composite nature."[13]

But if not distinct acts of will, these immediate antecedents of each movement of the chain are at any rate accompanied by consciousness of some kind. They are sensations to which we are usually inattentive, but which immediately call out attention if they go wrong. Schneider's account of these sensations deserves to be quoted. In the act of walking, he says, even when our attention is entirely off,

"we are continuously aware of certain muscular feelings; and we have, moreover, a feeling of certain impulses to keep our equilibrium and to set down one leg after another. It is doubtful whether we could preserve equilibrium if no sensation of our body's attitude were there, and doubtful whether we should advance our leg if we had no sensation of its movements as executed, and not even a minimal feeling of impulse to set it down. Knitting appears altogether mechanical, and the knitter keeps up her knitting even while she reads or is engaged in lively talk. But if we ask her how this be possible, she will hardly reply that the knitting goes on of itself. She will rather say that she has a feeling of it, that she feels in her hands that she knits and how she must knit, and that therefore the movements of knitting are called forth and regulated by the sensations associated therewithal, even when the attention is called away.

"So of every one who practises, apparently automatically, a long-familiar handicraft. The smith turning his tongs as he smites the iron, the carpenter wielding his plane, the lace-maker with her bobbin, the weaver at his loom, all will answer the same question in the same way by saying that they have a feeling of the proper management of the implement in their hands.

"In these cases, the feelings which are conditions of the appropriate acts are very faint. But none the less are they necessary. Imagine your hands not feeling; your movements could then only be provoked by ideas, and if your ideas were then diverted away, the movements ought to come to a standstill, which is a consequence that seldom occurs."[14]

Again:

"An idea makes you take, for example, a violin into your left hand. But it is not necessary that your idea remain fixed on the contraction of the muscles of the left hand and fingers in order that the violin may continue to be held fast and not let fall. The sensations themselves which the holding of the instrument awakens in the hand, since they are associated with the motor impulse of grasping, are sufficient to cause this impulse, which then lasts as long as the feeling itself lasts, or until the impulse is inhibited by the idea of some antagonistic motion."

And the same may be said of the manner in which the right hand holds the bow:

"It sometimes happens, in beginning these simultaneous combinations, that one movement or impulse will cease if the consciousness turn particularly toward another, because at the outset the guiding sensations must all be strongly felt. The bow will perhaps slip from the fingers, because some of the muscles have relaxed. But the slipping is a cause of new sensations starting up in the hand, so that the attention is in a moment brought back to the grasping of the bow.

"The following experiment shows this well: When one begins to play on the violin, to keep him from raising his right elbow in playing a book is placed under his right armpit, which he is ordered to hold fast by keeping the upper arm tight against his body. The muscular feelings, and feelings of contact connected with the book, provoke an impulse to press it tight. But often it happens that the beginner, whose attention gets absorbed in the production of the notes, lets drop the book. Later, however, this never happens; the faintest sensations of contact suffice to awaken the impulse to keep it in its place, and the attention may be wholly absorbed by the notes and the fingering with the left hand. The simultaneous combination of movements is thus in the first instance conditioned by the facility with which in us, alongside of intellectual processes, processes of inattentive feeling may still go on."[15]

This brings us by a very natural transition to the ethical implications of the law of habit. They are numerous and momentous. Dr. Carpenter, from whose 'Mental Physiology' we have quoted, has so prominently enforced the principle that our organs grow to the way in which they have been exercised, and dwelt upon its consequences, that his book almost deserves to be called a work of edification, on this account alone. We need make no apology, then, for tracing a few of these consequences ourselves:

"Habit a second nature! Habit is ten times nature," the Duke of Wellington is said to have exclaimed; and the degree to which this is true no one can probably appreciate as well as one who is a veteran soldier himself. The daily drill and the years of discipline end by fashioning a man completely over again, as to most of the possibilities of his conduct.

"There is a story, which is credible enough, though it may not be true, of a practical joker, who, seeing a discharged veteran carrying home his dinner, suddenly called out, 'Attention!' whereupon the man instantly brought his hands down, and lost his mutton and potatoes in the gutter. The drill had been thorough, and its effects had become embodied in the man's nervous structure."[16]

Riderless cavalry-horses, at many a battle, have been seen to come together and go through their customary evolutions at the sound of the bugle-call. Most trained domestic animals, dogs and oxen, and omnibus- and car-horses, seem to be machines almost pure and simple, undoubtingly, unhesitatingly doing from minute to minute the duties they have been taught, and giving no sign that the possibility of an alternative ever suggests itself to their mind. Men grown old in prison have asked to be readmitted after being once set free. In a railroad accident to a travelling menagerie in the United States some time in 1884, a tiger, whose cage had broken open, is said to have emerged, but presently crept back again, as if too much bewildered by his new responsibilities, so that he was without difficulty secured.

Habit is thus the enormous fly-wheel of society, its most precious conservative agent. It alone is what keeps us all within the bounds of ordinance, and saves the children of fortune from the envious uprisings of the poor. It alone prevents the hardest and most repulsive walks of life from being deserted by those brought up to tread therein. It keeps the fisherman and the deck-hand at sea through the winter; it holds the miner in his darkness, and nails the countryman to his log-cabin and his lonely farm through all the months of snow; it protects us from invasion by the natives of the desert and the frozen zone. It dooms us all to fight out the battle of life upon the lines of our nurture or our early choice, and to make the best of a pursuit that disagrees, because there is no other for which we are fitted, and it is too late to begin again. It keeps different social strata from mixing. Already at the age of twenty-five you see the professional mannerism settling down on the young commercial traveller, on the young doctor, on the young minister, on the young counsellor-at-law. You see the little lines of cleavage running through the character, the tricks of thought, the prejudices, the ways of the 'shop,' in a word, from which the man can by-and-by no more escape than his coat-sleeve can suddenly fall into a new set of folds. On the whole, it is best he should not escape. It is well for the world that in most of us, by the age of thirty, the character has set like plaster, and will never soften again.

If the period between twenty and thirty is the critical one in the formation of intellectual and professional habits, the period below twenty is more important still for the fixing of personal habits, properly so called, such as vocalization and pronunciation, gesture, motion, and address. Hardly ever is a language learned after twenty spoken without a foreign accent; hardly ever can a youth transferred to the society of his betters unlearn the nasality and other vices of speech bred in him by the associations of his growing years. Hardly ever, indeed, no matter how much money there be in his pocket, can he even learn to dress like a gentleman-born. The merchants offer their wares as eagerly to him as to the veriest 'swell,' but he simply cannot buy the right things. An invisible law, as strong as gravitation, keeps him within his orbit, arrayed this year as he was the last; and how his better-bred acquaintances contrive to get the things they wear will be for him a mystery till his dying day.

The great thing, then, in all education, is to make our nervous system our ally instead of our enemy. It is to fund and capitalize our acquisitions, and live at ease upon the interest of the fund. For this we must make automatic and habitual, as early as possible, as many useful actions as we can, and guard against the growing into ways that are likely to be disadvantageous to us, as we should guard against the plague. The more of the details of our daily life we can hand over to the effortless custody of automatism, the more our higher powers of mind will be set free for their own proper work. There is no more miserable human being than one in whom nothing is habitual but indecision, and for whom the lighting of every cigar, the drinking of every cup, the time of rising and going to bed every day, and the beginning of every bit of work, are subjects of express volitional deliberation. Full half the time of such a man goes to the deciding, or regretting, of matters which ought to be so ingrained in him as practically not to exist for his consciousness at all. If there be such daily duties not yet ingrained in any one of my readers, let him begin this very hour to set the matter right.

In Professor Bain's chapter on 'The Moral Habits' there are some admirable practical remarks laid down. Two great maxims emerge from his treatment. The first is that in the acquisition of a new habit, or the leaving off of an old one, we must take care to launch ourselves with as strong and decided an initiative as possible. Accumulate all the possible circumstances which shall re-enforce the right motives; put yourself assiduously in conditions that encourage the new way; make engagements incompatible with the old; take a public pledge, if the case allows; in short, envelop your resolution with every aid you know. This will give your new beginning such a momentum that the temptation to break down will not occur as soon as it otherwise might; and every day during which a breakdown is postponed adds to the chances of its not occurring at all.

The second maxim is: Never suffer an exception to occur till the new habit is securely rooted in your life. Each lapse is like the letting fall of a ball of string which one is carefully winding up; a single slip undoes more than a great many turns will wind again. Continuity of training is the great means of making the nervous system act infallibly right. As Professor Bain says:

"The peculiarity of the moral habits, contradistinguishing them from the intellectual acquisitions, is the presence of two hostile powers, one to be gradually raised into the ascendant over the other. It is necessary, above all things, in such a situation, never to lose a battle. Every gain on the wrong side undoes the effect of many conquests on the right. The essential precaution, therefore, is so to regulate the two opposing powers that the one may have a series of uninterrupted successes, until repetition has fortified it to such a degree as to enable it to cope with the opposition, under any circumstances. This is the theoretically best career of mental progress."

The need of securing success at the outset is imperative. Failure at first is apt to dampen the energy of all future attempts, whereas past experience of success nerves one to future vigor. Goethe says to a man who consulted him about an enterprise but mistrusted his own powers: "Ach! you need only blow on your hands!" And the remark illustrates the effect on Goethe's spirits of his own habitually successful career. Prof. Baumann, from whom I borrow the anecdote,[17] says that the collapse of barbarian nations when Europeans come among them is due to their despair of ever succeeding as the new-comers do in the larger tasks of life. Old ways are broken and new ones not formed.

The question of 'tapering-off,' in abandoning such habits as drink and opium-indulgence, comes in here, and is a question about which experts differ within certain limits, and in regard to what may be best for an individual case. In the main, however, all expert opinion would agree that abrupt acquisition of the new habit is the best way, if there be a real possibility of carrying it out. We must be careful not to give the will so stiff a task as to insure its defeat at the very outset; but, provided one can stand it, a sharp period of suffering, and then a free time, is the best thing to aim at, whether in giving up a habit like that of opium, or in simply changing one's hours of rising or of work. It is surprising how soon a desire will die of inanition if it be never fed.

"One must first learn, unmoved, looking neither to the right nor left, to walk firmly on the straight and narrow path, before one can begin 'to make one's self over again.' He who every day makes a fresh resolve is like one who, arriving at the edge of the ditch he is to leap, forever stops and returns for a fresh run. Without unbroken advance there is no such thing as accumulation of the ethical forces possible, and to make this possible, and to exercise us and habituate us in it, is the sovereign blessing of regular work."[18]

A third maxim may be added to the preceding pair: Seize the very first possible opportunity to act on every resolution you make, and on every emotional prompting you may experience in the direction of the habits you aspire to gain. It is not in the moment of their forming, but in the moment of their producing motor effects, that resolves and aspirations communicate the new 'set' to the brain. As the author last quoted remarks:
"The actual presence of the practical opportunity alone furnishes the fulcrum upon which the lever can rest, by means of which the moral will may multiply its strength, and raise itself aloft. He who has no solid ground to press against will never get beyond the stage of empty gesture-making."
No matter how full a reservoir of maxims one may possess, and no matter how good one's sentiments may be, if one have not taken advantage of every concrete opportunity to act, one's character may remain entirely unaffected for the better. With mere good intentions, hell is proverbially paved. An this is an obvious consequence of the principles we have laid down. A 'character,' as J.S. Mill says, 'is a completely fashioned will'; and a will, in the sense in which he means it, is an aggregate of tendencies to act in a firm and prompt and definite way upon all the principal emergencies of life. A tendency to act only becomes effectively ingrained in us in proportion to the uninterrupted frequency with which the actions actually occur, and the brain 'grows' to their use. Every time a resolve or a fine glow of feeling evaporates without bearing practical fruit is worse than a chance lost; it works so as positively to hinder future resolutions and emotions from taking the normal path of discharge. There is no more contemptible type of human character than that of the nerveless sentimentalist and dreamer, who spends his life in a weltering sea of sensibility and emotion, but who never does a manly concrete deed. Rousseau, inflaming all the mothers of France, by his eloquence, to follow Nature and nurse their babies themselves, while he sends his own children to the foundling hospital, is the classical example of what I mean. But every one of us in his measure, whenever, after glowing for an abstractly formulated Good, he practically ignores some actual case, among the squalid 'other particulars' of which that same Good lurks disguised, treads straight on Rousseau's path. All Goods are disguised by the vulgarity of their concomitants, in this work-a-day world; but woe to him who can only recognize them when he thinks them in their pure and abstract form! The habit of excessive novel-reading and theatre-going will produce true monsters in this line. The weeping of a Russian lady over the fictitious personages in the play, while her coach-man is freezing to death on his seat outside, is the sort of thing that everywhere happens on a less glaring scale. Even the habit of excessive indulgence in music, for those who are neither performers themselves nor musically gifted enough to take it in a purely intellectual way, has probably a relaxing effect upon the character. One becomes filled with emotions which habitually pass without prompting to any deed, and so the inertly sentimental condition is kept up. The remedy would be, never to suffer one's self to have an emotion at a concert, without expressing it afterward in some active way.[19] Let the expression be the least thing in the world -speaking genially to one's aunt, or giving up one's seat in a horse-car, if nothing more heroic offers - but let it not fail to take place.
These latter cases make us aware that it is not simply particular lines of discharge, but also general forms of discharge, that seem to be grooved out by habit in the brain. Just as, if we let our emotions evaporate, they get into a way of evaporating; so there is reason to suppose that if we often flinch from making an effort, before we know it the effort-making capacity will be gone; and that, if we suffer the wandering of our attention, presently it will wander all the time. Attention and effort are, as we shall see later, but two names for the same psychic fact. To what brain-processes they correspond we do not know. The strongest reason for believing that they do depend on brain-processes at all, and are not pure acts of the spirit, is just this fact, that they seem in some degree subject to the law of habit, which is a material law. As a final practical maxim, relative to these habits of the will, we may, then, offer something like this: Keep the faculty of effort alive in you by a little gratuitous exercise every day. That is, be systematically ascetic or heroic in little unnecessary points, do every day or two something for no other reason than that you would rather not do it, so that when the hour of dire need draws nigh, it may find you not unnerved and untrained to stand the test. Asceticism of this sort is like the insurance which a man pays on his house and goods. The tax does him no good at the time, and possibly may never bring him a return. But if the fire does come, his having paid it will be his salvation from ruin. So with the man who has daily inured himself to habits of concentrated attention, energetic volition, and self-denial in unnecessary things. He will stand like a tower when everything rocks around him, and when his softer fellow-mortals are winnowed like chaff in the blast.
The physiological study of mental conditions is thus the most powerful ally of hortatory ethics. The hell to be endured hereafter, of which theology tells, is no worse than the hell we make for ourselves in this world by habitually fashioning our characters in the wrong way. Could the young but realize how soon they will become mere walking bundles of habits, they would give more heed to their conduct while in the plastic state. We are spinning our own fates, good or evil, and never to be undone. Every smallest stroke of virtue or of vice leaves its never so little scar. The drunken Rip Van Winkle, in Jefferson's play, excuses himself for every fresh dereliction by saying, 'I won't count this time!' Well! he may not count it, and a kind Heaven may not count it; but it is being counted none the less. Down among his nerve-cells and fibres the molecules are counting it, registering and storing it up to be used against him when the next temptation comes. Nothing we ever do is, in strict scientific literalness, wiped out. Of course, this

has its good side as well as its bad one. As we become permanent drunkards by so many separate drinks, so we become saints in the moral, and authorities and experts in the practical and scientific spheres, by so many separate acts and hours of work. Let no youth have any anxiety about the upshot of his education, whatever the line of it may be. If he keep faithfully busy each hour of the working-day, he may safely leave the final result to itself. He can with perfect certainty count on waking up some fine morning, to find himself one of the competent ones of his generation, in whatever pursuit he may have singled out. Silently, between all the details of his business, the power of judging in all that class of matter will have built itself up within him as a possession that will never pass away. Young people should know this truth in advance. The ignorance of it has probably engendered more discouragement and faint-heartedness in youths embarking on arduous careers than all other causes put together.

Notes

[1] This chapter has already appeared in the Popular Science Monthly for February 1887.
[2] In the sense above explained, which applies to inner structure as well as to outer form.
[3] Revue Philosophique, I, 324.
[4] Some paths, to be sure, are banked up by bodies moving through them under too great pressure, and made impervious. These special cases we disregard.
[5] We cannot say the will, for, though many, perhaps most, human habits were once voluntary actions, no action, as we shall see in a later chapter, can be primarily such. While an habitual action may once have been voluntary, the voluntary action must before that, at least once, have been impulsive or reflex. It is this very first occurrence of all that we consider in the text.
[6] Those who desire a more definite formulation may consult J. Fiske's 'Cosmic Philosophy,' vol. II. pp. 142-146 and Spencer's 'Principles of Biology,' sections 302 and 303, and the part entitled 'Physical Synthesis' of his 'Principles of Psychology.' Mr. Spencer there tries, not only to show how new actions may arise in nervous systems and form new reflex arcs therein, but even how nervous tissue may actually be born by the passage of new waves of isometric transformation through an originally indifferent mass. I cannot help thinking that Mr. Spencer's data, under a great show of precision, conceal vagueness and improbability, and even self-contradiction.
[7] 'Mental Physiology' (1874,) pp. 339-345.
[8] [See, later, Masius in Van Benedens' and Van Bambeke's 'Archives de Biologie,' vol. I (Liége, 1880). - W.J.]
[9] G. H. Schneider: 'Der menschliche Wille' (1882), pp. 417-419 (freely translated). For the drain-simile, see also Spencer's 'Psychology,' part V, chap. VIII.
[10] Physiology of Mind, p. 155.
[11] Carpenter's 'Mental Physiology' (1874), pp. 217, 218.
[12] Von Hartmann devotes a chapter of his 'Philosophy of the Unconscious' (English translation, vol. I. p. 72) to proving that they must be both ideas and unconscious.
[13] 'Mental Physiology,' p. 20.
[14] 'Der menschliche Willie,' pp. 447, 448.
[15] 'Der menschliche Wille,' p. 439. The last sentence is rather freely translated - the sense is unaltered.
[16] Huxley's 'Elementary Lessons in Physiology,' lesson XII.
[17] See the admirable passage about success at the outset, in his Handbuch der Moral (1878), pp. 38-43.
[18] J. Bahnsen: 'Beiträge zu Charakterologie' (1867), vol. I. p. 209.
[19] See for remarks on this subject a readable article by Miss V. Scudder on 'Musical Devotees and Morals,' in the Andover Review for January 1887.

Chapter V - The Automaton-Theory

In describing the functions of the hemispheres a short way back, we used language derived from both the bodily and the mental life, saying now that the animal made indeterminate and unforeseeable reactions, and anon that he was swayed by considerations of future good and evil; treating his hemispheres sometimes as the seat of memory and ideas in the psychic sense, and sometimes talking of them as simply a complicated addition to his reflex machinery. This sort of vacillation in the point of view is a fatal incident of all ordinary talk about these questions; but I must now settle my scores with those readers to whom I already dropped a word in passing and who have probably been dissatisfied with my conduct ever since.

Suppose we restrict our view to facts of one and the same plane, and let that be the bodily plane: cannot all the outward phenomena of intelligence still be exhaustively described? Those mental images, those 'considerations,' whereof we spoke, - presumably they do not arise without neural processes arising simultaneously with them, and presumably each consideration corresponds to a process sui generis, and unlike all the rest. In other words, however numerous and delicately differentiated the train of ideas may be, the train of brain-events that runs alongside of it must in both respects be exactly its match, and we must postulate a neural machinery that offers a living counterpart for every shading, however fine, of the history of its owner's mind. Whatever degree of complication the latter may reach, the complication of the machinery must be quite as extreme, otherwise we should have to admit that there may be mental events to which no brain-events correspond. But such an admission as this the physiologist is reluctant to make. It would violate all his beliefs. 'No psychosis without neurosis,' is one form which the principle of continuity takes in his mind.

But this principle forces the physiologist to make still another step. If neural action is as complicated as mind; and if in the sympathetic system and lower spinal cord we see what, so far as we know, is unconscious neural action executing deeds that to all outward intent may be called intelligent; what is there to hinder us from supposing that even where we know consciousness to be there, the still more complicated neural action which we believe to be its inseparable companion is alone and of itself the real agent of whatever intelligent deeds may appear? "As actions of a certain degree of complexity are brought about by mere mechanism, why may not actions of a still greater degree of complexity be the result of a more refined mechanism?" The conception of reflex action is surely one of the best conquests of physiological theory; why not be radical with it? Why not say that just as the spinal cord is a machine with few reflexes, so the hemispheres are a machine with many, and that that is all the difference? The principle of continuity would press us to accept this view.

But what on this view could be the function of the consciousness itself? Mechanical function it would have none. The sense-organs would awaken the brain-cells; these would awaken each other in rational and orderly sequence, until the time for action came; and then the last brain-vibration would discharge downward into the motor tracts. But this would be a quite autonomous chain of occurrences, and whatever mind went with it would be there only as an 'epiphenomenon,' an inert spectator, a sort of 'foam, aura, or melody' as Mr. Hodgson says, whose opposition or whose furtherance would be alike powerless over the occurrences themselves. When talking, some time ago, we ought not, accordingly, as physiologists, to have said anything about 'considerations' as guiding the animal. We ought to have said 'paths left in the hemispherical cortex by former currents,' and nothing more.

Now so simple and attractive is this conception from the consistently physiological point of view, that it is quite wonderful to see how late it was stumbled on in philosophy, and how few people, even when it has been explained to them, fully and easily realize its import. Much of the polemic writing against it is by men who have as yet failed to take it into their imaginations. Since this has been the case, it seems worth while to devote a few more words to making it plausible, before criticising it ourselves.

To Descartes belongs the credit of having first been bold enough to conceive of a completely self-sufficing nervous mechanism which should be able to perform complicated and apparently intelligent acts. By a singularly arbitrary restriction, however, Descartes stopped short at man, and while contending that in beasts the nervous machinery was all, he held that the higher acts of man were the result of the agency of his rational soul. The opinion that beasts have no consciousness at all was of course too paradoxical to maintain itself long as anything more than a curious item in the history of philosophy. And with its abandonment the very notion that the nervous system per se might work the work of intelligence, which was an integral, though detachable part of the whole theory, seemed also to slip out of men's conception, until, in this century, the elaboration of the doctrine of reflex action made it possible and natural that it should again arise. But it was not till 1870, I believe, that Mr. Hodgson made the decisive step, by saying that feelings, no matter how intensely they may be present, can have no causal efficacy whatever, and comparing them to the colors laid on the surface of a mosaic, of which the events in the nervous system are represented by the stones.[1] Obviously the stones are held in place by each other and not by the several colors which they support.

About the same time Mr. Spalding, and a little later Messrs. Huxley and Clifford, gave great publicity to an identical doctrine, though in their case it was backed by less refined metaphysical considerations.[2]

A few sentences from Huxley and Clifford may be subjoined to make the matter entirely clear. Professor Huxley says: "The consciousness of brutes would appear to be related to the mechanism of their body simply as a collateral product of its working, and to be as completely without any power of modifying that working as the steam-whistle which accompanies the work of a locomotive engine is without influence on its machinery. Their volition, if they have any, is an emotion indicative of physical changes, not a cause of such changes... The soul stands related to the body as the bell of a clock to the works, and consciousness answers to the sound which the bell gives out when it is struck... Thus far I have strictly confined myself to the automatism of brutes... It is quite true that, to the best of my judgment, the argumentation which applies to brutes holds equally good of men; and, therefore, that all states of consciousness in us, as in them, are immediately caused by molecular changes of the brain-substance. It seems to me that in men, as in brutes, there is no proof that any state of consciousness is the cause of change in the motion of the matter of the organism. If these positions are well based, it follows that our mental conditions are simply the symbols in consciousness of the changes which take place automatically in the organism; and that, to take an extreme illustration, the feeling we call volition is not the cause of a voluntary act, but the symbol of that state of the brain which is the immediate cause of that act. We are conscious automata."

Professor Clifford writes:

"All the evidence that we have goes to show that the physical world gets along entirely by itself, according to practically universal rules.... The train of physical facts between the stimulus sent into the eye, or to any one of our senses, and the exertion which follows it, and the train of physical facts which goes on in the brain, even when there is no stimulus and no exertion, - these are perfectly complete physical trains, and every step is fully accounted for by mechanical conditions.... The two things are on utterly different platforms - the physical facts go along by themselves, and the mental facts go along by themselves. There is a parallelism between them, but there is no interference of one with the other. Again, if anybody says that the will influences matter, the statement is not untrue, but it is nonsense. Such an assertion belongs to the crude materialism of the savage. The only thing which influences matter is the position of surrounding matter or the motion of surrounding matter.... The assertion that another man's volition, a feeling in his consciousness that I cannot perceive, is part of the train of physical facts which I may perceive, - this is neither true non untrue, but nonsense; it is a combination of words whose corresponding ideas will not go together.... Sometimes one series is known better, and sometimes the other; so that in telling a story we speak sometimes of mental and sometimes of material facts. A feeling of chill made a man run; strictly speaking, the nervous disturbance which coexisted with that feeling of chill made him run, if we want to talk about material facts; or the feeling of chill produced the form of sub-consciousness which coexists with the motion of legs, if we want to talk about mental facts....When, therefore, we ask: 'What is the physical link between the ingoing message from chilled skin and the outgoing message which moves the leg?' and the answer is, 'A man's will,' we have as much right to be amused as if we had asked our friend with the picture what pigment was used in painting the cannon in the foreground, and received the answer, 'Wrought iron.' It will be found excellent practice in the mental operations required by this doctrine to imagine a train, the fore part of which is an engine and three carriages linked with iron couplings, and the hind part three other carriages linked with iron couplings; the bond between the two parts being made up out of the sentiments of amity subsisting between the stoker and the guard."

To comprehend completely the consequences of the dogma so confidently enunciated, one should unflinchingly apply it to the most complicated examples. The movements of our tongues and pens, the flashings of our eyes in conversation, are of course events of a material order, and as such their causal antecedents must be exclusively material. If we knew thoroughly the nervous system of Shakespeare, and as thoroughly all his environing conditions, we should be able to show why at a certain period of his life his hand came to trace on certain sheets of paper those crabbed little black marks which we for shortness' sake call the manuscript of Hamlet. We should understand the rationale of every erasure and alteration therein, and we should understand all this without in the slightest degree acknowledging the existence of the thoughts in Shakespeare's mind. The words and sentences would be taken, not as signs of anything beyond themselves, but as little outward facts, pure and simple. In like manner we might exhaustively write the biography of those two hundred pounds, more or less, of warmish albuminoid matter called Martin Luther, without ever implying that it felt.

But, on the other hand, nothing in all this could prevent us from giving an equally complete account of either Luther's or Shakespeare's spiritual history, an account in which every gleam of thought and emotion should find its place. The mind-history would run alongside of the body-history of each man, and each point in the one would correspond to, but not react upon, a point in the other. So the melody floats from the harp-string, but neither checks nor quickens its vibrations; so the shadow runs alongside the pedestrian, but in no way influences his steps.

Another inference, apparently more paradoxical still, needs to be made, though, as far as I am aware, Dr. Hodgson is the only writer who has explicitly drawn it. That inference is that feelings, not causing nerve-actions, cannot even cause each other. To ordinary common sense, felt pain is, as such, not only the cause of outward tears and cries, but also the cause of such inward events as sorrow, compunction, desire, or inventive thought. So the consciousness of good news is the direct producer of the feeling of joy, the awareness of premises that of the belief in conclusions. But according to the automaton-theory, each of the feelings mentioned is only the correlate of some nerve-movement whose cause lay wholly in a previous nerve-movement. The first nerve-movement called up the second; whatever feeling was attached to the second consequently found itself following upon the feeling that was attached to the first. If, for example, good news was the consciousness correlated with the first movement, then joy turned out to be the correlate in consciousness of the second. But all the while the items of the nerve series were the only ones in causal continuity; the items of the conscious series, however inwardly rational their sequence, were simply juxtaposed.

Reasons for the Theory

The 'conscious automaton-theory,' as this conception is generally called, is thus a radical and simple conception of the manner in which certain facts may possibly occur. But between conception and belief, proof ought to lie. And when we ask, 'What proves that all this is more than a mere conception of the possible?' it is not easy to get a sufficient reply. If we start from the frog's spinal cord and reason by continuity, saying, as that acts so intelligently, though unconscious, so the higher centres, though conscious, may have the intelligence they show quite as mechanically based; we are immediately met by the exact counter-argument from continuity, an argument actually urged by such writers as Pflüger and Lewes, which starts from the acts of the hemispheres, and says: "As these owe their intelligence to the consciousness which we know to be there, so the intelligence of the spinal cord's acts must really be due to the invisible presence of a consciousness lower in degree." All arguments from continuity work in two ways, you can either level up or level down by their means; and it is clear that such arguments as these can eat each other up to all eternity.

There remains a sort of philosophic faith, bred like most faiths from an aesthetic demand. Mental and physical events are, on all hands, admitted to present the strongest contrast in the entire field of being. The chasm which yawns between them is less easily bridged over by the mind than any interval we know. Why, then, not call it an absolute chasm, and say not only that the two worlds are different, but that they are independent? This gives us the comfort of all simple and absolute formulas, and it makes each chain homogeneous to our consideration. When talking of nervous tremors and bodily actions, we may feel secure against intrusion from an irrelevant mental world. When, on the other hand, we speak of feelings, we may with equal consistency use terms always of one denomination, and never be annoyed by what Aristotle calls 'slipping into another kind.' The desire on the part of men educated in laboratories not to have their physical reasonings mixed up with such incommensurable factors as feelings is certainly very strong. I have heard a most intelligent biologist say: "It is high time for scientific men to protest against the recognition of any such thing as consciousness in a scientific investigation." In a word, feeling constitutes the 'unscientific' half of existence, and any one who enjoys calling himself a 'scientist' will be too happy to purchase an untrammelled homogeneity of terms in the studies of his predilection, at the slight cost of admitting a dualism which, in the same breath that it allows to mind an independent status of being, banishes it to a limbo of causal inertness, from whence no intrusion or interruption on its part need ever be feared.

Over and above this great postulate that matters must be kept simple, there is, it must be confessed, still another highly abstract reason for denying causal efficacy to our feelings. We can form no positive image of the modus operandi of a volition or other thought affecting the cerebral molecules.

"Let us try to imagine an idea, say of food, producing a movement, say of carrying food to the mouth.... What is the method of its action? Does it assist the decomposition of the molecules of the gray matter, or does it retard the process, or does it alter the direction in which the shocks are distributed? Let us imagine the molecules of the gray matter combined in such a way that they will fall into simpler combinations on the impact of an incident force. Now suppose the incident force, in the shape of a shock from some other centre, to impinge upon these molecules. By hypothesis it will decompose them, and they will fall into the simpler combination. How is the idea of food to prevent this decomposition? Manifestly it can do so only by increasing the force which binds the molecules together. Good! Try to imagine the idea of a beefsteak binding two molecules together. It is impossible. Equally impossible is it to imagine a similar idea loosening the attractive force between two molecules."[3]

This passage from an exceedingly clever writer expresses admirably the difficulty to which I allude. Combined with a strong sense of the 'chasm' between the two worlds, and with a lively faith in reflex machinery, the sense of this difficulty can hardly fail to make one turn consciousness out of the door as a superfluity so far as one's explanations go. One may bow her out politely, allow her to remain as a 'concomitant,' but one insists that matter shall hold all the power.

"Having thoroughly recognized the fathomless abyss that separates mind from matter, and having so blended the very notion into his very nature that there is no chance of his ever forgetting it or failing to saturate with it all his meditations, the student of psychology has next to appreciate the association between these two orders of phenomena.... They are associated in a manner so intimate that some of the greatest thinkers consider them different aspects of the same process.... When the rearrangement of molecules takes place in the higher regions of the brain, a change of consciousness simultaneously occurs.... The change of consciousness never takes place without the change in the brain; the change in the brain never ... without the change in consciousness. But why the two occur together, or what the link is which connects them, we do not know, and most authorities believe that we never shall and never can know. Having firmly and tenaciously grasped these two notions, of the absolute separateness of mind and matter, and of the invariable concomitance of a mental change with a bodily change, the student will enter on the study of psychology with half his difficulties surmounted."[4]

Half his difficulties ignored, I should prefer to say. For this 'concomitance' in the midst of 'absolute separateness' is an utterly irrational notion. It is to my mind quite inconceivable that consciousness should have nothing to do with a business which it so faithfully attends. And the question, 'What has it to do?' is one which psychology has no right to 'surmount,' for it is her plain duty to consider it. The fact is that the whole question of interaction and influence between things is a metaphysical question, and cannot be discussed at all by those who are unwilling to go into matters thoroughly. It is truly enough hard to imagine the 'idea of a beefsteak binding two molecules together;' but since Hume's time it has been equally hard to imagine anything binding them together. The whole notion of 'binding' is a mystery, the first step towards the solution of which is to clear scholastic rubbish out of the way. Popular science talks of 'forces,' 'attractions' or 'affinities' as binding the molecules; but clear science, though she may use such words to abbreviate discourse, has no use for the conceptions, and is satisfied when she can express in simple 'laws' the bare space-relations of the molecules as functions of each other and of time. To the more curiously inquiring mind, however, this simplified expression of the bare facts is not enough; there must be a 'reason' for them, and something must 'determine' the laws. And when one seriously sits down to consider what sort of a thing one means when one asks for a 'reason,' one is led so far afield, so far away from popular science and its scholasticism, as to see that even such a fact as the existence or non-existence in the universe of 'the idea of a beefsteak' may not be wholly indifferent to other facts in the same universe, and in particular may have something to do with determining the distance at which two molecules in that universe shall lie apart. If this is so, then common-sense, though the intimate nature of causality and of the connection of things in the universe lies beyond her pitifully bounded horizon, has the root and gist of the truth in her hands when she obstinately holds to it that feelings and ideas are causes. However inadequate our ideas of causal efficacy may be, we are less wide of the mark when we say that our ideas and feelings have it, than the Automatists are when they say they haven't it. As in the night all cats are gray, so in the darkness of metaphysical criticism all causes are obscure. But one has no right to pull the pall over the psychic half of the subject only, as the automatists do, and to say that that causation is unintelligible, whilst in the same breath one dogmatizes about material causation as if Hume, Kant, and Lotze had never been born. One cannot thus blow hot and cold. One must be impartially naif or impartially critical. If the latter, the reconstruction must be thorough-going or 'metaphysical,' and will probably preserve the common-sense view that ideas are forces, in some translated form. But Psychology is a mere natural science, accepting certain terms uncritically as her data, and stopping short of metaphysical reconstruction. Like physics, she must be naïve; and if she finds that in her very peculiar field of study ideas seem to be causes, she had better continue to talk of them as such. She gains absolutely nothing by a breach with common-sense in this matter, and she loses, to say the least, all naturalness of speech. If feelings are causes, of course their effects must be furtherances and checkings of internal cerebral motions, of which in themselves we are entirely without knowledge. It is probable that for years to come we shall have to infer what happens in the brain either from our feelings or from motor effects which we observe. The organ will be for us a sort of vat in which feelings and motions somehow go on stewing together, and in which innumerable things happen of which we catch but the statistical result. Why, under these circumstances, we should be asked to forswear the language of our childhood I cannot well imagine, especially as it is perfectly compatible with the language of physiology. The feelings can produce nothing absolutely new, they can only reinforce and inhibit reflex currents, and the original organization by physiological forces of these in paths must always be the ground-work of the psychological scheme. My conclusion is that to urge the automaton-theory upon us, as it is now urged, on purely a priori and quasi-metaphysical grounds, is an unwarrantable impertinence in the present state of psychology.

Reasons Against the Theory

But there are much more positive reasons than this why we ought to continue to talk in psychology as if consciousness had causal efficacy. The particulars of the distribution of consciousness, so far as we know them, point to its being efficacious. Let us trace some of them.

It is very generally admitted, though the point would be hard to prove, that consciousness grows the more complex and intense the higher we rise in the animal kingdom. That of a man must exceed that of an oyster. From this point of view it seems an organ, superadded to the other organs which maintain the animal in the struggle for existence; and the presumption of course is that is helps him in some way in the struggle, just as they do. But it cannot help him without being in some way efficacious and influencing the course of his bodily history. If now it could be shown in what way consciousness might help him, and if, moreover, the defects of his other organs (where consciousness is most developed) are such as to make them need just the kind of help that consciousness would bring provided it were efficacious; why, then the plausible inference would be that it came just because of its efficacy - in other words, its efficacy would be inductively proved.

Now the study of the phenomena of consciousness which we shall make throughout the rest of this book will show us that consciousness is at all times primarily a selecting agency.[5] Whether we take it in the lowest sphere of sense, or in the highest of intellection, we find it always doing one thing, choosing one out of several of the materials so presented to its notice, emphasizing and accentuating that and suppressing as far as possible all the rest. The item emphasized is always in close connection with some interest felt by consciousness to be paramount at the time.

But what are now the defects of the nervous system in those animals whose consciousness seems most highly developed? Chief among them must be instability. The cerebral hemispheres are the characteristically 'high' nerve-centres, and we saw how indeterminate and unforeseeable their performances were in comparison with those of the basal ganglia and the cord. But this very vagueness constitutes their advantage. They allow their possessor to adapt his conduct to the minutest alterations in the environing circumstances, any one of which may be for him a sign, suggesting distant motives more powerful than any present solicitations of sense. It seems as if certain mechanical conclusions should be drawn from this state of things. An organ swayed by slight impressions is an organ whose natural state is one of unstable equilibrium. We may imagine the various lines of discharge in the cerebrum to be almost on a par in point of permeability - what discharge a given small impression will produce may be called accidental, in the sense in which we say it is a matter of accident whether a rain-drop falling on a mountain ridge descend the eastern or the western slope. It is in this sense that we may call it a matter of accident whether a child be a boy or a girl. The ovum is so unstable a body that certain causes too minute for our apprehension may at a certain moment tip it one way or the other. The natural law of an organ constituted after this fashion can be nothing but a law of caprice. I do not see how one could reasonably expect from it any certain pursuance of useful lines of reaction, such as the few and fatally determined performances of the lower centres constitute within their narrow sphere. The dilemma in regard to the nervous system seems, in short, to be of the following kind. We may construct one which will react infallibly and certainly, but it will then be capable of reacting to very few changes in the environment - it will fail to be adapted to all the rest. We may, on the other hand, construct a nervous system potentially adapted to respond to an infinite variety of minute features in the situation; but its fallibility will then be as great as its elaboration. We can never be sure that its equilibrium will be upset in the appropriate direction. In short, a high brain may do many things, and may do each of them at a very slight hint. But its hair-trigger organization makes of it a happy-go-lucky, hit-or-miss affair. It is as likely to do the crazy as the sane thing at any given moment. A low brain does few things, and in doing them perfectly forfeits all other use. The performances of a high brain are like dice thrown forever on a table. Unless they be loaded, what chance is there that the highest number will turn up oftener than the lowest?

All this is said of the brain as a physical machine pure and simple. Can consciousness increase its efficiency by loading its dice? Such is the problem.

Loading its dice would mean bringing a more or less constant pressure to bear in favor of those of its performances which make for the most permanent interests of the brain's owner; it would mean a constant inhibition of the tendencies to stray aside.

Well, just such pressure and such inhibition are what consciousness seems to be exerting all the while. And the interests in whose favor it seems to exert them are its interests and its alone, interests which it creates, and which, but for it, would have no status in the realm of being whatever. We talk, it is true, when we are darwinizing, as if the mere body that owns the brain had interests; we speak about the utilities of its various organs and how they help or hinder the body's survival; and we treat the survival as if it were an absolute end, existing as such in the physical world, a sort of actual should-be, presiding over the animal and judging his reactions, quite apart from the presence of any commenting intelligence outside. We forget that in the absence of some such superadded commenting intelligence (whether it be that of the animal itself, or only ours or Mr. Darwin's), the reactions cannot be properly talked of as 'useful' or 'hurtful' at all. Considered merely physically, all that can be said of them is that if they occur in a certain way survival will as a matter of fact prove to be their incidental consequence. The organs themselves, and all the rest of the physical world, will, however, all the time be quite indifferent to this consequence, and would quite as cheerfully, the circumstances changed, compass the animal's destruction. In a word, survival can enter into a purely physiological discussion only as an hypothesis made by an onlooker about the future. But the moment you bring a consciousness into the midst, survival ceases to be a mere hypothesis. No longer is it, "if survival is to occur, then so and so must brain and other organs work." It has now become an imperative decree: "Survival shall occur, and therefore organs must so work!" Real ends appear for the first time now upon the world's stage. The conception of consciousness as a purely cognitive form of being, which is the pet way of regarding it in many idealistic-modern as well as ancient schools, is thoroughly anti-psychological, as the remainder of this book will show. Every actually existing consciousness seems to itself at any rate to be a fighter for ends, of which many, but for its presence, would not be ends at all. Its powers of cognition are mainly subservient to these ends, discerning which facts further them and which do not.

Now let consciousness only be what it seems to itself, and it will help an instable brain to compass its proper ends. The movements of the brain per se yield the means of attaining these ends mechanically, but only out of a lot of other ends, if so they may be called, which are not the proper ones of the animal, but often quite opposed. The brain is an instrument of possibilities, but of no certainties. But the consciousness, with its own ends present to it, and knowing also well which possibilities lead thereto and which away, will, if endowed with causal efficacy, reinforce the favorable possibilities and repress the unfavorable or indifferent ones. The nerve-currents, coursing through the cells and fibres, must in this case be supposed strengthened by the fact of their awaking one consciousness and dampening by awakening another. How such reaction of the consciousness upon the currents may occur must remain at present unsolved: it is enough for my purpose to have shown that it may not uselessly exist, and that the matter is less simple than the brain-automatists hold.

All the facts of the natural history of consciousness lend color to this view. Consciousness, for example, is only intense when nerve-processes are hesitant. In rapid, automatic, habitual action it sinks to a minimum. Nothing could be more fitting than this, if consciousness have the teleological function we suppose; nothing more meaningless, if not. Habitual actions are certain, and being in no danger of going astray from their end, need no extraneous help. In hesitant action, there seem many alternative possibilities of final nervous discharge. The feeling awakened by the nascent excitement of each alternative nerve-tract seems by its attractive or repulsive quality to determine whether the excitement shall abort or shall become complete. Where indecision is great, as before a dangerous leap, consciousness is agonizingly intense. Feeling, from this point of view, may be likened to a cross-section of the chain of nervous discharge, ascertaining the links already laid down, and groping among the fresh ends presented to it for the one which seems best to fit the case.

The phenomena of 'vicarious function' which we studied in Chapter II seems to form another bit of circumstantial evidence. A machine in working order acts fatally in one way. Our consciousness calls this the right way. Take out a valve, throw a wheel out of gear or bend a pivot, and it becomes a different machine, acting just as fatally in another way which we call the wrong way. But the machine itself knows nothing of wrong or right: matter has no ideals to pursue. A locomotive will carry its train through an open drawbridge as cheerfully as to any other destination.

A brain with part of it scooped out is virtually a new machine, and during the first days after the operation functions in a thoroughly abnormal manner. As a matter of fact, however its performances become from day to day more normal, until at last a practised eye may be needed to suspect anything wrong. Some of the restoration is undoubtedly due to 'inhibitions' passing away. But if the consciousness which goes with the rest of the brain, be there not only in order to take cognizance of each functional error, but also to exert an efficient pressure to check it if it be a sin of commission, and to lend a strengthening hand if it be a weakness or sin of omission, - nothing seems more natural than that the remaining parts, assisted in this way, should by virtue of the principle of habit grow back to the old teleological modes of exercise for which they were at first incapacitated. Nothing, on the contrary, seems at first sight more unnatural than that they should vicariously take up the duties of a part now lost without those duties as such exerting any persuasive or coercive force. At the end of Chapter XXVI I shall return to this again.

There is yet another set of facts which seem explicable on the supposition that consciousness has causal efficacy. It is a well-known fact that pleasures are generally associated with beneficial, pains with detrimental, experiences. All the fundamental vital processes illustrate this law. Starvation, suffocation, privation of food, drink and sleep, work when exhausted, burns, wounds, inflammation, the effects of poison, are as disagreeable as filling the hungry stomach, enjoying rest and sleep after fatigue, exercise after rest, and a sound skin and unbroken bones at all times, are pleasant. Mr. Spencer and others have suggested that these coincidences are due, not to any pre-established harmony, but to the mere action of natural selection which would certainly kill off in the long-run any breed of creatures to whom the fundamentally noxious experience seemed enjoyable. An animal that should take pleasure in a feeling of suffocation would, if that pleasure were efficacious enough to make him immerse his head in water, enjoy a longevity of four or five minutes. But if pleasures and pains have no efficacy, one does not see (without some such à priori rational harmony as would be scouted by the 'scientific' champions of the automaton-theory) why the most noxious acts, such as burning, might not give thrills of delight, and the most necessary ones, such as breathing, cause agony. The exceptions to the law are, it is true, numerous, but relate to experiences that are either not vital or not universal. Drunkenness, for instance, which though noxious, is to many persons delightful, is a very exceptional experience. But, as the excellent physiologist Fick remarks, if all rivers and springs ran alcohol instead of water, either all men would now be born to hate it or our nerves would have been selected so as to drink it with impunity. The only considerable attempt, in fact, that has been made to explain the distribution of our feelings is that of Mr. Grant Allen in his suggestive little work Physiological Aesthetics; and his reasoning is based exclusively on that causal efficacy of pleasures and pains which the 'double-aspect' partisans so strenuously deny.

Thus, them, from every point of view the circumstantial evidence against that theory is strong. A priori analysis of both brain-action and conscious action shows us that if the latter were efficacious it would, by its selective emphasis, make amends for the indeterminateness of the former; whilst the study a posteriori of the distribution of consciousness shows it to be exactly such as we might expect in an organ added for the sake of steering a nervous system grown too complex to regulate itself. The conclusion that it is useful is, after all this, quite justifiable. But, if it is useful, it must be so through its causal efficaciousness, and the automaton-theory must succumb to the theory of commonsense. I, at any rate (pending metaphysical reconstructions not yet successfully achieved), shall have no hesitation in using the language of common-sense throughout this book.

Notes

[1] *The Theory of Practice.*

[2] *The present writer recalls how in 1869, when still a medical student, he began to write an essay showing how almost every one who speculated about brain-processes illicitly interpolated into his account of them links derived from the entirely heterogeneous universe of Feeling. Spencer, Hodgson (in his Time and Space), Maudsley, Lockhart Clarke, Bain, Dr. Carpenter, and other authors were cited as having been guilty of the confusion. The writing was soon stopped because he perceived that the view which he was upholding against these authors was a pure conception, with no proofs to be adduced of its reality. Later it seemed to him that whatever proofs existed really told in favor of their view.*

[3] *Chas. Mercier: The Nervous System and the Mind (1888). p. 9.*

[4] *Op. cit. p. 11.*

[5] *See in particular the end of Chapter IX.*

Chapter VI - The Mind-Stuff Theory

The reader who found himself swamped with too much metaphysics in the last chapter will have a still worse time of it in this one, which is exclusively metaphysical. Metaphysics means nothing but an unusually obstinate effort to think clearly. The fundamental conceptions of psychology are practically very clear to us, but theoretically they are very confused, and one easily makes the obscurest assumptions in this science without realizing, until challenged, what internal difficulties they involve. When these assumptions have once established themselves (as they have a way of doing in our very descriptions of the phenomenal facts) it is almost impossible to get rid of them afterwards or to make any one see that they are not essential features of the subject. The only way to prevent this disaster is to scrutinize them beforehand and make them give an articulate account of themselves before letting them pass. One of the obscurest of the assumptions of which I speak is the assumption that our mental states are composite in structure, made up of smaller states conjoined. This hypothesis has outward advantages which make it almost irresistibly attractive to the intellect, and yet it is inwardly quite unintelligible. Of its unintelligibility, however, half the writers on psychology seem unaware. As our own aim is to understand if possible, I make no apology for singling out this particular notion for very explicit treatment before taking up the descriptive part of our work. The theory of 'mind-stuff' is the theory that our mental states are compounds, expressed in its most radical form.

Evolutionary Psychology Demands a Mind-Dust

In a general theory of evolution the inorganic comes first, then the lowest forms of animal and vegetable life, then forms of life that possess mentality, and finally those like ourselves that possess it in a high degree. As long as we keep to the consideration of purely outward facts, even the most complicated facts of biology, our task as evolutionists is comparatively easy. We are dealing all the time with matter and its aggregations and separations; and although our treatment must perforce be hypothetical, this does not prevent it from being continuous. The point which as evolutionists we are bound to hold fast to is that all the new forms of being that make their appearance are really nothing more than results of the redistribution of the original and unchanging materials. The self-same atoms which, chaotically dispersed, made the nebula, now, jammed and temporarily caught in peculiar positions, form our brains; and the 'evolution' of the brains, if understood, would be simply the account of how the atoms came to be so caught and jammed. In this story no new natures, no factors not present at the beginning, are introduced at any later stage.
But with the dawn of consciousness an entirely new nature seems to slip in, something whereof the potency was not given in the mere outward atoms of the original chaos.
The enemies of evolution have been quick to pounce upon this undeniable discontinuity in the data of the world, and many of them, from the failure of evolutionary explanations at this point, have inferred their general incapacity all along the line. Every one admits the entire incommensurability of feeling as such with material motion as such. "A motion became a feeling!" - no phrase that our lips can frame is so devoid of apprehensible meaning. Accordingly, even the vaguest of evolutionary enthusiasts, when deliberately comparing material with mental facts, have been as forward as any one else to emphasize the 'chasm' between the inner and the outer worlds.
"Can the oscillations of a molecule," says Mr. Spencer, "be represented side by side with a nervous shock [he means a mental shock], and the two be recognized as one? No effort enables us to assimilate them. That a unit of feeling has nothing in common with a unit of motion becomes more than ever manifest when we bring the two into juxtaposition." [1]
And again:
"Suppose it to have become quite clear that a shock in consciousness and a molecular motion are the subjective and objective faces of the same thing; we continue utterly incapable of uniting the two, so as to conceive that reality of which they are the opposite faces." [2]
In other words, incapable of perceiving in them any common character. So Tyndall, in that lucky paragraph which has been quoted so often that every one knows it by heart:
"The passage from the physics of the brain to the corresponding facts of consciousness is unthinkable. Granted that a definite thought and a definite molecular action in the brain occur simultaneously; we do not possess the intellectual organ, nor apparently any rudiment of the organ, which would enable us to pass, by a process of reasoning, from one to the other." [3]
Or in this other passage:

"We can trace the development of a nervous system and correlate with it the parallel phenomena of sensation and thought. We see with undoubting certainty that they go hand in hand. But we try to soar in a vacuum the moment we seek to comprehend the connection between them ... There is no fusion possible between the two classes of facts - no motor energy in the intellect of man to carry it without logical rupture from the one to the other." [4]

None the less easily, however, when the evolutionary afflatus is upon them, do the very same writers leap over the breach whose flagrancy they are the foremost to announce, and talk as if mind grew out of body in a continuous way. Mr. Spencer, looking back on his review of mental evolution, tells us how "in tracing up the increase we found ourselves passing without break from the phenomena of bodily life to the phenomena of mental life." [5] And Mr. Tyndall, in the same Belfast Address from which we just quoted, delivers his other famous passage:

"Abandoning all disguise, the confession that I feel bound to make before you is that I prolong the vision backward across the boundary of the experimental evidence, and discern in that matter which we, in our ignorance and notwithstanding our professed reverence for its Creator, have hitherto covered with opprobrium the promise and potency of every form and quality of life." [6] mental life included, as a matter of course.

So strong a postulate is continuity! Now this book will tend to show that mental postulates are on the whole to be respected. The demand for continuity has, over large tracts of science, proved itself to possess true prophetic power. We ought therefore ourselves sincerely to try every possible mode of conceiving the dawn of consciousness so that it may not appear equivalent to the irruption into the universe of a new nature, non-existent until then.

Merely to call the consciousness 'nascent' will not serve our turn.[7] It is true that the word signifies not yet quite born, and so seems to form a sort of bridge between existence and nonentity. But that is a verbal quibble. The fact is that discontinuity comes in if a new nature comes in at all. The quantity of the latter is quite immaterial. The girl in 'Midshipman Easy' could not excuse the illegitimacy of her child by saying, 'it was a very small one.' And Consciousness, however small, is an illegitimate birth in any philosophy that starts without it, and yet professes to explain all facts by continuous evolution.

If evolution is to work smoothly, consciousness in some shape must have been present at the very origin of things. Accordingly we find that the more clear-sighted evolutionary philosophers are beginning to posit it there. Each atom of the nebula, they suppose, must have had an aboriginal atom of consciousness linked with it; and, just as the material atoms have formed bodies and brains by massing themselves together, so the mental atoms, by an analogous process of aggregation, have fused into those larger consciousnesses which we know in ourselves and suppose to exist in our fellow-animals. Some such doctrine of atomistic hylozoism as this is an indispensable part of a thorough-going philosophy of evolution. According to it there must be an infinite number of degrees of consciousness, following the degrees of complication and aggregation of the primordial mind-dust. To prove the separate existence of these degrees of consciousness by indirect evidence, since direct intuition of them is not to be had, becomes therefore the first duty of psychological evolutionism.

Some Alleged Proofs that Mind-Dust Exists

Some of this duty we find already performed by a number of philosophers who, though not interested at all in evolution, have nevertheless on independent grounds convinced themselves of the existence of a vast amount of sub-conscious mental life. The criticism of this general opinion and its grounds will have to be postponed for a while. At present let us merely deal with the arguments assumed to prove aggregation of bits of mind-stuff into distinctly sensible feelings. They are clear and admit of a clear reply.

The German physiologist A. Fick, in 1862, was, so far as I know, the first to use them. He made experiments on the discrimination of the feelings of warmth and of touch, when only a very small portion of the skin was excited through a hole in a card, the surrounding parts being protected by the card. He found that under these circumstances mistakes were frequently made by the patient,[8] and concluded that this must be because the number of sensations from the elementary nerve-tips affected was too small to sum itself distinctly into either of the qualities of feeling in question. He tried to show how a different manner of the summation might give rise in one case to the heat and in another to the touch.

" A feeling of temperatures," he says," arises when the intensities of the units of feeling are evenly gradated, so that between two elements a and b no other unit can spatially intervene whose intensity is not also between that of a and b. A feeling of contact perhaps arises when this condition is not fulfilled. Both kinds of feeling, however, are composed of the same units."

But it is obviously far clearer to interpret such a gradation of intensities as a brain-fact than as a mind-fact. If in the brain a tract were first excited in one of the ways suggested by Prof. Fick, and then again in the other, it might very well happen, for aught we can say to the contrary, that the psychic accompaniment in the one case would be heat, and in the other pain. The pain and the heat would, however, not be composed of psychic units, but would each be the direct result of one total brain-process. So long as this latter interpretation remains open, Fick cannot be held to have proved psychic summation.

Later, both Spencer and Taine, independently of each other, took up the same line of thought. Mr. Spencer's reasoning is worth quoting in extenso. He writes:

"Although the individual sensations and emotions, real or ideal, of which consciousness is built up, appear to be severally simple, homogeneous, unanalyzable, or of inscrutable natures, yet they are not so. There is at least one kind of feeling which, as ordinarily experienced, seems elementary, that is demonstrably not elementary. And after resolving it into its proximate components, we can scarcely help suspecting that other apparently-elementary feelings are also compound, and may have proximate components like those which we can in this one instance identify.

"Musical sound is the name we give to this seemingly simple feeling which is clearly resolvable into simpler feelings. Well known experiments prove that when equal blows or taps are made one after another at a rate not exceeding some sixteen per second, the effect of each is perceived as a separate noise; but when the rapidity with which the blows follow one another exceeds this, the noises are no longer identified in separate states of consciousness, and there arises in place of them a continuous state of consciousness, called a tone. In further increasing the rapidity of the blows, the tone undergoes the change of quality distinguished as rise in pitch; and it continues to rise in pitch as the blows continue to increase in rapidity, until it reaches an acuteness beyond which it is no longer appreciable as a tone. So that out of units of feeling of the same kind, many feelings distinguishable from one another in quality result, according as the units are more or less integrated.

"This is not all. The inquiries of Professor Helmholtz have shown that when, along with one series of these rapidly-recurring noises, there is generated another series in which the noises are more rapid though not so loud, the effect is a change in that quality known as its timbre. As various musical instruments show us, tones which are alike in pitch and strength are distinguishable by their harshness or sweetness, their ringing or their liquid characters; and all their specific peculiarities are proved to arise from the combination of one, two, three, or more, supplementary series of recurrent noises with the chief series of recurrent noises. So that while the unlikenesses of feeling known as differences of pitch in tones are due to differences of integration among the recurrent noises of one series, the unlikenesses of feeling known as differences of timbre, are due to the simultaneous integration with this series of other series having other degrees of integration. And thus an enormous number of qualitatively-contrasted kinds of consciousness that seem severally elementary prove to be composed of one simple kind of consciousness, combined and recombined with itself in multitudinous ways.

"Can we stop short here? If the different sensations known as sounds are built out of a common unit, is it not to be rationally inferred that so likewise are the different sensations known as tastes, and the different sensations known as odors, and the different sensations known as colors? Nay, shall we not regard it as probable that there is a unit common to all these strongly-contrasted classes of sensations? If the unlikenesses among the sensations of each class may be due to unlikenesses among the modes of aggregation of a unit of consciousness common to them all; so too may the much greater unlikenesses between the sensations of each class and those of other classes. There may be a single primordial element of consciousness, and the countless kinds of consciousness may be produced by the compounding of this element with itself and the recompounding of its compounds with one another in higher and higher degrees; so producing increased multiplicity, variety, and complexity.

"Have we any clue to this primordial element? I think we have. That simple mental impression which proves to be the unit of composition of the sensation of musical tone, is allied to certain other simple mental impressions differently originated. The subjective effect produced by a crack or noise that has no appreciable duration is little else than a nervous shock. Though we distinguish such a nervous shock as belonging to what we call sounds, yet it does not differ very much from nervous shocks of other kinds. An electric discharge sent through the body causes a feeling akin to that which a sudden loud report causes. A strong unexpected impression made through the eyes, as by a flash of lightning, similarly gives rise to a start or shock; and though the feeling so named seems, like the electric shock, to have the body at large for its seat, and may therefore be regarded as the correlative rather of the efferent than of the afferent disturbance yet on remembering the mental change that results from the instantaneous transit of an object across the field of vision, I think it may be perceived that the feeling accompanying the efferent disturbance is itself reduced very nearly to the same form. The state of consciousness so generated is, in fact, comparable in quality to the initial state of consciousness caused by a blow (distinguishing it from the pain or other feeling that commences the instant after); which state of consciousness caused by a blow may be taken as the primitive and typical form of the nervous shock. The fact that sudden brief disturbances thus set up by different stimuli through different sets of nerves cause feelings scarcely distinguishable in quality will not appear strange when we recollect that distinguishableness of feeling implies appreciable duration; and that when the duration is greatly abridged, nothing more is known than that some mental change has occurred and ceased. To have a sensation of redness, to know a tone as acute or grave, to be conscious of a taste as sweet, implies in each case a considerable continuity of state. If the state does not last long enough to admit of its being contemplated, it cannot be classed as of this or that kind; and becomes a momentary modification very similar to momentary modifications otherwise caused.

"It is possible, then - may we not even say probable? - that something of the same order as that which we call nervous shock is the ultimate unit of consciousness, and that all the unlikenesses among our feelings result from unlike modes of integration of this ultimate unit. I say of the same order, because there are discernible differences among nervous shocks that are differently caused; and the primitive nervous shock probably differs somewhat form each of them. And I say of the same order, for the further reason that while we may ascribe to them a general likeness in nature, we must suppose a great unlikeness in degree. The nervous shocks recognized as such are violent - must be violent before they can be perceived amid the procession of multitudinous vivid feelings suddenly interrupted by them. But the rapidly-recurring nervous shocks of which the different forms of feeling consist, we must assume to be of comparatively moderate, or even of very slight intensity. Were our various sensations and emotions composed of rapidly-recurring shocks as strong as those ordinarily called shocks, they would be unbearable; indeed life would cease at once. We must think of them rather as successive faint pulses of subjective change, each having the same quality as the strong pulse of subjective change distinguished as a nervous shock." [9]

Refutation of These Proofs.

Convincing as this argument of Mr. Spencer's may appear on a first reading, it is singular how weak it really is.[10] We do, it is true, when we study the connection between a musical note and its outward cause, find the note simple and continuous while the cause is multiple and discrete. Somewhere, then, there is a transformation, reduction, or fusion.

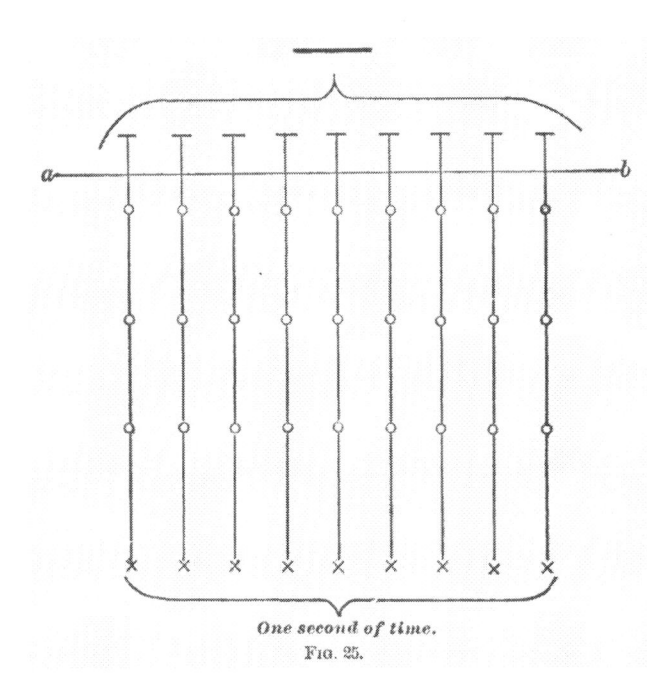

One second of time.
Fig. 25.

The question is, Where - in the nerve-world or in the mind-world? Really we have no experimental proof by which to decide; and if decide we must, analogy and a priori probability can alone guide us. Mr. Spencer assumes that the fusion must come to pass in the mental world, and that the physical processes get through air and ear, auditory nerve and medulla, lower brain and hemispheres, without their number being reduced. Figure 25, above, will make the point clear.

Let the line a - b represent the threshold of consciousness: then everything drawn below that line will symbolize a physical process, everything above it will mean a fact of mind. Let the crosses stand for the physical blows, the circles for the events in successively higher orders of nerve-cells, and the horizontal marks for the facts of feeling. Spencer's argument implies that each order of cells transmits just as many impulses as it receives to the cells above it; so that if the blows come at the rate of 20,000 in a second the cortical cells discharge at the same rate, and one unit of feeling corresponds to each one of the 20,000 discharges. Then, and only then, does 'integration' occur, by the 20,000 units of feeling 'compounding with themselves' into the 'continuous state of consciousness' represented by the short line at the top of the figure.

Now such an interpretation as this flies in the face of physical analogy, no less than of logical intelligibility. Consider physical analogy first.

A pendulum may be deflected by a single blow, and swing back. Will it swing back the more often the more we multiply the blows? No; for it they rain upon the pendulum too fast, it will not swing at all but remain deflected in a sensibly stationary state. In other words, increasing the cause numerically need not equally increase numerically the effect. Blow through a tube: you get a certain musical note; and increasing the blowing increases for a certain time the loudness of the note. Will this be true indefinitely? No; for when a certain force is reached, the note, instead of growing louder, suddenly disappears and is replaced by its higher octave. Turn on the gas slightly and light it: you get a tiny flame. Turn on more gas, and the breadth of the flame increases. Will this relation increase indefinitely? No, again; for at a certain moment up shoots the flame into a ragged streamer and begins to hiss. Send slowly through the nerve of a frog's gastrocnemius muscle a succession of galvanic shocks: you get a succession of twitches. Increasing the number of shocks does not increase the twitching; on the contrary, it stops it, and we have the muscle in the apparently stationary state of contraction called tetanus. This last fact is the true analogue of what must happen between the nerve-cell and the sensory fibre. It is certain that cells are more inert than fibres, and that rapid vibrations in the latter can only arouse relatively simple processes or states in the former. The higher cells may have even a slower rate of explosion than the lower, and so the twenty thousand supposed blows of the outer air may be 'integrated' in the cortex into a very small number of cell-discharges in a second.

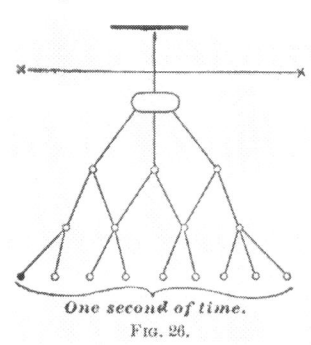

This other diagram will serve to contrast this supposition with Spencer's. In Fig. 26 all 'integration' occurs below the threshold of consciousness. The frequency of cell-events becomes more and more reduced as we approach the cells to which feeling is most directly attached, until at last we come to a condition of things symbolized by the larger ellipse, which may be taken to stand for some rather massive and slow process of tension and discharge in the cortical centres, to which, as a whole, the feeling of musical tone symbolized by the line at the top of the diagram simply and totally corresponds. It is as if a long file of men were to start one after the other to reach a distant point. The road at first is good and they keep their original distance apart. Presently it is intersected by bogs each worse than the last, so that the front men get so retarded that the hinder ones catch up with them before the journey is done, and all arrive together at the goal.[11]

One second of time.
FIG. 26.

On this supposition there are no unperceived units of mind-stuff preceding and composing the full consciousness. The latter is itself an immediate psychic fact and bears an immediate relation to the neural state which is its unconditional accompaniment. Did each neural shock give rise to its own psychic shock, and the psychic shocks then combine, it would be impossible to understand why severing one part of the central nervous system from another should break up the integrity of the consciousness. The cut has nothing to do with the psychic world. The atoms of mind-stuff ought to float off from the nerve-matter on either side of it, and come together over it and fuse, just as well as if it had not been made. We know, however, that they do not; that severance of the paths of conduction between a man's left auditory centre or optical centre and the rest of his cortex will sever all communication between the words which he hears or sees written and the rest of his ideas.

Moreover, if feelings can mix into a tertium quid, why do we not take a feeling of greenness and a feeling of redness, and make a feeling of yellowness out of them? Why has optics neglected the open road to truth, and wasted centuries in disputing about theories of color-composition which two minutes of introspection would have settled forever?[12] We cannot mix feelings as such, though we may mix the objects we feel, and from their mixture get new feelings. We cannot even (as we shall later see) have two feelings in our mind at once. At most we can compare together objects previously presented to us in distinct feelings; but then we find each object stubbornly maintaining its separate identity before consciousness, whatever the verdict of the comparison may be.[13]

Self-Compounding of Mental Facts is Inadmissible.

But there is a still more fatal objection to the theory of mental units 'compounding with themselves' or 'integrating.' It is logically unintelligible; it leaves out the essential feature of all the 'combinations' we actually know.

All the 'combinations' which we actually know are EFFECTS, wrought by the units said to be 'combined,' UPON SOME ENTITY OTHER THAN THEMSELVES. Without this feature of a medium or vehicle, the notion of combination has no sense.

"A multitude of contractile units, by joint action, and by being all connected, for instance, with a single tendon, will pull at the same, and will bring about a dynamical effect which is undoubtedly the resultant of their combined individual energies.... On the whole, tendons are to muscular fibres, and bones are to tendons, combining recipients of mechanical energies. A medium of composition is indispensable to the summation of energies. To realize the complete dependence of mechanical resultants on a combining substratum, one may fancy for a moment all the individually contracting muscular elements severed from their attachments. They might then still be capable of contracting with the same energy as before, yet no co-operative result would be accomplished. The medium of dynamical combination would be wanting. The multiple energies, singly exerted on no common recipient, would lose themselves on entirely isolated and disconnected efforts."[14]

In other words, no possible number of entities (call them as you like, whether forces, material particles, or mental elements) can sum themselves together. Each remains, in the sum, what it always was; and the sum itself exists only for a bystander who happens to overlook the units and to apprehend the sum as such; or else it exists in the shape of some other effect on an entity external to the sum itself. Let it not be objected that H2 and O combine of themselves into 'water,' and thenceforward exhibit new properties. They do not. The 'water' is just the old atoms in the new position, H-O-H; the 'new properties' are just their combined effects, when in this position, upon external media, such as our sense-organs and the various reagents on which water may exert its properties and be known.

"Aggregations are organized wholes only when they behave as such in the presence of other things. A statue is an aggregation of particles of marble; but as such it has no unity. For the spectator it is one; in itself it is an aggregate; just as, to the consciousness of an ant crawling over it, it may again appear a mere aggregate. No summing up of parts can make an unity of a mass of discrete constituents, unless this unity exist for some other subject, not for the mass itself."[15]

Just so, in the parallelogram of forces, the 'forces' themselves do not combine into the diagonal resultant; a body is needed on which they may impinge, to exhibit their resultant effect. No more do musical sounds combine per se into concords or discords. Concord and discord are names for their combined effects on that external medium, the ear. Where the elemental units are supposed to be feelings, the case is in no wise altered. Take a hundred of them, shuffle them and pack them as close together as you can (whatever that may mean); still each remains the same feeling it always was, shut in its own skin, windowless, ignorant of what the other feelings are and mean. There would be a hundred-and-first feeling there, if, when a group or series of such feelings were set up, a consciousness belonging to the group as such should emerge. And this 101st feeling would be a totally new fact; the 100 original feelings might, by a curious physical law, be a signal for its creation, when they came together; but they would have no substantial identity with it, nor it with them, and one could never deduce the one from the others, or (in any intelligible sense) say that they evolved it.

Take a sentence of a dozen words, and take twelve men and tell to each one word. Then stand the men in a row or jam them in a bunch, and let each think of his word as intently as he will; nowhere will there be a consciousness of the whole sentence.[16] We talk of the 'spirit of the age,' and the 'sentiment of the people,' and in various ways we hypostatize 'public opinion.' But we know this to be symbolic speech, and never dream that the spirit, opinion, sentiment, etc., constitute a consciousness other than, and additional to, that of the several individuals whom the words 'age,' 'people,' or 'public' denote. The private minds do not agglomerate into a higher compound mind. This has always been the invincible contention of the spiritualists against the associationists in Psychology, - a contention which we shall take up at greater length in Chapter X. The associationists say the mind is constituted by a multiplicity of distinct 'ideas' associated into a unity. There is, they say, an idea of a, and also an idea of b. Therefore, they say, there is an idea of a + b, or of a and b together. Which is like saying that the mathematical square of a plus that of b is equal to the square of a + b, a palpable untruth. Idea of a + idea of b is not identical with idea of (a + b). It is one, they are two; in it, what knows a also knows b; in them, what knows a is expressly posited as not knowing b; etc. In short, the two separate ideas can never by any logic be made to figure as one and the same thing as the 'associated' idea.

This is what the spiritualists keep saying; and since we do, as a matter of fact, have the 'compounded' idea, and do know a and b together, they adopt a farther hypothesis to explain that fact. The separate ideas exist, they say, but affect a third entity, the soul. This has the 'compounded' idea, if you please so to call it; and the compounded idea is an altogether new psychic fact to which the separate ideas stand in the relation, not of constituents, but of occasions of production.

This argument of the spiritualists against the associationists has never been answered by the latter. It holds good against any talk about self-compounding amongst feelings, against any 'blending,' or 'complication,' or 'mental chemistry,' or 'psychic synthesis,' which supposes a resultant consciousness to float off from the constituents per se, in the absence of a supernumerary principle of consciousness which they may affect. The mind-stuff theory, in short, is unintelligible. Atoms of feeling cannot compose higher feelings, any more than atoms of matter can compose physical things! The 'things,' for a clear-headed atomistic evolutionist, are not. Nothing is but the everlasting atoms. When grouped in a certain way, we name them this 'thing' or that; but the thing we name has no existence out of our mind. So of the states of mind which are supposed to be compound because they know many different things together. Since indubitably such states do exist, they must exist as single new facts, effects, possibly, as the spiritualists say, on the Soul (we will not decide that point here), but at any rate independent and integral, and not compounded of psychic atoms.[17]

Can States of Mind be Unconscious?

The passion for unity and smoothness is in some minds so insatiate that, in spite of the logical clearness of these reasonings and conclusions, many will fail to be influenced by them. They establish a sort of disjointedness in things which in certain quarters will appear intolerable. They sweep away all chance of 'passing without break' either from the material to the mental, or from the lower to the higher mental; and they thrust us back into a pluralism of consciousness - each arising discontinuity in the midst of two disconnected worlds, material and mental - which is even worse than the old notion of the separate creation of each particular soul. But the malcontents will hardly try to refute our reasonings by direct attack. It is more probable that, turning their back upon them altogether, they will devote themselves to sapping and mining the region roundabout until it is a bog of logical liquefaction, into the midst of which all definite conclusions of any sort may be trusted ere long to sink and disappear.

Our reasonings have assumed that the 'integration' of a thousand psychic units must be either just the units over again, simply rebaptized, or else something real, but then other than and additional to those units; that if a certain existing fact is that of a thousand feelings, it cannot at the same time be that of ONE feeling; for the essence of feeling is to be felt, and as a psychic existent feels, so it must be. If the one feeling feels like no one of the thousand, in what sense can it be said to be the thousand? These assumptions are what the monists will seek to undermine. The Hegelizers amongst them will take high ground at once, and say that the glory and beauty of the psychic life is that in it all contradictions find their reconciliation; and that it is just because the facts we are considering are facts of the self that they are both one and many at the same time. With this intellectual temper I confess that I cannot contend. As in striking at some unresisting gossamer with a club, one but overreaches one's self, and the thing one aims at gets no harm. So I leave this school to its devices.

The other monists are of less deliquescent frame, and try to break down distinctness among metal states by making a distinction. This sounds paradoxical, but it is only ingenious. The distinction is that between the unconscious and the conscious being of the mental state. It is the sovereign means for believing what one likes in psychology, and of turning what might become a science into a tumbling-ground for whimsies. It has numerous champions, and elaborate reasons to give for itself. We must therefore accord it due consideration. In discussing the question:

Do Unconscious Mental States Exist?

it will be best to give the list of so-called proofs as briefly as possible, and to follow each by its objection, as in scholastic books.[18]

First Proof. The minimum visible, the minimum audible, are objects composed of parts. How can the whole affect the sense unless each part does? And yet each part does so without being separately sensible. Leibnitz calls the total consciousness an 'aperception,' the supposed insensible consciousness by the name of 'petites perceptions.'

"To judge of the latter," he says, "I am accustomed to use the example of the roaring of the sea with which one is assailed when near the shore. To hear this noise as one does, on must hear the parts which compose its totality, that is, the noise of each wave, . . . although this noise would not be noticed if its wave were alone. One must be affected a little by the movement of one wave, one must have some perception of each several noise, however small it be. Otherwise one would not hear that of 100,000 waves, for of 100,000 zeros one can never make a quantity."[19]

Reply. This is an excellent example of the so-called 'fallacy of division,' or predicating what is true only of a collection, of each member of the collection distributively. It no more follows that if a thousand things together cause sensation, one thing alone must cause it, than it follows that if one pound weight moves a balance, then one ounce weight must move it too, in less degree. One ounce weight does not move it at all; its movement begins with the pound. At most we can say that each ounce affects it in some way which helps the advent of that movement. And so each infra-sensible stimulus to a nerve no doubt affects the nerve and helps the birth of sensation when the other stimuli come. But this affection is a nerve-affection, and there is not the slightest ground for supposing it to be a 'perception' unconscious of itself. "A certain quantity of the cause may be a necessary condition to the production of any of the effect,"[20] when the latter is a mental state.

Second Proof. In all acquired dexterities and habits, secondarily automatic performances as they are called, we do what originally required a chain of deliberately conscious perceptions and volitions. As the actions still keep their intelligent character, intelligence must still preside over their execution. But since our consciousness seems all the while elsewhere engaged, such intelligence must consist of unconscious perceptions, inferences, and volitions.

Reply. There is more than one alternative explanation in accordance with larger bodies of fact. One is that the perceptions and volitions in habitual actions may be performed consciously, only so quickly and inattentively that no memory of them remains. Another is that the consciousness of these actions exists, but is split-off from the rest of the consciousness of the hemispheres. We shall find in Chapter X numerous proofs of the reality of this split-off condition of portions of consciousness. Since in man the hemispheres indubitably co-operate in these secondarily automatic acts, it will not do to say either that they occur without consciousness or that their consciousness is that of the lower centres, which we know nothing about. But either lack of memory or split-off cortical consciousness will certainly account for all of the facts.[21]

Third Proof. Thinking of A, we presently find ourselves thinking of C. Now B is the natural logical link between A and C, but we have no consciousness of having thought of B. It must have been in our mind 'unconsciously,' and in that state affected the sequence of our ideas.

Reply. Here again we have a choice between more plausible explanations. Either B was consciously there, but the next instant forgotten, or its brain-tract alone was adequate to do the whole work of coupling A with C, without the idea B being aroused at all, whether consciously or 'unconsciously.'

Fourth Proof. Problems unsolved when we go to bed are found solved in the morning when we wake. Somnambulists do rational things. We awaken punctually at an hour predetermined overnight, etc. Unconscious thinking, volition, time-registration, etc., must have presided over these acts.

Reply. Consciousness forgotten, as in the hypnotic trance.

Fifth Proof. Some patients will often, in an attack of epileptiform unconsciousness, go through complicated processes, such as eating a dinner in a restaurant and paying for it, or making a violent homicidal attack. In trance, artificial or pathological, long and complex performances, involving the use of the reasoning powers, are executed, of which the patient is wholly unaware on coming to.

Reply. Rapid and complete oblivescence is certainly the explanation here. The analogue again is hypnoticism. Tell the subject of an hypnotic trance, during his trance, that he will remember, and he may remember everything perfectly when he awakes, though without your telling him no memory would have remained. The extremely rapid oblivescence of common dreams is a familiar fact.

Sixth Proof. In a musical concord the vibrations of the several notes are in relatively simple ratios. The mind must unconsciously count the vibrations, and be pleased by the simplicity which it finds.

Reply. The brain-process produced by the simple ratios may be as directly agreeable as the conscious process of comparing them would be. No counting, either conscious or 'unconscious,' is required.

Seventh Proof. Every hour we make theoretic judgments and emotional reactions, and exhibit practical tendencies, for which we can give no explicit logical justification, but which are good inferences from certain premises. We know more than we can say. Our conclusions run ahead of our power to analyze their grounds. A child, ignorant of the axiom that two things equal to the same are equal to each other, applies it nevertheless in his concrete judgments unerringly. A boor will use the dictum de omni et nullo who is unable to understand it in abstract terms.

"We seldom consciously think how our house is painted, what the shade of it is, what the pattern of our furniture is, or whether the door opens to the right or left, or out or in. But how quickly should we notice a change in any of these things! Think of the door you have most often opened, and tell, if you can, whether it opens to the right or left, out or in. Yet when you open the door you never put the hand on the wrong side to find the latch, nor try to push it when it opens with a pull.... What is the precise characteristic in your friend's step that enables you to recognize it when he is coming? Did you ever consciously think the idea, 'if I run into a solid piece of matter I shall get hurt, or be hindered in my progress'? and do you avoid running into obstacles because you ever distinctly conceived, or consciously acquired and thought, that idea?"[22]

Most of our knowledge is at all times potential. We act in accordance with the whole drift of what we have learned, but few items rise into consciousness at the time. Many of them, however, we may recall at will. All this co-operation of unrealized principles and facts, of potential knowledge, with our actual thought is quite inexplicable unless we suppose the perpetual existence of an immense mass of ideas in an unconscious state, all of them exerting a steady pressure and influence upon our conscious thinking, and many of them in such continuity with it as ever and anon to become conscious themselves.

Reply. No such mass of ideas is supposable. But there are all kinds of short-cuts in the brain; and processes not aroused strongly enough to give any 'idea' distinct enough to be a premise, may, nevertheless, help to determine just that resultant process of whose psychic accompaniment the said idea would be a premise, if the idea existed at all. A certain overtone may be a feature of my friend's voice, and may conspire with the other tones thereof to arouse in my brain the process which suggests to my consciousness his name. And yet I may be ignorant of the overtone per se, and unable, even when he speaks, to tell whether it be there or no. It leads me to the idea of the name; but it produces in me no such cerebral process as that to which the idea of the overtone would correspond. And similarly of our learning. Each subject we learn leaves behind it a modification of the brain, which makes it impossible for the latter to react upon things just as it did before; and the result of the difference may be a tendency to act, though with no idea, much as we should if we were consciously thinking about the subject. The becoming conscious of the latter at will is equally readily explained as a result of the brain-modification. This, as Wundt phrases it, is a 'predisposition' to bring forth the conscious idea of the original subject, a predisposition which other stimuli and brain-processes may convert into an actual result. But such a predisposition is no 'unconscious idea;' it is only a particular collocation of the molecules in certain tracts of the brain.

Eighth Proof. Instincts, as pursuits of ends by appropriate means, are manifestations of intelligence; but as the ends are not foreseen, the intelligence must be unconscious.

Reply. Chapter XXIV will show that all the phenomena of instinct are explicable as actions of the nervous system, mechanically discharged by stimuli to the senses.

Ninth Proof. In sense-perception we have results in abundance, which can only be explained as conclusions drawn by a process of unconscious inference from data given to sense. A small human image on the retina is referred, not to a pygmy, but to a distant man of normal size. A certain gray patch is inferred to be a white object seen in a dim light. Often the inference leads us astray: e.g., pale gray against pale green looks red, because we take a wrong premise to argue from. We think a green film is spread over everything; and knowing that under such a film a red thing would look gray, we wrongly infer from the gray appearance that a red thing must be there. Our study of space-perception in Chapter XVIII will give abundant additional examples both of the truthful and illusory percepts which have been explained to result from unconscious logic operations.

Reply. That chapter will also in many cases refute this explanation. Color- and light-contrast are certainly purely sensational affairs, in which inference plays no part. This has been satisfactorily proved by Hering,[23] and shall be treated of again in Chapter XVII. Our rapid judgments of size, shape, distance, and the like, are best explained as processes of simple cerebral association. Certain sense-impressions directly stimulate brain-tracts, of whose activity ready-made conscious percepts are the immediate psychic counterparts. They do this by a mechanism either connate or acquired by habit. It is to be remarked that Wundt and Helmholtz, who in their earlier writings did more than any one to give vogue to the notion that unconscious inference is a vital factor in sense-perception, have seen fit on later occasions to modify their views and to admit that results like those of reasoning may accrue without any actual reasoning process unconsciously taking place.[24] Maybe the excessive and riotous applications made by Hartmann of their principle have led them to this change. It would be natural to feel towards him as the sailor in the story felt towards the horse who got his foot into the stirrup, - "If you're going to get on, I must get off."

Hartmann fairly boxes the compass of the universe with the principle of unconscious thought. For him there is no namable thing that does not exemplify it. But his logic is so lax and his failure to consider the most obvious alternatives so complete that it would, on the whole, be a waste of time to look at his arguments in detail. The same is true of Schopenhauer, in whom the mythology reaches its climax. The visual perception, for example, of an object in space results, according to him, from the intellect performing the following operations, all unconscious. First, it apprehends the inverted retinal image and turns it right side up, constructing flat space as a preliminary operation; then it computes from the angle of convergence of the eyeballs that the two retinal images must be the projection of but a single object; thirdly, it constructs the third dimension and sees this object solid; fourthly, it assigns its distance; and fifthly, in each and all of these operations it gets the objective character of what it 'constructs' by unconsciously inferring it as the only possible cause of some sensation which it unconsciously feels.[25] Comment on this seems hardly called for. It is, as I said, pure mythology.

None of these facts, then, appealed to so confidently in proof of the existence of ideas in an unconscious state, prove anything of the sort. They prove either that conscious ideas were present which the next instant were forgotten; or they prove that certain results, similar to results of reasoning, may be wrought out by rapid brain-processes to which no ideation seems attached. But there is one more argument to be alleged, less obviously insufficient than those which we have reviewed, and demanding a new sort of reply.

Tenth Proof. There is a great class of experiences in our mental life which may be described as discoveries that a subjective condition which we have been having is really something different from what we had supposed. We suddenly find ourselves bored by a thing which we thought we were enjoying well enough; or in love with a person whom we imagined we only liked. Or else we deliberately analyze our motives, and find that at bottom they contain jealousies and cupidities which we little suspected to be there. Our feelings towards people are perfect wells of motivation, unconscious of itself, which introspection brings to light. And our sensations likewise: we constantly discover new elements in sensations which we have been in the habit of receiving all our days, elements, too, which have been there from the first, since otherwise we should have been unable to distinguish the sensations containing them from others nearly allied. The elements must exist, for we use them to discriminate by; but they must exist in an unconscious state, since we so completely fail to single them out.[26] The books of the analytic school of psychology abound in examples of the kind. Who knows the countless associations that mingle with his each and every thought? Who can pick apart all the nameless feelings that stream in at every moment from his various internal organs, muscles, heart, glands, lungs, etc., and compose in their totality his sense of bodily life? Who is aware of the part played by feelings of innervation and suggestions of possible muscular exertion in all his judgments of distance, shape, and size? Consider, too, the difference between a sensation which we simply have and one which we attend to. Attention gives results that seem like fresh creations; and yet the feelings and elements of feeling which it reveals must have been already there - in an unconscious state. We all know practically the difference between the so-called sonant and the so-called surd consonants, between D, B, Z, G, V, and T, P, S, K, F, respectively. But comparatively few persons know the difference theoretically, until their attention has been called to what it is, when they perceive it readily enough. The sonants are nothing but the surds plus a certain element, which is alike in all, superadded. That element is the laryngeal sound with which they are uttered, surds having no such accompaniment. When we hear the sonant letter, both its component elements must really be in our mind; but we remain unconscious of what they really are, and mistake the letter for a simple quality of sound until an effort of attention teaches us its two components. There exist a host of sensations which most men pass through life and never attend to, and consequently have only in an unconscious way. The feelings of opening and closing the glottis, of making tense the tympanic membrane, of accommodating for near vision, of intercepting the passage from the nostrils to the throat, are instances of what I mean. Every one gets these feelings many times an hour; but few readers, probably, are conscious of exactly what sensations are meant by the names I have just used. All these facts, and an enormous number more, seem to prove conclusively that, in addition to the fully conscious way in which an idea may exist in the mind, there is also an unconscious way; that it is unquestionably the same identical idea which exists in these two ways; and that therefore any arguments against the mind-stuff theory, based on the notion that esse in our mental life is sentiri, and that an idea must consciously be felt as what it is, fall to the ground.

Objection. These reasonings are one tissue of confusion. Two states of mind which refer to the same external reality, or two states of mind the later one of which refers to the earlier, are described as the same state of mind, or 'idea,' published as it were in two editions; and then whatever qualities of the second edition are found openly lacking in the first are explained as having really been there, only in an 'unconscious' way. It would be difficult to believe that intelligent men could be guilty of so patent a fallacy, were not the history of psychology there to give the proof. The psychological stock-in-trade of some authors is the belief that two thoughts about one thing are virtually the same thought, and that this same thought may in subsequent reflections become more and more conscious of what it really was all along from the first. But once make the distinction between simply having an idea at the moment of its presence and subsequently knowing all sorts of things about it; make moreover that between a state of mind itself, taken as a subjective fact, on the one hand, and the objective thing it knows, on the other, and one has no difficulty in escaping from the labyrinth.

Take the latter distinction first: Immediately all the arguments based on sensations and the new features in them which attention brings to light fall to the ground. The sensations of the B and the V when we attend to these sounds and analyze out the laryngeal contribution which makes them differ from P and F respectively, are different sensations from those of the B and the V taken in a simple way. They stand, it is true, for the same letters, and thus mean the same outer realities; but they are different mental affections, and certainly depend on widely different processes of cerebral activity. It is unbelievable that two mental states so different as the passive reception of a sound as a whole, and the analysis of that whole into distinct ingredients by voluntary attention, should be due to processes at all similar. And the subjective difference does not consist in that the first-named state is the second in an 'unconscious' form. It is an absolute psychic difference, even greater than that between the states to which two different surds will give rise. The same is true of the other sensations chosen as examples. The man who learns for the first time how the closure of his glottis feels, experiences in this discovery an absolutely new psychic modification, the like of which he never had before. He had another feeling before, a feeling incessantly renewed, and of which the same glottis was the organic starting point; but that was not the later feeling in an 'unconscious' state; it was a feeling sui generis altogether, although it took cognizance of the same bodily part, the glottis. We shall see, hereafter, that the same reality can be cognized by an endless number of psychic states, which may differ toto coelo among themselves, without ceasing on that account to refer to the reality in question. Each of them is a conscious fact; none of them has any mode of being whatever except a certain way of being felt at the moment of being present. It is simply unintelligible and fantastical to say, because they point to the same outer reality, that they must therefore be so many editions of the same 'idea,' now in conscious and now in an 'unconscious' phase. There is only one 'phase' in which an idea can be, and that is a fully conscious condition. If it is not in that condition, then it is not at all. Something else is, in its place. The something else may be a merely physical brain-process, or it may be another conscious idea. Either of these things may perform much the same function as the first idea, refer to the same object, and roughly stand in the same relations to the upshot of our thought. But that is no reason why we should throw away the logical principle of identity in psychology, and say that, however it may fare in the outer world, the mind at any rate is a place in which a thing can be all kinds of other things without ceasing to be itself as well.

Now take the other cases alleged, and the other distinction, that namely between having a mental state and knowing all about it. The truth is here even simpler to unravel. When I decide that I have, without knowing it, been for several weeks in love, I am simply giving a name to a state which previously I have not named, but which was fully conscious; which had no residual mode of being except the manner in which it was conscious; and which, though it was a feeling towards the same person for whom I now have much more inflamed feeling, and though it continuously led into the latter, and is similar enough to be called by the same name, is yet in no sense identical with the latter, and least of all in an 'unconscious' way. Again, the feelings from our viscera and other dimly-felt organs, the feelings of innervation (if such there be), and those of muscular exertion which, in our spatial judgments, are supposed unconsciously to determine what we shall perceive, are just exactly what we feel them, perfectly determinate conscious states, not vague editions of other conscious states. They may be faint and weak; they may be very vague cognizers of the same realities which other conscious states cognize and name exactly; they may be unconscious of much in the reality which the other states are conscious of. But that does not make them in themselves a whit dim or vague or unconscious. They are eternally as they feel when they exist, and can, neither actually nor potentially, be identified with anything else than their own faint selves. A faint feeling may be looked back upon and classified and understood in its relations to what went before or after it in the stream of thought. But it, on the one hand, and the later state of mind which knows all these things about it, on the other, are surely not two conditions, one conscious and the other 'unconscious,' of the same identical psychic fact. It is the destiny of thought that, on the whole, our early ideas are superseded by later ones, giving fuller accounts of the same realities. But none the less do the earlier and the later ideas preserve their own several substantive identities as so many several successive states of mind. To believe the contrary would make any definite science of psychology impossible. The only identity to be found among our successive ideas is their similarity of cognitive or representative function as dealing with the same objects. Identity of being, there is none; and I believe that throughout the rest of this volume the reader will reap the advantages of the simpler way of formulating the facts which is here begun.[27]

So we seem not only to have ascertained the unintelligibility of the notion that a mental fact can be two things at once, and that what seems like one feeling, of blueness for example, or of hatred, may really and 'unconsciously' be ten thousand elementary feelings which do not resemble blueness or hatred at all, but we find that we can express all the observed facts in other ways. The mind-stuff theory, however, though scotched, is, we may be sure, not killed. If we ascribe consciousness to unicellular animalcules, then single cells can have it, and analogy should make us ascribe it to the several cells of the brain, each individually taken. And what a convenience would it not be for the psychologist if, by the adding together of various doses of this separate-cell-consciousness, he could treat thought as a kind of stuff or material, to be measured out in great or small amount, increased and subtracted from and baled about at will! He feels an imperious craving to be allowed to construct synthetically the successive mental states which he describes. The mind-stuff theory so easily admits of the construction being made, that it seems certain that 'man's unconquerable mind' will devote much future pertinacity and ingenuity to setting it on its legs again and getting it into some sort of plausible working-order. I will therefore conclude the chapter with some consideration of the remaining difficulties which beset the matter as it at present stands.

Difficulty of Stating the Connection Between Mind and Brain.

It will be remembered that in our criticism of the theory of the integration of successive conscious units into a feeling of musical pitch, we decided that whatever integration there was was that of the air-pulses into a simpler and simpler sort of physical effect, as the propagations of material change got higher and higher in the nervous system. At last, we said, there results some simple and massive process in the auditory centres of the hemispherical cortex, to which, as a whole, the feeling of musical pitch directly corresponds. Already, in discussing the localization of functions in the brain, I had said that consciousness accompanies the stream of innervation through that organ and varies in quality with the character of the currents, being mainly of things seen if the occipital lobes are much involved, of things heard if the action is focalized in the temporal lobes, etc., etc.; and I had added that a vague formula like this was as much as one could safely venture on in the actual state of physiology. The facts of mental deafness and blindness, of auditory and optical aphasia, show us that the whole brain must act together if certain thoughts are to occur. The consciousness, which is itself an integral thing not made of parts, 'corresponds' to the entire activity of the brain, whatever that may be, at the moment. This is a way of expressing the relation of mind and brain from which I shall not depart during the remainder of the book, because it expresses the bare phenomenal fact with no hypothesis, and is exposed to no such logical objections as we have found to cling to the theory of ideas in combination.

Nevertheless, this formula which is so unobjectionable if taken vaguely, positivistically, or scientifically, as a mere empirical law of concomitance between our thoughts and our brain, tumbles to pieces entirely if we assume to represent anything more intimate or ultimate by it. The ultimate of ultimate problems, of course, in the study of the relations of thought and brain, is to understand why and how such disparate things are connected at all. But before that problem is solved (if it ever is solved) there is a less ultimate problem which must first be settled. Before the connection of thought and brain can be explained, it must at least be stated in an elementary form; and there are great difficulties about so stating it. To state it in elementary form one must reduce it to its lowest terms and know which mental fact and which cerebral fact are, so to speak, in immediate juxtaposition. We must find the minimal mental fact whose being reposes directly on a brain-fact; and we must similarly find the minimal brain-event which will have a mental counterpart at all. Between the mental and the physical minima thus found there will be an immediate relation, the expression of which, if we had it, would be the elementary psycho-physic law.

Our own formula escapes the unintelligibility of psychic atoms by taking the entire thought (even of a complex object) as the minimum with which it deals on the mental side. But in taking the entire brain-process as its minimal fact on the material side it confronts other difficulties almost as bad.

In the first place, it ignores analogies on which certain critics will insist, those, namely, between the composition of the total brain-process and that of the object of the thought. The total brain-process is composed of parts, of simultaneous processes in the seeing, the hearing, the feeling, and other centres. The object thought of is also composed of parts, some of which are seen, others heard, others perceived by touch and muscular manipulation. "How then," these critics will say, "should the thought not itself be composed of parts, each the counterpart of a part of the object and of a part of the brain-process?" So natural is this way of looking at the matter that it has given rise to what is on the whole the most flourishing of all psychological systems - that of the Lockian school of associated ideas - of which school the mind-stuff theory is nothing but the last and subtlest offshoot.

The second difficulty is deeper still. The 'entire brain-process' is not a physical fact at all. It is the appearance to an onlooking mind of a multitude of physical facts. 'Entire brain' is nothing but our name for the way in which a million of molecules arranged in certain positions may affect our sense. On the principles of the corpuscular or mechanical philosophy, the only realities are the separate molecules, or at most the cells. Their aggregation into a 'brain' is a fiction of popular speech. Such a fiction cannot serve as the objectively real counterpart to any psychic state whatever. Only a genuinely physical fact can so serve. But the molecular fact is the only genuine physical fact - whereupon we seem, if we are to have an elementary psycho-physic law at all, thrust right back upon something like the mind-stuff theory, for the molecular fact, being an element of the 'brain,' would seem naturally to correspond, not to the total thoughts, but to elements in the thought.

What shall we do? Many would find relief at this point in celebrating the mystery of the Unknowable and the 'awe' which we should feel at having such a principle to take final charge of our perplexities. Others would rejoice that the finite and separatist view of things with which we started had at last developed its contradictions, and was about to lead us dialectically upwards to some 'higher synthesis' in which inconsistencies cease from troubling and logic is at rest. It may be a constitutional infirmity, but I can take no comfort in such devices for making a luxury of intellectual defeat. They are but spiritual chloroform. Better live on the ragged edge, better gnaw the file forever!

The Material - Monad Theory.

The most rational thing to do is to suspect that there may be a third possibility, an alternative supposition which we have not considered. Now there is an alternative supposition - a supposition moreover which has been frequently made in the history of philosophy, and which is freer from logical objections than either of the views we have ourselves discussed. It may be called the theory of polyzoism or multiple monadism; and it conceives the matter thus:

Every brain-cell has its own individual consciousness, which no other cell knows anything about, all individual consciousness being 'ejective' to each other. There is, however, among the cells one central or pontifical one to which our consciousness is attached. But the events of all the other cells physically influence this arch-cell; and through producing their joint effects on it, these other cells may be said to 'combine.' The arch-cell is, in fact, one of those 'external media' without which we saw that no fusion or integration of a number of things can occur. The physical modifications of the arch-cell thus form a sequence of results in the production whereof every other cell has a share, so that, as one might say, every other cell is represented therein. And similarly, the conscious correlates to these physical modifications form a sequence of thoughts or feelings, each one of which is, as to its substantive being, an integral and uncompounded psychic thing, but each one of which may (in the exercise of its cognitive function) be aware of THINGS many and complicated in proportion to the number of other cells that have helped to modify the central cell.

By a conception of this sort, one incurs neither of the internal contradictions which we found to beset the other two theories. One has no unintelligible self-combining of psychic units to account for on the one hand; and on the other hand, one need not treat as the physical counterpart of the stream of consciousness under observation, a 'total brain-activity' which is non-existent as a genuinely physiological fact. But, to offset these advantages, one has physiological difficulties and improbabilities. There is no cell or group of cells in the brain of such anatomical or functional pre-eminence as to appear to be the keystone or centre of gravity of the whole system. And even if there were such a cell, the theory of multiple monadism would, in strictness of thought, have no right to stop at it and treat it as a unit. The cell is no more a unit, materially considered, than the total brain is a unit. It is a compound of molecules, just as the brain is a compound of cells and fibres. And the molecules, according to the prevalent physical theories, are in turn compounds of atoms. The theory in question, therefore, if radically carried out, must set up for its elementary and irreducible psycho-physic couple, not the cell and its consciousness, but the primordial and eternal atom and its consciousness. We are back at Leibnitzian monadism, and therewith leave physiology behind us and dive into regions inaccessible to experience and verification; and our doctrine, although not self-contradictory, becomes so remote and unreal as to be almost as bad as if it were. Speculative minds alone will take an interest in it; and metaphysics, not psychology, will be responsible for its career. That the career may be a successful one must be admitted as a possibility - a theory which Leibnitz, Herbart, and Lotze have taken under their protection must have some sort of a destiny.

The Soul – Theory.

But is this my last word? By no means. Many readers have certainly been saying to themselves for the last few pages: "Why on earth doesn't the poor man say the Soul and have done with it?" Other readers, of antispiritualistic training and prepossessions, advanced thinkers, or popular evolutionists, will perhaps be a little surprised to find this much-despised word now sprung upon them at the end of so physiological a train of thought. But the plain fact is that all the arguments for a 'pontifical cell' or an 'arch-monad' are also arguments for that well-known spiritual agent in which scholastic psychology and common-sense have always believed. And my only reason for beating the bushes so, and not bringing it in earlier as a possible solution of our difficulties, has been that by this procedure I might perhaps force some of these materialistic minds to feel the more strongly the logical respectability of the spiritualistic position. The fact is that one cannot afford to despise any of these great traditional objects of belief. Whether we realize it or not, there is always a great drift of reasons, positive and negative, towing us in their direction. If there be such entities as Souls in the universe, they may possibly be affected by the manifold occurrences that go on in the nervous centres. To the state of the entire brain at a given moment they may respond by inward modifications of their own. These changes of state may be pulses of consciousness, cognitive of objects few or many, simple or complex. The soul would be thus a medium upon which (to use our earlier phraseology) the manifold brain-processes combine their effects. Not needing to consider it as the 'inner aspect' of any arch-molecule or brain-cell, we escape that physiological improbability; and as its pulses of consciousness are unitary and integral affairs from the outset, we escape the absurdity of supposing feelings which exist separately and then 'fuse together' by themselves. The separateness is in the brain-world, on this theory, and the unity in the soul-world; and the only trouble that remains to haunt us is the metaphysical one of understanding how one sort of world or existent thing can affect or influence another at all. This trouble, however, since it also exists inside of both worlds, and involves neither physical improbability nor logical contradiction, is relatively small.
I confess, therefore, that to posit a soul influenced in some mysterious way by the brain-states and responding to them by conscious affections of its own, seems to me the line of least logical resistance, so far as we yet have attained.
If it does not strictly explain anything, it is at any rate less positively objectionable than either mind-stuff or a material-monad creed. The bare PHENOMENON, however, the IMMEDIATELY KNOWN thing which on the mental side is in apposition with the entire brain-process is the state of consciousness and not the soul itself. Many of the stanchest believers in the soul admit that we know it only as an inference from experiencing its states. In Chapter X, accordingly, we must return to its consideration again, and ask ourselves whether, after all, the ascertainment of a blank unmediated correspondence, term for term, of the succession of states of consciousness with the succession of total brain-processes, be not the simplest psycho-physic formula, and the last word of a psychology which contents itself with verifiable laws, and seeks only to be clear, and to avoid unsafe hypotheses. Such a mere admission of the empirical parallelism will there appear the wisest course. By keeping to it, our psychology will remain positivistic and non-metaphysical; and although this is certainly only a provisional halting-place, and things must some day be more thoroughly thought out, we shall abide there in this book, and just as we have rejected mind-dust, we shall take no account of the soul. The spiritualistic reader may nevertheless believe in the soul if he will; whilst the positivistic one who wishes to give a tinge of mystery to the expression of his positivism can continue to say that nature in her unfathomable designs has mixed us of clay and flame, of brain and mind, that the two things hang indubitably together and determine each other's being, but how or why, no mortal may ever know.

Notes

[1] Psychol. § 62.
[2] Ibid. § 272.
[3] Fragments of Science, 5th ed., p. 420.
[4] Belfast Address, 'Nature,' August 20, 1874, p. 318. I cannot help remarking that the disparity between motions and feelings on which these authors lay so much stress, is somewhat less absolute than at first sight it seems. There are categories common to the two worlds. Not only temporal succession (as Helmholtz admits, Physiol. Optik, p. 445), but such attributes as intensity, volume, simplicity or complication, smooth or impeded change, rest or agitation, are habitually predicated of both physical facts and mental facts. Where such analogies obtain, the things do have something in common.
[5] Psychology, § 131.
[6] 'Nature,' as above.
[7] 'Nascent' is Mr. Spencer's great word. In showing how at a certain point consciousness must appear upon the evolving scene this author fairly outdoes himself in vagueness.
"In its higher forms, Instinct is probably accompanied by a rudimentary consciousness. There cannot be co-ordination of many stimuli without some ganglion through which they are all brought into relation. In the process of bringing them into relation, this ganglion must be subject to the influence of each - must undergo many changes. And the quick succession of changes in a ganglion, implying as it does perpetual experiences of differences and likenesses, constitutes the *raw material* of consciousness. The *implication* is that as fast as Instinct is developed, some kind of consciousness becomes nascent." (Psychology, § 195.)
The words 'raw material' and 'implication' which I have italicized are the words which do the evolving. They are supposed to have all the rigor which the 'synthetic philosophy' requires. In the following passage, when 'impressions' pass through a common 'centre of communication' in succession (much as people might pass into a theatre through a turnstile) consciousness, non-existent until then, is supposed to result:
"Separate impressions are received by the senses - by different parts of the body. If they go no further than the places at which they are received, they are useless. Or if only some of them are brought into relation with one another, they are useless. That an effectual adjustment may be made, they must be all brought into relation with one another. But this implies some centre of communication common to them all, through which they severally pass; and as they cannot pass through it simultaneously, they must pass through it in succession. So that as the external phenomena responded to become greater in number and more complicated in kind, the variety and rapidity of the changes to which this common centre of communication is subject must increase - there must result an unbroken series of these changes - there must arise a consciousness.
"Hence the progress of the correspondence between the organism and its environment necessitates a gradual reduction of the sensorial changes to a succession; and by so doing evolves a distinct consciousness - a consciousness that becomes higher as the succession becomes more rapid and the correspondence more complete." (Ibid. § 179.)
It is true that in the Fortnightly Review (vol. XIV. p. 716) Mr. Spencer denies that he means by this passage to tell us anything about the origin of consciousness at all. It resembles, however, too many other places in his Psychology (e.g. §§ 43, 110, 244) not to be taken as a serious attempt to explain how consciousness must at a certain point be 'evolved.' That, when a critic calls his attention to the inanity of his words, Mr. Spencer should say he never meant anything particular by them, is simply an example of the scandalous vagueness with which this sort of 'chromo-philosophy' is carried on.
[8] His own words are: "Mistakes are made in the sense that he admits having been touched, when in reality it was radiant heat that affected his skin. In our own before-mentioned experiments there was never any deception on the entire palmar side of the hand or on the face. On the back of the hand in one case in a series of 60 stimulations 4 mistakes occurred, in another case 2 mistakes in 45 stimulations. On the extensor side of the upper arm 3 deceptions out of 48 stimulations were noticed, and in the case of another individual, 1 out of 31. In one case over the spine 3 deceptions in a series of 11 excitations were observed; in another, 4 out of 19. On the lumbar spine 6 deceptions came among 29 stimulations, and again 4 out of 7. There is certainly not yet enough material on which to rest a calculation of probabilities, but any one can easily convince himself that on the back there is no question of even a moderately accurate discrimination between warmth and a light pressure so far as but small portions of skin come into play. It has been as yet impossible to make corresponding experiments with regard to sensibility to cold." (Lehrb. d. Anat. u. Physiol. d. Sinnesorgane (1862), p. 29.)
[9] Principles of Psychology, § 60.
[10] Oddly enough, Mr. Spencer seems quite unaware of the general function of the theory of elementary units of mind-stuff in the evolutionary philosophy. We have seen it to be absolutely indispensable, if that philosophy is to work, to postulate consciousness in the nebula, - the simplest way being, of course, to suppose every atom animated. Mr. Spencer, however, will have it (e.g. First Principles, § 71) that consciousness is only the occasional result of the 'transformation' of a certain amount of 'physical force' to which it is 'equivalent.' Presumably a brain must already be there before any such 'transformation' can take place; and so the argument quoted in the text stands as a mere local detail, without general bearings.
[11] The compounding of colors may be dealt with in an identical way. Helmholtz has shown that if green light and red light fall simultaneously on the retina, we see the color yellow. The mind-stuff theory would interpret this as a case where the feeling green and the feeling red 'combine' into the tertium quid of feeling, yellow. What really occurs is no doubt that a third

kind of nerve-process is set up when the combined lights impinge on the retina, - not simply the process of red plus the process of green, but something quite different from both or either. Of course, then, there are no feelings, either of red or of green, present to the mind at all; but the feeling of yellow which is there, answers as directly to the nerve-process which momentarily then exists, as the feelings of green and red would answer to their respective nerve-processes did the latter happen to be taking place.

[12] *Cf. Mill's Logic, book VI. chap. IV. § 3.*

[13] *I find in my students an almost invincible tendency to think that we can immediately perceive that feelings do combine. "What!" they say, "is not the taste of lemonade composed of that of lemon plus that of sugar?" This is taking the combining of objects for that of feelings. The physical lemonade contains both the lemon and the sugar, but its taste does not contain their tastes, for if there are any two things which are certainly not present in the taste of lemonade, those are the lemon-sour on the one hand and the sugar-sweet on the other. These tastes are absent utterly. The entirely new taste which is present resembles, it is true, both those tastes; but in Chapter XIII we shall see that resemblance can not always be held to involve partial identity.*

[14] *E. Montgomery, in 'Mind,' V. 18-19. See also pp. 24-5.*

[15] *J. Royce, 'Mind,' VI. p. 376. Lotze has set forth the truth of this law more clearly and copiously than any other writer. Unfortunately he is too lengthy to quote. See his Microcosmus, bk. II. ch. I. § 5; Metaphysik, §§ 242, 260; Outlines of Metaphysics, part II. chap. I. §§ 3, 4, 5. Compare also Reid's Intellectual Powers, essay V, chap. III ad fin.; Bowne's Metaphysics, pp. 361-76; St. J. Mivart: Nature and Thought, pp. 98-101; E. Gurney: 'Monism,' in 'Mind,' VI. 153; and the article by Prof. Royce, just quoted, on 'Mind-stuff and Reality.'*

In defence of the mind-stuff view, see W. K. Clifford: 'Mind,' III. 57 (reprinted in his 'Lectures and Essays,' II. 71); G. T. Fechner, Psychophysik, Bd. II. cap. XLV; H. Taine: on Intelligence, bk. III; E. Haeckel. 'Zellseelen u. Seelenzellen ' in Gesammelte pop. Vorträge, Bd. I. p. 143; W. S. Duncan. Conscious Matter, passim; H. Zollner; Natur d. Cometen, pp. 320 ff.; Alfred Barratt: 'Physical Ethic' and Physical Metempiric,' passum' J. Soury: 'Hylozoismus,' in Kosmos,' V. Jahrg., Heft X. p. 241; A. Main: 'Mind,' I. 292, 431, 566; II. 129, 402; Id. Revue Philos., II. 86, 88, 419; III. 51, 502; IV. 402; F. W. Frankland: 'Mind,' VI. 116; Whittaker: 'Mind,' VI. 498 (historical); Morton Prince: The Nature of Mind and Human Automatism (1885); A. Riehl: Der philosophische Kriticismus, Bd. II. Theil 2, 2ter Abschnitt, 2tes Cap. (1887). The clearest of all these statements is, as far as it goes, that of Prince.

[16] *"Someone might say that although it is true that neither a blind man nor a deaf man by himself can compare sounds with colors, yet since one hears and the other sees they might do so both together.... But whether they are apart or close together makes no difference; not even if they permanently keep house together; no, not if they were Siamese twins, or more than Siamese twins, and were inseparably grown together, would it make the assumption any more possible. Only when sound and color are represented in the same reality is it thinkable that they should be compared." (Brentano; Psychologie, p. 209.)*

[17] *The reader must observe that we are reasoning altogether about the logic of the mind-stuff theory, about whether it can explain the constitution of higher mental states by viewing them as identical with lower ones summed together. We say the two sorts of fact are not identical: a higher state is not a lot of lower states; it is itself. When, however, a lot of lower states have come together, or when certain brain-conditions occur together which, if they occurred separately, would produce a lot of lower states, we have not for a moment pretended that a higher state may not emerge. In fact it does emerge under those conditions; and our Chapter IX will be mainly devoted to the proof of this fact. But such emergence is that of a new psychic entity, and is toto coelo different from such an 'integration' of the lower states as the mind-stuff theory affirms.*

It may seem strange to suppose that anyone should mistake criticism of a certain theory about a fact for doubt of the fact itself. And yet the confusion is made in high quarters enough to justify our remarks. Mr. J. Ward, in his article Psychology in the Encyclopaedia Britannica, speaking of the hypothesis that "a series of feelings can be aware of itself as a series," says (p. 39): "Paradox is too mild a word for it, even contradiction will hardly suffice." Whereupon, Professor Bain takes him thus to task: "As to 'a series of states being aware of itself, I confess I see no insurmountable difficulty. It may be a fact, or not a fact; it may be a very clumsy expression for what it is applied to; but it is neither paradox nor contradiction. A series merely contradicts an individual, or it may be two or more individuals as coexisting; but that is too general to exclude the possibility of self-knowledge. It certainly does not bring the property of self-knowledge into the foreground, which, however, is not the same as denying it. An algebraic series might know itself, without any contradiction: the only thing against it is the want of evidence of the fact." ('Mind,' XI, 459). Prof. Bain thinks, then, that all the bother is about the difficulty of seeing how a series of feelings can have the knowledge of itself added to it!!! As if anybody ever was troubled about that. That, notoriously enough, is a fact: our consciousness is a series of feelings to which every now and then is added a retrospective consciousness that they have come and gone. What Mr. Ward and I are troubled about is merely the silliness of the mind-stuffists and associationists continuing to say that the 'series of states' is the 'awareness of itself;' that if the states be posited severally, their collective consciousness is eo ipso given; and that we need no farther explanation, or 'evidence of the fact.'

[18] *The writers about 'unconscious cerebration' seem sometimes to mean that and sometimes unconscious thought. The arguments which follow are culled from various quarters. The reader will find them most systematically urged by E. von Hartmann: Philosophy of the Unconscious, vol. I, and by E. Colsenet: La vie Inconsciente de l'Esprit (1880). Consult also T. Laycock: Mind and Brain, vol, I. chap. V (1860); W. B. Carpenter: Mental Physiology, chap. XIII; F. P. Cobbe: Darwinism in Morals and other Essays, essay XI, Unconscious Cerebration (1872); F. Bowen: Modern Philosophy, pp. 428-480; R. H. Hutton: Contemporary Review, vol. XXIV. p. 201; J. S. Mill: Exam. of Hamilton, chap. XV; G. H. Lewes; Problems of life and Mind, 3d*

series, Prob. II. chap. X, and also Prob. III. chap. II; D. G. Thompson: A System of Psychology, chap. XXXIII; J. M. Baldwin, Handbook of Psychology, chap. IV.
[19] Nouveaux Essais, Avant-propos.
[20] J. S. Mill, Exam of Hamilton, chap. XV.
[21] Cf. Dugald Stewart, Elements, chap. II.
[22] J. E. Maude: 'The Unconscious in Education,' in 'Education' vol. I. p. 401 (1882).
[23] Zur Lehre vom Lichtsinne (1878).
[24] Cf. Wundt: Ueber den Einfluss der Philosophie, etc. - Antrittsrede (1876), pp. 10-11; - Helmholtz: Die Thatsachen in der Wahrnehmung, (1879), p. 27.
[25] Cf. Satz vom Grunde, pp. 59-65. Compare also F. Zöllner's Natur der Kometen, pp. 342 ff., and 425.
[26] Cf. the statements from Helmholtz to be found later in Chapter XIII.
[27] The text was written before Professor Lipps's Grundtatsachen des Seelenlebens (1883) came into my hands. In Chapter III of that book the notion of unconscious thought is subjected to the clearest and most searching criticism which it has yet received, [sic] Some passages are so similar to what I have myself written that I must quote them in a note. After proving that dimness and clearness, incompleteness and completeness do not pertain to a state of mind as such - since every state of mind must be exactly what it is, and nothing else - but only pertain to the way in which states of mind stand for objects, which they more or less dimly, more or less clearly, represent; Lipps takes the case of those sensations which attention is said to make more clear. "I perceive an object," he says, "now in clear daylight, and again at night. Call the content of the day-perception a, and that of the evening-perception a1. There will probably be a considerable difference between a and a1. The colors of a will be varied and intense, and will be sharply bounded by each other; those of a1 will be less luminous, and less strongly contrasted, and will approach a common gray or brown, and merge more into each other. Both percepts, however, as such, are completely determinate and distinct from all others. The colors of a1 appear before my eye neither neither more nor less decidedly dark and blurred than the colors of a appear bright and sharply bounded. But now I know, or believe I know, that one and the same real Object A corresponds to both a and a1. I am convinced, moreover, that a represents A better than does a1. Instead, however, of giving to my conviction this, its only correct, expression, and keeping the content of the consciousness, and the real object, the representation and what it means, distinct from each other, I substitute the real object for the content of the consciousness, and talk of the experience as if it consisted in one and the same object (namely, the surreptitiously introduced real one), constituting twice over the content of my consciousness, once in a clear and distinct, the other time in an obscure and vague fashion. I talk now of a distincter and of a less distinct consciousness of A, whereas I am only justified in talking of two consciousnesses, a and a1, equally distinct in se, but to which the supposed external object A corresponds with different degrees of distinctness." (P. 38-9.)

Chapter VII - The Methods and Snares of Psychology

We have now finished the physiological preliminaries of our subject and must in the remaining chapters study the mental states themselves whose cerebral conditions and concomitants we have been considering hitherto. Beyond the brain, however, there is an outer world to which the brain-states themselves 'correspond.' And it will be well, ere we advance farther, to say a word about the relation of the mind to this larger sphere of physical fact.

Psychology is a Natural Science.

That is, the mind which the psychologist studies is the mind of distinct individuals inhabiting definite portions of a real space and of a real time. With any other sort of mind, absolute Intelligence, Mind unattached to a particular body, or Mind not subject to the course of time, the psychologist as such has nothing to do. 'Mind,' in his mouth, is only a class name for minds. Fortunate will it be if his more modest inquiry result in any generalizations which the philosopher devoted to absolute Intelligence as such can use.

To the psychologist, then, the minds he studies are objects, in a world of other objects. Even when he introspectively analyzes his own mind, and tells what he finds there, he talks about it in an objective way. He says, for instance, that under certain circumstances the color gray appears to him green, and calls the appearance an illusion. This implies that he compares two objects, a real color seen under conditions, and a mental perception which he believes to represent it, and that he declares the relation between them to be of a certain kind. In making this critical judgment, the psychologist stands as much outside of the perception which he criticises as he does of the color. Both are his objects. And if this is true of him when he reflects on his own conscious states, how much truer is it when he treats of those of others! In German philosophy since Kant the word Erkenntnisstheorie, criticism of the faculty of knowledge, plays a great part. Now the psychologist necessarily becomes such an Erkenntnisstheoretiker. But the knowledge he theorizes about is not the bare function of knowledge which Kant criticises - he does not inquire into the possibility of knowledge überhaupt. He assumes it to be possible, he does not doubt its presence in himself at the moment he speaks. The knowledge he criticises is the knowledge of particular men about the particular things that surround them. This he may, upon occasion, in the light of his own unquestioned knowledge, pronounce true or false, and trace the reasons by which it has become one or the other.

It is highly important that this natural-science point of view should be understood at the outset. Otherwise more may be demanded of the psychologist than he ought to be expected to perform.

A diagram will exhibit more emphatically what the assumptions of Psychology must be:

1	2	3	4
The Psychologist	The Thought Studied	The Thought's Object	The Psychologist's Reality

These four squares contain the irreducible data of psychology. No. 1, the psychologist, believes Nos. 2, 3, and 4, which together form his total object, to be realities, and reports them and their mutual relations as truly as he can without troubling himself with the puzzle of how he can report them at all. About such ultimate puzzles he in the main need trouble himself no more than the geometer, the chemist, or the botanist do, who make precisely the same assumptions as he.[1]

Of certain fallacies to which the psychologist is exposed by reason of his peculiar point of view - that of being a reporter of subjective as well as of objective facts, we must presently speak. But not until we have considered the methods he uses for ascertaining what the facts in question are.

The Methods of Investigation.

Introspective Observation is what we have to rely on first and foremost and always. The word introspection need hardly be defined - it means, of course, the looking into our own minds and reporting what we there discover. Every one agrees that we there discover states of consciousness. So far as I know, the existence of such states has never been doubted by any critic, however sceptical in other respects he may have been. That we have cogitations of some sort is the inconcussum in a world most of whose other facts have at some time tottered in the breath of philosophic doubt. All people unhesitatingly believe that they feel themselves thinking, and that they distinguish the mental state as an inward activity or passion, from all the objects with which it may cognitively deal. I regard this belief as the most fundamental of all the postulates of Psychology, and shall discard all curious inquiries about its certainty as too metaphysical for the scope of this book.

A Question of Nomenclature. We ought to have some general term by which to designate all states of consciousness merely as such, and apart from their particular quality or cognitive function. Unfortunately most of the terms in use have grave objections. 'Mental state,' 'state of consciousness,' 'conscious modification,' are cumbrous and have no kindred verbs. The same is true of 'subjective condition.' 'Feeling' has the verb 'to feel,' both active and neuter, and such derivatives as 'feelingly,' 'felt,' 'feltness,' etc., which make it extremely convenient. But on the other hand it has specific meanings as well as its generic one, sometimes standing for pleasure and pain, and being sometimes a synonym of 'sensation' as opposed to thought ; whereas we wish a term to cover sensation and thought indifferently. Moreover, 'feeling' has acquired in the hearts of platonizing thinkers a very opprobrious set of implications ; and since one of the greatest obstacles to mutual understanding in philosophy is the use of words eulogistically and disparagingly, impartial terms ought always, if possible, to be preferred. The word psychosis has been proposed by Mr. Huxley. It has the advantage of being correlative to neurosis (the name applied by the same author to the corresponding nerve-process), and is moreover technical and devoid of partial implications. But it has no verb or other grammatical form allied to it. The expressions 'affection of the soul,' 'modification of the ego,' are clumsy, like 'state of consciousness,' and they implicitly assert theories which it is not well to embody in terminology before they have been openly discussed and approved. 'Idea' is a good vague neutral word, and was by Locke employed in the broadest generic way ; but notwithstanding his authority it has not domesticated itself in the language so as to cover bodily sensations. It has no opprobrious connotation such as 'feeling' has, and it immediately suggests the omnipresence of cognition (or reference to an object other than the mental state itself), which we shall soon see to be of the mental life's essence. But can the expression 'thought of a toothache' ever suggest to the reader the actual present pain itself? It is hardly possible ; and we thus seem about to be forced back on some pair of terms like Hume's 'impression and idea,' or Hamilton's 'presentation and representation,' or the ordinary 'feeling and thought,' if we wish to cover the whole ground.

In this quandary we can make no definitive choice, but must, according to the convenience of the context, use sometimes one, sometimes another of the synonyms that have been mentioned. My own partiality is for either FEELING or THOUGHT. I shall probably often use both words in a wider sense than usual, and alternately startle two classes of readers by their unusual sound ; but if the connection makes it clear that mental states at large, irrespective of their kind, are meant, this will do no harm, and may even do some good.[2]

The inaccuracy of introspective observation has been made a subject of debate. It is important to gain some fixed ideas on this point before we proceed.

The commonest spiritualistic opinion is that the Soul or Subject of the mental life is a metaphysical entity, inaccessible to direct knowledge, and that the various mental states and operations of which we reflectively become aware are objects of an inner sense which does not lay hold of the real agent in itself, any more than sight or hearing gives us direct knowledge of matter in itself. From this point of view introspection is, of course, incompetent to lay hold of anything more than the Soul's phenomena. But even then the question remains, How well can it know the phenomena themselves?

Some authors take high ground here and claim for it a sort of infallibility. Thus Ueberweg:

"When a mental image, as such, is the object of my apprehension, there is no meaning in seeking to distinguish its existence in my consciousness (in me) from its existence out of my consciousness (in itself) ; for the object apprehended is, in this case, one which does not even exist, as the objects of external perception do, in itself outside of my consciousness. It exists only within me."[3]

And Brentano:

"The phenomena inwardly apprehended are true in themselves. As they appear - of this the evidence with which they are apprehended is a warrant - so they are in reality. Who, then, can deny that in this a great superiority of Psychology over the physical sciences comes to light?"

And again:

"No one can doubt whether the psychic condition he apprehends in himself be, and be so, as he apprehends it. Whoever should doubt this would have reached that finished doubt which destroys itself in destroying every fixed point from which to make an attack upon knowledge."[4]

Others have gone to the opposite extreme, and maintained that we can have no introspective cognition of our own minds at all. A deliverance of Auguste Comte to this effect has been so often quoted as to be almost classical ; and some reference to it seems therefore indispensable here.

Philosophers, says Comte,[5] have

"in these latter days imagined themselves able to distinguish, by a very singular subtlety, two sorts of observation of equal importance, one external, the other internal, the latter being solely destined for the study of intellectual phenomena.... I limit myself to pointing out the principal consideration which proves clearly that this pretended direct contemplation of the mind by itself is a pure illusion.... It is in fact evident that, by an invincible neccessity, [sic] the human mind can observe directly all phenomena except its own proper states. For by whom shall the observation of these be made? It is conceivable that a man might observe himself with respect to the passions that animate him, for the anatomical organs of passion are distinct from those whose function is observation. Though we have all made such observations on ourselves, they can never have much scientific value, and the best mode of knowing the passions will always be that of observing them from without ; for every strong state of passion ... is necessarily incompatible with the state of observation. But, as for observing in the same way intellectual phenomena at the time of their actual presence, that is a manifest impossibility. The thinker cannot divide himself into two, of whom one reasons whilst the other observes him reason. The organ observed and the organ observing being, in this case, identical, how could observation take place? This pretended psychological method is then radically null and void. On the one hand, they advise you to isolate yourself, as far as possible, from every external sensation, especially every intellectual work, - for if you were to busy yourself even with the simplest calculation, what would become of internal observation? - on the other hand, after having with the utmost care attained this state of intellectual slumber, you must begin to contemplate the operations going on in your mind, when nothing there takes place! Our descendants will doubtless see such pretensions some day ridiculed upon the stage. The results of so strange a procedure harmonize entirely with its principle. For all the two thousand years during which metaphysicians have thus cultivated psychology, they are not agreed about one intelligible and established proposition. 'Internal observation' gives almost as many divergent results as there are individuals who think they practise it."

Comte hardly could have known anything of the English, and nothing of the German, empirical psychology. The 'results' which he had in mind when writing were probably scholastic ones, such as principles of internal activity, the faculties, the ego, the liberum arbitrium indifferentioe, etc. John Mill, in replying to him,[6] says:

"It might have occurred to M. Comte that a fact may be studied through the medium of memory, not at the very moment of our perceiving it, but the moment after : and this is really the mode in which our best knowledge of our intellectual acts is generally acquired. We reflect on what we have been doing when the act is past, but when its impression in the memory is still fresh. Unless in one of these ways, we could not have acquired the knowledge which nobody denies us to have, of what passes in our minds. M. Comte would scarcely have affirmed that we are not aware of our own intellectual operations. We know of our observings and our reasonings, either at the very time, or by memory the moment after ; in either case, by direct knowledge, and not (like things done by us in a state of somnambulism) merely by their results. This simple fact destroys the whole of M. Comte's argument. Whatever we are directly aware of, we can directly observe."

Where now does the truth lie? Our quotation from Mill is obviously the one which expresses the most of practical truth about the matter. Even the writers who insist upon the absolute veracity of our immediate inner apprehension of a conscious state have to contrast with this the fallibility of our memory or observation of it, a moment later. No one has emphasized more sharply than Brentano himself the difference between the immediate feltness of a feeling, and its perception by a subsequent reflective act. But which mode of consciousness of it is that which the psychologist must depend on? If to have feelings or thoughts in their immediacy were enough, babies in the cradle would be psychologists, and infallible ones. But the psychologist must not only have his mental states in their absolute veritableness, he must report them and write about them, name them, classify and compare them and trace their relations to other things. Whilst alive they are their own property ; it is only post-mortem that they become his prey.[7] And as in the naming, classing, and knowing of things in general we are notoriously fallible, why not also here? Comte is quite right in laying stress on the fact that a feeling, to be named, judged, or perceived, must be already past. No subjective state, whilst present, is its own object ; its object is always something else. There are, it is true, cases in which we appear to be naming our present feeling, and so to be experiencing and observing the same inner fact at a single stroke, as when we say 'I feel tired,' 'I am angry,' etc. But these are illusory, and a little attention unmasks the illusion. The present conscious state, when I say 'I feel tired,' is not the direct state of tire ; when I say "I feel angry,' it is not the direct state of anger. It is the state of saying-I-feel-tired, of saying-I-feel-angry, - entirely different matters, so different that the fatigue and anger apparently included in them are considerable modifications of the fatigue and anger directly felt in the previous instant. The act of naming them has momentarily detracted from their force.[8]

The only sound grounds on which the infallible veracity of the introspective judgment might be maintained are empirical. If we had reason to think it has never yet deceived us, we might continue to trust it. This is the ground actually maintained by Herr Mohr.

"The illusions of our senses." says this author," have undermined our belief in the reality of the outer world ; but in the sphere of inner observation our confidence is intact, for we have never found ourselves to be in error about the reality of an act of thought or feeling. We have never been misled into thinking we were not in doubt or in anger when these conditions were really states of our consciousness."[9]

But sound as the reasoning here would be, were the premises correct, I fear the latter cannot pass. However it may be with such strong feelings as doubt or anger, about weaker feelings, and about the relations to each other of all feelings, we find ourselves in continual error and uncertainty so soon as we are called on to name and class, and not merely to feel. Who can be sure of the exact order of his feelings when they are excessively rapid? Who can be sure, in his sensible perception of a chair, how much comes from the eye and how much is supplied out of the previous knowledge of the mind? Who can compare with precision the quantities of disparate feelings even where the feelings are very much alike. For instance, where an object is felt now against the back and now against the cheek, which feeling is most extensive? Who can be sure that two given feelings are or are not exactly the same? Who can tell which is briefer or longer than the other when both occupy but an instant of time? Who knows, of many actions, for what motive they were done, or if for any motive at all? Who can enumerate all the distinct ingredients of such a complicated feeling as anger? and who can tell offhand whether or no a perception of distance be a compound or a simple state of mind. The whole mind-stuff controversy would stop if we could decide conclusively by introspection that what seem to us elementary feelings are really elementary and not compound.

Mr. Sully, in his work on Illusions, has a chapter on those of Introspection from which we might now quote. But, since the rest of this volume will be little more than a collection of illustrations of the difficulty of discovering by direct introspection exactly what our feelings and their relations are, we need not anticipate our own future details, but just state our general conclusion that introspection is difficult and fallible ; and that the difficulty is simply that of all observation of whatever kind. Something is before us ; we do our best to tell what it is, but in spite of our good will we may go astray, and give a description more applicable to some other sort of thing. The only safeguard is in the final consensus of our farther knowledge about the thing in question, later views correcting earlier ones, until at last the harmony of a consistent system is reached. Such a system, gradually worked out, is the best guarantee the psychologist can give for the soundness of any particular psychologic observation which he may report. Such a system we ourselves must strive, as far as may be, to attain.

The English writers on psychology, and the school of Herbart in Germany, have in the main contented themselves with such results as the immediate introspection of single individuals gave, and shown what a body of doctrine they may make. The works of Locke, Hume, Reid, Hartley, Stewart Brown, the Mills, will always be classics in this line ; and in Professor Brain's Treatises we have probably the last word of what this method taken mainly by itself can do - the last monument of the youth of our science, still untechnical and generally intelligible, like the Chemistry of Lavoisier, or Anatomy before the microscope was used.

The Experimental Method. But psychology is passing into a less simple phase. Within a few years what one may call a microscopic psychology has arisen in Germany, carried on by experimental methods, asking of course every moment for introspective data, but eliminating their uncertainty by operating on a large scale and taking statistical means. This method taxes patience to the utmost, and could hardly have arisen in a country whose natives could be bored. Such Germans as Weber, Fechner, Vierordt, and Wundt obviously cannot ; and their success has brought into the field an array of younger experimental psychologists, bent on studying the elements of the mental life, dissecting them out from the gross results in which they are embedded, and as far as possible reducing them to quantitative scales. The simple and open method of attack having done what it can, the method of patience, starving out, and harassing to death is tried ; the Mind must submit to a regular siege, in which minute advantages gained night and day by the forces that hem her in must sum themselves up at last into her overthrow. There is little of the grand style about these new prism, pendulum, and chronograph-philosophers. They mean business, not chivalry. What generous divination, and that superiority in virtue which was thought by Cicero to give a man the best insight into nature, have failed to do, their spying and scraping, their deadly tenacity and almost diabolic cunning, will doubtless some day bring about.

No general description of the methods of experimental psychology would be instructive to one unfamiliar with the instances of their application, so we will waste no words upon the attempt. The principal fields of experimentation so far have been : 1) the connection of conscious states with their physical conditions, including the whole of brain-physiology, and the recent minutely cultivated physiology of the sense-organs, together with what is technically known as 'psycho-physics,' or the laws of correlation between sensations and the outward stimuli by which they are aroused ; 2) the analysis of space-perception into its sensational elements ; 3) the measurement of the duration of the simplest mental processes ; 4) that of the accuracy of reproduction in the memory of sensible experiences and of intervals of space and time ; 5) that of the manner in which simple mental states influence each other, call each other up, or inhibit each other's reproduction ; 6) that of the number of facts which consciousness can simultaneously discern ; finally, 7) that of the elementary laws of oblivescence and retention. It must be said that in some of these fields the results have as yet borne little theoretic fruit commensurate with the great labor expended in their acquisition. But facts are facts, and if we only get enough of them they are sure to combine. New ground will from year to year be broken, and theoretic results will grow. Meanwhile the experimental method has quite changed the face of the science so far as the latter is a record of mere work done.

The comparative method, finally, supplements the introspective and experimental methods. This method presupposes a normal psychology of introspection to be established in its main features. But where the origin of these features, or their dependence upon one another, is in question, it is of the utmost importance to trace the phenomenon considered through all its possible variations of type and combination. So it has come to pass that instincts of animals are ransacked to throw light on our own ; and that the reasoning faculties of bees and ants, the minds of savages, infants, madmen, idiots, the deaf and blind, criminals, and eccentrics, are all invoked in support of this or that special theory about some part of our own mental life. The history of sciences, moral and political institutions, and languages, as types of mental product, are pressed into the same service. Messrs. Darwin and Galton have set the example of circulars of questions sent out by the hundred to those supposed able to reply. The custom has spread, and it will be well for us in the next generation if such circulars be not ranked among the common pests of life. Meanwhile information grows, and results emerge. There are great sources of error in the comparative method. The interpretation of the 'psychoses' of animals, savages, and infants is necessarily wild work, in which the personal equation of the investigator has things very much its own way. A savage will be reported to have no moral or religious feeling if his actions shock the observer unduly. A child will be assumed without self-consciousness because he talks of himself in the third person, etc., etc. No rules can be laid down in advance. Comparative observations, to be definite, must usually be made to test some pre-existing hypothesis ; and the only thing then is to use as much sagacity as you possess, and to be as candid as you can.

The Sources Of Error in Psychology.

The first of them arises from the Misleading Influence of Speech. Language was originally made by men who were not psychologists, and most men to-day employ almost exclusively the vocabulary of outward things. The cardinal passions of our life, anger, love, fear, hate, hope, and the most comprehensive divisions of our intellectual activity, to remember, expect, think, know, dream, with the broadest genera of aesthetic feeling, joy, sorrow, pleasure, pain, are the only facts of a subjective order which this vocabulary deigns to note by special words. The elementary qualities of sensation, bright, loud, red, blue, hot, cold, are, it is true, susceptible of being used in both an objective and a subjective sense. They stand for outer qualities and for the feelings which these arouse. But the objective sense is the original sense ; and still to-day we have to describe a large number of sensations by the name of the object from which they have most frequently been got. An orange color, an odor of violets, a cheesy taste, a thunderous sound, a fiery smart, etc., will recall what I mean. This absence of a special vocabulary for subjective facts hinders the study of all but the very coarsest of them. Empiricist writers are very fond of emphasizing one great set of delusions which language inflicts on the mind. Whenever we have made a word, they say, to denote a certain group of phenomena, we are prone to suppose a substantive entity existing beyond the phenomena, of which the word shall be the name. But the lack of a word quite as often leads to the directly opposite error. We are then prone to suppose that no entity can be there ; and so we come to overlook phenomena whose existence would be patent to us all, had we only grown up to hear it familiarly recognized in speech.[10] It is hard to focus our attention on the nameless, and so there results a certain vacuousness in the descriptive parts of most psychologies.

But a worse defect than vacuousness comes from the dependence of psychology on common speech. Naming our thought by its own objects, we almost all of us assume that as the objects are, so the thought must be. The thought of several distinct things can only consist of several distinct bits of thought, or 'ideas ;' that of an abstract or universal object can only be an abstract or universal idea. As each object may come and go, be forgotten and then thought of again, it is held that the thought of it has a precisely similar independence, self-identity, and mobility. The thought of the object's recurrent identity is regarded as the identity of its recurrent thought ; and the perceptions of multiplicity, of coexistence, of succession, are severally conceived to be brought about only through a multiplicity, a coexistence, a succession, of perceptions. The continuous flow of the mental stream is sacrificed, and in its place an atomism, a brickbat plan of construction, is preached, for the existence of which no good introspective grounds can be brought forward, and out of which presently grow all sorts of paradoxes and contradictions, the heritage of woe of students of the mind.

These words are meant to impeach the entire English psychology derived from Locke and Hume, and the entire German psychology derived from Herbart, so far as they both treat 'ideas' as separate subjective entities that come and go. Examples will soon make the matter clearer. Meanwhile our psychologic insight is vitiated by still other snares.

'The Psychologist's Fallacy.' The great snare of the psychologist is the confusion of his own standpoint with that of the mental fact about which he is making his report. I shall hereafter call this the 'psychologist's fallacy' par excellence. For some of the mischief, here too, language is to blame. The psychologist, as we remarked above, stands outside of the mental state he speaks of. Both itself and its object are objects for him. Now when it is a cognitive state (percept, thought, concept, etc.), he ordinarily has no other way of naming it than as the thought, percept, etc., of that object. He himself, meanwhile, knowing the self-same object in his way, gets easily led to suppose that the thought, which is of it, knows it in the same way in which he knows it, although this is often very far from being the case.[11] The most fictitious puzzles have been introduced into our science by this means. The so-called question of presentative or representative perception, of whether an object is present to the thought that thinks it by a counterfeit image of itself, or directly and without any intervening image at all ; the question of nominalism and conceptualism, of the shape in which things are present when only a general notion of them is before the mind ; are comparatively easy questions when once the psychologist's fallacy is eliminated from their treatment, - as we shall ere long see (in Chapter XII).

Another variety of the psychologist' fallacy is the assumption that the mental state studied must be conscious of itself as the psychologist is conscious of it. The mental state is aware of itself only from within ; it grasps what we call its own content, and nothing more. The psychologist, on the contrary, is aware of it from without, and knows its relations with all sorts of other things. What the thought sees is only its own object ; what the psychologist sees is the thought's object, plus the thought itself, plus possibly all the rest of the world. We must be very careful therefore, in discussing a state of mind from the psychologist's point of view, to avoid foisting into its own ken matters that are only there for ours. We must avoid substituting what we know the consciousness is, for what it is a consciousness of, and counting its outward, and so to speak physical, relations with other facts of the world, in among the objects of which we set it down as aware. Crude as such a confusion of standpoints seems to be when abstractly stated, it is nevertheless a snare into which no psychologist has kept himself at all times from falling, and which forms almost the entire stock-in-trade of certain schools. We cannot be too watchful against its subtly corrupting influence.

Summary. To sum up the chapter, Psychology assumes that thoughts successively occur, and that they know objects in a world which the psychologist also knows. These thoughts are the subjective data of which he treats, and their relations to their objects, to the brain, and to the rest of the world constitute the subject-matter of psychologic science. Its methods are introspection, experimentation, and comparison. But introspection is no sure guide to truths about our mental states ; and in particular the poverty of the psychological vocabu. [sic] lary leads us to drop out certain states from our consideration, and to treat others as if they knew themselves and their objects as the psychologist knows both, which is a disastrous fallacy in the science.

Notes

[1] On the relation between Psychology and General Philosophy, see G. C. Robertson, 'Mind,' vol. VIII. p. 1, and J. Ward, ibid. p. 153 ; J. Dewey, ibid. vol. IX. p. 1.
[2] Compare some remarks in Mill's Logic, bk. I. chap. III. §§ 2, 3.
[3] Logic, § 40.
[4] Psychologie, bk. II. chap. III. §§ 1, 2.
[5] Cours de Philosophie Positive, I. 34-8.
[6] Auguste Comte and Positivism, 3d edition (1882), p. 64.
[7] Wundt says: "The first rule for utilizing inward observation consists in taking, as far as possible, experiences that are accidental, unexpected, and not intentionally brought about. . . . First it is best as far as possible to rely on Memory and not on immediate Apprehension. . . . Second, internal observation is better fitted to grasp clearly conscious states, especially voluntary mental acts: such inner processes as are obscurely conscious and involuntary will almost entirely elude it, because the effort to observe interferes with them, and because they seldom abide in memory." (Logik, II. 432.)
[8] In cases like this, where the state outlasts the act of naming it, exists before it, and recurs when it is past, we probably run little practical risk of error when we talk as if the state knew itself. The state of feeling and the state of naming the feeling are continuous, and the infallibility of such prompt introspective judgments is probably great. But even here the certainty of our knowledge ought not to be argued on the a priori ground that percipi and esse are in psychology the same. The states are really two ; the naming state and the named state are apart ; percipi is esse' is not the principle that applies.
[9] J. Mohr : Grundlage der Empirischen Psychologie (Leipzig, 1882), p. 47.
[10] In English we have not even the generic distinction between the-thing-thought-of and the-thought-thinking-it, which in German is expressed by the opposition between Gedachtes and Gedanke, in Latin by that between cogitatum and cogitatio.
[11] Compare B. P. Bowne's Metaphysics (1882), p. 408.

Chapter VIII - The Relations of Minds to Other Things

Since, for psychology, a mind is an object in a world of other objects, its relation to those other objects must next be surveyed. First of all, to its...

Time-Relations

Minds, as we know them, are temporary existences. Whether my mind had a being prior to the birth of my body, whether it shall have one after the latter's decease, are questions to be decided by my general philosophy or theology rather than by what we call 'scientific facts' - I leave out the facts of so-called spiritualism, as being still in dispute. Psychology, as a natural science, confines itself to the present life, in which every mind appears yoked to a body through which its manifestations appear. In the present world, then, minds precede, succeed, and coexist with each other in the common receptacle of time, and of their collective relations to the latter nothing more can be said. The life of the individual consciousness in time seems, however, to be an interrupted one, so that the question: Are we ever wholly unconscious?

becomes one which must be discussed. Sleep, fainting, coma, epilepsy, and other 'unconscious' conditions are apt to break in upon and occupy large durations of what we nevertheless consider the mental history of a single man. And, the fact of interruption being admitted, is it not possible that it may exist where we do not suspect it, and even perhaps in an incessant and fine-grained form?

This might happen, and yet the subject himself never know it. We often take ether and have operations performed without a suspicion that our consciousness has suffered a breach. The two ends join each other smoothly over the gap; and only the sight of our wound assures us that we must have been living through a time which for our immediate consciousness was non-existent. Even in sleep this sometimes happens: We think we have had no nap, and it takes the clock to assure us that we are wrong.[1] We thus may live through a real outward time, a time known by the psychologist who studies us, and yet not feel the time, or infer it from any inward sign. The question is, how often does this happen? Is consciousness really discontinuous, incessantly interrupted and recommencing (from the psychologist's point of view)? and does it only seem continuous to itself by an illusion analogous to that of the zoetrope? Or is it at most times as continuous outwardly as it inwardly seems?

It must be confessed that we can give no rigorous answer to this question. Cartesians, who hold that the essence of the soul is to think, can of course solve it a priori, and explain the appearance of thoughtless intervals either by lapses in our ordinary memory, or by the sinking of consciousness to a minimal state, in which perhaps all that it feels is a bare existence which leaves no particulars behind to be recalled. If, however, one have no doctrine about the soul or its essence, one is free to take the appearances for what they seem to be, and to admit that the mind, as well as the body, may go to sleep.

Locke was the first prominent champion of this latter view, and the pages in which he attacks the Cartesian belief are as spirited as any in his Essay. "Every drowsy nod shakes their doctrine who teach that their soul is always thinking." He will not believe that men so easily forget. M. Jouffroy and Sir W. Hamilton, attacking the question in the same empirical way, are led to an opposite conclusion. Their reasons, briefly stated, are these:

In somnambulism, natural or induced, there is often a great display of intellectual activity, followed by complete oblivion of all that has passed.[2]

On being suddenly awakened from a sleep, however profound, we always catch ourselves in the middle of a dream. Common dreams are often remembered for a few minutes after waking, and then irretrievably lost.

Frequently, when awake and absent-minded, we are visited by thoughts and images which the next instant we cannot recall.

Our insensibility to habitual noises, etc., whilst awake, proves that we can neglect to attend to that which we nevertheless feel. Similarly in sleep, we grow inured, and sleep soundly in presence of sensations of sound, cold, contact, etc., which at first prevented our complete repose. We have learned to neglect them whilst asleep as we should whilst awake. The mere sense-impressions are the same when the sleep is deep as when it is light; the difference must lie in a judgment on the part of the apparently slumbering mind that they are not worth noticing. This discrimination is equally shown by nurses of the sick and mothers of infants, who will sleep through much noise of an irrelevant sort, but waken at the slightest stirring of the patient or the babe. This last fact shows the sense-organ to be pervious for sounds.

Many people have a remarkable faculty of registering when asleep the flight of time. They will habitually wake up at the same minute day after day, or will wake punctually at an unusual hour determined upon overnight. How can this knowledge of the hour (more accurate often than anything the waking consciousness shows) be possible without mental activity during the interval?

Such are what we may call the classical reasons for admitting that the mind is active even when the person afterwards ignores the fact.[3] Of late years, or rather, one may say, of late months, they have been reinforced by a lot of curious observations made on hysterical and hypnotic subjects, which prove the existence of a highly developed consciousness in places where it has hitherto not been suspected at all. These observations throw such a novel light upon human nature that I must give them in some detail. That at least four different and in a certain sense rival observers should agree in the same conclusion justifies us in accepting the conclusion as true.

'Unconsciousness' in Hysterics.

One of the most constant symptoms in persons suffering from hysteric disease in its extreme forms consists in alterations of the natural sensibility of various parts and organs of the body. Usually the alteration is in the direction of defect, or anaesthesia. One or both eyes are blind, or color-blind, or there is hemianopsia (blindness to one half the field of view), or the field is contracted. Hearing, taste, smell may similarly disappear, in part or in totality. Still more striking are the cutaneous anaesthesias. The old witch-finders looking for the 'devil's seals' learned well the existence of those insensible patches on the skin of their victims, to which the minute physical examinations of recent medicine have but recently attracted attention again. They may be scattered anywhere, but are very apt to affect one side of the body. Not infrequently they affect an entire lateral half, from head to foot; and the insensible skin of, say, the left side will then be found separated from the naturally sensitive skin of the right by a perfectly sharp line of demarcation down the middle of the front and back. Sometimes, most remarkable of all, the entire skin, hands, feet, face, everything, and the mucous membranes, muscles and joints so far as they can be explored, become completely insensible without the other vital functions becoming gravely disturbed.

These hysterical anaesthesias can be made to disappear more or less completely by various odd processes. It has been recently found that magnets, plates of metal, or the electrodes of a battery, placed against the skin, have this peculiar power. And when one side is relieved in this way, the anaesthesia is often found to have transferred itself to the opposite side, which until then was well. Whether these strange effects of magnets and metals be due to their direct physiological action, or to a prior effect on the patient's mind ('expectant attention' or 'suggestion') is still a mooted question. A still better awakener of sensibility is the hypnotic trance, into which many of these patients can be very easily placed, and in which their lost sensibility not infrequently becomes entirely restored. Such returns of sensibility succeed the times of insensibility and alternate with them. But Messrs. Pierre Janet[4] and A. Binet[5] have shown that during the times of anaesthesia, and coexisting with it, sensibility to the anaesthetic parts is also there, in the form of a secondary consciousness entirely cut off from the primary or normal one, but susceptible of being tapped and made to testify to its existence in various odd ways.

Chief amongst these is what M. Janet calls 'the method of distraction.' These hysterics are apt to possess a very narrow field of attention, and to be unable to think of more than one thing at a time. When talking with any person they forget everything else. "When Lucie talked directly with any one," says M. Janet, "she ceased to be able to hear any other person. You may stand behind her, call her by name, shout abuse into her ears, without making her turn round; or place yourself before her, show her objects, touch her, etc., without attracting her notice. When finally she becomes aware of you, she thinks you have just come into the room again, and greets you accordingly. This singular forgetfulness makes her liable to tell all her secrets aloud, unrestrained by the presence of unsuitable auditors."

Now M. Janet found in several subjects like this that if he came up behind them whilst they were plunged in conversation with a third party, and addressed them in a whisper, telling them to raise their hand or perform other simple acts, they would obey the order given, although their talking intelligence was quite unconscious of receiving it. Leading them from one thing to another, he made them reply by signs to his whispered questions, and finally made them answer in writing, if a pencil were placed in their hand. The primary consciousness meanwhile went on with the conversation, entirely unaware of these performances on the hand's part. The consciousness which presided over these latter appeared in its turn to be quite as little disturbed by the upper consciousness's concerns. This proof by 'automatic' writing, of a secondary consciousness's existence, is the most cogent and striking one; but a crowd of other facts prove the same thing. If I run through them rapidly, the reader will probably be convinced. The apparently anaesthetic hand of these subjects, for one thing, will often adapt itself discriminatingly to whatever object may be put into it. With a pencil it will make writing movements; into a pair of scissors it will put its fingers and will open and shut them, etc., etc. The primary consciousness, so to call it, is meanwhile unable to say whether or no anything is in the hand, if the latter be hidden from sight. "I put a pair of eyeglasses into Léonie's anaesthetic hand, this hand opens it and raises it towards the nose, but half way thither it enters the field of vision of Léonie, who sees it and stops stupefied: 'Why,' says she, 'I have an eyeglass in my left hand!'" M. Binet found a very curious sort of connection between the apparently anaesthetic skin and the mind in some Salpêtrière-subjects. Things placed in the hand were not felt, but thought of (apparently in visual terms) and in no wise referred by the subject to their starting point in the hand's sensation. A key, a knife, placed in the hand occasioned ideas of a key or a knife, but the hand felt nothing. Similarly the subject thought of the number 3, 6, etc., if the hand or finger was bent three or six times by the operator, or if he stroked it three, six, etc., times.

In certain individuals there was found a still odder phenomenon, which reminds one of that curious idiosyncrasy of 'colored hearing' of which a few cases have been lately described with great care by foreign writers. These individuals, namely, saw the impression received by the hand, but could not feel it; and the thing seen appeared by no means associated with the hand, but more like an independent vision, which usually interested and surprised the patient. Her hand being hidden by a screen, she was ordered to look at another screen and to tell of any visual image which might project itself thereon. Numbers would then come, corresponding to the number of times the insensible member was raised, touched, etc. Colored lines and figures would come, corresponding to similar ones traced on the palm; the hand itself or its fingers would come when manipulated; and finally objects placed in it would come; but on the hand itself nothing would ever be felt. Of course simulation would not be hard here; but M. Binet disbelieves this (usually very shallow) explanation to be a probable one in cases in question.[6]

The usual way in which doctors measure the delicacy of our touch is by the compass-points. Two points are normally felt as one whenever they are too close together for discrimination; but what is 'too close' on one part of the skin may seem very far apart on another. In the middle of the back or on the thigh, less than 3 inches may be too close; on the finger-tip a tenth of an inch is far enough apart. Now, as tested in this way, with the appeal made to the primary consciousness, which talks through the mouth and seems to hold the field alone, a certain person's skin may be entirely anaesthetic and not feel the compass-points at all; and yet this same skin will prove to have a perfectly normal sensibility if the appeal be made to that other secondary or sub-consciousness, which expresses itself automatically by writing or by movements of the hand. M. Binet, M. Pierre Janet, and M. Jules Janet have all found this. The subject, whenever touched, wonld [sic] signify 'one point' or 'two points,' as accurately as if she were a normal person. She would signify it only by these movements; and of the movements themselves her primary self would be as unconscious as of the facts they signified, for what the submerged consciousness makes the hand do automatically is unknown to the consciousness which uses the mouth.

Messrs. Bernheim and Pitres have also proved, by observations too complicated to be given in this spot, that the hysterical blindness is no real blindness at all. The eye of an hysteric which is totally blind when the other or seeing eye is shut, will do its share of vision perfectly well when both eyes are open together. But even where both eyes are semi-blind from hysterical disease, the method of automatic writing proves that their perceptions exist, only cut off from communication with the upper consciousness. M. Binet has found the hand of his patients unconsciously writing down words which their eyes were vainly endeavoring to 'see,' i.e., to bring to the upper consciousness. Their submerged consciousness was of course seeing them, or the hand could not have written as it did. Colors are similarly perceived by the sub-conscious self, which the hysterically color-blind eyes cannot bring to the normal consciousness. Pricks, burns, and pinches on the anaesthetic skin, all unnoticed by the upper self, are recollected to have been suffered, and complained of, as soon as the under self gets a chance to express itself by the passage of the subject into hypnotic trance.

It must be admitted, therefore, that in certain persons, at least, the total possible consciousness may be split into parts which coexist but mutually ignore each other, and share the objects of knowledge between them. More remarkable still, they are complementary. Give an object to one of the consciousnesses, and by that fact you remove it from the other or others. Barring a certain common fund of information, like the command of language, etc., what the upper self knows the under self is ignorant of, and vice versa. M. Janet has proved this beautifully in his subject Lucie. The following experiment will serve as the type of the rest: In her trance he covered her lap with cards, each bearing a number. He then told her that on waking she should not see any card whose number was a multiple of three. This is the ordinary so-called 'post-hypnotic suggestion,' now well known, and for which Lucie was a well-adapted subject. Accordingly, when she was awakened and asked about the papers on her lap, she counted and said she saw those only whose number was not a multiple of 3. To the 12, 18, 9, etc., she was blind. But the hand, when the sub-conscious self was interrogated by the usual method of engrossing the upper self in another conversation, wrote that the only cards in Lucie's lap were those numbered 12, 18, 9, etc., and on being asked to pick up all the cards which were there, picked up these and let the others lie. Similarly when the sight of certain things was suggested to the sub-conscious Lucie, the normal Lucie suddenly became partially or totally blind. "What is the matter? I can't see!" the normal personage suddenly cried out in the midst of her conversation, when M. Janet whispered to the secondary personage to make use of her eyes. The anaesthesias, paralyses, contractions and other irregularities from which hysterics suffer seem then to be due to the fact that their secondary personage has enriched itself by robbing the primary one of a function which the latter ought to have retained. The curative indication is evident: get at the secondary personage, by hypnotization or in whatever other way, and make her give up the eye, the skin, the arm, or whatever the affected part may be. The normal self thereupon regains possession, sees, feels, or is able to move again. In this way M. Jules Janet easily cured the well-known subject of the Salpêtrière, Wit., of all sorts of afflictions which, until he discovered the secret of her deeper trance, it had been difficult to subdue. "Cessez cette mauvaise plaisanterie," he said to the secondary self - and the latter obeyed. The way in which the various personages share the stock of possible sensations between them seems to be amusingly illustrated in this young woman. When awake, her skin is insensible everywhere except on a zone about the arm where she habitually wears a gold bracelet. This zone has feeling; but in the deepest trance, when all the rest of her body feels, this particular zone becomes absolutely anaesthetic.

Sometimes the mutual ignorance of the selves leads to incidents which are strange enough. The acts and movements performed by the sub-conscious self are withdrawn from the conscious one, and the subject will do all sorts of incongruous things of which he remains quite unaware. "I order Lucie [by the method of distraction] to make a pied de nez, and her hands go forthwith to the end of her nose. Asked what she is doing, she replies that she is doing nothing, and continues for a long time talking, with no apparent suspicion that her fingers are moving in front of her nose. I make her walk about the room; she continues to speak and believes herself sitting down."

M. Janet observed similar acts in a man in alcoholic delirium. Whilst the doctor was questioning him, M. J. made him by whispered suggestion walk, sit, kneel, and even lie down on his face on the floor, he all the while believing himself to be standing beside his bed. Such bizarreries sound incredible, until one has seen their like. Long ago, without understanding it, I myself saw a small example of the way in which a person's knowledge may be shared by the two selves. A young woman who had been writing automatically was sitting with a pencil in her hand, trying to recall at my request the name of a gentleman whom she had once seen. She could only recollect the first syllable. Her hand meanwhile, without her knowledge, wrote down the last two syllables. In a perfectly healthy young man who can write with the planchette, I lately found the hand to be entirely anaesthetic during the writing act; I could prick it severely without the Subject knowing the fact. The writing on the planchette, however, accused me in strong terms of hurting the hand. Pricks on the other (non-writing) hand, meanwhile, which awakened strong protest from the young man's vocal organs, were denied to exist by the self which made the planchette go.[7]

We get exactly similar results in the so-called post-hypnotic suggestion. It is a familiar fact that certain subjects, when told during a trance to perform an act or to experience an hallucination after waking, will when the time comes, obey the command. How is the command registered? How is its performance so accurately timed? These problems were long a mystery, for the primary personality remembers nothing of the trance or the suggestion, and will often trump up an improvised pretext for yielding to the unaccountable impulse which possesses the man so suddenly and which he cannot resist. Edmund Gurney was the first to discover, by means of automatic writing, that the secondary self is awake, keeping its attention constantly fixed on the command and watching for the signal of its execution. Certain trance-subjects who were also automatic writers, when roused from trance and put to the planchette, - not knowing then what they wrote, and having their upper attention fully engrossed by reading aloud, talking, or solving problems in mental arithmetic, - would inscribe the orders which they had received, together with notes relative to the time elapsed and the time yet to run before the execution.[8] It is therefore to no 'automatism' in the mechanical sense that such acts are due: a self presides over them, a split-off, limited and buried, but yet a fully conscious, self. More than this, the buried self often comes to the surface and drives out the other self whilst the acts are performing. In other words, the subject lapses into trance again when the moment arrives for execution, and has no subsequent recollection of the act which he has done. Gurney and Beaunis established this fact, which has since been verified on a large scale; and Gurney also showed that the patient became suggestible again during the brief time of the performance. M. Janet's observations, in their turn, well illustrate the phenomenon.

"I tell Lucie to keep her arms raised after she shall have awakened. Hardly is she in the normal state, when up go her arms above her head, but she pays no attention to them. She goes, comes, converses, holding her arms high in the air. If asked what her arms are doing, she is surprised at such a question, and says very sincerely: 'My hands are doing nothing; they are just like yours.' ... I command her to weep, and when awake she really sobs, but continues in the midst of her tears to talk of very gay matters. The sobbing over, there remained no trace of this grief, which seemed to have been quite sub-conscious."

The primary self often has to invent an hallucination by which to mask and hide from its own view the deeds which the other self is enacting. Léonie 3 [9] writes real letters, whilst Léonie 1 believes that she is knitting; or Lucie 3 really comes to the doctor's office, whilst Lucie 1 believes herself to be at home. This is a sort of delirium. The alphabet, or the series of numbers, when handed over to the attention of the secondary personage may for the time be lost to the normal self. Whilst the hand writes the alphabet, obediently to command, the 'subject,' to her great stupefaction, finds herself unable to recall it, etc. Few things are more curious than these relations of mutual exclusion, of which all gradations exist between the several partial consciousnesses.

How far this splitting up of the mind into separate consciousnesses may exist in each one of us is a problem. M. Janet holds that it is only possible where there is abnormal weakness, and consequently a defect of unifying or co-ordinating power. An hysterical woman abandons part of her consciousness because she is too weak nervously to hold it together. The abandoned part meanwhile may solidify into a secondary or sub-conscious self. In a perfectly sound subject, on the other hand, what is dropped out of mind at one moment keeps coming back at the next. The whole fund of experiences and knowledges remains integrated, and no split-off portions of it can get organized stably enough to form subordinate selves. The stability, monotony, and stupidity of these latter is often very striking. The post-hypnotic sub-consciousness seems to think of nothing but the order which it last received; the cataleptic sub-consciousness, of nothing but the last position imprinted on the limb. M. Janet could cause definitely circumscribed reddening and tumefaction of the skin on two of his subjects, by suggesting to them in hypnotism the hallucination of a mustard-poultice of any special shape. "J'ai tout le temps pensé à votre sinapisme," says the subject, when put back into trance after the suggestion has taken effect. A man N.,... whom M. Janet operated on at long intervals, was betweenwhiles tampered with by another operator, and when put to sleep again by M. Janet, said he was 'too far away to receive orders, being in Algiers.' The other operator, having suggested that hallucination, had forgotten to remove it before waking the subject from his trance, and the poor passive trance-personality had stuck for weeks in the stagnant dream. Léonie's sub-conscious performances having been illustrated to a caller, by a 'pied de nez' executed with her left hand in the course of conversation, when, a year later, she meets him again, up goes the same hand to her nose again, without Léonie's normal self suspecting the fact.

All these facts, taken together, form unquestionably the beginning of an inquiry which is destined to throw a new light into the very abysses of our nature. It is for that reason that I have cited them at such length in this early chapter of the book. They prove one thing conclusively, namely, that we must never take a person's testimony, however sincere, that he has felt nothing, as proof positive that no feeling has been there. It may have been there as part of the consciousness of a 'secondary personage,' of whose experiences the primary one whom we are consulting can naturally give no account. In hypnotic subjects (as we shall see in a later chapter) just as it is the easiest thing in the world to paralyze a movement or member by simple suggestion, so it is easy to produce what is called a systematized anaesthesia by word of command. A systematized anaesthesia means an insensibility, not to any one element of things, but to some one concrete thing or class of things. The subject is made blind or deaf to a certain person in the room and to no one else, and thereupon denies that that person is present, or has spoken, etc. M. P. Janet's Lucie, blind to some of the numbered cards in her lap, is a case in point. Now when the object is simple, like a red wafer or a black cross, the subject, although he denies that he sees it when he looks straight at it, nevertheless gets a 'negative after-image' of it when he looks away again, showing that the optical impression of it has been received. Moreover reflection shows that such a subject must distinguish the object from others like it in order to be blind to it. Make him blind to one person in the room, set all the persons in a row, and tell him to count them. He will count all but that one. But how can he tell which one not to count without recognizing who he is? In like manner, make a stroke on paper or blackboard, and tell him it is not there, and he will see nothing but the clean paper or board. Next (he not looking) surround the original stroke with other strokes exactly like it, and ask him what he sees. He will point out one by one all the new strokes, and omit the original one every time, no matter how numerous the new strokes may be, or in what order they are arranged. Similarly, if the original single stroke to which he is blind be doubled by a prism of some sixteen degrees placed before one of his eyes (both being kept open), he will say that he now sees one stroke, and point in the direction in which the image seen through the prism lies, ignoring still the original stroke.

Obviously, then, he is not blind to the kind of stroke in the least. He is blind only to one individual stroke of that kind in a particular position on the board or paper - that is to a particular complex object; and, paradoxical as it may seem to say so, he must distinguish it with great accuracy from others like it, in order to remain blind to it when the others are brought near. He discriminates it, as a preliminary to not seeing it at all.

Again, when by a prism before one eye a previously invisible line has been made visible to that eye, and the other eye is thereupon closed or screened, its closure makes no difference; the line still remains visible. But if then the prism be removed, the line will disappear even to the eye which a moment ago saw it, and both eyes will revert to their original blind state.

We have, then, to deal in these cases neither with a blindness of the eye itself, nor with a mere failure to notice, but with something much more complex; namely, an active counting out and positive exclusion of certain objects. It is as when one 'cuts' an acquaintance, 'ignores' a claim, or 'refuses to be influenced' by a consideration. But the perceptive activity which works to this result is disconnected from the consciousness which is personal, so to speak, to the subject, and makes of the object concerning which the suggestion is made, its own private possession and prey.[10] The mother who is asleep to every sound but the stirrings of her babe, evidently has the babe-portion of her auditory sensibility systematically awake. Relatively to that, the rest of her mind is in a state of systematized anaesthesia. That department, split off and disconnected from the sleeping part, can none the less wake the latter up in case of need. So that on the whole the quarrel between Descartes and Locke as to whether the mind ever sleeps is less near to solution than ever. On a priori speculative grounds Locke's view that thought and feeling may at times wholly disappear seems the more plausible. As glands cease to secrete and muscles to contract, so the brain should sometimes cease to carry currents, and with this minimum of its activity might well coexist a minimum of consciousness. On the other hand, we see how deceptive are appearances, and are forced to admit that a part of consciousness may sever its connections with other parts and yet continue to be. On the whole it is best to abstain from a conclusion. The science of the near future will doubtless answer this question more wisely than we can now. Let us turn now to consider the...

Relations of Consciousness to Space.

This is the problem known in the history of philosophy as the question of the seat of the soul. It has given rise to much literature, but we must ourselves treat it very briefly. Everything depends on what we conceive the soul to be, an extended or an inextended entity. If the former, it may occupy a seat. If the latter, it may not; though it has been thought that even then it might still have a position. Much hair-splitting has arisen about the possibility of an inextended thing nevertheless being present throughout a certain amount of extension. We must distinguish the kinds of presence. In some manner our consciousness is 'present' to everything with which it is in relation. I am cognitively present to Orion whenever I perceive that constellation, but I am not dynamically present there, I work no effects. To my brain, however, I am dynamically present, inasmuch as my thought and feelings seem to react upon the processes thereof. If, then, by the seat of the mind is meant nothing more than the locality with which it stands in immediate dynamic relations, we are certain to be right in saying that its seat is somewhere in the cortex of the brain. Descartes, as is well known, thought that the inextended soul was immediately present to the pineal gland. Others, as Lotze in his earlier days, and W. Volkmann, think its position must be at some point of the structureless matrix of the anatomical brain-elements, at which point they suppose that all nerve-currents may cross and combine. The scholastic doctrine is that the soul is totally present, both in the whole and in each and every part of the body. This mode of presence is said to be due to the soul's inextended nature and to its simplicity. Two extended entities could only correspond in space with one another, part to part, - but not so does the soul, which has no parts, correspond with the body. Sir Wm. Hamilton and Professor Bowen defend something like this view. I. H. Fichte, Ulrici, and, among American philosophers, Mr. J. E. Walter,[11] maintain the soul to be a space-filling principle. Fichte calls it the inner body, Ulrici likens it to a fluid of non-molecular composition. These theories remind us of the 'theosophic' doctrines of the present day, and carry us back to times when the soul as vehicle of consciousness was not discriminated , as it now is, from the vital principle presiding over the formation of the body. Plato gave head, breast, and abdomen to the immortal reason, the courage, and the appetites, as their seats respectively. Aristotle argues that the heart is the sole seat. Elsewhere we find the blood, the brain, the lungs, the liver the kidneys even, in turn assigned as seat of the whole or part of the soul.[12]

The truth is that if the thinking principle is extended we neither know its form nor its seat; whilst if unextended, it is absurd to speak of its having any space-relations at all. Space-relations we shall see hereafter to be sensible things. The only objects that can have mutual relations of position are objects that are perceived coexisting in the same felt space. A thing not perceived at all, such as the inextended soul must be, cannot coexist with any perceived objects in this way. No lines can be felt stretching from it to the other objects. It can form no terminus to any space-interval. It can therefore in no intelligible sense enjoy position. Its relations cannot be spatial, but must be exclusively cognitive or dynamic, as we have seen. So far as they are dynamic to talk of the soul being 'present' is only a figure of speech. Hamilton's doctrine that the soul is present to the whole body is at any rate false: for cognitively its presence extends far beyond the body, and dynamically it does not extent beyond the brain.[13]

The Relations of Minds to Other Objects

...are either relations to other minds, or to material things. The material things are either the mind's own brain, on the one hand, or anything else, on the other. The relations of a mind to its own brain are of a unique and utterly mysterious sort; we discussed them in the last two chapters, and can add nothing to that account.

The mind's relations to other objects than the brain are cognitive and emotional relations exclusively, so far as we know. It knows them, and it inwardly welcomes or rejects them, but it has no other dealings with them. When it seems to act upon them, it only does so through the intermediary of its own body, so that not it but the body is what acts on them, and the brain must first act upon the body. The same is true when other things seem to act on it - they only act on its body, and through that on its brain.[14] All that it can do directly is to know other things, misknow or ignore them, and to find that they interest it, in this fashion or in that.

Now the relation of knowing is the most mysterious thing in the world. If we ask how one thing can know another we are led into the heart of Erkenntnisstheorie and metaphysics. The psychologist, for his part, does not consider the matter so curiously as this. Finding a world before him which he cannot but believe that he knows, and setting himself to study his own past thoughts, or someone else's thoughts, of what he believes to be that same world; he cannot but conclude that those other thoughts know it after their fashion even as he knows it after his. Knowledge becomes for him an ultimate relation that must be admitted, whether it be explained or not, just like difference or resemblance, which no one seeks to explain.

Were our topic Absolute Mind instead of being the concrete minds of individuals dwelling in the natural world, we could not tell whether that Mind had the function of knowing or not, as knowing is commonly understood. We might learn the complexion of its thoughts; but, as we should have no realities outside of it to compare them with, - for if we had, the Mind would not be Absolute, - we could not criticise them, and find them either right or wrong; and we should have to call them simply the thoughts, and not the knowledge, of the Absolute Mind. Finite minds, however, can be judged in a different way, because the psychologist himself can go bail for the independent reality of the objects of which they think. He knows these to exist outside as well as inside the minds in question; he thus knows whether the minds think and know, or only think; and though his knowledge is of course that of a fallible mortal, there is nothing in the conditions that should make it more likely to wrong in this case than in any other.

Now by what tests does the psychologist decide whether the state of mind he is studying is a bit of knowledge, or only a subjective fact not referring to anything outside itself?

He uses the tests we all practically use. If the state of mind resembles his own idea of a certain reality; or if without resembling his idea of it, it seems to imply that reality and refer to it by operating upon it through the bodily organs; or even if it resembles and operates on some other reality that implies, and leads up to, and terminates in, the first one, - in either or all of these cases the psychologist admits that the state of mind takes cognizance, directly or remotely, distinctly or vaguely, truly or falsely, of the reality's nature and position in the world. If, on the other hand, the mental state under examination neither resembles nor operates on any of the realities known to the psychologist, he calls it a subjective state pure and simple, possessed of no cognitive worth. If, again, it resemble a reality or a set of realities as he knows them, but altogether fail to operate on them or modify their course by producing bodily motions which the psychologist sees, then the psychologist, like all of us, may be in doubt. Let the mental state, for example, occur during the sleep of its subject. Let the latter dream of the death of a certain man, and let the man simultaneously die. Is the dream a mere coincidence, or a veritable cognition of the death? Such puzzling cases are what the Societies for 'Psychical Research' are collecting and trying to interpret in the most reasonable way.

If the dream were the only one of the kind the subject ever had in his life, if the context of the death in the dream differed in many particulars from the real death's context, and if the dream led to no action about the death, unquestionably we should all call it a strange coincidence, and naught besides. But if the death in the dream had a long context, agreeing point for point with every feature that attended the real death; if the subject were constantly having such dreams, all equally perfect, and if on awaking he had a habit of acting immediately as if they were true and so getting 'the start' of his more tardily informed neighbors, - we should probably all have to admit that he had some mysterious kind of clairvoyant power, that his dreams in an inscrutable way knew just those realities which they figured, and that the word 'coincidence' failed to touch the root of the matter. And whatever doubts any one preserved would completely vanish if it should appear that from the midst of his dream he had the power of interfering with the course of the reality, and making the events in it turn this way or that, according as he dreamed they should. Then at least it would be certain that he and the psychologist were dealing with the same. It is by such tests as these that we are convinced that the waking minds of our fellows and our own minds know the same external world.

The psychologist's attitude towards cognition will be so important in the sequel that we must not leave it until it is made perfectly clear. It is a thoroughgoing dualism. It supposes two elements, mind knowing and thing known, and treats them as irreducible. Neither gets out of itself or into the other, neither in any way is the other, neither makes the other. They just stand face to face in a common world, and one simply knows, or is known unto, its counterpart. This singular relation is not to be expressed in any lower terms, or translated into any more intelligible name. Some sort of signal must be given by the thing to the mind's brain, or the knowing will not occur - we find as a matter of fact that the mere existence of a thing outside the brain is not a sufficient cause for our knowing it: it must strike the brain in some way, as well as be there, to be known. But the brain being struck, the knowledge is constituted by a new construction that occurs altogether in the mind. The thing remains the same whether known or not.[15] And when once there, the knowledge may remain there, whatever becomes of the thing.

By the ancients, and by unreflecting people perhaps today, knowledge is explained as the passage of something from without into the mind - the latter, so far, at least, as its sensible affections go, being passive and receptive. But even in mere sense-impression the duplication of the object by an inner construction must take place. Consider, with Professor Bowne, what happens when two people converse together and know each other's mind.

"No thoughts leave the mind of one and cross into the mind of the other. When we speak of an exchange of thought, even the crudest mind knows that this is a mere figure of speech.... To perceive another's thought, we must construct his thought within ourselves; . . . this thought is our own and is strictly original with us. At the same time we owe it to the other; and if it had not originated with him, it would probably not have originated with us. But what has the other done? . . . This: by an entirely mysterious world-order, the speaker is enabled to produce a series of signs which are totally unlike [the] thought, but which, by virtue of the same mysterious order, act as a series of incitements upon the hearer, so that he constructs within himself the corresponding mental state. The act of the speaker consists in availing himself of the proper incitements. The act of the hearer is immediately only the reaction of the soul against the incitement. . . . All communication between finite minds is of this sort. . . . Probably no reflecting person would deny this conclusion, but when we say that what is thus true of perception of another's thought is equally true of the perception of the outer world in general, many minds will be disposed to question, and not a few will deny it outright. Yet there is no alternative but to affirm that to perceive the universe we must construct it in thought, and that our knowledge of the universe is but the unfolding of the mind's inner nature. . . . By describing the mind as a waxen tablet, and things as impressing themselves upon it, we seem to get great insight until we think to ask where this extended tablet is, and how things stamp themselves on it, and how the perceptive act would be explained even if they did. . . . The immediate antecedents of sensation and perception are a series of nervous changes in the brain. Whatever we know of the outer world is revealed only in and through these nervous changes. But these are totally unlike the objects assumed to exist as their causes. If we might conceive the mind as in the light, and in direct contact with its objects, the imagination at least would be comforted; but when we conceive the mind as coming in contact with the outer world only in the dark chamber of the skull, and then not in contact with the objects perceived, but only with a series of nerve-changes of which, moreover, it knows nothing, it is plain that the object is a long way off. All talk of pictures, impressions, etc., ceases because of the lack of all the conditions to give such figures any meaning. It is not even clear that we shall ever find our way out of the darkness into the world of light and reality again. We begin with complete trust in physics and the senses, and are forthwith led away from the object into a nervous labyrinth, where the object is entirely displaced by a set of nervous changes which are totally unlike anything but themselves. Finally, we land in the dark chamber of the skull. The object has gone completely, and knowledge has not yet appeared. Nervous signs are the raw material of all knowledge of the outer world according to the most decided realism. But in order to pass beyond these signs into a knowledge of the outer world, we must posit an interpreter who shall read back these signs into their objective meaning. But that interpreter, again, must implicitly contain the meaning of the universe within itself; and these signs are really but excitations which cause the soul to unfold what is within itself. Inasmuch as by common consent the soul communicates with the outer world only through these signs, and never comes nearer to the object than such signs can bring it, it follows that the principles of interpretation must be in the mind itself, and that the resulting construction is primarily only an expression of the mind's own nature. All reaction is of this sort; it expresses the nature of the reacting agent, and knowledge comes under the same head. this [sic] fact makes it necessary for us either to admit a pre-established harmony between the laws and nature of thought and the laws and nature of things, or else to allow that the objects of perception, the universe as it appears, are purely phenomenal, being but the way in which the mind reacts against the ground of its sensations."[16]

The dualism of Object and Subject and their pre-established harmony are what the psychologist as such must assume, whatever ulterior monistic philosophy he may, as an individual who has the right also to be a metaphysician, have in reserve. I hope that this general point is now made clear, so that we may leave it, and descend to some distinctions of detail.

There are two kinds of knowledge broadly and practically distinguishable: we may call them respectively knowledge of acquaintance and knowledge-about. Most languages express the distinction; thus, g n v n a i , e i d e n a i ; noscere, scire; kennen, wissen; connaître, savoir.[17] I am acquainted with many people and things, which I know very little about, except their presence in the places where I have met them. I know the color blue when I see it, and the flavor of a pear when I taste it; I know an inch when I move my finger through it; a second of time, when I feel it pass; an effort of attention when I make it; a difference between two things when I notice it; but about the inner nature of these facts or what makes them what they are, I can say nothing at all. I cannot impart acquaintance with them to any one who has not already made it himself. I cannot describe them, make a blind man guess what blue is like, define to a child a syllogism, or tell a philosopher in just what respect distance is just what it is, and differs from other forms of relation. At most, I can say to my friends, Go to certain places and act in certain ways, and these objects will probably come. All the elementary natures of the world, its highest genera, the simple qualities of matter and mind, together with the kinds of relation that subsist between them, must either not be known at all, or known in this dumb way of acquaintance without knowledge-about. In minds able to speak at all there is, it is true, some knowledge about everything. Things can at least be classed, and the times of their appearance told. But in general, the less we analyze a thing, and the fewer of its relations we perceive, the less we know about it and the more our familiarity with it is of the acquaintance-type. The two kinds of knowledge are, therefore, as the human mind practically exerts them, relative terms. That is, the same thought of a thing may be called knowledge-about it in comparison with a simpler thought, or acquaintance with it in comparison with a thought of it that is more articulate and explicit still.

The grammatical sentence expresses this. Its 'subject' stands for an object of acquaintance which, by the addition of the predicate, is to get something known about it. We may already know a good deal, when we hear the subject named - its name may have rich connotations. But, know we much or little then, we know more still when the sentence is done. We can relapse at will into a mere condition of acquaintance with an object by scattering our attention and staring at it in a vacuous trance-like way. We can ascend to knowledge about it by rallying our wits and proceeding to notice and analyze and think. What we are only acquainted with is only present to our minds; we have it, or the idea of it. But when we know about it, we do more than merely have it; we seem, as we think over its relations, to subject it to a sort of treatment and to operate upon it with our thought. The words feeling and thought give voice to the antithesis. Through feelings we become acquainted with things, but only by our thoughts do we know about them. Feelings are the germ and starting point of cognition, thoughts the developed tree. The minimum of grammatical subject, of objective presence, of reality known about, the mere beginning of knowledge, must be named by the word that says the least. Such a word is the interjection, as lo! there! ecco! voilà! or the article or demonstrative pronoun introducing the sentence, as the, it, that. In Chapter XII we shall see a little deeper into what this distinction, between the mere mental having or feeling of an object and the thinking of it, portends.

The mental states usually distinguished as feelings are the emotions, and the sensations we get from skin, muscle, viscus, eye, ear, nose, and palate. The 'thoughts,' as recognized in popular parlance, are the conceptions and judgments. When we treat of these mental states in particular we shall have to say a word about the cognitive function and value of each. It may perhaps be well to notice now that our senses only give us acquaintance with facts of body, and that of the mental states of other persons we only have conceptual knowledge. Of our own past states of mind we take cognizance in a peculiar way. They are 'objects of memory,' and appear to us endowed with a sort of warmth and intimacy that makes the perception of them seem more like a process of sensation than like a thought.

Notes

[1] Messrs. Payton-Spence (Journal of Spec. Phil., X. 338, XIV. 286) and M. M. Garver (Amer. Jour. of Science, 3d series, XX. 189) argue, the one from speculative, the other from experimental grounds, that, the physical condition of consciousness being neural vibration, the consciousness must itself be incessantly interrupted by unconsciousness - about fifty times a second, according to Garver.

[2] That the appearance of mental activity here is real can be proved by suggesting to the 'hypnotized' somnambulist that he shall remember when he awakes. He will then often do so.

[3] For more details, cf. Malebranche, Rech. de la Verité, bk. III. chap. I; J. Locke, Essay conc. H. U., book II. ch. I; C. Wolf, Psychol. rationalis, § 59; Sir W. Hamilton, Lectures on Metaph., lecture XVII; J. Bascom, Science of Mind, § 12; Th. Jouffroy, Mélanges Philos., 'du Sommeil'; H. Holland, Chapters on Mental Physiol., p. 80; B. Brodie, Psychol. Researches, p. 147; E. M. Chesley, Journ. of Spec. Phil., vol. XI. p. 72; Th. Ribot, Maladies de la Personnalité, pp. 8-10; H. Lotze, Metaphysics, § 533.

[4] L'Automatisme Psychologique, Paris, 1889, passim.

[5] See his articles in the Chicago Open Court, for July, August and November, 1889. Also in the Revue Philosophique for 1889 and '90.

[6] This whole phenomena shows how an idea which remains itself below the threshold of a certain conscious self may occasion associative effects therein. The skin-sensations unfelt by the patient's primary consciousness awaken nevertheless their usual visual associates therein.

[7] See Proceedings of American Soc. for Psych. Research, vol. I. p. 548.

[8] Proceedings of the (London) Soc. for Psych. Research, May 1887, p. 268 ff.

[9] M. Janet designates by numbers the different personalities which the subject may display.

[10] How to conceive of this state of mind is not easy. It would be much simpler to understand the process, if adding new strokes made the first one visible. There would then be two different objects apperceived as totals, - paper with one stroke, paper with many strokes; and, blind to the former, he would see all that was in the latter, because he would have apperceived it as a different total in the first instance.

A process of this sort occurs sometimes (not always) when the new strokes, instead of being mere repetitions of the original one, are lines which combine with it into a total object, say a human face. The subject of the trance then may regain his sight of the line to which he had previously been blind, by seeing it as part of the face.

[11] Perception of Space and Matter, 1879, part II. chap. 3.

[12] For a very good condensed history of the various opinions, see W. Volkmann von Volkmar, Lehrbuch d. Psychologie, § 16. Anm. Complete references to Sir W. Hamilton are given in J. E. Walter, Perception of Space and Matter, pp. 65-6.

[13] Most contemporary writers ignore the question of the soul's seat. Lotze is the only one who seems to have been much concerned about it, and his views have varied. Cf. Medicinische Psychol., § 10. Microcosmus, bk. III. ch. 2. Metaphysic, bk. III. ch. 5. Outlines of Psychol., part II. ch. 3. See also G. T. Fechner, Psychophysik, chap. XXXVII.

[14] *I purposely ignore 'clairvoyance' and action upon distant things by 'mediums,' as not yet matters of common consent.*
[15] *I disregard consequences which may later come to the thing from the fact that it is known. The knowing per se in no wise affects the thing.*
[16] *B. P. Bowne: Metaphysics, pp. 407-10. Cf. also Lotze: Logik, §§ 308, 326-7.*
[17] *Cf. John Grote: Exploratio Philosophica, p. 60; H. Helmholtz, Popular Scientific Lectures, London, p. 308-9.*

Chapter IX - The Stream of Thought[1]

We now begin our study of the mind from within. Most books start with sensations, as the simplest mental facts, and proceed synthetically, constructing each higher stage from those below it. But this is abandoning the empirical method of investigation. No one ever had a simple sensation by itself. Consciousness, from our natal day, is of a teeming multiplicity of objects and relations, and what we call simple sensations are results of discriminative attention, pushed often to a very high degree. It is astonishing what havoc is wrought in psychology by admitting at the outset apparently innocent suppositions, that nevertheless contain a flaw. The bad consequences develop themselves later on, and are irremediable, being woven through the whole texture of the work. The notion that sensations, being the simplest things, are the first things to take up in psychology is one of these suppositions. The only thing which psychology has a right to postulate at the outset is the fact of thinking itself, and that must first be taken up and analyzed. If sensations then prove to be amongst the elements of the thinking, we shall be no worse off as respects them than if we had taken them for granted at the start.

The first fact for us, then, as psychologists, is that thinking of some sort goes on. I use the word thinking, in accordance with what was said, for every form of consciousness indiscriminately. If we could say in English 'it thinks,' as we say 'it rains' or 'it blows,' we should be stating the fact most simply and with the minimum of assumption. As we cannot, we must simply say that thought goes on.

Five Characters in Thought

How does it go on? We notice immediately five important characters in the process, of which it shall be the duty of the present chapter to treat in a general way:

1) Every thought tends to be part of a personal consciousness.
2) Within each personal consciousness thought is always changing.
3) Within each personal consciousness thought is sensibly continuous.
4) It always appears to deal with objects independent of itself.
5) It is interested in some parts of these objects to the exclusion of others, and welcomes or rejects - chooses from among them, in a word - all the while.

In considering these five points successively, we shall have to plunge in medias res as regards our vocabulary, and use psychological terms which can only be adequately defined in later chapters of the book. But every one knows what the terms mean in a rough way; and it is only in a rough way that we are now to take them. This chapter is like a painter's first charcoal sketch upon his canvas, in which no niceties appear.

1)   Thought tends to Personal Form.

When I say every thought is part of a personal consciousness, 'personal consciousness' is one of the terms in question, Its meaning we know so long as no one asks us to define it, but to give an accurate account of it is the most difficult of philosophic tasks. This task we must confront in the next chapter; here a preliminary word will suffice. In this room - this lecture-room, say - there are a multitude of thoughts, yours and mine, some of which cohere mutually, and some not. They are as little each-for-itself and reciprocally independent as they are all-belonging-together. They are neither: no one of them is separate, but each belongs with certain others and with none beside. My thought belongs with my other thoughts, and your thought with your other thoughts. Whether anywhere in the room there be a mere thought, which is nobody's thought, we have no means of ascertaining, for we have no experience of its like. The only states of consciousness that we naturally deal with are found in personal consciousnesses, minds, selves, concrete particular I's and you's.

Each of these minds keeps its own thoughts to itself. There is no giving or bartering between them. No thought even comes into direct sight of a thought in another personal consciousness than its own. Absolute insulation, irreducible pluralism, is the law. It seems as if the elementary psychic fact were not thought or this thought or that thought, but my thought, every thought being owned. Neither contemporaneity, nor proximity in space, nor similarity of quality and content are able to fuse thoughts together which are sundered by this barrier of belonging to different personal minds. The breaches between such thoughts are the most absolute breaches in nature. Everyone will recognize this to be true, so long as the existence of something corresponding to the term 'personal mind' is all that is insisted on, without any particular view of its nature being implied. On these terms the personal self rather than the thought might be treated as the immediate datum in psychology. The universal conscious fact is not 'feelings and thoughts exist,' but 'I think' and 'I feel.'[2] No psychology, at any rate, can question the existence of personal selves. The worst a psychology can do is so to interpret the nature of these selves as to rob them of their worth. A French writer, speaking of our ideas, says somewhere in a fit of anti-spiritualistic excitement that, misled by certain peculiaritities which they display, we 'end by personifying' the procession which they make, - such personification being regarded by him as a great philosophic blunder on our part. It could only be a blunder if the notion of personality meant something essentially different from anything to be found in the mental procession. But if that procession be itself the very 'original' of the notion of personality, to personify it cannot possibly be wrong. It is already personified. There are no marks of personality to be gathered aliunde, and then found lacking in the train of thought. It has them all already; so that to whatever farther analysis we may subject that form of personal selfhood under which thoughts appear, it is, and must remain, true that the thoughts which psychology studies do continually tend to appear as parts of personal selves.

I say 'tend to appear' rather than 'appear,' on account of those facts of sub-conscious personality, automatic writing, etc., of which we studied a few in the last chapter. The buried feelings and thoughts proved now to exist in hysterical anæsthetics, in recipients of post-hypnotic suggestion, etc.,themselves are parts of secondary personal selves. These selves are for the most part very stupid and contracted, and are cut off at ordinary times from communication with the regular and normal self of the individual; but still they form conscious unities, have continuous memories, speak, write, invent distinct names for themselves, or adopt names that are suggested; and, in short, are entirely worthy of that title of secondary personalities which is now commonly given them. According to M. Janet these secondary personalities are always abnormal, and result from the splitting of what ought to be a single complete self into two parts, of which one lurks in the background whilst the other appears on the surface as the only self the man or woman has. For our present purpose it is unimportant whether this account of the origin of secondary selves is applicable to all possible cases of them or not, for it certainly is true of a large number of them. Now although the size of a secondary self thus formed will depend on the number of thoughts that are thus split-off from the main consciousness, the form, of it tends to personality, and the later thoughts pertaining to it remember the earlier ones and adopt them as their own. M. Janet caught the actual moment of inspissation (so to speak) of one of these secondary personalities in his anæsthetic somnambulist Lucie. He found that when this young woman's attention was absorbed in conversation with a third party, her anæsthetic hand would write simple answers to questions whispered to her by himself. "Do you hear?" he asked. "No," was the unconsciously written reply. "But to answer you must hear." "Yes, quite so." "Then how do you manage?" "I don't know." "There must be some one who hears me." "Yes." "Who?" "Someone other than Lucie." "Ah! another person. Shall we give her a name?" "No." "Yes, it will be more convenient." "Well, Adrienne, then." "Once baptized, the subconscious personage," M. Janet continues, "grows more definitely outlined and displays better her psychological characters. In particular she shows us that she is conscious of the feelings excluded from the consciousness of the primary or normal personage. She it is who tells us that I am pinching the arm or touching the little finger in which Lucie for so long has had no tactile sensations."[3]

In other cases the adoption of the name by the secondary self is more spontaneous. I have seen a number of incipient automatic writers and mediums as yet imperfectly 'developed,' who immediately and of their own accord write and speak in the name of departed spirits. These may be public characters, as Mozart, Faraday, or real persons formerly known to the subject, or altogether imaginary beings. Without prejudicing the question of real 'spirit-control' in the more developed sorts of trance- utterance, I incline to think that these (often deplorably unintelligent) rudimentary utterances are the work of an inferior fraction of the subject's own natural mind, set free from control by the rest, and working after a set pattern fixed by the prejudices of the social environment. In a spiritualistic community we get optimistic messages, whilst in an ignorant Catholic village the secondary personage calls itself by the name of a demon,and proffers blasphemies and obscenities, instead of telling us how happy it is in the summer-land.[4]

Beneath these tracts of thought, which, however rudimentary, are still organized selves with a memory, habits, and sense of their own identity, M. Janet thinks that the facts of catalepsy in hysteric patients drive us to suppose that there are thoughts quite unorganized and impersonal. A patient in cataleptic trance (which can be produced artificially in certain hypnotized subjects) is without memory on waking, and seems insensible and unconscious as long as the cataleptic condition lasts. If, however, one raises the arm of such a subject it stays in that position, and the whole body can thus be moulded like wax under the hands of the operator, retaining for a considerable time whatever attitude he communicates to it. In hysterics whose arm, for example, is anæsthetic, the same thing may happen. The anæsthetic arm may remain passively in positions which it is made to assume; or if the hand be taken and made to hold a pencil and trace a certain letter, it will continue tracing that letter indefinitely on the paper. These acts, until recently, were supposed to be accompanied by no consciousness at all: they were physiological reflexes. M. Janet considers with much more plausibility that feeling escorts them. The feeling is probably merely that of the position or movement of the limb, and it produces no more than its natural effects when it discharges into the motor centres which keep the position maintained, or the movement incessantly renewed.[5] Such thoughts as these, says M. Janet, "are known by no one, for disaggregated sensations reduced to a state of mental dust are not synthetized in any personality."[6] He admits, however, that these very same unutterably stupid thoughts tend to develop memory, - the cataleptic ere long moves her arm at a bare hint; so that they form no important exception to the law that all thought tends to assume the form of personal consciousness.

2) Thought is in Constant Change.

I do not mean necessarily that no one state of mind has any duration - even if true, that would be hard to establish. The change which I have more particularly in view is that which takes place in sensible intervals of time; and the result on which I wish to lay stress is this, that no state once gone can recur and be identical with what it was before. Let us begin with Mr. Shadworth Hodgson's description:

"I go straight to the facts, without saying I go to perception, or sensation, or thought, or any special mode at all. What I find when I look at my consciousness at all is that what I cannot divest myself of, or not have in consciousness, if I have any consciousness at all, is a sequence of different feelings. I may shut my eyes and keep perfectly still, and try not to contribute anything of my own will; but whether I think or do not think, whether I perceive external things or not, I always have a succession of different feelings. Anything else that I may have also, of a more special character, comes in as parts of this succession. Not to have the succession of different feelings is not to be conscious at all… The chain of consciousness is a sequence of differents."[7]

Such a description as this can awaken no possible protest from any one. We all recognize as different great classes of our conscious states. Now we are seeing, now hearing; now reasoning, now willing; now recollecting, now expecting; now loving, now hating; and in a hundred other ways we know our minds to be alternately engaged. But all these are complex states. The aim of science is always to reduce complexity to simplicity; and in psychological science we have the celebrated 'theory of ideas' which, admitting the great difference among each other of what may be called concrete conditions of mind, seeks to show how this is all the resultant effect of variations in the combination of certain simple elements of consciousness that always remain the same. These mental atoms or molecules are what Locke called 'simple ideas.' Some of Locke's successors made out that the only simple ideas were the sensations strictly so called. Which ideas the simple ones may be does not, however, now concern us. It is enough that certain philosophers have thought they could see under the dissolving-view-appearance of the mind elementary facts of any sort that remained unchanged amid the flow.

And the view of these philosophers has been called little into question, for our common experience seems at first sight to corroborate it entirely. Are not the sensations we get from the same object, for example, always the same? Does not the same piano-key, struck with the same force, make us hear in the same way? Does not the same grass give us the same feeling of green, the same sky the same feeling of blue, and do we not get the same olfactory sensation no matter how many times we put our nose to the same flask of cologne? It seems a piece of metaphysical sophistry to suggest that we do not; and yet a close attention to the matter shows that there is no proof that the same bodily sensation is ever got by us twice.

What is got twice is the same OBJECT. We hear the same note over and over again; we see the same quality of green, or smell the same objective perfume, or experience the same species of pain. The realities, concrete and abstract, physical and ideal, whose permanent existence we believe in, seem to be constantly coming up again before our thought, and lead us, in our carelessness, to suppose that our 'ideas' of them are the same ideas. When we come, some time later, to the chapter on Perception, we shall see how inveterate is our habit of not attending to sensations as subjective facts, but of simply using them as stepping-stones to pass over to the recognition of the realities whose presence they reveal. The grass out of the window now looks to me of the same green in the sun as in the shade, and yet a painter would have to paint one part of it dark brown, another part bright yellow, to give its real sensational effect. We take no heed, as a rule, of the different way in which the same things look and sound and smell at different distances and under different circumstances. The sameness of the things is what we are concerned to ascertain; and any sensations that assure us of that will probably be considered in a rough way to be the same with each other. This is what makes off-hand testimony about the subjective identity of different sensations well-nigh worthless as a proof of the fact. The entire history of Sensation is a commentary on our inability to tell whether two sensations received apart are exactly alike. What appeals to our attention far more than the absolute quality or quantity of a given sensation is its ratio to whatever other sensations we may have at the same time. When everything is dark a somewhat less dark sensation makes us see an object white. Helmholtz calculates that the white marble painted in a picture representing an architectural view by moonlight is, when seen by daylight, from ten to twenty thousand times brighter than the real moonlit marble would be.[8]

Such a difference as this could never have been sensibly learned; it had to be inferred from a series of indirect considerations. There are facts which make us believe that our sensibility is altering all the time, so that the same object cannot easily give us the same sensation over again. The eye's sensibility to light is at its maximum when the eye is first exposed, and blunts itself with surprising rapidity. A long night's sleep will make it see things twice as brightly on wakening, as simple rest by closure will make it see them later in the day.[9] We feel things differently according as we are sleepy or awake, hungry or full, fresh or tired; differently at night and in the morning, differently in summer and in winter, and above all things differently in childhood, manhood, and old age. Yet we never doubt that our feelings reveal the same world, with the same sensible qualities and the same sensible things occupying it. The difference of the sensibility is shown best by the difference of our emotion about the things from one age to another, or when we are in different organic moods. What was bright and exciting becomes weary, flat, and unprofitable. The bird's song is tedious, the breeze is mournful, the sky is sad.

To these indirect presumptions that our sensations, following the mutations of our capacity for feeling, are always undergoing an essential change, must be added another presumption, based on what must happen in the brain. Every sensation corresponds to some cerebral action. For an identical sensation to recur it would have to occur the second time in an unmodified brain. But as this, strictly speaking, is a physiological impossibility, so is an unmodified feeling an impossibility; for to every brain-modification, however small, must correspond a change of equal amount in the feeling which the brain subserves.

All this would be true if even sensations came to us pure and single and not combined into 'things.' Even then we should have to confess that, however we might in ordinary conversation speak of getting the same sensation again, we never in strict theoretic accuracy could do so; and that whatever was true of the river of life, of the river of elementary feeling, it would certainly be true to say, like Heraclitus, that we never descend twice into the same stream.

But if the assumption of 'simple ideas of sensation' recurring in immutable shape is so easily shown to be baseless, how much more baseless is the assumption of immutability in the larger masses of our thought!

For there it is obvious and palpable that our state of mind is never precisely the same. Every thought we have of a given fact is, strictly speaking, unique, and only bears a resemblance of kind with our other thoughts of the same fact. When the identical fact recurs, we must think of it in a fresh manner, see it under a somewhat different angle, apprehend it in different relations from those in which it last appeared. And the thought by which we cognize it is the thought of it-in-those-relations, a thought suffused with the consciousness of all that dim context. Often we are ourselves struck at the strange differences in our successive views of the same thing. We wonder how we ever could have opined as we did last month about a certain matter. We have outgrown the possibility of that state of mind, we know not how. From one year to another we see things in new lights. What was unreal has grown real, and what was exciting is insipid. The friends we used to care the world for are shrunken to shadows; the women, once so divine, the stars, the woods, and the waters, how now so dull and common; the young girls that brought an aura, of infinity, at present hardly distinguishable existences; the pictures so empty; and as for the books, what was there to find so mysteriously significant in Goethe, or in John Mill so full of weight? Instead of all this, more zestful than ever is the work, the work; and fuller and deeper the import of common duties and of common goods.

But what here strikes us so forcibly on the flagrant scale exists on every scale, down to the imperceptible transition from one hour's outlook to that of the next. Experience is remoulding us every moment, and our mental reaction on every given thing is really a resultant of our experience of the whole world up to that date. The analogies of brain-physiology must again be appealed to to corroborate our view.

Our earlier chapters have taught us to believe that, whilst we think, our brain changes, and that, like the aurora borealis, its whole internal equilibrium shifts with every pulse of change. The precise nature of the shifting at a given moment is a product of many factors. The accidental state of local nutrition or blood-supply may be among them. But just as one of them certainly is the influence of outward objects on the sense-organs during the moment, so is another certainly the very special susceptibility in which the organ has been left at that moment by all it has gone through in the past. Every brain-state is partly determined by the nature of this entire past succession. Alter the latter in any part, and the brain-state must be somewhat different. Each present brain-state is a record in which the eye of Omniscience might read all the foregone history of its owner. It is out of the question, then, that any total brain-state should identically recur. Something like it may recur; but to suppose it to recur would be equivalent to the absurd admission that all the states that had intervened between its two appearances had been pure nonentities, and that the organ after their passage was exactly as it was before. And (to consider shorter periods) just as, in the senses, an impression feels very differently according to what has preceded it; as one color succeeding another is modified by the contrast, silence sounds delicious after noise, and a note, when the scale is sung up, sounds unlike itself when the scale is sung down; as the presence of certain lines in a figure changes the apparent form of the other lines, and as in music the whole æsthetic effect comes from the manner in which one set of sounds alters our feeling of another; so, in thought, we must admit that those portions of the brain that have just been maximally excited retain a kind of soreness which is a condition of our present consciousness, a codeterminant of how and what we now shall feel.[10]

Ever some tracts are waning in tension, some waxing, whilst others actively discharge. The states of tension have as positive an influence as any in determining the total condition, and in deciding what the psychosis shall be. All we know of submaximal nerve-irritations, and of the summation of apparently ineffective stimuli, tends to show that no changes in the brain are physiologically ineffective, and that presumably none are bare of psychological result. But as the brain-tension shifts from one relative state of equilibrium to another, like the gyrations of a kaleidoscope, now rapid and now slow, is it likely that its faithful psychic concomitant is heavier-footed than itself, and that it cannot match each one of the organ's irradiations by a shifting inward iridescence of its own? But if it can do this, its inward iridescences must be infinite, for the brain-redistributions are in infinite variety. If so coarse a thing as a telephone-plate can be made to thrill for years and never reduplicate its inward condition, how much more must this be the case with the infinitely delicate brain?

I am sure that this concrete and total manner of regarding the mind's changes is the only true manner, difficult as it may be to carry it out in detail. If anything seems obscure about it, it will grow clearer as we advance. Meanwhile, if it be true, it is certainly also true that no two 'ideas' are ever exactly the same, which is the proposition we started to prove. The proposition is more important theoretically than it at first sight seems. For it makes it already impossible for us to follow obediently in the footprints of either the Lockian or the Herbartian school, schools which have had almost unlimited influence in Germany and among ourselves. No doubt it is often convenient to formulate the mental facts in an atomistic sort of way, aud to treat the higher states of consciousness as if they were all built out of unchanging simple ideas. It is convenient often to treat curves as if they were composed of small straight lines, and electricity and nerve-force as if they were fluids. But in the one case as in the other we must never forget that we are talking symbolically, and that there is nothing in nature to answer to our words. A permanently existing 'idea' or 'Vorstellung' which makes its appearance before the footlights of consciousness at periodical intervals, is as mythological an entity as the Jack of Spades.

What makes it convenient to use the mythological formulas is the whole organization of speech, which, as was remarked a while ago, was not made by psychologists, but by men who were as a rule only interested in the facts their mental states revealed. They only spoke of their states as ideas of this or of that thing. What wonder, then, that the thought is most easily conceived under the law of the thing whose name it bears! If the thing is composed of parts, then we suppose that the thought of the thing must be composed of the thoughts of the parts. If one part of the thing have appeared in the same thing or in other things on former occasions, why then we must be having even now the very same 'idea' of that part which was there on those occasions. If the thing is simple, its thought is simple. If it is multitudinous, it must require a multitude of thoughts to think it. If a succession, only a succession of thoughts can know it. If permanent, its thought is permanent. And so on ad libitum. What after all is so natural as to assume that one object, called by one name, should be known by one affection of the mind? But, if language must thus influence us, the agglutinative languages, and even Greek and Latin with their declensions, would be the better guides. Names did not appear in them inalterable, but changed their shape to suit the context in which they lay. It must have been easier then that now to conceive of the same object as being thought of at different times in non-identical conscious states.

This, too, will grow clearer as we proceed. Meanwhile a necessary consequence of the belief in permanent self-identical psychic facts that absent themselves and recur periodically is the Humian doctrine that our thought is composed of separate independent parts and is not a sensibly continuous stream. That this doctrine entirely misrepresents the natural appearances is what I next shall try to show.

3) **Within each personal consciousness, thought is sensibly continuous.**

I can only define 'continuous' as that which is without breach, crack, or division. I have already said that the breach from one mind to another is perhaps the greatest breach in nature. The only breaches that can well be conceived to occur within the limits of a single mind would either be interruptions, time-gaps during which the consciousness went out altogether to come into existence again at a later moment; or they would be breaks in the quality, or content, of the thought, so abrupt that the segment that followed had no connection whatever with the one that went before. The proposition that within each personal consciousness thought feels continuous, means two things:

1. That even where there is a time-gap the consciousness after it feels as if it belonged together with the consciousness before it, as another part of the same self;
2. That the changes from one moment to another in the quality of the consciousness are never absolutely abrupt.

The case of the time-gaps, as the simplest, shall be taken first. And first of all, a word about time-gaps of which the consciousness may not be itself aware.

Earlier we saw that such time-gaps existed, and that they might be more numerous than is usually supposed. If the consciousness is not aware of them, it cannot feel them as interruptions. In the unconsciousness produced by nitrous oxide and other anæsthetics, in that of epilepsy and fainting, the broken edges of the sentient life may meet and merge over the gap, much as the feelings of space of the opposite margins of the 'blind spot' meet and merge over that objective interruption to the sensitiveness of the eye. Such consciousness as this, whatever it be for the onlooking psychologist, is for itself unbroken. It feels unbroken; a waking day of it is sensibly a unit as long as that day lasts, in the sense in which the hours themselves are units, as having all their parts next each other, with no intrusive alien substance between. To expect the consciousness to feel the interruptions of its objective continuity as gaps, would be like expecting the eye to feel a gap of silence because it does not hear, or the ear to feel a gap of darkness because it does not see. So much for the gaps that are unfelt.

With the felt gaps the case is different. On waking from sleep, we usually know that we have been unconscious, and we often have an accurate judgment of how long. The judgment here is certainly an inference from sensible signs, and its ease is due to long practice in the particular field.[11] The result of it, however, is that the consciousness is, for itself, not what it was in the former case, but interrupted and continuous, in the mere time-sense of the words. But in the other sense of continuity, the sense of the parts being inwardly connected and belonging together because they are parts of a common whole, the consciousness remains sensibly continuous and one. What now is the common whole? The natural name for it is myself, I, or me.

When Paul and Peter wake up in the same bed, and recognize that they have been asleep, each one of them mentally reaches back and makes connection with but one of the two streams of thought which were broken by the sleeping hours. As the current of an electrode buried in the ground unerringly finds its way to its own similarly buried mate, across no matter how much intervening earth; so Peter's present instantly finds out Peter's past, and never by mistake knits itself on to that of Paul. Paul's thought in turn is as little liable to go astray. The past thought of Peter is appropriated by the present Peter alone. He may have a knowledge, and a correct one too, of what Paul's last drowsy states of mind were as he sank into sleep, but it is an entirely different sort of knowledge from that which he has of his own last states. He remembers his own states, whilst he only conceives Paul's. Remembrance is like direct feeling; its object is suffused with a warmth and intimacy to which no object of mere conception ever attains. This quality of warmth and intimacy and immediacy is what Peter's present thought also possesses for itself. So sure as this present is me, is mine, it says, so sure is anything else that comes with the same warmth and intimacy and immediacy, me and mine. What the qualities called warmth and intimacy may in themselves be will have to be matter for future consideration. But whatever past feeling appear with those qualities must be admitted to receive the greeting of the present mental state, to be owned by it, and accepted as belonging together with it in a common self. This community of self is what the time-gap cannot break in twain, and is why a present thought, although not ignorant of the time-gap, can still regard itself as continuous with certain chosen portions of the past.

Consciousness, then, does not appear to itself chopped up in bits. Such words as 'chain' or 'train' do not describe it fitly as it presents itself in the first instance. It is nothing jointed; if flows. A 'river' or a 'stream' are the metaphors by which it is most naturally described. In talking of it hereafter, let us call it the stream of thought, of consciousness, or of subjective life. But now there appears, even within the limits of the same self, and between thoughts all of which alike have this same sense of belonging together, a kind of jointing and separateness among the parts, of which this statement seems to take no account. I refer to the breaks that are produced by sudden contrasts in the quality of the successive segments of the stream of thought. If the words 'chain' and 'train' had no natural fitness in them, how came such words to be used at all? Does not a loud explosion rend the consciousness upon which it abruptly breaks, in twain? Does not every sudden shock, appearance of a new object, or change in a sensation, create a real interruption, sensibly felt as such, which cuts the conscious stream across at the moment at which it appears? Do not such interruptions smite us every hour of our lives, and have we the right, in their presence, still to call our consciousness a continuous stream?

This objection is based partly on a confusion and partly on a superficial introspective view.

The confusion is between the thoughts themselves, taken as subjective facts, and the things of which they are aware. It is natural to make this confusion, but easy to avoid it when once put on one's guard. The things are discrete and discontinuous; they do pass before us in a train or chain, making often explosive appearances and rending each other in twain. But their comings and goings and contrasts no more break the flow of the thought that thinks them than they break the time and the space in which they lie. A silence may be broken by a thunder-clap, and we may be so stunned and confused for a moment by the shock as to give no instant account to ourselves of what has happened. But that very confusion is a mental state, and a state that passes us straight over from the silence to the sound. The transition between the thought of one object and the thought of another is no more a break in the thought than a joint in a bamboo is a break in the wood. It is a part of the consciousness as much as the joint is a part of the bamboo. The superficial introspective view is the overlooking, even when the things are contrasted with each other most violently, of the large amount of affinity that may still remain between the thoughts by whose means they are cognized. Into the awareness of the thunder itself the awareness of the previous silence creeps and continues; for what we hear when the thunder crashes is not thunder pure, but thunder-breaking-upon-silence-and-contrasting-with-it.[12] Our feeling of the same objective thunder, coming in this way, is quite different from what it would be were the thunder a continuation of previous thunder. The thunder itself we believe to abolish and exclude the silence; but the feeling of the thunder is also a feeling of the silence as just gone; and it would be difficult to find in the actual concrete consciousness of man a feeling so limited to the present as not to have an inkling of anything that went before. Here, again, language works against our perception of the truth. We name our thoughts simply, each after its thing, as if each knew its own thing and nothing else. What each really knows is clearly the thing it is named for, with dimly perhaps a thousand other things. It ought to be named after all of them, but it never is. Some of them are always things known a moment ago more clearly; others are things to be known more clearly a moment hence.[13] Our own bodily position, attitude, condition, is one of the things of which some awareness, however inattentive, invariably accompanies the knowledge of whatever else we know, We think; and as we think we feel our bodily selves as the seat of the thinking. If the thinking be our thinking, it must be suffused through all its parts with that peculiar warmth and intimacy that make it come as ours. Whether the

warmth and intimacy be anything more than the feeling of the same old body always there, is a matter for the next chapter to decide. Whatever the content of the ego may be, it is habitually felt with everything else by us humans, and must form a liaison between all the things of which we become successively aware.[14]

On this gradualness in the changes of our mental content the principles of nerve-action can throw some more light. When studying, in Chapter III, the summation of nervous activities, we saw that no state of the brain can be supposed instantly to die away. If a new state comes, the inertia of the old state will still be there and modify the result accordingly. Of course we cannot tell, in our ignorance, what in each instance the modifications ought to be. The commonest modifications in sense-perception are known as the phenomena of contrast. In æsthetics they are the feelings of delight or displeasure which certain particular orders in a series of impressions give. In thought, strictly and narrowly so called, they are unquestionably that consciousness of the whence and the whither that always accompanies its flows. If recently the brain-tract a was vividly excited, and then b, and now vividly c, the total present consciousness is not produced simply by c's excitement, but also by the dying vibrations of a and b as well. If we want to represent the brain-process we must write it thus: abc - three different processes coexisting, and correlated with them a thought which is no one of the three thoughts which they would have produced had each of them occurred alone. But whatever this fourth thought may exactly be, it seems impossible that it should not be something like each of the three other thoughts whose tracts are concerned in its production, though in a fast-waning phase.

It all goes back to what we said in another connection only a few pages ago. As the total neurosis changes, so does the total psychosis change. But as the changes of neurosis are never absolutely discontinuous, so must the successive psychoses shade gradually into each other, although their rate of change may be much faster at one moment than at the next.

This difference in the rate of change lies at the basis of a difference of subjective states of which we ought immediately to speak. When the rate is slow we are aware of the object of our thought in a comparatively restful and stable way. When rapid, we are aware of a passage, a relation, a transition from it, or between it and something else. As we take, in fact, a general view of the wonderful stream of our consciousness, what strikes us first is this different pace of its parts. Like a bird's life, it seems to be made of an alternation of flights and perchings. The rhythm of language expresses this, where every thought is expressed in a sentence, and every sentence closed by a period. The resting-places are usually occupied by sensorial imaginations of some sort, whose peculiarity is that they can be held before the mind for an indefinite time, and contemplated without changing; the places of flight are filled with thoughts of relations, static or dynamic, that for the most part obtain between the matters contemplated in the periods of comparative rest.

Let us call the resting-places the 'substantive parts,' and the places of flight the 'transitive parts,' of the stream of thought. It then appears that the main end of our thinking is at all times the attainment of some other substantive part than the one from which we have just been dislodged. And we may say that the main use of the transitive parts is to lead us from one substantive conclusion to another.

Now it is very difficult, introspectively, to see the transitive parts for what they really are. If they are but flights to a conclusion, stopping them to look at them before the conclusion is reached is really annihilating them. Whilst if we wait till the conclusion be reached, it so exceeds them in vigor and stability that it quite eclipses and swallows them up in its glare. Let anyone try to cut a thought across in the middle and get a look at its section, and he will see how difficult the introspective observation of the transitive tracts is. The rush of the thought is so headlong that it almost always brings us up at the conclusion before we can arrest it. Or if our purpose is nimble enough and we do arrest it, it ceases forthwith to be itself. As a snow-flake crystal caught in the warm hand is no longer a crystal but a drop, so, instead of catching the feeling of relation moving to its term, we find we have caught some substantive thing, usually the last word we were pronouncing, statically taken, and with its function, tendency, and particular meaning in the sentence quite evaporated. The attempt at introspective analysis in these cases is in fact like seizing a spinning top to catch its motion, or trying to turn up the gas quickly enough to see how the darkness looks. And the challenge to produce these psychoses, which is sure to be thrown by doubting psychologists at anyone who contends for their existence, is as unfair as Zeno's treatment of the advocates of motion, when, asking them to point out in what place an arrow is when it moves, he argues the falsity of their thesis from their inability to make to so preposterous a question an immediate reply.

The results of this introspective difficulty are baleful. If to hold fast and observe the transitive parts of thought's stream be so hard, then the great blunder to which all schools are liable must be the failure to register them, and the undue emphasizing of the more substantive parts of the stream. Were we not ourselves a moment since in danger of ignoring any feeling transitive between the silence and the thunder, and of treating their boundary as a sort of break in the mind? Now such ignoring as this has historically worked in two ways. One set of thinkers have been led by it to Sensationalism. Unable to lay their hands on any coarse feelings corresponding to the innumerable relations and forms of connection between the facts of the world, finding no named subjective modifications mirroring such relations, they have for the most part denied that feelings of relation exist, and many of them, like Hume, have gone so far as to deny the reality of most relations out of the mind as well as in it. Substantive psychoses, sensations and their copies and derivatives, juxtaposed like dominoes in a game, but really separate, everything else verbal illusion, - such is the upshot of this view.[15] The Intellectualists, on the other hand, unable to give up the reality of relations extra mentem, but equally unable to point to any distinct substantive feelings in which they were known, have made the same admission that the feelings do not exist. But they have drawn an opposite conclusion. The relations must be known, they say, in something that is no feeling, no mental modification continuous and consubstantial with the subjective tissue out of which sensations
and other substantive states are made. They are known, these relations, by something that lies on an entirely different plane, by an actus purus of Thought, Intellect, or Reason, all written with capitals and considered to mean something unutterably superior to any fact of sensibility whatever.
But from our point of view both Intellectualists and Sensationalists are wrong. If there be such things as feelings at all, then so surely as relations between objects exist in rerum naturâ, so surely, and more surely, do feelings exist to which these relations are known. There is not a conjunction or a preposition, and hardly an adverbial phrase, syntactic form, or inflection of voice, in human speech, that does not express some shading or other of relation which we at some moment actually feel to exist between the larger objects of our thought. If we speak objectively, it is the real relations that appear revealed; if we speak subjectively, it is the stream of consciousness that matches each of them by an inward coloring of its own. In either case the relations are numberless, and no existing language is capable of doing justice to all their shades.
We ought to say a feeling of and, a feeling of if, a feeling of but, and a feeling of by, quite as readily as we say a feeling of blue or a feeling of cold. Yet we do not: so inveterate has our habit become of recognizing the existence of the substantive parts alone, that language almost refuses to lend itself to any other use. The Empiricists have always dwelt on its influence in making us suppose that where we have a separate name, a separate thing must needs be there to correspond with it; and they have rightly denied the existence of the mob of abstract entities, principles, and forces, in whose favor no other evidence than this could be brought up. But they have said nothing of that obverse error, of which we said a word in Chapter VII, of supposing that where there is no name no entity can exist. All dumb or anonymous psychic states have, owing to this error, been coolly suppressed; or, if recognized at all, have been named after the substantive perception they led to, as thoughts 'about' this object or 'about' that, the stolid word about engulfing all their delicate idiosyncrasies in its monotonous sound. Thus the greater and greater accentuation and isolation of the substantive parts have continually gone on.
Once more take a look at the brain. We believe the brain to be an organ whose internal equilibrium is always in a state of change, - the change affecting every part. The pulses of change are doubtless more violent in one place than in another, their rhythm more rapid at this time than at that. As in a kaleidoscope revolving at a uniform rate, although the figures are always rearranging themselves, there are instants during which the transformation seems minute and interstitial and almost absent, followed by others when it shoots with magical rapidity, relatively stable forms thus alternating with forms we should not distinguish if seen again; so in the brain the perpetual rearrangement must result in some forms of tension lingering relatively long, whilst others simply come and pass. But if consciousness corresponds to the fact of rearrangement itself, why, if the rearrangement stop not, should the consciousness ever cease? And if a lingering rearrangement brings with it one kind of consciousness, why should not a swift rearrangement bring another kind of consciousness as peculiar as the rearrangement itself? The lingering consciousnesses, if of simple objects, we call 'sensations' or 'images,'
according as they are vivid or faint; if of complex objects, we call them 'percepts' when vivid, 'concepts' or 'thoughts' when faint. For the swift consciousnesses we have only those names of 'transitive states,' or 'feelings of relation,' which we have used.[16] As the brain-changes are continuous, so do all these consciousnesses melt into each other like dissolving views. Properly they are but one protracted consciousness, one unbroken stream.

Feelings of Tendency.

So much for the transitive states. But there are other unnamed states or qualities of states that are just as important and just as cognitive as they, and just as much unrecognized by the traditional sensationalist and intellectualist philosophies of mind. The first fails to find them at all, the second finds their cognitive function, but denies that anything in the way of feeling has a share in bringing it about. Examples will make clear what these inarticulate psychoses, due to waxing and waning excitements of the brain, are like.[17]

Suppose three successive persons say to us: 'Wait!' 'Hark!' 'Look!' Our consciousness is thrown into three quite different attitudes of expectancy, although no definite object is before it in any one of the three cases. Leaving out different actual bodily attitudes, and leaving out the reverberating images of the three words, which are of course diverse, probably no one will deny the existence of a residual conscious affection, a sense of the direction from which an impression is about to come, although no positive impression is yet there. Meanwhile we have no names for the psychoses in question but the names hark, look, and wait.

Suppose we try to recall a forgotten name, The state of our consciousness is peculiar. There is a gap therein; but no mere gap. It is a gap that is intensely active. A sort of wraith of the name is in it, beckoning us in a given direction, making us at moments tingle with the sense of our closeness, and then letting us sink back without the longed-for term. If wrong names are proposed to us, this singularly definite gap acts immediately so as to negate them. They do not fit into its mould. And the gap of one word does not feel like the gap of another, all empty of content as both might seem necessarily to be when described as gaps. When I vainly try to recall the name of Spalding, my consciousness is far removed from what it is when I vainly try to recall the name of Bowles. Here some ingenious persons will say: "How can the two consciousnesses be different when the terms which might make them different are not there? All that is there, so long as the effort to recall is vain, is the bare effort itself. How should that differ in the two cases? You are making it seem to differ by prematurely filling it out with the different names, although these, by the hypothesis, have not yet come. Stick to the two efforts as they are, without naming them after facts not yet existent, and you'll be quite unable to designate any point in which they differ," Designate, truly enough. We can only designate the difference by borrowing the names of objects not yet in the mind. Which is to say that our psychological vocabulary is wholly inadequate to name the differences that exist, even such strong differences as these. But namelessness is compatible with existence. There are innumerable consciousnesses of emptiness, no one of which taken in itself has a name, but all different from each other. The ordinary way is to assume that they are all emptinesses of consciousness, and so the same state. But the feeling of an absence is toto cœlo other than the absence of a feeling. It is an intense feeling. The rhythm of a lost word may be there without a sound to clothe it; or the evanescent sense of something which is the initial vowel or consonant may mock us fitfully, without growing more distinct. Every one must know the tantalizing effect of the blank rhythm of some forgotten verse, restlessly dancing in one's mind, striving to be filled out with words.

Again, what is the strange difference between an experience tasted for the first time and the same experience recognized as familiar, as having been enjoyed before, though we cannot name it or say where or when? A tune, an odor, a flavor sometimes carry this inarticulate feeling of their familiarity so deep into our consciousness that we are fairly shaken by its mysterious emotional power. But strong and characteristic as this psychosis is - it probably is due to the submaximal excitement of wide-spreading associational brain-tracts - the only name we have for all its shadings is 'sense of familiarity.'

When we read such phrases as 'naught but,' 'either one or the other,' 'a is b, but,' 'although it is, nevertheless,' 'it is an excluded middle, there is no tertium quid,' and a host of other verbal skeletons of logical relation, is it true that there is nothing more in our minds than the words themselves as they pass? What then is the meaning of the words which we think we understand as we read? What makes that meaning different in one phrase from what it is in the other? 'Who?' 'When?' 'Where?' Is the difference of felt meaning in these interrogatives nothing more than their difference of sound? And is it not (just like the difference of sound itself) known and understood in an affection of consciousness correlative to it, though so impalpable to direct examination? Is not the same true of such negatives as 'no,' 'never,' 'not yet'?

The truth is that large tracts of human speech are nothing but signs of direction in thought, of which direction we nevertheless have an acutely discriminate sense, though no definite sensorial image plays any part in it whatsoever. Sensorial images are stable psychic facts; we can hold them still and look at them as long as we like. These bare images of logical movement, on the contrary, are psychic transitions, always on the wing, so to speak, and not to be glimpsed except in flight. Their function is to lead from one set of images to another. As they pass, we feel both the waxing and the waning images in a way altogether peculiar and a way quite different from the way of their full presence. If we try to hold fast the feeling of direction, the full presence comes and the feeling of direction is lost. The blank verbal scheme of the logical movement gives us the fleeting sense of the movement as we read it, quite as well as does a rational sentence awakening definite imaginations by its words.

What is that first instantaneous glimpse of some one's meaning which we have, when in vulgar phrase we say we 'twig' it? Surely an altogether specific affection of our mind. And has the reader never asked himself what kind of a mental fact is his intention of saying a thing before he has said it? It is an entirely definite intention, distinct from all other intentions, an absolutely distinct state of consciousness, therefore; and yet how much of it consists of definite sensorial images, either of words or of things? Hardly anything! Linger, and the words and things come into the mind; the anticipatory intention, the divination is there no more. But as the words that replace it arrive, it welcomes them successively and calls them right if they agree with it, it rejects them and calls them wrong if they do not. If has therefore a nature of its own of the most positive sort, and yet what can we say about it without using words that belong to the later mental facts that replace it? The intention to-say-so-and-so is the only name it can receive. One may admit that a good third of our psychic life consists in these rapid premonitory perspective views of schemes of thought not yet articulate. How comes it about that a man reading something aloud for the first time is able immediately to emphasize all his words aright, unless from the very first he have a sense of at least the form of the sentence yet to come, which sense is fused with his consciousness of the present word, and modifies its emphasis in his mind so as to make him give it the proper accent as he utters it? Emphasis of this kind is almost altogether a matter of grammatical construction. If we read 'no more' we expect presently to come upon a 'than'; if we read 'however' at the outset of a sentence it is a 'yet,' a 'still,' or a 'nevertheless,' that we expect. A noun in a certain position demands a verb in a certain mood and number, in another position it expects a relative pronoun. Adjectives call for nouns, verbs for adverbs, etc., etc. And this foreboding of the coming grammatical scheme combined with each successive uttered word is so practically accurate that a reader incapable of understanding four ideas of the book he is reading aloud, can nevertheless read it with the most delicately modulated expression of intelligence. Some will interpret these facts by calling them all cases in which certain images, by laws of association, awaken others so very rapidly that we think afterwards we felt the very tendencies of the nascent images to arise, before they were actually there. For this school the only possible materials of consciousness are images of a perfectly definite nature. Tendencies exist, but they are facts for the outside psychologist rather than for the subject of the observation. The tendency is thus a psychical zero; only its results are felt.

Now what I contend for, and accumulate examples to show, is that 'tendencies' are not only descriptions from without, but that they are among the objects of the stream, which is thus aware of them from within, and must be described as in very large measure constituted of feelings of tendency, often so vague that we are unable to name them at all. It is in short, the re-instatement of the vague to its proper place in our mental life which I am so anxious to press on the attention. Mr. Galton and Prof. Huxley have, as we shall see in Chapter XVIII, made one step in advance in exploding the ridiculous theory of Hume and Berkeley that we can have no images but of perfectly definite things. Another is made in the overthrow of the equally ridiculous notion that, whilst simple objective qualities are revealed to our knowledge in subjective feelings, relations are not. But these reforms are not half sweeping and radical enough. What must be admitted is that the definite images of traditional psychology form but the very smallest part of our minds as they actually live. The traditional psychology talks like one who should say a river consists of nothing but pailsful, spoonsful, quartpotsful, barrelsful, and other moulded forms of water. Even were the pails and the pots all actually standing in the stream, still between them the free water would continue to flow. It is just this free water of consciousness that psychologists resolutely overlook. Every definite image in the mind is steeped and dyed in the free water that flows round it. With it goes the sense of its relations, near and remote, the dying echo of whence it came to us, the dawning sense of whither it is to lead. The significance, the value, of the image is all in this halo or penumbra that surrounds and escorts it, - or rather that is fused into one with it and has become bone of its bone and flesh of its flesh; leaving it, it is true, an image of the same thing it was before, but making it an image of that thing newly taken and freshly understood.

What is that shadowy scheme of the 'form' of an opera, play, or book, which remains in our mind and on which we pass judgment when the actual thing is done? What is our notion of a scientific or philosophical system? Great thinkers have vast premonitory glimpses of schemes of relation between terms, which hardly even as verbal images enter the mind, so rapid is the whole process.[18] We all of us have this permanent consciousness of whither our thought is going. It is a feeling like any other, a feeling of what thoughts are next to arise, before they have arisen. This field of view of consciousness varies very much in extent, depending largely on the degree of mental freshness or fatigue. When very fresh, our minds carry an immense horizon with them. The present image shoots its perspective far before it, irradiating in advance the regions in which lie the thoughts as yet unborn. Under ordinary conditions the halo of felt relations is much more circumscribed. And in states of extreme brain-fag the horizon is narrowed almost to the passing word, - the associative machinery, however, providing for the next word turning up in orderly sequence, until at last the tired thinker is led to some kind of a conclusion. At certain moments he may find himself doubting whether his thoughts have not come to a full stop; but the vague sense of a plus ultra makes him ever struggle on towards a more definite expression of what it may be; whilst the slowness of his utterance shows how difficult, under such conditions, the labor of thinking must be.

The awareness that our definite thought has come to a stop is an entirely different thing from the awareness that our thought is definitively completed. The expression of the latter state of mind is the falling inflection which betokens that the sentence is ended, and silence. The expression of the former state is 'hemming and hawing,' or else such phrases as 'et cetera,' or 'and so forth.' But notice that every part of the sentence to be left incomplete feels differently as it passes, by reason of the premonition we have that we shall be unable to end it. The 'and so forth' casts its shadow back, and is as integral a part of the object of the thought as the distinctest of images would be. Again, when we use a common noun, such as man, in a universal sense, as signifying all possible men, we are fully aware of this intention on our part, and distinguish it carefully from our intention when we mean a certain group of men, or a solitary individual before us. In the chapter on Conception we shall see how important this difference of intention is. It casts its influence over the whole of the sentence, both before and after the spot in which the word man is used.

Nothing is easier than to symbolize all these facts in terms of brain-action. Just as the echo of the whence, the sense of the starting point of our thought, is probably due to the dying excitement of processes but a moment since vividly aroused; so the sense of the whither, the fore-taste of the terminus, must be due to the waxing excitement of tracts or processes which, a moment hence, will be the cerebral correlatives of some thing which a moment hence will be vividly present to the thought. Represented by a curve, the neurosis underlying consciousness must at any moment be like this:

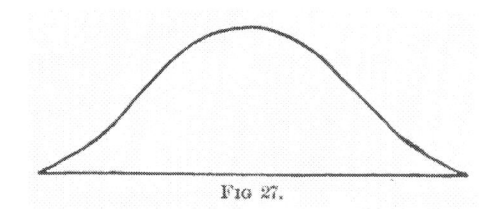

Fig 27.

Each point of the horizontal line stands for some brain-tract or process. The height of the curve above the line stands for the intensity of the process. All the processes are present, in the intensities shown by the curve. But those before the latter's apex were more intense a moment ago; those after it will be more intense a moment hence. If I recite a, b, c, d, e, f, g, at the moment of uttering d, neither a, b, c, nor e, f, g, are out of my consciousness altogether, but both, after their respective fashions, 'mix their dim lights' with the stronger one of the d, because their neuroses are both awake in some degree.

There is a common class of mistakes which shows how brain-processes begin to be excited before the thoughts attached to them are due-due, that is, in substantive and vivid form. I mean those mistakes of speech or writing by which, in Dr. Carpenter's words, "we mispronounce or misspell a word, by introducing into it a letter or syllable of some other, whose turn is shortly to come; or, it may be, the whole of the anticipated word is substituted for the one which ought to have been expressed."[19] In these cases one of two things must have happened: either some local accident of nutrition blocks the process that is due, so that other processes discharge that ought as yet to be but nascently aroused; or some opposite local accident furthers the latter processes and makes them explode before their time. In the chapter on Association of Ideas, numerous instances will come before us of the actual effect on consciousness of neuroses not yet maximally aroused.

It is just like the 'overtones' in music. Different instruments give the 'same note,' but each in a different voice, because each gives more than that note, namely, various upper harmonics of it which differ from one instrument to another. They are not separately heard by the ear; they blend with the fundamental note, and suffuse it, and alter it; and even so do the waxing and waning brain-processes at every moment blend with and suffuse and alter the psychic effect of the processes which are at their culminating point.

Let us use the words psychic overtone, suffusion, or fringe, to designate the influence of a faint brain-process upon our thought, as it makes it aware of relations and objects but dimly perceived.[20]

If we then consider the cognitive function of different states of mind, we may feel assured that the difference between those that are mere 'acquaintance,' and those that are 'knowledges-about' is reducible almost entirely to the absence or presence of psychic fringes or overtones. Knowledge about a thing is knowledge of its relations. Acquaintance with it is limitation to the bare impression which it makes. Of most of its relations we are only aware in the penumbral nascent way of a 'fringe' of unarticulated affinities about it. And, before passing to the next topic in order, I must say a little of this sense of affinity, as itself one of the most interesting features of the subjective stream. In all our voluntary thinking there is some topic or subject about which all the members of the thought revolve. Half the time this topic is a problem, a gap we cannot yet fill with a definite picture, word, or phrase, but which, in the manner described some time back, influences us in an intensely active and determinate psychic way. Whatever may be the images and phrases that pass before us, we feel their relation to this aching gap. To fill it up is our thought's destiny. Some bring us nearer to that consummation. Some the gap negates as quite irrelevant. Each swims in a felt fringe of relations of which the aforesaid gap is the term. Or instead of a definite gap we may merely carry a mood of interest about with us. Then, however vague the mood, it will still act in the same way, throwing a mantle of felt affinity over such representations, entering the mind, as suit it, and tingeing with the feeling of tediousness or discord all those with which it has no concern.

Relation, then, to our topic or interest is constantly felt in the fringe, and particularly the relation of harmony and discord, of furtherance or hindrance of the topic. When the sense of furtherance is there, we are 'all right;' with the sense of hindrance we are dissatisfied and perplexed, and cast about us for other thoughts. Now any thought the quality of whose fringe lets us feel ourselves 'all right,' is an acceptable member of our thinking, whatever kind of thought it may otherwise be. Provided we only feel it to have a place in the scheme of relations in which the interesting topic also lies, that is quite sufficient to make of it a relevant and appropriate portion of our train of ideas. For the important thing about a train of thought is its conclusion. That is the meaning, or, as we say, the topic of the thought. That is what abides when all its other members have faded from memory. Usually this conclusion is a word or phrase or particular image, or practical attitude or resolve, whether rising to answer a problem or fill a pre-existing gap that worried us, or whether accidentally stumbled on in revery. In either case it stands out from the other segments of the stream by reason of the peculiar interest attaching to it. This interest arrests it, makes a sort of crisis of it when it comes, induces attention upon it and makes us treat it in a substantive way.

The parts of the stream that precede these substantive conclusions are but the means of the latter's attainment. And, provided the same conclusion be reached, the means may be as mutable as we like, for the 'meaning' of the stream of thought will be the same. What difference does it make what the means are? "Qu'importe le flacon, pourvu qu'on ait l'ivresse?" The relative unimportance of the means appears from the fact that when the conclusion is there, we have always forgotten most of the steps preceding its attainment. When we have uttered a proposition, we are rarely able a moment afterwards to recall our exact words, though we can express it in different words easily enough. The practical upshot of a book we read remains with us, though we may not recall one of its sentences.

The only paradox would seem to lie in supposing that the fringe of felt affinity and discord can be the same in two heterogeneous sets of images. Take a train of words passing through the mind and leading to a certain conclusion on the one hand, and on the other hand an almost wordless set of tactile, visual and other fancies leading to the same conclusion. Can the halo, fringe, or scheme in which we feel the words to lie be the same as that in which we feel the images to lie? Does not the discrepancy of terms involve a discrepancy of felt relations among them?

If the terms be taken quâ mere sensations, it assuredly does. For instance, the words may rhyme with each other, - the visual images can have no such affinity as that. But quâ thoughts, quâ sensations understood, the words have contracted by long association fringes of mutual repugnance or affinity with each other and with the conclusion, which run exactly parallel with like fringes in the visual, tactile and other ideas. The most important element of these fringes is, I repeat, the mere feeling of harmony or discord, of a right or wrong direction in the thought. Dr. Campbell has, so far as I know, made the best analysis of this fact, and his words, often quoted, deserve to be quoted again. The chapter is entitled "What is the cause that nonsense so often escapes being detected, both by the writer and by the reader?" The author, in answering this question, makes (inter alia) the following remarks:[21]

"That connection [he says] or relation which comes gradually to subsist among the different words of a language, in the minds of those who speak it, ... is merely consequent on this, that those words are employed as signs of connected or related things. It is an axiom in geometry that things equal to the same thing are equal to one another. It may, in like manner, be admitted as an axiom in psychology that ideas associated by the same idea will associate one another. Hence it will happen that if, from experiencing the connection of two things, there results, as infallibly there will result, an association between the ideas or notions annexed to them, as each idea will moreover be associated by its sign, there will likewise be an association between the ideas of the signs. Hence the sounds considered as signs will be conceived to have a connection analogous to that which subsisteth among the things signified; I say, the sounds considered as signs; for this way of considering them constantly attends us in speaking, writing, hearing, and reading. When we purposely abstract from it, and regard them merely as sounds, we are instantly sensible that they are quite unconnected, and have no other relation than what ariseth from similitude of tone or accent. But to consider them in this manner commonly results from previous design, and requires a kind of effort which is not exerted in the ordinary use of speech. In ordinary use they are regarded solely as signs, or, rather, they are confounded with the things they signify; the consequence of which is that, in the manner just now explained, we come insensibly to conceive a connection among them of a very different sort from that of which sounds are naturally susceptible.

"Now this conception, habit, or tendency of the mind, call it which you please, is considerably strengthened by the frequent use of language and by the structure of it. Language is the sole channel through which we communicate our knowledge and discoveries to others, and through which the knowledge and discoveries of others are communicated to us. By reiterated recourse to this medium, if necessarily happens that when things are related to each other, the words signifying those things are more commonly brought together in discourse. Hence the words and names by themselves, by customary vicinity, contract in the fancy a relation additional to that which they derive purely from being the symbols of related things. Farther, this tendency is strengthened by the structure of language. All languages whatever, even the most barbarous, as far as hath yet appeared, are of a regular and analogical make. The consequence is that similar relations in things will be expressed similarly; that is, by similar inflections, derivations, compositions, arrangement of words, or juxtaposition of particles, according to the genius or grammatical form of the particular tongue. Now as, by the habitual use of a language (even though it were quite irregular), the signs would insensibly become connected in the imagination wherever the things signified are connected in nature, so, by the regular structure of a language, this connection among the signs is conceived as analogous to that which subsisteth among their archetypes."

If we know English and French and begin a sentence in French, all the later words that come are French; we hardly ever drop into English. And this affinity of the French words for each other is not something merely operating mechanically as a brain-law, it is something we feel at the time. Our understanding of a French sentence heard never falls to so low an ebb that we are not aware that the words linguistically belong together. Our attention can hardly so wander that if an English word be suddenly introduced we shall not start at the change. Such a vague sense as this of the words belonging together is the very minimum of fringe that can accompany them, if 'thought' at all. Usually the vague perception that all the words we hear belong to the same language and to the same special vocabulary in that language, and that the grammatical sequence is familiar, is practically equivalent to an admission that what we hear is sense. But if an unusual foreign word be introduced, if the grammar trip, or if a term from an incongruous vocabulary suddenly appear, such as 'rat-trap' or 'plumber's bill' in a philosophical discourse, the sentence detonates, as it were, we receive a shock from the incongruity, and the drowsy assent is gone. The feeling of rationality in these cases seems rather a negative than a positive thing, being the mere absence of shock, or sense of discord, between the terms of thought.

So delicate and incessant is this recognition by the mind of the mere fitness of words to be mentioned together that the slightest misreading, such as 'casualty' for 'causality,' or 'perpetual' for 'perceptual,' will be corrected by a listener whose attention is so relaxed that he gets no idea of the meaning of the sentence at all.

Conversely, if words do belong to the same vocabulary, and if the grammatical structure is correct, sentences with absolutely no meaning may be uttered in good faith and pass unchallenged. Discourses at prayer-meetings, re-shuffling the same collection of cant phrases, and the whole genus of penny-a-line-isms and newspaper-reporter's flourishes give illustrations of this. "The birds filled the tree-tops with their morning song, making the air moist, cool, and pleasant," is a sentence I remember reading once in a report of some athletic exercises in Jerome Park. It was probably written unconsciously by the hurried reporter, and read uncritically by many readers. An entire volume of 784 pages lately published in Boston[22] is composed of stuff like this passage picked out at random:

"The flow of the efferent fluids of all these vessels from their outlets at the terminal loop of each culminate link on the surface of the nuclear organism is continuous as their respective atmospheric fruitage up to the altitudinal limit of their expansibility, whence, when atmosphered by like but coalescing essences from higher altitudes, - those sensibly expressed as the essential qualities of external forms, - they descend, and become assimilated by the afferents of the nuclear organism."[23]

There are every year works published whose contents show them to be by real lunatics. To the reader, the book quoted from seems pure nonsense from beginning to end. It is impossible to divine, in such a case, just what sort of feeling of rational relation between the words may have appeared to the author's mind. The border line between objective sense and nonsense is hard to draw; that between subjective sense and nonsense, impossible. Subjectively, any collocation of words may make sense - even the wildest words in a dream - if one only does not doubt their belonging together. Take the obscurer passages in Hegel: it is a fair question whether the rationality included in them be anything more than the fact that the words all belong to a common vocabulary, and are strung together on a scheme of predication and relation, - immediacy, self-relation, and what not, - which has habitually recurred. Yet there seems no reason to doubt that the subjective feeling of the rationality of these sentences was strong in the writer as he penned them, or even that some readers by straining may have reproduced it in themselves.

To sum up, certain kinds of verbal associate, certain grammatical expectations fulfilled, stand for a good part of our impression that a sentence has a meaning and is dominated by the Unity of one Thought. Nonsense in grammatical form sounds half rational; sense with grammatical sequence upset sounds nonsensical; e.g., "Elba the Napoleon English faith had banished broken to he Saint because Helena at." Finally, there is about each word the psychic 'overtone' of feeling that it brings us nearer to a forefelt conclusion. Suffuse all the words of a sentence, as they pass, with these three fringes or haloes of relation, let the conclusion seem worth arriving at, and all will admit the sentence to be an expression of thoroughly continuous, unified, and rational thought.[24]

Each word, in such a sentence, is felt, not only as a word, but as having a meaning. The 'meaning' of a word taken thus dynamically in a sentence may be quite different from its meaning when taken statically or without context. The dynamic meaning is usually reduced to the bare fringe we have described, of felt suitability or unfitness to the context and conclusion. The static meaning, when the word is concrete, as 'table,' 'Boston,' consists of sensory images awakened; when it is abstract, as 'criminal legislation,' 'fallacy,' the meaning consists of other words aroused, forming the so-called 'definition.'

Hegel's celebrated dictum that pure being is identical with pure nothing results from his taking the words statically, or without the fringe they wear in a context. Taken in isolation, they agree in the single point of awakening no sensorial images. But taken dynamically, or as significant, - as thought, - their fringes of relation, their affinities and repugnances, their function and meaning, are felt and understood to be absolutely opposed.

Such considerations as these remove all appearance of paradox from those cases of extremely deficient visual imagery of whose existence Mr. Galton has made us aware (see below). An exceptionally intelligent friend informs me that he can frame no image whatever of the appearance of his breakfast-table. When asked how he then remembers it at all, he says he simple 'knows' that it seated four people, and was covered with a white cloth on which were a butter-dish, a coffee-pot, radishes, and so forth. The mind-stuff of which this 'knowing' is made seems to be verbal images exclusively. But if the words 'coffee,' 'bacon,' 'muffins,' and 'eggs' lead a man to speak to his cook, to pay his bills, and to take measures for the morrow's meal exactly as visual and gustatory memories would, why are they not, for all practical intents and purposes, as good a kind of material in which to think? In fact, we may suspect them to be for most purposes better than terms with a richer imaginative coloring. The scheme of relationship and the conclusion being the essential things in thinking, that kind of mind-stuff which is handiest will be the best for the purpose. Now words, uttered or unexpressed, are the handiest mental elements we have. Not only are they very rapidly revivable, but they are revivable as actual sensations more easily than any other items of our experience. Did they not possess some such advantage as

this, it would hardly be the case that the older men are and the more effective as thinkers, the more, as a rule, they have lost their visualizing power and depend on words. This was ascertained by Mr. Galton to be the case with members of the Royal Society. The present writer observes it in his own person most distinctly.

On the other hand, a deaf and dumb man can weave his tactile and visual images into a system of thought quite as effective and rational as that of a word-user. The question whether thought is possible without language has been a favorite topic of discussion among philosophers. Some interesting reminiscences of his childhood by Mr. Ballard, a deaf-mute instructor in the National College at Washington, show it to be perfectly possible. A few paragraphs may be quoted here.

"In consequence of the loss of my hearing in infancy, I was debarred from enjoying the advantages which children in the full possession of their senses derive from the exercises of the common primary school, from the every-day talk of their school-fellows and playmates, and from the conversation of their parents and other grown-up persons.

"I could convey my thoughts and feelings to my parents and brothers by natural signs or pantomime, and I could understand what they said to me by the same medium; our intercourse being, however, confined to the daily routine of home affairs and hardly going beyond the circle of my own observation....

"My father adopted a course which he thought would, in some measure, compensate me for the loss of my hearing. It was that of taking me with him when business required him to ride abroad; and he took me more frequently than he did my brothers; giving, as the reason for his apparent partiality, that they could acquire information through the ear, while I depended solely upon my eye for acquaintance with affairs of the outside world....

"I have a vivid recollection of the delight I felt in watching the different scenes we passed through, observing the various phases of nature, both animate and inanimate; though we did not, owing to my infirmity, engage in conversation. It was during those delightful rides, some two or three years before my initiation into the rudiments of written language, that I began to ask myself the question: How came the world into being? When this question occurred to my mind, I set myself to thinking it over a long time. My curiosity was awakened as to what was the origin of human life in its first appearance upon the earth, and of vegetable life as well, and also the cause of the existence of the earth, sun, moon, and stars.

"I remember at one time when my eye fell upon a very large old stump which we happened to pass in one of our rides, I asked myself, 'Is it possible that the first man that ever came into the world rose out of that stump? But that stump is only a remnant of a once noble magnificent tree, and how came that tree? Why, it came only by beginning to grow out of the ground just like those little trees now coming up.' And I dismissed from my mind, as an absurd idea, the connection between the origin of man and a decaying old stump....

"I have no recollection of what it was that first suggested to me the question as to the origin of things. I had before this time gained ideas of the descent from parent to child, of the propagation of animals, and of the production of plants from seeds. The question that occurred to my mind was: whence came the first man, the first animal, and the first plant, at the remotest distance of time, before which there was no man, no animal, no plant; since I knew they all had a beginning and an end.

"It is impossible to state the exact order in which these different questions arose, i.e., about men, animals, plants, the earth, sun, moon, etc. The lower animals did not receive so much thought as was bestowed upon man and the earth; perhaps because I put man and beast in the same class, since I believed that man would be annihilated and there was no resurrection beyond the grave, - though I am told by my mother that, in answer to my question, in the case of a deceased uncle who looked to me like a person in sleep, she had tried to make me understand that he would awake in the far future. It was my belief that man and beast derived their being from the same source and were to be laid down in the dust in a state of annihilation. Considering the brute animal as of secondary importance, and allied to man on a lower level, man and the earth were the two things on which my mind dwelled most.

"I think I was five years old, when I began to understand the descent from parent to child and the propagation of animals. I was nearly eleven years old, when I entered the Institution where I was educated; and I remember distinctly that it was at least two years before this time that I began to ask myself the question as to the origin of the universe. My age was then about eight, not over nine years.

"Of the form of the earth, I had no idea in my childhood, except that, from a look at a map of the hemispheres, I inferred there were two immense disks of matter lying near each other. I also believed the sun and moon to be round, flat plates of illuminating matter; and for those luminaries I entertained a sort of reverence on account of their power of lighting and heating the earth. I thought from their coming up and going down, travelling across the sky in so regular a manner that there must be a certain something having power to govern their course. I believed the sun went into a hole at the west and came out of another at the east, travelling through a great tube in the earth, describing the same curve as it seemed to describe in the sky. The stars seemed to me to be tiny lights studded in the sky.

"The source from which the universe came was the question about which my mind revolved in a vain struggle to grasp it, or rather to fight the way up to attain to a satisfactory answer. When I had occupied myself with this subject a considerable time, I perceived that it was a matter much greater than my mind could comprehend; and I remember well that I became so appalled at its mystery and so bewildered at my inability to grapple with it that I laid the subject aside and out of my mind, glad to escape being, as it were, drawn into a vortex of inextricable confusion. Though I felt relieved at this escape, yet I could not resist the desire to know the truth; and I returned to the subject; but as before, I left it, after thinking it over for some time. In this state of perplexity, I hoped all the time to get at the truth, still believing that the more I gave thought to the subject, the more my mind would penetrate the mystery. Thus I was tossed like a shuttlecock, returning to the subject and recoiling from it, till I came to school.

"I remember that my mother once told me about a being up above, pointing her finger towards the sky and with a solemn look on her countenance. I do not recall the circumstance which led to this communication. When she mentioned the mysterious being up in the sky, I was eager to take hold of the subject, and plied her with questions concerning the form and appearance of this unknown being, asking if it was the sun, moon, or one of the stars. I knew she meant that there was a living one somewhere up in the sky; but when I realized that she could not answer my questions, I gave it up in despair, feeling sorrowful that I could not obtain a definite idea of the mysterious living one up in the sky.

"One day, while we were haying in a field, there was a series of heavy thunder-claps. I asked one of my brothers where they came from. He pointed to the sky and made a zigzag motion with his finger, signifying lightning. I imagined there was a great man somewhere in the blue vault, who made a loud noise with his voice out of it; and each time I heard[25] a thunder-clap I was frightened, and looked up at the sky, fearing he was speaking a threatening word."[26]

Here we may pause. The reader sees by this time that it makes little or no difference in what sort of mind-stuff, in what quality of imagery, his thinking goes on. The only images intrinsically important are the halting-places, the substantive conclusions, provisional or final, of the thought. Throughout all the rest of the stream, the feelings of relation are everything, and the terms related almost naught. These feelings of relation, these psychic overtones, halos, suffusions, or fringes about the terms, may be the same in very different systems of imagery. A diagram may help to accentuate this indifference of the mental means where the end is the same. Let A be some experience from which a number of thinkers start. Let Z be the practical conclusion rationally inferrible from it. One gets to the conclusion by one line, another by another; one follows a course of English, another of German, verbal imagery. With one, visual images predominate; with another, tactile. Some trains are tinged with emotions, others not; some are very abridged, synthetic and rapid, others, hesitating and broken into many steps. But when the penultimate terms of all the trains, however differing inter se, finally shoot into the same conclusion, we say and rightly say, that all the thinkers have had substantially the same thought. It would probably astound each of them beyond measure to be let into his neighbor's mind and to find how different the scenery there was from that in his own.

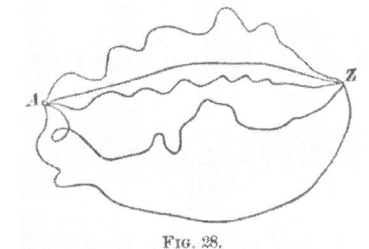

FIG. 28.

Thought is in fact a kind of Algebra, as Berkeley long ago said, "in which, though a particular quantity be marked by each letter, yet to proceed right, it is not requisite that in every step each letter suggest to your thoughts that particular quantity it was appointed to stand for." Mr. Lewes has developed this algebra-analogy so well that I must quote his words:

"The leading characteristic of algebra is that of operation on relations. This also is the leading characteristic of Thought. Algebra cannot exist without values, nor Thought without Feelings. The operations are so many blank forms till the values are assigned. Words are vacant sounds, ideas are blank forms, unless they symbolize images and sensations which are their values. Nevertheless it is rigorously true, and of the greatest importance, that analysts carry on very extensive operations with blank forms, never pausing to supply the symbols with values until the calculation is completed; and ordinary men, no less than philosophers, carry on long trains of thought without pausing to translate their ideas (words) into images. . . . Suppose some one from a distance shouts 'a lion!' At once the man starts in alarm. . . . To the man the word is not only an. . . . expression of all that he has seen and heard of lions, capable of recalling various experiences, but is also capable of taking its place in a connected series of thoughts without recalling any of those experiences, without reviving an image, however faint, of the lion - simply as a sign of a certain relation included in the complex so named. Like an algebraic symbol it may be operated on without conveying other significance than an abstract relation: it is a sign of Danger, related to fear with all its motor sequences. Its logical position suffices. . . . Ideas are substitutions which require a secondary process when what is symbolized by them is translated into the images and experiences it replaces; and this secondary process is frequently not performed at all, generally only performed to a very small extent. Let anyone closely examine what has passed in his mind when he has constructed a chain of reasoning, and he will be surprised at the fewness and faintness of the images which have accompanied the ideas. Suppose you inform me that 'the blood rushed violently from the man's heart, quickening his pulse at the sight of his enemy.' Of the many latent images in this phrase, how many were salient in your mind and in mine? Probably two - the man and his enemy - and these images were faint. Images of blood, heart, violent rushing, pulse, quickening, and sight, were either not revived at all, or were passing shadows. Had any such images arisen, they would have hampered thought, retarding the logical process of judgment by irrelevant connections. The symbols had substituted relations for these values. . . . There are no images of two things and three things, when I say 'two and three equal five;' there are simply familiar symbols having precise relations. . . .The verbal symbol 'horse,' which stands for all our experiences of horses, serves all the purposes of Thought, without recalling one of the images clustered in the perception of horses, just as the sight of a horse's form serves all the purposes of recognition without recalling the sound of its neighing or its tramp, its qualities as an animal of draught, and so forth.[27]

It need only be added that as the Algebrist, though the sequence of his terms is fixed by their relations rather than by their several values, must give a real value to the final one he reaches; so the thinker in words must let his concluding word or phrase be translated into its full sensible-image-value, under penalty of the thought being left unrealized and pale.

This is all I have to say about the sensible continuity and unity of our thought as contrasted with the apparent discreteness of the words, images, and other means by which it seems to be carried on. Between all their substantive elements there is 'transitive' consciousness, and the words and images are 'fringed,' and not as discrete as to a careless view they seem. Let us advance now to the next head in our description of Thought's stream.

4. Human thought appears to deal with objects independent of itself; that is, it is cognitive, or possesses the function of knowing.

For Absolute Idealism, the infinite Thought and its objects are one. The Objects are, through being thought; the eternal Mind is, through thinking them. Were a human thought alone in the world there would be no reason for any other assumption regarding it. Whatever it might have before it would be its vision, would be there, in its 'there,' or then, in its 'then'; and the question would never arise whether an extra-mental duplicate of it existed or not. The reason why we all believe that the objects of our thoughts have a duplicate existence outside, is that there are many human thoughts, each with the same objects, as we cannot help supposing. The judgment that my thought has the same object as his thought is what makes the psychologist call my thought cognitive of an outer reality. The judgment that my own past thought and my own present thought are of the same object is what makes me take the object out of either and project it by a sort of triangulation into an independent position, from which it may appear to both. Sameness in a multiplicity of objective appearances is thus the basis of our belief in realities outside of thought.[28] In Chapter XII we shall have to take up the judgment of sameness again.

To show that the question of reality being extra-mental or not is not likely to arise in the absence of repeated experiences of the same, take the example of an altogether unprecedented experience, such as a new taste in the throat. Is it a subjective quality of feeling, or an objective quality felt? You do not even ask the question at this point. It is simply that taste. But if a doctor hears you describe it, and says: "Ha! Now you know what heartburn is," then it becomes a quality already existent extra mentem tuam; which you in turn have come upon and learned. The first spaces, times, things, qualities, experienced by the child probably appear, like the first heartburn, in this absolute way, as simple beings, neither in nor out of thought. But later, by having other thoughts than this present one, and making repeated judgments of sameness among their objects, he corroborates in himself the notion of realities, past and distant as well as present, which realities no one single thought either possesses or engenders, but which all may contemplate and know. This, as was stated in the last chapter, is the psychological point of view, the relatively uncritical non-idealistic point of view of all natural science, beyond which this book cannot go. A mind which has become conscious of its own cognitive function, plays what we have called 'the psychologist' upon itself. It not only knows the things that appear before it; it knows that it knows them. This stage of reflective condition is, more or less explicitly, our habitual adult state of mind.

It cannot, however, be regarded as primitive. The consciousness of objects must come first. We seem to lapse into this primordial condition when consciousness is reduced to a minimum by the inhalation of anæsthetics or during a faint. Many persons testify that at a certain stage of the anaesthetic process objects are still cognized whilst the thought of self is lost. Professor Herzen says:[29]

"During the syncope there is absolute psychic annihilation, the absence of all consciousness; then at the beginning of coming to, one has at a certain moment a vague, limitless, infinite feeling - a sense of existence in general without the least trace of distinction between the me and the not-me."

Dr. Shoemaker of Philadelphia describes during the deepest conscious stage of ether-intoxication a vision of "two endless parallel lines in swift longitudinal motion....on a uniform misty background....together with a constant sound or whirr, not loud but distinct.... which seemed to be connected with the parallel lines....These phenomena occupied the whole field. There were present no dreams or visions in any way connected with human affairs, no ideas or impressions akin to anything in past experience, no emotions, of course no idea of personality. There was no conception as to what being it was that was regarding the two lines, or that there existed any such thing as such a being; the lines and waves were all."[30]

Similarly a friend of Mr. Herbert Spencer, quoted by him in 'Mind' (vol. III. p. 556), speaks of "an undisturbed empty quiet everywhere except that a stupid presence lay like a heavy intrusion somewhere - a blotch on the calm." This sense of objectivity and lapse of subjectivity, even when the object is almost indefinable, is, it seems to me, a somewhat familiar phase in chloroformization, though in my own case it is too deep a phase for any articulate after-memory to remain. I only know that as it vanishes I seem to wake to a sense of my own existence as something additional to what had previously been there.[31]

Many philosophers, however, hold that the reflective consciousness of the self is essential to the cognitive function of thought. They hold that a thought, in order to know a thing at all, must expressly distinguish between the thing and its own self.[32] This is a perfectly wanton assumption, and not the faintest shadow of reason exists for supposing it true. As well might I contend that I cannot dream without dreaming that I dream, swear without swearing that I swear, deny without denying that I deny, as maintain that I cannot know without knowing that I know. I may have either acquaintance-with, or knowledge-about, an object O without think about myself at all. It suffices for this that I think O, and that it exist. If, in addition to thinking O, I also think that I exist and that I know O, well and good; I then know one more thing, a fact about of which I previously was unmindful. That, however, does not prevent me from having already known it a good deal. O per se, or O plus P, are as good objects of knowledge as O plus me is. The philosophers in question simply substitute one particular object for all others, and call it the object par excellence. It is a case of the 'psychologist's fallacy'. They know the object to be one thing and the thought another; and they forthwith foist their own knowledge into that of the thought of which they pretend to give a true account. To conclude, then, thought may, but need not, in knowing, discriminate between its object and itself.

We have been using the word Object. Something must now be said about the proper use of the term in Psychology. In popular parlance the word object is commonly taken without reference to the act of knowledge, and treated as synonymous with individual subject of existence. Thus if anyone ask what is the mind's object when you say 'Columbus discovered America in 1492,' most people will reply 'Columbus,' or 'America,' or, at most, 'the discovery of America.' They will name a substantive kernel or nucleus of the consciousness, and say the thought is 'about' that, - as indeed it is, - and they will call that your thought's 'object.' Really that is usually only the grammatical object, or more likely the grammatical subject, of your sentence. It is at most your 'fractional object;' or you may call it the 'topic' of your thought, or the 'subject of your discourse.' But the Object of your thought is really its entire content or deliverance, neither more nor less. It is a vicious use of speech to take out a substantive kernel from its content and call that its object; and it is an equally vicious use of speech to add a substantive kernel not articulately included in its content, and to call that its object. Yet either one of these two sins we commit, whenever we content ourselves with saying that a given thought is simply 'about' a certain topic, or that that topic is its 'object.' The object of my thought in the previous sentence, for example, is strictly speaking neither Columbus, nor America, nor its discovery. It is nothing short of the entire sentence, 'Columbus-
discovered-America-in-1492.' And if we wish to speak of it substantively, we must make a substantive of it by writing it out thus with hyphens between all its words. Nothing but this can possibly name its delicate idiosyncrasy. And if we wish to feel that idiosyncrasy we must reproduce the thought as it was uttered, with every word fringed

and the whole sentence bathed in that original halo of obscure relations, which, like an horizon, then spread about its meaning.

Our psychological duty is to cling as closely as possible to the actual constitution of the thought we are studying. We may err as much by excess as by defect. If the kernel or 'topic,' Columbus, is in one way less than the thought's object, so in another way it may be more. That is, when named by the psychologist, it may mean much more than actually is present to the thought of which he is reporter. Thus, for example, suppose you should go on to think: 'He was a daring genius!' An ordinary psychologist would not hesitate to say that the object of your thought was still 'Columbus.' True, your thought is about Columbus. It 'terminates' in Columbus, leads from and to the direct idea of Columbus. But for the moment it is not fully and immediately Columbus, it is only 'he,' or rather 'he-was-a-daring-genius;' which, though it may be an unimportant difference for conversational purposes, is, for introspective psychology, as great a differences as there can be.

The object of every thought, then, is neither more nor less than all that the thought thinks, exactly as thought thinks it, however complicated the matter, and however symbolic the manner of the thinking may be. It is needless to say that memory can seldom accurately reproduce such an object, when once it has passed from before the mind. It either makes too little or too much of it. Its best plan is to repeat the verbal sentence, if there was one, in which the object was expressed. But for inarticulate thoughts there is not even this resource, and introspection must confess that the task exceeds her powers. The mass of our thinking vanishes for ever, beyond hope of recovery, and psychology only gathers up a few of the crumbs that fall from the feast. The next point to make clear is that, however complex the object may be, the thought of it is one undivided state of consciousness. As Thomas Brown says:[33]

"I have already spoken too often to require again to caution you against the mistake into which, I confess, that the terms which the poverty of our language obliges us to use might of themselves very naturally lead you; the mistake of supposing that the most complex states of mind are not truly, in their very essence, as much one and indivisible as those which we term simple - the complexity and seeming coexistence which they involve being relative to our feeling[34] only, not to their own absolute nature. I trust I need not repeat to you that, in itself, every notion, however seemingly complex, is, and must be, truly simple - being one state or affection, of one simple substance, mind. Our conception of a whole army, for example, is as truly this one mind existing in this one state, as our conception of any of the individuals that compose an army. Our notion of the abstract numbers, eight, four, two, is as truly one feeling of the mind as our notion of simple unity."

The ordinary associationist-psychology supposes, in contrast with this, that whenever an object of thought contains many elements, the thought itself must be made up of just as many ideas, one idea for each element, and all fused together in appearance, but really separate.[35] The enemies of this psychology find (as we have already seen) little trouble in showing that such a bundle of separate ideas would never form one thought at all, and they contend that an Ego must be added to the bundle to give it unity, and bring the various ideas into relation with each other.[36] We will not discuss the ego just yet, but it is obvious that if things are to be thought in relation, they must be thought together, and in one something, be that something ego, psychosis, state of consciousness, or whatever you please. If not thought with each other, things are not thought in relation at all. Now most believers in the ego make the same mistake as the associationists and sensationists whom they oppose. Both agree that the elements of the subjective stream are discrete and separate and constitute what Kant calls a 'manifold.' But while the associationists think that a 'manifold' can form a single knowledge, the egoists deny this, and say that the knowledge comes only when the manifold is subjected to the synthetizing activity of an ego. Both make an identical initial hypothesis; but the egoist, finding it won't express the facts, adds another hypothesis to correct it. Now I do not wish just yet to 'commit myself' about the existence or non-existence of the ego, but I do contend that we need not invoke it for this particular reason - namely, because the manifold of ideas has to be reduced to unity. There is no manifold of coexisting ideas; the notion of such a thing is a chimera. Whatever things are thought in relation are thought from the outset in a unity, in a single pulse of subjectivity, a single psychosis, feeling, or state of mind.

The reason why this fact is so strangely garble in the books seems to be what on an earlier page I called the psychologist's fallacy. We have the inveterate habit, whenever we try introspectively to describe one of our thoughts, of dropping the thought as it is in itself and talking of something else. We describe the things that appear to the thought, and we describe other thoughts about those things - as if these and the original thought were the same. If, for example, the thought be 'the pack of cards is on the table,' we say, "Well, isn't it a thought of the pack of cards? Isn't it of the cards as included in the pack? Isn't it of the table? And of the legs of the table as well? The table has legs - how can you think the table without virtually thinking its legs? Hasn't our thought then, all these parts - one part for the pack and another for the table? And within the pack-part a part for each card, as within the table-part a part for each leg? And isn't each of these parts an idea? And can our thought, then, be anything but an assemblage or pack of ideas, each answering to some element of what it knows?"

Now not one of these assumptions is true. The thought taken as an example is, in the first place, not of 'a pack of cards.' It is of 'the-pack-of-cards-is-on-the-table,' an entirely different subjective phenomenon, whose Object implies the pack, and every one of the cards in it, but whose conscious constitution bears very little resemblance to that of the thought of the pack per se. What a thought is, and what it may be developed into, or explained to stand for, and be equivalent to, are two things, not one.[37]

An analysis of what passes through the mind as we utter the phrase the pack of cards is on the table will, I hope, make this clear, and may at the same time condense into a concrete example a good deal of what has gone before.

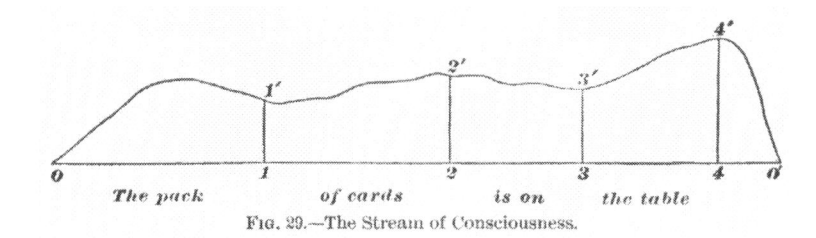

FIG. 29.—The Stream of Consciousness.

It takes time to utter the phrase. Let the horizontal line in Fig. 29 represent time. Every part of it will then stand for a fraction, every point for an instant, of the time. Of course the thought has time-parts. The part 2-3 of it, though continuous with 1-2, is yet a different part from 1-2. Now I say of these time-parts that we cannot take any one of them so short that it will not after some fashion or other be a thought of the whole object 'the pack of cards is on the table.' They melt into each other like dissolving views, and no two of them feel the object just alike, but each feels the total object in a unitary undivided way. This is what I mean by denying that in the thought any parts can be found corresponding to the object's parts. Time-parts are not such parts

Now let the vertical dimensions of the figure stand for the objects or contents of the thoughts. A line vertical to any point of the horizontal, as 1-1', will then symbolize the object in the mind at the instant 1; a space above the horizontal, as 1-1'-2'-2, will symbolize all that passes through the mind during the time 1-2 whose line it covers. The entire diagram from 0 to 0' represents a finite length of thought's stream.

Can we now define the psychic constitution of each vertical section of this segment? We can, though in a very rough way. Immediately after 0, even before we have opened our mouths to speak, the entire thought is present to our mind in the form of an intention to utter that sentence. This intention, though it has no simple name, and though it is a transitive state immediately displaced by the first word, is yet a perfectly determinate phase of thought, unlike anything else. Again, immediately before 0', after the last word of the sentence is spoken, all will admit that we again think its entire content as we inwardly realize its completed deliverance. All vertical sections made through any other parts of the diagram will be respectively filled with other ways of feeling the sentence's meaning. Through 2, for example, the cards will be the part of the object most emphatically present to the mind; through 4, the table. The stream is made higher in the drawing at its end than at its beginning, because the final way of feeling the content is fuller and richer than the initial way. As Joubert says, "we only know just what we meant to say, after we have said it." And as M. V. Egger remarks, "before speaking, one barely knows what one intends to say, but afterwards one is filled with admiration and surprise at having said and thought it so well."

This latter author seems to me to have kept at much closer quarters with the facts than any other analyst of consciousness.[38] But even he does not quite hit the mark, for, as I understand him, he thinks that each word as it occupies the mind displaces the rest of the thought's content. He distinguishes the 'idea' (what I have called the total object or meaning) from the consciousness of the words, calling the former a very feeble state, and contrasting it with the liveliness of the words, even when these are only silently rehearsed. "The feeling," he says, "of the words makes ten or twenty times more noise in our consciousness than the sense of the phrase, which for consciousness is a very slight matter."[39] And having distinguished these two things, he goes on to separate them in time, saying that the idea may either precede or follow the words, but that it is a 'pure illusion' to suppose them simultaneous.[40]

Now I believe that in all cases where the words are understood, the total idea may be and usually is present not only before and after the phrase has been spoken, but also whilst each separate word is uttered.[41] It is the overtone, halo, or fringe of the word as spoken in that sentence. It is never absent; no word in an understood sentence comes to consciousness as a mere noise. We feel its meaning as it passes; and although our object differs from one moment to another as to its verbal kernel or nucleus, yet it is similar throughout the entire segment of the stream. The same object is known everywhere, now from the point of view, if we may so call it, of this word, now from the point of view of that. And in our feeling of each word there chimes an echo or foretaste of every other. The consciousness of the 'Idea' and that of the words are thus consubstantial. They are made of the same 'mind-stuff,' and form an unbroken stream. Annihilate a mind at any instant, cut its thought through whilst yet uncompleted, and examine the object present to the cross-section thus suddenly made; you will find, not the bald word in process of utterance, but that word suffused with the whole idea. The word may be so loud, as M. Egger would say, that we cannot tell just how its suffusion, as such, feels, or how it differs from the suffusion of the next word. But it does differ; and we may be sure that, could we see into the brain, we should find the same processes active through the entire sentence in different degrees, each one in turn becoming maximally excited and then yielding the momentary verbal 'kernel,' to the thought's content, at other times being only sub-excited, and then combining with the other sub-excited processes to give the overtone or fringe.[42]

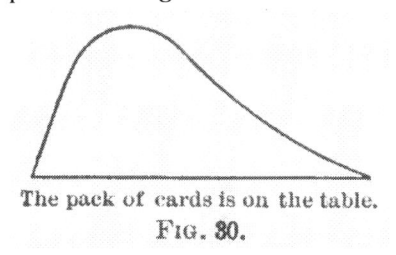

We may illustrate this by a farther development of the diagram Fig 29. Let the objective content of any vertical section through the stream be represented no longer by a line, but by a plane figure, highest opposite whatever part of the object is most prominent in consciousness at the moment when the section is made. This part, in verbal thought, will usually be some word. A series of sections 1-1', taken at the moments 1, 2, 3, would then look like this:

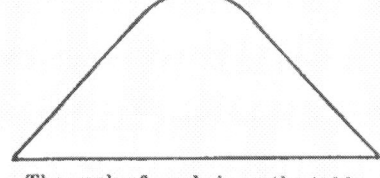

The pack of cards is on the table.
FIG. 30.

The pack of cards is on the table.
FIG. 31.

The horizontal breadth stands for the entire object in each of the figures; the height of the curve above each part of that object marks the relative prominence of that part in the thought. At the moment symbolized by the first figure pack is the prominent part; in the third figure it is table, etc.

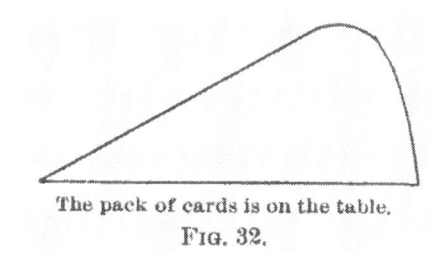

We can easily add all these plane sections together to make a solid, one of whose solid dimensions will represent time, whilst a cut across this at right angles will give the thought's content at the moment when the cut is made.

Let it be the thought, 'I am the same I that I was yesterday.' If at the fourth moment of time we annihilate the thinker and examine how the last pulsation of his consciousness was made, we find that it was an awareness of the whole content with same most prominent, and the other parts of the thing known relatively less distinct.

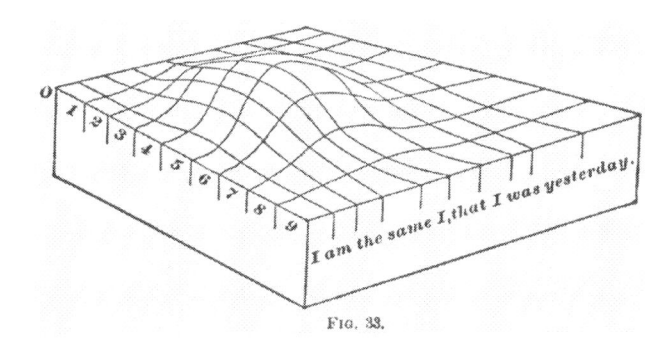

The pack of cards is on the table.
FIG. 32.

FIG. 33.

With each prolongation of the scheme in the time-direction, the summit of the curve of section would come further towards the end of the sentence. If we make a solid wooden frame with the sentence written on its front, and the time-scale on one of its sides, if we spread flatly a sheet of India rubber over its top, on which rectangular co-ordinates are painted, and slide a smooth ball under the rubber in the direction from 0 to 'yesterday,' the bulging of the membrane along this diagonal at successive moments will symbolize the changing of the thought's content in a way plain enough, after what has been said, to call for no more explanation. Or to express it in cerebral terms, it will show the relative intensities, at successive moments, of the several nerve-processes to which the various parts of the thought-object correspond.

The last peculiarity of consciousness to which attention is to be drawn in this first rough description of its stream is that

5) It is always interested more in one part of its object than in another, and welcomes and rejects, or chooses, all the while it thinks.

The phenomena of selective attention and of deliberative will are of course patent examples of this choosing activity. But few of us are aware how incessantly it is at work in operations not ordinarily called by these names.

Accentuation and Emphasis are present in every perception we have. We find it quite impossible to disperse our attention impartially over a number of impressions. A monotonous succession of sonorous strokes is broken up into rhythms, now of one sort, now of another, by the different accent which we place on different strokes. The simplest of these rhythms is the double one, tick-tóck, tick-tock, tick-tóck. Dots dispersed on a surface are perceived in rows and groups. Lines separate into diverse figures. The ubiquity of the distinctions, this and that, here and there, now and then, in our minds is the result of our laying the same selective emphasis on parts of place and time.

But we do far more than emphasize things, and unite some, and keep others apart. We actually ignore most of the things before us. Let me briefly show how this goes on.

To begin at the bottom, what are our very senses themselves but organs of selection? Out of the infinite chaos of movements, of which physics teaches us that the outer world consists, each sense-organ picks out those which fall within certain limits of velocity. To these it responds, but ignores the rest as completely as if they did not exist. It thus accentuates particular movements in a manner for which objectively there seems no valid ground; for, as Lange says, there is no reason whatever to think that the gap in Nature between the highest sound-waves and the lowest heat-waves is an abrupt break like that of our sensations; or that the difference between violet and ultra-violet rays has anything like the objective importance subjectively represented by that between light and darkness. Out of what is in itself an undistinguishable, swarming continuum, devoid of distinction or emphasis, our senses make for us, by attending to this motion and ignoring that, a world full of contrasts, of sharp accents, of abrupt changes, of picturesque light and shade.

If the sensations we receive from a given organ have their causes thus picked out for us by the conformation of the organ's termination, Attention, on the other hand, out of all the sensations yielded, picks out certain ones as worthy of its notice and suppresses all the rest. Helmholtz's work on Optics is little more than a study of those visual sensations of which common men never become aware - blind spots, muscœ volitantes, after images, irradiation, chromatic fringes, marginal changes of color, double images, astigmatism, movements of accommodation and convergence, retinal rivalry, and more besides. We do not even know without special training on which of our eyes an image falls. So habitually ignorant are most men of this that one may be blind for years of a single eye and never know the fact.

Helmholtz says that we notice only those sensations which are signs to us of things. But what are things? Nothing, as we shall abundantly see, but special groups of sensible qualities, which happen practically or aesthetically to interest us, to which we therefore give substantive names, and which we exalt to this exclusive status of independence and dignity. But in itself, apart from my interest, a particular dust-wreath on a windy day is just as much of an individual thing, and just as much or as little deserves an individual name, as my own body does.

And then, among the sensations we get from each separate thing, what happens? The mind selects again. It chooses certain of the sensations to represent the thing most truly, and considers the rest as its appearances, modified by the conditions of the moment. Thus my table-top is named square, after but one of an infinite number of retinal sensations which it yields, the rest of them being sensations of two acute and two obtuse angles; but I call the latter perspective views, and the four right angles the true form of the table, and erect the attribute squareness into the table's essence, for aesthetic reasons of my own In like manner, the real form of the circle is deemed to be the sensation it gives when the line of vision is perpendicular to its centre - all its other sensations are signs of this sensation. The real sound of the cannon is the sensation it makes when the ear is close by. The real color of the brick is the sensation it gives when the eye looks squarely at it from a near point, out of the sunshine and yet not in the gloom; under other circumstances it gives us other color-sensations which are but signs of this - we then see it looks pinker or blacker than it really is. The reader knows no object which lie does not represent to himself by preference as in some typical attitude, of some normal size, at some characteristic distance, of some standard tint, etc., etc. But all these essential characteristics, which together form for us the genuine objectivity of the thing and are contrasted with what we call the subjective sensations it may yield us at a given moment, are mere sensations like the latter. The mind chooses to suit itself, and decides what particular sensation shall be held more real and valid than all the rest.

Thus perception involves a twofold choice. Out of all present sensations, we notice mainly such as are significant of absent ones; and out of all the absent associates which these suggest, we again pick out a very few to stand for the objective reality par excellence. We could have no more exquisite example of selective industry.

That industry goes on to deal with the things thus given in perception. A man's empirical thought depends on the things he has experienced, but what these shall be is to a large extent determined by his habits of attention. A thing may be present to him a thousand times, but if he persistently fails to notice it, it cannot be said to enter into his experience. We are all seeing flies, moths, and beetles by the thousand, but to whom, save an entomologist, do they say anything distinct? On the other hand, a thing met only once in a lifetime may leave an indelible experience in the memory. Let four men make a tour in Europe. One will bring home only picturesque impressions - costumes and colors, parks and views and works of architecture, pictures and statues. To another all this will be non-existent; and distances and prices, populations and drainage-arrangements, door-and window-fastenings, and other useful statistics will take their place. A third will give a rich account of the theatres, restaurants, and public balls, and naught beside; whilst the fourth will perhaps have been so wrapped in his own subjective broodings as to tell little more than a few names of places through which he passed. Each has selected, out of the same mass of presented objects, those which suited his private interest and has made his experience thereby.

If, now, leaving the empirical combination of objects, we ask how the mind proceeds rationally to connect them, we find selection again to be omnipotent. In a future chapter we shall see that all Reasoning depends on the ability of the mind to break up the totality of the phenomenon reasoned about, into parts, and to pick out from among these the particular one which, in our given emergency, may lead to the proper conclusion. Another predicament will need another conclusion, and require another element to be picked out. The man of genius is he who will always stick in his bill at the right point, and bring it out with the right element - 'reason' if the emergency be theoretical, 'means' if it be practical - transfixed upon it. I here confine myself to this brief statement, but it may suffice to show that Reasoning is but another form of the selective activity of the mind.

If now we pass to its æsthetic department, our law is still more obvious. The artist notoriously selects his items, rejecting all tones, colors, shapes, which do not harmonize with each other and with the main purpose of his work. That unity, harmony, 'convergence of characters,' as M. Taine calls it, which gives to works of art their superiority over works of nature, is wholly due to elimination. Any natural subject will do, if the artist has wit enough to pounce upon some one feature of it as characteristic, and suppress all merely accidental items which do not harmonize with this.

Ascending, still higher, we reach the plane of Ethics, where choice reigns notoriously supreme. An act has no ethical quality whatever unless it be chosen out of several all equally possible. To sustain the arguments for the good course and keep them ever before us, to stifle our longing for more flowery ways, to keep the foot unflinchingly on the arduous path, these are characteristic ethical energies. But more than these; for these but deal with the means of compassing interests already felt by the man to be supreme. The ethical energy par excellence has to go farther and choose which interest out of several, equally coercive, shall become supreme. The issue here is of the utmost pregnancy, for it decides a man's entire career. When he debates, Shall I commit this crime? choose that profession? accept that office, or marry this fortune? - his choice really lies between one of several equally possible future Characters. What he shall become is fixed by the conduct of this moment. Schopenhauer, who enforces his determinism by the argument that with a given fixed character only one reaction is possible under given circumstances, forgets that, in these critical ethical moments, what consciously seems to be in question is the complexion of the character itself. The problem with the man is less what act he shall now choose to do, than what being he shall now resolve to become.

Looking back, then, over this review, we see that the mind is at every stage a theatre of simultaneous possibilities. Consciousness consists in the comparison of these with each other, the selection of some, and the suppression of the rest by the reinforcing and inhibiting agency of attention. The highest and most elaborated mental products are filtered from the data chosen by the faculty next beneath, out of the mass offered by the faculty below that, which mass in turn was sifted from a still larger amount of yet simpler material, and so on. The mind, in short, works on the data it receives very much as a sculptor works on his block of stone. In a sense the statue stood there from eternity. But there were a thousand different ones beside it, and the sculptor alone is to thank for having extricated this one from the rest. Just so the world of each of us, howsoever different our several views of it may be, all lay embedded in the primordial chaos of sensations, which gave the mere matter to the thought of all of us indifferently. We may, if we like, by our reasonings unwind things back to that black and jointless continuity of space and moving clouds of swarming atoms which science calls the only real world. But all the while the world we feel and live in will be that which our ancestors and we, by slowly cumulative strokes of choice, have extricated out of this, like sculptors, by simply rejecting certain portions of the given stuff. Other sculptors, other statues from the same stone! Other minds, other worlds from the same monotonous and inexpressive chaos ! My world is but one in a million alike embedded, alike real to those who may abstract them. How different must be the worlds in the consciousness of ant, cuttle-fish, or crab!

But in my mind and your mind the rejected portions and the selected portions of the original world-stuff are to a great extent the same. The human race as a whole largely agrees as to what it shall notice and name, and what not. And among the noticed parts we select in much the same way for accentuation and preference or subordination and dislike. There is, however, one entirely extraordinary case in which no two men ever are known to choose alike. One great splitting of the whole universe into two halves is made by each of us; and for each of us almost all of the interest attaches to one of the halves; but we all draw the line of division between them in a different place. When I say that we all call the two halves by the same names, and that those names are 'me' and 'not-me' respectively, it will at once be seen what I mean. The altogether unique kind of interest which each human mind feels in those parts of creation which it can call me or mine may be a moral riddle, but it is a fundamental psychological fact. No mind can take the same interest in his neighbor's me as in his own. The neighbor's me falls together with all the rest of things in one foreign mass, against which his own me stands out in startling relief. Even the trodden worm, as Lotze somewhere says, contrasts his own suffering self with the whole remaining universe, though he have no clear conception either of himself or of what the universe may be. He is for me a mere part of the world; for him it is I who am the mere part. Each of us dichotomizes the Kosmos in a different place.

Descending now to finer work than this first general sketch, let us in the next chapter try to trace the psychology of this fact of self-consciousness to which we have thus once more been led.

Notes

[1] A good deal of this chapter is reprinted from an article 'On some Omissions of Introspective Psychology' which appeared in 'Mind' for January 1884.
[2] B. P. Bowne: Metaphysics, p. 362.
[3] L'Automatisme Psychologique, p. 318.
[4] Cf. A. Constans: Relation sur une Epidémie d'hystero-demonopathie en 1861. 2me ed. Paris, 1863. -Chiap e Franzolini: L'Epidemia d'isterodemonopatie in Verzegnis. Reggio, 1879. - See also J. Kerner's little work: Nachricht von dem Vorkommen des Besessenseins. 1836.
[5] For the Physiology of this compare the chapter on the Will.
[6] Loc. cit. p. 316.
[7] The Philosophy of Reflection, I. 248, 290.
[8] Populäre Wissenschaftliche Vorträge, Drittes Heft (1876), p. 72.
[9] Fick, in L. Hermann's Handb. d. Physiol., Bd. III. Th. I. p. 225.
[10] It need of course not follow, because a total brain-state does not recur, that no point of the brain can ever be twice in the same condition. That would be as improbable a consequence as that in the sea a wave-crest should never come twice at the same point of space. What can hardly come twice is an identical combination of wave-forms all with their crests and hollows reoccupying identical places. For such a total combination as this is the analogue of the brain-state to which our actual consciousness at any moment is due.
[11] The accurate registration of the 'how long' is still a little mysterious.
[12] Cf. Brentano; Psychologie, vol. I. pp. 219-20. Altogether this chapter of Brentano's on the Unity of Consciousness is as good as anything with which I am acquainted.
[13] Honor to whom honor is due! The most explicit acknowledgment I have anywhere found of all this is in a buried and forgotten paper by the Rev. Jas. Wills, on 'Accidental Association,' in the Transactions of the Royal Irish Academy, vol. XXI. part I (1846). Mr. Wills writes:
"At every instant of conscious thought there is a certain sum of perceptions, or reflections, or both together, present, and together constituting one whole state of apprehension. Of this some definite portion may be far more distinct than all the rest; and the rest be in consequence proportionably vague, even to the limit of obliteration. But still, within this limit, the most dim shade of perception enters into, and in some infinitesimal degree modifies, the whole existing state. This state will thus be in some way modified by any sensation or emotion, or act of distinct attention, that may give prominence to any part of it; so that the actual result is capable of the utmost variation, according to the person or the occasion.
. . . To any portion of the entire scope here described there may be a special direction of the attention, and this special direction is recognized as strictly what is recognized as the idea present to the mind. This idea is evidently not commensurate with the entire state of apprehension, and much perplexity has arisen from not observing this fact. However deeply we may suppose the attention to be engaged by any thought, any considerable alteration of the surrounding phenomena would still be perceived; the most abstruse demonstration in this room would not prevent a listener, however absorbed, from noticing the sudden extinction of the lights. Our mental states have always an essential unity, such that each state of apprehension, however variously compounded, is a single whole, of which every component is, therefore, strictly apprehended (so far as it is apprehended) as a part. Such is the elementary basis from which all our intellectual operations commence."
[14] Compare the charming passage in Taine on Intelligence (N.Y. ed.), I. 83-4.
[15] E.g.: "The stream of thought is not a continuous current, but a series of distinct ideas, more or less rapid in their succession; the rapidity being measurable by the number that pass through the mind in a given time." (Bain: E. and W., 29.)
[16] Few writers have admitted that we cognize relations through feeling. The intellectualists have explicitly denied the possibility of such a thing - e.g., Prof. T. H. Green ('Mind,' vol. VII. p. 28): "No feeling, as such or as felt, is [of?] a relation. . . . Even a relation between feelings is not itself a feeling or felt." On the other hand, the sensationalists have either smuggled in the cognition without giving any account of it, or have denied the relations to be cognized, or even to exist, at all. A few honorable exceptions, however, deserve to be named among the sensationalists. Destutt de Tracy, Laromiguière, Cardaillac, Brown, and finally Spencer, have explicitly contended for feelings of relation, consubstantial with our feelings or thoughts of the terms 'between' which they obtain. Thus Destutt de Tracy says (Eléments d'Idéologie, T. Ier, chap. IV): "The faculty of judgment is itself a sort of sensibility, for it is the faculty of feeling the relations among our ideas; and to feel relations is to feel." Laromiguière writes (LeÇons de Philosophie, IIme Partie, 3me LeÇon):
"There is no one whose intelligence does not embrace simultaneously many ideas, more or less distinct, more or less confused. Now, when we have many ideas at once, a peculiar feeling arises in us: we feel, among these ideas, resemblances, differences, relations. Let us call this mode of feeling, common to us all, the feeling of relation, or relation-feeling (sentiment-rapport). One

sees immediately that these relation-feelings, resulting from the propinquity of ideas, must be infinitely more numerous than the sensation-feelings (sentiments-sensations) or the feelings we have of the action of our faculties. The slightest knowledge of the mathematical theory of combinations will prove this. . . . Ideas of relation originate in feelings of relation. They are the effect of our comparing them and reasoning about them."

Similarly, de Cardaillac (Études Élementaires de Philosophie, Section I. chap. VII):

"By a natural consequence, we are led to suppose that at the same time that we have several sensations or several ideas in the mind, we feel the relations which exist between these sensations, and the relations which exist between these ideas. . . . If the feeling of relations exists in us, . . . it is necessarily the most varied and the most fertile of all human feelings: 1o the most varied, because, relations being more numerous than beings, the feelings of relation must be in the same proportion more numbers than the sensations whose presence gives rise to their formulation; 2o, the most fertile, for the relative ideas of which the feeling-of-relation is the source . . . are more important than absolute ideas, if such exist. . . . If we interrogate common speech, we find the feeling of relation expressed there in a thousand different ways. If it is easy to seize a relation, we say that it is sensible, to distinguish it from one which, because its terms are too remote, cannot be as quickly perceived. A sensible difference, or resemblance. . . . What is taste in the arts, in intellectual productions? What but the feeling of those relations among the parts which constitutes their merit? . . . Did we not feel relations and should never attain to true knowledge, . . . for almost all our knowledge is of relations. . . . We never have an isolated sensation; . . . we are therefore never without the feeling of relation. . . . An object strikes our sense; we see in it only a sensation. . . . The relative is so near the absolute, the relation-feeling so near the sensation-feeling, the two are so intimately fused in the composition of the object, that the relation appears to us as part of the sensation itself. It is doubtless to this sort of fusion between sensations and feelings of relation that the silence of metaphysicians as to the latter is due; and it is for the same reason that they have obstinately persisted in asking from sensation alone those ideas of relation which it was powerless to give."

Dr. Thomas Brown writes (Lectures, XLV. init.): "There is an extensive order of our feelings which involve this notion of relation, and which consist indeed in the mere perception of a relation of some sort. . . . Whether the relation be of two or of many external objects, or of two or many affections of the mind, the feeling of this relation . . . is what I term a relative suggestion; that phrase being the simplest which it is possible to employ, for expressing, without any theory, the mere fact of the rise of certain feelings of relation, after certain other feelings which precede them; and therefore, as involving no particular theory, and simply expressive of an undoubted fact. . . . . That the feelings of relation are states of the mind essentially different from our simple perceptions, or conceptions of the objects, . . . that they are not what Condillac terms transformed sensations, I proved in a former lecture, when I combated the excessive simplification of that ingenious but not very accurate philosopher. There is an original tendency or susceptibility of the mind, by which, on perceiving together different objects, we are instantly, without the intervention of any other mental process, sensible of their relation in certain respects, as truly as there is an original tendency or susceptibility by which, when external objects are present and have produced a certain affection of our sensorial organ, we are instantly affected with the primary elementary feelings of perception; and, I may add, that as our sensations or perceptions are of various species, so are there various species of relations; - the number of relations, indeed, even of external things, being almost infinite, while the number of perceptions is, necessarily, limited by that of the objects which have the power of producing some affection of our organs of sensation. . . . Without that susceptibility of the mind by which it has the feeling of relation, our consciousness would be as truly limited to a single point, as our body would become, were it possible to fetter it to a single atom."

Mr. Spencer is even more explicit. His philosophy is crude in that he seems to suppose that it is only in transitive states that outward relations are known; whereas in truth space-relations, relations of contrast, etc., are felt along with their terms, in substantive states as well as in transitive states, as we shall abundantly see. Nevertheless Mr. Spencer's passage is so clear that it also deserves to be quoted in full (Principles of Psychology, § 65):

"The proximate components of Mind are of two broadly-contrasted kinds - Feelings and the relations between feelings. Among the members of each group there exist multitudinous unlikenesses, many of which are extremely strong; but such unlikenesses are small compared with those which distinguish members of the one group from members of the other. Let us, in the first place, consider what are the characters which all Relations between feelings have in common.

"Each feeling, as we here define it, is any portion of consciousness which occupies a place sufficiently large to give it a perceivable individuality; which has its individually marked off from adjacent portions of consciousness by qualitative contrasts; and which, when introspectively contemplated, appears to be homogeneous. These are the essentials. Obviously if, under introspection, a state of consciousness is decomposable into unlike parts that exist either simultaneously or successively, it is not one feeling but two or more. Obviously if it is indistinguishable from an adjacent portion of consciousness, it forms one with that portion - is not an individual feeling, but part of one. And obviously if it does not occupy in consciousness an appreciable area, or an appreciable duration, it cannot be known as a feeling.

"A Relation between feelings is, on the contrary, characterized by occupying no appreciable part of consciousness. Take away the terms it unites, and it disappears along with them; having no independent place, no individuality of its own. It is true that, under an ultimate analysis, what we call a relation proves to be itself a kind of feeling - the momentary feeling accompanying the transition from one conspicuous feeling to an adjacent conspicuous feeling. And it is true that, notwithstanding its extreme brevity, its qualitative character is appreciable; for relations are (as we shall hereafter see) distinguishable from one another only by the unlikenesses of the feelings which accompany the momentary transitions. Each relational feeling may, in fact, be regarded as one of those nervous shocks which we suspect to be the units of composition of feelings; and, though instantaneous, it is known as of greater or less strength, and as taking place with greater or less facility. But the contrast between these relational feelings and what we ordinarily call feelings is so strong that we must class them apart. Their extreme brevity, their small variety, and their dependence on the terms they unite, differentiate them in an unmistakable way. "Perhaps it will be well to recognize more fully the truth that this distinction cannot be absolute. Besides admitting that, as an element of consciousness, a relation is a momentary feeling, we must also admit that just as a relation can have no existence apart from the feelings which form its terms, so a feeling can exist only by relations to other feelings which limit it in space or time or both. Strictly speaking, neither a feeling nor a relation is an independent element of consciousness: there is throughout a dependence such that the appreciable areas of consciousness occupied by feelings can no more possess individualities apart from the relations which link them, than these relations can possess individualities apart from the feelings they link. The essential distinction between the two, then, appears to be that whereas a relational feeling is a portion of consciousness inseparable into parts, a feeling, ordinarily so called, is a portion of consciousness that admits imaginary division into like parts which are related to one another in sequence or coexistence. A feeling proper is either made up of like parts that occupy time, or it is made up of like parts that occupy space, or both. In any case, a feeling proper is an aggregate of related like parts, while a relational feeling is undecomposable. And this is exactly the contrast between the two which must result if, as we have inferred, feelings are composed of units of feelings, or shocks."

[17] M. Paulhan (Revue Philosophique, XX. 455-6), after speaking of the faint mental images of objects and emotions, says: "We find other vaguer states still, upon which attention seldom rests, except in persons who by nature or profession are addicted to internal observation. It is even difficult to name them precisely, for they are little known and not classed; but we may cite as an example of them that peculiar impression which we feel when, strongly preoccupied by a certain subject, we nevertheless are engaged with, and have our attention almost completely absorbed by, matters quite disconnected therewithal. We do not then exactly think of the object of our preoccupation; we do not represent it in a clear manner; and yet our mind is not as it would be without this preoccupation. Its object, absent from consciousness, is nevertheless represented there by a peculiar unmistakable impression, which often persists long and is a strong feeling, although so obscure for our intelligence." "A mental sign of the kind is the unfavorable disposition left in our mind towards an individual by painful incidents erewhile experienced and now perhaps forgotten. The sign remains, but is not understood; its definite meaning is lost." (P. 458.)

[18] Mozart describes thus his manner of composing: First bits and crumbs of the piece come and gradually join together in his mind; then the soul getting warmed to the work, the thing grows more and more, "and I spread it out broader and clearer, and at last it gets almost finished in my head, even when it is a long piece, so that I can see the whole of it at a single glance in my mind, as if it were a beautiful painting or a handsome human being; in which way I do not hear it in my imagination at all as a succession - the way it must come later - but all at once, as it were. It is a rare feast! All the inventing and making goes on in me as in a beautiful strong dream. But the best of all is the hearing of it all at once."

[19] Mental Physiology, § 236. Dr. Carpenter's explanation differs materially from that given in the text.

[20] Cf. also S. Stricker: Vorlesungen über allg. u. exp. Pathologie (1879), pp. 462-3, 501, 547; Romanes: Origin of Human Faculty, p. 82. It is so hard to make one's self clear that I may advert to a misunderstanding of my views by the late Prof. Thos. Maguire of Dublin (Lectures on Philosophy, 1885). This author considers that by the 'fringe' I mean some sort of psychic material by which sensations in themselves separate are made to cohere together, and wittily says that I ought to "see that uniting sensations by their 'finges' is more vague than to construct the universe out of oysters by platting their beards" (p. 211). But the fringe, as I use the word, means nothing like this; it is part of the object cognized, - substantive qualities and things appearing to the mind in a fringe of relations. Some parts - the transitive parts - of our stream of thought cognize the relations rather than the things; but both the transitive and the substantive parts form one continuous stream, with no discrete 'sensations' in it such as Prof. Maguire supposes, and supposes me suppose, to be there.

[21] George Campbell: Philosophy of Rhetoric, book II. chap. VII.

[22] Substantialism or Philosophy of Knowledge, by 'Jean Story' (1879).

[23] [Classics Editor's Note: the symbol for this footnote does not appear in the main text of the Dover edition; however it does appear in Miller's (1981) edition.]

M. G. Tarde, quoting (in Delboeuf, Le Sommeil et les Rêves (1885), p. 226) some nonsense-verses from a dream, says they show how prosodic forms may subsist in a mind from which logical rules are effaced.... I was able, in dreaming, to preserve the faculty of finding two words which rhymed, to appreciate the rhyme, to fill up the verse as it first presented itself with other words which, added, gave the right number of syllables, and yet I was ignorant of the sense of the words.... Thus we have the extraordinary fact that the words called each other up, without calling up their sense.... Even when awake, it is more difficult to ascend to the meaning of a word than to pass from one word to another; or to put it otherwise, it is harder to be a thinker than to be a rhetorician, and on the whole nothing is commoner than trains of words not understood."

[24] We think it odd that young children should listen with such rapt attention to the reading of stories expressed in words half of which they do not understand, and of none of which they ask the meaning. But their thinking is in form just what ours is when it is rapid. Both of us make flying leaps over large portions of the sentences uttered and we give attention only to substantive starting points, turning points, and conclusions here and there. All the rest, 'substantive' and separately intelligible as it may potentially be, actually serves only as so much transitive material. It is internodal consciousness, giving us the sense of continuity, but having no significance apart from its mere gap-filling function. The children probably feel no gap when through a lot of unintelligible words they are swiftly carried to a familiar and intelligible terminus.

[25] Not literally heard, of course. Deaf mutes are quick to perceive shocks and jars that can be felt, even when so slight as to be unnoticed by those who can hear.
[26] Quoted by Samuel Porter: 'Is Thought possible without Language?' in Princeton Review, 57th year, pp. 108-12 (Jan. 1881 ?). Cf. also W. W. Ireland: The Blot upon the Brain (1886), Paper X, part II; G. J. Romanes: Mental Evolution in Man, pp. 81-83, and references therein made. Prof. Max Müller gives a very complete history of this controversy in pp. 30-64 of his 'Science of Thought' (1887). His own view is that Thought and Speech are inseparable; but under speech he includes any conceivable sort of symbolism or even mental imagery, and he makes no allowance for the wordless summary glimpses which we have of systems of relation and direction.
[27] Problems of Life and Mind, 3d Series, Problem IV, chapter 5. Compare also Victor Egger: La Parole Intérieure (Paris, 1881), chap. VI.
[28] If but one person sees an apparition we consider it his private hallucination. If more than one, we begin to think it may be a real external presence.
[29] Revue Philosophique, vol. XXI. p. 671.
[30] Quoted from the Therapeutic Gazette, by the N. Y. Semi-weekly Evening Post for Nov. 2, 1886.
[31] In half-stunned states self-consciousness may lapse. A friend writes me: "We were driving back from ---- in a wagonette. The door flew open and X., alias 'Baldy,' fell out on the road. We pulled up at once, and then he said, 'Did anybody fall out?' or 'Who fell out?' - I don't exactly remember the words. When told that Baldy fell out, he said, 'Did Baldy fall out? Poor Baldy!'"
[32] Kant originated this view. I subjoin a few English statements of it. J. Ferrier, Institutes of Metaphysic, Proposition I: "Along with whatever any intelligence knows it must, as the ground or condition of its knowledge, have some knowledge of itself.: Sir Wm. Hamilton, Discussions, p. 47: "We know, and we know that we know, - these propositions, logically distinct, are really identical; each implies the other. . . . So true is the scholastic brocard: non sentimus nisi sentiamus nos sentire." H. S. Mansel, Metaphysics, p. 58: "Whatever variety of materials may exist within reach of my mind, I can become conscious of them only by recognizing them as mine. . . . Relation to the conscious self is thus the permanent and universal feature which every state of consciousness as such must exhibit." T. H. Green, Introduction to Hume, p. 12: "A consciousness by the man . . . of himself, in negative relation to the thing that is his object, and this consciousness must be taken to go along with the perceptive act itself. Not less than this indeed can be involved in any act that is to be the beginning of knowledge at all. It is the minimum of possible thought or intelligence."
[33] Lectures on the Philosophy of the Human Mind, Lecture 45.
[34] Instead of saying to our feeling only, he should have said, to the object only.
[35] "There can be no difficulty in admitting that association does form the ideas of an indefinite number of individuals into one complex idea; because it is an acknowledged fact. Have we not the idea of an army? And is not that precisely the ideas of an indefinite number of men formed into one idea?" (Jas. Mill's Analysis of the Human Mind (J. S. Mill's Edition, vol. I. p. 264)
[36] For their arguments, see above, Chapter VI.
[37] I know there are readers whom nothing can convince that the thought of a complex object has not as many parts as are discriminated in the object itself. Well, then, let the word parts pass. Only observe that these parts are not the separate 'ideas' of traditional psychology. No one of them can live out of that particular thought, any more than my head can live off of my particular shoulders. In a sense a soap-bubble has parts; it is a sum of juxtaposed spherical triangles. But these triangles are not separate realities; neither are the 'parts' of the thought separate realities. Touch the bubble and the triangles are no more. Dismiss the thought and out go its parts. You can no more make a new thought out of 'ideas' that have once served than you can make a new bubble out of old triangles. Each bubble, each thought, is a fresh organic unity, sui generis.
[38] In his work, La Parole Intérieure (Paris, 1881), especially chapters VI and VII.
[39] Page 301.
[40] Page 218. To prove this point, M. Egger appeals to the fact that we often hear some one speak whilst our mind is preoccupied, but do not understand him until some moments afterwards, when we suddenly 'realize' what he meant. Also to our digging out the meaning of a sentence in an unfamiliar tongue, where the words are present to us long before the idea is taken in. In these special cases the word does indeed precede the idea. The idea, on the contrary, precedes the word whenever we try to express ourselves with effort, as in a foreign tongue, or in an unusual field of intellectual invention. Both sets of cases, however, are exceptional, and M. Egger would probably himself admit, on reflection, that in the former class there is some sort of a verbal suffusion, however evanescent, of the idea, when it is grasped - we hear the echo of the words as we catch their meaning. And he would probably admit that in the second class of cases the idea persists after the words that came with so much effort are found. In normal cases the simultaneity, as he admits, is obviously there.
[41] A good way to get the words and the sense separately is to inwardly articulate word for word the discourse of another. One then finds that the meaning will often come to the mind in pulses, after clauses or sentences are finished.
[42] The nearest approach (with which I am acquainted) to the doctrine set forth here is in O. Liebmann's Zur Analysis der Wirklichkeit, pp. 427-438.

Chapter X - The Consciousness of Self

Let us begin with the Self in its widest acceptation, and follow it up to its most delicate and subtle form, advancing from the study of the empirical, as the Germans call it, to that of the pure, Ego.

The Empirical Self or Me.

The Empirical Self of each of us is all that he is tempted to call by the name of me. But it is clear that between what a man calls me and what he simply calls mine the line is difficult to draw. We feel and act about certain things that are ours very much as we feel and act about ourselves. Our fame, our children, the work of our hands, may be as dear to us as our bodies are, and arouse the same feelings and the same acts of reprisal if attacked. And our bodies themselves, are they simply ours, or are they us? Certainly men have been ready to disown their very bodies and to regard them as mere vestures, or even as prisons of clay from which they should some day be glad to escape.
We see then that we are dealing with a fluctuating material. The same object being sometimes treated as a part of me, at other times as simply mine, and then again as if I had nothing to do with it at all. In its widest possible sense, however, a man's Self is the sum total of all that he CAN call his, not only his body and his psychic powers, but his clothes and his house, his wife and children, his ancestors and friends, his reputation and works, his lands and horses, and yacht and bank-account. All these things give him the same emotions. If they wax and prosper, he feels triumphant; if they dwindle and die away, he feels cast down, - not necessarily in the same degree for each thing, but in much the same way for all. Understanding the Self in this widest sense, we may begin by dividing the history of it into three parts, relating respectively to –

1. Its constituents;
2. The feelings and emotions they arouse, -- Self-feelings;
3. The actions to which they prompt, -- Self-seeking and Self-preservation.

1. The constituents of the Self may be divided into two classes, those which make up respectively -
(a) The material Self;
(b) The social Self;
(c) The spiritual Self; and
(d) The pure Ego.

(a) The body is the innermost part of the material Self in each of us; and certain parts of the body seem more intimately ours than the rest. The clothes come next. The old saying that the human person is composed of three parts - soul, body and clothes - is more than a joke. We so appropriate our clothes and identify ourselves with them that there are few of us who, if asked to choose between having a beautiful body clad in raiment perpetually shabby and unclean, and having an ugly and blemished form always spotlessly attired, would not hesitate a moment before making a decisive reply.[1] Next, our immediate family is a part of ourselves. Our father and mother, our wife and babes, are bone of our bone and flesh of our flesh. When they die, a part of our very selves is gone. If they do anything wrong, it is our shame. If they are insulted, our anger flashes forth as readily as if we stood in their place. Our home comes next. Its scenes are part of our life; its aspects awaken the tenderest feelings of affection; and we do not easily forgive the stranger who, in visiting it, finds fault with its arrangements or treats it with contempt. All these different things are the objects of instinctive preferences coupled with the most important practical interests of life. We all have a blind impulse to watch over our body, to deck it with clothing of an ornamental sort, to cherish parents, wife and babes, and to find for ourselves a home of our own which we may live in and 'improve.'
An equally instinctive impulse drives us to collect property; and the collections thus made become, with different degrees of intimacy, parts of our empirical selves. The parts of our wealth most intimately ours are those which are saturated with our labor. There are few men who would not feel personally annihilated if a life-long construction of their hands or brains - say an entomological collection or an extensive work in manuscript - were suddenly swept away. The miser feels similarly towards his gold, and although it is true that a part of our depression at the loss of possessions is due to our feeling that we must now go without certain goods that we expected the possessions to bring in their train, yet in every case there remains, over and above this, a sense of the shrinkage of our personality, a partial conversion of ourselves to nothingness, which is a psychological phenomenon by itself. We are all at once assimilated to the tramps and poor devils whom we so despise, and at the same time removed farther than ever away from the happy sons of earth who lord it over land and sea and men in the full-blown lustihood that wealth and

power can give, and before whom, stiffen ourselves as we will by appealing to anti-snobbish first principles, we cannot escape an emotion, open or sneaking, of respect and dread.

(b) A man's Social Self is the recognition which he gets from his mates. We are not only gregarious animals, liking to be in sight of our fellows, but we have an innate propensity to get ourselves noticed, and noticed favorably, by our kind. No more fiendish punishment could be devised, were such a thing physically possible, than that one should be turned loose in society and remain absolutely unnoticed by all the members thereof. If no one turned round when we entered, answered when we spoke, or minded what we did, but if every person we met 'cut us dead,' and acted as if we were non-existing things, a kind of rage and impotent despair would ere long well up in us, from which the cruellest bodily tortures would be a relief; for these would make us feel that, however bad might be our plight, we had not sunk to such a depth as to be unworthy of attention at all.

Properly speaking, a man has as many social selves as there are individuals who recognize him and carry an image of him in their mind. To wound any one of these his images is to wound him.[2] But as the individuals who carry the images fall naturally into classes, we may practically say that he has as many different social selves as there are distinct groups of persons about whose opinion he cares. He generally shows a different side of himself to each of these different groups. Many a youth who is demure enough before his parents and teachers, swears and swaggers like a pirate among his 'tough' young friends. We do not show ourselves to our children as to our club-companions, to our customers as to the laborers we employ, to our own masters and employers as to our intimate friends. From this there results what practically is a division of the man into several selves; and this may be a discordant splitting, as where one is afraid to let one set of his acquaintances know him as he is elsewhere; or it may be a perfectly harmonious division of labor, as where one tender to his children is stern to the soldiers or prisoners under his command.

The most peculiar social self which one is apt to have is in the mind of the person one is in love with. The good or bad fortunes of this self cause the most intense elation and dejection - unreasonable enough as measured by every other standard than that of the organic feeling of the individual. To his own consciousness he is not, so long as this particular social self fails to get recognition, and when it is recognized his contentment passes all bounds.

A man's fame, good or bad, and his honor or dishonor, are names for one of his social selves. The particular social self of a man called his honor is usually the result of one of those splittings of which we have spoken. It is his image in the eyes of his own 'set,' which exalts or condemns him as he conforms or not to certain requirements that may not be made of one in another walk of life. Thus a layman may abandon a city infected with cholera; but a priest or a doctor would think such an act incompatible with his honor. A soldier's honor requires him to fight or to die under circumstances where another man can apologize or run away with no stain upon his social self. A judge, a statesman, are in like manner debarred by the honor of their cloth from entering into pecuniary relations perfectly honorable to persons in private life. Nothing is commoner than to hear people discriminate between their different selves of this sort: "As a man I pity you, but as an official I must show you no mercy; as a politician I regard him as an ally, but as a moralist I loathe him;" etc., etc. What may be called 'club-opinion' is one of the very strongest forces in life.[3] The thief must not steal from other thieves; the gambler must pay his gambling-debts, though he pay no other debts in the world. The code of honor of fashionable society has throughout history been full of permissions as well as of vetoes, the only reason for following either of which is that so we best serve one of our social selves. You must not lie in general, but you may lie as much as you please if asked about your relations with a lady; you must accept a challenge from an equal, but if challenged by an inferior you may laugh him to scorn: these are examples of what is meant.

(c) By the Spiritual Self, so far as it belongs to the Empirical Me, I mean a man's inner or subjective being, his psychic faculties or dispositions, taken concretely; not the bare principle of personal Unity, or 'pure' Ego, which remains still to be discussed. These psychic dispositions are the most enduring and intimate part of the self, that which we most verily seem to be. We take a purer self-satisfaction when we think of our ability to argue and discriminate, of our moral sensibility and conscience, of our indomitable will, than when we survey any of our other possessions. Only when these are altered is a man said to be alienatus a se.

Now this spiritual self may be considered in various ways. We may divide it into faculties, as just instanced, isolating them one from another, and identifying ourselves with either in turn. This is an abstract way of dealing with consciousness, in which, as it actually presents itself, a plurality of such faculties are always to be simultaneously found; or we may insist on a concrete view, and then the spiritual self in us will be either the entire stream of our personal consciousness, or the present 'segment' or 'section' of that stream, according as we take a broader or a narrower view - both the stream and the section being concrete existences in time, and each being a unity after its own peculiar kind. But whether we take it abstractly or concretely, our considering the spiritual self at all is a reflective process, is the result of our abandoning the outward-looking point of view, and of our having become able to think of subjectivity as such, to think ourselves as thinkers.

This attention to thought as such, and the identification of ourselves with it rather than with any of the objects which it reveals, is a momentous and in some respects a rather mysterious operation, of which we need here only say that as a matter of fact it exists; and that in everyone, at an early age, the distinction between thought as such, and what it is 'of' or 'about,' has become familiar to the mind. The deeper grounds for this discrimination may possibly be hard to find; but superficial grounds are plenty and near at hand. Almost anyone will tell us that thought is a different sort of existence from things, because many sorts of thought are of no things - e.g., pleasures, pains, and emotions; others are of non-existent things - errors and fictions; others again of existent things, but in a form that is symbolic and does not resemble them - abstract ideas and concepts; whilst in the thoughts that do resemble the things they are 'of' (percepts, sensations), we can feel, alongside of the thing known, the thought of it going on as an altogether separate act and operation in the mind.

Now this subjective life of ours, distinguished as such so clearly from the objects known by its means, may, as aforesaid, be taken by us in a concrete or in an abstract way. Of the concrete way I will say nothing just now, except that the actual 'section' of the stream will ere long, in our discussion of the nature of the principle of unity in consciousness, play a very important part. The abstract way claims our attention first. If the stream as a whole is identified with the Self far more than any outward thing, a certain portion of the stream abstracted from the rest is so identified in an altogether peculiar degree, and is felt by all men as a sort of innermost centre within the circle, of sanctuary within the citadel, constituted by the subjective life as a whole. Compared with this element of the stream, the other parts, even of the subjective life, seem transient external possessions, of which each in turn can be disowned, whilst that which disowns them remains. Now, what is this self of all the other selves?

Probably all men would describe it in much the same way up to a certain point. They would call it the active element in all consciousness; saying that whatever qualities a man's feelings may possess, or whatever content his thought may include, there is a spiritual something in him which seems to go out to meet these qualities and contents, whilst they seem to come in to be received by it. It is what welcomes or rejects. It presides over the perception of sensations, and by giving or withholding its assent it influences the movements they tend to arouse. It is the home of interest, - not the pleasant or the painful, not even pleasure or pain, as such, but that within us to which pleasure and pain, the pleasant and the painful, speak. It is the source of effort and attention, and the place from which appear to emanate the fiats of the will. A physiologist who should reflect upon it in his own person could hardly help, I should think, connecting it more or less vaguely with the process by which ideas or incoming sensations are 'reflected' or pass over into outward acts. Not necessarily that it should be this process or the mere feeling of this process, but that it should be in some close way related to this process; for it plays a part analogous to it in the psychic life, being a sort of junction at which sensory ideas terminate and from which motor ideas proceed, and forming a kind of link between the two. Being more incessantly there than any other single element of the mental life, the other elements end by seeming to accrete round it and to belong to it. It becomes opposed to them as the permanent is opposed to the changing and inconstant.

One may, I think, without fear of being upset by any future Galtonian circulars, believe that all men must single out from the rest of what they call themselves some central principle of which each would recognize the foregoing to be a fair general description, - accurate enough, at any rate, to denote what is meant, and keep it unconfused with other things. The moment, however, they came to closer quarters with it, trying to define more accurately its precise nature, we should find opinions beginning to diverge. Some would say that it is a simple active substance, the soul, of which they are thus conscious; others, that it is nothing but a fiction, the imaginary being denoted by the pronoun I; and between these extremes of opinion all sorts of intermediaries would be found.

Later we must ourselves discuss them all, and sufficient to that day will be the evil thereof. Now, let us try to settle for ourselves as definitely as we can, just how this central nucleus of the Self may feel, no matter whether it be a spiritual substance or only a delusive word.

For this central part of the Self is felt. It may be all that Transcendentalists say it is, and all that Empiricists say it is into the bargain, but it is at any rate no mere ens rationis, cognized only in an intellectual way, and no mere summation of memories or mere sound of a word in our ears. It is something with which we also have direct sensible acquaintance, and which is as fully present at any moment of consciousness in which it is present, as in a whole lifetime of such moments. When, just now, it was called an abstraction, that did not mean that, like some general notion, it could not be presented in a particular experience. It only meant that in the stream of consciousness it never was found all alone. But when it is found, it is felt; just as the body is felt, the feeling of which is also an abstraction, because never is the body felt all alone, but always together with other things. Now can we tell more precisely in what the feeling of this central active self consists, - not necessarily as yet what the active self is, as a being or principle, but what we feel when we become aware of its existence?

I think I can in my own case; and as what I say will be likely to meet with opposition if generalized (as indeed it may be in part inapplicable to other individuals), I had better continue in the first person, leaving my description to be accepted by those to whose introspection it may commend itself as true, and confessing my inability to meet the demands of others, if others there be.

First of all, I am aware of a constant play of furtherances and hindrances in my thinking, of checks and releases, tendencies which run with desire, and tendencies which run the other way. Among the matters I think of, some range themselves on the side of the thought's interests, whilst others play an unfriendly part thereto. The mutual inconsistencies and agreements, reinforcements and obstructions, which obtain amongst these objective matters reverberate backwards and produce what seem to be incessant reactions of my spontaneity upon them, welcoming or opposing, appropriating or disowning, striving with or against, saying yes or no. This palpitating inward life is, in me, that central nucleus which I just tried to describe in terms that all men might use. But when I forsake such general descriptions and grapple with particulars, coming to the closest possible quarters with the facts, it is difficult for me to detect in the activity any purely spiritual element at all. Whenever my introspective glance succeeds in turning round quickly enough to catch one of these manifestations of spontaneity in the act, all it can ever feel distinctly is some bodily process, for the most part taking place within the head. Omitting for a moment what is obscure in these introspective results, let me try to state those particulars which to my own consciousness seem indubitable and distinct.

In the first place, the acts of attending, assenting, negating, making an effort, are felt as movements of something in the head. In many cases it is possible to describe these movements quite exactly. In attending to either an idea or a sensation belonging to a particular sense-sphere, the movement is the adjustment of the sense-organ, felt as it occurs. I cannot think in visual terms, for example, without feeling a fluctuating play of pressures, convergences, divergences, and accommodations in my eyeballs. The direction in which the object is conceived to lie determines the character of these movements, the feeling of which becomes, for my consciousness, identified with the manner in which I make myself ready to receive the visible thing. My brain appears to me as if all shot across with lines of direction, of which I have become conscious as my attention has shifted from one sense-organ to another, in passing to successive outer things, or in following trains of varying sense-ideas.

When I try to remember or reflect, the movements in question, instead of being directed towards the periphery, seem to come from the periphery inwards and feel like a sort of withdrawal from the outer world. As far as I can detect, these feelings are due to an actual rolling outwards and upwards of the eyeballs, such as I believe occurs in me in sleep, and is the exact opposite of their action in fixating a physical thing. In reasoning, I find that I am apt to have a kind of vaguely localized diagram in my mind, with the various fractional objects of the thought disposed at particular points thereof; and the oscillations of my attention from one of them to another are most distinctly felt as alternations of direction in movements occurring inside the head.[4]

In consenting and negating, and in making a mental effort, the movements seem more complex, and I find them harder to describe. The opening and closing of the glottis play a great part in these operations, and, less distinctly, the movements of the soft palate, etc., shutting off the posterior nares of the mouth. My glottis is like a sensitive valve, intercepting my breath instantaneously at every mental hesitation or felt aversion to the objects of my thought, and as quickly opening, to let the air pass through my throat and nose, the moment the repugnance is overcome. The feeling of the movement of this air is, in me, one strong ingredient of the feeling of assent. The movements of the muscles of the brow and eyelids also respond very sensitively to every fluctuation in the agreeableness or disagreeableness of what comes before my mind.

In effort of any sort, contractions of the jaw-muscles and of those of respiration are added to those of the brow and glottis, and thus the feeling passes out of the head properly so called. It passes out of the head whenever the welcoming or rejecting of the object is strongly felt. Then a set of feelings pour in from many bodily parts, all 'expressive' of my emotion, and the head-feelings proper are swallowed up in this larger mass.

In a sense, then, it may be truly said that, in one person at least, the 'Self of selves,' when carefully examined, is found to consist mainly of the collection of these peculiar motions in the head or between the head and throat. I do not for a moment say that this is all it consists of, for I fully realize how desperately hard is introspection in this field. But I feel quite sure that these cephalic motions are the portions of my innermost activity of which I am most distinctly aware. If the dim portions which I cannot yet define should prove to be like unto these distinct portions in me, and I like other men, it would follow that our entire feeling of spiritual activity, or what commonly passes by that name, is really a feeling of bodily activities whose exact nature is by most men overlooked.

Now, without pledging ourselves in any way to adopt this hypothesis, let us dally with it for a while to see to what consequences it might lead if it were true.

In the first place, the nuclear part of the Self, intermediary between ideas and overt acts, would be a collection of activities physiologically in no essential way different from the overt acts themselves. If we divide all possible physiological acts into adjustments and executions, the nuclear self would be the adjustments collectively considered; and the less intimate, more shifting self, so far as it was active, would be the executions. But both adjustments and executions would obey the reflex type. Both would be the result of sensorial and ideational processes discharging either into each other within the brain, or into muscles and other parts outside. The peculiarity of the adjustments would be that they are minimal reflexes, few in number, incessantly repeated, constant amid great fluctuations in the rest of the mind's content, and entirely unimportant and uninteresting except through their uses in furthering or inhibiting the presence of various things, and actions before consciousness. These characters would naturally keep us from introspectively paying much attention to them in detail, whilst they would at the same time make us aware of them as a coherent group of processes, strongly contrasted with all the other things consciousness contained, - even with the other constituents of the 'Self,' material, social, or spiritual, as the case might be. They are reactions, and they are primary reactions. Everything arouses them; for objects which have no other effects will for a moment contract the brow and make the glottis close. It is as if all that visited the mind had to stand an entrance-examination, and just show its face so as to be either approved or sent back. These primary reactions are like the opening or the closing of the door. In the midst of psychic change they are the permanent core of turnings-towards and trunings-from, of yieldings and arrests, which naturally seem central and interior in comparison with the foreign matters, apropos to which they occur, and hold a sort of arbitrating, decisive position, quite unlike that held by any of the other constituents of the Me. It would not be surprising, then, if we were to feel them as the birthplace of conclusions and the starting point of acts, or if they came to appear as what we called a while back the 'sanctuary within the citadel' of our personal life.[5]

If they really were the innermost sanctuary, the ultimate one of all the selves whose being we can ever directly experience, it would follow that all that is experienced is, strictly considered, objective; that this Objective falls asunder into two contrasted parts, one realized as 'Self,' the other as 'not-Self;' and that over and above these parts there is nothing save the fact that they are known, the fact of the stream of thought being there as the indispensable subjective condition of their being experienced at all. But this condition of the experience is not one of the things experienced at the moment; this knowing is not immediately known. It is only known in subsequent reflection. Instead, then, of the stream of thought being one of con-sciousness, "thinking its own existence along with whatever else it thinks," (as Ferrier says) it might be better called a stream of Sciousness pure and simple, thinking objects of some of which it makes what it calls a 'Me,' and only aware of its 'pure' Self in an abstract, hypothetic or conceptual way. Each 'section' of the stream would then be a bit of sciousness or knowledge of this sort, including and contemplating its 'me' and its 'not-me' as objects which work out their drama together, but not yet including or contemplating its own subjective being. The sciousness in question would be the Thinker, and the existence of this thinker would be given to us rather as a logical postulate than as that direct inner perception of spiritual activity which we naturally believe ourselves to have. 'Matter,' as something behind physical phenomena, is a postulate of this sort. Between the postulated Matter and the postulated Thinker, the sheet of phenomena would then swing, some of them (the 'realities') pertaining more to the matter, others (the fictions, opinions, and errors) pertaining more to the Thinker. But who the Thinker would be, or how many distinct Thinkers we ought to suppose in the universe, would all be subjects for an ulterior metaphysical inquiry.

Speculations like this traverse common-sense; and not only do they traverse common sense (which in philosophy is no insuperable objection) but they contradict the fundamental assumption of every philosophic school. Spiritualists, transcendentalists, and empiricists alike admit in us a continual direct perception of the thinking activity in the concrete. However they may otherwise disagree, they vie with each other in the cordiality of their recognition of our thoughts as the one sort of existent which skepticism cannot touch.[6] I will therefore treat the last few pages as a parenthetical digression, and from now to the end of the volume revert to the path of common-sense again. I mean by this that I will continue to assume (as I have assumed all along, especially in the last chapter) a direct awareness of the process of our thinking as such, simply insisting on the fact that it is an even more inward and subtle phenomenon than most of us suppose. At the conclusion of the volume, however, I may permit myself to revert again to the doubts here provisionally mooted, and will indulge in some metaphysical reflections suggested by them.

At present, then, the only conclusion I come to is the following: That (in some persons at least) the part of the innermost Self which is most vividly felt turns out to consist for the most part of a collection of cephalic movements of 'adjustments' which, for want of attention and reflection, usually fail to be perceived and classed as what they are; that over and above these there is an obscurer feeling of something more; but whether it be of fainter physiological processes, or of nothing objective at all, but rather of subjectivity as such, of thought become 'its own object,' must at present remain an open question, - like the question whether it be an indivisible active soul-substance, or the question whether it be a personification of the pronoun I, or any other of the guesses as to what its nature may be. Farther than this we cannot as yet go clearly in our analysis of the Self's constituents. So let us proceed to the emotions of Self which they arouse.

2. Self-Feeling.

These are primarily self-complacency and self-dissatisfaction. Of what is called 'self-love,' I will treat a little farther on. Language has synonyms enough for both primary feelings. Thus pride, conceit, vanity, self-esteem, arrogance, vainglory, on the one hand; and on the other modesty, humility, confusion, diffidence, shame, mortification, contrition, the sense of obloquy and personal despair. These two opposite classes of affection seem to be direct and elementary endowments of our nature. Associationists would have it that they are, on the other hand, secondary phenomena arising from a rapid computation of the sensible pleasures or pains to which our prosperous or debased personal predicament is likely to lead, the sum of the represented pleasures forming the self-satisfaction, and the sum of the represented pains forming the opposite feeling of shame. No doubt, when we are self-satisfied, we do fondly rehearse all possible rewards for our desert, and when in a fit of self-despair we forebode evil. But the mere expectation of reward is not the self-satisfaction, and the mere apprehension of the evil is not the self-despair, for there is a certain average tone of self-feeling which each one of us carries about with him, and which is independent of the objective reasons we may have for satisfaction or discontent. That is, a very meanly-conditioned man may abound in unfaltering conceit, and one whose success in life is secure and who is esteemed by all may remain diffident of his powers to the end.

One may say, however, that the normal provocative of self-feeling is one's actual success or failure, and the good or bad actual position one holds in the world. "He put in his thumb and pulled out a plum, and said what a good boy am I." A man with a broadly extended empirical Ego, with powers that have uniformly brought him success, with place and wealth and friends and fame, is not likely to be visited by the morbid diffidences and doubts about himself which he had when he was a boy. "Is not this great Babylon, which I have planted?"[7] Whereas he who has made one blunder after another, and still lies in middle life among the failures at the foot of the hill, is liable to grow all sicklied o'er with self-distrust, and to shrink from trials with which his powers can really cope.

The emotions themselves of self-satisfaction and abasement are of a unique sort, each as worthy to be classed as a primitive emotional species as are, for example, rage or pain. Each has its own peculiar physiognomical expression. In self-satisfaction the extensor muscles are innervated, the eye is strong and glorious, the gait rolling and elastic, the nostril dilated, and a peculiar smile plays upon the lips. This whole complex of symptoms is seen in an exquisite way in lunatic asylums, which always contain some patients who are literally mad with conceit, and whose fatuous expression and absurdly strutting or swaggering gait is in tragic contrast with their lack of any valuable personal quality. It is in these same castles of despair that we find the strongest examples of the opposite physiognomy, in good people who think they have committed 'the unpardonable sin' and are lost forever, who crouch and cringe and slink from notice and are unable to speak aloud or look us in the eye. Like fear and like anger, in similar morbid conditions, these opposite feelings of Self may be aroused with no adequate exciting cause. And in fact we ourselves know how the barometer of our self-esteem and confidence rises and falls from one day to another through causes that seem to be visceral and organic rather than rational, and which certainly answer to no corresponding variations in the esteem in which we are held by our friends. Of the origin of these emotions in the race, we can speak better when we have treated of -

3. Self-Seeking and Self-Preservation.

These words cover a large number of our fundamental instinctive impulses. We have those of bodily self-seeking, those of social self-seeking, and those of spiritual self-seeking.

All the ordinary useful reflex actions and movements of alimentation and defence are acts of bodily self-preservation. Fear and anger prompt to acts that are useful in the same way. Whilst if by self-seeking we mean the providing for the future as distinguished from maintaining the present, we must class both anger and fear with the hunting, the acquisitive, the home-constructing and the tool-constructing instincts, as impulses to self-seeking of the bodily kind. Really, however, these latter instincts, with amativeness, parental fondness, curiosity and emulation, seek not only the development of the bodily Self, but that of the material Self in the widest possible sense of the word.

Our social self-seeking, in turn, is carried on directly through our amativeness and friendliness, our desire to please and attract notice and admiration, our emulation and jealousy, our love of glory, influence, and power, and indirectly through whichever of the material self-seeking impulses prove serviceable as means to social ends. That the direct social self-seeking impulses are probably pure instincts is easily seen. The noteworthy thing about the desire to be 'recognized' by others is that its strength has so little to do with the worth of the recognition computed in sensational or rational terms. We are crazy to get a visiting-list which shall be large, to be able to say when any one is mentioned, "Oh! I know him well," and to be bowed to in the street by half the people we meet. Of course distinguished friends and admiring recognition are the most desirable - Thackeray somewhere asks his readers to confess whether it would not give each of them an exquisite pleasure to be met walking down Pall Mall with a duke on either arm. But in default of dukes and envious salutations almost anything will do for some of us; and there is a whole race of beings to-day whose passion is to keep their names in the newspapers, no matter under what heading, 'arrivals and departures,' 'personal paragraphs,' 'interviews,' - gossip, even scandal, will suit them if nothing better is to be had. Guiteau, Garfield's assassin, is an example of the extremity to which this sort of craving for the notoriety of print may go in a pathological case. The newspapers bounded his mental horizon; and in the poor wretch's prayer on the scaffold, one of the most heartfelt expressions was: "The newspaper press of this land has a big bill to settle with thee, O Lord!"

Not only the people but the places and things I know enlarge my Self in a sort of metaphoric social way. 'Çame connaît,' as the French workman says of the implement he can use well. So that is comes about that persons for whose opinion we care nothing are nevertheless persons whose notice we woo; and that many a man truly great, many a woman truly fastidious in most respects, will take a deal of trouble to dazzle some insignificant cad whose whole personality they heartily despise.

Under the head of spiritual self-seeking ought to be included every impulse towards psychic progress, whether intellectual, moral, or spiritual in the narrow sense of the term. It must be admitted, however, that much that commonly passes for spiritual self-seeking in this narrow sense is only material and social self-seeking beyond the grave. In the Mohammedan desire for paradise and the Christian aspiration not to be damned in hell, the materiality of the goods sought is undisguised. In the more positive and refined view of heaven many of its goods, the fellowship of the saints and of our dead ones, and the presence of God, are but social goods of the most exalted kind. It is only the search of the redeemed inward nature, the spotlessness from sin, whether here or hereafter, that can count as spiritual self-seeking pure and undefiled.

But this broad external review of the facts of the life of the Self will be incomplete without some account of the

Rivalry and Conflict of the Different Selves.

With most objects of desire, physical nature restricts our choice to but one of many represented goods, and even so it is here. I am often confronted by the necessity of standing by one of my empirical selves and relinquishing the rest. Not that I would not, if I could, be both handsome and fat and well dressed, and a great athlete, and make a million a year, be a wit, a bon-vivant, and a lady-killer, as well as a philosopher; a philanthropist, statesman, warrior, and African explorer, as well as a 'tone-poet' and saint. But the thing is simply impossible. The millionaire's work would run counter to the saint's; the bon-vivant and the philanthropist would trip each other up; the philosopher and the lady-killer could not well keep house in the same tenement of clay. Such different characters may conceivably at the outset of life be alike possible to a man. But to make any one of them actual, the rest must more or less be suppressed. So the seeker of his truest, strongest, deepest self must review the list carefully, and pick out the one on which to stake his salvation. All other selves thereupon become unreal, but the fortunes of this self are real. Its failures are real failures, its triumphs real triumphs, carrying shame and gladness with them. This is as strong an example as there is of that selective industry of the mind on which I insisted some pages back. Our thought, incessantly deciding, among many things of a kind, which ones for it shall be realities, here chooses one of many possible selves or characters, and forthwith reckons it no shame to fail in any of those not adopted expressly as its own.

I, who for the time have staked my all on being a psychologist, am mortified if others know much more psychology than I. But I am contented to wallow in the grossest ignorance of Greek. My deficiencies there give me no sense of personal humiliation at all. Had I 'pretensions' to be a linguist, it would have been just the reverse. So we have the paradox of a man shamed to death because he is only the second pugilist or the second oarsman in the world. That he is able to beat the whole population of the globe minus one is nothing; he has 'pitted' himself to beat that one; and as long as he doesn't do that nothing else counts. He is to his own regard as if he were not, indeed he is not. Yonder puny fellow, however, whom every one can beat, suffers no chagrin about it, for he has long ago abandoned the attempt to 'carry that line,' as the merchants say, of self at all. With no attempt there can be no failure; with no failure no humiliation. So our self-feeling in this world depends entirely on what we back ourselves to be and do. It is determined by the ratio of our actualities to our supposed potentialities; a fraction of which our pretensions are the denominator and the numerator our success: thus, Self-esteem = Success / Pretensions. Such a fraction may be increased as well by diminishing the denominator as by increasing the numerator.[8] To give up pretensions is as blessed a relief as to get them gratified; and where disappointment is incessant and the struggle unending, this is what men will always do. The history of evangelical theology, with its conviction of sin, its self-despair, and its abandonment of salvation by works, is the deepest of possible examples, but we meet others in every walk of life. There is the strangest lightness about the heart when one's nothingness in a particular line is once accepted in good faith. All is not bitterness in the lot of the lover sent away by the final inexorable 'No.' Many Bostonians, crede experto (and inhabitants of other cities, too, I fear), would be happier women and men to-day, if they could once for all abandon the notion of keeping up a Musical Self, and without shame let people hear them call a symphony a nuisance. How pleasant is the day when we give up striving to be young, - or slender! Thank God! we say, those illusions are gone. Everything added to the Self is a burden as well as a pride. A certain man who lost every penny during our civil war went and actually rolled in the dust, saying he had not felt so free and happy since he was born.

Once more, then, our self-feeling is in our power. As Carlyle says: "Make thy claim of wages a zero, then hast thou the world under thy feet. Well did the wisest of our time write, it is only with renunciation that life, properly speaking, can be said to begin."

Neither threats nor pleadings can move a man unless they touch some one of his potential or actual selves. Only thus can we, as a rule, get a 'purchase' on another's will. The first care of diplomatists and monarchs and all who wish to rule or influence is, accordingly, to find out their victim's strongest principle of self-regard, so as to make that the fulcrum of all appeals. But if a man has given up those things which are subject to foreign fate, and ceased to regard them as parts of himself at all, we are well-nigh powerless over him. The Stoic receipt for contentment was to dispossess yourself in advance of all that was out of your own power, - then fortune's shocks might rain down unfelt. Epictetus exhorts us, by thus narrowing and at the same time solidifying our Self to make it invulnerable: "I must die; well, but must I die groaning too? I will speak what appears to be right, and if the despot says, then I will put you to death, I will reply, 'When did I ever tell you that I was immortal? You will do your part and I mine; it is yours to kill and mine to die intrepid; yours to banish, mine to depart untroubled.' How do we act in a voyage? We choose the pilot, the sailors, the hour. Afterwards comes a storm. What have I to care for? My part is performed. This matter belongs to the pilot. But the ship is sinking; what then have I to do? That which alone I can do - submit to being drowned without fear, without clamor or accusing of God, but as one who knows that what is born must likewise die."[9]

This Stoic fashion, though efficacious and heroic enough in its place and time, is, it must be confessed, only possible as an habitual mood of the soul to narrow and unsympathetic characters. It proceeds altogether by exclusion. If I am a Stoic, the goods I cannot appropriate cease to be my goods, and the temptation lies very near to deny that they are goods at all. We find this mode of protecting the Self by exclusion and denial very common among people who are in other respects not Stoics. All narrow people intrench their Me, they retract it, - from the region of what they cannot securely possess. People who don't resemble them, or who treat them with indifference, people over whom they gain no influence, are people on whose existence, however meritorious it may intrinsically be, they look with chill negation, if not with positive hate. Who will not be mine I will exclude from existence altogether; that is, as far as I can make it so, such people shall be as if they were not.[10] Thus may a certain absoluteness and definiteness in the outline of my Me console me for the smallness of its content.

Sympathetic people, on the contrary, proceed by the entirely opposite way of expansion and inclusion. The outline of their self often gets uncertain enough, but for this the spread of its content more than atones. Nil humani a me alienum. Let them despise this little person of mine, and treat me like a dog, I shall not negate them so long as I have a soul in my body. They are realities as much as I am. What positive good is in them shall be mine too, etc., etc. The magnanimity of these expansive natures is often touching indeed. Such persons can feel a sort of delicate rapture in thinking that, however sick, ill-favored, mean-conditioned, and generally forsaken they may be, they yet are integral parts of the whole of this brave world, have a fellow's share in the strength of the dray-horses, the happiness of the young people, the wisdom of the wise ones, and are not altogether without part or lot in the good fortunes of the Vanderbilts and the Hohenzollerns themselves. Thus either by negating or by embracing, the Ego may seek to establish itself in reality. He who, with Marcus Aurelius, can truly say, "O Universe, I wish all that thou wishest," has a self from which every trace of negativeness and obstructiveness has been removed - no wind can blow except to fill its sails.

A tolerably unanimous opinion ranges the different selves of which a man may be 'seized and possessed,' and the consequent different orders of his self-regard, in an hierarchical scale, with the bodily Self at the bottom, the spiritual Self at the top, and the extracorporeal material selves and the various social selves between. Our merely natural self-seeking would lead us to aggrandize all these selves; we give up deliberately only those among them which we find we cannot keep. Our unselfishness is thus apt to be a 'virtue of necessity'; and it is not without all show of reason that cynics quote the fable of the fox and the grapes in describing our progress therein. But this is the moral education of the race; and if we agree in the result that on the whole the selves we can keep are the intrinsically best, we need not complain of being led to the knowledge of their superior worth in such a tortuous way.

Of course this is not the only way in which we learn to subordinate our lower selves to our higher. A direct ethical judgment unquestionably also plays its part, and last, not least, we apply to our own persons judgments originally called forth by the acts of others. It is one of the strangest laws of our nature that many things which we are well satisfied with in ourselves disgust us when seen in others. With another man's bodily 'hoggishness' hardly anyone has any sympathy; - almost as little with his cupidity, his social vanity and eagerness, his jealousy, his despotism, and his pride. Left absolutely to myself I should probably allow all these spontaneous tendencies to luxuriate in me unchecked, and it would be long before I formed a distinct notion of the order of their subordination. But having constantly to pass judgment on my associates, I come ere long to see, as Herr Horwicz says, my own lusts in the mirror of the lusts of others, and to think about them in a very different way from that in which I simply feel. Of course, the moral generalities which from childhood have been instilled into me accelerate enormously the advent of this reflective judgment on myself.

So it comes to pass that, as aforesaid, men have arranged the various selves which they may seek in an hierarchical scale according to their worth. A certain amount of bodily selfishness is required as a basis for all the other selves. But too much sensuality is despised, or at best condoned on account of the other qualities of the individual. The wider material selves are regarded as higher than the immediate body. He is esteemed a poor creature who is unable to forego a little meat and drink and warmth and sleep for the sake of getting on in the world. The social self as a whole, again, ranks higher than the material self

as a whole. We must care more for our honor, our friends, our human ties, than for a sound skin or wealth. And the spiritual self is so supremely precious that, rather than lose it, a man ought to be willing to give up friends and good fame, and property, and life itself.

In each kind of self, material, social, and spiritual, men distinguish between the immediate and actual, and the remote and potential, between the narrower and the wider view, to the detriment of the former and advantage of the latter. One must forego a present bodily enjoyment for the sake of one's general health; one must abandon the dollar in the hand for the sake of the hundred dollars to come; one must make an enemy of his present interlocutor if thereby one makes friends of a more valued circle; one must go without learning and grace, and wit, the better to compass one's soul's salvation.

Of all these wider, more potential selves, the potential social self is the most interesting, by reason of certain apparent paradoxes to which it leads in conduct, and by reason of its connection with our moral and religious life. When for motives of honor and conscience I brave the condemnation of my own family, club, and 'set'; when, as a protestant, I turn catholic; as a catholic, freethinker; as a 'regular practitioner,' homoeopath, or what not, I am always inwardly strengthened in my course and steeled against the loss of my actual social self by the thought of other and better possible social judges than those whose verdict goes against me now. The ideal social self which I thus seek in appealing to their decision may be very remote: it may be represented as barely possible. I may not hope for its realization during my lifetime; I may even expect the future generations, which would approve me if they knew me, to know nothing about me when I am dead and gone. Yet still the emotion that beckons me on is indubitably the pursuit of an ideal social self, of a self that is at least worthy of approving recognition by the highest possible judging companion, if such companion there be.[11] This self is the true, the intimate, the ultimate, the permanent Me which I seek. This judge is God, the Absolute Mind, the 'Great Companion.' We hear, in these days of scientific enlightenment, a great deal of discussion about the efficacy of prayer; and many reasons are given us why we should not pray, whilst others are given us why we should. But in all this very little is said of the reason why we do pray, which is simply that we cannot help praying. It seems probable that, in spite of all that 'science' may do to the contrary, men will continue to pray to the end of time, unless their mental nature changes in a manner which nothing we know should lead us to expect. The impulse to pray is a necessary consequence of the fact that whilst the innermost of the empirical selves of a man is a Self of the social sort, it yet can find its only adequate Socius in an ideal world.

All progress in the social Self is the substitution of higher tribunals for lower; this ideal tribunal is the highest; and most men, either continually or occasionally, carry a reference to it in their breast. The humblest outcast on this earth can feel himself to be real and valid by means of this higher recognition. And, on the other hand, for most of us, a world with no such inner refuge when the outer social self failed and dropped from us would be the abyss of horror. I say 'for most of us,' because it is probable that individuals differ a good deal in the degree in which they are haunted by this sense of an ideal spectator. It is a much more essential part of the consciousness of some men that of others. Those who have the most of it are possibly the most religious men. But I am sure that even those who say they are altogether without it deceive themselves, and really have it in some degree. Only a non-gregarious animal could be completely without it. Probably no one can make sacrifices for 'right,' without to some degree personifying the principle of right for which the sacrifice is made, and expecting thanks from it. Complete social unselfishness, in other words, can hardly exist; complete social suicide hardly occur to a man's mind. Even such texts as Job's, "Though He slay me yet will I trust Him," or Marcus Aurelius's, "If gods hate me and my children, there is a reason for it," can least of all be cited to prove the contrary. For beyond all doubt Job revelled in the thought of Jehovah's recognition of the worship after the slaying should have been done; and the Roman emperor felt sure the Absolute Reason would not be all indifferent to his acquiescence in the gods' dislike. The old test of piety, "Are you willing to be damned for the glory of God?" was probably never answered in the affirmative except by those who felt sure in their heart of hearts that God would 'credit' them with their willingness, and set more store by them thus than if in His unfathomable scheme He had not damned them at all.

All this about the impossibility of suicide is said on the supposition of positive motives. When possessed by the emotion of fear, however, we are in a negative state of mind; that is, our desire is limited to the mere banishing of something, without regard to what shall take its place. In this state of mind there can unquestionably be genuine thoughts, and genuine acts, of suicide, spiritual and social, as well as bodily. Anything, anything, at such times, so as to escape and not to be! But such conditions of suicidal frenzy are pathological in their nature and run dead against everything that is regular in the life of the Self in man.

What Self is Loved in 'Self-Love'?

We must now try to interpret the facts of self-love and self-seeking a little more delicately from within.
A man in whom self-seeking of any sort is largely developed is said to be selfish.[12] He is on the other hand called unselfish if he shows consideration for the interest of other selves than his own. Now what is the intimate nature of the selfish emotion in him? and what is the primary object of its regard? We have described him pursuing and fostering as his self first one set of things and then another: we have seen the same set of facts gain or lose interest in his eyes, leave him indifferent, or fill him either with triumph or despair according as he made pretensions to appropriate them, treated them as if they were potentially or actually parts of himself, or not. We know how little it matters to us whether some man, a man taken at large and in the abstract, prove a failure or succeed in life, - he may be hanged for aught we care, - but we know the utter momentousness and terribleness of the alternative when the man is the one whose name we ourselves bear. I must not be a failure, is the very loudest of the voices that clamor in each of our breasts: let fail who may, I at least must succeed. Now the first conclusion which these facts suggest is that each of us is animated by a direct feeling of regard for his own pure principle of individual existence, whatever that may be, taken merely as such. It appears as if all our concrete manifestations of selfishness might be the conclusions of as many syllogisms, each with this principle as the subject of its major premiss, thus: Whatever is me is precious; this is me; therefore this is precious; whatever is mine must not fail; this is mine; therefore this must not fail, etc. It appears, I say, as if this principle inoculated all it touched with its own intimate quality of worth; as if, previous to the touching, everything might be matter of indifference, and nothing interesting in its own right; as if my regard for my own body even were an interest not simply in this body, but in this body only so far as it is mine. But what is this abstract numerical principle of identity, this 'Number One' within me, for which, according to proverbial philosophy, I am supposed to keep so constant a 'lookout'? Is it the inner nucleus of my spiritual self, that collection of obscurely felt 'adjustments,' plus perhaps that still more obscurely perceived subjectivity as such, of which we recently spoke? Or is it perhaps the concrete stream of my thought in its entirety, or some one section of the same? Or may it be the indivisible Soul-Substance, in which, according to the orthodox tradition, my faculties inhere? Or, finally, can it be the mere pronoun I? Surely it is none of these things, that self for which I feel such hot regard. Though all of them together were put within me, I should still be cold, and fail to exhibit anything worthy of the name of selfishness or of devotion to 'Number One.' To have a self that I can care for, nature must first present me with some object interesting enough to make me instinctively wish to appropriate it for its own sake, and out of it to manufacture one of those material, social, or spiritual selves, which we have already passed in review. We shall find that all the facts of rivalry and substitution that have so struck us, all the shiftings and expansions and contractions of the sphere of what shall be considered me and mine, are but results of the fact that certain things appeal to primitive and instinctive impulses of our nature, and that we follow their destinies with an excitement that owes nothing to a reflective source. These objects our consciousness treats as the primordial constituents of its Me. Whatever other objects, whether by association with the fate of these, or in any other way, come to be followed with the same sort of interest, form our remoter and more secondary self. The words ME, then, and SELF, so far as they arouse feeling and connote emotional worth, are OBJECTIVE designations, meaning ALL THE THINGS which have the power to produce in a stream of consciousness excitement of a certain peculiar sort. Let us try to justify this proposition in detail.
The most palpable selfishness of a man is his bodily selfishness; and his most palpable self is the body to which that selfishness relates. Now I say that he identifies himself with this body because he loves it, and that he does not love it because he finds it to be identified with himself. Reverting to natural history-psychology will help us to see the truth of this. In the chapter on Instincts we shall learn that every creature has a certain selective interest in certain portions of the world, and that this interest is as often connate as acquired. Our interest in things means the attention and emotion which the thought of them will excite, and the actions which their presence will evoke. Thus every species is particularly interested in its own prey or food, its own enemies, its own sexual mates, and its own young. These things fascinate by their intrinsic power to do so; they are cared for for their own sakes.
Well, it stands not in the least otherwise with our bodies. They too are percepts in our objective field - they are simply the most interesting percepts there. What happens to them excites in us emotions and tendencies to action more energetic and habitual than any which are excited by other portions of the 'field.' What my comrades call my bodily selfishness or self-love, is nothing but the sum of all the outer acts which this interest in my body spontaneously draws from me. My 'selfishness' is here but a descriptive name for grouping together the outward symptoms which I show. When I am led by self-love to keep my seat whilst ladies stand, or to grab something first

and cut out my neighbor, what I really love is the comfortable seat, is the thing itself which I grab. I love them primarily, as the mother loves her babe, or a generous man an heroic deed. Wherever, as here, self-seeking is the outcome of simple instinctive propensity, it is but a name for certain reflex acts. Something rivets my attention fatally, and fatally provokes the 'selfish' response. Could an automaton be so skilfully constructed as to ape these acts, it would be called selfish as properly as I. It is true that I am no automaton, but a thinker. But my thoughts, like my acts, are here concerned only with the outward things. They need neither know nor care for any pure principle within. In fact the more utterly 'selfish' I am in this primitive way, the more blindly absorbed my thought will be in the objects and impulses of my lusts, and the more devoid of any inward looking glance. A baby, whose consciousness of the pure Ego, of himself as a thinker, is not usually supposed developed, is, in this way, as some German has said, 'der vollendeteste Egoist.' His corporeal person, and what ministers to its needs, are the only self he can possibly be said to love. His so-called self-love is but a name for his insensibility to all but this one set of things. It may be that he needs a pure principle of subjectivity, a soul or pure Ego (he certainly needs a stream of thought) to make him sensible at all to anything, to make him discriminate and love uberhaupt, - how that may be, we shall see ere long; but this pure Ego, which would then be the condition of his loving, need no more be the object of his love than it need be the object of his thought. If his interests were altruistic and all his acts suicidal, still he would need a principle of consciousness just as he does now. Such a principle cannot then be the principle of his bodily selfishness any more than it is the principle of any other tendency he may show.

So much for the bodily self-love. But my social self-love, my interest in the images other men have framed of me, is also an interest in a set of objects external to my thought. These thoughts in other men's minds are out of my mind and 'ejective' to me. They come and go, and grow and dwindle, and I am puffed up with pride, or blush with shame, at the result, just as at my success or failure in the pursuit of a material thing. So that here again, just as in the former case, the pure principle seems out of the game as an object of regard, and present only as the general form or condition under which the regard and the thinking go on in me at all.

But, it will immediately be objected, this is giving a mutilated account of the facts. Those images of me in the minds of other men are, it is true, things outside of me, whose changes I perceive just as I perceive any other outward change. But the pride and shame which I feel are not concerned merely with those changes. I feel as if something else had changed too, when I perceived my image in your mind to have changed for the worse, something in me to which that image belongs, and which a moment ago I felt inside of me, big and strong and lusty, but now weak, contracted, and collapsed. Is not this latter change the change I feel the shame about? Is not the condition of this thing inside of me the proper object of my egoistic concern, of my self-regard? And is it not, after all, my pure Ego, my bare numerical principle of distinction from other men, and no empirical part of me at all?

No, it is no such pure principle, it is simply my total empirical selfhood again, my historic Me, a collection of objective facts, to which the depreciated image in your mind 'belongs.' In what capacity is it that I claim and demand a respectful greeting from you instead of this expression of disdain? It is not as being a bare I that I claim it; it is as being an I who has always been treated with respect, who belongs to a certain family and 'set,' who has certain powers, possessions, and public functions, sensibilities, duties, and purposes, and merits and deserts. All this is what your disdain negates and contradicts; this is 'the thing inside of me' whose changed treatment I feel the shame about; this is what was lusty, and now, in consequence of your conduct, is collapsed; and this certainly is an empirical objective thing. Indeed, the thing that is felt modified and changed for the worse during my feeling of shame is often more concrete even than this, - it is simply my bodily person, in which your conduct immediately and without any reflection at all on my part works those muscular, glandular, and vascular changes which together make up the 'expression' of shame. In this instinctive, reflex sort of shame, the body is just as much the entire vehicle of the self-feeling as, in the coarser cases which we first took up, it was the vehicle of the self-seeking. As, in simple 'hoggishness,' a succulent morsel gives rise, by the reflex mechanism, to behavior which the bystanders find 'greedy,' and consider to flow from a certain sort of 'self-regard;' so here your disdain gives rise, by a mechanism quite as reflex and immediate, to another sort of behavior, which the bystanders call 'shame-faced' and which they consider due to another kind of self-regard. But in both cases there may be no particular self regarded at all by the mind; and the name self-regard may be only a descriptive title imposed from without the reflex acts themselves, and the feelings that immediately result from their discharge.

After the bodily and social selves come the spiritual. But which of my spiritual selves do I really care for? My Soul-substance? my 'transcendental Ego, or Thinker'? my pronoun I? my subjectivity as such? my nucleus of cephalic adjustments? or my more phenomenal and perishable powers, my loves and hates, willingnesses and sensibilities, and the like? Surely the latter. But they, relatively to the central principle, whatever it may be, are external and objective. They come and go, and it remains - "so shakes the magnet, and so stands the pole." It may indeed have to be there for them to be loved, but being there is not identical with being loved itself.

To sum up, then, we see no reason to suppose that self-love' is primarily, or secondarily, or ever, love for one's mere principle of conscious identity. It is always love for something which, as compared with that principle, is superficial, transient, liable to be taken up or dropped at will.

And zoological psychology again comes to the aid of our understanding and shows us that this must needs be so. In fact, in answering the question what things it is that a man loves in his self-love, we have implicitly answered the farther question, of why he loves them.

Unless his consciousness were something more than cognitive, unless it experienced a partiality for certain of the objects, which, in succession, occupy its ken, it could not long maintain itself in existence; for, by an inscrutable necessity, each human mind's appearance on this earth is conditioned upon the integrity of the body with which it belongs, upon the treatment which that body gets from others, and upon the spiritual dispositions which use it as their tool, and lead it either towards longevity or to destruction. Its own body, then, first of all, its friends next, and finally its spiritual dispositions, MUST be the supremely interesting OBJECTS for each human mind. Each mind, to begin with, must have a certain minimum of selfishness in the shape of instincts of bodily self-seeking in order to exist. This minimum must be there as a basis for all farther conscious acts, whether of self-negation or of a selfishness more subtle still. All minds must have come, by the way of survival of the fittest, if by no director path, to take an intense interest in the bodies to which they are yoked, altogether apart from any interest in the pure Ego which they also possess.

And similarly with the images of their person in the minds of others. I should not be extant now had I not become sensitive to looks of approval or disapproval on the faces among which my life is cast. Looks of contempt cast on other persons need affect me in no such peculiar way. Were my mental life dependent exclusively on some other person's welfare, either directly or in an indirect way, then natural selection would unquestionably have brought it about that I should be as sensitive to the social vicissitudes of that other person as I now am to my own. Instead of being egoistic I should be spontaneously altruistic, then. But in this case, only partially realized in actual human conditions, though the self I empirically love would have changed, my pure Ego or Thinker would have to remain just what it is now.

My spiritual powers, again, must interest me more than those of other people, and for the same reason. I should not be here at all unless I had cultivated them and kept them from decay. And the same law which made me once care for them makes me care for them still.

My own body and what ministers to its needs are thus the primitive object, instinctively determined, of my egoistic interests. Other objects may become interesting derivatively through association with any of these things, either as means or as habitual concomitants; and so in a thousand ways the primitive sphere of the egoistic emotions may enlarge and change its boundaries.

This sort of interest is really the meaning of the word 'my.' Whatever has it is eo ipso a part of me. My child, my friend dies, and where he goes I feel that part of myself now is and evermore shall be:

"For this losing is true dying;
This is lordly man's down-lying;
This his slow but sure reclining,
Star by star his world resigning."

The fact remains, however, that certain special sorts of thing tend primordially to possess this interest, and form the natural me. But all these things are objects, properly so called, to the subject which does the thinking.[13] And this latter fact upsets at once the dictum of the old-fashioned sensationalist psychology, that altruistic passions and interests are contradictory to the nature of things, and that if they appear anywhere to exist, it must be as secondary products, resolvable at bottom into cases of selfishness, taught by experience a hypocritical disguise. If the zoological and evolutionary point of view is the true one, there is no reason why any object whatever might not arouse passion and interest as primitively and instinctively as any other, whether connected or not with the interests of the me. The phenomenon of passion is in origin and essence the same, whatever be the target upon which it is discharged; and what the target actually happens to be is solely a question of fact. I might conceivably be as much fascinated, and as primitively so, by the care of my neighbor's body as by the care of my own. The only check to such exuberant altruistic interests is natural selection, which would weed out such as were very harmful to the individual or to his tribe. Many such interests, however, remain unweeded out - the interest in the opposite sex, for example, which seems in mankind stronger than is called for by its utilitarian need; and alongside of them remain interests, like that in alcoholic intoxication, or in musical sounds, which, for aught we can see, are without any utility whatever. The sympathetic instincts and the egoistic ones are thus co-ordinate. They arise, so far as we can tell, on the same psychologic level. The only difference between them is, that the instincts called egoistic form much the larger mass.

The only author whom I know to have discussed the question whether the 'pure Ego,' per se, can be an object of regard, is Herr Horwicz, in his extremely able and acute Psychologische Analysen. He too says that all self-regard is regard for certain objective things. He disposes so well of one kind of objection that I must conclude by quoting a part of his own words:

First, the objection:

"The fact is indubitable that one's own children always pass for the prettiest and brightest, the wine from one's own cellar for the best - at least for its price, - one's own house and horses for the finest. With what tender admiration do we con over our own little deed of benevolence! our own frailties and misdemeanors, how ready we are to acquit ourselves for them, when we notice them at all, on the ground of 'extenuating circumstances'! How much more really comic are our own jokes than those of others, which, unlike ours, will not bear being repeated ten or twelve times over! How eloquent, striking, powerful, our own speeches are! How appropriate our own address! In short, how much more intelligent, soulful, better, is everything about us than in anyone else. The sad chapter of artists' and authors' conceit and vanity belongs here.

"The prevalence of this obvious preference which we feel for everything of our own is indeed striking. Does it not look as if our dear Ego must first lend its color and flavor to anything in order to make it please us? . . . Is it not the simplest explanation for all these phenomena, so consistent among themselves, to suppose that the Ego, the self, which forms the origin and centre of our thinking life, is at the same time the original and central object of our life of feeling, and the ground both of whatever special ideas and of whatever special feelings ensue?"

Herr Horwicz goes on to refer to what we have already noticed, that various things which disgust us in others do not disgust us at all in ourselves.

"To most of us even the bodily warmth of another, for example the chair warm from another's sitting, is felt unpleasantly, whereas there is nothing disagreeable in the warmth of the chair in which we have been sitting ourselves."

After some further remarks, he replies to these facts and reasonings as follows:

"We may with confidence affirm that our own possessions in most cases please us better [not because they are ours], but simply because we know them better, 'realize' them more intimately, feel them more deeply. We learn to appreciate what is ours in all its details and shadings, whilst the goods of others appear to us in coarse outlines and rude averages. Here are some examples: A piece of music which one plays one's self is heard and understood better than when it is played by another. We get more exactly all the details, penetrate more deeply into the musical thought. We may meanwhile perceive perfectly well that the other person is the better performer, and yet nevertheless - at times get more enjoyment from our own playing because it brings the melody and harmony so much nearer home to us. This case may almost be taken as typical for the other cases of self-love. On close examination, we shall almost always find that a great part of our feeling about what is ours is due to the fact that we live closer to our own things, and so feel them more thoroughly and deeply. As a friend of mine was about to marry, he often bored me by the repeated and minute way in which he would discuss the details of his new household arrangements. I wondered that so intellectual a man should be so deeply interested in things of so external a nature. But as I entered, a few years later, the same condition myself, these matters acquired for me an entirely different interest, and it became my turn to turn them over and talk of them unceasingly. . . . The reason was simply this, that in the first instance I understood nothing of these things and their importance for domestic comfort, whilst in the latter case they came home to me with irresistible urgency, and vividly took possession of my fancy. So it is with many a one who mocks at decorations and titles, until he gains one himself. And this is also surely the reason why one's own portrait or reflection in the mirror is so peculiarly interesting a thing to contemplate . . . not on account of any absolute 'c'est moi,' but just as with the music played by ourselves. What greets our eyes is what we know best, most deeply understand; because we ourselves have felt it and lived through it. We know what has ploughed these furrows, deepened these shadows, blanched this hair; and other faces may be handsomer, but none can speak to us or interest us like this."[14]

Moreover, this author goes on to show that our own things are fuller for us than those of others because of the memories they awaken and the practical hopes and expectations they arouse. This alone would emphasize them, apart from any value derived from their belonging to ourselves. We may conclude with him, then, that an original central self-feeling can never explain the passionate warmth of our self-regarding emotions, which must, on the contrary, be addressed directly to special things less abstract and empty of content. To these things the name of 'self' may be given, or to our conduct towards them the name of 'selfishness,' but neither in the self nor the selfishness does the pure Thinker play the 'title-rôle.'

Only one more point connected with our self-regard need be mentioned. We have spoken of it so far as active instinct or emotion. It remains to speak of it as cold intellectual self-estimation. We may weigh our own Me in the balance of praise and blame as easily as we weigh other people, - though with difficulty quite as fairly. The just man is the one who can weigh himself impartially. Impartial weighing presupposes a rare faculty of abstraction from the vividness with which, as Herr Horwicz has pointed out, things known as intimately as our own possessions and performances appeal to our imagination; and an equally rare power of vividly representing the affairs of others. But, granting these rare powers, there is no reason why a man should not pass judgment on himself quite as objectively and well as on anyone else. No matter how he feels about himself, unduly elated or unduly depressed, he may still truly know his own worth by measuring it by the outward standard he applies to other men, and counteract the injustice of the feeling he cannot wholly escape. This self-measuring process has nothing to do with the instinctive self-regard we have hitherto been dealing with. Being merely one application of intellectual comparison, it need no longer detain us here. Please note again, however, how the pure Ego appears merely as the vehicle in which the estimation is carried on, the objects estimated being all of them facts of an empirical sort,[15] one's body, one's credit, one's fame, one's intellectual ability, one's goodness, or whatever the case may be.

The empirical life of Self is divided, as below, into:

	MATERIAL.	SOCIAL.	SPIRITUAL.
SELF-SEEKING.	Bodily Appetites and Instincts Love of Adornment, Foppery, Acquisitiveness, Constructiveness, Love of Home, etc.	Desire to please, be noticed, admired, etc. Sociability, Emulation, Envy, Love, Pursuit of Honor, Ambition, etc.	Intellectual, Moral and Religious Aspiration, Conscientiousness
SELF-ESTIMATION.	Personal Vanity, Modesty, etc. Pride of Wealth, Fear of Poverty	Social and Family Pride, Vainglory, Snobbery, Humility, Shame, etc.	Sense of Moral or Mental Superiority, Purity, etc. Sense of Inferiority or of Guilt

The Pure Ego.

Having summed up in the above table the principal results of the chapter thus far, I have said all that need be said of the constituents of the phenomenal self, and of the nature of self-regard. Our decks are consequently cleared for the struggle with that pure principle of personal identity which has met us all along our preliminary exposition, but which we have always shied from and treated as a difficulty to be postponed. Ever since Hume's time, it has been justly regarded as the most puzzling puzzle with which psychology has to deal; and whatever view one may espouse, one has to hold his position against heavy odds. If, with the Spiritualists, one contend for a substantial soul, or transcendental principle of unity, one can give no positive account of what that may be. And if, with the Humians, one deny such a principle and say that the stream of passing thoughts is all, one runs against the entire common-sense of mankind, of which the belief in a distinct principle of selfhood seems an integral part. Whatever solution be adopted in the pages to come, we may as well make up our minds in advance that it will fail to satisfy the majority of those to whom it is addressed. The best way of approaching the matter will be to take up first -

The Sense of Personal Identity.

In the last chapter it was stated in as radical a way as possible that the thoughts which we actually know to exist do not fly about loose, but seem each to belong to some one thinker and not to another. Each thought, out of a multitude of other thoughts of which it may think, is able to distinguish those which belong to its own Ego from those which do not. The former have a warmth and intimacy about them of which the latter are completely devoid, being merely conceived, in a cold and foreign fashion, and not appearing as blood-relatives, bringing their greetings to us from out of the past.

Now this consciousness of personal sameness may be treated either as a subjective phenomenon or as an objective deliverance, as a feeling, or as a truth. We may explain how one bit of thought can come to judge other bits to belong to the same Ego with itself; or we may criticise its judgment and decide how far it may tally with the nature of things. As a mere subjective phenomenon the judgment presents no difficulty or mystery peculiar to itself. It belongs to the great class of judgments of sameness; and there is nothing more remarkable in making a judgment of sameness in the first person than in the second or the third. The intellectual operations seem essentially alike, whether I say 'I am the same,' or whether I say 'the pen is the same, as yesterday.' It is as easy to think this as to think the opposite and say 'neither I nor the pen is the same.'

This sort of bringing of things together into the object of a single judgment is of course essential to all thinking. The things are conjoined in the thought, whatever may be the relation in which they appear to the thought. The thinking them is thinking them together, even if only with the result of judging that they do not belong together. This sort of subjective synthesis, essential to knowledge as such (whenever it has a complex object), must not be confounded with objective synthesis or union instead of difference or disconnection, known among the things.[16] The subjective synthesis is involved in thought's mere existence. Even a really disconnected world could only be known to be such by having its parts temporarily united in the Object of some pulse of consciousness.[17]

The sense of personal identity is not, then, this mere synthetic form essential to all thought. It is the sense of a sameness perceived by thought and predicated of things thought-about. These things are a present self and a self of yesterday. The thought not only thinks them both, but thinks that they are identical. The psychologist, looking on and playing the critic, might prove the thought wrong, and show there was no real identity, - there might have been no yesterday, or, at any rate, no self of yesterday; or, if there were, the sameness predicated might not obtain, or might be predicated on insufficient grounds. In either case the personal identity would not exist as a fact; but it would exist as a feeling all the same; the consciousness of it by the thought would be there, and the psychologist would still have to analyze that, and show where its illusoriness lay. Let us now be the psychologist and see whether it be right or wrong when it says, I am the same self that I was yesterday.

We may immediately call it right and intelligible so far as it posits a past time with past thoughts or selves contained therein - these were data which we assumed at the outset of the book. Right also and intelligible so far as it thinks of a present self - that present self we have just studied in its various forms. The only question for us is as to what the consciousness may mean when it calls the present self the same with one of the past selves which it has in mind.

We spoke a moment since of warmth and intimacy. This leads us to the answer sought. For, whatever the thought we are criticising may think about its present self, that self comes to its acquaintance, or is actually felt, with warmth and intimacy. Of course this is the case with the bodily part of it; we feel the whole cubic mass of our body all the while, it gives us an unceasing sense of personal existence. Equally do we feel the inner 'nucleus of the spiritual self,' either in the shape of yon faint physiological adjustments, or (adopting the universal psychological belief), in that of the pure activity of our thought taking place as such. Our remoter spiritual, material, and social selves, so far as they are realized, come also with a glow and a warmth; for the thought of them infallibly brings some degree of organic emotion in the shape of quickened heart-beats, oppressed breathing, or some other alteration, even though it be a slight one, in the general bodily tone. The character of 'warmth,' then, in the present self, reduces itself to either of two things, - something in the feeling which we have of the thought itself, as thinking, or else the feeling of the body's actual existence at the moment, - or finally to both. We cannot realize our present self without simultaneously feeling one or other of these two things. Any other fact which brings these two things with it into consciousness will be thought with a warmth and an intimacy like those which cling to the present self.

Any distinct self which fulfills this condition will be thought with such warmth and intimacy. But which distant selves do fulfil the condition, when represented?

Obviously those, and only those, which fulfilled it when they were alive. Them we shall imagine with the animal warmth upon them, to them may possibly cling the aroma, the echo of the thinking taken in the act. And by a natural consequence, we shall assimilate them to each other and to the warm and intimate self we now feel within us as we think, and separate them as a collection from whatever selves have not this mark, much as out of a herd of cattle let loose for the winter on some wide western prairie the owner picks out and sorts together when the time for the round-up comes in the spring, all the beasts on which he finds his own particular brand.

The various members of the collection thus set apart are felt to belong with each other whenever they are thought at all. The animal warmth, etc., is their herd-mark, the brand from which they can never more escape. It runs through them all like a thread through a chaplet and makes them into a whole, which we treat as a unit, no matter how much in other ways the parts may differ inter se. Add to this character the farther one that the distant selves appear to our thought as having for hours of time been continuous with each other, and the most recent ones of them continuous with the Self of the present moment, melting into it by slow degrees; and we get a still stronger bond of union. As we think we see an identical bodily thing when, in spite of changes of structure, it exists continuously before our eyes, or when, however interrupted its presence, its quality returns unchanged; so here we think we experience an identical Self when it appears to us in an analogous way. Continuity makes us unite what dissimilarity might otherwise separate; similarity makes us unite what discontinuity might hold apart. And thus it is, finally, that Peter, awakening in the same bed with Paul, and recalling what both had in mind before they went to sleep, reidentifies and appropriates the 'warm' ideas as his, and is never tempted to confuse them with those cold and pale-appearing ones which he ascribes to Paul. As well might he confound Paul's body, which he only sees, with his own body, which he sees but also feels. Each of us when he awakens says, Here's the same old self again, just as he says, Here's the same old bed, the same old room, the same old world.

The sense of our own personal identity, then, is exactly like any one of our other perceptions of sameness among phenomena. It is a conclusion grounded either on the resemblance in a fundamental respect, or on the continuity before the mind, of the phenomena compared.

And it must not be taken to mean more than these grounds warrant, or treated as a sort of metaphysical or absolute Unity in which all differences are overwhelmed. The past and present selves compared are the same just so far as they are the same, and no farther. A uniform feeling of 'warmth,' of bodily existence (or an equally uniform feeling of pure psychic energy?) pervades them all; and this is what gives them a generic unity, and makes them the same in kind. But this generic unity coexists with generic differences just as real as the unity. And if from the one point of view they are one self, from others they are as truly not one but many selves. And similarly of the attribute of continuity; it gives its own kind of unity to the self - that of mere connectedness, or unbrokenness, a perfectly definite phenomenal thing - but it gives not a jot or tittle more. And this unbrokenness in the stream of selves, like the unbrokenness in an exhibition of 'dissolving views,' in no wise implies any farther unity or contradicts any amount of plurality in other respects.

And accordingly we find that, where the resemblance and the continuity are no longer felt, the sense of personal identity goes too. We hear from our parents various anecdotes about our infant years, but we do not appropriate them as we do our own memories. Those breaches of decorum awaken no blush, those bright sayings no self-complacency. That child is a foreign creature with which our present self is no more identified in feeling than it is with some stranger's living child to-day. Why? Partly because great time-gaps break up all these early years - we cannot ascend to them by continuous memories; and partly because no representation of how the child felt comes up with the stories. We know what he said and did; but no sentiment of his little body, of his emotions, of his psychic strivings as they felt to him, comes up to contribute an element of warmth and intimacy to the narrative we hear, and the main bond of union with our present self thus disappears. It is the same with certain of our dimly-recollected experiences. We hardly know whether to appropriate them or to disown them as fancies, or things read or heard and not lived through. Their animal heat has evaporated; the feelings that accompanied them are so lacking in the recall, or so different from those we now enjoy, that no judgment of identity can be decisively cast.

Resemblance among the parts of a continuum of feelings (especially bodily feelings) experienced along with things widely different in all other regards, thus constitutes the real and verifiable 'personal identity' which we feel. There is no other identity than this in the 'stream' of subjective consciousness which we described in the last chapter. Its parts differ, but under all their differences they are knit in these two ways; and if either way of knitting disappears, the sense of unity departs. If a man wakes up some fine day unable to recall any of his past experiences, so that he has to learn his biography afresh, or if he only recalls the facts of it in a cold abstract way as things that he is sure once happened; or if, without this loss of memory, his bodily and spiritual habits all change during the night, each organ giving a different tone, and the act of thought becoming aware of itself in a different way; he feels, and he says, that he is a changed person. He disowns his former me, gives himself a new name, identifies his present life with nothing from out of the older time. Such cases are not rare in mental pathology; but, as we still have some reasoning to do, we had better give no concrete account of them until the end of the chapter.

This description of personal identity will be recognized by the instructed reader as the ordinary doctrine professed by the empirical school. Associationists in England and France, Herbartians in Germany, all describe the Self as an aggregate of which each part, as to its being, is a separate fact. So far so good, then; thus much is true whatever farther things may be true; and it is to the imperishable glory of Hume and Herbart and their successors to have taken so much of the meaning of personal identity out of the clouds and made of the Self an empirical and verifiable thing.

But in leaving the matter here, and saying that this sum of passing things is all, these writers have neglected certain more subtle aspects of the Unity of Consciousness, to which we next must turn.

Our recent simile of the herd of cattle will help us. It will be remembered that the beasts were brought together into one herd because their owner found on each of them his brand. The 'owner' symbolized here that 'section' of consciousness, or pulse of thought, which we have all along represented as the vehicle of the judgment of identity; and the 'brand' symbolizes the characters of warmth and continuity, by reason of which the judgment is made. There is found a self-brand, just as there is found a herd-brand. Each brand, so far, is the mark, or cause of our knowing, that certain things belong-together. But if the brand is the ratio cognoscendi of the belonging, the belonging, in the case of the herd, is in turn the ratio existendi of the brand. No beast would be so branded unless he belonged to the owner of the herd. They are not his because they are branded; they are branded because they are his. So that it seems as if our description of the belonging-together of the various selves, as a belonging-together which is merely represented, in a later pulse of thought, had knocked the bottom out of the matter, and omitted the most characteristic one of all the features found in the herd - a feature which common-sense finds in the phenomenon of personal identity as well, and for our omission of which she will hold us to a strict account. For common-sense insists that the unity of all the selves is not a mere appearance of similarity or continuity, ascertained after the fact. She is sure that it involves a real belonging to a real Owner, to a pure spiritual entity of some kind. Relation to this entity is what makes the self's constituents stick together as they do for thought. The individual beasts do not stick together, for all that they wear the same brand. Each wanders with whatever accidental mates it finds. The herd's unity is only potential, its centre ideal, like the 'centre of gravity' in physics, until the herdsman or owner comes. He furnishes a real centre of accretion to which the beasts are driven and by which they are held. The beasts stick together by sticking severally to him. Just so, common-sense insists, there must be a real proprietor in the case of the selves, or else their actual accretion into a 'personal consciousness' would never have taken place.

To the usual empiricist explanation of personal consciousness this is a formidable reproof, because all the individual thoughts and feelings which have succeeded each other 'up to date' are represented by ordinary Associationism as in some inscrutable way 'integrating' or gumming themselves together on their own account, and thus fusing into a stream. All the incomprehensibilities which in Chapter VI we saw to attach to the idea of things fusing without a medium apply to the empiricist description of personal identity.

But in our own account the medium is fully assigned, the herdsman is there, in the shape of something not among the things collected, but superior to them all, namely, the real, present onlooking, remembering, 'judging thought' or identifying 'section' of the stream. This is what collects, - 'owns' some of the past facts which it surveys, and disowns the rest, - and so makes a unity that is actualized and anchored and does not merely float in the blue air of possibility. And the reality of such pulses of thought, with their function of knowing, it will be remembered that we did not seek to deduce or explain, but simply assumed them as the ultimate kind of fact that the psychologist must admit to exist.

But this assumption, though it yields much, still does not yield all that common-sense demands. The unity into which the Thought - as I shall for a time proceed to call, with a capital T, the present mental state - binds the individual past facts with each other and with itself, does not exist until the Thought is there. It is as if wild cattle were lassoed by a newly-created settler and then owned for the first time. But the essence of the matter to common-sense is that the past thoughts never were wild cattle, they were always owned. The Thought does not capture them, but as soon as it comes into existence it finds them already its own. How is this possible unless the Thought have a substantial identity with a former owner, - not a mere continuity or a resemblance, as in our account, but a real unity? Common-sense in fact would drive us to admit what we may for the moment call an Arch-Ego, dominating the entire stream of thought and all the selves that may be represented in it, as the ever self-same and changeless principle implied in their union. The 'Soul' of Metaphysics and the 'Transcendental Ego' of the Kantian Philosophy, are, as we shall soon see, but attempts to satisfy this urgent demand of common-sense. But, for a time at least, we can still express without any such hypotheses that appearance of never-lapsing ownership for which common-sense contends.

For how would it be if the Thought, the present judging Thought, instead of being in any way substantially or transcendentally identical with the former owner of the past self, merely inherited his 'title,' and thus stood as his legal representative now? It would then, if its birth coincided exactly with the death of another owner, find the past self already its own as soon as it found it at all, and the past self would thus never be wild, but always owned, by a title that never lapsed. We can imagine a long succession of herdsmen coming rapidly into possession of the same cattle by transmission of an original title by bequest. May not the 'title' of a collective self be passed from one Thought to another in some analogous way?

It is a patent fact of consciousness that a transmission like this actually occurs. Each pulse of cognitive consciousness, each Thought, dies away and is replaced by another. The other, among the things it knows, knows its own predecessor, and finding it 'warm,' in the way we have described, greets it, saying: "Thou art mine, and part of the same self with me." Each later Thought, knowing and including thus the Thoughts which went before, is the final receptacle - and appropriating them is the final owner - of all that they contain and own. Each Thought is thus born an owner, and dies owned, transmitting whatever it realized as its Self to its own later proprietor. As Kant says, it is as if elastic balls were to have not only motion but knowledge of it, and a first ball were to transmit both its motion and its consciousness to a second, which took both up into its consciousness and passed them to a third, until the last ball held all that the other balls had held, and realized it as its own. It is this trick which the nascent thought has of immediately taking up the expiring thought and 'adopting' it, which is the foundation of the appropriation of most of the remoter constituents of the self. Who owns the last self owns the self before the last, for what possesses the possessor possesses the possessed.

It is impossible to discover any verifiable features in personal identity, which this sketch does not contain, impossible to imagine how any transcendent non-phenomenal sort of an Arch-Ego, were he there, could shape matters to any other result, or be known in time by any other fruit, than just this production of a stream of consciousness each 'section' of which should know, and knowing, hug to itself and adopt, all those that went before, - thus standing as the representative of the entire past stream; and which should similarly adopt the objects already adopted by any portion of this spiritual stream. Such standing-as-representative, and such adopting, are perfectly clear phenomenal relations. The Thought which, whilst it knows another Thought and the Object of that Other, appropriates the Other and the Object which the Other appropriated, is still a perfectly distinct phenomenon form that Other; it may hardly resemble it; it may be far removed from it in space and time.

The only point that is obscure is the act of appropriation itself. Already in enumerating the constituents of the self and their rivalry, I had to use the word appropriate. And the quick-witted reader probably noticed at the time, in hearing how one constituent was let drop and disowned and another one held fast to and espoused, that the phrase was meaningless unless the constituents were objects in the hands of something else. A thing cannot appropriate itself; it is itself; and still less can it disown itself. There must be an agent of the appropriating and disowning; but that agent we have already named. It is the Thought to whom the various 'constituents' are known. That Thought is a vehicle of choice as well as of cognition; and among the choices it makes are these appropriations, or repudiations, of its 'own.' But the Thought never is an object in its own hands, it never appropriates or disowns itself. It appropriates to itself, it is the actual focus of accretion, the hook from which the chain of past selves dangles, planted firmly in the Present, which alone passes for real, and thus keeping the chain from being a purely ideal thing. Anon the hook itself will drop into the past with all it carries, and then be treated as an object and appropriated by a new Thought in the new present which will serve as living hook in turn. The present moment of consciousness is thus, as Mr. Hodgson says, the darkest in the whole series. It may feel its own immediate existence - we have all along admitted the possibility of this, hard as it is by direct introspection to ascertain the fact - but nothing can be known about it till it be dead and gone. Its appropriations are therefore less to itself than to the most intimately felt part of its present Object, the body, and the central adjustments, which accompany the act of thinking, in the head. These are the real nucleus of our personal identity, and it is their actual existence, realized as a solid present fact, which makes us say 'as sure as I exist, those past facts were part of myself.' They are the kernel to which the represented parts of the Self are assimilated, accreted, and knit on; and even were Thought entirely unconscious of itself in the act of thinking, these 'warm' parts of its present object would be a firm basis on which the consciousness of personal identity would rest.[18] Such consciousness, then, as a psychologic fact, can be fully described without supposing any other agent than a succession of perishing thoughts, endowed with the functions of appropriation and rejection, and of which some can know and appropriate or reject objects already known, appropriated, or rejected by the rest.

To illustrate by diagram, let A, B, and C stand for three successive thoughts, each with its object inside of it.

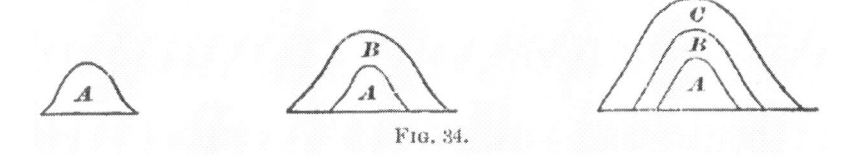

FIG. 34.

If B's object be A, and C's object be B; then A, B, and C would stand for three pulses in a consciousness of personal identity. Each pulse would be something different from the others; but B would know and adopt A, and C would know and adopt A and B. Three successive states of the same brain, on which each experience in passing leaves its mark, might very well engender thoughts differing from each other in just such a way as this.

The passing Thought then seems to be the Thinker; and though there may be another non-phenomenal Thinker behind that, so far we do not seem to need him to express the facts. But we cannot definitively make up our mind about him until we have heard the reasons that have historically been used to prove his reality.

The Pure Self or Inner Principle of Personal Unity.

To a brief survey of the theories of the Ego let us then next proceed. They are three in number, as follows:

1) The Spiritualist theory;
2) The Associationist theory;
3) The Transcendentalist theory.

The Theory of the Soul.

In Chapter VI we were led ourselves to the spiritualist theory of the 'Soul,' as a means of escape from the unintelligibilities of mind-stuff 'integrating' with itself, and from the physiological improbability of a material monad, with thought attached to it, in the brain. But at the end of the chapter we said we should examine the 'Soul' critically in a later place, to see whether it had any other advantages as a theory over the simple phenomenal notion of a stream of thought accompanying a stream of cerebral activity, by a law yet unexplained.

The theory of the Soul is the theory of popular philosophy and of scholasticism, which is only popular philosophy made systematic. It declares that the principle of individuality within us must be substantial, for psychic phenomena are activities, and there can be no activity without a concrete agent. This substantial agent cannot be the brain but must be something immaterial; for its activity, thought, is both immaterial, and takes cognizance of immaterial things, and of material things in general and intelligible, as well as in particular and sensible ways, - all which powers are incompatible with the nature of matter, of which the brain is composed. Thought moreover is simple, whilst the activities of the brain are compounded of the elementary activities of each of its parts. Furthermore, thought is spontaneous or free, whilst all material activity is determined ab extra; and the will can turn itself against all corporeal goods and appetites, which would be impossible were it a corporeal function. For these objective reasons the principle of psychic life must be both immaterial and simple as well as substantial, must be what is called a Soul. The same consequence follows from subjective reasons. Our consciousness of personal identity assures us of our essential simplicity: the owner of the various constituents of the self, as we have seen them, the hypothetical Arch-Ego whom we provisionally conceived as possible, is a real entity of whose existence self-consciousness makes us directly aware. No material agent could thus turn round and grasp itself - material activities always grasp something else than the agent. And if a brain could grasp itself and be self-conscious, it would be conscious of itself as a brain and not as something of an altogether different kind. The Soul then exists as a simple spiritual substance in which the various psychic faculties, operations, and affections inhere.

If we ask what a Substance is, the only answer is that it is a self-existent being, or one which needs no other subject in which to inhere. At bottom its only positive determination is Being, and this is something whose meaning we all realize even though we find it hard to explain. The Soul is moreover an individual being, and if we ask what that is, we are told to look in upon our Self, and we shall learn by direct intuition better than through any abstract reply. Our direct perception of our own inward being is in fact by many deemed to be the original prototype out of which our notion of simple active substance in general is fashioned. The consequences of the simplicity and substantiality of the Soul are its incorruptibility and natural immortality - nothing but God's direct fiat can annihilate it - and its responsibility at all times for whatever it may have ever done.

This substantialist view of the soul was essentially the view of Plato and of Aristotle. It received its completely formal elaboration in the middle ages. It was believed in by Hobbes, Descartes, Locke, Leibnitz, Wolf, Berkeley, and is no defended by the entire modern dualistic or spiritualistic or common-sense school. Kant held to it while denying its fruitfulness as a premise for deducing consequences verifiable here below. Kant's successors, the absolute idealists, profess to have discarded it, - how that may be we shall inquire ere long. Let us make up our minds what to think of it ourselves.

It is at all events needless for expressing the actual subjective phenomena of consciousness as they appear. We have formulated them all without its aid, by the supposition of a stream of thoughts, each substantially different from the rest, but cognitive of the rest and 'appropriative' of each other's content. At least, if I have not already succeeded in making this plausible to the reader, I am hopeless of convincing him by anything I could add now. The unity, the identity, the individuality, and the immateriality that appear in the psychic life are thus accounted for as phenomenal and temporal facts exclusively, and with no need of reference to any more simple or substantial agent than the present Thought or 'section' of the stream. We have seen it to be single and unique in the sense of having no separable parts - perhaps that is the only kind of simplicity meant to be predicated of the soul. The present Thought also has being, - at least all believers in the Soul believe so - and if there be no other Being in which it 'inheres,' it ought itself to be a 'substance'. If this kind of simplicity and substantiality were all that is predicated of the Soul, then it might appear that we had been talking of the soul all along, without knowing it, when we treated the present Thought as an agent, an owner, and the like. But the Thought is a perishing and not an immortal or incorruptible thing. Its successors may continuously succeed to it, resemble it, and appropriate it, but they are not it, whereas the Soul-Substance is supposed to be a fixed unchanging thing. By the Soul is always meant something behind the present Thought, another kind of substance, existing on a non-phenomenal plane.

When we brought in the Soul at the end of the Chapter VI, as an entity which the various brain-processes were supposed to affect simultaneously, and which responded to their combined influence by single pulses of its thought, it was to escape integrated mind-stuff on the one hand, and an improbable cerebral monad on the other. But when (as now, after all we have been through since that earlier passage) we take the two formulations, first of a brain to whose processes pulses of thought simply correspond, and second, of one to whose processes pulses of thought in a Soul correspond, and compare them together, we see that at bottom the second formulation is only a more roundabout way than the first, of expressing the same bald fact. That bald fact is that when the brain acts, a thought occurs. The spiritualistic formulation says that the brain-processes knock the thought, so to speak, out of a Soul which stands there to receive their influence. The simpler formulation says that the thought simply comes. But what positive meaning has the Soul, when scrutinized, but the ground of possibility of the thought? And what is the 'knocking' but the determining of the possibility to actuality? And what is this after all but giving a sort of concreted form to one's belief that the coming of the thought, when the brain-processes occur, has some sort of ground in the nature of things? If the world Soul be understood merely to express that claim, it is a good word to use. But if it be held to do more, to gratify the claim, - for instance, to connect rationally the thought which comes, with the processes which occur, and to mediate intelligibly between their two disparate natures, - then it is an illusory term. It is, in fact, with the word Soul as with the word Substance in general. To say that phenomena inhere in a Substance is at bottom only to record one's protest against the notion that the bare existence of the phenomena is the total truth. A phenomenon would not itself be, we insist, unless there were something more than the phenomenon. To the more we give the provisional name of Substance. So, in the present instance, we ought certainly to admit that there is more than the bare fact of coexistence of a passing thought with a passing brain-state. But we do not answer the question 'What is that more?' when we say that it is a 'Soul' which the brain-state affects. This kind of more explains nothing; and when we are once trying metaphysical explanations we are foolish not to go as far as we can. For my own part I confess that the moment I become metaphysical and try to define the more, I find the notion of some sort of an anima mundi thinking in all of us to be a more promising hypothesis, in spite of all its difficulties, than that of a lot of absolutely individual souls. Meanwhile, as psychologists, we need not be metaphysical at all. The phenomena are enough, the passing Thought itself is the only verifiable thinker, and its empirical connection with the brain-process is the ultimate known law.

To the other arguments which would prove the need of a soul, we may also turn a deaf ear. The argument from free-will can convince only those who believe in free-will; and even they will have to admit that spontaneity is just as possible, to say the least, in a temporary spiritual agent like our 'Thought' as in a permanent one like the supposed Soul. The same is true of the argument from the kinds of things cognized. Even if the brain could not cognize universals, immaterials, or its 'Self,' still the 'Thought' which we have relied upon in our account is not the brain, closely as it seems connected with it; and after all, if the brain could cognize at all, one does not well see why it might not cognize one sort of thing as well as another. The great difficulty is in seeing how a thing can cognize anything. This difficulty is not in the least removed by giving to the thing that cognizes the name of Soul. The Spiritualists do not deduce any of the properties of the mental life from otherwise known properties of the soul. They simply find various characters ready-made in the mental life, and these they clap into the Soul, saying, "Lo! behold the source from whence they flow!" The merely verbal character of this 'explanation' is obvious. The Soul invoked, far from making the phenomena more intelligible, can only be made intelligible itself by borrowing their form, - it must be represented, if at all, as a transcendent stream of consciousness duplicating the one we know.

Altogether, the Soul is an outbirth of that sort of philosophizing whose great maxim, according to Dr. Hodgson, is: "Whatever you are totally ignorant of, assert to be the explanation of everything else."

Locke and Kant, whilst still believing in the soul, began the work of undermining the notion that we know anything about it. Most modern writers of the mitigated, spiritualistic, or dualistic philosophy - the Scotch school, as it is often called among us - are forward to proclaim this ignorance, and to attend exclusively to the verifiable phenomena of self-consciousness, as we have laid them down. Dr. Wayland, for example, begins his Elements of Intellectual Philosophy with the phrase "Of the essence of Mind we know nothing," and goes on: "All that we are able to affirm of it is that it is something which perceives, reflects, remembers, imagines, and wills; but what that something is which exerts these energies we know not. It is only as we are conscious of the action of these energies that we are conscious of the existence of mind. It is only by the exertion of its own powers that the mind becomes cognizant of their existence. The cognizance of its powers, however, gives us no knowledge of that essence of which they are predicated. In these respects our knowledge of mind is precisely analogous to our knowledge of matter." This analogy of our two ignorances is a favorite remark in the Scotch school. It is but a step to lump them together into a single ignorance, that of the 'Unknowable' to which any one fond of superfluities in philosophy may accord the hospitality of his belief, if it so please him, but which any one else may as freely ignore and reject.

The Soul-theory is, then, a complete superfluity, so far as accounting for the actually verified facts of conscious experience goes. So far, no one can be compelled to subscribe to it for definite scientific reasons. The case would rest here, and the reader be left free to make his choice, were it not for other demands of a more practical kind.

The first of these is Immortality, for which the simplicity and substantiality of the Soul seem to offer a solid guarantee. A 'stream' of thought, for aught that we see to be contained in its essence, may come to a full stop at any moment; but a simple substance is incorruptible and will, by its own inertia, persist in Being so long as the Creator does not by a direct miracle snuff it out. Unquestionably this is the stronghold of the spiritualistic belief, - as indeed the popular touchstone for all philosophies is the question, "What is their bearing on a future life?"

The Soul, however, when closely scrutinized, guarantees no immortality of a sort we care for. The enjoyment of the atom-like simplicity of their substance in soecula soeculorum would not to most people seem a consummation devoutly to be wished. The substance must give rise to a stream of consciousness continuous with the present stream, in order to arouse our hope, but of this the mere persistence of the substance per se offers no guarantee. Moreover, in the general advance of our moral ideas, there has come to be something ridiculous in the way our forefathers had of grounding their hopes of immortality on the simplicity of their substance. The demand for immortality is nowadays essentially teleological. We believe ourselves immortal because we believe ourselves fit for immortality. A 'substance, ought surely to perish, we think, if not worthy to survive, and an insubstantial 'stream' to prolong itself, provided it be worthy, if the nature of Things is organized in the rational way in which we trust it is. Substance or no substance, soul or 'stream,' what Lotze says of immortality is about all that human wisdom can say: "We have no other principle for deciding it than this general idealistic belief: that every created thing will continue whose continuance belongs to the meaning of the world, and so long as it does so belong; whilst every one will pass away whose reality is justified only in a transitory phase of the world's course. That this principle admits of no further application in human hands need hardly be said. We surely know not the merits which may give to one being a claim on eternity, nor the defects which would cut others off."[19]

A second alleged necessity for a soul-substance is our forensic responsibility before God. Locke caused an uproar when he said that the unity of consciousness made a man the same person, whether supported by the same substance or no, and that God would not, in the great day, make a person answer for what he remembered nothing of. It was supposed scandalous that our forgetfulness might thus deprive God of the chance of certain retributions, which otherwise would have enhanced his 'glory.' This is certainly a good speculative ground for retaining the Soul - at least for those who demand a plenitude of retribution. The mere stream of consciousness, with its lapses of memory, cannot possibly be as 'responsible' as a soul which is at the judgment day all that it ever was. To modern readers, however, who are less insatiate for retribution than their grandfathers, this argument will hardly be as convincing as it seems once to have been.

One great use of the Soul has always been to account for, and at the same time to guarantee, the closed individuality of each personal consciousness. The thoughts of one soul must unite into one self, it was supposed, and must be eternally insulated from those of every other soul. But we have already begun to see that, although unity is the rule of each man's consciousness, yet in some individuals, at least, thoughts may split away from the others and form separate selves. As for insulation, it would be rash, in view of the phenomena of thought-transference, mesmeric influence and spirit-control, which are being alleged nowadays on better authority than ever before, to be too sure about that point either. The definitively closed nature of our personal consciousness is probably an average statistical resultant of many conditions, but not an elementary force or fact; so that, if one wishes to preserve the Soul, the less he draws his arguments from that quarter the better. So long as our self, on the whole, makes itself good and practically maintains itself as a closed individual, why, as Lotze says, is not that enough? And why is the being-an-individual in some inaccessible metaphysical way so much prouder an achievement?[20]

My final conclusion, then, about the substantial Soul is that it explains nothing and guarantees nothing. Its successive thoughts are the only intelligible and verifiable things about it, and definitely to ascertain the correlations of these with brain-processes is as much as psychology can empirically do. From the metaphysical point of view, it is true that one may claim that the correlations have a rational ground; and if the word Soul could be taken to mean merely some such vague problematic ground, it would be unobjectionable. But the trouble is that it professes to give the ground in positive terms of a very dubiously credible sort. I therefore feel entirely free to discard the word Soul from the rest of this book. If I ever use it, it will be in the vaguest and most popular way. The reader who finds any comfort in the idea of the Soul, is, however, perfectly free to continue to believe in it; for our reasonings have not established the non-existence of the Soul; they have only proved its superfluity for scientific purposes.

The next theory of the pure Self to which we pass is

The Associationist Theory.

Locke paved the way for it by the hypothesis he suggested of the same substance having two successive consciousnesses, or of the same consciousness being supported by more than one substance. He made his readers feel that the important unity of the Self was its verifiable and felt unity, and that a metaphysical or absolute unity would be insignificant, so long as a consciousness of diversity might be there.

Hume showed how great the consciousness of diversity actually was. In the famous chapter on Personal Identity, in his Treatise on Human Nature, he writes as follows:

"There are some philosophers who imagine we are every moment intimately conscious of what we call our SELF; that we feel its existence and its continuance in existence, and are certain, beyond the evidence of a demonstration, both of its perfect identity and simplicity.... Unluckily all these positive assertions are contrary to that very experience which is pleaded for them, nor have we any idea of Self, after the manner it is here explained.... It must be some one impression that gives rise to every real idea.... If any impression gives rise to the idea of Self, that impression must continue invariably the same through the whole course of our lives, since self is supposed to exist after that manner. But there is no impression constant and invariable. Pain and pleasure, grief and joy, passions and sensations succeed each other, and never all exist at the same time.... For my part, when I enter most intimately into what I call myself, I always stumble on some particular perception or other of heat or cold, light or shade, love or hatred, pain or pleasure. I never can catch myself at any time without a perception, and never can observe anything but the perception. When my perceptions are removed for any time, as by sound sleep, so long am I insensible of myself, and may truly be said not to exist. And were all my perceptions removed by death, and could I neither think, nor feel, nor see, nor love, nor hate after the dissolution of my body, I should be entirely annihilated, nor do I conceive what is farther requisite to make me a perfect non-entity. If anyone, upon serious and unprejudiced reflection, thinks he has a different notion of himself, I must confess I can reason no longer with him. All I can allow him is, that he may be in the right as well as I, and that we are essentially different in this particular. He may, perhaps, perceive something simple and continued which he calls himself; though I am certain there is no such principle in me.

"But setting aside some metaphysicians of this kind, I may venture to affirm of the rest of mankind that they are nothing but a bundle or collection of different perceptions, which succeeded each other with an inconceivable rapidity, and are in a perceptual flux and movement. Our eyes cannot turn in their sockets without varying our perceptions. Our thought is still more variable than our sight; and all our other senses and faculties contribute to this change; nor is there any single power of the soul which remains unalterably the same, perhaps for one moment. The mind is a kind of theatre, where several perceptions successively make their appearance; pass, repass, glide away and mingle in an infinite variety of postures and situations. There is properly no simplicity in it at one time, nor identity in different; whatever natural propension we may have to imagine that simplicity and identity. The comparison of the theatre must not mislead us. They are the successive perceptions only, that constitute the mind; nor have we the most distant notion of the place where these scenes are represented, nor of the material of which it is composed."

But Hume, after doing this good piece of introspective work, proceeds to pour out the child with the bath, and to fly to as great an extreme as the substantialist philosophers. As they say the Self is nothing but Unity, unity abstract and absolute, so Hume says it is nothing but Diversity, diversity abstract and absolute; whereas in truth it is that mixture of unity and diversity which we ourselves have already found so easy to pick apart. We found among the objects of the stream certain feelings that hardly changed, that stood out warm and vivid in the past just as the present feeling does now; and we found the present feeling to be the centre of accretion to which, de proche en proche, these other feelings are, by the judging Thought, felt to cling. Hume says nothing of the judging Thought; and he denies this thread of resemblance, this core of sameness running through the ingredients of the Self, to exist even as a phenomenal thing. To him there is no tertium quid between pure unity and pure separateness. A succession of ideas "connected by a close relation affords to an accurate view as perfect a notion of diversity as if there was no manner of relation" at all.

"All our distinct perceptions are distinct existences, and the mind never perceives any real connection among distinct existences. Did our perceptions either inhere in something simple or individual, or did the mind perceive some real connection among them, there would be no difficulty in the case. For my part, I must plead the privilege of a sceptic and confess that this difficulty is too hard for my understanding. I pretend not, however, to pronounce it insuperable. Others, perhaps, ... may discover some hypothesis that will reconcile these contradictions."[21]

Hume is at bottom as much of a metaphysician as Thomas Aquinas. No wonder he can discover no 'hypothesis.' The unity of the parts of the stream is just as 'real' a connection as their diversity is a real separation; both connection and separation are ways in which the past thoughts appear to the present Thought; - unlike each other in respect of date and certain qualities - this is the separation; alike in other qualities, and continuous in time - this is the connection. In demanding a more 'real' connection than this obvious and verifiable likeness and continuity, Hume seeks 'the world behind the looking-glass,' and gives a striking example of that Absolutism which is the great disease of philosophic Thought.

The chain of distinct existences into which Hume thus chopped up our 'stream' was adopted by all of his successors as a complete inventory of the facts. The associationist Philosophy was founded. Somehow, out of 'ideas,' each separate, each ignorant of its mates, but sticking together and calling each other up according to certain laws, all the higher forms of consciousness were to be explained, and among them the consciousness of our personal identity. The task was a hard one, in which what we called the psychologist's fallacy bore the brunt of the work. Two ideas, one of 'A,' succeeded by another of 'B,' were transmuted into a third idea of 'A after B.' An idea from last year returning now was taken to be an idea of last year; two similar ideas stood for an idea of similarity, and the like; palpable confusions, in which certain facts about the ideas, possible only to an outside knower of them, were put into the place of the ideas' own proper and limited deliverance and content. Out of such recurrences and resemblances in a series of discrete ideas and feelings a knowledge was somehow supposed to be engendered in each feeling that it was recurrent and resembling, and that it helped to form a series to whose unity the name I came to be joined. In the same way, substantially, Herbart,[22] in Germany, tried to show how a conflict of ideas would fuse into a manner of representing itself for which I was the consecrated name.[23]

The defect of all these attempts is that the conclusion pretended to follow from certain premises is by no means rationally involved in the premises. A feeling of any kind, if it simply returns, ought to be nothing else than what it was at first. If memory of previous existence and all sorts of other cognitive functions are attributed to it when it returns, it is no longer the same, but a wholly different feeling, and ought to be so described. We have so described it with the greatest explicitness. We have said that feelings never do return. We have not pretended to explain this; we have recorded it as an empirically ascertained law, analogous to certain laws of brain-physiology; and, seeking to define the way in which new feelings do differ from the old, we have found them to be cognizant and appropriative of the old, whereas the old were always cognizant and appropriative of something else. Once more, this account pretended to be nothing more than a complete description of the facts. It explained them no more than the associationist account explains them. But the latter both assumes to explain them and in the same breath falsifies them, and for each reason stands condemned.

It is but just to say that the associationist writers as a rule seem to have a lurking bad conscience about the Self; and that although they are explicit enough about what it is, namely, a train of feelings or thoughts, they are very shy about openly tackling the problem of how it comes to be aware of itself. Neither Bain nor Spencer, for example, directly touch this problem. As a rule, associationist writers keep talking about 'the mind' and about what 'we' do; and so, smuggling in surreptitiously what they ought avowedly to have postulated in the form of a present 'judging Thought,' they either trade upon their reader's lack of discernment or are undiscerning themselves.

Mr. D. G. Thompson is the only associationist writer I know who perfectly escapes this confusion, and postulates openly what he needs. "All states of consciousness," he says, "imply and postulate a subject Ego, whose substance is unknown and unknowable, to which [why not say by which?] states of consciousness are referred as attributes, but which in the process of reference becomes objectified and becomes itself an attribute of a subject Ego which lies still beyond, and which ever eludes cognition though ever postulated for cognition.'[24] This is exactly our judging and remembering present 'Thought,' described in less simple terms.

After Mr. Thompson, M. Taine and the two Mills deserve credit for seeking to be as clear as they can. Taine tells us in the first volume of his 'Intelligence' what the Ego is, - a continuous web of conscious events no more really distinct from each other[25] than rhomboids, triangles, and squares marked with chalk on a plank are really distinct, for the plank itself is one. In the second volume he says all these parts have a common character embedded in them, that of being internal [this is our character of 'warmness,' otherwise named]. This character is abstracted and isolated by a mental fiction, and is what we are conscious of as our self - 'this stable within is what each of us calls I or me.' Obviously M. Taine forgets to tell us what this 'each of us' is, which suddenly starts up and performs the abstraction and 'calls' its product I or me. The character does not abstract itself. Taine means by 'each of us' merely the present 'judging Thought' with its memory and tendency to appropriate, but he does not name it distinctly enough, and lapses into the fiction that the entire series of thoughts, the entire 'plank,' is the reflecting psychologist.

James Mill, after defining Memory as a train of associated ideas beginning with that of my past self and ending with that of my present self, defines my Self as a train of ideas of which Memory declares the first to be continuously connected with the last. The successive associated ideas 'run, as it were, into a single point of consciousness.'[26] John Mill, annotating this account, says:

"The phenomenon of Self and that of Memory are merely two sides of the same fact, or two different modes of viewing the same fact. We may, as psychologists, set out from either of them, and refer the other to it. . . . But it is hardly allowable to do both. At least it must be said that by doing so we explain neither. We only show that the two things are essentially the same; that my memory of having ascended Skiddaw on a given day, and my consciousness of being the same person who ascended Skiddaw on that day, are two modes of stating the same fact: a fact which psychology has as yet failed to resolve into anything more elementary. In analyzing the complex phenomena of consciousness, we must come to something ultimate; and we seem to have reached two elements which have a good prima facie claim to that title. There is, first, . . . the difference between a fact and the Thought of that fact: a distinction which we are able to cognize in the past, and which then constitutes Memory, and in the future, when it constitutes Expectation; but in neither case can we give any account of it except that it exists. . . . Secondly, in addition to this, and setting out from the belief . . . that the idea I now have was derived from a previous sensation . . . there is the further conviction that this sensation . . . was my own; that it happened to my self. In other words, I am aware of a long and uninterrupted succession of past feelings, going back as far as memory reaches, and terminating with the sensations I have at the present moment, all of which are connected by an inexplicable tie, that distinguishes them not only from any succession or combination in mere thought, but also from the parallel succession of feelings which I believe, on satisfactory evidence, to have happened to each of the other beings, shaped like myself, whom I perceive around me. This succession of feelings, which I call my memory of the past, is that by which I distinguish my Self. Myself is the person who had that series of feelings, and I know nothing of myself, by direct knowledge, except that I had them. But there is a bond of some sort among all the parts of the series, which makes me say that they were feelings of a person who was the same person throughout [according to us this is their 'warmth' and resemblance to the 'central spiritual self' now actually felt] and a different person from those who had any of the parallel successions of feelings; and this bond, to me, constitutes my Ego. Here I think the question must rest, until some psychologist succeeds better than anyone else has done, in showing a mode in which the analysis can be carried further."[27]

The reader must judge of our own success in carrying the analysis farther. The various distinctions we have made are all part of an endeavor so to do. John Mill himself, in a later-written passage, so far from advancing in the line of analysis, seems to fall back upon something perilously near to the Soul. He says:

"The fact of recognizing a sensation, . . . remembering that it has been felt before, is the simplest and most elementary fact of memory: and the inexplicable tie . . . which connects the present consciousness with the past one of which it reminds me, is as near as I think we can get to a positive conception of Self. That there is something real in this tie, real as the sensations themselves, and not a mere product of the laws of thought without any fact corresponding to it, I hold to be indubitable . . . This original element, . . . to which we cannot give any name but its own peculiar one, without implying some false or ungrounded theory, is the Ego, or Self. As such I ascribe a reality to the Ego - to my own mind - different from that real existence as a Permanent Possibility, which is the only reality I acknowledge in Matter. . . . We are forced to apprehend every part of the series as linked with the other parts by something in common which is not the feelings themselves, any more than the succession of the feelings is the feelings themselves; and as that which is the same in the first as in the second, in the second as in the third, in the third as in the fourth, and so on, must be the same in the first and in the fiftieth, this common element is a permanent element. But beyond this we can affirm nothing of it except the states of consciousness themselves. The feelings or consciousnesses which belong or have belonged to it, and its possibilities of having more, are the only facts there are to be asserted of Self - the only positive attributes, except permanence, which we can ascribe to it."[28]

Mr. Mill's habitual method of philosophizing was to affirm boldly some general doctrine derived from his father, and then make so many concessions of detail to its enemies as practically to abandon it altogether.[29] In this place the concessions amount, so far as they are intelligible, to the admission of something very like the Soul. This 'inexplicable tie' which connects the feelings, this 'something in common' by which they are linked and which is not the passing feelings themselves, but something 'permanent,' of which we can 'affirm nothing' save its attributes and its permanence, what is it but metaphysical Substance come again to life? Much as one must respect the fairness of Mill's temper, quite as much must one regret his failure of acumen at this point. At bottom he makes the same blunder as Hume: the sensations per se, he thinks, have no 'tie.' The tie of resemblance and continuity which the remembering Thought finds among them is not a 'real tie' but 'a mere product of the laws of thought;' and the fact that the present Thought 'appropriates' them is also no real tie. But whereas Hume was contended to say that there might after all be no 'real tie,' Mill, unwilling to admit this possibility, is driven, like any scholastic, to place it in a non-phenomenal world.

John Mill's concessions may be regarded as the definitive bankruptcy of the associationist description of the consciousness of self, starting, as it does, with the best intentions, and dimly conscious of the path, but 'perplexed in the extreme' at last with the inadequacy of those 'simple feelings,' non-cognitive, non-transcendent of themselves, which were the only baggage it was willing to take along. One must beg memory, knowledge on the part of the feelings of something outside themselves. That granted, every other true thing follows naturally, and it is hard to go astray. The knowledge the present feeling has of the past
ones is a real tie between them, so is their resemblance; so is their continuity; so is the one's 'appropriation' of the other: all are real ties, realized in the judging Thought of every moment, the only place where disconnections could be realized, did they exist. Hume and Mill both imply that a disconnection can be realized there, whilst a tie cannot. But the ties and the disconnections are exactly on a par, in this matter of self-consciousness. The way in which the present Thought appropriates the past is a real way, so long as no other owner appropriates it in a more real way, and so long as the Thought has no grounds for repudiating it stronger than those which lead to its appropriation. But no other owner ever does in point of fact present himself for my past; and the grounds which I perceive for appropriating it - - viz., continuity and resemblance with the present - outweigh those I perceive for disowning it - - viz., distance in time. My present Thought stands thus in the plenitude of ownership of the train of my past selves, is owner not only de facto, but de jure, the most real owner there can be, and all without the supposition of any 'inexplicable tie,' but in a perfectly verifiable and phenomenal way.

Turn we now to what we may call...

The Transcendentalist Theory.

which owes its origin to Kant. Kant's own statements are too lengthy and obscure for verbatim quotation here, so I must give their substance only. Kant starts, as I understand him, from a view of the Object essentially like our own description of it on p. 275 ff., that is, it is a system of things, qualities or facts in relation. "Object is that in the knowledge (Begriff) of which the Manifold of a given Perception is connected."[30] But whereas we simple begged the vehicle of this connected knowledge in the shape of what we call the present Thought, or section of the Stream of Consciousness (which we declared to be the ultimate fact for psychology), Kant denies this to be an ultimate fact and insists on analyzing it into a large number of distinct, though equally essential, elements. The 'Manifoldness' of the Object is due to Sensibility, which per se is chaotic, and the unity is due to the synthetic handling which this Manifold receives from the higher faculties of Intuition, Apprehension, Imagination, Understanding, and Apperception. It is the one essential spontaneity of the Understanding which, under these different names, brings unity into the manifold of sense.

"The Understanding is, in fact, nothing more than the faculty of binding together a priori, and of bringing the Manifold of given ideas under the unity of Apperception, which consequently is the supreme principle of all human knowledge" (§ 16).

The material connected must be given by lower faculties to the Understanding, for the latter is not an intuitive faculty, but by nature 'empty.' And the bringing of this material 'under the unity of Apperception' is explained by Kant to mean the thinking it always so that, whatever its other determinations be, it may be known as thought by me.[31] Though this consciousness, that I think it, need not be at every moment explicitly realized, it is always capable of being realized. For if an object incapable of being combined with the idea of a thinker were there, how could it be known, how related to other objects, how form part of 'experience' at all?

The awareness that I think is therefore implied in all experience. No connected consciousness of anything without that of Self as its presupposition and 'transcendental' condition! All things, then, so far as they are intelligible at all, are so through combination with pure consciousness of Self, and apart from this, at least potential, combination nothing is knowable to us at all.

But this self, whose consciousness Kant thus established deductively as a conditio sine quâ non of experience, is in the same breath denied by him to have any positive attributes. Although Kant's name for it - the 'original transcendental synthetic Unity of Apperception' - is so long, our consciousness about it is, according to him, short enough. Self-consciousness of this 'transcendental' sort tells us, 'not how we appear, not how we inwardly are, but only that we are' (§ 25). At the basis of our knowledge of our selves there lies only "the simple and utterly empty idea: I; of which we cannot even say we have a notion, but only a consciousness which accompanies all notions. In this I, or he or it (the thing) which thinks, nothing more is represented than the bare transcendental Subject of the knowledge = x, which is only recognized by the thoughts which are its predicates, and of which, taken by itself, we cannot form the least conception" (ibid. 'Paralogisms'). The pure Ego of all apperception is thus for Kant not the soul, but only that 'Subject' which is the necessary correlate of the Object in all knowledge. There is a soul, Kant thinks, but this mere ego-form of our consciousness tells us nothing about it, neither whether it be substantial, nor whether it be immaterial, nor whether it be simple, nor whether it be permanent. These declarations on Kant's part of the utter barrenness of the consciousness of the pure Self, and of the consequent impossibility of any deductive or 'rational' psychology, are what, more than anything else, earned for him the title of the 'all-destroyer.' The only self we know anything positive about, he thinks, is the empirical me, not the pure I; the self which is an object among other objects and the 'constituents' of which we ourselves have seen, and recognized to be phenomenal things appearing in the form of space as well as time.

This, for our purposes, is a sufficient account of the 'transcendental' Ego.

Those purposes go no farther than to ascertain whether anything in Kant's conception ought to make us give up our own, of a remembering and appropriating Thought incessantly renewed. In many respects Kant's meaning is obscure, but it will not be necessary for us to squeeze the texts in order to make sure what it actually and historically was. If we can define clearly two or three things which it may possibly have been, that will help us just as much to clear our own ideas.

On the whole, a defensible interpretation of Kant's view would take somewhat the following shape. Like ourselves he believes in a Reality outside the mind of which he writes, but the critic who vouches for that reality does so on grounds of faith, for it is not a verifiable phenomenal thing. Neither is it manifold. The 'Manifold' which the intellectual functions combine is a mental manifold altogether, which thus stands between the Ego of Apperception and the outer Reality, but still stands inside the mind. In the function of knowing there is a multiplicity to be connected, and Kant brings this multiplicity inside the mind. The Reality becomes a mere empty locus, or unknowable, the so-called Noumenon; the manifold phenomenon is in the mind. We, on the contrary, put the

Multiplicity with the Reality outside, and leave the mind simple. Both of us deal with the same elements - thought and object - the only question is in which of them the multiplicity shall be lodged. Wherever it is lodged it must be 'synthetized' when it comes to be thought. And that particular way of lodging it will be the better, which, in addition to describing the facts naturally, makes the 'mystery of synthesis' least hard to understand.

Well, Kant's way of describing the facts is mythological. The notion of our thought being this sort of an elaborate internal machine-shop stands condemned by all we said in favor of its simplicity. Our Thought is not composed of parts, however so composed its objects may be. There is no originally chaotic manifold in it to be reduced to order. There is something almost shocking in the notion of so chaste a function carrying this Kantian hurlyburly in her womb. If we are to have a dualism of Thought and Reality at all, the multiplicity should be lodged in the latter and not in the former member of the couple of related terms. The parts and the relations surely belong less to the knower than to what is known.

But even were all the mythology true, the process of synthesis would in no whit be explained by calling the inside of the mind its seat. No mystery would be made lighter by such means. It is just as much a puzzle how the 'Ego' can employ the productive Imagination to make the Understanding use the categories to combine the data which Recognition, Association, and Apprehension receive from sensible Intuition, as how the Thought can combine the objective facts. Phrase it as one may, the difficulty is always the same: the Many known by the One. Or does one seriously think he understands better how the knower 'connects' its objects, when one calls the former a transcendental Ego and the latter a 'Manifold of Intuition' than when one calls them Thought and Things respectively? Knowing must have a vehicle. Call the vehicle Ego, or call it Thought, Psychosis, Soul, Intelligence, Consciousness, Mind, Reason, Feeling, - what you like - it must know. The best grammatical subject for the verb know would, if possible, be one from whose other properties the knowing could be deduced. And if there be no such subject, the best one would be that with the fewest ambiguities and the least pretentious name. By Kant's confession, the transcendental Ego has no properties, and from it nothing can be deduced. Its name is pretentious, and, as we shall presently see, has its meaning ambiguously mixed up with that of the substantial soul. So on every possible account we are excused from using it instead of our own term of the present passing 'Thought,' as the principle by which the Many is simultaneously known.

The ambiguity referred to in the meaning of the transcendental Ego is as to whether Kant signified by it an Agent, and by the Experience it helps to constitute, an operation; or whether the experience is an event produced in an unassigned way, and the Ego a mere indwelling element therein contained. If an operation be meant, then Ego and Manifold must both be existent prior to that collision which results in the experience of one by the other. If a mere analysis is meant, there is no such prior existence, and the elements only are in so far as they are in union. Now Kant's tone and language are everywhere the very words of one who is talking of operations and the agents by which they are performed.[32] And yet there is reason to think that at bottom he may have had nothing of the sort in mind.[33] In this uncertainty we need again do no more than decide what to think of his transcendental Ego if it be an agent.

Well, if it be so, Transcendentalism is only Substantialism grown shame-faced, and the Ego only a 'cheap and nasty' edition of the soul. All our reasons for preferring the 'Thought' to the 'Soul' apply with redoubled force when the Soul is shrunk to this estate. The Soul truly explained nothing; the 'syntheses,' which she performed, were simply taken ready-made and clapped on to her as expressions of her nature taken after the fact; but at least she had some semblance of nobility and outlook. She was called active; might select; was responsible, and permanent in her way. The Ego is simply nothing: as ineffectual and windy an abortion as Philosophy can show. It would indeed by one of Reason's tragedies if the good Kant, with all his honesty and strenuous pains, should have deemed this conception an important outbirth of his thought.

But we have seen that Kant deemed it of next to no importance at all. It was reserved for his Fichtean and Hegelian successors to call it the first Principle of Philosophy, to spell its name in capitals and pronounce it with adoration, to act, in short, as if they were going up in a balloon, whenever the notion of it crossed their mind. Here again, however, I am uncertain of the facts of history, and know that I may not read my authors aright. The whole lesson of Kantian and post-Kantian speculation is, it seems to me, the lesson of simplicity. With Kant, complication both of thought and statement was an inborn infirmity, enhanced by the musty academicism of his Königsberg existence. With Hegel is was a raging fever. Terribly, therefore, do the sour grapes which these fathers of philosophy have eaten set our teeth on edge. We have in England and America, however, a contemporary continuation of Hegelism from which, fortunately, somewhat simpler deliverances come; and, unable to find any definite psychology in what Hegel, Rosenkranz, or Erdmann tells us of the Ego, I turn to Caird and Green.

The great difference, practically, between these authors and Kant is their complete abstraction from the onlooking Psychologist and from the Reality he thinks he knows; or rather it is the absorption of both of these outlying terms into the proper topic of Psychology, viz., the mental experience of the mind under observation. The Reality coalesces with the connected Manifold, the Psychologist with the Ego, knowing becomes 'connecting,' and there results no longer a finite or criticisable, but an 'absolute' Experience, of which the Object and the Subject are always the same. Our finite 'Thought' is virtually and potentially this eternal (or rather this 'timeless'), absolute Ego, and only provisionally and speciously the limited thing which it seems primâ facie to be. The later 'sections' of our 'Stream,' which come and appropriate the earlier ones, are those earlier ones, just as in substantialism the Soul is throughout all time the same.[34] This 'solipsistic' character of an Experience conceived as absolute really annihilates psychology as a distinct body of science.

Psychology is a natural science, an account of particularly finite streams of thought, coexisting and succeeding in time. It is of course conceivable (though far from clearly so) that in the last metaphysical resort all these streams of thought may be thought by one universal All-thinker. But in this metaphysical notion there is no profit for psychology; for grant that one Thinker does think in all of us, still what He thinks in me and what in you can never be deduced from the bare idea of Him. The idea of Him seems even to exert a positively paralyzing effect on the mind. The existence of finite thoughts is suppressed altogether. Thought's characteristics, as Professor Green says, are "not to be sought in the incidents of individual lives which last but for a day.... No knowledge, nor any mental act involved in knowledge, can properly be called a 'phenomenon of consciousness.'... For a phenomenon is a sensible event, related in the way of antecedence or consequence to other sensible events, but the consciousness which constitutes a knowledge . . . is not an event so related nor made up of such events."

Again, if

"we examine the constituents of any perceived object, . . . we shall find alike that it is only for consciousness that they can exist, and that the consciousness for which they thus exist cannot be merely a series of phenomena or a succession of states.... It then becomes clear that there is a function of consciousness, as exercised in the most rudimentary experience [namely, the function of synthesis] which is incompatible with the definition of consciousness as any sort of succession of any sort of phenomena."[35]

Were we to follow these remarks, we should have to abandon our notion of the 'Thought' (perennially renewed in time, but always cognitive thereof), and to espouse instead of it an entity copied from thought in all essential respects, but differing from it in being 'out of time.' What psychology can gain by this barter would be hard to divine. Moreover this resemblance of the timeless Ego to the Soul is completed by other resemblances still. The monism of the post-Kantian idealists seems always lapsing into a regular old-fashioned spiritualistic dualism. They incessantly talk as if, like the Soul, their All-thinker were an Agent, operating on detached materials of sense. This may come from the accidental fact that the English writings of the school have been more polemic than constructive, and that a reader may often take for a positive profession a statement ad hominem meant as part of a reduction to the absurd, or mistake the analysis of a bit of knowledge into elements for a dramatic myth about its creation. But I think the matter has profounder roots. Professor Green constantly talks of the 'activity' of Self as a 'condition' of knowledge taking place. Facts are said to become incorporated with other facts only through the 'action of a combining self-consciousness upon data of sensation.'

"Every object we perceive . . . requires, in order to its presentation, the action of a principle of consciousness, not itself subject to conditions of time, upon successive appearances, such action as may hold the appearances together, without fusion, in an apprehended fact."[36]

It is needless to repeat that the connection of things in our knowledge is in no whit explained by making it the deed of an agent whose essence is self-identity and who is out of time. The agency of phenomenal thought coming and going in time is just as easy to understand. And when it is furthermore said that the agent that combines is the same 'self-distinguishing subject' which 'in another mode of its activity' presents the manifold object to itself, the unintelligibilities become quite paroxysmal, and we are forced to confess that the entire school of thought in question, in spite of occasional glimpses of something more refined, still dwells habitually in that mythological stage of thought where phenomena are explained as results of dramas enacted by entities which but reduplicate the characters of the phenomena themselves. The self must not only know its object, - that is too bald and dead a relation to be written down and left in its static state. The knowing must be painted as a 'famous victory' in which the object's distinctness is in some way 'overcome.'

"The self exists as one self only as it opposes itself, as object, to itself as subject, and immediately denies and transcends that opposition. Only because it is such a concrete unity, which has in itself a resolved contradiction, can the intelligence cope with all the manifoldness and division of the mighty universe, and hope to master its secrets. As the lightning sleeps in the dew-drop, so in the simple and transparent unity of self-consciousness there is held in equilibrium that vital antagonism of opposites which . . . seems to rend the world asunder. The intelligence is able to understand the world, or, in other words, to break down the barrier itself and things and find itself in them, just because its own existence is implicitly the solution of all the division and conflict of things."[37]

This dynamic (I had almost written dynamitic) way of representing knowledge has the merit of not being tame. To turn from it to our own psychological formulation is like turning from the fireworks, trap-doors, and transformations of the pantomime into the insipidity of the midnight, where...

*"ghastly through the drizzling rain,
On the bald street breaks the blank day!"*[38]

And yet turn we must, with the confession that our 'Thought' - a cognitive phenomenal event in time - is, if it exist at all, itself the only Thinker which the facts require. The only service that transcendental egoism has done to psychology has been by its protests against Hume's 'bundle' - theory of mind. But this service has been ill-performed; for the Egoists themselves, let them say what they will, believe in the bundle, and in their own system merely tie it up, with their special transcendental string, invented for that use alone. Besides, they talk as if, with this miraculous tying or 'relating,' the Ego's duties were done. Of its far more important duty of choosing some of the things it ties and appropriating them, to the exclusion of the rest, they tell us never a word. To sum up, then, my own opinion of the transcendentalist school, it is (whatever ulterior metaphysical truth it may divine) a school in which psychology at least has naught to learn, and whose deliverances about the Ego in particular in no wise oblige us to revise our own formulation of the Stream of Thought.[39]

With this, all possible rival formulations have been discussed. The literature of the Self is large, but all its authors may be classed as radical or mitigated representatives of the three schools we have named, substantialism, associationism, or transcendentalism. Our own opinion must be classed apart, although it incorporates essential elements from all three schools. There need never have been a quarrel between associationism and its rivals if the former had admitted the indecomposable unity of every pulse of thought, and the latter been willing to allow that 'perishing' pulses of thought might recollect and know.

We may sum up by saying that personality implies the incessant presence of two elements, and objective person, known by a passing subjective Thought and recognized as continuing in time. Hereafter let us see the words ME and I for the empirical person and the judging Thought.

Certain vicissitudes in the me demand our notice.

In the first place, although its changes are gradual, they become in time great. The central part of the me is the feeling of the body and of the adjustments in the head; and in the feeling of the body should be included that of the general emotional tones and tendencies, for at bottom these are but the habits in which organic activities and sensibilities run. Well, from infancy to old age, this assemblage of feelings, most constant of all, is yet a prey to slow mutation. Our powers, bodily and mental, change at least as fast.[40] Our possessions notoriously are perishable facts.

The identity which the I discovers, as it surveys this long procession, can only be a relative identity, that of a slow shifting in which there is always some common ingredient retained.[41] The commonest element of all, the most uniform, is the possession of the same memories. However different the man may be from the youth, both look back on the same childhood, and call it their own.

Thus the identity found by the I in its me is only a loosely construed thing, an identity 'on the whole,' just like that which any outside observer might find in the same assemblage of facts. We often say of a man 'he is so changed one would not know him'; and so does a man, less often, speak of himself. These changes in the me, recognized by the I, or by outside observers, may be grave or slight. They deserve some notice here.

The Mutations of the Self.

...may be divided into two main classes:

1. Alterations of memory; and
2. Alterations in the present bodily and spiritual selves.

1. Alterations of memory are either losses or false recollections. In either case the me is changed. Should a man be punished for what he did in his childhood and no longer remembers? Should he be punished for crimes enacted in post-epileptic unconsciousness, somnambulism, or in any involuntarily induced state of which no recollection is retained? Law, in accord with common-sense, says: "No; he is not the same person forensically now which he was then." These losses of memory are a normal incident of extreme old age, and the person's me shrinks in the ratio of the facts that have disappeared.

In dreams we forget our waking experiences; they are as if they were not. And the converse is also true. As a rule, no memory is retained during the waking state of what has happened during mesmeric trance, although when again entranced the person may remember it distinctly, and may then forget facts belonging to the waking state. We thus have, within the bounds of healthy mental life, an approach to an alteration of me's.

False memories are by no means rare occurrences in most of us, and, whenever they occur, they distort the consciousness of the me. Most people, probably, are in doubt about certain matters ascribed to their past. They may have seen them, may have said them, done them, or they may only have dreamed or imagined they did so. The content of a dream will oftentimes insert itself into the stream of real life in a most perplexing way. The most frequent source of false memory is the accounts we give to others of our experiences. Such accounts we almost always make both more simple and more interesting than the truth. We quote what we should have said or done, rather than what we really said or did; and in the first telling we may be fully aware of the distinction. But ere long the fiction expels the reality from memory and reigns in its stead alone. This is one great source of the fallibility of testimony meant to be quite honest. Especially where the marvellous is concerned, the story takes a tilt that way, and the memory follows the story. Dr. Carpenter quotes from Miss Cobbe the following, as in instance of a very common sort:

"It happened once to the Writer to hear a most scrupulously conscientious friend narrate an incident of table-turning, to which she appended an assurance that the table rapped when nobody was within a yard of it. The writer being confounded by this latter fact, the lady, though fully satisfied of the accuracy of her statement, promised to look at the note she had made ten years previously of the transaction. The note was examined, and was found to contain the distinct statement that the table rapped when the hands of six persons rested on it! The lady's memory as to all other points proved to be strictly correct; and in this point she had erred in entire good faith."[42]

It is next to impossible to get a story of this sort accurate in all its details, although it is the inessential details that suffer most change.[43] Dickens and Balzac were said to have constantly mingled their fictions with their real experiences. Every one must have known some specimen of our mortal dust so intoxicated with the thought of his own person and the sound of his own voice as never to be able even to think the truth when his autobiography was in question. Amiable, harmless, radiant J. V.! mayst thou ne'er wake to the difference between thy real and thy fondly-imagined self![44]

2. When we pass beyond alterations of memory to abnormal alterations in the present self we have still graver disturbances. These alterations are of three main types, from the descriptive point of view. But certain cases unite features of two or more types; and our knowledge of the elements and causes of these changes of personality is so slight that the division into types must not be regarded as having any profound significance. The types are:

(1)   Insane delusions;
(2)   Alternating selves;
(3)   Mediumships or possessions.

1)   In insanity we often have delusions projected into the past, which are melancholic or sanguine according to the character of the disease. But the worst alterations of the self come from present perversions of sensibility and impulse which leave the past undisturbed, but induce the patient to think that the present me is an altogether new personage. Something of this sort happens normally in the rapid expansion of the whole character, intellectual as well as volitional, which takes place after the time of puberty. The pathological cases are curious enough to merit longer notice.

The basis of our personality, as M. Ribot says, is that feeling of our vitality which, because it is so perpetually present, remains in the background of our consciousness.

"It is the basis because, always present, always acting, without peace or rest, it knows neither sleep nor fainting, and lasts as long as life itself, of which it is one form. It serves as a support to that self-conscious me which memory constitutes, it is the medium of association among its other parts. . . . Suppose now that it were possible at once to change our body and put another into its place: skeleton, vessels, viscera, muscles, skin, everything made new, except the nervous system with its stored-up memory of the past. There can be no doubt that in such a case the afflux of unaccustomed vital sensations would produce the gravest disorders. Between the old sense of existence engraved on the nervous system, and the new one acting with all the intensity of its reality and novelty, there would be irreconcilable contradiction."[45]

With the beginnings of cerebral disease there often happens something quite comparable to this:

"Masses of new sensation, hitherto foreign to the individual, impulses and ideas of the same inexperienced kind, for example terrors, representations of enacted crime, of enemies pursuing one, etc. At the outset, these stand in contrast with the old familiar me, as a strange, often astonishing and abhorrent thou.[46] Often their invasion into the former circle of feelings is felt as if the old self were being taken possession of by a dark overpowering might, and the fact of such 'possession' is described in fantastic images. Always this doubleness, this struggle of the old self against the new discordant forms of experience, is accompanied with painful mental conflict, with passion, with violent emotional excitement. This is in great part the reason for the common experience, that the first stage in the immense majority of cases of mental disease is an emotional alteration particularly of a melancholic sort. If now the brain-affection, which is the immediate cause of the new abnormal train of ideas, be not relieved, the latter becomes confirmed. It may gradually contract associations with the trains of ideas which characterized the old self, or portions of the latter may be extinguished and lost in the progress of the cerebral malady, so that little by little the opposition of the two conscious me's abates, and the emotional storms are calmed. But by that time the old me itself has been falsified and turned into another by those associations, by that reception into itself of the abnormal elements of feeling and of will. The patient may again be quiet, and his thought sometimes logically correct, but in it the morbid erroneous ideas are always present, with the adhesions they have contracted, as uncontrollable premises, and the man is no longer the same, but a really new person, his old self transformed."[47]

But the patient himself rarely continues to describe the change in just these terms unless new bodily sensations in him or the loss of old ones play a predominant part. Mere perversions of sight and hearing, or even of impulse, soon cease to be felt as contradictions of the unity of the me.

What the particular perversions of the bodily sensibility may be, which give rise to there contradictions, is for the most part impossible for a sound-minded person to conceive. One patient has another self that repeats all his thoughts for him. Others, among whom are some of the first characters in history, have familiar daemons who speak with them, and are replied to. In another someone 'makes' his thoughts for him. Another has two bodies, lying in different beds. Some patients feel as if they had lost parts of their bodies, teeth, brain, stomach, etc. In some it is made of wood, glass, butter, etc. In some it does not exist any longer, or is dead, or is a foreign object quite separate from the speaker's self. Occasionally, parts of the body lose their connection for consciousness with the rest, and are treated as belonging to another person and moved by a hostile will. Thus the right hand may fight with the left as with an enemy.[48] Or the cries of the patient himself are assigned to another person with whom the patient expresses sympathy. The literature of insanity is filled with narratives of such illusions as these. M. Taine quotes from a patient of Dr. Krishaber an account of sufferings, from which it will be seen how completely aloof from what is normal a man's experience may suddenly become:

"After the first or second day it was for some weeks impossible to observe or analyze myself. The suffering - angina pectoris - was too overwhelming. It was not till the first days of January that I could give an account to myself of what I experienced. . . . Here is the first thing of which I retain a clear rememberance. I was alone, and already a prey to permanent visual trouble, when I was suddenly seized with a visual trouble infinitely more pronounced. Objects grew small and receded to infinite distances - men and things together. I was myself immeasurably far away. I looked about me with terror and astonishment; the world was escaping from me. . . . I remarked at the same time that my voice was extremely far away from me, that it sounded no longer as if mine. I struck the ground with my foot, and perceived its resistance; but this resistance seemed illusory - not that the soil was soft, but that the weight of my body was reduced to almost nothing. . . . I had the feeling of being without weight. . " In addition to being so distant, "objects appeared to me flat. When I spoke with anyone, I saw him like an image cut out of paper with no relief. . . . This sensation lasted intermittently for two years. . . . Constantly it seemed as if my legs did not belong to me. It was almost as bad with my arms. As for my head, it seemed no longer to exist. . . . I appeared to myself to act automatically, by an impulsion foreign to myself. . . . There was inside of me a new being, and another part of myself, the old being, which took no interest in the new-comer. I distinctly remember saying to myself that the sufferings of this new being were to me indifferent. I was never really dupe of these illusions, but my mind grew often tired of incessantly correcting the new impressions, and I let myself go an lived the unhappy life of this new entity. I had an ardent desire to see my old world again, to get back to my old self. This desire kept me from killing myself. . . . I was another, and I hated, I despised this other; he was perfectly odious to me; it was certainly another who had taken my form and assumed my functions."[49]

In cases similar to this, it is as certain that the I is unaltered as that the me is changed. That is to say, the present Thought of the patient is cognitive of both the old me and the new, so long as its memory holds good. Only, within that objective sphere which formerly lent itself so simply to the judgment of recognition and of egoistic appropriation, strange perplexities have arisen. The present and the past both seen therein will not unite. Where is my old me? What is this new one? Are they the same? Or have I two? Such questions, answered by whatever theory the patient is able to conjure up as plausible, form the beginning of his insane life.[50]

A case with which I am acquainted through Dr. C. J. Fisher of Tewksbury has possibly its origin in this way. The woman, Bridget F.,

"has been many years insane, and always speaks of her supposed self as 'the rat,' asking me to 'bury the little rat,' etc. Her real self she speaks of in the third person as 'the good woman,' saying, 'The good woman knew Dr. F. and used to work for him,' etc. Sometimes she sadly asks: 'Do you think the good woman will ever come back?' She works at needlework, knitting, laundry, etc., and shows her work, saying, 'Isn't that good for only a rat?' She has, during periods of depression, hid herself under buildings, and crawled into holes and under boxes. 'She was only a rat, and wants to die,' she would say when we found her."

2. The phenomenon of altering personality in its simplest phases seems based on lapses of memory. Any man becomes, as we say, inconsistent with himself if he forgets his engagements, pledges, knowledges, and habits; and it is merely a question of degree at what point we shall say that his personality is changed. In the pathological cases known as those of double or alternate personality the lapse of memory is abrupt, and is usually preceded by a period of unconsciousness or syncope lasting a variable length of time. In the hypnotic trance we can easily produce an alteration of the personality, either by telling the subject to forget all that has happened to him since such or such a date, in which case he becomes (it may be) a child again, or by telling him he is another altogether imaginary personage, in which case all facts about himself seem for the time being to lapse from out his mind, and he throws himself into the new character with a vivacity proportionate to the amount of histrionic imagination which he possesses.[51] But in the pathological cases the transformation is spontaneous. The most famous case, perhaps, on record is that of Fèlida X., reported by Dr. Azam of Bordeaux.[52] At the age of fourteen this woman began to pass into a 'secondary' state characterized by a change in her general disposition and character, as if certain 'inhibitions,' previously existing, were suddenly removed. During the secondary state she remembered the first state, but on emerging from it into the first state she remembered nothing of the second. At the age of forty-four the duration of the secondary state (which was on the whole superior in quality to the original state) had gained upon the latter so much as to occupy most of her time. During it she remembers the events belonging to the original state, but her complete oblivion of the secondary state when the original state recurs is often very distressing to her, as, for example, when the transition takes place in a carriage on her way to a funeral, and she hasn't the least idea which one of her friends may be dead. She actually became pregnant during one of her early secondary states, and during her first state had no knowledge of how it had come to pass. Her distress at these blanks of memory is sometimes intense and once drove her to attempt suicide.

To take another example, Dr. Rieger gives an account[53] of an epileptic man who for seventeen years had passed his life alternately free, in prisons, or in asylums, his character being orderly enough in the normal state, but alternating with periods, during which he would leave his home for several weeks, leading the life of a thief and vagabond, being sent to jail, having epileptic fits and excitement, being accused of malingering, etc., etc., and with never a memory of the abnormal conditions which were to blame for all his wretchedness.

"I have never got from anyone," says Dr. Rieger, "so singular an impression as from this man, of whom it could not be said that he had any properly conscious past at all.... It is really impossible to think one's self into such a state of mind. His last larceny had been performed in Nürnberg, he knew nothing of it, and saw himself before the court and then in the hospital, but without in the least understanding the reason why. That he had epileptic attacks, he knew. But it was impossible to convince him that for hours together he raved and acted in an abnormal way."

Another remarkable case is that of Mary Reynolds, lately republished again by Dr. Weir Mitchell.[54] This dull and melancholy young woman, inhabiting the Pennsylvania wilderness in 1811,

"was found one morning, long after her habitual time for rising, in a profound sleep from which it was impossible to arouse her. After eighteen or twenty hours of sleeping she awakened, but in a state of unnatural consciousness. Memory had fled. To all intents and purposes she was as a being for the first time ushered into the world. 'All of the past that remained to her was the faculty of pronouncing a few words, and this seems to have been as purely instinctive as the wailings of an infant; for at first the words which she uttered were connected with no ideas in her mind.' Until she was taught their significance they were unmeaning sounds.

"'Her eyes were virtually for the first time opened upon the world. Old things had passed away; all things had become new.' Her parents, brothers, sisters, friends, were not recognized or acknowledged as such by her. She had never seen them before, - never known them, - was not aware that such persons had been. Now for the first time she was introduced to their company and acquaintance. To the scenes by which she was surrounded she was a perfect stranger. The house, the fields, the forest, the hills, the vales, the streams, - all were novelties. The beauties of the landscape were all unexplored.

"She had not the slightest consciousness that she had ever existed previous to the moment in which she awoke from that mysterious slumber. 'In a word, she was an infant, just born, yet born in a state of maturity, with a capacity for relishing the rich, sublime, luxuriant wonders of created nature.'

"The first lesson in her education was to teach her by what ties she was bound to those by whom she was surrounded, and the duties devolving upon her accordingly. This she was very slow to learn, and, 'indeed, never did learn, or, at least, never would acknowledge the ties of consanguinity, or scarcely those of friendship. She considered those she had once known as for the most part strangers and enemies, among whom she was, by some remarkable and unaccountable means, transplanted, though from what region or state of existence was a problem unsolved.'

"The next lesson was to re-teach her the arts of reading and writing. She was apt enough, and made such rapid progress in both that in a few weeks she had readily re-learned to read and write. In copying her name which her brother had written for her as a first lesson, she took her pen in a very awkward manner and began to copy from right to left in the Hebrew mode, as though she had been transplanted from an Eastern soil...

"The next thing that is noteworthy is the change which took place in her disposition. Instead of being melancholy she was now cheerful to extremity. Instead of being reserved she was buoyant and social. Formerly taciturn and retiring, she was now merry and jocose. Her disposition was totally and absolutely changed. While she was, in this second state, extravagantly found of company, she was much more enamoured of nature's works, as exhibited in the forests, hills, vales, and water-courses. She used to start in the morning, either on foot or horseback, and ramble until nightfall over the whole country; nor was she at all particular whether she were on a path or in the trackless forest. Her predilection for this manner of life may have been occasioned by the restraint necessarily imposed upon her by her friends, which caused her to consider them her enemies and not companions, and she was glad to keep out of their way.

"She knew no fear, and as bears and panthers were numerous in the woods, and rattlesnakes and copperheads abounded everywhere, her friends told her of the danger to which she exposed herself, but it produced no other effect than to draw forth a contemptuous laugh, as she said, 'I know you only want to frighten me and keep me at home, but you miss it, for I often see your bears and I am perfectly convinced that they are nothing more than black hogs.'

"One evening, after her return from her daily excursion, she told the following incident: 'As I was riding to-day along a narrow path a great black hog came out of the woods and stopped before me. I never saw such an impudent black hog before. It stood up on its hind feet and grinned and gnashed its teeth at me. I could not make the horse go on. I told him he was a fool to be frightened at a hog, and tried to whip him past, but he would not go an wanted to turn back. I told the hog to get out of the way, but he did not mind me. "Well," said I, "if you won't for words, I'll try blows;" so I got off and took a stick, and walked up toward it. When I got pretty close by, it got down on all fours and walked away slowly and sullenly, stopping every few steps and looking back and grinning and growling. Then I got on my horse and rode on.'...

"Thus it continued for five weeks, when one morning, after a protracted sleep, she awoke and was herself again. She recognized the parental, the brotherly, and sisterly ties as though nothing had happened, and immediately went about the performance of duties incumbent upon her, and which she had planned five weeks previously. Great was her surprise at the change which one night (as she supposed) had produced. Nature bore a different aspect. Not a trace was left in her mind of the giddy scenes through which she had passed. Her ramblings through the forest, her tricks and humor, all were faded from her memory, and not a shadow left behind. Her parents saw their child; her brothers and sisters saw their sister. She now had all the knowledge that she had possessed in her first state previous to the change, still fresh and in as vigorous exercise as though no change had been. But any new acquisitions she had made, and any new ideas she had obtained, were lost to her now - yet not lost, but laid up out of sight in safe-keeping for future use. Of course her natural disposition returned; her melancholy was deepened by the information of what had occurred. All went on in the old-fashioned way, and it was fondly hoped that the mysterious occurrences of those five weeks would never be repeated, but these anticipations were not to be realized. After the lapse of a few weeks she fell into a profound sleep, and awoke in her second state, taking up her new life again precisely where she had left it when she before passed from that state. She was not now a daughter or a sister. All the knowledge she possessed was that acquired during the few weeks of her former period of second consciousness. She knew nothing of the intervening time. Two periods widely separated were brought into contact. She thought it was but one night.

"In this state she came to understand perfectly the facts of her case, not from memory, but from information. Yet her buoyancy of spirits was so great that no depression was produced. On the contrary, it added to her cheerfulness, and was made the foundation, as was everything else, of mirth.

"These alternations from one state to another continued at intervals of varying length for fifteen or sixteen years, but finally ceased when she attained the age of thirty-five or thirty-six, leaving her permanently in her second state. In this she remained without change for the last quarter of a century of her life."

The emotional opposition of the two states seems, however, to have become gradually effaced in Mary Reynolds:

"The change from a gay, hysterical, mischievous woman, fond of jests and subject to absurd beliefs or delusive convictions, to one retaining the joyousness and love of society, but sobered down to levels of practical usefulness, was gradual. The most of the twenty-five years which followed she was as different from her melancholy, morbid self as from the hilarious condition of the early years of her second state. Some of her family spoke of it as her third state. She is described as becoming rational, industrious, and very cheerful, yet reasonably serious; possessed of a well-balanced temperament, and not having the slightest indication of an injured or disturbed mind. For some years she taught school, and in that capacity was both useful and acceptable, being a general favorite with old and young.

"During these last twenty-five years she lived in the same house with the Rev. Dr. John Reynolds, her nephew, part of that time keeping house for him, showing a sound judgment and a thorough acquaintance with the duties of her position.

"Dr. Reynolds, who is still living in Meadville," says Dr. Mitchell, "and who has most kindly placed the facts at my disposal, states in his letter to me of January 4, 1888, that at a later period of her life she said she did sometimes seem to have a dim, dreamy idea of a shadowy past, which she could not fully grasp, and could not be certain whether it originated in a partially restored memory or in the statements of the events by others during her abnormal state.

"Miss Reynolds died in January, 1854, at the age of sixty-one. On the morning of the day of her death she rose in her usual health, at her breakfast, and superintended household duties. While thus employed she suddenly raised her hands to her head and exclaimed: 'Oh! I wonder what is the matter with my head!' and immediately fell to the floor. When carried to a sofa she gasped once or twice and died."

In such cases as the preceding, in which the secondary character is superior to the first, there seems reason to think that the first one is the morbid one. The word inhibition describes its dulness and melancholy. Félida X.'s original character was dull and melancholy in comparison with that which she later acquired, and the change may be regarded as the removal of inhibitions which had maintained themselves from earlier years. Such inhibitions we all know temporarily, when we can not recollect or in some other way command our mental resources. The systematized amnesias (losses of memory) of hypnotic subjects ordered to forget all nouns, or all verbs, or a particular letter of the alphabet, or all that is relative to a certain person, are inhibitions of the sort on a more extensive scale. They sometimes occur spontaneously as symptoms of disease.[55] Now M. Pierre Janet has shown that such inhibitions when they bear on a certain class of sensations (making the subject anaesthetic thereto) and also on the memory of such sensations, are the basis of changes of personality. The anaesthetic and 'amnesic' hysteric is one person; but when you restore her inhibited sensibilities and memories by plunging her into the hypnotic trance - in other words, when

you rescue them from their 'dissociated' and split-off condition, and make them rejoin the other sensibilities and memories - she is a different person. As said above the hypnotic trance is one method of restoring sensibility in hysterics. But one day when the hysteric anaesthetic named Lucie was already in the hypnotic trance, M. Janet for a certain reason continued to make passes over her for a full half-hour as if she were not already asleep. The result was to throw her into a sort of syncope from which, after half an hour, she revived in a second somnambulic condition entirely unlike that which had characterized her thitherto - different sensibilities, a different memory, a different person, in short. In the waking state the poor young woman was anaesthetic all over, nearly deaf, and with a badly contracted field of vision. Bad as it was, however, sight was her best sense, and she used it as a guide in all her movements. With her eyes bandaged she became entirely helpless, and like other persons of a similar sort whose cases have been recorded, she almost immediately fell asleep in consequence of the withdrawal of her last sensorial stimulus. M. Janet calls this waking or primary (one can hardly in such a connection say 'normal') state by the name of Lucie 1. In Lucie 2, her first sort of hypnotic trance, the anaesthesias were diminished but not removed. In the deeper trance, 'Lucie 3,' brought about as just described, no trace of them remained. Her sensibility became perfect, and instead of being an extreme example of the 'visual' type, she was transformed into what in Prof. Charcot's terminology is known as a motor. That is to say, that whereas when awake she had thought in visual terms exclusively, and could imagine things only by remembering how they looked, now in this deeper trance her thoughts and memories seemed to M. Janet to be largely composed of images of movement and of touch.

Having discovered this deeper trance and change of personality in Lucie, M. Janet naturally became eager to find it in his other subjects. He found it in Rose, in Marie, and in Léonie; and his brother, Dr. Jules Janet, who was interne at the Salpétrière Hospital, found it in the celebrated subject Wit . . . . whose trances had been studied for years by the various doctors of that institution without any of them having happened to awaken this very peculiar individuality.[56]

With the return of all the sensibilities in the deeper trance, these subjects turned, as it were, into normal persons. Their memories in particular grew more extensive, and hereupon M. Janet spins a theoretic generalization. When a certain kind of sensation, he says, is abolished in an hysteric patient, there is also abolished along with it all recollection of past sensations of that kind. If, for example, hearing be the anaesthetic sense, the patient becomes unable even to imagine sounds and voices, and has to speak (when speech is till possible) by means of motor or articulatory cues. If the motor sense be abolished, the patient must will the movements of his limbs by first defining them to his mind in visual terms, and must innervate his voice by premonitory ideas of the way in which the words are going to sound. The practical consequences of this law would be great, for all experiences belonging to a sphere of sensibility which afterwards became anaesthetic, as, for example, touch, would have been stored away and remembered in tactile terms, and be incontinently forgotten as soon as the cutaneous and muscular sensibility should come to be cut out in the course of disease. Memory of them would be restored again, on the other hand, as soon as the sense of touch came back. Now, in the hysteric subjects on whom M. Janet experimented, touch did come back in the state of trance. The result was that all sorts of memories, absent in the ordinary condition, came back too, and they could then go back and explain the origin of many otherwise inexplicable things in their life. One stage in the great convulsive crisis of hystero-epilepsy, for example, is what French writers call the phase des attitudes passionelles, in which the patient, without speaking or giving any account of herself, will go through the outward movements of fear, anger, or some other emotional state of mind. Usually this phase is, with each patient, a thing so stereotyped as to seem automatic, and doubts have even been expressed as to whether any consciousness exists whilst it lasts. When, however, the patient Lucie's tactile sensibility came back in the deeper trance, she explained the origin of her hysteric crisis in a great fright which she had had when a child, on a day when certain men, hid behind the curtains, had jumped out upon her; she told how she went through this scene again in all her crises; she told of her sleep-walking fits through the house when a child, and how for several months she had been shut in a dark room because of a disorder of the eyes. All these were things of which she recollected nothing when awake, because they were records of experiences mainly of motion and of touch.

But M. Janet's subject Léonie is interesting, and shows best how with the sensibilities and motor impulses the memories and character will change.

"This woman, whose life sounds more like an improbable romance than a genuine history, has had attacks of natural somnambulism since the age of three years. She has been hypnotized constantly by all sorts of persons from the age of sixteen upwards, and she is now forty-five. Whilst her normal life developed in one way in the midst of her poor country surroundings, her second life was passed in drawing-rooms and doctors' offices, and naturally took an entirely different direction. Today, when in her normal state, this poor peasant woman is a serious and rather sad person, calm and slow, very mild with every one, and extremely timid: to look at her one would never suspect the personage which she contains. But hardly is she put to sleep hypnotically when a metamorphosis occurs. Her face is no longer the same. She keeps her eyes closed, it is true, but the acuteness of her other senses supplies their place. She is gay, noisy, restless, sometimes insupportably so. She remains good-natured, but has acquired a singular tendency to irony and sharp jesting. Nothing is more curious than to hear her after a sitting when she has received a visit from strangers who wished to see her asleep. She gives a word-portrait of them, apes their manners, pretends to know their little ridiculous aspects and passions, and for each invents a romance. To this character must be added the possession of an enormous number of recollections, whose existence she does not even suspect when awake, for her amnesia is then complete.... She refuses the name of Léonie and takes that of Léontine (Léonie 2) to which her first magnetizers had accustomed her. 'That good woman is not myself,' she says, 'she is too stupid!' To herself, Léontine or Léonie 2, she attributes all the sensations and all the actions, is a word all the conscious experiences which she has undergone in somnambulism, and knits them together to make the history of her already long life. To Léonie 1 (as M. Janet calls the waking woman] on the other hand, she exclusively ascribes the events lived through in waking hours. I was at first struck by an important exception to the rule, and was disposed to think that there might be something arbitrary in this partition of her recollections. In the normal state Léonie has a husband and children; but Léonie 2, the somnambulist, whilst acknowledging the children as her own, attributes the husband to 'the other.' This choice, was perhaps explicable, but it followed no rule. It was not till later that I learned that her magnetizers in early days, as audacious as certain hypnotizers of recent date, had somnambulized her for her first accouchements, and that she had lapsed into that state spontaneously in the later ones. Léonie 2 was thus quite right in ascribing to herself the children - it was she who had had them, and the rule that her first trance-state forms a different personality was not broken. But it is the same with her second or deepest state of trance. When after the renewed passes, syncope, etc., she reaches the condition which I have called Léonie 3, she is another person still. Serious and grave, instead of being a restless child, she speaks slowly and moves but little. Again she separates herself from the waking Léonie 1. 'A good but rather stupid woman,' she says, 'and not me.' And she also separates herself from Léonie 2: 'How can you see anything of me in that crazy creature?' she says. 'Fortunately I am nothing for her.'"

Léonie 1 knows only of herself; Léonie 2 of herself and of Léonie 1; Léonie 3 knows of herself and of both the others. Léonie 1 has a visual consciousness; Léonie 2 has one both visual and auditory; in Léonie 3 it is at once visual, auditory, and tactile. Prof. Janet thought at first that he was Léonie 3's discoverer. But she told him that she had been frequently in that condition before. A former magnetizer had hit upon her just as M. Janet had, in seeking by means of passes to deepen the sleep of Léonie 2.

"This resurrection of a somnambulic personage who had been extinct for twenty years is curious enough; and in speaking to Léonie 3, I naturally now adopt the name of Léonore which was given her by her first master."

The most carefully studies case of multiple personality is that of the hysteric youth Louis V. about whom MM. Bourru and Burot have written a book.[57] The symptoms are too intricate to be reproduced here with detail. Suffice it that Louis V. had led an irregular life, in the army, in hospitals, and in houses of correction, and had had numerous hysteric anaesthesias, paralyses, and contractures attacking him differently at different times and when he lived at different places. At eighteen, at an agricultural House of Correction he was bitten by a viper, which brought on a convulsive crisis and left both of his legs paralyzed for three years. During this condition he was gentle, moral, and industrious. But suddenly at last, after a long convulsive seizure, his paralysis disappeared, and with it his memory for all the time during which it had endured. His character also changed: he became quarrelsome, gluttonous, impolite, stealing his comrades' wine, and money from an attendant, and finally escaped from the establishment and fought furiously when he was overtaken and caught. Later, when he first fell under the observation of the authors, his right side was half paralyzed and insensible, and his character intolerable; the application of metals transferred the paralysis to the left side, abolished his recollections of the other condition, and carried him psychically back to the hospital of Bicêtre where he had been treated for a similar physical condition. His character, opinions, education, all underwent a concomitant transformation. He was no longer the personage of the moment before. It appeared ere long that any present nervous disorder in him could be temporarily removed by metals, magnets, electric or other baths, etc.; and that any past disorder could be brought back by hypnotic suggestion. He also went through a rapid spontaneous repetition of his series of past disorders after each of the convulsive attacks which occurred in him at intervals. It was observed that each physical state in which he found himself, excluded certain memories and brought with it a definite modification of character.

"The law of these changes," say the authors, "is quite clear. There exist precise, constant, and necessary relations between the bodily and the mental state, such that it is impossible to modify the one without modifying the other in a parallel fashion."[58]

The case of this proteiform individual would seem, then, nicely to corroborate M. P. Janet's law that anaesthesias and gaps in memory go together. Coupling Janet's law with Locke's that changes of memory bring changes of personality, we should have an apparent explanation of some cases at least of alternate personality. But mere anaesthesia does not sufficiently explain the changes of disposition, which are probably due to modifications in the perviousness of motor and associative paths, co-ordinate with those of the sensorial paths rather than consecutive upon them. And indeed a glance at other cases than M. Janet's own, suffices to show us that sensibility and memory are not coupled in any invariable way.[59] M. Janet's law, true of his own cases, does not seem to hold good in all.

Of course it is mere guesswork to speculate on what may be the cause of the amnesias which lie at the bottom of changes in the Self. Changes of blood-supply have naturally been invoked. Alternate action of the two hemispheres was long ago proposed by Dr. Wigan in his book on the Duality of the Mind. I shall revert to this explanation after considering the third class of alterations of the Self, those, namely, which I have called 'possessions.'

I have myself become quite recently acquainted with the subject of a case of alternate personality of the 'ambulatory' sort, who has given me permission to name him in these pages.[60]

The Rev. Ansel Bourne, of Greene, R. I., was brought up to the trade of a carpenter; but, in consequence of a sudden temporary loss of sight and hearing under very peculiar circumstances, he became converted from Atheism to Christianity just before his thirtieth year, and has since that time for the most part lived the life of an itinerant preacher. He has been subject to headaches and temporary fits of depression of spirits during most of his life, and has had a few fits of unconsciousness lasting an hour or less. He also has a region of somewhat diminished cutaneous sensibility on the left thigh. Otherwise his health is good, and his muscular strength and endurance excellent. He is of a firm and self-reliant disposition, a man whose yea is yea and his nay, nay; and his character for uprightness is such in the community that no person who knows him will for a moment admit the possibility of his case not being perfectly genuine.

On January 17, 1887, he drew 551 dollars from a bank in Providence with which to pay for a certain lot of land in Greene, paid certain bills, and got into a Pawtucket horse-car. This is the last incident which he remembers. He did not return home that day, and nothing was heard of him for two months. He was published in the papers as missing, and foul play being suspected, the police sought in vain his whereabouts. On the morning of March 14th, however, at Norristown, Pennsylvania, a man calling himself A. J. Brown, who had rented a small shop six weeks previously stocked it with stationery, confectionery, fruit and small articles, and carried on his quiet trade without seeming to any one unnatural or eccentric, woke up in a fright and called in the people of the house to tell him where he was. He said that his name was Ansel Bourne, that he was entirely ignorant of Norristown, that he knew nothing of shop-keeping, and that the last thing he remembered - it seemed only yesterday - was drawing the money from the bank, etc., in Providence. He would not believe that two months had elapsed. The people of the house thought him insane; and so, at first, did Dr. Louis H. Read, whom they called in to see him. But on telegraphing to Providence, confirmatory messages came, and presently his nephew, Mr. Andrew Harris, arrived upon the scene, made everything straight, and took him home. He was very weak, having lost apparently over twenty pounds of flesh during his escapade, and had such a horror of the idea of the candy-store that he refused to set foot in it again.

The first two weeks of the period remained unaccounted for, as he had no memory, after he had once resumed his normal personality, of any part of the time, and no one who knew him seems to have seen him after he left home. The remarkable part of the change is, of course, the peculiar occupation which the so-called Brown indulged in. Mr. Bourne has never in his life had the slightest contract with trade. 'Brown' was described by the neighbors as taciturn, orderly in his habits, and in no way queer. He went to Philadelphia several times; replenished his stock; cooked for himself in the back shop, where he also slept; went regularly to church; and once at a prayer-meeting made what was considered by the hearers a good address, in the course of which he related an incident which he had witnessed in his natural state of Bourne.

This was all that was known of the case up to June 1890, when I induced Mr. Bourne to submit to hypnotism, so as to see whether, in the hypnotic trance, his 'Brown' memory would not come back. It did so with surprising readiness; so much so indeed that it proved quite impossible to make him whilst in the hypnosis remember any of the facts of his normal life. He had heard of Ansel Bourne, but "didn't know as he had ever met the man." When confronted with Mrs. Bourne he said that he had "never seen the woman before," etc. On the other hand, he told of his peregrinations during the lost fortnight,[61] and gave all sorts of details about the Norristown episode. The whole thing was prosaic enough; and the Brown-personality seems to be nothing but a rather shrunken, dejected, and amnesic extract of Mr. Bourne himself. He gives no motive for the wandering except that there was 'trouble back there' and he 'wanted rest.' During the trance he looks old, the corners of his mouth are drawn down, his voice is slow and weak, and he sits screening his eyes and trying vainly to remember what lay before and after the two months of the Brown experience. "I'm all hedged in," he says: "I can't get out at either end. I don't know what set me down in that Pawtucket horse-car, and I don't know how I ever left that store, or what became of it." His eyes are practically normal, and all his sensibilities (save for tardier response) about the same in hypnosis as in waking. I had hoped by suggestion, etc., to run the two personalities into one, and make the memories continuous, but no artifice would avail to accomplish this, and Mr. Bourne's skull to-day still covers two distinct personal selves.

The case (whether it contain an epileptic element or not) should apparently be classed as one of spontaneous hypnotic trance, persisting for two months. The peculiarity of it is that nothing else like it ever occurred in the man's life, and that no eccentricity of character came out. In most similar cases, the attacks recur, and the sensibilities and conduct markedly change.[62]

3. In 'mediumships' or 'possessions' the invasion and the passing away of the secondary state are both relatively abrupt, and the duration of the state is usually short - i.e., from a few minutes to a few hours. Whenever the secondary state is well developed no memory for aught that happened during it remains after the primary consciousness comes back. The subject during the secondary consciousness speaks, writes, or acts as if animated by a foreign person, and often names this foreign person and gives his history. In old times the foreign 'control' was usually a demon, and is so now in communities which favor that belief. With us he gives himself out at the worst for an Indian or other grotesquely speaking but harmless personage. Usually he purports to be the spirit of a dead person known or unknown to those present, and the subject is then what we call a 'medium.' Mediumistic possession in all its grades seems to form a perfectly natural special type of alternate personality, and the susceptibility to it in some form is by no means an uncommon gift, in persons who have no other obvious nervous anomaly. The phenomena are very intricate, and are only just beginning to be studied in a proper scientific way. The lowest phase of mediumship is automatic writing, and the lowest grade of that is where the Subject knows what words are coming, but feels impelled to write them as if from without. Then comes writing unconsciously, even whilst engaged in reading or talk. Inspirational speaking, playing on musical instruments, etc., also belong to the relatively lower phases of possession, in which the normal self is not excluded from conscious participation in the performance, though their initiative seems to come from elsewhere. In the highest phase the trance is complete, the voice, language, and everything are changed, and there is no after-memory whatever until the next trance comes. One curious thing about trance-utterances is their generic similarity in different individuals. The 'control' here in America is either a grotesque, slangy, and flippant personage ('Indian' controls, calling the ladies 'squaws,' the men 'braves,' the house a 'wigwam,' etc., etc., are excessively common); or, if he ventures on higher intellectual flights, he abounds in a curiously vague optimistic philosophy-and-water, in which phrases about spirit, harmony, beauty, law, progression, development, etc., keep recurring. It seems exactly as if one author composed more than half of the trance-messages, no matter by whom they are uttered. Whether all sub-conscious selves are peculiarly susceptible to a certain stratum of the Zeitgeist, and get their inspiration from it, I know not; but this is obviously the case with the secondary selves which become 'developed' in spiritualist circles. There the beginnings of the medium trance are indistinguishable from effects of hypnotic suggestion. The subject assumes the role of a medium simply because opinion expects it of him under the conditions which are present; and carries it out with a feebleness or a vivacity proportionate to his histrionic gifts. But the odd thing is that persons unexposed to spiritualist traditions will so often act in the same way when they become entranced, speak in the name of the departed, go through the motions of their several death-agonies, send messages about their happy home in the summer-land, and describe the ailments of those present. I have no theory to publish of these cases, several of which I have personally seen.

As an example of the automatic writing performances I will quote from an account of his own case kindly furnished me by Mr. Sidney Dean of Warren, R. I., member of Congress from Connecticut from 1855 to 1859, who has been all his life a robust and active journalist, author, and man of affairs. He has for many years been a writing subject, and has a large collection of manuscript automatically produced.

"Some of it," he writes us, "is in hieroglyph, or strange compounded arbitrary characters; each series possessing a seeming unity in general design or character, followed by what purports to be a translation or rendering into mother English. I never attempted the seemingly impossible feat of copying the characters. They were cut with the precision of a graver's tool, and generally with a single rapid stroke of the pencil. Many languages, some obsolete and passed from history, and professedly given. To see them would satisfy you that no one could copy them except by tracing.

"These, however, are but a small part of the phenomena. The 'automatic' has given place to the impressional, and when the work is in progress I am in the normal condition, and seemingly two minds, intelligences, persons, are practically engaged. The writing is in my own hand but the dictation not of my own mind and will, but that of another, upon subjects of which I can have no knowledge and hardly a theory; and I, myself, consciously criticise the thought, fact, mode of expressing it, etc., while the hand is recording the subject-matter and even the words impressed to be written. If I refuse to write the sentence, or even the word, the impression instantly ceases, and my willingness must be mentally expressed before the work is resumed, and it is resumed at the point of cessation, even if it should be in the middle of a sentence. Sentences are commenced without knowledge of mine as to their subject or ending. In fact, I have never known in advance the subject of disquisition.

"There is in progress now, at uncertain times, not subject to my will, a series of twenty-four chapters upon the scientific features of life, moral, spiritual, eternal. Seven have already been written in the manner indicated. These were preceded by twenty-four chapters relating generally to the life beyond material death, its characteristics, etc. Each chapter is signed by the name of some person who has lived on earth, - some with whom I have been personally acquainted, others known in history. . . . I know nothing of the alleged authorship of any chapter until it is completed and the name impressed and appended. . . . I am interested not only in the reputed authorship, - of which I have nothing corroborative, - but in the philosophy taught, of which I was in ignorance until these chapters appeared. From my standpoint of life - which has been that of biblical orthodoxy - the philosophy is new, seems to be reasonable, and is logically put. I confess to an inability to successfully controvert it to my own satisfaction.

"It is an intelligent ego who writes, or else the influence assumes individuality, which practically makes of the influence a personality. It is not myself; of that I am conscious at every step of the process. I have also traversed the whole field of the claims of 'unconscious cerebration,' so called, so far as I am competent to critically examine it, and it fails, as a theory, in numberless points, when applied to this strange work through me. It would be far more reasonable and satisfactory for me to accept the silly hypothesis of re-incarnation, - the old doctrine of metempsychosis, - as taught by some spiritualists to-day, and to believe that I lived a former life here, and that once in a while it dominates my intellectual powers, and writes chapters upon the philosophy of life, or opens a post-office for spirits to drop their effusions, and have them put into English script. No; the easiest and most natural solution to me is to admit the claim made, i.e., that it is a decarnated intelligence who writes. But who? that is the question. The names of scholars and thinkers who once lived are affixed to the most ungrammatical and weakest of bosh. . .

"It seems reasonable to me - upon the hypothesis that it is a person using another's mind or brain - that there must be more or less of that other's style or tone incorporated in the message, and that to the unseen personality, i.e., the power which impresses, the thought, the fact, or the philosophy, and not the style or tone, belongs. For instance, while the influence is impressing my brain with the greatest force and rapidity, so that my pencil fairly flies over the paper to record the thoughts, I am conscious that, in many cases, the vehicle of the thought, i.e., the language, is very natural and familiar to me, as if, somehow, my personality as a writer was getting mixed up with the message. And, again, the style, language, everything, is entirely foreign to my own style."

I am myself persuaded by abundant acquaintance with the trances of one medium that the 'control' may be altogether different from any possible waking self of the person. In the case I have in mind, if professes to be a certain departed French doctor; and is, I am convinced, acquainted with facts about the circumstances, and the living and dead relatives and acquaintances, of numberless sitters whom the medium never met before, and of whom she has never heard the names. I record my bare opinion here unsupported by the evidence, not, of course, in order to convert anyone to my view, but because I am persuaded that a serious study of these trance-phenomena is one of the greatest needs of psychology, and think that my personal confession may possibly draw a reader or two into a field which the soidisant 'scientist' usually refuses to explore.

Many persons have found evidence conclusive to their minds that in some cases the control is really the departed spirit whom it pretends to be. The phenomena shade off so gradually into cases where this is obviously absurd, that the presumption (quite apart from a priori 'scientific' prejudice) is great against its being true. The case of Lurancy Vennum is perhaps as extreme a case of 'possession' of the modern sort as one can find.[63] Lurancy was a young girl of fourteen, living with her parents at Watseka, Ill., who (after various distressing hysterical disorders and spontaneous trances, during which she was possessed by departed spirits of a more or less grotesque sort) finally declared herself to be animated by the spirit of Mary Roff (a neighbor's daughter, who had died in an insane asylum twelve years before) and insisted on being sent 'home' to Mr. Roff's house. After a week of 'homesickness' and importunity on her part, her parents agreed, and the Roffs, who pitied her, and who were spiritualists into the bargain, took her in. Once there, she seems to have convinced the family that their dead Mary had exchanged habitations with Lurancy. Lurancy was said to be temporarily in heaven, and Mary's spirit now controlled her organism, and lived again in her former earthly home.

"The girl, now in her new home, seemed perfectly happy and content, knowing every person and everything that Mary knew when in her original body, twelve to twenty-five years ago, recognizing and calling by name those who were friends and neighbors of the family from 1852 to 1865, when Mary died, calling attention to scores, yes, hundreds of incidents that transpired during her natural life. During all the period of her sojourn at Mr. Roff's she had no knowledge of, and did not recognize, any of Mr. Vennum's family, their friends or neighbors, yet Mr. and Mrs. Vennum and their children visited her and Mr. Roff's people, she being introduced to them as to any strangers. After frequent visits, and hearing them often and favorably spoken of, she learned to love them as acquaintances, and visited them with Mrs. Roff three times. From day to day she appeared natural, easy, affable, and industrious, attending diligently and faithfully to her household duties, assisting in the general work of the family as a faithful, prudent daughter might be supposed to do, singing, reading, or conversing as opportunity offered, upon all matters of private or general interest to the family."

The so-called Mary whilst at the Roffs' would sometimes 'go back to heaven,' and leave the body in a 'quiet trance,' i.e., without the original personality of Lurancy returning. After eight or nine weeks however, the memory and manner of Lurancy would sometimes partially, but not entirely, return for a few minutes. Once Lurancy seems to have taken full possession for a short time. At last, after some fourteen weeks, comformably to the prophecy which 'Mary' had made when she first assumed 'control,' she departed definitively and the Lurancy-consciousness came back for good. Mr. Roff writes:

"She wanted me to take her home, which I did. She called me Mr. Roff, and talked with me as a young girl would, not being acquainted. I asked her how things appeared to her - if they seemed natural. She said it seemed like a dream to her. She met her parents and brothers in a very affectionate manner, hugging and kissing each one in tears of gladness. She clasped her arms around her father's neck a long time, fairly smothering him with kisses. I saw her father just now (eleven o'clock). He says she has been perfectly natural, and seems entirely well."

Lurancy's mother writes, a couple of months later, that she was

"perfectly and entirely well and natural. For two or three weeks after her return home, she seemed a little strange to what she had been before she was taken sick last summer, but only, perhaps, the natural change that had taken place with the girl, and except it seemed to her as though she had been dreaming or sleeping, etc. Lurancy has been smarter, more intelligent, more industrious, more womanly, and more polite than before. We give the credit of her complete cure and restoration to her family, to Dr. E. W. Stevens, and Mr. and Mrs. Roff, by their obtaining her removal to Mr. Roff's, where her cure was perfected. We firmly believe that, had she remained at home, she would have died, or we would have been obliged to send her to the insane asylum; and if so, that she would have died there; and further, that I could not have lived a short time with the care and trouble devolving on me. Several of the relatives of Lurancy, including ourselves, now believe she was cured by spirit power, and that Mary Roff controlled the girl."

Eight years later, Lurancy was reported to be married and a mother, and in good health. She had apparently outgrown the mediumistic phase of her existence.[64]

On the condition of the sensibility during these invasions, few observations have been made. I have found the hands of two automatic writers anaesthetic during the act. In two others I have found this not to be the case. Automatic writing is usually preceded by shooting pains along the arm-nerves and irregular contractions of the arm-muscles. I have found one medium's tongue and lips apparently insensible to pin-pricks during her (speaking) trance.

If we speculate on the brain-condition during all these different perversions of personality, we see that it must be supposed capable of successively changing all its modes of action, and abandoning the use for the time being of whole sets of well organized association-paths. In no other way can we explain the loss of memory in passing from one alternating condition to another. And not only this, but we must admit that organized systems of paths can be thrown out of gear with others, so that the processes in one system give rise to one consciousness, and those of another system to another simultaneously existing consciousness. Thus only can we understand the facts of automatic writing, etc., whilst the patient is out of trance, and the false anaesthesias and amnesias of the hysteric type. But just what sort of dissociation the phrase 'thrown out of gear' may stand for, we cannot even conjecture; only I think we ought not to talk of the doubling of the self as if it consisted in the failure to combine on the part of certain systems of ideas which usually do so. It is better to talk of objects usually combined, and which are now divided between the two 'selves,' in the hysteric and automatic cases in question. Each of the selves is due to a system of cerebral paths acting by itself. If the brain acted normally, and the dissociated systems came together again, we should get a new affection of consciousness in the form of a third 'Self' different from the other two, but knowing their objects together, as the result. - After all I have said in the last chapter, this hardly needs further remark.

Some peculiarities in the lower automatic performances suggest that the systems thrown out of gear with each other are contained one in the right and the other in the left hemisphere. The subjects, e.g., often write backwards, or they transpose letters, or they write mirror-script. All these are symptoms of agraphic disease. The left hand, if left to its natural impulse, will in most people write mirror-script more easily than natural script. Mr. F. W. H. Myers has laid stress on these analogies.[65] He has also called attention to the usual inferior moral tone of ordinary planchette writing. On Hughlings Jackson's principles, the left hemisphere, being the more evolved organ, at ordinary times inhibits the activity of the right one; but Mr. Myers suggests that during the automatic performances the usual inhibition may be removed and the right hemisphere set free to act all by itself. This is very likely to some extent to be the case. But the crude explanation of 'two' selves by 'two' hemispheres is of course far from Mr. Myers's thought. The selves may be more than two, and the brain-systems severally used for each must be conceived as interpenetrating each other in very minute ways.

Summary.

To sum up now this long chapter. The consciousness of Self involves a stream of thought, each part of which as 'I' can 1) remember those which went before, and know the things they knew; and 2) emphasize and care paramountly for certain ones among them as 'me,' and appropriate to these the rest. The nucleus of the 'me' is always the bodily existence felt to be present at the time. Whatever remembered-past-feelings resemble this present feeling are deemed to belong to the same me with it. Whatever other things are perceived to be associated with this feeling are deemed to form part of that me's experience; and of them certain ones (which fluctuate more or less) are reckoned to be themselves constituents of the me in a larger sense, - such are the clothes, the material possessions, the friends, the honors and esteem which the person receives or may receive. This me is an empirical aggregate of things objectively known. The I which knows them cannot itself be an aggregate, neither for psychological purposes need it be considered to be an unchanging metaphysical entity like the Soul, or a principle like the pure Ego, viewed as 'out of time.' It is a Thought, at each moment different from that of the last moment, but appropriative of the latter, together with all that the latter called its own. All the experiential facts find their place in this description, unencumbered with any hypothesis save that of the existence of passing thoughts or states of mind. The same brain may subserve many conscious selves, either alternate or coexisting; but by what modifications in its action, or whether ultra-cerebral conditions may intervene, are questions which cannot now be answered.

If anyone urge that I assign no reason why the successive passing thoughts should inherit each other's possessions, or why they and the brain-states should be functions (in the mathematical sense) of each other, I reply that the reason, if there be any, must lie where all real reasons lie, in the total sense or meaning of the world. If there be such a meaning, or any approach to it (as we are bound to trust there is), it alone can make clear to us why such finite human streams of thought are called into existence in such functional dependence upon brains. This is as much as to say that the special natural science of psychology must stop with the mere functional formula. If the passing thought be the directly verifiable existent which no school has hitherto doubted it to be, then that thought is itself the thinker, and psychology need not look beyond. The only pathway that I can discover for bringing in a more transcendental thinker would be to deny that we have any direct knowledge of the thought as such. The latter's existence would then be reduced to a postulate, an assertion that there must be a knower correlative to all this known; and the problem who that knower is would have become a metaphysical problem. With the question once stated in these terms, the spiritualist and transcendentalist solutions must be considered as prima facie on a par with our own psychological one, and discussed impartially. But that carries us beyond the psychological or naturalistic point of view.

Notes

[1] *See, for a charming passage on the Philosophy of Dress, H. Lotze's Microcosmus, Eug. tr. vol. I. p. 592 ff.*
[2] *"Who filches from me my good name," etc.*
[3] *"He who imagines commendation and disgrace not to be strong motives on men . . . seems little skilled in the nature and history of mankind; the greatest part whereof he shall find to govern themselves chiefly, if not solely, by this law of fashion; and so they do that which keeps them in reputation with their company, little regard the laws of God or the magistrate. The penalties that attend the breach of God's laws some, nay, most, men seldom seriously reflect on; and amongst those that do, many, whilst they break the laws, entertain thoughts of future reconciliation, and making their peace for such breaches: and as to the punishments due from the laws of the commonwealth, they frequently flatter themselves with the hope of impunity. But no man escapes the punishment of their censure and dislike who offends against the fashion and opinion of the company*

he keeps, and would recommend himself to. Nor is there one in ten thousand who is stiff and insensible enough to bear up under the constant dislike and condemnation of his own club. He must be of a strange and unusual constitution who can content himself to live in constant disgrace and disrepute with his own particular society. Solitude many men have sought and been reconciled to; but nobody that has the least thought or sense of a man about him can live in society under the constant dislike and ill opinion of his familiars and those he converses with. This is a burden too heavy for human sufferance: and he must be made up of irreconcilable contradictions who can take pleasure in company and yet be insensible of contempt and disgrace from his companions." (Locke's Essay, book II. ch. XXVIII.§ 12.)

[4] For some farther remarks on these feelings of movement see the next chapter.

[5] Wundt's account of Self-consciousness deserves to be compared with this. What I have called 'adjustments' he calls processes of 'Apperception.' "In this development (of consciousness) one particular group of percepts claims a prominent significance, namely, those of which the spring lies in ourselves. The images of feelings we get from our own body, and the representations of our own movements distinguish themselves from all others by forming a permanent group. As there are always some muscles in a state either of tension or of activity it follows that we never lack a sense, either dim or clear, of the positions or movements of our body.... This permanent sense, moreover, has this particularity, that we are aware of our power at any moment voluntarily to arouse any one of its ingredients. We excite the sensations of movement immediately by such impulses of the will as shall arouse the movements themselves; and we excite the visual and tactile feelings of our body by the voluntary movement of our organs of sense. So we come to conceive this permanent mass of feeling as immediately or remotely subject to our will, and call it the consciousness of ourself. This self-consciousness is, at the outset, thoroughly sensational, ... only gradually the second-named of its characters, its subjection to our will, attains predominance. In proportion as the apperception of all our mental objects appears to us as an inward exercise of will, does our self-consciousness begin both to widen itself and to narrow itself at the same time. It widens itself in that every mental act, whatever comes to stand in relation to our will; and it narrows itself in that it concentrates itself more and more upon the inner activity of apperception, over against which our own body and all the representations connected with it appear as external objects, different from our proper self. This consciousness, contracted down to the process of apperception, we call our Ego; and the apperception of mental objects in general, may thus, after Leibnitz, be designated as the raising of them into our self-consciousness. Thus the natural development of self-consciousness implicitly involves the most abstract forms in which this faculty has been described in philosophy; only philosophy is fond of placing the abstract ego at the outset, and so reversing the process of development. Nor should we overlook the fact that the completely abstract ego [as pure activity], although suggested by the natural development of our consciousness, is never actually found therein. The most speculative of philosophers is incapable of disjoining his ego form those bodily feelings and images which form the incessant background of his awareness of himself. The notion of his ego as such is, like every notion, derived from sensibility, for the process of apperception itself comes to our knowledge chiefly through those feelings of tension [what I have above called inward adjustments] which accompany it." (Physiologische Psychologie, 2te Aufl. Bd. II. pp. 217-19.)

[6] The only exception I know of is M. J. Souriau, in his important article in the Revue Philosophique, vol. XXII. p. 449. M. Souriau's conclusion is 'que la conscience n'existe pas' (p. 472).

[7] See the excellent remarks by Prof. Bain on the 'Emotion of Power' in his 'Emotions and the Will.'

[8] Cf. Carlyle: Sartor Resartus, 'The Everlasting Yea.' "I tell thee, blockhead, it all comes of thy vanity; of what thou fanciest those same deserts of thine to be. Fancy that thou deservest to be hanged (as is most likely), thou wilt feel it happiness to be only shot: fancy that thou deservest to be hanged in a hair halter, it will be luxury to die in hemp.... What act of legislature was there that thou shouldst be happy? A little while ago thou hadst no right to be at all," etc. etc.

[9] T. W. Higginson's translation (1866), p. 105.

[10] "The usual mode of lessening the shock of disappointment or disesteem is to contract, if possible, a low estimate of the persons that inflict it. This is our remedy for the unjust censures of party spirit, as well as of personal malignity." (Bain: Emotion and Will, p. 209.)

[11] It must be observed that the qualities of the Self thus ideally constituted are all qualities approved by my actual fellows in the first instance; and that my reason for now appealing from their verdict to that of the ideal judge lies in some outward peculiarity of the immediate case. What once was admired in me as courage has now become in the eyes of men 'impertinence'; what was fortitude is obstinacy; what was fidelity is now fanaticism. The ideal judge alone, I now believe, can read my qualities, my willingnesses, my powers, or what they truly are. My fellows, misled by interest and prejudice, have gone astray.

[12] The kind of selfishness varies with the self that is sought. If it be the mere bodily self; if a man grabs the best food the warm corner, the vacant seat; if he makes room for no one, spits about, and belches in our faces, - we call it hoggishness. If it be the social self, in the form of popularity or influence, for which he is greedy, he may in material ways subordinate himself to others as the best means to his end; and in this case he is very apt to pass for a disinterested man. If it be the 'other-worldly' self which he seeks, and if he seeks it ascetically, - even though he would rather see all mankind damned eternally than lose his individual soul, - 'saintliness' will probably be the name by which his selfishness will be called.

[13] Lotze, Med. Psych. 498-501; Microcosmus, bk. II. chap. V §§ 3, 4.

[14] Psychologische Analyzen auf Physiologischer Grundlage. Theil II. IIte Hälfte, § 11. The whole section ought to be read.

[15] Professor Bain, in his chapter on 'Emotions of Self,' does scant justice to the primitive nature of a large part of our self-feeling, and seems to reduce it to reflective self-estimation of this sober intellectual sort, which certainly most of it is not. He

says that when the attention is turned inward upon self as a Personality, "we are putting forth towards ourselves the kind of exercise that properly accompanies our contemplation of other persons. We are accustomed to scrutinize the actions and conduct of those about us, to set a higher value upon one man than upon another, by comparing the two; to pity one in distress; to feel complacency towards a particular individual; to congratulate a man on some good fortune that it pleases us to see him gain; to admire greatness or excellence as displayed by any of our fellows. All these exercises are intrinsically social, like Love and Resentment; an isolated individual could never attain to them, nor exercise them. By what means, then, through what fiction [!] can we turn round and play them off upon self? Or how comes it that we obtain any satisfaction by putting self in the place of the other party? Perhaps the simplest form of the reflected act is that expressed by Self-worth and Self-estimation, based and begun upon observation of the ways and conduct of our fellow-beings. We soon make comparisons among the individuals about us; we see that one is stronger and does more work than another, and, in consequence perhaps, receives more pay. We see one putting forth perhaps more kindness than another, and in consequence receiving more love. We see some individuals surpassing the rest in astonishing feats, and drawing after them the gaze and admiration of a crowd. We acquire a series of fixed associations towards persons so situated; favorable in the case of the superior, and unfavorable to the inferior. To the strong and laborious man we attach an estimate of greater reward, and feel that to be in his place would be a happier lot than falls to others. Desiring, as we do, from the primary motives of our being, to possess good things, and observing these to come by a man's superior exertions, we feel a respect for such exertion and a wish that it might be ours. We know that we also put forth exertions for our share of good things; and on witnessing others, we are apt to be reminded of ourselves and to make comparisons with ourselves, which comparisons derive their interest from the substantial consequences. Having thus once learned to look at other persons as performing labors, greater or less, and as realizing fruits to accord; being, moreover, in all respects like our fellows, - we find it an exercise neither difficult nor unmeaning to contemplate self as doing work and receiving the reward. . . . As we decide between one man and another, - which is worthier, . . . so we decide between self and all other men; being, however, in this decision under the bias of our own desires." A couple of pages farther on we read: "By the terms Self-complacency, Self-gratulation, is indicated a positive enjoyment in dwelling upon our own merits and belongings. As in other modes, so here, the starting point is the contemplation of excellence or pleasing qualities in another person, accompanied more or less with fondness or love." Self-pity is also regarded by Professor Bain, in this place, as an emotion diverted to ourselves from a more immediate object, "in a manner that we may term fictitious and unreal. Still, as we can view self in the light of another person, we can feel towards it the emotion of pity called forth by others in our situation."

This account of Professor Bain's is, it will be observed a good specimen of the old-fashioned mode of explaining the several emotions as rapid calculations of results, and the transfer of feeling from one object to another, associated by contiguity or similarity with the first. Zoological evolutionism, which came up since Professor Bain first wrote, has made us see, on the contrary, that many emotions must be primitively aroused by special objects. None are more worthy of being ranked primitive than the self-gratulation and humiliation attendant on our own successes and failures in the main functions of life. We need no borrowed reflection for these feelings. Professor Bain's account applied to but that small fraction of our self-feeling which reflective criticism can add to, or subtract from, the total mass. - Lotze has some pages on the modifications of our self-regard by universal judgments, in Microcosmus, book V. chap. V. § 5.

[16] "Also nur dadurch, dass ich ein Mannigfaltiges gegebener Vorstellungen in einem Bewusstsein verbinden kann, ist es möglich dass ich die Identität des Bewusstseins in diesen Vorstellungen selbst vorstelle, d. h. die analytische Einheit der Apperception ist nur unter der Voraussetzung irgend einer synthetischen möglich." In this passage (Kritik der reinen Vernunft, 2te Aufl. § 16) Kant calls by the names of analytic and synthetic apperception what we here mean by objective and subjective synthesis respectively. It were much to be desired that some one might invent a good pair of terms in which to record the distinction - those used in the text are certainly very bad, but Kant's seem to me still worse. 'Categorical unity' and 'transcendental synthesis' would also be good Kantian, but hardly good human, speech.

[17] So that we might say, by a sort of bad pun, "only a connected world can be known as disconnected." I say bad pun, because the point of view shifts between the connectedness and the disconnectedness. The disconnectedness is of the realities known; the connectedness is of the knowledge of them; and reality and knowledge of it are, from the psychological point of view held fast to in these pages, two different facts.

[18] Some subtle reader will object that the Thought cannot call any part of its Object 'I' and knit other parts on to it, without first knitting that part on to Itself; and that it cannot knit it on to Itself without knowing Itself; - so that our supposition that the Thought may conceivably have no immediate knowledge of Itself is thus overthrown. To which the reply is that we must take care not to be duped by words. The words I and me signify nothing mysterious and unexampled - they are at bottom only names of emphasis; and Thought is always emphasizing something. Within a tract of space which it cognizes, it contrasts a here with a there; within a tract of time a now with a then; of a pair of things it calls one this, the other that. I and thou, I and it, are distinctions exactly on a par with these, - distinctions possible in an exclusively objective field of knowledge, the 'I' meaning for the Thought nothing but the bodily life which it momentarily feels. The sense of my bodily existence, however obscurely recognized as such, may then be the absolute original of my conscious selfhood, the fundamental perception that I am. All appropriations may be made to it, by a Thought not at the moment immediately cognized by itself. Whether these are not only logical possibilities but actual facts is something not yet dogmatically decided in the text.

[19] Metaphysik, § 245fin. This writer, who in his early work, the Medizinische Psychologie, was (to my reading) a strong defender of the Soul-Substance theory, has written in §§ 243-5 of his Metaphysik the most beautiful criticism of this theory which exists.
[20] On the empirical and transcendental conceptions of the self's unity, see Lotze, Metaphysic, § 244.
[21] Appendix to book I of Hume's Treatise on Human Nature.
[22] Herbart believed in the Soul, too; but for him the 'Self' of which we are 'conscious' is the empirical Self - not the soul.
[23] Compare again the remarks in Chapter VI.
[24] System of Psychology (1884). vol. I. p. 114.
[25] 'Distinct only to observation,' he adds. To whose observation? the outside psychologist's, the Ego's, their own, or the plank's? Darauf kommt es an!
[26] Analysis, etc., J. S. Mill's Edition, vol. I. p. 331. The 'as it were' is delightfully characteristic of the school.
[27] J. Mill's Analysis, vol. II. p. 175.
[28] Examination of Hamilton, 4th ed. p. 263.
[29] His chapter on the Psychological Theory of Mind is a beautiful case in point, and his concessions there have become so celebrated that they must be quoted for the reader's benefit. He ends the chapter with these words (loc. cit. p. 247): "The theory, therefore, which resolves Mind into a series of feelings, with a background of possibilities of feeling, can effectually withstand the most invidious of the arguments directed against it. But groundless as are the extrinsic objections, the theory has intrinsic difficulties which we have not set forth, and which it seems to me beyond the power of metaphysical analysis to remove. . . .
"The thread of consciousness which composes the mind's phenomenal life consist not only of present sensations, but likewise, in part, of memories and expectations. Now what are these? In themselves, they are present feelings, states of present consciousness, and in that respect not distinguished from sensations. They all, moreover, resemble some given sensations or feelings, of which we have previously had experience. But they are attended with the peculiarity that each of them involves a belief in more than its own present existence. A sensation involves only this; but a remembrance of sensation, even if not referred to any particular date, involves the suggestion and belief that a sensation, of which it is a copy or representation, actually existed in the past; and an expectation involves the belief, more or less positive, that a sensation or other feeling to which it directly refers will exist in the future. Nor can the phenomena involved in these two states of consciousness be adequately expressed, without saying that the belief they include is, that I myself formerly had, or that I myself, and no other, shall hereafter have, the sensations remembered or expected. The fact believed is, that the sensations did actually form, or will hereafter form, part of the self-same series of states, or thread of consciousness, of which the remembrance or expectation of those sensations is the part now present. If, therefore, we speak of the mind as a series of feelings we are obliged to complete the statement by calling it a series of feelings which is aware of itself as past and future; and we are reduced to the alternative of believing that the mind, or Ego, is something different from any series of feelings, or possibilities of them, or of accepting the paradox that something which ex hypothesi is but a series of feelings, can be aware of itself as a series.
"The truth is, that we are here face to face with that final inexplicability, at which, as Sir W. Hamilton observes, we inevitably arrive when we reach ultimate facts; and in general, one mode of stating it only appears more incomprehensible than another, because the whole of human language is accommodated to the one, and is so incongruous with the other that it cannot be expressed in any terms which do not deny its truth. The real stumbling-block is perhaps not in any theory of the fact, but in the fact itself. The true incomprehensibility perhaps is, that something which has ceased, or is not yet in existence, can still be, in a manner, present; that a series of feelings, the infinitely greater part of which is past or future, can be gathered up, as it were, into a simple present conception, accompanied by a belief or reality. I think by far the wisest thing we can do is to accept the inexplicable fact, without any theory of how it takes place; and when we are obliged to speak of it in terms which assume a theory, to use them with a reservation as to their meaning."
In a later place in the same book (p. 561) Mill, speaking of what may rightly be demanded of a theorist, says: "He is not entitled to frame a theory from one class of phenomena, extend it to another class which it does not fit, and excuse himself by saying that if we cannot make it fit, it is because ultimate facts are inexplicable." The class of phenomena which the associationist school takes to frame its theory of the Ego are feelings unaware of each other. The class of phenomena the Ego presents are feelings of which the later ones are intensely aware of those that went before. The two classes do not 'fit,' and no exercise of ingenuity can ever make them fit. No shuffling of unaware feelings can make them aware. To get the awareness we must openly beg it by postulating a new feeling which has it. This new feeling is no 'Theory' of the phenomena, but a simple statement of them; and as such I postulate in the text the present passing Thought as a psychic integer, with its knowledge of so much that has gone before.
[30] Kritik d. reinen Vernunft, 2te Aufl. § 17.
[31] It must be noticed, in justice to what was said above that neither Kant nor his successors anywhere discriminate between the presence of the apperceiving Ego to the combined object, and the awareness by that Ego of its own presence and of its distinctness from what it apperceives. That the Object must be known to something which thinks, and that it must be known to something which thinks that it thinks, are treated by them as identical necessities, - by what logic, does not appear. Kant tries to soften the jump in the reasoning by saying the thought of itself on the part of the Ego need only be potential - "the 'I think' must be capable of accompanying all other knowledge" - but a thought which is only potential is actually no thought at all, which practically gives up the case.

[32] "As regards the soul, now, or the 'I,' the 'thinker,' the whole drift of Kant's advance upon Hume and sensational psychology is towards the demonstration that the subject of knowledge is an Agent." (G. S. Morris, Kant's Critique, etc. (Chicago, 1882), p. 224.)

[33] "In Kant's Prolegomena," says II. Cohen, - I do not myself find the passage, - "it is expressly said that the problem is not to show how experience arises (ensteht), but of what it consists (besteht)." (Kant's Theorie d. Erfahrung (1871), p. 138.)

[34] The contrast between the Monism thus reached and our own psychological point of view can be exhibited schematically thus, the terms in squares standing for what, for us, are the ultimate irreducible data of psychological science, and the vincula above it symbolizing the reductions which post-Kantian idealism performs:
These reductions account for the ubiquitousness of the 'psychologist's fallacy' (bk. II. ch. I. p. 32) in the modern monistic writings. For us it is an unpardonable logical sin, when talking of a thought's knowledge (either of an object or of itself), to change the terms without warning, and, substituting the psychologist's knowledge therefor, [sic] still make as if we were continuing to talk of the same thing. For monistic idealism, this is the very enfranchisement of philosophy, and of course cannot be too much indulged in.

[35] T. H. Green, Prolegomena to Ethics, §§ 57, 61, 64.

[36] Loc. cit. § 64.

[37] E. Caird: Hegel (1883), p. 149.

[38] One is almost tempted to believe that the pantomime-state of mind and that of the Hegelian dialectics are, emotionally considered, one and the same thing. In the pantomime all common things are represented to happen in impossible ways, people jump down each other's throats, houses turn inside out, old women become young men, everything 'passes into its opposite' with inconceivable celerity and skill; and this, so far from producing perplexity, brings rapture to the beholder's mind. And so in the Hegelian logic, relations elsewhere recognized under the insipid name of distinctions (such as that between knower and object, many and one) must first be translated into impossibilities and contradictions, then 'transcended' and identified by miracle, ere the proper temper is induced for thoroughly enjoying the spectacle they show.

[39] The reader will please understand that I am quite willing to leave the hypothesis of the transcendental Ego as a substitute for the passing Thought open to discussion on general speculative grounds. Only in this book I prefer to stick by the common-sense assumption that we have successive conscious states, because all psychologists make it, and because one does not see how there can be a Psychology written which does not postulate such thoughts as its ultimate data. The data of all natural sciences become in turn subjects of a critical treatment more refined than that which the sciences themselves accord; and so it may fare in the end with our passing Thought. We have ourselves seen that the sensible certainty of its existence is less strong than is usually assumed. My quarrel with the transcendental Egoists is mainly about their grounds for their belief. Did they consistently propose it as a substitute for the passing Thought, did they consistently deny the latter's existence, I should respect their position more. But so far as I can understand them, they habitually believe in the passing Thought also. They seem even to believe in the Lockian stream of separate ideas, for the chief glory of the Ego in their pages is always its power to 'overcome' this separateness and unite the naturally disunited, 'synthesizing,' 'connecting,' or 'relating' the ideas together being used as synonyms, by transcendentalist writers, for knowing various objects at once. Not the being conscious at all, but the being conscious of many things together is held to be the difficult thing, in our psychic life, which only the wonder-working Ego can perform. But on what slippery ground does one get the moment one changes the definite notion of knowing an object into the altogether vague one of uniting or synthesizing the ideas of its various parts! - In the chapters on Sensation we shall come upon all this again.

[40] "When we compare the listless inactivity of the infant, slumbering from the moment at which he takes his milky food to the moment at which he wakes to require it again, with the restless energies of that mighty being which he is to become in his maturer years, pouring truth after truth, in rapid and dazzling profusion, upon the world, or grasping in his single hand the destiny of empires, how few are the circumstances of resemblance which we can trace, of all that intelligence which is afterwards to be displayed; how little more is seen than what serves to give feeble motion to the mere machinery of life! . . . Every age, if we may speak of many ages in the few years of human life, seems to be marked with a distinct character. Each has its peculiar objects which excite lively affections; and in each, exertion is excited by affections, which in other periods terminate without inducing active desire. The boy finds a world in less space than that which bounds his visible horizon; he wanders over his range of field and exhausts his strength in the pursuit of objects which, in the years that follow, are seen only to be neglected; while to him the objects that are afterwards to absorb his whole soul are as indifferent as the objects of his present passions are destined then to appear. . . . How many opportunities must every one have had of witnessing the progress of intellectual decay, and the coldness that steals upon the once benevolent heart! We quit our country, perhaps at an early period of life, and after an absence of many years we return with all the rememberances of past pleasure which grow more tender as they approach their objects. We eagerly seek him to whose paternal voice we have been accustomed to listen with the same reverence as if its predictions had possessed oracular certainty, - who first led us into knowledge, and whose image has been constantly joined in our mind with all that veneration which does not forbid love. We find him sunk, perhaps, in the imbecility of idiotism, unable to recognize us, - ignorant alike of the past and of the future, and living only in the sensibility of animal gratification. We seek the favorite companion of our childhood, whose tenderness of heart, etc. . . . We find him hardened into a man, meeting us scarcely with the cold hypocrisy of dissembled friendship - in his general relations to the world careless of the misery he is not to feel.

... When we observe all this, ... do we use only a metaphor of little meaning when we say of him that he is become a different person, and that his mind and character are changed? In what does the identity consist?

... The supposed test of identity, when applied to the mind in these cases, completely fails. It neither affects, nor is affected, in the same manner in the same circumstances. It therefore, if the test be a just one, is not the same identical mind." (T. Brown: Lectures on the Philosophy of the Human Mind, 'on Mental Identity.'

[41] *"Sir John Cutler had a pair of black worsted stockings, which his maid darned so often with silk that they became at last a pair of silk stockings. Now, supposing these stockings of Sir John's endued with some degree of consciousness at every particular darning, they would have been sensible that they were the same individual pair of stockings both before and after the darning; and this sensation would have continued in them through all the succession of darnings; and yet after the last of all, there was not perhaps one thread left of the first pair of stockings: but they were grown to be silk stockings, as was said before." (Pope's Martinus Scriblerus, quoted by Brown, ibid.)*

[42] *Hours of Work and Play, p. 100.*

[43] *For a careful study of the errors in narratives, see E. Gurney: Phantasms of the Living, vol. I. pp. 126-158. In the Proceedings of the Society for Psychical Research for May 1887 Mr. Richard Hodgson shows by an extraordinary array of instances how utterly inaccurate everyone's description from memory of a rapid series of events is certain to be.*

[44] *See Josiah Royce (Mind, vol. 13, p. 244, and Proceedings of Am. Soc. of Psych. Research, vol. I. p. 366), for evidence that a certain sort of hallucination of memory which he calls 'pseudo-presentiment' is no uncommon phenomenon.*

[45] *Maladies de la Mémoire, p. 85. The little that would be left of personal consciousness if all our senses stopped their work is ingeniously shown in the remark of the extraordinary anaesthetic youth whose case Professor Strümpell reports (in the Deutsches Archiv f. klin. Med., XXII. 347, 1878). This boy, whom we shall later find instructive in many connections, was totally anaesthetic without and (so far as could be tested) within, save for the sight of one eye and the hearing of one ear. When his eye was closed, he said: "Wenn ich nicht sehen kann, da BIN ich gar nicht - I no longer am."*

[46] *"One can compare the state of the patient to nothing so well as to that of a caterpillar, which, keeping all its caterpillar's ideas and remembrances, should suddenly become a butterfly with a butterfly's sense and sensations. Between the old and the new state, between the first self, that of the caterpillar, and second self, that of the butterfly, there is a deep scission, a complete rupture. The new feelings find no anterior series to which they can knit themselves on; the patient can neither interpret nor use them; he does not recognize them; they are unknown. Hence two conclusions, the first which consists in his saying, I no longer am; the second, somewhat later, which consists in his saying, I am another person." (H. Taine: de l'Intelligence, 3me édition (1878), p. 462.*

[47] *W. Griesinger: Mental Diseases, § 29.*

[48] *See the interesting case of 'old Stump' in the Proceedings of the Am. Soc. for Psych. Research, p. 552.*

[49] *De l'Intelligence, 3me édition (1878), vol. II, note, p. 461. Krishaber's book (La Névropathie Cérébro-cardiaque, 1873) is full of similar observations.*

[50] *Sudden alterations in outward fortune often produce such a change in the empirical me as almost to amount to a pathological disturbance of self-consciousness. When a poor man draws the big prize in a lottery, or unexpectedly inherits an estate; when a man high in fame is publicly disgraced, a millionaire becomes a pauper, or a loving husband and father sees his family perish at one fell swoop, there is temporarily such a rupture between all past habits, whether of an active or a passive kind, and the exigencies and possibilities of the new situation, that the individual may find no medium of continuity or association to carry him over from the one phase to the other of his life. Under these conditions mental derangement is no unfrequent result.*

[51] *The number of subjects who can do this with any fertility and exuberance is relatively quite small.*

[52] *First in the Revue Scientifique for May 26, 1876, then in his book, Hypnotisme, Double Conscience, et Altérations de la Personnalité (Paris, 1887).*

[53] *Der Hypnotismus (1884), pp. 109-15.*

[54] *Transactions of the College of Physicians of Philadelphia, April 4, 1888. Also, less complete, in Harper's Magazine, May 1860.*

[55] *Cf. Ribot's Diseases of Memory for cases. See also a large number of them in Forbes Winslow's Obscure Diseases of the Brain and Mind, chapters XIII - XVII.*

[56] *See the interesting account by M. J. Janet in the Revue Scientifique, May 19, 1888.*

[57] *Variations de la Personnalité (Paris, 1888).*

[58] *Op. cit. p. 84. In this work and in Dr. Azam's (cited on a previous page), as well as in Prof. Th. Ribot's Maladies de la Personnalité (1885), the reader will find information and references relative to the other known cases of the kind.*

[59] *His own brother's subject Wit. . . . , although in her anaesthetic waking state she recollected nothing of either of her trances, yet remembered her deeper trance (in which her sensibilities became perfect) when she was in her lighter trance. Nevertheless in the latter she was as anaesthetic as when awake. (Loc. cit. p. 619.) - It does not appear that there was an important difference in the sensibility of Félida X. between her two states - as far as one can judge from M. Azam's account she was to some degree anaesthetic in both (op. cit. pp. 71, 96). - In the case of double personality reported by M. Dufay (Revue Scientifique, vol. XVIII. p. 69), the memory seems to have been best in the more anaesthetic condition. - Hypnotic subjects made blind do not necessarily lose their visual ideas. It appears, then, both that amnesias may occur without anaesthesias,*

and anaesthesias without amnesias, though they may also occur in combination. Hypnotic subjects made blind by suggestion will tell you that they clearly imagine the things which they can no longer see.

[60] *A full account of the case, by Mr. R. Hodgson, will be found in the Proceedings of the Society for Psychical Research for 1890.*

[61] *He had spent an afternoon in Boston, a night in New York, an afternoon in Newark, and ten days or more in Philadelphia, first in a certain hotel and next in a certain boarding-house, making no acquaintances, 'resting,' reading, and 'looking round.' I have unfortunately been unable to get independent corroboration of these details, as the hotel registers are destroyed, and the boarding-house named by him has been pulled down. He forgets the name of the two ladies who kept it.*

[62] *The details of the case, it will be seen, are all compatible with simulation. I can only say of that, that no one who has examined Mr. Bourne (including Dr. Read, Dr. Weir Mitchell, Dr. Guy Hindsdale, and Mr. R. Hodgson) practically doubts his ingrained honesty, nor, so far as I can discover, do any of his personal acquaintances indulge in a sceptical view.*

[63] *The Watseka Wonder, by E. W. Stevens. Chicago, Religio-Philosophical Publishing House, 1887.*

[64] *My friend Mr. R. Hodgson informs me that he visited Watseka in April 1889, and cross-examined the principal witnesses of this case. His confidence in the original narrative was strengthened by what he learned; and various unpublished facts were ascertained, which increased the plausibility of the spiritualistic interpretation of the phenomenon.*

[65] *See his highly important series of articles on Automatic Writing, etc., in the Proceedings of the Soc. for Psych. Research, especially Article II (May 1885). Compare also Dr. Maudsley's instructive article in Mind, vol. XIV. p. 161, and Luys's essay, 'Sur le Dédoublement,' etc., in l'Encéphale for 1889.*

Chapter XI – Attention

Strange to say, so patent a fact as the perpetual presence of selective attention has received hardly any notice from psychologists of the English empiricist school. The Germans have explicitly treated of it, either as a faculty or as a resultant, but in the pages of such writers as Locke, Hume, Hartley, the Mills, and Spencer the word hardly occurs, or if it does so, it is parenthetically and as if by inadvertence.[1] The motive of this ignoring of the phenomenon of attention is obvious enough. These writers are bent on showing how the higher faculties of the mind are pure products of 'experience;' and experience is supposed to be of something simply given. Attention, implying a degree of reactive spontaneity, would seem to break through the circle of pure receptivity which constitutes 'experience,' and hence must not be spoken of under penalty of interfering with the smoothness of the tale.

But the moment one thinks of the matter, one sees how false a notion of experience that is which would make it tantamount to the mere presence to the senses of an outward order. Millions of items of the outward order are present to my senses which never properly enter into my experience. Why? Because they have no interest for me. My experience is what I agree to attend to. Only those items which I notice shape my mind - without selective interest, experience is an utter chaos. Interest alone gives accent and emphasis, light and shade, background and foreground - intelligible perspective, in a word. It varies in every creature, but without it the consciousness of every creature would be a gray chaotic indiscriminateness, impossible for us even to conceive. Such an empiricist writer as Mr. Spencer, for example, regards the creature as absolutely passive clay, upon which 'experience' rains down. The clay will be impressed most deeply where the drops fall thickest, and so the final shape of the mind is moulded. Give time enough, and all sentient things ought, at this rate, to end by assuming an identical mental constitution - for 'experience,' the sole shaper, is a constant fact, and the order of its items must end by being exactly reflected by the passive mirror which we call the sentient organism. If such an account were true, a race of dogs bred for generations, say in the Vatican, with characters of visual shape, sculptured in marble, presented to their eyes, in every variety of form and combination, ought to discriminate before long the finest shades of these peculiar characters. In a word, they ought to become, if time were given, accomplished connoisseurs of sculpture. Anyone may judge of the probability of this consummation. Surely an eternity of experience of the statues would leave the dog as inartistic as he was at first, for the lack of an original interest to knit his discriminations on to. Meanwhile the odors at the bases of the pedestals would have organized themselves in the consciousness of this breed of dogs into a system of 'correspondences' to which the most heredity caste of custodi would never approximate, merely because to them, as human beings, the dog's interest in those smells would for ever be an inscrutable mystery. These writers have, then, utterly ignored the glaring fact that subjective interest may, by laying its weighty index-finger on particular items of experience, so accent them as to give to the least frequent associations far more power to shape our thought than the most frequent ones possess. The interest itself, though its genesis is doubtless perfectly natural, makes experience more than it is made by it.

Every one knows what attention is. It is the taking possession by the mind, in clear and vivid form, of one out of what seem several simultaneously possible objects or trains of thought. Focalization, concentration, of consciousness are of its essence. It implies withdrawal from some things in order to deal effectively with others, and is a condition which has a real opposite in the confused, dazed, scatterbrained state which in French is called distraction, and Zerstreutheit in German.

We all know this latter state, even in its extreme degree. Most people probably fall several times a day into a fit of something like this: The eyes are fixed on vacancy, the sounds of the world melt into confused unity, the attention is dispersed so that the whole body is felt, as it were, at once, and the foreground of consciousness is filled, if by anything, by a sort of solemn sense of surrender to the empty passing of time. In the dim background of our mind we know meanwhile what we ought to be doing: getting up, dressing ourselves, answering the person who has spoken to us, trying to make the next step in our reasoning. But somehow we cannot start; the pensée de derrière la tête fails to pierce the shell of lethargy that wraps our state about. Every moment we expect the spell to break, for we know no reason why it should continue. But it does continue, pulse after pulse, and we float with it, until - also without reason that we can discover - an energy is given, something - we know not what - enables us to gather ourselves together, we wink our eyes, we shake our heads, the background-ideas become effective, and the wheels of life go round again.

This curious state or inhibition can for a few moments be produced at will by fixing the eyes on vacancy. Some persons can voluntarily empty their minds and 'think of nothing.' With many, as Professor Exner remarks of himself, this is the most efficacious means of falling asleep. It is difficult not to suppose something like this scattered condition of mind to be the usual state of brutes when not actively engaged in some pursuit. Fatigue, monotonous mechanical occupations that end by being automatically carried on, tend to reproduce it in men. It is not sleep; and yet when aroused from such a state, a person will often hardly be able to say what he has been thinking about. Subjects of the hypnotic trance seem to lapse into it when left to themselves; asked what they are thinking of, they reply, 'of nothing particular'![2]

The abolition of this condition is what we call the awakening of the attention. One principal object comes then into the focus of consciousness, others are temporarily suppressed. The awakening may come about either by reason of a stimulus from without, or in consequence of some unknown inner alteration; and the change it brings with it amounts to a concentration upon one single object with exclusion of aught besides, or to a condition anywhere between this and the completely dispersed state.

To How Many Things Can we Attend at Once?

The question of the 'span' of consciousness has often been asked and answered - sometimes a priori, sometimes by experiment. This seems the proper place for us to touch upon it; and our answer, according to the principles laid down in Chapter IX, will not be difficult. The number of things we may attend to is altogether indefinite, depending on the power of the individual intellect, on the form of the apprehension, and on what the things are. When apprehended conceptually as a connected system, their number may be very large. But however numerous the things, they can only be known in a single pulse of consciousness for which they form one complex 'object' so that properly speaking there is before the mind at no time a plurality of ideas, properly so called.

The 'unity of the soul' has been supposed by many philosophers, who also believed in the distinct atomic nature of 'ideas,' to preclude the presence to it of more than one objective fact, manifested in one idea, at a time. Even Dugald Stuart opines that every minimum visible of a pictured figure

"constitutes just as distinct an object of attention to the mind as if it were separated by an interval of empty space from the rest. . . . It is impossible for the mind to attend to more than one of these points at once; and as the perception of the figure implies a knowledge of the relative situation of the different points with respect to each other, we must conclude that the perception of figure by the eye is the result of a number of different acts of attention. These acts of attention, however, are performed with such rapidity, that the effect, with respect to us, is the same as if the perception were instantaneous."[3]

Such glaringly artificial views can only come from fantastic metaphysics or from the ambiguity of the word 'idea,' which, standing sometimes for mental state and sometimes for things known, leads men to ascribe to the thing, not only the unity which belongs to the mental state, but even the simplicity which is thought to reside in the Soul. When the things are apprehended by the senses, the number of them that can be attended to at once is small, "Pluribus intentus, minor est ad singula sensus."

"By Charles Bonnet the Mind is allowed to have a distinct notion of six objects at once; by Abraham Tucker the number is limited to four; while Destutt Tracy again amplifies it to six. The opinion of the first and last of these philosophers" [continues Sir Wm. Hamilton] "seems to me correct. You can easily make the experiments for yourselves, but you must beware of grouping the objects into classes. If you throw a handful of marbles on the floor, you will find it difficult to view at once more than six, or seven at most, without confusion; but if you group them into twos, or threes, or fives, you can comprehend as many groups as you can units; because the mind considers these groups only as units - it views them as wholes, and throws their parts out of consideration."[4]

Professor Jevons, repeating this observation, by counting instantaneously beans thrown into a box, found that the number 6 was guessed correctly 120 times out of 147, 5 correctly 102 times out of 107, and 4 and 3 always right.[5] It is obvious that such observations decide nothing at all about our attention, properly so called. They rather measure in part the distinctness of our vision - especially of the primary-memory-image[6] - in part the amount of association in the individual between seen arrangements and the names of numbers.[7]

Each number-name is a way of grasping the beans as one total object. In such a total object, all the parts converge harmoniously to the one resultant concept; no single bean has special discrepant associations of its own; and so, with practice, they may grow quite numerous ere we fail to estimate them aright. But where the 'object' before us breaks into parts disconnected with each other, and forming each as it were a separate object or system, not conceivable in union with the rest, it becomes harder to apprehend all these parts at once, and the mind tends to let go of one whilst it attends to another. Still, within limits this can be done. M. Paulhan has experimented carefully on the matter by declaiming one poem aloud whilst he repeated a different one mentally, or by writing one sentence whilst speaking another, or by performing calculations on paper whilst reciting poetry.[8] He found that "the most favorable condition for the doubling of the mind was its sinultaneous [sic] application to two easy and heterogeneous operations. Two operations of the same sort, two multiplications, two recitations, or the reciting one poem and writing another, render the process more uncertain and difficult."

The attention often, but not always, oscillates during these performances; and sometimes a word from one part of the task slips into another. I myself find when I try to simultaneously recite one thing and write another that the beginning of each word or segment of a phrase is what requires the attention. Once started, my pen runs on for a word or two as if by its own momentum. M. Paulhan compared the time occupied by the same two operations done simultaneously or in succession, and found that there was often a considerable gain of time from doing them simultaneously. For instance:

" I write the first four verses of Athalie, whilst reciting eleven of Musset. The whole performance occupies 40 seconds. But reciting alone takes 22 and writing alone takes 31, or 53 altogether, so that there is a difference in favor of the simultaneous operations."

Or again:

"I multiply 421 312 212 by 2; the operation takes 6 seconds; the recitation of 4 verses also takes 6 seconds. But the two operations done at once only take 6 seconds, so that there is no loss of time from combining them."

Of course these time-measurements lack precision. With three systems of objects (writing with each hand whilst reciting) the operation became much more difficult.

If, then, by the original question, how many ideas or things can we attend to at once, be meant how many entirely disconnected systems or processes of conception can go on simultaneously, the answer is, not easily more than one, unless the processes are very habitual; but then two, or even three, without very much oscillation of the attention. Where, however, the processes are less automatic, as in the story of Julius Caesar dictating four letters whilst he writes a fifth,[9] there must be a rapid oscillation of the mind from one to the next, and no consequent gain of time. Within any one of the systems the parts may be numberless, but we attend to them collectively when we conceive the whole which they form.

When the things to be attended to are small sensations, and when the effort is to be exact in noting them, it is found that attention to one interferes a good deal with the perception of the other. A good deal of fine work has been done in this field, of which I must give some account.

It has long been noticed, when expectant attention is concentrated upon one of two sensations, that the other one is apt to be displaced from consciousness for a moment and to appear subsequent; although in reality the two may have been contemporaneous events. Thus, to use the stock example of the books, the surgeon would sometimes see the blood flow from the arm of the patient whom he was bleeding, before he saw the instrument penetrate the skin. Similarly the smith may see the sparks fly before he sees the hammer smite the iron, etc. There is thus a certain difficulty in perceiving the exact date of two impressions when they do not interest our attention equally, and when they are of a disparate sort.

Professor Exner, whose experiments on the minimal perceptible succession in time of two sensations we shall have to quote in another chapter, makes some noteworthy remarks about the way in which the attention must be set to catch the interval and the right order of the sensations, when the time is exceeding small. The point was to tell whether two signals were simultaneous or successive; and, if successive, which one of them came first.

The first way of attending which he found himself to fall into, was when the signals did not differ greatly - when, e.g., they were similar sounds heard each by a different ear. Here he lay in wait for the first signal, whichever it might be, and identified it the next moment in memory. The second, which could then always be known by default, was often not clearly distinguished in itself. When the time was too short, the first could not be isolated from the second at all. The second way was to accommodate the attention for a certain sort of signal, and the next moment to become aware in memory of whether it came before or after its mate.

"This way brings great uncertainty with it. The impression not prepared for comes to us in the memory more weak than the other, obscure as it were, badly fixed in time. We tend to take the subjectively stronger stimulus, that which we were intent upon, for the first, just as we are apt to take an objectively stronger stimulus to be the first. Still, it may happen otherwise. In the experiments from touch to sight it often seemed to me as if the impression for which the attention was not prepared were there already when the other came."

Exner found himself employing this method oftenest when the impressions differed strongly.[10]

In such observations (which must not be confounded with those where the two signals were identical and their successiveness known as mere doubleness, without distinction of which came first), it is obvious that each signal must combine stably in our perception with a different instant of time. It is the simplest possible case of two discrepant concepts simultaneously occupying the mind. Now the case of the signals being simultaneous seems of a different sort. We must turn to Wundt for observations fit to cast a nearer light thereon.

The reader will remember the reaction-time experiments of which we treated in Chapter III. It happened occasionally in Wundt's experiments that the reaction-time was reduced to zero or even assumed a negative value, which, being translated into common speech, means that the observer was sometimes so intent upon the signal that his reaction actually coincided in time with it, or even preceded it, instead of coming a fraction of a second after it, as in the nature of things it should. More will be said of these results anon. Meanwhile Wundt, in explaining them, says this:

"In general we have a very exact feeling of the simultaneity of two stimuli, if they do not differ much in strength. And in a series of experiments in which a warning precedes, at a fixed interval, the stimulus, we involuntarily try to react, not only as promptly as possible, but also in such wise that our movement may coincide with the stimulus itself. We seek to make our own feelings of touch and innervation [muscular contraction] objectively contemporaneous with the signal which we hear; and experience shows that in many cases we approximately succeed. In these cases we have a distinct consciousness of hearing the signal, reacting upon it, and feeling our reaction take place, - all at one and the same moment."[11]

In another place, Wundt adds:

"The difficulty of these observations and the comparative infrequency with which the reaction-time can be made thus to disappear shows how hard it is, when our attention is intense, to keep it fixed even on two different ideas at once. Note besides that when this happens, one always tries to bring the ideas into a certain connection, to grasp them as components of a certain complex representation. Thus in the experiments in question, it has often seemed to me that I produced by my own recording movement the sound which the ball made in dropping on the board."[12]

The 'difficulty,' in the cases of which Wundt speaks, is that of forcing two non-simultaneous events into apparent combination with the same instant of time. There is no difficulty, as he admits, in so dividing our attention between two really simultaneous impressions as to feel them to be such. The cases he describes are really cases of anachronistic perception, of subjective time-displacement, to use his own term. Still more curious cases of it have been most carefully studied by him. They carry us a step farther in our research, so I will quote them, using as far as possible his exact words:

"The conditions become more complicated when we receive a series of impressions separated by distinct intervals, into the midst of which a heterogeneous impression is suddenly brought. Then comes the question, with which member of the series do we perceive the additional impression to coincide? with that member with whose presence it really coexists, or is there some aberration? . . . If the additional stimulus belongs to a different sense very considerable aberrations may occur.

"The best way to experiment is with a number of visual impressions (which one can easily get from a moving object) for the series, and with a sound as the disparate impression. Let, e.g., an index-hand move over a circular scale with uniform and sufficiently slow velocity, so that the impressions it gives will not fuse, but permit its position at any instant to be distinctly seen. Let the clockwork which turns it have an arrangement which rings a bell once in every revolution, but at a point which can be varied, so that the observer need never know in advance just when the bell-stroke takes place. In such observations three cases are possible. The bell-stroke can be perceived either exactly at the moment to which the index points when it sounds - in this case there will be no time-displacement; or we can combine it with a later position of the index - . . . positive time-displacement, as we shall call it; or finally we can combine it with a position of the index earlier than that at which the sounds occurred - and this we will call a negative displacement. The most natural displacement would apparently be the positive, since for apperception a certain time is always required. . . . But experience shows that the opposite is the case: it happens most frequently that the sound appears earlier than its real date - far less often coincident with it, or later. It should be observed that in all these experiments it takes some time to get a distinctly perceived combination of the sound with a particular position of the index, and that a single revolution of the latter is never enough for the purpose. The motion must go on long enough for the sounds themselves to form a regular series - the outcome being a simultaneous perception of two distinct series of events, of which either may by changes in its rapidity modify the result. The first thing one remarks is that the sound belongs in a certain region of the scale; only gradually is it perceived to combine with a particular position of the index. But even a result gained by observation of many revolutions may be deficient in certainty, for accidental combinations of attention have a great influence upon it. If we deliberately try to combine the bell-stroke with an arbitrarily chosen position of the index, we succeed without difficulty, provided this position be not too remote from the true one. If, again, we cover the whole scale, except a single division over which we may see the index pass, we have a strong tendency to combine the bell-stroke with this actually seen position; and in so doing may easily overlook more than ¼ of a second of time. Results, therefore, to be of any value, must be drawn from long-continued and very numerous observations, in which such irregular oscillations of the attention neutralize each other according to the law of great numbers, and allow the true laws to appear. Although my own experiments extend over many years (with interruption), they are not even yet numerous enough to exhaust the subject - still, they bring out the principal laws which the attention follows under such conditions."[13]

Wundt accordingly distinguishes the direction from the amount of the apparent displacement in time of the bell-stroke. The direction depends on the rapidity of the movement of the index and (consequently) on that of the succession of the bell-strokes. The moment at which the bell struck was estimated by him with the least tendency to error, when the revolutions took place once in a second. Faster than this, positive errors began to prevail; slower, negative ones almost always were present. On the other hand, if the rapidity went quickening, errors became

negative; if slowing, positive. The amount of error is, in general, the greater the slower the speed and its alterations. Finally, individual differences prevail, as well as differences in the same individual at different times.[14]
Wundt's pupil von Tschisch has carried out these experiments on a still more elaborate scale,[15] using, not only the single bell-stroke, but 2, 3, 4, or 5 simultaneous impressions, so that the attention had to note the place of the index at the moment when a whole group of things was happening. The single bell-stroke was always heard too early by von Tschisch - the displacement was invariably 'negative.' As the other simultaneous impressions were added, the displacement first became zero and finally positive, i.e. the impressions were connected with a position of the index that was too late. This retardation was greater when the simultaneous impressions were disparate (electric tactile stimuli on different places, simple touch-stimuli, different sounds) than when they were all of the same sort. The increment of retardation became relatively less with each additional impression, so that it is probable that six impressions would have given almost the same result as five, which was the maximum number used by Herr von T. Wundt explains all these results by his previous observation that a reaction sometimes antedates the signal. The mind, he supposes, is so intent upon the bell-strokes that its 'apperception' keeps ripening periodically after each stroke in anticipation of the next. Its most natural rate of ripening may be faster or slower than the rate at which the strokes come. If faster, then it hears the stroke too early; if slower, it hears it too late. The position of the index on the scale, meanwhile, is noted at the moment, early or late, at which the bell-stroke is subjectively heard. Substituting several impressions for the single bell-stroke makes the ripening of the perception slower, and the index is seen too late. So, at least, do I understand the explanations which Herren Wundt and v. Tschisch give.[16]
This is all I have to say about the difficulty of having two discrepant concepts together, and about the number of things to which we can simultaneously attend.

The Varieties of Attention.

The things to which we attend are said to interest us. Our interest in them is supposed to be the cause of our attending. What makes an object interesting we shall see presently; and later inquire in what sense interest may cause attention. Meanwhile
Attention may be divided into kinds in various ways.
It is either to

a) Objects of sense (sensorial attention); or to
b) Ideal or represented objects (intellectual attention).

It is either

c) Immediate; or
d) Derived: immediate, when the topic or stimulus is interesting in itself, without relation to anything else; derived, when it owes its interest to association with some other immediately interesting thing. What I call derived attention has been named 'apperceptive' attention. Furthermore, Attention may be either
e) Passive, reflex, non-voluntary, effortless; or
f) Active and voluntary.

Voluntary attention is always derived; we never make an effort to attend to an object except for the sake of some remote interest which the effort will serve. But both sensorial and intellectual attention may be either passive or voluntary.
In passive immediate sensorial attention the stimulus is a sense-impression, either very intense, voluminous, or sudden, - in which case it makes no difference what its nature may be, whether sight, sound, smell, blow, or inner pain, - or else it is an instinctive stimulus, a perception which, by reason of its nature rather than its mere force, appeals to some one of our normal congenital impulses and has a directly exciting quality. In the chapter on Instinct we shall see how these stimuli differ from one animal to another, and what most of them are in man: strange things, moving things, wild animals, bright things, pretty things, metallic things, words, blows, blood, etc., etc., etc. Sensitiveness to immediately exciting sensorial stimuli characterizes the attention of childhood and youth. In mature age we have generally selected those stimuli which are connected with one or more so-called permanent interests, and our attention has grown irresponsive to the rest.[17] But childhood is characterized by great active energy, and has few organized interests by which to meet new impressions and decide whether they are worthy of notice or not, and the consequence is that extreme mobility of the attention with which we are all familiar in children, and which makes their first lessons such rough affairs. Any strong sensation whatever produces accommodation of the organs which perceive it, and absolute oblivion, for the time being, of the task in hand. This reflex and passive character of

the attention which, as a French writer says, makes the child seem to belong less to himself than to every object which happens to catch his notice, is the first thing which the teacher must overcome. It never is overcome in some people, whose work, to the end of life, gets done in the interstices of their mind-wandering.

The passive sensorial attention is derived when the impression, without being either strong or of an instinctively exciting nature, is connected by previous experience and education with things that are so. These things may be called the motives of the attention. The impression draws an interest from them, or perhaps it even fuses into a single complex object with them; the result is that it is brought into the focus of the mind. A faint tap per se is not an interesting sound; it may well escape being discriminated from the general rumor of the world. But when it is a signal, as that of a lover on the window-pane, it will hardly go unperceived. Herbart writes:

"How a bit of bad grammar wounds the ear of the purist! How a false note hurts the musician! or an offence against good manners the man of the world! How rapid is progress in a science when its first principles have been so well impressed upon us that we reproduce them mentally with perfect distinctness and ease! How slow and uncertain, on the other hand, is our learning of the principles themselves, when familiarity with the still more elementary percepts connected with the subject has not given us an adequate predisposition! - Apperceptive attention may be plainly observed in very small children when, hearing the speech of their elders, as yet unintelligible to them, they suddenly catch a single known word here and there, and repeat it to themselves; yes! even in the dog who looks round at us when we speak of him and pronounce his name. Not far removed is the talent which mind-wandering school-boys display during the hours of instruction, of noticing every moment in which the teacher tells a story. I remember classes in which, instruction being uninteresting, and discipline relaxed, a buzzing murmur was always to be heard, which invariably stopped for as long a time as an anecdote lasted. How could the boys, since they seemed to hear nothing, notice when the anecdote began? Doubtless most of them always heard something of the teacher's talk; but most of it had no connection with their previous knowledge and occupations, and therefore the separate words no sooner entered their consciousness than they fell out of it again; but, on the other hand, no sooner did the words awaken old thoughts, forming strongly-connected series with which the new impression easily combined, than out of new and old together a total interest resulted which drove the vagrant ideas below the threshold of consciousness, and brought for a while settled attention into their place."[18]

Passive intellectual attention is immediate when we follow in thought a train of images exciting or interesting per se; derived, when the images are interesting only as means to a remote end, or merely because they are associated with something which makes them dear. Owing to the way in which immerse numbers of real things become integrated into single objects of thought for us, there is no clear line to be drawn between immediate and derived attention of an intellectual sort. When absorbed in intellectual attention we may become so inattentive to outer things as to be 'absent-minded,,' 'abstracted,' or 'distraits.' All revery or concentrated meditation is apt to throw us into this state.

"Archimedes, it is well known, was so absorbed in geometrical meditation that he was first aware of the storming of Syracuse by his own death-wound, and his exclamation on the entrance of the Roman soldiers was: Noli turbare circulos meos! In like manner Joseph Scaliger, the most learned of men, when a Protestant student in Paris, was so engrossed in the study of Homer that he became aware of the massacre of St. Bartholomew, and of his own escape, only on the day subsequent to the catastrophe. The philosopher Carneades was habitually liable to fits of meditation so profound that, to prevent him sinking from inanition, his maid found it necessary to feed him like a child. And it is reported of Newton that, while engaged in his mathematical researches, he sometimes forgot to dine. Cardan, one of the most illustrious of philosophers and mathematicians, was once, upon a journey, so lost in thought that he forgot both his way and the object of his journey. To the questions of his driver whether he should proceed, he make no answer; and when he came to himself at nightfall, he was surprised to find the carriage at a standstill, and directly under a gallows. The mathematician Vieta was sometimes so buried in meditation that for hours he bore more resemblance to a dead person than to a living, and was then wholly unconscious of everything going on around him. On the day of his marriage the great Budæus forgot everything in his philological speculations, and he was only awakened to the affairs of the external world by a tardy embassy from the marriage-party, who found him absorbed in the composition of his Commentarii."[19]

The absorption may be so deep as not only to banish ordinary sensations, but even the severest pain. Pascal, Wesley, Robert Hall, are said to have had this capacity. Dr. Carpenter says of himself that

"he has frequently begun a lecture whilst suffering neuralgic pain so severe as to make him apprehend that he would find it impossible to proceed; yet no sooner has he by a determined effort fairly launched himself into the stream of thought, than he has found himself continuously borne along without the least distraction, until the end has come, and the attention has been released; when the pain has recurred with a force that has overmastered all resistance, making him wonder how he could have ever ceased to feel it."[20]

Dr. Carpenter speaks of launching himself by a determined effort. This effort characterizes what we called active or voluntary attention. It is a feeling which every one knows, but which most people would call quite indescribable. We get it in the sensorial sphere whenever we seek to catch an impression of extreme faintness, be it of sight, hearing, taste, smell, or touch; we get it whenever we seek to discriminate a sensation merged in a mass of others that are similar; we get it whenever we resist the attractions of more potent stimuli and keep our mind occupied with some object that is naturally unimpressive. We get it in the intellectual sphere under exactly similar conditions: as we strive to sharpen and make distinct an idea which we but vaguely seem to have; or painfully discriminate a shade of meaning from its similars; or resolutely hold fast to a thought so discordant with our impulses that, if left unaided, it would quickly yield place to images of an exciting and impassioned kind. All forms of attentive effort would be exercised at once by one whom we might suppose at a dinner-party resolutely to listen to a neighbor giving him insipid and unwelcome advice in a low voice, whilst all around the guests were loudly laughing and talking about exciting and interesting things.

There is no such thing as voluntary attention sustained for more than a few seconds at a time. What is called sustained voluntary attention is a repetition of successive efforts which bring back the topic to the mind.[21] The topic once brought back, if a congenial one, develops; and if its development is interesting it engages the attention passively for a time. Dr. Carpenter, a moment back, described the stream of thought, once entered, as 'bearing him along.' This passive interest may be short or long. As soon as it flags, the attention is diverted by some irrelevant thing, and then a voluntary effort may bring it back to the topic again; and so on, under favorable conditions, for hours together. During all this time, however, note that it is not an identical object in the psychological sense but a succession of mutually related objects forming an identical topic only, upon which the attention is fixed. No one can possibly attend continuously to an object that does not change.

Now there are always some objects that for the time being will not develop. They simply go out; and to keep the mind upon anything related to them requires such incessantly renewed effort that the most resolute Will ere long gives out and let its thoughts follow the more stimulating solicitations after it has withstood them for what length of time it can. There are topics known to every man from which he shies like a frightened horse, and which to get a glimpse of is to shun. Such are his ebbing assets to the spendthrift in full career. But why single out the spendthrift when to every man actuated by passion the thought of interests which negate the passion can hardly for more than a fleeting instant stay before the mind? It is like 'memento mori' in the heyday of the pride of life. Nature rises at such suggestions, and excludes them from the view: - How long, O healthy reader, can you now continue thinking of your tomb? - In milder instances the difficulty is as great, especially when the brain is fagged. One snatches at any and every passing pretext, no matter how trivial or external, to escape from the odiousness of the matter in hand. I know a person, for example, who will poke the fire, set chairs straight, pick dust-specks from the floor, arrange his table, snatch up the newspaper, take down any book which catches his eye, trim his nails, waste the morning anyhow, in short, and all without premeditation, - simply because the only thing he ought to attend to is the preparation of a noonday lesson in formal logic which he detests. Anything but that!

Once more, the object must change. When it is one of sight, it will actually become invisible; when of hearing, inaudible, - if we attend to it too unmovingly. Helmholtz, who has put his sensorial attention to the severest tests, by using his eyes on objects which in common life are expressly overlooked, makes some interesting remarks on this point in his chapter on retinal rivalry.[22] The phenomenon called by that name is this, that if we look with each eye upon a different picture (as in the annexed stereoscopic slide), sometimes one picture, sometimes the other, or parts of both, will come to consciousness, hardly ever both combined.

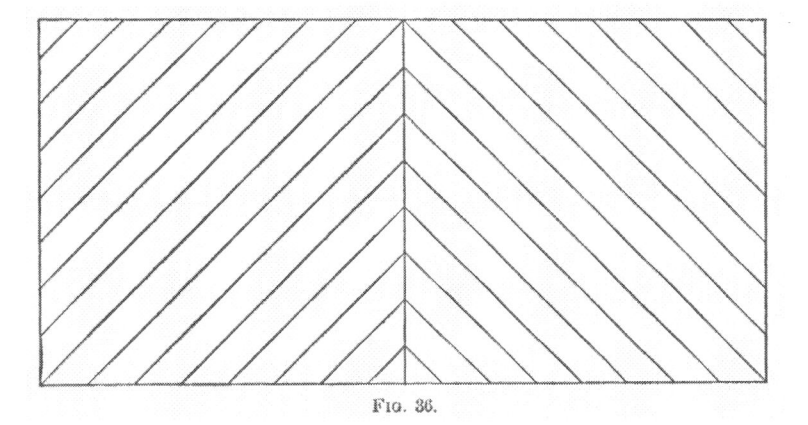

Fig. 36.

Helmholtz now says:
"I find that I am able to attend voluntarily, now to one and now to the other system of lines; and that then this system remains visible alone for a certain time, whilst the other completely vanishes. This happens, for example, whenever I try to count the lines first of one and then of the other system.... But it is extremely hard to chain the

attention down to one of the systems for long, unless we associate with our looking some distinct purpose which keeps the activity of the attention perpetually renewed. Such a one is counting the lines, comparing their intervals, or the like. An equilibrium of the attention, persistent for any length of time, is under no circumstances attainable. The natural tendency of attention when left to itself is to wander to ever new things; and so soon as the interest of its object is over, so soon as nothing new is to be noticed there, it passes, in spite of our will, to something else. If we wish to keep it upon one and the same object, we must seek constantly to find out something new about the latter, especially if other powerful impressions are attracting us away."

And again criticising an author who had treated of attention as an activity absolutely subject to the conscious will, Helmholtz writes:

"This is only restrictedly true. We move our eyes by our will; but one without training cannot so easily execute the intention of making them converge. At any moment, however, he can execute that of looking at a near object, in which act convergence is involved. Now just as little can we carry out our purpose to keep our attention steadily fixed upon a certain object, when our interest in the object is exhausted, and the purpose is inwardly formulated in this abstract way. But we can set ourselves new questions about the object, so that a new interest in it arises, and then the attention will remain riveted. The relation of attention to will is, then, less one of immediate than of mediate control."

These words of Helmholtz are of fundamental importance. And if true of sensorial attention, how much more true are they of the intellectual variety! The conditio sine quâ non of sustained attention to a given topic of thought is that we should roll it over and over incessantly and consider different aspects and relations of it in turn. Only in pathological states will a fixed and ever monotonously recurring idea possess the mind.

And now we can see why it is that what is called sustained attention is the easier, the richer in acquisitions and the fresher and more original the mind. In such minds, subjects bud and sprout and grow At every moment, they please by a new consequence and rivet the attention afresh. But an intellect unfurnished with materials, stagnant, unoriginal, will hardly be likely to consider any subject long. A glance exhausts its possibilities of interest. Geniuses are commonly believed to excel other men in their power of sustained attention.[23] In most of them, it is to be feared, the so-called 'power' is of the passive sort. Their ideas coruscate, every subject branches infinitely before their fertile minds, and so for hours they may be rapt. But it is their genius making them attentive, not their attention making geniuses of them. And, when we come down to the root of the matter, we see that they differ from ordinary men less in the character of their attention than in the nature of the objects upon which it is successively bestowed. In the genius, these form a concatenated series, suggesting each other mutually by some rational law. Therefore we call the attention 'sustained' and the topic of meditation for hours 'the same.' In the common man the series is for the most part incoherent, the objects have no rational bond, and we call the attention wandering and unfixed.

It is probable that genius tends actually to prevent a man from acquiring habits of voluntary attention, and that moderate intellectual endowments are the soil in which we may best expect, here as elsewhere, the virtues of the will, strictly so called, to thrive. But, whether the attention come by grace of genius or by dint of will, the longer one does attend to a topic the more mastery of it one has. And the faculty of voluntarily bringing back a wandering attention, over and over again, is the very root of judgment, character, and will. No one is compos sui if he have it not. An education which should improve this faculty would be the education par excellence. But it is easier to define this ideal than to give practical directions for bringing it about. The only general pedagogic maxim bearing on attention is that the more interest the child has in advance in the subject, the better he will attend. Induct him therefore in such a way as to knit each new thing on to some acquisition already there; and if possible awaken curiosity, so that the new thing shall seem to come as an answer, or part of an answer, to a question pre-existing in his mind.

At present having described the varieties, let us turn to...

The Effects of Attention

Its remote effects are too incalculable to be recorded. The practical and theoretical life of whole species, as well as of individual beings, results from the selection which the habitual direction of their attention involves. In Chapters XIV and XV some of these consequences will come to light. Suffice it meanwhile that each of us literally chooses, by his ways of attending to things, what sort of a universe he shall appear to himself to inhabit.

The immediate effects of attention are to make us:

a) perceive-
b) conceive-
c) distinguish-
d) remember-better than otherwise we could - both more successive things and each thing more clearly. It also

e) shortens 'reaction-time.'

a and b. Most people would say that a sensation attended to becomes stronger than it otherwise would be. This point is, however, not quite plain, and has occasioned some discussion[24] >From the strength or intensity of a sensation must be distinguished its clearness; and to increase this is, for some psychologists, the utmost that attention can do. When the facts are surveyed, however, it must be admitted that to some extent the relative intensity of two sensations may be changed when one of them is attended to and the other not. Every artist knows how he can make a scene before his eyes appear warmer or colder in color, according to the way he sets his attention. If for warm, he soon begins to see the red color start out of everything; if for cold, the blue. Similarly in listening for certain notes in a chord, or overtones in a musical sound, the one we attend to sounds probably a little more loud as well as more emphatic than it did before. When we mentally break a series of monotonous strokes into a rhythm, by accentuating every second or third one, etc., the stroke on which the stress of attention is laid seems to become stronger as well as more emphatic. The increased visibility of optical after-images and of double images, which close attention brings about, can hardly be interpreted otherwise than as a real strengthening of the retinal sensations themselves. And this view is rendered particularly probable by the fact that an imagined visual object may, if attention be concentrated upon it long enough, acquire before the mind's eye almost the brilliancy of reality, and (in the case of certain exceptionally gifted observers) leave a negative after-image of itself when it passes away (see Chapter XVIII). Confident expectation of a certain intensity or quality of impression will often make us sensibly see or hear it in an object which really falls far short of it. In face of such facts it is rash to say that attention cannot make a sense-impression more intense.

But, on the other hand, the intensification which may be brought about seems never to lead the judgment astray. As we rightly perceive and name the same color under various lights, the same sound at various distances; so we seem to make an analogous sort of allowance for the varying amounts of attention with which objects are viewed; and whatever changes of feeling the attention may bring we charge, as it were, to the attention's account, and still perceive and conceive the object as the same.

"A gray paper appears to us no lighter, the pendulum-beat of a clock no louder, no matter how much we increase the strain of our attention upon them. No one, by doing this, can make the gray paper look white, or the stroke of the pendulum sound like the blow of a strong hammer, - everyone, on the contrary, feels the increase as that of his own conscious activity turned upon the thing."[25]

Were it otherwise, we should not be able to note intensities by attending to them. Weak impressions would, as Stumpf says,[26] become stronger by the very fact of being observed.

"I should not be able to observe faint sounds at all, but only such as appeared to me of maximal strength, or at least of a strength that increased with the amount of my observation. In reality, however, I can, with steadily increasing attention, follow a diminuendo perfectly well."

The subject is one which would well repay exact experiment, if methods could be devised. Meanwhile there is no question whatever that attention augments the clearness of all that we perceive or conceive by its aid. But what is meant by clearness here?

c. Clearness, so far as attention produces it, means distinction from other things and internal analysis or subdivision. These are essentially products of intellectual discrimination, involving comparison, memory, and perception of various relations. The attention per se does not distinguish and analyze and relate. The most we can say is that it is a condition of our doing so. And as these processes are to be described later, the clearness they produce had better not be farther discussed here. The important point to notice here is that it is not attention's immediate fruit.[27]

d. Whatever future conclusion we may reach as to this, we cannot deny that an object once attended to will remain in the memory, whilst one inattentively allowed to pass will leave no traces behind. Already in Chapter VI we discussed whether certain states of mind were 'unconscious,' or whether they were not rather states to which no attention had been paid, and of whose passage recollection could afterwards find no vestiges. Dugald Stewart says:[28] "The connection between attention and memory has been remarked by many authors." He quotes Quintilian, Locke, and Helvetius; and goes on at great length to explain the phenomena of 'secondary automatism' by the presence of a mental action grown so inattentive as to preserve no memory of itself. In our chapter on Memory, later on, the point will come up again.

e. Under this head, the shortening of reaction-time, there is a good deal to be said of Attention's effects. Since Wundt has probably worked over the subject more thoroughly than any other investigator and made it peculiarly his own, what follows had better, as far as possible, be in his words. The reader will remember the method and results of experimentation on 'reaction-time,' as given in Chapter III.

The facts I proceed to quote may also be taken as a supplement to that chapter. Wundt writes:

"When we wait with strained attention for a stimulus, it will often happen that instead of registering the stimulus, we react upon some entirely different impression, - and this not through confounding the one with the other. On the contrary, we are perfectly well aware at the moment of making the movement that we respond to the wrong stimulus. Sometimes even, though not so often, the latter may be another kind of sensation altogether, - one may, for example, in experimenting with sound, register a flash of light, produced either by accident or design. We cannot well explain these results otherwise than by assuming that the strain of the attention towards the impression we expect coexists with a preparatory innervation of the motor centre for the reaction, which innervation the slightest shock then suffices to turn into an actual discharge. This shock may be given by any chance impression, even by one to which we never intended to respond. When the preparatory innervation has once reached this pitch of intensity, the time that intervenes between the stimulus and the contraction of the muscles which react, may become vanishingly small."[29]

"The perception of an impression is facillitated when the impression is preceded by a warning which announces beforehand that it is about to occur. This case is realized whenever several stimuli follow each other at equal intervals, - when, e.g. we note pendulum movements by the eye, or pendulum-strokes by the ear. Each single stroke forms here the signal for the next, which is thus met by a fully prepared attention. The same thing happens when the stimulus to be perceived is preceded, at a certain interval, by a single warning: the time is always notably shortened. . . . I have made comparative observations on reaction-time with and without a warning signal. The impression to be reacted on was the sound made by the dropping of a ball on the board of the 'drop apparatus.' . . . . In a first series no warning preceded the stroke of the ball; in the second, the noise made by the apparatus in liberating the ball served as a signal. . . . Here are the averages of two series of such experiments:

Height of Fall.		Average.	Mean Error.	No. of Expts.
25 cm.	No warning	0.253	0.051	13
	Warning	0.076	0.060	17
5 cm.	No warning	0.266	0.036	14
	Warning	0.175	0.035	17

". . . In a long series of experiments, (the interval between warning and stimulus remaining the same) the reaction-time grows less and less, and it is possible occasionally to reduce it to a vanishing quantity (a few thousandths of a second), to zero, or even to a negative value.[30] . . . The only ground that we can assign for this phenomenon is the preparation (vorbereitende Spannung) of the attention. It is easy to understand that the reaction-time should be shortened by this means; but that is should sometimes sink to zero and even assume negative values, may appear surprising. Nevertheless this latter case is also explained by what happens in the simple reaction-time experiments" just referred to, in which, "when the strain of the attention has reached
its climax, the movement we stand ready to execute escapes from the control of our will, and we register a wrong signal. In these other experiments, in which a warning foretells the moment of the stimulus, it is also plain that attention accommodates itself so exactly to the latter's reception that no sooner is it objectively given than it is fully apperceived, and with the apperception the motor discharge coincides."[31]

Usually, when the impression is fully anticipated, attention prepares the motor centres so completely for both stimulus and reaction that the only time lost is that of the physiological conduction downwards. But even this interval may disappear, i.e. the stimulus and reaction may become objectively contemporaneous; or more remarkable still, the reaction may be discharged before the stimulus has actually occurred.[32] Wundt, as we saw some pages back explains this by the effort of the mind so to react that we may feel our own movement and the signal which prompts it, both at the same instant. As the execution of the movement must precede our feeling of it, so it must also precede the stimulus, if that and our movement are to be felt at once.

The peculiar theoretic interest of these experiments lies in their showing expectant attention and sensation to be continuous or identical processes, since they may have identical motor effects. Although other exceptional observations show them likewise to be continuous subjectively. Wundt's experiments do not: he seems never, at the moment of reacting prematurely, to have been misled into the belief that the real stimulus was there.

As concentrated attention accelerates perception, so, conversely, perception of a stimulus is retarded by anything which either baffles or distracts the attention with which we await it.

"If, e.g., we make reactions on a sound in such a way that weak and strong stimuli irregularly alternate so that the observer can never expect a determinate strength with any certainty, the reaction-time for all for various signals is increased, - and so is the average error. I append two examples. . . . In Series I a strong and a weak sound alternated regularly, so that the intensity was each time known in advance. In II they came irregularly.

"Still greater is the increase of the time when, unexpectedly into a series of strong impressions, a weak one is interpolated, or vice versâ. In this way I have seen the time of reaction upon a sound so weak as to be barely perceived rise to 0.4" or 0.5", and for a strong sound to 0.25". It is also matter of general experience that a stimulus expected in a general way, but for whose intensity attention cannot be adapted in advance, demands a longer reaction-time.

I. *Regular Alternation.*

	Average Time.	Average Error.	No. of Expts.
Strong sound	0.116"	0.010"	18
Weak sound	0.127"	0.012"	9

II. *Irregular Alternation.*

	Average Time.	Average Error.	No. of Expts.
Strong sound	0.189"	0.038"	9
Weak sound	0.298"	0.076"	15

In such cases ... the reason for the difference can only lie in the fact that wherever a preparation of the attention is impossible, the time of both perception and volition is prolonged. Perhaps also the conspicuously large reaction-times which are got with stimuli so faint as to be just perceptible may be explained by the attention tending always to adapt itself for something more than this minimal amount of stimulus, so that a state ensues similar to that in the case of unexpected stimuli.... Still more than by previously unknown stimuli is the reaction-time prolonged by wholly unexpected impressions. This is sometimes accidentally brought about, when the observer's attention, instead of being concentrated on the coming signal, is dispersed. It can be realized purposely by suddenly thrusting into a long series of equidistant stimuli a much shorter interval which the observer does not expect. The mental effect here is like that of being startled; - often the startling is outwardly visible. The time of reaction may then easily be lengthened to one quarter of a second with strong signals, or with weak ones to a half-second. Slighter, but still very noticeable, is the retardation when the experiment is so arranged that the observer, ignorant whether the stimulus is to be an impression of light, sound, or touch, cannot keep his attention turned to any particular sense-organ in advance. One notices then at the same time a peculiar unrest, as the feeling of strain which accompanies the attention keeps vacillating between the several senses.

"Complications of another sort arise when what is registered is an impression anticipated both in point of quality and strength, but accompanied by other stimuli which make the concentration of the attention difficult. The reaction-time is here always more or less prolonged. The simplest case of the sort is where a momentary impression is registered in the midst of another, and continuous, sensorial-stimulation of considerable strength. The continuous stimulus may belong to the same sense as the stimulus to be reacted on, or to another. When it is of the same sense, the retardation it causes may be partly due to the distraction of the attention by it, but partly also to the fact that the stimulus to be reacted on stands out less strongly than if alone, and practically becomes a less intense sensation. But other factors in reality are present; for we find the reaction-time more prolonged by the concomitant stimulation when the stimulus is weak than when it is strong. I made experiments in which the principal impression, or signal for reaction, was a bell-stroke whose strength could be graduated by a spring against the hammer with a movable counterpoise. Each set of observations comprised two series; in one of which the bell-stroke was registered in the ordinary way, whilst in the other a toothed wheel belonging to the chronometric apparatus made during the entire experiment a steady noise against a metal spring. In one half of the latter series (A) the bell-stroke was only moderately strong, so that the accompanying noise diminished it considerably, without, however, making it indistinguishable. In the other half (B) the bell-sound was so loud as to be heard with perfect distinctness above the noise.

		Mean.	Maximum.	Minimum.	No. of Experiments.
A (Bell-stroke moderate)	Without noise	0.189	0.244	0.156	21
	With noise	0.313	0.499	0.183	16
B (Bell-stroke loud)	Without noise	0.158	0.206	0.133	20
	With noise	0.203	0.295	0.140	19

"Since, in these experiments, the sound B even with noise made a considerably stronger impression than the sound A without, we must see in the figures a direct influence of the disturbing noise on the process of reaction. This influence is freed from mixture with other factors when the momentary stimulus and the concomitant disturbance appeal to different senses. I chose, to test this, sight and hearing. The momentary signal was an induction-spark leaping from one platinum point to another against a dark background. The steady stimulation was the noise above described.

Spark.	Mean.	Maximum.	Minimum.	No. of Expts.
Without noise	0.222	0.284	0.158	20
With noise	0.300	0.390	0.250	18

"When one reflects that in the experiments with one and the same sense the relative intensity of the signal is always depressed [which by itself is a retarding condition] the amount of retardation in these last observations makes it probable that the disturbing influence upon attention is greater when the stimuli are disparate than when they belong to the same sense. One does not, in fact, find it particularly hard to register immediately, when the bell rings in the midst of the noise; but when the spark is the signal one has a feeling of being coerced, as one turns away from the noise towards it. This fact is immediately connected with other properties of our attention. The effort of the latter is accompanied by various corporeal sensations, according to the sense which is engaged. The innervation which exists during the effort of attention is therefore probably a different one for each sense-organ."[33]
Wundt then, after some theoretical remarks which we need not quote now, gives a table of retardations, as follows:
Retardation.

1. Unexpected strength of impression:
    a) Unexpectedly strong sound 0.073
    b) Unexpectedly weak sound.. 0.171
2. Interference by like stimulus (sound by sound) ....0.045[34]
3. Interference by unlike stimulus (light by sound)............................ 0.078

It seems probable, from these results obtained with elementary processes of mind, that all processes, even the higher ones of reminiscence, reasoning, etc., whenever attention is concentrated upon them instead of being diffused and languid, are thereby more rapidly performed.[35]
Still more interesting reaction-time observations have been made by Münsterberg. The reader will recollect the fact noted in Chapter III that reaction-time is shorter when one concentrates his attention on the expected movement than when one concentrates it on the expected signal. Herr Münsterberg found that this is equally the case when the reaction is no simple reflex, but can take place only after an intellectual operation. In a series of experiments the five fingers were used to react with, and
the reacter had to use a different finger according as the signal was of one sort or another. Thus when a word in the nominative case was called out he used the thumb, for the dative he used another finger; similarly adjectives, substantives, pronouns, numerals, etc., or, again, towns, rivers, beasts, plants, elements; or poets, musicians, philosophers, etc., were co-ordinated each with its finger, so that when a world belonging to either of these classes was mentioned, a particular finger and no other had to perform the reaction. In a second series of experiments the reaction consisted in the utterance of a word in answer to a question, such as "name an edible fish," etc.; or "name the first drama of Schiller," etc.; or "which is greater, Hume or Kant?" etc.; or (first naming apples and cherries, and several other fruits) "which do you prefer, apples or cherries?" etc.; or "which is Goethe's finest drama?" etc.; or "which letter comes the later in the alphabet, the letter L or the first letter of the most beautiful tree?" etc.; or "which is less, 15 or 20 minus 8?"[36] etc. etc. etc. Even in this series of reactions the time was much quicker when the reacter turned his attention in advance towards the answer than when he turned it towards the question. The shorter reaction-time was seldom more than one fifth of a second; the longer, from four to eight times as long.
To understand such results, one must bear in mind that in these experiments the reacter always knew in advance in a general way the kind of question which he was to receive, and consequently the sphere within which his possible answer lay.[37] In turning his attention, therefore, from the outset towards the answer, those brain-processes in him which were connected with this entire 'sphere' were kept sub-excited, and the question could then discharge with a minimum amount of lost time that particular answer out of the 'sphere' which belonged especially to it. When, on the contrary, the attention was kept looking towards the question exclusively and averted from the possible reply, all this preliminary sub-excitement of motor tracts failed to occur, and the entire process of answering had to be gone through with after the question was heard. No wonder that the time was prolonged. It is a beautiful example of the summation of stimulations, and of the way in which expectant attention, even when not very strongly focalized, will prepare the motor centres, and shorten the work which a stimulus has to perform on them, in order to produce a given effect when it comes.

The Intimate Nature Of The Attentive Process.

We have now a sufficient number of facts to warrant our considering this more recondite question. And two physiological processes, of which we have got a glimpse, immediately suggest themselves as possibly forming in combination a complete reply. I mean

1. The accommodation or adjustment of the sensory organs; and
2. The anticipatory preparation from within of the ideational centres concerned with the object to which the attention is paid.

1. The sense-organ and the bodily muscles which favor their exercise are adjusted most energetically in sensorial attention, whether immediate and reflex, or derived. But there are good grounds for believing that even intellectual attention, attention to the idea of a sensible object, is also accompanied with some degree of excitement of the sense-organs to which the object appeals. The preparation of the ideational centres exists, on the other hand, wherever our interest in the object - be it sensible or ideal - is derived from, or in any way connected with, other interests, or the presence of other objects, in the mind. It exists as well when the attention thus derived is classed as passive as when it is classed as voluntary. So that on the whole we may confidently conclude - since in mature life we never attend to anything without our interest in it being in some degree derived from its connection with other objects - that the two processes of sensorial adjustment and ideational preparation probably coexist in all our concrete attentive acts.

The two points must now be proved in more detail. First, as respects the sensorial adjustment.

That it is present when we attend to sensible things is obvious. When we look or listen we accommodate our eyes and ears involuntarily, and we turn our head and body as well; when we taste or smell we adjust the tongue, lips and respiration to the object; in feeling a surface we move the palpatory organ in a suitable way; in all these acts, besides making involuntary muscular contractions of a positive sort, we inhibit others which might interfere with the result - we close the eyes in tasting, suspend the respiration in listening, etc. The result is a more or less massive organic feeling that attention is going on. This organic feeling comes, in the way described earlier, to be contrasted with that of the objects which it accompanies, and regarded as peculiarly ours, whilst the objects form the not-me. We treat it as a sense of our own activity, although it comes in to us from our organs after they are accommodated, just as the feeling of any object does. Any object, if immediately exciting, causes a reflex accommodation of the sense-organ, and this has two results - first, the object's increase in clearness; and second, the feeling of activity in question. Both are sensations of an 'afferent' sort.

But in intellectual attention, as we have already seen, similar feelings of activity occur. Fechner was the first, I believe, to analyze these feelings, and discriminate them from the stronger ones just named. He writes:

"When we transfer the attention from objects of one sense to those of another, we have an indescribable feeling (though at the same time one perfectly determinate, and reproducible at pleasure), of altered direction or differently localized tension (Spannung). We feel a strain forward in the eyes, one directed sidewise in the ears, increasing with the degree of our attention, and changing according as we look at an object carefully, or listen to something attentively; and we speak accordingly of straining the attention. The difference is most plainly felt when the attention oscillates rapidly between eye and ear; and the feeling localizes itself with most decided difference in regard to the various sense-organs, according as we wish to discriminate a thing delicately by touch, taste, or smell.

"But now I have, when I try to vividly recall a picture of memory or fancy, a feeling perfectly analogous to that which I experience when I seek to apprehend a thing keenly by eye or ear; and this analogous feeling is very differently localized. While in sharpest possible attention to real objects (as well as to after-images) the strain is plainly forwards, and when the attention changes from one sense to another only alters its direction between the several external sense-organs, leaving the rest of the head free from strain, the case is different in memory or fancy, for here the feeling withdraws entirely from the external sense-organs, and seems rather to take refuge in that part of the head which the brain fills; if I wish, for example, to recall a place or person it will arise before me with vividness, not according as I strain my attention forwards, but rather in proportion as I, so to speak, retract it backwards."[38]

In myself the 'backward retraction' which is felt during attention to ideas of memory, etc., seems to be principally constituted by the feeling of an actual rolling outwards and upwards of the eyeballs, such as occurs in sleep, and in the exact opposite of their behavior when we look at a physical thing. I have already spoken of this feeling earlier.[39] The reader who doubts the presence of these organic feelings is requested to read the whole of that passage again.

It has been said, however, that we may attend to an object on the periphery of the visual field and yet not accommodate the eye for it. Teachers thus notice the acts of children in the school-room at whom they appear not to be looking. Women in general train their peripheral visual attention more than men. This would be an objection to the invariable and universal presence of movements of adjustment as ingredients of the attentive process. Usually, as is well known, no object lying in the marginal portions of the field of vision can catch our attention without at the same time 'catching our eye' - that is, fatally provoking such movements of rotation and accommodation as will focus its image on the fovea, or point of greatest sensibility. Practice, however, enables us, with effort, to attend to a marginal object whilst keeping the eyes immovable. The object under these circumstances never becomes perfectly distinct - the place of its image on the retina makes distinctness impossible - but (as anyone can satisfy himself by trying) we become more vividly conscious of it than we were before the effort was made. Helmholtz states the fact so strikingly that I will quote his observation in full. He was trying to combine in a single solid percept pairs of stereoscopic pictures illuminated instantaneously by the electric spark. The pictures were in a dark box which the spark from time to time lighted up; and, to keep the eyes from wandering betweenwhiles, a pin-hole was pricked through the middle of each picture, through which the light of the room came, so that each eye had presented to it during the dark intervals a single bright point. With parallel optical axes the points combined into a single image; and the slightest movement of the eyeballs was betrayed by this image at once becoming double. Helmholtz now found that simple linear figures could, when the eyes were thus kept immovable, be perceived as solids at a single flash of the spark. But when the figures were complicated photographs, many successive flashes were required to grasp their totality.

"Now it is interesting," he says, "to find that, although we keep steadily fixating the pin-holes and never allow their combined image to break into two, we can, nevertheless, before the spark comes, keep our attention voluntarily turned to any particular portion we please of the dark field, so as then, when the spark comes, to receive an impression only from such parts of the picture as lie in this region. In this respect, then, our attention is quite independent of the position and accommodation of the eyes, and of any known alteration in these organs; and free to direct itself by a conscious and voluntary effort upon any selected portion of a dark and undifferentiated field of view. This is one of the most important observations for a future theory of attention."[40]

Hering, however, adds the following detail:

"Whilst attending to the marginal object we must always," he says, "attend at the same time to the object directly fixated. If even for a single instant we let the latter slip out of our mind, our eye moves towards the former, as may be easily recognized by the after-images produced, or by the muscular sounds heard. The case is then less properly to be called one of translocation, than one of unusually wide dispersion, of the attention, in which dispersion the largest share still falls upon the thing directly looked at,"[41]

and consequently directly accommodated for. Accommodation exists here, then, as it does elsewhere, and without it we should lose a part of our sense of attentive activity. In fact, the strain of that activity (which is remarkably great in the experiment) is due in part to unusually strong contractions of the muscles needed to keep the eyeballs still, which produce unwonted feelings of pressure in those organs.

2. But if the peripheral part of the picture in this experiment be not physically accommodated for, what is meant by its sharing our attention? What happens when we 'distribute' or 'disperse' the latter upon a thing for which we remain unwilling to 'adjust'? This leads us to that second feature in the process, the 'ideational preparation' of which we spoke. The effort to attend to the marginal region of the picture consists in nothing more nor less than the effort to form as clear an idea as is possible of what is there portrayed. The idea is to come to the help of the sensation and make it more distinct. It comes with effort, and such a mode of coming in the remaining part of what we know as our attention's 'strain' under the circumstances. Let us show how universally present in our acts of attention this reinforcing imagination, this inward reproduction, this anticipatory thinking of the thing we attend to, is.

It must as a matter of course be present when the attention is of the intellectual variety, for the thing attended to then is nothing but an idea, an inward reproduction or conception. If then we prove ideal construction of the object to be present in sensorial attention, it will be present everywhere. When, however, sensorial attention is at its height, it is impossible to tell how much of the percept comes from without and how much from within; but if we find that the preparation we make for it always partly consists of the creation of an imaginary duplicate of the object in the mind, which shall stand ready to receive the outward impression as if in a matrix, that will be quite enough to establish the point in dispute.

In Wundt's and Exner's experiments quoted above, the lying in wait for the impressions, and the preparation to react, consist of nothing but the anticipatory imagination of what the impressions or the reactions are to be. Where the stimulus is unknown and the reaction undetermined, time is lost, because no stable image can under such circumstances be formed in advance. But where both nature and time of signal and reaction are foretold, so completely does the expectant attention consist in premonitory imagination that, as we have seen, it may mimic the intensity of reality, or at any rate produce reality's motor effects. It is impossible to read Wundt's and Exner's pages of description and not to interpret the 'Apperception' and 'Spannung' and other terms as equivalents of imagination. With Wundt, in particular, the word Apperception (which he sets great store by) is quite interchangeable with both imagination and attention. All three are names for the excitement from within of ideational brain-centres, for which Mr. Lewes's name of preperception seems the best possible designation.

Where the impression to be caught is very weak, the way not to miss it is to sharpen our attention for it by preliminary contact with it in a stronger form.

"If we wish to begin to observe overtones, it is advisable, just before the sound which is to be analyzed, to sound very softly the note of which we are in search.... The piano and harmonium are well fitted for this use, as both give overtones that are strong. Strike upon the piano first the g' [of a certain musical example previously given in the text]; then, when it vibrations have objectively ceased, strike powerfully the note c, in whose sound g' is the third overtone, and keep your attention steadily bent upon the pitch of the just heard g'; you will now hear this tone sounding in the midst of the c.... If you place the resonator which corresponds to a certain overtone, for example g' of the sound c, against your ear, and then make the note c sound, you will hear g' much strengthened by the reasonator.... This strengthening by the resonator can be used to make the naked ear attentive to the sound which it is to catch. For when the resonator is gradually removed, the g' grows weaker; but the attention, once directed to it, holds it now more easily fast, and the observer hears the tone g' now in the natural unaltered sound of the note with his unaided ear."[42]

Wundt, commenting on experiences of this sort, says that

"on carefully observing, one will always find that one tries first to recall the image in memory of the tone to be heard, and that then one hears it in the total sound. The same thing is to be noticed in weak or fugitive visual impressions. Illuminate a drawing by electric sparks separated by considerable intervals, and after the first, and often after the second and third spark, hardly anything will be recognized. But the confused image is held fast in memory; each successive illumination completes it; and so at last we attain to a clearer perception. The primary motive to this inward activity proceeds usually from the outer impression itself. We hear a sound in which, from certain associations, we suspect a certain overtone; the next thing is to recall the overtone in memory; and finally we catch it in the sound we hear. Or perhaps we see some mineral substance we have met before; the impression awakens the memory-image, which again more or less completely melts with the impression itself. In this way every idea takes a certain time to penetrate to the focus of consciousness. And during this time we always find in ourselves the peculiar feeling of attention.... The phenomena show that an adaptation of attention to the impression takes place. The surprise which unexpected impressions give us is due essentially to the fact that our attention, at the moment when the impression occurs, is not accommodated for it. The accommodation itself is of the double sort, relating as it does to the intensity as well as to the quality of the stimulus. Different qualities of impression require disparate adaptations. And we remark that our feeling of the strain of our inward attentiveness increases with every increase in the strength of the impressions of whose perceptions we are intent."[43]

The natural way of conceiving all this is under the symbolic form of a brain-cell played upon from two directions. Whilst the object excites it from without, other brain-cells, or perhaps spiritual forces, arouse it from within. The latter influence is the 'adaptation of the attention.' The plenary energy of the brain-cell demands the co-operation of both factors: not when merely present, but when both present and attended to, is the object fully perceived.

A few additional experiences will now be perfectly clear. Helmholtz, for instance, adds this observation to the passage we quoted a while ago concerning the stereoscopic pictures lit by the electric spark.

"These experiments," he says, "are interesting as regards the part which attention plays in the matter of double images.... For in pictures so simple that it is relatively difficult for me to see them double, I can succeed in seeing them double, even when the illumination is only instantaneous, the moment I strive to imagine in a lively way how they ought then to look. The influence of attention is here pure; for all eye movements are shut out."[44]

In another place[45] the same writer says:

"When I have before my eyes a pair of stereoscopic drawings which are hard to combine, it is difficult to bring the lines and points that correspond, to cover each other, and with every little motion of the eyes they glide apart. But if I chance to gain a lively mental image (Anschauungsbild) of the represented solid form (a thing that often occurs by lucky chance), I then move my two eyes with perfect certainty over the figure without the picture separating again."

Again, writing of retinal rivalry, Helmholtz says:

"It is not a trial of strength between two sensations, but depends on our fixing or failing to fix the attention. Indeed, there is scarcely any phenomenon so well fitted for the study of the causes which are capable of determining the attention. It is not enough to form the conscious intention of seeing first with one eye then with the other; we must form as clear a notion as possible of what we expect to see. Then it will actually appear."[46]

In figures 37 and 38, where the result is ambiguous, we can make the change from one apparent form to the other by imagining strongly in advance the form we wish to see. Similarly in those puzzles where certain lines in a picture form by their combination an object that has no connection with what the picture ostensibly represents; or indeed in every case where an object is inconspicuous and hard to discern from the background; we may not be able to see it for a long time; but, having once seen it, we can attend to it again whenever we like, on account of the mental duplicate of it which our imagination now bears.

In the meaningless French words 'pas de lieu Rhône que nous,' who can recognize immediately the English 'paddle your own canoe'?[47] But who that has once noticed the identity can fail to have it arrest his attention again? When watching for the distant clock to strike, our mind is so filled with its image that at every moment we think we hear the longed-for dreaded sound. So of an awaited footstep. Every stir in the wood is for the hunter his game; for the fugitive his pursuers. Every bonnet in the street is momentarily taken by the lover to enshroud the head of his idol.

The image in the mind is the attention; the preperception, as Mr. Lewes calls it, is half of the perception of the looked-for thing.[48]

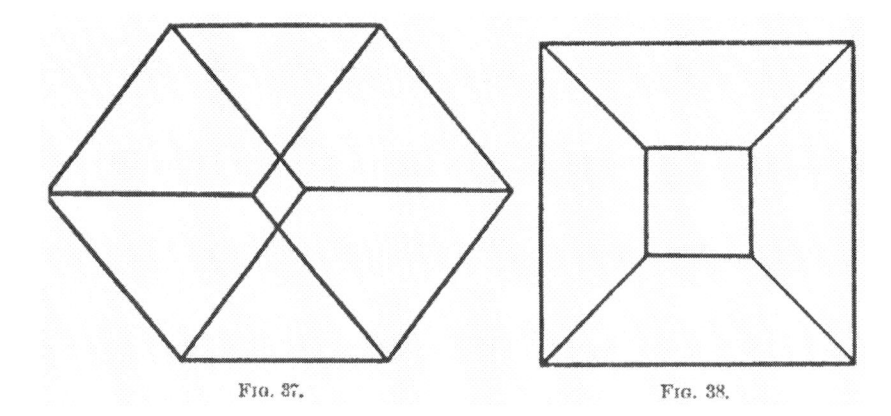

Fig. 37.   Fig. 38.

It is for this reason that men have no eyes but for those aspects of things which they have already been taught to discern. Any one of us can notice a phenomenon after it has once been pointed out, which not one in ten thousand could ever have discovered for himself. Even in poetry and the arts, some one has to come and tell us what aspects we may single out, and what effects we may admire, before our æsthetic nature can 'dilate' to its full extent and never 'with the wrong emotion.' In kindergarten instruction one of the exercises is to make the children see how many features they can point out in such an object as a flower or a stuffed bird. They readily name the features they know already, such as leaves, tail, bill, feet. But they may look for hours without distinguishing nostrils, claws, scales, etc., until their attention is called to these details; thereafter, however, they see them every time. In short, the only things which we commonly see are those which we preperceive, and the only things which we preperceive are those which have been labelled for us, and the labels stamped into our mind. If we lost our stock of labels we should be intellectually lost in the midst of the world.

Organic adjustment, then, and ideational preparation or preperception are concerned in all attentive acts. An interesting theory is defended by no less authorities than Professors Bain[49] and Ribot,[50] and still more ably advocated by Mr. N. Lange,[51] who will have it that the ideational preparation itself is a consequence of muscular adjustment, so that the latter may be called the essence of the attentive process throughout. This at least is what the theory of these authors practically amounts to, though the former two do not state it in just these terms. The proof consists in the exhibition of cases of intellectual attention which organic adjustment accompanies, or of objects in thinking which we have to execute a movement. Thus Lange says that when he tries to imagine a certain colored circle, he finds himself first making with his eyes the movement to which the circle corresponds, and then imagining the color, etc., as a consequence of the movement.

"Let my reader," he adds, "close his eyes and think of an extended object, for instance a pencil. He will easily notice that he first makes a slight movement [of the eyes] corresponding to the straight line, and that he often gets a weak feeling of innervation of the hand as if touching the pencil's surface. So, in thinking of a certain sound, we turn towards its direction or repeat muscularly its rhythm, or articulate an imitation of it."[52]

But it is one thing to point out the presence of muscular contractions as constant concomitants of our thoughts, and another thing to say, with Herr Lange, that thought is made possible by muscular contraction alone. It may well be that where the object of thought consists of two parts, one perceived by movement and another not, the part perceived by movement is habitually called up first and fixed in the mind by the movement's execution, whilst the other part comes secondarily as the movement's mere associate. But even were this the rule with all men (which I doubt[53]), it would only be a practical habit, not an ultimate necessity. In the chapter on the Will we shall learn that movements themselves are results of images coming before the mind, images sometimes of feelings in the moving part, sometimes of the movement's effects on eye and ear, and sometimes (if the movement be originally reflex or instinctive), of its natural stimulus or exciting cause. It is, in truth, contrary to all wider and deeper analogies to deny that any quality of feeling whatever can directly rise up in the form of an idea, and to assert that only ideas of movement can call other ideas to the mind.

So much for adjustment and preperception. The only third process I can think of as always present is the inhibition of irrelevant movements and ideas. This seems, however, to be a feature incidental to voluntary attention rather than the essential feature of attention at large,[54] and need not concern us particularly now. Noting merely the intimate connection which our account so far establishes between attention, on the one hand, and imagination, discrimination, and memory, on the other, let us draw a couple of practical inferences, and then pass to the more speculative problem that remains.

The practical inferences are pedagogic. First, to strengthen attention in children who care nothing for the subject they are studying and let their wits go wool-gathering. The interest here must be 'derived' from something that the teacher associates with the task, a reward or a punishment if nothing less external comes to mind. Prof. Ribot says: "A child refuses to read; he is incapable of keeping his mind fixed on the letters, which have no attraction for him; but he looks with avidity upon the pictures contained in a book. 'What do they mean?' he asks. The father replies: 'When you can read, the book will tell you.' After several colloquies like this, the child resigns himself and falls to work, first slackly, then the habit grows, and finally he shows an ardor which has to be restrained. This is a case of the genesis of voluntary attention. An artificial and indirect desire has to be grafted on a natural and direct one. Reading has no immediate attractiveness, but is has a borrowed one, and that is enough. The child is caught in the wheelwork, the first step is made."

I take another example, from M. B. Perez:[55]

"A child of six years, habitually prone to mind-wandering, sat down one day to the piano of his own accord to repeat an air by which his mother had been charmed. His exercises lasted an hour. The same child at the age of seven, seeing his brother busy with tasks in vacation, went and sat at his father's desk. 'What are you doing there?' his nurse said, surprised at so finding him. 'I am,' said the child, 'learning a page of German; it isn't very amusing, but it is for an agreeable surprise to mamma.'"

Here, again, a birth of voluntary attention, grafted this time on a sympathetic instead of a selfish sentiment like that of the first example. The piano, the German, awaken no spontaneous attention; but they arouse and maintain it by borrowing a force from elsewhere.[56]

Second, take that mind-wandering which at a later age may trouble us whilst reading or listening to a discourse. If attention be the reproduction of the sensation from within, the habit of reading not merely with the eye, and of listening not merely with the ear, but of articulating to one's self the words seen or heard, ought to deepen one's attention to the latter. Experience shows that this is the case. I can keep my wandering mind a great deal more closely upon a conversation or a lecture if I actively re-echo to myself the words than if I simply hear them; and I find a number of my students who report benefit from voluntarily adopting a similar course.[57]

Second, a teacher who wishes to engage the attention of his class must knit his novelties on to things of which they already have preperceptions. The old and familiar is readily attended to by the mind and helps to hold in turn the new, forming, in Herbartian phraseology, an 'Apperceptionsmasse' for it. Of course it is in every case a very delicate problem to know what 'Apperceptionsmasse' to use. Psychology can only lay down the general rule.

Is Voluntary Attention a Resultant or a Force?

When, a few pages back, I symbolized the 'ideational preparation' element in attention by a brain-cell played upon from within, I added 'by other brain-cells, or by some spiritual force,' without deciding which. The question 'which?' is one of those central psychologic mysteries which part the schools. When we reflect that the turnings of our attention form the nucleus of our inner self; when we see (as in the chapter on the Will we shall see) that volition is nothing but attention; when we believe that our autonomy in the midst of nature depends on our not being pure effect, but a cause,-

Principium quoddam quod fati fœdera rumpat,
Ex infinito ne causam causa sequatur

- we must admit that the question whether attention involve such a principle of spiritual activity or not is metaphysical as well as psychological, and is well worthy of all the pains we can bestow on its solution. It is in fact the pivotal question of metaphysics, the very hinge on which our picture of the world shall swing from materialism, fatalism, monism, towards spiritualism, freedom, pluralism, - or else the other way.

It goes back to the automaton-theory. If feeling is an inert accompaniment, then of course the brain-cell can be played upon only by other brain-cells, and the attention which we give at any time to any subject, whether in the form of sensory adaptation or of 'preperception,' is the fatally predetermined effect of exclusively material laws. If, on the other hand, the feeling which coexists with the brain-cells' activity reacts dynamically upon that activity, furthering or checking it, then the attention is in part, at least, a cause. It does not necessarily follow, of course, that this reactive feeling should be 'free' in the sense of having its amount and direction undetermined in advance, for it might very well be predetermined in all these particulars. If it were so, our attention would not be materially determined, nor yet would it be 'free' in the sense of being spontaneous or unpredictable in advance. The question is of course a purely speculative one, for we have no means of objectively ascertaining whether our feelings react on our nerve-processes or not; and those who answer the question in either way do so in consequence of general analogies and presumptions drawn from other fields. As mere conceptions, the effect-theory and the cause-theory of attention are equally clear; and whoever affirms either conception to be true must do so on metaphysical or universal rather than on scientific or particular grounds.

As regards immediate sensorial attention hardly any one is tempted to regard it as anything but an effect.[58] We are 'evolved' so as to respond to special stimuli by special accommodative acts which produce clear perceptions on the one hand in us, and on the other hand such feelings of inner activity as were above described. The accommodation and the resultant feeling are the attention. We don't bestow it, the object draws it from us. The object has the initiative, not the mind.

Derived attention, where there is no voluntary effort, seems also most plausibly to be a mere effect. The object again takes the initiative and draws our attention to itself, not by reason of its own intrinsic interest, but because it is connected with some other interesting thing. Its brain-process is connected with another that is either excited, or tending to be excited, and the liability to share the excitement and become aroused is the liability to 'preperception' in which the attention consists. If I have received an insult, I may not be actively thinking of it all the time, yet the thought of it is in such a state of heightened irritability, that the place where I received it or the man who inflicted it cannot be mentioned in my hearing without my attention bounding, as it were, in that direction, as the imagination of the whole transaction revives. Where such a stirring-up occurs, organic adjustment must exist as well, and the ideas must innervate to some degree the muscles. Thus the whole process of involuntary derived attention is accounted for if we grant that there is something interesting enough to arouse and fix the thought of whatever may be connected with it. This fixing is the attention; and it carries with it a vague sense of activity going on, and of acquiescence, furtherance, and adoption, which makes us feel the activity to be our own.

This reinforcement of ideas and impressions by the pre-existing contents of the mind was what Herbart had in mind when he gave the name of apperceptive attention to the variety we describe. We easily see now why the lover's tap should be heard - it finds a nerve-centre half ready in advance to explode. We see how we can attend to a companion's voice in the midst of noises which pass unnoticd [sic] though objectively much louder than the words we hear. Each word is doubly awakened; once from without by the lips of the talker, but already before that from within by the premonitory processes irradiating from the previous words, and by the dim arousal of all processes that are connected with the 'topic' of the talk. The irrelevant noises, on the other hand, are awakened only once. They form an unconnected train. The boys at school, inattentive to the teacher except when he begins an anecdote, and then all pricking up their ears, are as easily explained. The words of the anecdote shoot into association with exciting objects which react and fix them; the other words do not. Similarly with the gramma heard by the purist and Herbart's other examples quoted.

Even where the attention is voluntary, it is possible to conceive of it as an effect, and not a cause, a product and not an agent, The things we attend to come to us by their own laws. Attention creates no idea; an idea must already be there before we can attend to it. Attention only fixes and retains what the ordinary laws of association bring 'before the footlights' of consciousness. But the moment we admit this we see that the attention per se, the feeling of attending need no morc fix and retain the ideas than it need bring them. The associates which bring them also fix them by the interest which they lend. In short, voluntary and involuntary attention may be essentially the same. It is true that where the ideas are intrinsically very unwelcome and the effort to attend to them is great, it seems to us as if the frequent renewal of the effort were the very cause by which they are held fast, and we naturally think of the effort of an original force. In fact it is only to the effort to attend, not to the mere attending, that we are seriously tempted to ascribe spontaneous power. We think we can make more of it if we will; and the amount which we make does not seem a fixed function of the ideas themselves, as it would necessarily have to be if our effort were an effect and not a spiritual force. But even here it is possible to conceive the facts mechanically and to regard the effort as a mere effect.

Effort is felt only where there is a conflict of interests in the mind. The idea A may be intrinsically exciting to us. The idea Z may derive its interest from association with some remoter good. A may be our sweetheart, Z may be some condition of our soul's salvation. Under these circumstances, if we succeed in attending to Z at all it is always with expenditure of effort. The 'ideational prepararation,' the 'preperception' of A keeps going on of its own accord, whilst that of Z need incessant pulses of voluntary reinforcement - that is, we have the feeling of voluntary reinforcement (or effort) at each successive moment in which the thought of Z flares brightly up in our mind. Dynamically, however, that may mean only this: that the associative processes which make Z triumph are really the stronger, and in A's absence would make us give a 'passive' and unimpeded attention to Z; but, so long as A is present, some of their force is used to inhibit the processes concerned with A. Such inhibition is a partial neutralization of the brain-energy which would otherwise be available for fluent thought. But what is lost for thought is converted into feeling, in this case into the peculiar feeling of effort, difficulty, or strain.

The stream of our thought is like a river. On the whole easy simple flowing predominates in it, the drift of things is with the pull of gravity, and effortless attention is the rule. But at intervals an obstruction, a set-back, a log-jam occurs, stops the current, creates an eddy, and makes things temporarily move the other way. If a real river could feel, it would feel these eddies and set-backs as places of effort. "I am here flowing," it would say, "in the direction of greatest resistance, instead of flowing, as usual, in the direction of least. My effort is what enables me to perform this feat." Really, the effort would only be a passive index that the feat was being performed. The agent would all the while be the total downward drift of the rest of the water, forcing some of it upwards in this spot; and although, on the average, the direction of least resistance is downwards, that would be no reason for its not being upwards now and then. Just so with our voluntary acts of attention. They are momentary arrests, coupled with a peculiar feeling, or portions of the stream. But the arresting force, instead of being this peculiar feeling itself, may be nothing but the processes by which the collision is produced. The feeling of effort may be 'an accompaniment,' as Mr. Bradley says,' more or less superfluous,' and no more contribute to the result than the pain in a man's finger, when a hammer falls on it, contributes to the hammer's weight. Thus the notion that our effort in attending is an original faculty, a force additional to the others of which brain and mind are the seat, may be an abject superstition. Attention may have to go, like many a faculty once deemed essential, like many a verbal phantom, like many an idol of the tribe. It may be an excrescence on Psychology. No need of it to drag ideas before consciousness or fix them, when we see how perfectly they drag and fix each other there.

I have stated the effect-theory as persuasively as I can.[59] It is a clear, strong, well-equipped conception, and like all such, is fitted to carry conviction, where there is no contrary proof. The feeling of effort certainly may be an inert accompaniment and not the active element which it seems. No measurements are as yet performed (it is safe to say none ever will be performed) which can show that it contributes energy to the result. We may then regard attention as a superfluity, or a 'Luxus,' and dogmatize against its causal function with no feeling in our hearts but one of pride that we are applying Occam's razor to an entity that has multiplied itself 'beyond necessity.'

But Occam's razor, though a very good rule of method, is certainly no law of nature. The laws of stimulation and of association may well be indispensable actors in all attention's performances, and may even be a good enough 'stock-company' to carry on many performances without aid; and yet they may at times simply form the background for a 'star-performer,' who is no more their 'inert accompaniment' or their 'incidental product' than Hamlet is Horatio's and Ophelia's. Such a star-performer would be the voluntary effort to attend, if it were an original psychic force. Nature may, I say, indulge in these complications; and the conception that she has done so in this case is, I think, just as clear (if not as 'parsimonious' logically) as the conception that she has not. To justify this assertion, let us ask just what the effort to attend would effect if it were an original force.

It would deepen and prolong the stay in consciousness of innumerable ideas which else would fade more quickly away. The delay thus gained might not be more than a second in duration - but that second might be critical; for in the constant rising and falling of considerations in the mind, where two associated systems of them are nearly in equilibrium it is often a matter of but a second more or less of attention at the outset, whether one system shall gain force to occupy the field and develop itself, and exclude the other, or be excluded itself by the other. When developed, it may make us act; and that act may seal our doom. When we come to the chapter on the Will, we shall see that the whole drama of the voluntary life hinges on the amount of attention, slightly more or slightly less, which rival motor ideas may receive. But the whole feeling of reality, the whole sting and excitement of our voluntary life, depends on our sense that in it things are really being decided from one moment to another, and that it is not the dull rattling off of a chain that was forged innumerable ages ago. This appearance, which makes life and history tingle with such a tragic zest, may not be an illusion. As we grant to the advocate of the mechanical theory that it may be one, so he must grant to us that it may not. And the result is two conceptions of possibility face to face with no facts definitely enough known to stand as arbiter between them.

Under these circumstances, one can leave the question open whilst waiting for light, or one can do what most speculative minds do, that is, look to one's general philosophy to incline the beam. The believers in mechanism do so without hesitation, and they ought not to refuse a similar privilege to the believers in a spiritual force. I count myself among the latter, but as my reasons are ethical they are hardly suited for introduction into a psychological work.[60] The last word of psychology here is ignorance, for the 'forces' engaged are certainly too delicate and numerous to be followed in detail. Meanwhile, in view of the strange arrogance with which the wildest materialistic speculations persist in calling themselves 'science,' it is well to recall just what the reasoning is, by which the effect-theory of attention is confirmed. It is an argument from analogy, drawn from rivers, reflex actions and other material phenomena where no consciousness appears exist at all, and extended to cases where consciousness seems the phenomenon's essential feature. The consciousness doesn't count, these reasoners say; it doesn't exist for science, it is nil; you mustn't think about it at all. The intensely reckless character of all this needs no comment. It is making the mechanical theory true per fas aut nefas. For the sake of that theory we make inductions from phenomena to others that are startingly unlike them; and we assume that a complication which Nature has introduced (the presence of feeling and of effort, namely) is not worthy of scientific recognition at all. Such conduct may conceivably be wise, though I doubt it; but scientific, as contrasted with metaphysical, it cannot seriously be called.[61]

Inattention.

Having spoken fully of attention, let me add a word about inattention.

We do not notice the ticking of the clock, the noise of the city streets, or the roaring of the brook near the house; and even the din of a foundry or factory will not mingle with the thoughts of its workers, if they have been there long enough. When we first put on spectacles, especially if they be of certain curvatures, the bright reflections they give of the windows, etc., mixing with the field of view, are very disturbing. In a few days we ignore them altogether. Various entoptic images, muscœ volitantes, etc., although constantly present, are hardly even known. The pressure of our clothes and shoes, the beating of our hearts and arteries, our breathing, certain steadfast bodily pains, habitual odors, tastes in the mouth, etc., are examples from other senses, of the same lapse into unconsciousness of any too unchanging content - a lapse which Hobbes has expressed in the well-known phrase, "Semper idem sentire ac non sentire ad idem revertunt."

The cause of the unconciousness is certainly not the mere blunting of the sense-organs. Were the sensation important, we should notice it well enough; and we can at any moment notice it by expressly throwing our attention upon it,[62] provided it have not become so inveterate that inattention to it is ingrained in our very constitution, as in the case of the muscœ volitantes the double retinal images, etc. But even in these cases artificial conditions of observation and patience soon give us command of the impression which we seek. The inattentiveness must then be a habit grounded on higher conditions than mere sensorial fatigue.

Helmholtz has formulated a general law of inattention which we shall have to study in the next chapter but one. Helmholtz's law is that we leave all impressions unnoticed which are valueless to us as signs by which to discriminate things. At most such impressions fuse with their consorts into an aggregate effect. The upper partial tones which make human voices differ make them differ as wholes only - we cannot dissociate the tones themselves. The odors which form integral parts of the characteristic taste of certain substances, meat, fish, cheese, butter, wine, do not come as odors to our attention. The various muscular and tactile feelings that make up the perception of the attributes 'wet,' 'elastic,' 'doughy,' etc., are not singled out separately for what they are. And all this is due to an inveterate habit we have contracted, of passing from them immediately to their import and letting their substantive nature alone. They have formed connections in the mind which it is now difficult to break; they are constituents of processes which it is hard to arrest, and which differ altogether from what the processes of catching the attention would be. In the cases Helmholtz has in mind, not only we but our ancestors have formed these habits. In the cases we started from, however, of the mill-wheel, the spectacles, the factory, din, the tights shoes, etc., the habits of inattention are more recent, and the manner of their genesis seems susceptible, hypothetically at least, of being traced.

How can impressions that are not needed by the intellect be thus shunted off from all relation to the rest of consciousness? Professor G. E. Müller has made a plausible reply to this question, and most of what follows is borrowed from him.[63] He begins with the fact that

"When we first come out of a mill or factory, in which we have remained long enough to get wonted to the noise, we feel as if something were lacking. Our total feeling of existence is different from what it was when we were in the mill. . . . A friend writes to me: 'I have in my room a little clock which does not run quite twenty-four hours without winding. In consequence of this, it often stops. So soon as this happens, I notice it, whereas I naturally fail to notice it when going. When this first began to happen, there was this modification: I suddenly felt an undefined uneasiness or sort of void, without being able to say what was the matter; and only after some consideration did I find the cause in the stopping of the clock.'"

That the stopping of an unfelt stimulus may itself be felt is a well-known fact: the sleeper in church who wakes when the sermon ends; the miller who does the same when his wheel stands still, are stock examples. Now (since every impression falling on the nervous system must propagate itself somewhither), Müller suggests that impressions which come to us when the thought-centres are preoccupied with other matters may thereby be blocked or inhibited from invading these centres, and may then overflow into lower paths of discharge. And he farther suggests that if this process recur often enough, the side-track thus created will grow so permeable as to be used, no matter what may be going on in the centres above. In the acquired inattention mentioned, the constant stimulus always caused disturbance at first; and consciousness of it was extruded successfully only when the brain was strongly excited about other things. Gradually the extrusion became easier, and at last automatic.

The side-tracks which thus learn to draft off the stimulations that interfere with thought cannot be assigned with any precision. They probably terminate in organic processes, or insignificant muscular contractions which, when stopped by the cessation of their instigating cause, immediately give us the feeling that something is gone from our existence (as Müller says), or (as his friend puts it) the feeling of a void.[64]

Müller's suggestion awakens another. It is a well-known fact that persons striving to keep their attention on a difficult subject will resort to movements of various unmeaning kinds, such as pacing the room, drumming with the fingers, playing with keys or watch-chain, scratching head, pulling mustache, vibrating foot, or what not, according to the individual. There is an anecdote of Sir W. Scott, when a boy, rising to the head of his class by cutting off from the jacket of the usual head-boy a button which the latter was in the habit of twirling in his fingers during the lesson. The button gone, its owner's power of reciting also departed. - Now much of this activity is unquestionably due to the overflow of emotional excitement during anxious and concentrated thought. It drains away nerve-currents which if pent up within the thought-centres would very likely make the confusion there worse confounded. But may it not also be a means of drafting off all the irrelevant sensations of the moment, and so keeping the attention more exclusively concentrated upon its inner task? Each individual usually has his own peculiar habitual movement of this sort. A downward nerve-path is thus kept constantly open during concentrated thought; and as it seems to be a law of frequent (if not of universal) application, that incidental stimuli tend to discharge through paths that are already discharging rather than through others, the whole arrangement might protect the thought-centres from interference from without. Were this the true rationale of these peculiar movements, we should have to suppose that the sensations produced by each phase of the movement itself are also drafted off immediately by the next phase and help to keep the circular process agoing. I offer the suggestion for what it is worth; the connection of the movements themselves with the continued effort of attention is certainly a genuine and curious fact.

Notes

[1] Bain mentions attention in the Senses and the Intellect, p. 558, and even gives a theory of it on pp. 370-374 of the Emotions of the Will. I shall recur to this theory later on.

[2] "The first and most important, but also the most difficult, task at the outset of an education is to overcome gradually the inattentive dispersion of mind which shows itself wherever the organic life preponderates over the intellectual. The training of animals ... must be in the first instance based on the awakening of attention (cf. Adrian Leonard, Essai sur l'Education des Animaux, Lille, 1842), that is to say, we must seek to make them gradually perceive separately things which, if left to themselves, would not be attended to, because they would fuse with a great sum of other sensorial stimuli to a confused total impression of which each separate item only darkens and interferes with the rest. Similarly at first with the human child. The enormous difficulties of deaf-mute- and especially of idiot-instruction is principally due to the slow and painful manner in which we succeed in bringing out from the general confusion of perception single items with sufficient sharpness." (Waitz, Lehrb. d. Psychol., p. 632.)

[3] Elements, part I. chap. II. fin.

[4] Lectures on Metaphysics, lecture XIV.

[5] Nature, vol. III. p. 281 (1871).

[6] If a lot of dots or strokes on a piece of paper be exhibited for a moment to a person in normal condition, with the request that he say how many are there, he will find that they break into groups in his mind's eye, and that whilst he is analyzing and counting one group in his memory the others dissolve. In short, the impression made by the dots changes rapidly into something else. In the trance-subject, on the contrary, it seems to stick; I find that persons in the hypnotic state easily count the dots in the mind's eye so long as they do not much exceed twenty in number.

[7] Mr. Cattell made Jevon's experiment in a much more precise way (Philosophische Studien, III. 121 ff.). Cards were ruled with short lines, varying in number from four to fifteen, and exposed to the eye for a hundredth of a second. When the number was but four or five, no mistakes as a rule were made. For higher numbers the tendency was to under- rather than over-estimate. Similar experiments were tried with letters and figures, and gave the same result. When the letters formed familiar words, three times as many of them could be named as when their combination was meaningless. If the words formed a sentence, twice as many of them could be caught as when they had no connection. "The sentence was then apprehended as a whole. If not apprehended thus, almost nothing is apprehended of the several words; but if the sentence as a whole is apprehended, then the words appear very difficult." - Wundt and his pupil Dietze had tried similar experiments on rapidly repeated strokes of sound. Wundt made them follow each other in groups, and found that groups of twelve strokes at most could be recognized and identified when they succeeded each other at the most favorable rate, namely, from three to five tenths of a second (Phys. Psych., II. 215). Dietze found that by mentally subdividing the groups into sub-groups as one listened, as many as forty strokes could be identified as a whole. They were then grasped as eight sub-groups of five, or as five of eight strokes each. (Philosophische Studien, II. 362.) - Later in Wundt's Laboratory, Bechterew made observations on two simultaneously elapsing series of metronome strokes, of which one contained one stroke more than the other. The most favorable rate of succession was 0.3 sec., and he then discriminated a group of 18 from one of 18 + 1, apparently. (Neurologisches Centralblatt, 1889, 272.)

[8] Revue Scientifique, vol. 39, p. 684 (May 28, 1887).

[9] Cf. Chr. Wolff: Psychologia Empirica, § 245. Wolff's account of the phenomena of attention is in general excellent.

[10] Pflüger's Archiv, XI. 429-31.

[11] *Physiol. Psych., 2d ed. II. pp. 238-40.*
[12] *Ib. p. 262.*
[13] *Physiol. Psych., 2d ed. II. 264-6.*
[14] *This was the original 'personal equation' observation of Bessel. An observer looked through his equatorial telescope to note the moment at which a star crossed the meridian, the latter being marked in the telescopic field of view by a visible thread, beside which other equidistant threads appear. "Before the star reached the thread he looked at the clock, and then, with eye at telescope, counted the seconds by the beat of the pendulum.*

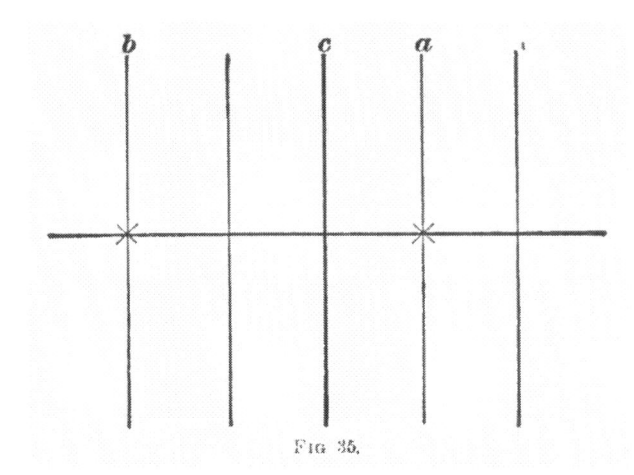

FIG. 35.

Since the star seldom passed the meridian at the exact moment of a beat, the observer, in order to estimate fractions, had to note its position at the stroke before and at the stroke after the passage, and to divide the time as the meridian-line seemed to divide the space. If, e.g., one had counted 20 seconds, and at the 21st the star seemed removed by ac from the meridian-thread c, whilst at the 22nd it was at the distance bc; then, if ac: bc :: 1 : 2, the star would have passed at 21 1/3 seconds. The conditions resemble those in our experiment: the star is the index-hand, the threads are the scale; and a time-displacement is to be expected, which with high rapidities may be positive, and negative with low. The astronomic observations do not permit us to measure its absolute amount; but that it exists is made certain by the fact than after all other possible errors are eliminated, there still remains between different observers a personal difference which is often much larger than that between mere reaction-times, amounting . . . sometimes to more than a second." (Op. cit. p. 270.)
[15] *Philosophische Studien, II. 601.*
[16] *Physiol. Psych., 2d ed. II. 273-4; 3d. II. 339; Philosophische Studien, II. 621 ff. - I know that I am stupid, but I confess I find these theoretical statements, especially Wundt's, a little hazy. Herr v. Tschisch considers it impossible that the perception of the index's position should come in too late, and says it demands no particular attention (p. 622). It seems, however, that this can hardly be the case. Both observers speak of the difficulty of seeing the index at the right moment. The case is quite different from that of distributing the attention impartially over simultaneous momentary sensations. The bell or other signal gives a momentary sensation, the index a continuous one, of motion. To note any one position of the latter is to interrupt this sensation of motion and to substitute an entirely different percept - one, namely, of position - for it, during a time however brief. This involves a sudden change in the manner of attending to the revolutions of the index; which change ought to take place neither sooner nor later than the momentary impression, and fix the index as it is then and there visible. Now this is not a case of simply getting two sensations at once and so feeling them - which would be an harmonious act; but of stopping one and changing it into another, whilst we simultaneously get a third. Two of these acts are discrepant, and the whole three rather interfere with each other. It becomes hard to 'fix' the index at the very instant that we catch the momentary impression; so we fall into a way of fixing it either at the last possible moment before, or at the first possible moment after, the impression comes.*

This at least seems to me the more probable state of affairs. If we fix the index before the impression really comes, that means that we perceive it too late. But why do we fix it before when the impressions come slow and simple, and after when they come rapid and complex? And why under certain conditions is there no displacement at all? The answer which suggests itself is that when there is just enough leisure between the impressions for the attention to adapt itself comfortably both to them and to the index (one second in W.'s experiments), it carries on the two processes at once; when the leisure is excessive, the attention, following its own laws of ripening, and being ready to note the index before the other impression comes, notes it then, since that is the moment of easiest action, whilst the impression, which comes a moment later, interferes with noting it again; and finally, that when the leisure is insufficient, the momentary impressions, being the more fixed data, are attended to first, and the index is fixed a little later on. The noting of the index at too early a moment would be the noting of a real fact, with its analogue in many other rhythmical experiences. In reaction-time experiments, for example, when, in a regularly recurring series, the stimulus is once in a while omitted, the observer sometimes reacts as if it came. Here, as Wundt somewhere observes, we catch ourselves acting merely because our inward preparation is complete. The 'fixing' of the index is a sort of action; so that my interpretation tallies with facts recognized elsewhere; but Wundt's explanation (if I understand it) of the experiments requires us to believe that an observer like v. Tschisch shall steadily and without exception get an hallucination of a bell-stroke before the later occurs, and not hear the real bell-stroke afterwards. I doubt whether this is possible, and I can think of no analogue to it in the rest of our experience. The whole subject deserves to be gone over again. To Wundt is due the highest credit for his patience in working out the facts. His explanation of them in his earlier work (Vorlesungen üb. Menschen und Thierseele, I. 37-42, 365-371) consisted merely in the appeal to the unity of consciousness, and may be considered quite crude.

[17] *Note that the permanent interests are themselves grounded in certain objects and relations in which our interest is immediate and instinctive.*

[18] *Herbart: Psychologie als Wissenschaft, §128.*

[19] *Sir W. Hamilton: Metaphysics, lecture XIV.*

[20] *Mental Physiol., § 124. The oft-cited case of soldiers not perceiving that they are wounded is of an analogous sort.*

[21] *Prof. J. M. Cattell made experiments to which we shall refer further on, on the degree to which reaction-times might be shortened by distracting or voluntarily concentrating the attention. He says of the latter series that "the averages show that the attention can be kept strained, that is, the centres kept in a state of unstable equilibrium, for one second" (Mind, XI. 240).*

[22] *Physiologische Optik, § 32.*

[23] *"'Genius,' says Helvetius, ' is nothing but a continued attention (une attention suivie).' 'Genius,' says Buffon, 'is only a protracted patience (une longue patience).' 'In the exact sciences, at least,' says Cuvier, 'it is the patience of a sound intellect, when invincible, which truly constitutes genius.' And Chesterfield has also observed that 'the power of applying an attention, steady and undissipated, to a single object, is the sure mark of a superior genius." (Hamilton: Lect. on Metaph., lecture XIV.)*

[24] *See, e.g., Ulrici: Leib u. Seele, II. 28; Lotze: Metaphysik, § 273; Fechner: Revision d. Psychophysik, XIX; G. E. Müller: Zur Theorie d. sinnl. Aufmerksamkeit, § 1; Stumpf: Tonpsychologie, I. 71.*

[25] *Fechner, op. cit. p. 271.*

[26] *Tonpsychologie, I. p. 71.*

[27] *Compare, on clearness as the essential fruit of attention, Lotze's Metaphysic, § 273.*

[28] *Elements, part I. chap. II.*

[29] *Physiol. Psych., 2d ed. II. 226.*

[30] *By a negative value of the reaction-time Wundt means the case of the reactive movement occurring before the stimulus.*

[31] *Op. cit. II. 239.*

[32] *The reader must not suppose this phenomenon to be of frequent occurrence. Experienced observers, like Exner and Cattell, deny having met with it in their personal experience.*

[33] *Op. cit. pp. 241-5.*

[34] *It should be added that Mr. J. M. Cattell (Mind, XI. 33) found, on repeating Wundt's experiments with a disturbing noise upon two practised observers, that the simple reaction-time either for light or sound was hardly perceptibly increased. Making strong voluntary concentration of attention shortened it by about 0.013 seconds on an average (p. 240). Performing mental additions whilst waiting for the stimulus lengthened it more than anything, apparently. For other, less careful, observations, compare Obersteiner, in Brain, I. 439. Cattell's negative results show how far some persons can abstract their attention from stimuli by which others would be disturbed. - A. Bartels (Versuche über die Ablenkung d. Aufmerksamkeit, Dorpat, 1889) found that a stimulus to one eye sometimes prevented, sometimes improved, the perception of a quickly ensuing very faint stimulus to the other.*

[35] *Cf. Wundt, Physiol. Psych., 1st ed.p. 794.*

[36] *Beiträge zur Experimentellen Psychologie, Heft I. pp. 73-106 (1889).*

[37] *To say the very least, he always brought his articulatory innervation close to the discharging point. Herr M. describes a tightening of the head-muscles as characteristic of the attitude of attention to the reply.*

[38] *Psychophysik, Bd. II. pp. 475-6.*

[39] *I must say that I am wholly unconscious of the peculiar feelings in the scalp which Fechner goes on to describe. "The feeling of strained attention in the different sense-organs seems to be only a muscular one produced in using these various organs by setting in motion, by a sort of reflex action, the muscles which belong to them. One can ask, then, with what particular muscular contraction the sense of strained attention in the effort to recall something is associated? On this question my own feeling gives me a decided answer; it comes to me distinctly, not as a sensation of tension in the inside of the head, but as a feeling of strain and contraction in the scalp with a pressure from without inwards over the whole cranium, undoubtedly caused by a contraction of the muscles of the scalp. The harmonizes very well with the German popular expression den Kopf zusammennehmen, etc., etc. In a former illness, in which I could not endure the slightest effort of continuous thought, and had no theoretical bias on this question, the muscles of the scalp, especially those of the occiput, assumed a fairly morbid degree of sensibility whenever I tried to think." (Ibid. pp. 490-491.) In an early writing by Professor Mach, after speaking of the way in which by attention we decompose complex musical sounds into their elements, this investigator continues: "It is more than a figure of speech when one says that we 'search' among the sounds. This hearkening search is very observably a bodily activity, just like attentive looking in the case of the eye. If, obeying the drift of physiology, we understand by attention nothing mystical, but a bodily disposition, it is most natural to seek it in the variable tension of the muscles of the ear. Just so, what common men call attentive looking reduces itself mainly to accommodating and setting of the optic axes. . . . According to this, it seems to me a very plausible view that quite generally Attention has its seat in the*

mechanism of the body. If nervous work is being done through certain channels, that by itself is a mechanical ground for other channels being closed." (Wien. Sitzungsberichte, Math. Naturw., XLVIII. 2. 297, 1863.)
[40] Physiol. Optik, p. 741.
[41] Hermann's Handbuch, III. I. 548.
[42] Helmholtz: Tonempfindungen, 3d ed. 85-9 (Engl. tr., 2d ed. 50, 51; see also pp. 60-1).
[43] Physiol. Psych., II. 209.
[44] Physiol. Optik, 741.
[45] P. 728.
[46] Popular Scientific Lectures, Eng. Trans., p. 295.
[47] Similarly in the verses which some one tried to puzzle me with the other day: "Gui n'a beau dit, qui sabot dit, nid a beau dit elle?"
[48] I cannot refrain from referring in a note to an additional set of facts instanced by Lotze in his Medizinische Psychologie, § 431, although I am not satisfied with the explanation, fatigue of the sense-organ, which he gives. "In quietly lying and contemplating a wall-paper pattern, sometimes it is the ground, sometimes the design, which is clearer and consequently comes nearer. . . . Arabesques of monochromic many-convoluted lines now strike us as composed of one, now of another connected linear system, and all without any intention on our part. [This is beautifully seen in Moorish patterns; but a simple diagram like Fig. 39 also shows it well. We see it sometimes as two large triangles superposed, sometimes as a hexagon with angles spanning its sides, sometimes as six small triangles stuck together at their corners.] . . . Often it happens in revery that when we stare at a picture, suddenly some one of its features will be lit up with especial clearness, although neither its optical character nor its meaning discloses any motive for such an arousal of the attention. . . . To one in process of becoming drowsy the surroundings alternately fade into darkness and abruptly brighten up. The talk of the bystanders seems now to come from indefinite distances; but at the next moment it startles us by its threatening loudness at our very ear," etc. These variations, which everyone will have noticed, are, it seems to me, easily explicable by the very unstable equilibrium of our ideational centres, of which constant change is the law. We conceive one set of lines as object, the other as background, and forthwith the first set becomes the set we see. There need be no logical motive for the conceptual change, the irradiations of brain-tracts by each other, according to accidents of nutrition, 'like sparks in burnt-up paper,' suffice. The changes during drowsiness are still more obviously due to this cause.

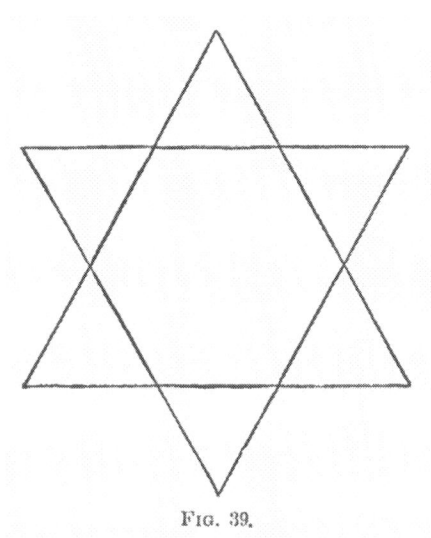

FIG. 39.

[49] The Emotions and the Will, 3d. p. 370.
[50] Psychologie de l'Attention (1889), p. 32 ff.
[51] Philosophische Studien, IV. 413 ff.
[52] See Lange, loc. cit. p. 417, for another proof of his view, drawn from the phenomenon of retinal rivalry.
[53] Many of my students have at my request experimented with imagined letters of the alphabet and syllables, and they tell me that they can see them inwardly as total colored pictures without following their outlines with the eye. I am myself a bad visualizer, and make movements all the while. - M. L. Marillier, in an article of eminent introspective power which appeared after my text was written (Remarques sur le Mécanisme de l'Attention, in Revue Philosophique, vol. XXVII. p. 566), has contended against Ribot and others for the non-dependence of sensory upon motor images in their relations to attention. I am glad to cite him as an ally.
[54] Drs. Ferrier (Functions of the Brain, §§ 102-3) and Obersteiner (Brain, I, 439 ff.) treat it as the essential feature. The author whose treatment of the subject is by far the most thorough and satisfactory is Prof. G. E. Müller, whose little work Zur Theorie der sinnlichen Aufmerksamkeit, Inauguraldissertation, Leipzig, Edelmann (1874?), is for learning and acuteness a model of what a monograph should be. I should like to have quoted from it, but the Germanism of its composition makes quotation quite impossible. See also G. H. Lewes: Problems of Life and Mind, 3d Series, Prob. 2, chap. 10, G. H. Schneider: Der menschliche Wille, 294 ff., 309 ff., C. Stumpf: Tonpsychologie, I. 67-75; W. B. Carpenter: Mental Physiology. chap. 3; Cappie in 'Brain,' July 1886 (hyperæmia-theory); J. Sully in 'Brain,' Oct. 1890.
[55] L'Enfant de trois à sept Ans, p. 108.
[56] Psychologie de l'Attention, p. 53.
[57] Repetition of this sort does not confer intelligence of what is said, it only keeps the mind from wandering into other channels. The intelligence sometimes comes in beats, as it were, at the end of sentences, or in the midst of words which were mere words until then.
[58] The reader will please observe that I am saying all that can possibly be said in favor of the effect-theory, since, inclining as I do myself to the cause-theory, I do not want to undervalue the enemy. As a matter of fact, one might begin to take one's stand against the effect-theory at the outset, with the phenomenon of immediate sensorial attention. One might say that attention causes the movements of adjustment of the eyes, for example, and is not merely their effect. Hering writes most emphatically to this effect: "The movements from one point of fixation to another are occasioned and regulated by the

changes of place of the attention. When an object, seen at first indirectly, draws our attention to itself, the corresponding movement of the eye follows without further ado, as a consequence of the attention's migration and of our effort to make the object distinct. The wandering of the attention entails that of the fixation point. Before its movement begins, its goal is already in consciousness and grasped by the attention, and the location of this spot in the total space seen is what determines the direction and amount of the movement of the eye." (Hermann's Handbuch, p. 534.) I do not here insist on this, because it is hard to tell whether the attention or the movement comes first (Hering's reasons, pp. 535-6, also 544-6, seem to me ambiguous), and because, even if the attention to the object does come first, it may be a mere effect of stimulus and association. Mach's theory that the will to look is the space-feeling itself may be compared with Hering's in this place." See Mach's Beiträge zur Analyse der Empfindungen (1886), pp. 55 ff.

[59] F. H. Bradley, "Is there a Special Activity of Attention?" in 'Mind,' XI. 305, and Lipps, Grundtatsachen, chaps. IV and XXIX, have stated it similarly.

[60] More will be said of the matter when we come to the chapter on the Will.

[61] See, for a defence of the notion of inward activity, Mr. James Ward's searching articles in 'Mind,' XII. 45 and 564.

[62] It must be admitted that some little time will often elapse before this effort succeeds. As a child, I slept in a nursery with a very loud-ticking clock, and remember my astonishment more than once, on listening for its tick, to find myself unable to catch it for what seemed a long space of time; then suddenly it would break into my consciousness with an almost startling loudness. - M. Delbœuf somewhere narrates how, sleeping in the country near a mill-dam, he woke in the night and thought the water had ceased to flow, but on looking out of the open window saw it flowing in the moonlight, and then heard it too.

[63] Zur Theorie d. sinnl. Aufmerksamkeit, p. 128 foll.

[64] I have begun to inquire experimentally whether any of the measurable functions of the workmen change after the din of machinery stops at a workshop. So far I have found no constant results as regards either pulse, breathing, or strength of squeeze by the hand. I hope to prosecute the inquiry farther (May, 1890).

Chapter XII – Conception - The Sense Of Sameness

In Chapter VIII the distinction was drawn between two kinds of knowledge of things, bare acquaintance with them and knowledge about them. The possibility of two such knowledges depends on a fundamental psychical peculiarity which may be entitled "the principle of constancy in the mind's meanings," and which may be thus expressed: "The same matters can be thought of in successive portions of the mental stream, and some of these portions can know that they mean the same matters which the other portions meant." One might put it otherwise by saying that "the mind can always intend, and know when it intends, to think of the Same."

This sense of sameness is the very keel and backbone of our thinking. We saw in Chapter X how the consciousness of personal identity reposed on it, the present thought finding in its memories a warmth and intimacy which it recognizes as the same warmth and intimacy it now feels. This sense of identity of the knowing subject is held by some philosophers to be the only vehicle by which the world hangs together. It seems hardly necessary to say that a sense of identity of the known object would perform exactly the same unifying function, even if the sense of subjective identity were lost. And without the intention to think of the same outer things over and over again, and the sense that we were doing so, our sense of our own personal sameness would carry us but a little way towards making a universe of our experience.

Note, however, that we are in the first instance speaking of the sense of sameness from the point of view of the mind's structure alone, and not from the point of view of the universe. We are psychologizing, not philosophizing. That is, we do not care whether there be any real sameness in things or not, or whether the mind be true or false in its assumptions of it. Our principle only lays it down that the mind makes continual use of the notion of sameness, and if deprived of it, would have a different structure from what it has. In a word, the principle that the mind can mean the Same is true of its meanings, but not necessarily of aught besides.[1] The mind must conceive as possible that the Same should be before it, for our experience to be the sort of thing it is. Without the psychological sense of identity, sameness might rain down upon us from the outer world for ever and we be none the wiser. With the psychological sense, on the other hand, the outer world might be an unbroken flux, and yet we should perceive a repeated experience. Even now, the world may be a place in which the same thing never did and never will come twice. The thing we mean to point at may change from top to bottom and we be ignorant of the fact. But in our meaning itself we are not deceived; our intention is to think of the same. The name which I have given to the principle, in calling it the law of constancy in our meanings, accentuates its subjective character, and justifies us in laying it down as the most important of all the features of our mental structure.

Not all psychic life need be assumed to have the sense of sameness developed in this way. In the consciousness of worms and polyps, though the same realities may frequently impress it, the feeling of sameness may seldom emerge. We, however, running back and forth, like spiders on the web they weave, feel ourselves to be working over identical materials and thinking them in different ways. And the man who identifies the materials most is held to have the most philosophic human mind.

Conception Defined.

The function by which we thus identify a numerically distinct and permanent subject of disclosure is called CONCEPTION; and the thoughts which are its vehicles are called concepts. But the word 'concept' is often used as if it stood for the object of discourse itself; and this looseness feeds such evasiveness in discussion that I shall avoid the use of the expression concept altogether, and speak of 'conceiving state of mind,' or something similar, instead. The word 'conception' is unambiguous. It properly denotes neither the mental state nor what the mental state signifies, but the relation between the two, namely, the function of the mental state in signifying just that particular thing. It is plain that one and the same mental state can be the vehicle of many conceptions, can mean a particular thing, and a great deal more besides. If it has such a multiple conceptual function, it may be called an act of compound conception.

We may conceive realities supposed to be extra-mental, as steam-engine; fictions, as mermaid; or mere entia rationis, like difference or nonentity. But whatever we do conceive, our conception is of that and nothing else - nothing else, that is, instead of that, though it may be of much else in addition to that. Each act of conception results from our attention singling out some one part of the mass of matter for thought which the world presents, and holding fast to it, without confusion.[2] Confusion occurs when we do not know whether a certain object proposed to us is the same with one of our meanings or not; so that the conceptual function requires, to be complete, that the thought should not only say 'I mean this,' but also say 'I don't mean that.'[3]

Each conception thus eternally remains what it is, and never can become another. The mind may change its states, and its meanings, at different times; may drop one conception and take up another, but the dropped conception can in no intelligible sense be said to change into its successor. The paper, a moment ago white, I may now see to have been scorched black. But my conception 'white' does not change into my conception 'black.' On the contrary, it stays alongside of the objective blackness, as a different meaning in my mind, and by so doing lets me judge the blackness as the paper's change. Unless it stayed, I should simply say 'blackness' and know no more. Thus, amid the flux of opinions and of physical things, the world of conceptions, or things intended to be thought about, stands stiff and immutable, like Plato's Realm of Ideas.[4]

Some conceptions are of things, some of events, some of qualities. Any fact, be it thing, event, or quality, may be conceived sufficiently for purposes of identification, if only it be singled out and marked so as to separate it from other things. Simply calling it 'this' or 'that' will suffice. To speak in technical language, a subject may be conceived by its denotation, with no connotation, or a very minimum of connotation, attached. The essential point is that it should be re-identified by us as that which the talk is about; and no full representation of it is necessary for this, even when it is a fully representable thing.

In this sense, creatures extremely low in the intellectual scale may have conception. All that is required is that they should recognize the same experience again. A polyp would be a conceptual thinker if a feeling of 'Hollo! thingumbob again!' ever flitted through its mind.

Most of the objects of our thought, however, are to some degree represented as well as merely pointed out. Either they are things and events perceived or imagined, or they are qualities apprehended in a positive way. Even where we have no intuitive acquaintance with the nature of a thing, if we know any of the relations of it at all, anything about it, that is enough to individualize and distinguish it from all the other things which we might mean. Many of our topics of discourse are thus problematical, or defined by their relations only. We think of a thing about which certain facts must obtain, but we do not yet know how the thing will look when it is realized. Thus we conceive of a perpetual-motion machine. It is a quœsitum of a perfectly definite kind, - we can always tell whether the actual machines offered us do or do not agree with what we mean by it. The natural possibility or impossibility of the thing does not touch the question of its conceivability in this problematic way. 'Round square,' 'black-white-thing,' are absolutely definite conceptions; it is a mere accident, as far as conception goes, that they happen to stand for things which nature lets us sensibly perceive.[5]

Conceptions Are Unchangeable.

The fact that the same real topic of discourse is at one time conceived as a mere 'that' or 'that which, etc.,' and is at another time conceived with additional specifications, has been treated by many authors as a proof that conceptions themselves are fertile and self-developing. A conception, according to the Hegelizers in philosophy, 'develops its own significance,' 'makes explicit what it implicitly contained,' passes, on occasion, 'over into its opposite,' and in short loses altogether the blankly self-identical character we supposed it to maintain. The figure we viewed as a polygon appears to us now as a sum of juxtaposed triangles; the number hitherto conceived as thirteen is at last noticed to be six plus seven, or prime; the man thought honest is believed a rogue. Such changes of our opinion are viewed by these thinkers as evolutions of our conception, from within.

The facts are unquestionable; our knowledge does grow and change by rational and inward processes, as well as by empirical discoveries. Where the discoveries are empirical, no one pretends that the propulsive agency, the force that makes the knowledge develop, is mere conception. All admit it to be our continued exposure to the thing, with its power to impress our senses. Thus strychnin, which tastes bitter, we find will also kill, etc. Now I say that where the new knowledge merely comes from thinking, the facts are essentially the same, and that to talk of self-development on the part of our conceptions is a very bad way of stating the case. Not new sensations, as in the empirical instance, but new conceptions, are the indispensable conditions of advance.

For if the alleged cases of self-development be examined it will be found, I believe, that the new truth affirms in every case a relation between the original subject of conception and some new subject conceived later on. These new subjects of conception arise in various ways. Every one of our conceptions is of something which our attention originally tore out of the continuum of felt experience, and provisionally isolated so as to make of it an individual topic of discourse. Every one of them has a way, if the mind is left alone with it, of suggesting other parts of the continuum from which it was torn, for conception to work upon in a similar way. This 'suggestion' is often no more than what we shall later know as the association of ideas. Often, however, it is a sort of invitation to the mind to play, add lines, break number-groups, etc. Whatever it is, it brings new conceptions into consciousness, which latter thereupon may or may not expressly attend to the relation in which the new stands to the old. Thus I have a conception of equidistant lines. Suddenly, I know not whence, there pops into my head the conception of their meeting. Suddenly again I think of the meeting and the equidistance both together, and perceive them incompatible.

"Those lines will never meet," I say. Suddenly again the word 'parallel' pops into my head. 'They are parallels,' I continue; and so on. Original conceptions to start with; adventitious conceptions pushed forward by multifarious psychologic causes; comparisons and combinations of the two; resultant conceptions to end with; which latter may be of either rational or empirical relations.

As regards these relations, they are conceptions of the second degree, as one might say, and their birthplace is the mind itself. In Chapter XXVIII I shall at considerable length defend the mind's claim to originality and fertility in bringing them forth. But no single one of the mind's conceptions is fertile of itself, as the opinion which I criticise pretends. When the several notes of a chord are sounded together, we get a new feeling from their combination. This feeling is due to the mind reacting upon that

group of sounds in that determinate way, and no one would think of saying of any single note of the chord that it 'developed' of itself into the other notes or into the feeling of harmony. So of Conceptions. No one of them develops into any other. But if two of them are thought at once, their relation may come to consciousness, and form matter for a third conception.

Take 'thirteen' for example, which is said to develop into 'prime.' What really happens is that we compare the utterly changeless conception of thirteen with various other conceptions, those of the different multiples of two, three, four, five, and six, and ascertain that it differs from them all. Such difference is a freshly ascertained relation. It is only for mere brevity's sake that we call it a property of the original thirteen, the property of being prime. We shall see in the next chapter that (if we count out æsthetic and moral relations between things) the only important relations of which the mere inspection of conceptions makes us aware are relations of comparison, that is, of difference and no-difference, between them. The judgment $6 + 7 = 13$ expresses the relation of equality between two ideal objects, 13 on the one hand and $6 + 7$ on the other, successively conceived and compared. The judgments $6 + 7 > 12$, or $6 + 7 < 14$, express in like manner relations of inequality between ideal objects. But if it be unfair to say that the conception of $6 + 7$ generates that of 12 or of 14, surely it is as unfair to say that it generates that of 13.

The conceptions of 12, 13, and 14 are each and all generated by individual acts of the mind, playing with its materials. When, comparing two ideal objects, we find them equal, the conception of one of them may be that of a whole and of the other that of all its parts. This particular case is, it seems to me, the only case which makes the notion of one conception evolving into another sound plausible. But even in this case the conception, as such, of the whole does not evolve into the conception, as such, of the parts. Let the conception of some object as a whole be given first. To begin with, it points to and identifies for future thought a certain that. The 'whole' in question might be one of those mechanical puzzles of which the difficulty is to unlock the parts. In this case, nobody would pretend that the richer and more elaborate conception which we gain of the puzzle after solving it came directly out of our first crude conception of it, for it is notoriously the outcome of experimenting with our hands. It is true that, as they both mean that same puzzle, our earlier thought and our later thought have one conceptual function, are vehicles of one conception. But in addition to being the vehicle of this bald unchanging conception, 'that same puzzle,' the later thought is the vehicle of all those other conceptions which it took the manual experimentation to acquire. Now, it is just the same where the whole is mathematical instead of being mechanical. Let it be a polygonal space, which we cut into triangles, and of which we then affirm that it is those triangles. Here the experimentation (although usually done by a pencil in the hands) may be done by the unaided imagination. We hold the space, first conceived as polygonal simply, in our mind's eye until our attention wandering to and fro within it has carved it into the triangles. The triangles are a new conception, the result of this new operation. Having once conceived them, however, and compared them with the old polygon which we originally conceived and which we have never ceased conceiving, we judge them to fit exactly into its area. The earlier and later conceptions, we say, are of one and the same space. But this relation between triangles and polygon which the mind cannot help finding if it compares them at all, is very badly expressed by saying that the old conception has developed into the new. New conceptions come from new sensations, new movements, new emotions, new associations, new acts of attention, and new comparisons of old conceptions, and not in other ways, Endogenous prolification is not a mode of growth to which conceptions can lay claim.

I hope, therefore, that I shall not be accused of huddling mysteries out of sight, when I insist that the psychology of conception is not the place in which to treat of those of continuity and change. Conceptions form the one class of entities that cannot under any circumstances change. They can cease to be, altogether; or they can stay, as what they severally are; but there is for them no middle way. They form an essentially discontinuous system, and translate the process of our perceptual experience, which is naturally a flux, into a set of stagnant and petrified terms. The very conception of flux itself is an absolutely changeless meaning in the mind: it signifies just that one thing, flux, immovably. - And, with this, the doctrine of the flux of the concept may be dismissed, and need not occupy our attention again.[6]

'Abstract' Ideas.

We have now to pass to a less excusable mistake. There are philosophers who deny that associated things can be broken asunder at all, even provisionally, by the conceiving mind. The opinion known as Nominalism says that we really never frame any conception of the partial elements of an experience, but are compelled, whenever we think it, to think it in its totality, just as it came.

I will be silent of mediæval Nominalism, and begin with Berkeley, who is supposed to have rediscovered the doctrine for himself. His asseverations against 'abstract ideas' are among the oftenest quoted passages in philosophic literature.

"It is agreed," he says, "on all hands that the qualities or modes of things do never really exist each of them apart by itself, and separated from all others, but are mixed, as it were, and blended together, several in the same object. But, we are told, the mind being able to consider each quality singly, or abstracted from those other qualities with which it is united, does by that means frame to itself abstract ideas.... After this manner, it is said, we come by the abstract idea of man, or, if you please, humanity, or human nature; wherein it is true there is included color, because there is no man but has some color, but then it can be neither white, nor black, nor any particular color, because there is no one particular color wherein all men partake. So likewise there is included stature, but then it is neither tall stature nor low stature, nor yet middle stature, but something abstracted from all these. And so of the rest.....Whether others have this wonderful faculty of abstracting their ideas, they best can tell: for myself, I find indeed I have a faculty of imagining or representing to myself the ideas of those particular things I have perceived and of variously compounding and dividing them.... I can consider the hand, the eye, the nose, each by itself abstracted or separated from the rest of the body. But then, whatever hand or eye I imagine, it must have some particular shape and color. Likewise the idea of man that I frame to myself must be either of a white, or a black, or a tawny, a straight, or a crooked, a tall, or a low, or a middle-sized man. I cannot by any effort of thought conceive the abstract idea above described. And it is equally impossible for me to form the abstract idea of motion distinct from the body moving, and which is neither swift nor slow, curvilinear nor rectilinear; and the like may be said of all other abstract general ideas whatsoever.... And there is ground to think most men will acknowledge themselves to be in my case. The generality of men which are simple and illiterate never pretend to abstract notions. It is said they are difficult, and not to be attained without pains and study.... Now I would fain know at what time it is men are employed in surmounting that difficulty, and furnishing themselves with those necessary helps for discourse. It cannot be when they are grown up, for then it seems they are not conscious of any such painstaking; it remains therefore to be the business of their childhood. And surely the great and multiplied labor of framing abstract notions will be found a hard task for that tender age. Is it not a hard thing to imagine that a couple of children cannot prate together of their sugar-plums and rattles and the rest of their little trinkets, till they have first tacked together numberless inconsistencies, and so framed in their minds abstract general ideas, and annexed them to every common name they make use of?"[7]

The note, so bravely struck by Berkeley, could not, however, be well sustained in face of the fact patent to every human being that we can mean color without meaning any particular color, and stature without meaning any particular height. James Mill, to be sure, chimes in heroically in the chapter on Classification of his 'Analysis'; but in his son John the nominalistic voice has grown so weak that, although 'abstract ideas' are repudiated as a matter of traditional form, the opinions uttered are really nothing but a conceptualism ashamed to call itself by its own legitimate name.[8] Conceptualism says the mind can conceive any quality or relation it pleases, and mean nothing but it, in isolation from everything else in the world. This is, of course, the doctrine which we have professed. John Mill says:

"The formation of a Concept does not consist in separating the attributes which are said to compose it from all other attributes of the same object, and enabling us to conceive those attributes, disjoined from any others. We neither conceive them, nor think them, nor cognize them in any way, as a thing apart, but solely as forming, in combination with numerous other attributes, the idea of an individual object. But, though meaning them only as part of a larger agglomeration, we have the power of fixing out attention on them, to the neglect of the other attributes with which we think them combined. While the concentration of attention lasts, if it is sufficiently intense, we may be temporarily unconscious of any of the other attributes, and may really, for a brief interval, have nothing present to our mind but the attributes constituent of the concept.... General concepts, therefore, we have, properly speaking, none; we have only complex ideas of objects in the concrete: but we are able to attend exclusively to certain parts of the concrete idea: and by that exclusive attention we enable those parts to determine exclusively the course of our thoughts as subsequently called up by association; and are in a condition to carry on a train of meditation or reasoning relating to those parts only, exactly as if we were able to conceive them separately from the rest."[9]

This is a lovely example of Mill's way of holding piously to his general statements, but conceding in detail all that their adversaries ask. If there be a better description extant, of a mind in possession of an 'abstract idea,' than is contained in the words I have italicized, I am unacquainted with it. The Berkeleyan nominalism thus breaks down. It is easy to lay bare the false assumption which underlies the whole discussion of the question as hitherto carried on. That assumption is that ideas, in order to know, must be cast in the exact likeness of whatever things they know, and that the only things that can be known are those which ideas can resemble. The error has not been confined to nominalists. Omnis cognito fit per assimilationem cognoscentis et cogniti has been the maxim, more or less explicitly assumed, of writers of every school. Practically it amounts to saying that an idea must be a duplicate edition of what it knows[10] - in other words, that it can only know itself - or, more shortly still, that knowledge in any strict sense of the word, as a self-transcendent function, is impossible.

Now our own blunt statements about the ultimateness of the cognitive relation, and the difference between the 'object' of the thought and its mere 'topic' or 'subject of discourse' (cf. pp. 275 ff.), are all at variance with any such theory; and we shall find more and more occasion, as we advance in this book, to deny its general truth. All that a state of mind need do, in order to take cognizance of a reality, intend it, or be 'about' it, is to lead to a remoter state of mind which either acts upon the reality or resembles it. The only class of thoughts which can with any show of plausibility be said to resemble their objects are sensations. The stuff of which all our other thoughts are composed is symbolic, and a thought attests its pertinency to a topic by simply terminating, sooner or later, in a sensation which resembles the latter.

But Mill and the rest believe that a thought must be what it means, and mean what it is, and that if it be a picture of an entire individual, it cannot mean any part of him to the exclusion of the rest. I say nothing here of the preposterously false descriptive psychology involved in the statement that the only things we can mentally picture are individuals completely determinate in all regards. Chapter XVIII will have something to say on that point, and we can ignore it here. For even if it were true that our images were always of concrete individuals, it would not in the least follow that our meanings were of the same.

The sense of our meaning is an entirely peculiar element of the thought. It is one of those evanescent and 'transitive' facts of mind which introspection cannot turn round upon, and isolate and hold up for examination, as an entomologist passes round an insect on a pin. In the (somewhat clumsy) terminology I have used, it pertains to the 'fringe' of the subjective state, and is a 'feeling of tendency,' whose neural counterpart is undoubtedly a lot of dawning and dying processes too faint and complex to be traced. The geometer, with his one definite figure before him, knows perfectly that his thoughts apply to countless other figures as well, and that although he sees lines of a certain special bigness, direction, color, etc., he means not one of these details. When I use the word man in two different sentences, I may have both times exactly the same sound upon my lips and the same picture in my mental eye, but I may mean, and at the very moment of uttering the word and imagining the picture, know that I mean, two entirely different things. Thus when I say: "What a wonderful man Jones is!" I am perfectly aware that I mean by man to exclude Napoleon Bonaparte or Smith. But when I say: "What a wonderful thing Man is!" I am equally well aware that I mean to include not only Jones, but Napoleon and Smith as well. This added consciousness is an absolutely positive sort of feeling, transforming what would otherwise be mere noise or vision into something understood; and determining the sequel of my thinking, the later words and images, in a perfectly definite way. We saw in Chapter IX that the image per se, the nucleus, is functionally the least important part of the thought. Our doctrine, therefore, of the 'fringe' leads to a perfectly satisfactory decision of the nominalistic and conceptualistic controversy, so far as it touches psychology. We must decide in favor of the conceptualists, and affirm that the power to think things, qualities, relations, or whatever other elements there may be, isolated and abstracted from the total experience in which they appear, is the most indisputable function of our thought.

Universals.

After abstractions, universals! The 'fringe,' which lets us believe in the one, lets us believe in the other too. An individual conception is of something restricted, in its application, to a single case. A universal or general conception is of an entire class, or of something belonging to an entire class, of things. The conception of an abstract quality is, taken by itself, neither universal nor particular.[11] If I abstract white from the rest of the wintry landscape this morning, it is a perfectly definite conception, a self-identical quality which I may mean again; but, as I have not yet individualized it by expressly meaning to restrict it to this particular snow, nor thought at all of the possibility of other things to which it may be applicable, it is so far nothing but a 'that,' a 'floating adjective,' as Mr. Bradley calls it, or a topic broken out from the rest of the world. Properly it is, in this state, a singular - I have 'singled it out;' and when, later, I universalize or individualize its application, and my thought turns to mean either this white or all possible whites, I am in reality meaning two new things and forming two new conceptions.[12] Such an alteration of my meaning has nothing to do with any change in the image I may have in my mental eye, but solely with the vague consciousness that surrounds the image, of the sphere to which is is intended to apply. We can give no more definite account of this vague consciousness than has been given on pp. 249-266. But that is no reason for denying its presence.[13]

But the nominalists and traditional conceptualists find matter for an inveterate quarrel in these simple facts. Full of their notion that an idea, feeling, or state of consciousness can at bottom only be aware of its own quality; and agreeing, as they both do, that such an idea or state of consciousness is a perfectly determinate, singular, and transitory thing; they find it impossible to conceive how it should become the vehicle of a knowledge of anything permanent or universal. "To know a universal, it must be universal; for like can only be known by like," etc. Unable to reconcile these incompatibles, the knower and the known, each side immolates one of them to save the other. The nominalists 'settle the hash' of the thing known by denying it to be ever a genuine universal; the conceptualists despatch the knower by denying it to be a state of mind, in the sense of being a perishing segment of thoughts' stream, consubstantial with other facts of sensibility. They invent, instead of it, as the vehicle of the knowledge of universals, an actus purus intellectûs, or an Ego, whose function is treated as quasi-miraculous and nothing if not awe-inspiring, and which it is a sort of blasphemy to approach with the intent to explain and make common, or reduce to lower terms. Invoked in the first instance as a vehicle for the knowledge of universals, the higher principle presently is made the indispensible vehicle of all thinking whatever, for, it is contended, "a universal element is present in every thought." The nominalists meanwhile, who dislike actus puros and awe-inspiring principles and despise the reverential mood, content themselves with saying that we are mistaken in supposing we ever get sight of the face of an universal; and that what deludes us is nothing but the swarm of 'individual ideas' which may at any time be awakend by the hearing of a name.

If we open the pages of either school, we find it impossible to tell, in all the whirl about universal and particular, when the author is talking about universals in the mind, and when about objective universals, so strangely are the two mixed together. James Ferrier, for example, is the most brilliant of anti-nominalist writers. But who is nimble-witted enough to count, in the following sentences from him, the number of times he steps from the known to the knower, and attributes to both whatever properties he finds in either one?

"To think is to pass from the singular or particular to the idea [concept] or universal.... Ideas are necessary because no thinking can take place without them. They are universal, inasmuch as they are completely divested of the particularity which characterizes all the phenomena of mere sensation. To grasp the nature of this universality is not easy. Perhaps the best means by which this end may be compassed is by contrasting it with the particular. It is not difficult to understand that a sensation, a phenomenon of sense, is never more than the particular which it is. As such, that is, in its strict particularity, it is absolutely unthinkable. In the very act of being thought, something more than it emerges, and this something more cannot be again the particular.... Ten particulars per se cannot be thought of any more than one particular can be thought of; ... there always emerges in thought an additional something, which is the possibility of other particulars to an indefinite extent.....The indefinite additional something which they are instances of is a universal.... The idea or universal cannot possibly be pictured in the imagination, for this would at once reduce it to the particular.... This inability to form any sort of picture or representation of an idea does not proceed from any imperfection or limitation of our faculties, but is a quality inherent in the very nature of intelligence. A contradiction is involved in the supposition that an idea or a universal can become the object either of sense or of the imagination. An idea is thus diametrically opposed to an image."[14]

The nominalists, on their side, admit a quasi-universal, something which we think as if it were universal, though it is not; and in all that they say about this something, which they explain to be 'an indefinite number of particular ideas,' the same vacillation between the subjective and the objective points of view appears. The reader never can tell whether an 'idea' spoken of is supposed to be a knower or a known. The authors themselves do not distinguish. They want to get something in the mind which shall resemble what is out of the mind, however vaguely, and they think that when that fact is accomplished, no farther questions will be asked. James Mill writes:[15]

"The word, man, we shall say, is first applied to an individual; it is first associated with the idea of that individual, and acquires the power of calling up the idea of him; it is next applied to another individual and acquires the power of calling up the idea of him; so of another and another, till it has become associated with an indefinite number, and has acquired the power of calling up an indefinite number of those ideas indifferently. What happens? It does call up an indefinite number of the ideas of individuals as often as it occurs; and calling them in close connection, it forms a species of complex idea of them.... It is also a fact, that when an idea becomes to a certain extent complex, from the multiplicity of the ideas it comprehends, it is of necessity indistinct; ... and this indistinctness has, doubtless, been a main cause of the mystery which has appeared to belong to it.... It thus appears that the word man is not a word having a very simple idea, as was the opinion of the realists; nor a word having no idea at all, as was that of the [earlier] nominalists; but a word calling up an indefinite number of ideas, by the irresistible laws of association, and forming them into one very complex and distinct, but not therefore unintelligible, idea."

Berkeley had already said:[16]

"A word becomes general by being made the sign, not of an abstract general idea, but of many several particular ideas, any one of which it indifferently suggests to the mind. An idea which, considered in itself, is particular, becomes general by being made to represent or stand for all other particular ideas of the same sort."

'Stand for,' not know; 'becomes general,' not becomes aware of something general; 'particular ideas,' not particular things - everywhere the same timidity about begging the fact of knowing, and the pitifully impotent attempt to foist it in the shape of a mode of being of 'ideas.' If the fact to be conceived be the indefinitely numerous actual and possible members of a class, then it is assumed that if we can only get enough ideas to huddle together for a moment in the mind, the being of each several one of them there will be an equivalent for the knowing, or meaning, of one member of the class in question; and their number will be so large as to confuse our tally and leave it doubtful whether all the possible members of the class have thus been satisfactorily told off or not.

Of course this is nonsense. An idea neither is what it knows, nor knows what it is; nor will swarms of copies of the same 'idea,' recurring in stereotyped form, or 'by the irresistible laws of association formed into one idea,' ever be the same thing as a thought of 'all the possible members' of a class. We must mean that by an altogether special bit of consciousness ad hoc. But it is easy to translate Berkeley's, Hume's, and Mill's notion of a swarm of ideas into cerebral terms, and so to make them stand for something real; and, in this sense, I think the doctrine of these authors less hollow than the opposite one which makes the vehicle of universal conceptions to be an actus purus of the soul. If each 'idea' stand for some special nascent nerve-process, then the aggregate of these nascent processes might have for its conscious correlate a psychic 'fringe,' which should be just that universal meaning, or intention that the name or mental picture employed should mean all the possible individuals of the class. Every peculiar complication of brain-processes must have some peculiar correlate in the soul. To one set of processes will correspond the thought of an indefinite taking of the extent of a word like man; to another set that of a particular taking; and to a third set that of a universal taking, of the extent of the same word. The thought corresponding to either set of processes, is always itself a unique and singular event, whose dependence on its peculiar nerve-process I of course am far from professing to explain.[17]

Truly in comparison with the fact that every conception, whatever it be of, is one of the mind's immutable possessions, the question whether a single thing, or a whole class of things, or only an unassigned quality, be meant by it, is an insignificant matter of detail. Our meanings are of singulars, particulars, indefinites, and universals, mixed together in every way. A singular individual is as much conceived when he is isolated and identified away from the rest of the world in my mind, as is the most rarefied and universally applicable quality he may possess - being, for example, when treated in the same way.[18] From every point of view, the overwhelming and portentous character ascribed to universal conceptions is surprising. Why, from Plato and Aristotle downwards, philosophers should have vied with each other in scorn of the knowledge of the particular, and in adoration of that of the general, is hard to understand, seeing that the more adorable knowledge ought to be that of the more adorable things, and that the things of worth are all concretes and singulars. The only value of universal characters is that they help us, by reasoning, to know new truths about individual things. The restriction of one's meaning, moreover, to an individual thing, probably requires even more complicated brain-processes than its extension to all the instances of a kind; and the mere mystery, as such, of the knowledge, is equally great, whether generals or singulars be the things known. In sum, therefore, the traditional universal-worship can only be called a bit of perverse sentimentalism, a philosophic 'idol of the cave.'

It may seem hardly necessary to add (what follows as a matter of course from pp. 229-237, and what has been implied in our assertions all along) that nothing can be conceived twice over without being conceived in entirely different states of mind. Thus, my arm-chair is one of the things of which I have a conception; I knew it yesterday and recognized it when I looked at it. But if I think of it to-day as the same arm-chair which I looked at yesterday, it is obvious that the very conception of it as the same is an additional complication to the thought, whose inward constitution must alter in consequence. In short, it is logically impossible that the same thing should be known as the same by two successive copies of the same thought. As a matter of fact, the thoughts by which we know that we mean the same thing are apt to be very different indeed from each other. We think the thing now in one context, now in another; now in a definite image, now in a symbol. Sometimes our sense of its identity pertains to the mere fringe, sometimes it involves the nucleus, of our thought. We never can break the thought asunder and tell just which one of its bits is the part that lets us know which subject is referred to; but nevertheless we always do know which of all possible subjects we have in mind. Introspective psychology must here throw up the sponge; the fluctuations of subjective life are too exquisite to be arrested by its coarse means. It must confine itself to bearing witness to the fact that all sorts of different subjective states do form the vehicle by which the same is known; and it must contradict the opposite view.

The ordinary Psychology of 'ideas' constantly talks as if the vehicle of the same thing-known must be the same recurrent state of mind, and as if the having over again of the same 'idea' were not only a necessary but a sufficient condition for meaning the same thing twice. But this recurrence of the same idea would utterly defeat the existence of a repeated knowledge of anything. It would be a simple reversion into a pre-existant state, with nothing gained in the interval, and with complete unconsciousness of the state having existed before. Such is not the way in which we think. As a rule we are fully aware that we have thought before of the thing we think of now. The continuity and permanency of the topic is of the essence of our intellection. We recognize the old problem, and the old solutions; and we go on to alter and improve and substitute one predicate for another without ever letting the subject change. This is what is meant when it is said that thinking consists in making judgments. A succession of judgments may all be about the same thing. The general practical postulate which encourages us to keep thinking at all is that by going on to do so we shall judge better of the same things than if we do not.[19] In the successive judgments, all sorts of new operations are performed on the things, and all sorts of new results brought out, without the sense of the main topic ever getting lost. At the outset, we merely have the topic; then we operate on it; and finally we have it again in a richer and truer way. A compound conception has been substituted for the simple one, but with full consciousness that both are of the Same.

The distinction between having and operating is as natural in the mental as in the material world. As our hands may hold a bit of wood and a knife, and yet do naught with either; so our mind may simply be aware of a thing's existence, and yet neither attend to it nor discriminate it, neither locate nor count nor compare nor like nor dislike nor deduce it, nor recognize it articulately as having been met with before. At the same time we know that, instead of staring at it in this entranced and senseless way, we may rally our activity in a moment, and locate, class, compare, count, and judge it. There is nothing involved in all this which we did not postulate at the very outset of our introspective work: realities, namely, extra mentem, thoughts, and possible relations of cognition between the two. The result of the thoughts' operating on the data given to sense is to transform the order in which experience comes into an entirely different order, that of the conceived world. There is no spot of light, for example, which I pick out and proceed to define as a pebble, which is not thereby torn from its mere time- and space-neighbors, and thought in conjunction with things physically parted from it by the width of nature. Compare the form in which facts appear in a text-book of physics, as logically subordinated laws, with that in which we naturally make their acquaintance. The conceptual scheme is a sort of sieve in which we try to gather up the world's contents. Most facts and relations fall through its meshes, being either too subtle or insignificant to be fixed in any conception. But whenever a physical reality is caught and identified as the same with something already conceived, it remains on the sieve, and all the predicates and relations of the conception with which it is identified become its predicates and relations too; it is subjected to the sieve's network, in other words. Thus comes to pass what Mr. Hodgson calls the translation of the perceptual into the conceptual order of the world.[20]

In Chapter XXII we shall see how this translation always takes place for the sake of some subjective interest, and how the conception with which we handle a bit of sensible experience is really nothing but a teleological instrument. This whole function of conceiving, of fixing, and holding fast to meanings, has no significance apart from the fact that the conceiver is a creature with partial purposes and private ends. There remains, therefore, much more to be said about conception, but for the present this will suffice.

Notes

[1] There are two other 'principles of identity' in philosophy. The ontological one asserts that every real thing is what it is, that a is a, and b, b. The logical one says that what is once true of the subject of a judgment is always true of that subject. The ontological law is a tautological truism; the logical principle is already more, for it implies subjects unalterable by time. The psychological law also implies facts which might not be realized: there might be no succession of thoughts; or if there were, the later ones might not think of the earlier; or if they did, they might not recall the content thereof; or, recalling the content, they might not take it as 'the same' with anything else.

[2] In later chapters we shall see that determinate relations exist between the various data thus fixed upon by the mind. These are called a priori or axiomatic relations. Simple inspection of the data enables us to perceive them; and one inspection is as effective as a million for engendering in us the conviction that between those data that relation must always hold. To change the relation we should have to make the data different. 'The guarantee for the uniformity and adequacy' of the data can only be the mind's own power to fix upon any objective content, and to mean that content as often as it likes. This right of the mind to 'construct' permanent ideal objects for itself out of the data of experience seems, singularly enough, to be a stumbling-block to many. Professor Robertson in his clear and instructive article 'Axioms' in the Encyclopedia Britannica (9th edition) suggests that it may only be where movements enter into the constitution of the ideal object (as they do in geometrical figures) that we can "make the ultimate relations to be what for us they must be in all circumstances." He makes, it is true, a concession in favor of conceptions of number abstracted from "subjective occurrences succeeding each other in time" because these also are acts "of construction, dependent on the power we have of voluntarily determining the flow of subjective consciousness." "The content of passive sensation," on the other hand, "may indefinitely vary beyond any control of ours." What if it do vary, so long as we can continue to think of and mean the qualities it varied from? We can 'make' ideal objects for ourselves out of

irrecoverable bits of passive experience quite as perfectly as out of easily repeatable active experiences. And when we have got our objects together and compared them, we do not make, but find, their relations.

[3] Cf. Hodgson, Time and Space, § 46. Lotze, Logic, § 11.

[4] "For though a man in a fever should from sugar have a bitter taste, which at another time would produce a sweet one, yet the idea of bitter in that man's mind would be as distinct as if he had tasted only gall." (Locke's Essay, bk. II. chap. XI. § 3. Read the whole section!)

[5] Black round things, square white things, per contra, Nature gives us freely enough. But the combinations which she refuses to realize may exist as distinctly, in the shape of postulates, as those which she gives may exist in the shape of positive images, in our mind. As a matter of fact, she may realize a warm cold thing whenever two points of the skin, so near together as not to be locally distinguished, are touched, the one with a warm, the other with a cold, piece of metal. The warmth and the cold are then often felt as if in the same objective place. Under similar conditions two objects, one sharp and the other blunt, may feel like one sharp blunt thing. The same space may appear of two colors if, by optical artifice, one of the colors is made to appear as if seen through the other - Whether any two attributes whatever shall be compatible or not, in the sense of appearing or not to occupy the same place and moment, depends simply on de facto peculiarities of natural bodies of our sense-organs. Logically, any one combination of qualities is to the full as conceivable as any other, and has as distinct a meaning for thought. What necessitates this remark is the confusion deliberately kept up by certain authors (e.g., Spencer, Psychology, §§ 426-7) between the inconceivable and the not-distinctly-imaginable. How do we know which things we cannot imagine unless by first conceiving them, meaning them and not other things?

[6] Arguments seldom make converts in matters philosophical; and some readers, I know, who find that they conceive a certain matter differently from what they did, will still prefer saying they have two different editions of the same conception, one evolved from the other, to saying they have two different conceptions of the same thing. It depends, after all, on how we define conception. We ourselves defined it as the function by which a state of mind means to think the same whereof it thought on a former occasion. Two states of mind will accordingly be two editions of the same conception just so far as either does mean to think what the other thought; but no farther. If either mean to think what the other did not think, it is a different conception from the other. And if either mean to think all that the other thought, and more, it is a different conception, so far as the more goes. In this last case one state of mind has two conceptual functions. Each thought decides, by its own authority, which, out of all the conceptive functions open to it, it shall now renew; with which other thought it shall identify itself as a conceiver, and just how far. "The same A which I once meant," it says, "I shall now mean again, and mean it with C as its predicate (or what not) instead of B, as before." In all this, therefore, there is absolutely no changing, but only uncoupling and re-coupling of conceptions. Compound conceptions come, as functions of new states of mind. Some of these functions are the same with previous ones, some not. Any changed opinion, then, partly contains new editions (absolutely identical with the old, however) of former conceptions, partly absolutely new conceptions. The division is a perfectly easy one to make in each particular case.

[7] Principles of Human Knowledge, Introduction, §§ 10, 14.

[8] 'Conceptualisme honteux,' Rabier, Psychologie, 310.

[9] Exam. of Hamilton, p. 393. Cf. also Logic, bk. II. chap. v § 1. and bk. IV. chap. II. § 1.

[10] E.g.: "The knowledge of things must mean that the mind finds itself in them, or that, in some way, the difference between them and the mind is dissolved." (E. Caird, Philosophy of Kant, first edition, p. 553.)

[11] The traditional conceptualist doctrine is that an abstract must eo ipso be a universal. Even modern and independent authors like Prof. Dewey (Psychology, 207) obey the tradition: "The mind seizes upon some one aspect, . . . abstracts or prescinds it. This very seizure of some one element generalizes the one abstracted. . . . Attention, in drawing it forth, makes it a distinct content of consciousness and thus universalizes it; it is considered no longer in its particular connection with the object, but on its own account; that is, as an idea, or what it signifies to the mind; and significance is always universal."

[12] C. F. Reid's Intellectual Powers, Essay v. chap. III. - Whiteness is one thing, the whiteness of this sheet of paper another thing.

[13] Mr. F. H. Bradley says the conception or the 'meaning' "consists of a part of the content, cut off, fixed by the mind, and considered apart from the existence of the sign. It would not be correct to add, and referred away to another real subject; for where we think without judging, and where we deny, that description would not be applicable." This seems to be the same doctrine as ours; the application to one or to all subjects of the abstract fact conceived (i.e. its individuality or its universality), constituting a new conception. I am, however, not quite sure that Mr. Bradley steadily maintains this ground. Cf. the first chapter of his Principles of Logic. The doctrine I defend is stoutly upheld in Rosmini's Philosophical System, Introduction by Thomas Davidson, p. 43 (London, 1882).

[14] Lectures on Greek Philosophy, pp. 33-39.

[15] Analysis, chap. VIII.

[16] Principles of Human Knowledge, Introduction, §§ 11, 12.

[17] It may add to the effect of the text to quote a passage from the essay in 'Mind,' referred to on p. 224.
"Why may we not side with the conceptualists in saying that the universal sense of a word does correspond to a mental fact of some kind, but at the same time, agreeing with the nominalists that all mental facts are modifications of subjective sensibility, why may we not call that fact a 'feeling'? Man meant for mankind is in short a different feeling from man as a mere noise, or from man meant for that man, to wit, John Smith alone. Not that the difference consists simply in the fact that, when taken

universally, the word has one of Mr. Galton's 'blended' images of man associated with it. Many persons have seemed to think that these blended or, as Prof. Huxley calls them, 'generic' images are equivalent to concepts. But, in itself, a blurred thing is just as particular as a sharp thing; and the generic character of either sharp image or blurred image depends on its being felt with its representative function. This function is the mysterious plus, the understood meaning. But it is nothing applied to the image from above, no pure act of reason inhabiting a supersensible and semi-supernatural plane. It can be diagrammatized as continuous with all the other segments of the subjective stream. It is just that staining, fringe, or halo of obscurely felt relation to masses of other imagery about to come, but not yet distinctly in focus, which we have so absolutely set forth [in Chapter IX].

"If the image come unfringed, it reveals but a simple quality, thing, or event; if it come fringed, it may reveal something expressly taken universally or in a scheme of relations. The difference between thought and feeling thus reduces itself, in the last subjective analysis, to the presence or absence of 'fringe.' And this in turn reduces itself, with much probability, in the last physiological analysis, to the absence or presence of sub-excitements in other convolutions of the brain than those whose discharges underlie the more definite nucleus, the substantive ingredient, of the thought, - in this instance, the word or image it may happen to arouse.

"The contrast is not, then, as the Platonists would have it, between certain subjective facts called images and sensations, and others called acts of relating intelligence; the former being blind perishing things, knowing not even their own existence as such, whilst the latter combine the poles in the mysterious synthesis of their cognitive sweep. The contrast is really between two aspects, in which all mental facts without exception may be taken; their structural aspect, as being subjective, and their functional aspect, as being cognitions. In the former aspect, the highest as well as the lowest is a feeling, a peculiarly tinged segment of the stream. This tingeing is its sensitive body, the wie ihm zu Muthe ist, the way it feels whilst passing. In the latter aspect, the lowest mental fact as well as the highest may grasp some bit of truth as its content, even though that truth were as relationless a matter as a bare unlocalized and undated quality of pain. From the cognitive point of view, all mental facts are intellections. From the subjective point of view all are feelings. Once admit that the passing and evanescent are as real parts of the stream as the distinct and comparatively abiding; once allow that fringes and halos, inarticulate perceptions, whereof the objects are as yet unnamed, mere nascencies of cognition, premonitions, awarenesses of direction, are thoughts sui generis, as much as articulate imaginings and propositions are; once restore, I say, the vague to its psychological rights, and the matter presents no further difficulty.

"And then we see that the current opposition of Feeling to Knowledge is quite a false issue. If every feeling is at the same time a bit of knowledge, we ought no longer to talk of mental states differing by having more or less of the cognitive quality; they only differ in knowing more or less, in having much fact or little fact for their object. The feeling of a broad scheme of relations is a feeling that knows much; the feeling of a simple quality is a feeling that knows little. But the knowing itself, whether of much or of little, has the same essence, and is as good knowing in the one case as in the other. Concept and image, thus discriminated through their objects, are consubstantial in their inward nature, as modes of feeling. The one, as particular, will no longer be held to be a relatively base sort of entity, to be taken as a matter of course, whilst the other, as universal, is celebrated as a sort of standing miracle, to be adored but not explained. Both concept and image, quâ subjective, are singular and particular. Both are moments of the stream, which come and in an instant are no more. The word universality has no meaning as applied to their psychic body or structure, which is always finite. It only has a meaning when applied to their use, import, or reference to the kind of object they may reveal. The representation, as such, of the universal object is as particular as that of an object about which we know so little that the interjection 'Ha!' is all it can evoke from us in the way of speech. Both should be weighed in the same scales, and have the same measure meted out to them, whether of worship or of contempt." (Mind, IX. pp. 18-19.)

[18] Hodgson, Time and Space, p. 404.
[19] Compare the admirable passage in Hodgson's Time and Space, p. 310.
[20] Philosophy of Reflection, I. 273-308.

Chapter XIII - Discrimination and Comparison

It is a matter of popular observation that some men have sharper senses than others, and that some have acuter minds and are able to 'split hairs' and see two shades of meaning where the majority see but one. Locke long ago set apart the faculty of discrimination as one in which men differ individually. What he wrote is good enough to quote as an introduction to this chapter:

"Another faculty we may take notice of in our minds is that of discerning and distinguishing between the several ideas it has. It is not enough to have a confused perception of something in general: unless the mind had a distinct perception of different objects and their qualities, it would be capable of very little knowledge; though the bodies that affect us were as busy about us as they are now, and the mind were continually employed in thinking. On this faculty of distinguishing one thing from another depends the evidence and certainty of several even very general propositions, which have passed for innate truths; because men, overlooking the true cause why those propositions find universal assent, impute it wholly to native uniform impressions: whereas it in truth depends upon this clear discerning faculty of the mind, whereby it perceives two ideas to be the same or different. But of this more hereafter.

"How much the imperfection of accurately discriminating ideas one from another lies either in the dulness or faults of the organs of sense, or want of acuteness, exercise, or attention in the understanding, or hastiness and precipitancy natural to some tempers, I will not here examine: it suffices to take notice that this is one of the operations that the mind may reflect on and observe in itself. It is of that consequence to its other knowledge, that so far as this faculty is in itself dull, or not rightly made use of for the distinguishing one thing from another, so far our notions are confused, and our reason and judgment disturbed or misled. If in having our ideas in the memory ready at hand consists quickness of parts; in this of having them unconfused, and being able nicely to distinguish one thing from another where there is but the least difference, consists in a great measure the exactness of judgment and clearness of reason which is to be observed in one man above another. And hence, perhaps, may be given some reason of that common observation, -- that men who have a great deal of wit and prompt memories have not always the clearest judgment or deepest reason. For, wit lying most in the assemblage of ideas, and putting those together with quickness and variety wherein can be found any resemblance or congruity, thereby to make up pleasant pictures and agreeable visions in the fancy; judgment, on the contrary, lies quite on the other side, in separating carefully one from another ideas wherein can be found the least difference, thereby to avoid being misled by similitude and by affinity to take one thing for another. This is a way of proceeding quite contrary to metaphor and allusion, wherein for the most part lies that entertainment and pleasantry of wit which strikes so lively on the fancy, and therefore, so acceptable to all people because its beauty appears at first sight, and there is required no labor of thought to examine what truth or reason there is in it."[1]

But Locke's descendants have been slow to enter into the path whose fruitfulness was thus pointed out by their master, and have so neglected the study of discrimination that one might almost say that the classic English psychologists have, as a school, hardly recognized it to exist. 'Association' has proved itself in their hands the one all-absorbing power of the mind. Dr. Martineau, in his review of Bain, makes some very weighty remarks on this onesidedness of the Lockian school. Our mental history, says he, is, in its view,

"a perpetual formation of new compounds: and the words 'association,' 'cohesion,' 'fusion,' 'indissoluble connection,' all express the change from plurality of data to some unity of result. An explanation of the process therefore requires two things: a true enumeration of the primary constituents, and a correct statement of their laws of combination: just as, in chemistry, we are furnished with a list of the simple elements, and the with then principles of their synthesis. Now the latter of these two conditions we find satisfied by the association-psychologists: but not the former. They are not agreed upon their catalogue of elements, or the marks by which they may know the simple from the compound. The psychologic unit is not fixed; that which is called one impression by Hartley is treated as half-a-dozen or more by Mill: and the tendency of the modern teachers on this point is to recede more and more from the better chosen track of their master. Hartley, for example, regarded the whole present effect upon us of any single object—say, an orange—as a single sensation; and the whole vestige is left behind, as a single 'idea of sensation.' His modern disciples, on the other hand, consider this same effect as an aggregate from a plurality of sensations, and the ideal trace it leaves as highly compound. 'The idea of an object,' instead of being an elementary starting-point with them, is one of the elaborate results of repetition and experience; and is continually adduced as remarkably illustrating the fusing power of habitual association. Thus James Mill observes:

"'It is to this great law of association that we trace the formation of our ideas of what we call external objects; that is, the ideas of a certain number of sensations, received together so frequently that they coalesce as it were, and are spoken of under the idea of unity. Hence, what we call the idea of a tree, the idea of a stone, the idea of a horse, the idea of a man. In using the names, tree, horse, man, the names of what I call objects, I am referring, and can be referring, only to my own sensations; in fact, therefore, only naming a certain number of sensations regarded as in a particular state of combination, that is, concomitance. Particular sensations of sight, of touch, of the muscles, are the sensations to the ideas of which, color, extension, roughness, hardness, smoothness, taste, smell, so coalescing as to appear one idea, I give the name of the idea of a tree.'[2]

"To precisely the same effect Mr. Bain remarks:

"External objects usually affect us through a plurality of senses. The pebble on the sea-shore is pictured on the eye as form and color. We take it up in the hand and repeat the impression of form, with the additional feeling of touch. Knock two together, and there is a characteristic sound. To preserve the impression of an object of this kind, there must be an association of all these different effects. Such association, when matured and firm, is our idea, our intellectual grasp of the pebble. Passing to the organic world, and plucking a rose, we have the same effects of form to the eye and hand, color and touch, with new effects of odor and taste. A certain time is requisite for the coherence of all these qualities in one aggregate, so as to give us for all purposes the enduring image of the rose. When fully acquired, any one of the characteristic impressions will revive the others; the odor, the sight, the feeling of the thorny stalk—each of these by itself will hoist the entire impression into the view.'[3]

"Now, this order of derivation, making our objective knowledge begin with plurality of impression and arrive at unity, we take to be a complete inversion of our psychological history. Hartley, we think, was perfectly right in taking no notice of the number of inlets through which an object delivers its effects upon us, and, in spite of this circumstance, treating the effect as one.... Even now, after life has read us so many analytic lessons, in proportion as we can fix the attitude of our scene and ourselves, the sense of plurality in our impressions retreats, and we lapse into an undivided consciousness; losing, for instance, the separate notice of any uniform hum in the ear, or light in the eye, or weight of clothes on the body, though not one of them is inoperative on the complexion of our feeling. This law, once granted, must be carried far beyond Hartley's point. Not only must each object present itself to us integrally before it shells off into its qualities, but the whole scene around us must disengage for us object after object from its still background by emergence and change; and even our self-detachment from the world over against us must wait for the start of collision between the force we issue and that which we receive. To confine ourselves to the simplest case: when a red ivory ball, seen for the first time, has been withdrawn, it will leave a mental representation of itself, in which all that it simultaneously gave us will indistinguishably coexist. Let a white ball succeed to it; now, and not before, will an attribute detach itself, and the color, by force of contrast, be shaken out into the foreground. Let the white ball be replaced by an egg: and this new difference will bring the form into notice from its previous slumber. And thus, that which began by being simply an object, cut out from the surrounding scene, becomes for us first a red object, and then a red round object; and so on. Instead, therefore, of the qualities, as separately given, subscribing together and adding themselves up to present us with the object as their aggregate, the object is beforehand with them, and from its integrity delivers them out to our knowledge, one by one. In this disintegration, the primary nucleus never loses its substantive character or name; whilst the difference which it throws off appears as a mere attribute, expressed by an adjective. Hence it is that we are compelled to think of the object as having, not as being, its qualities; and can never heartily admit the belief of any loose lot of attributes really fusing themselves into a thing. The unity of the original whole is not felt to go to pieces and be resolved into the properties which it successively gives off; it retains a residuary existence, which constitutes it a substance, as against the emerging quality, which is only its phenomenal predicate. Were it not for this perpetual process of differentiation of self from the world, of object from its scene, of attribute from object, no step of Abstraction could be taken; no qualities could fall under our notice; and had we ten thousand senses, they would all converge and meet in but one consciousness. But if this be so, it is an utter falsification of the order of nature to speak of sensations grouping themselves into aggregates, and so composing for us the objects of which we think; and the whole language of the theory, in regard to the field of synchronous existences, is a direct inversion of the truth. Experience proceeds and intellect is trained, not by Association, but by Dissociation, not by reduction of pluralities of impression to one, but by the opening out of one into many; and a true psychological history must expound itself in analytic rather than synthetic terms. Precisely those ideas—of Substance, of Mind, of Cause, of Space—which this system treats as infinitely complex, the last result of myriads of confluent elements, are in truth the residuary simplicities of consciousness, whose stability the eddies and currents of phenomenal experience have left undisturbed."[4]

The truth is that Experience is trained by both association and dissociation, and that psychology must be writ both in synthetic and in analytic terms. Our original sensible totals are, on the one hand, subdivided by discriminative attention, and, on the other, united with other totals, -- either through the agency of our own movements, carrying our senses from one part of space to another, or because new objects come successively and replace those by which we were at first impressed. The 'simple impression' of Hume, the 'simple idea' of Locke are both abstractions, never realized in experience. Experience, from the very first, presents us with concreted objects, vaguely continuous with the rest of the world which envelops them in space and time, and potentially divisible into inward elements and parts. These objects we break asunder and reunite. We must treat them in both ways for our knowledge of them to grow; and it is hard to say, on the whole, which way preponderates. But since the elements with which the traditional associationism performs its constructions—'simple sensations,' namely—are all products of discrimination carried to a high pitch, it seems as if we ought to discuss the subject of analytic attention and discrimination first.

The noticing of any part whatever of our object is an act of discrimination. Already on p. 404 I have described the manner in which we often spontaneously lapse into the undiscriminating state, even with regard to objects which we have already learned to distinguish. Such anæsthetics as chloroform, nitrous oxide, etc., sometimes bring about transient lapses even more total, in which numerical discrimination especially seems gone; for one sees light and hears sound, but whether one or many lights and sounds is quite impossible to tell. Where the parts of an object have already been discerned, and each made the object of a special discriminative act, we can with difficulty feel the object again in its pristine unity; and so prominent may our consciousness of its composition be, that we may hardly believe that it ever could have appeared undivided. But this is an erroneous view, the undeniable fact being that any number of impressions, from any number of sensory sources, falling simultaneously on a mind WHICH HAS NOT YET EXPERIENCED THEM SEPARATELY, will fuse into a single undivided object for that mind. The law is that all things fuse that can fuse, and nothing separates except what must. What makes impressions separate we have to study in this chapter. Although they separate easier if they come in through distinct nerves, yet distinct nerves are not an unconditional ground of their discrimination, as we shall presently see. The baby, assailed by eyes, ears, nose, skin, and entrails at once, feels it all as one great blooming, buzzing confusion; and to the very end of life, our location of all things in one space is due to the fact that the original extents or bignesses of all the sensations which came to our notice at once, coalesced together into one and the same space. There is no other reason than this why "the hand I touch and see coincides spatially with the hand I immediately feel."[5]

It is true that we may sometimes be tempted to exclaim, when once a lot of hitherto unnoticed details of the object lie before us, "How could we ever have been ignorant of these things and yet have felt the object, or drawn the conclusion, as if it were a continuum, a plenum? There would have been gaps—but we felt no gaps; wherefore we must have seen and heard these details, leaned upon these steps; they must have been operative upon our minds, just as they are now, only unconsciously, or at least inattentively. Our first unanalyzed sensation was really composed of these elementary sensations, our first rapid conclusion was really based on these intermediate inferences, all the while, only we failed to note the fact." But this is nothing but the fatal 'psychologists fallacy' of treating an inferior state of mind as if it must somehow know implicitly all that is explicitly known about the same topic by superior states of mind. The thing thought of is unquestionably the same, but it is thought twice over in two absolutely different psychoses, -- once as an unbroken unit, and again as a sum of discriminated parts. It is not one thought in two editions, but two entirely distinct thoughts of one thing. And each thought is within itself a continuum, a plenum, needing no contributions from the other to fill up its gaps. As I sit here, I think objects, and I make inferences, which the future is sure to analyze and articulate and riddle with discriminations, showing me many things wherever I now notice one. Nevertheless, my thought feels quite sufficient unto itself for the time being; and ranges from pole to pole, as free, and as unconscious of having overlooked anything, as if it possessed the greatest discriminative enlightenment. We all cease analyzing the world at some point, and notice no more differences. The last units with which we stop are our objective elements of being. Those of a dog are different from those of a Humboldt; those of a practical man from those of a metaphysician. But the dog's and the practical man's thoughts feel continuous, though to the Humboldt or the metaphysician they would appear full of gaps and defects. And they are continuous, as thoughts. It is only as mirrors of things that the superior minds find them full of omissions. And when the omitted things are discovered and the unnoticed differences laid bare, it is not that the old thoughts split up, but that new thoughts supersede them, which make new judgments about the same objective world.

The Principle of Mediate Comparison.

When we discriminate an element, we may contrast it with the case of its own absence, of its simply not being there, without reference to what is there; or we may also take the latter into account. Let the first sort of discrimination be called existential, the latter differential discrimination. A peculiarity of differential discriminations is that they result in a perception of differences which are felt as greater or less one than the other. Entire groups of differences may be ranged in series: the musical scale, the color scale, are examples. Every department of our experience may have its data written down in an evenly gradated order, from a lowest to a highest member. And any one datum may be a term in several such orders. A given note may have a high place in the pitch-series, a low place in the loudness-series, and a medium place in the series of agreeableness. A given tint must, in order to be fully determined, have its place assigned in the series of qualities, in the series of purities (freedom from white), and in the series of intensities or brightnesses. It may be low in one of these respects, but high in another. In passing from term to term in any such series we are conscious not only of each step of difference being equal to (or greater or less than) the last, but we are conscious of proceeding in a uniform direction, different from other possible directions. This consciousness of serial increase of differences is one of the fundamental facts of our intellectual life. More, more, MORE, of the same kind of difference, we say, as we advance from term to term, and realize that the farther on we get the larger grows the breach between the term we are at and the one from which we started. Between any two terms of such a series the difference is greater than that between any intermediate terms, or than that between an intermediate term and either of the extremes. The louder than the loud is louder than the less loud; the farther than the far is farther than the less far; the earlier than the early is earlier than the late; the higher than the high is higher than the low; the bigger than the big is bigger than the small; or, to put it briefly and universally, the more than the more is more than the less; such is the great synthetic principle of mediate comparison which is involved in the possession by the human mind of the sense of serial increase. In Chapter XX we shall see the altogether overwhelming importance of this principle in the conduct of all our higher rational operations.

Are All Differences Differences of Composition?

Each of the differences in one of these uniform series feels like a definite sensible quantity, and each term seems like the last term with this quantity added. In many concrete objects which differ from one another we can plainly see that the difference does consist simply in the fact that one object is the same as the other plus something else, or that they both have an identical part, to which each adds a distinct remainder. Thus two pictures may be struck form the same block, but one of them may differ in having color added; or two carpets may show an identical pattern which in each is woven in distinct hues. Similarly, two classes of sensation may have the same emotional tone but negate each other in remaining respects—a dark color and a deep sound, for example; or two faces may have the same shape of nose but everything else unlike. The similarity of the same note sounded by instruments of different timbre is explained by the coexistence of a fundamental tone common to both, with over-tones in one which the other lacks. Dipping my hand into water and anon into a colder water, I may then observe certain additional feelings, broader and deeper irradiations of the cold, so to speak, which were not in the earlier experience, though for aught I can tell, the feelings may be otherwise the same. 'Hefting' first one weight, and then another, new feelings may start out in my elbow-joint, wrist, and elsewhere, and make me call the second weight the heavier of the twain. In all these cases each of the differing things may be represented by two parts, one that is common to it and the others, and another that is peculiar to itself. If they form a series, A, B, C, D, etc., and the common part be called X, whilst the lowest difference be called d, then the composition of the series would be as follows:

A = X + d;
B = (X + d) + d, or x + 2d;
C = X + 3d;
D = X + 4d;
. . . .

If X itself were ultimately composed of d's we should have the entire series explained as due to the varying combination and re-combination with itself of an unvarying element; and all the apparent differences of quality would be translated into differences of quantity alone. This is the sort of reduction which the atomic theory in physics and the mind-stuff theory in psychology regard as their ideal. So that, following the analogy of our instances, one might easily be tempted to generalize and to say that all difference is but addition and subtraction, and that what we called 'differential' discrimination is only 'existential' discrimination in disguise; that is to say, that where A and B differ, we merely discern something in the one which the other is without. Absolute identity in things up to a certain point, then absolute non-identity, would on this theory take the place of those ultimate qualitative unlikenesses between them, in which we naturally believe; and the mental function of discrimination, ceasing to be regarded as an ultimate one, would resolve itself into mere logical affirmation and negation, or perception that a feature found in one thing, in another does not exist.

Theoretically, however, this theory is full of difficulty. If all the differences which we feel were in one direction, so that all objects could be arranged in one series (however long), it might still work. But when we consider the notorious fact that objects differ from each other in divergent directions, it grows well nigh impossible to make it do so. For then, supposing that an object differed from things in one direction by the increment d, it would have to differ from things in another direction by a different sort of increment, call it d'; so that, after getting rid of qualitative unlikeness between objects, we should have it back on our hands again between their increments. We may of course re-apply our method, and say that the difference between d and d' is not a qualitative unlikeness, but a fact of composition, one of them being the same as the other plus an increment of still higher order, d for example, added.

But when we recollect that everything in the world can be compared with everything else, and that the number of directions of difference is indefinitely great, then we see that the complication of self-compoundings of the ultimate differential increment by which, on this theory, all the innumerable unlikenesses of the world are explained, in order to avoid writing any of them down as ultimate differences of kind, would beggar all conception. It is the mind-dust theory, with all its difficulties in a particularly uncompromising form; and all for the sake of the fantastic pleasure of being able arbitrarily to say that there is between the things in the world and between the 'ideas' in the mind nothing but absolute sameness and absolute not-sameness of elements, the not-sameness admitting no degrees. To me it seems much wiser to turn away from such transcendental extravagances of speculation, and to abide by the natural appearances. These would leave unlikeness as an indecomposable relation amongst things, and a relation moreover of which there were all degrees. Absolute not-sameness would be the maximal degree, absolute sameness the minimal degree of this unlikeness, the discernment of which would be one of our ultimate cognitive powers.[6] Certainly the natural appearances are dead against the notion that no qualitative differences exist. With the same clearness with which, in certain objects, we do feel a difference to be a mere matter of plus and minus, in other objects we feel that this is not the case. Contrast our feeling of the difference between the length of two lines with our feeling of the difference between blue and yellow, or with that between right and left. Is right equal to left with something added? Is blue yellow plus something? If so, plus what?[7] So long as we stick to verifiable psychology, we are forced to admit that differences of simple KIND form an irreducible sort of relation between some of the elements of our experience, and forced to deny that differential discrimination can everywhere be reduced to the mere ascertainment that elements present in one fact, in another fail to exist. The perception that an element exists in one thing and does not exist in another and the perception of qualitative difference are, in short, entirely disconnected mental functions.[8]

But at the same time that we insist on this, we must also admit that differences of quality, however abundant, are not the only distinctions with which our mind has to deal. Differences which seem of mere composition, of number, of plus and minus, also abound.[9] But it will be best for the present to disregard all these quantitative cases and, taking the others (which, by the least favorable calculation, will still be numerous enough), to consider next the manner in which we come to cognize simple differences of kind. We cannot explain the cognition; we can only ascertain the conditions by virtue of which it occurs.

The Conditions of Discrimination.

What, then, are the conditions under which we discriminate things differing in a simple way?

First, the things must BE different, either in time, or place, or quality. If the difference in any of these regards is sufficiently great, then we cannot overlook it, except by not noticing the things at all. No one can help singling out a black stripe on a white ground, or feeling the contrast between a bass note and a high one sounded immediately after it. Discrimination is here involuntary. But where the objective difference is less, discrimination need not so inevitably occur, and may even require considerable effort of attention to be performed at all.

Another condition which then favors it is that the sensations excited by the differing objects should not come to us simultaneously but fall in immediate SUCCESSION upon the same organ. It is easier to compare successive than simultaneous sounds, easier to compare two weights or two temperatures by testing one after the other with the same hand, than by using both hands and comparing both at once. Similarly it is easier to discriminate shades of light or color by moving the eye from one to the other, so that they successively stimulate the same retinal tract. In testing the local discrimination of the skin, by applying compass-points, it is found that they are felt to touch different spots much more readily when set down one after the other than when both are applied at once. In the latter case they may be two or three inches apart on the back, thighs, etc., and still feel as if they were set down in one spot. Finally, in the case of smell and taste it is well-nigh impossible to compare simultaneous impressions at all. The reason why successive impression so much favors the result seems to be that there is a real sensation of difference, aroused by the shock of transition from one perception to another which is unlike the first. This sensation of difference has its own peculiar quality, as difference, which remains sensible, no matter of what sort the terms may be, between which it obtains. It is, in short, one of those transitive feelings, or feelings of relation, of which I treated in a former place and, when once aroused, its object lingers in the memory along with the substantive terms which precede and follow, and enables our judgments of comparison to be made. We shall soon see reason to believe that no two terms can possibly be simultaneously perceived to differ, unless, in a preliminary operation, we have successively attended to each, and, in so doing, had the transitional sensation of difference between them aroused. A field of consciousness, however complex, is never analyzed unless some of its ingredients have changed. We now discern, 'tis true, a multitude of coexisting things about us at every moment: but this is because we have had a long education, and each thing we now see distinct has been already differentiated from its neighbors by repeated appearances in successive order. To the infant, sounds, sights, touches, and pains, form probably one unanalyzed bloom of confusion.[10]

Where the difference between the successive sensations is but slight, the transition between them must be made as immediate as possible, and both must be compared in memory, in order to get the best results. One cannot judge accurately of the difference between two similar wines, whilst the second is still in one's mouth. So of sounds, warmths, etc.—we must get the dying phases of both sensations of the pair we are comparing. Where, however, the difference is strong, this condition is immaterial, and we can then compare a sensation actually felt with another carried in memory only. The longer the interval of time between the sensations, the more uncertain is their discrimination.

The difference, thus immediately felt between two terms, is independent of our ability to identify either of the terms by itself. I can feel two distinct spots to be touched on my skin, yet not know which is above and which below. I can observe two neighboring musical tones to differ, and still not know which of the two is the higher in pitch. Similarly I may discriminate two neighboring tints, whilst remaining uncertain which is the bluer or the yellower, or how either differs from its mate.[11]

With such direct perceptions of difference as this, we must not confound those entirely unlike cases in which we infer that two things must differ because we know enough about each of them taken by itself to warrant our classing them under distinct heads. It often happens, when the interval is long between two experiences, that our judgments are guided, not so much by a positive image or copy of the earlier one, as by our recollection of certain facts about it. Thus I know that the sunshine to-day is less bright than on a certain day last week, because I then said it was quite dazzling, a remark I should not now care to make. Or I know myself to feel better now than I was last summer, because I can now psychologize, and then I could not. We are constantly busy comparing feelings with whose quality our imagination has no sort of acquaintance at the time—pleasures, or pains, for example. It is notoriously hard to conjure up in imagination a lively image of either of these classes of feeling. The associationists may prate of an idea of pleasure being a pleasant idea, of an idea of pain being a painful one, but the unsophisticated sense of mankind is against them, agreeing with Homer that the memory of griefs when past may be a joy, and with Dante that there is no greater sorrow than, in misery, to recollect one's happier time.

Feelings remembered in this imperfect way must be compared with present or recent feelings by the aid of what we know about them. We identify the remote experience in such a case by conceiving it. The most perfect way of conceiving it is by defining it in terms of some standard scale. If I know the thermometer to stand at zero to-day and to have stood at 32o last Sunday, I know to-day to be colder, and I know just how much colder, than it was last Sunday. If I know that a certain note was c, and that this note is d, I know that this note must be the higher of the two.

The inference that two things differ because their concomitants, effects, names, kinds, or—to put it generally—their signs, differ, is of course susceptible of unlimited complication. The sciences furnish examples, in the way in which men are led, by noticing differences in effects, to assume new hypothetical causes, differing from any known heretofore. But no matter how many may be the steps by which such inferential discriminations are made, they all end in a direct intuition of difference somewhere. The last ground for inferring that A and B differ must be that, whilst A is an m, B is an n, and that m and n are seen to differ. Let us then neglect the complex cases, the A's and the B's, and go back to the study of the unanalyzable perception of difference between their signs, the m's and the n's, when these are seemingly simple terms.

I said that in their immediate succession the shock of their difference was felt. It is felt repeatedly when we go back and forth from m to n; and we make a point of getting it thus repeatedly (by alternating our attention at least) whenever the shock is so slight as to be with difficulty perceived. But in addition to being felt at the brief instant of transition, the difference also feels as if incorporated and taken up into the second term, which feels 'different-from-the-first' even while it lasts. It is obvious that the 'second term' of the mind in this case is not bald n, but a very complex object; and that the sequence is not simply first 'm,' then 'difference,' then 'n'; but first 'm,' then 'difference,' then 'n-different-from-m.' The several thoughts, however, to which these three several objects are revealed, are three ordinary 'segments' of the mental 'stream.'

As our brains and minds are actually made, it is impossible to get certain m's and n's in immediate sequence and to keep them pure. If kept pure, it would mean that they remained uncompared. With us, inevitably, by a mechanism which we as yet fail to understand, the shock of difference is felt between them, and the second object is not n pure, but n-as-different-from-m.[12] It is no more a paradox that under these conditions this cognition of m and n in mutual relation should occur, than that under other condtitions the cognition of m's or n's simple quality should occur. But as it has been treated as a paradox, and as a spiritual agent, not itself a portion of the stream, has been invoked to account for it, a word of further remark seems desirable.

My account, it will be noted, is merely a description of the facts as they occur: feelings (or thoughts) each knowing something, but the later one knowing, if preceded by a certain earlier one, a more complicated object than it would have known had the earlier one not been there. I offer no explanation of such a sequence of cognitions. The explanation (I devoutly expect) will be found some day to depend on cerebral conditions. Until it is forthcoming, we can only treat the sequence as a special case of the general law that every experience undergone by the brain leaves in it a modification which is one factor in determining what manner of experiences the following ones shall be (cf. pp. 232-236). To anyone who denies the possibility of such a law I have nothing to say, until he brings his proofs. The sentationalists and the spiritualists meanwhile (filled both of them with their notion that the mind must in some fashion contain what it knows) begin by giving a cooked account of the facts. Both admit that for m and n to be known in any way whatever, little rounded and finished off duplicates of each must be contained in the mind as separate entities. These pure ideas, so called, of m and n respectively, succeed each other there. And since they are distinct, say the sensationalists, they are eo ipso distinguished. "To have ideas different and ideas distinguished, are synonymous expressions; different and distinguished meaning exactly the same thing," says James Mill.[13] "Distinguished!" say the spiritualists, "distinguished by what, forsooth? Truly the respective ideas of m and of n in the mind are distinct. But for that very reason neither can distinguish itself from the other, for to do that it would have to be aware of the other, and thus for the time being become the other, and that would be to get mixed up with the other and to lose its own distinctness. Distinctness of ideas and idea of distinctness, are not one thing, but two. This last is a relation. Only a relating principle, opposed in nature to all facts of feeling, an Ego, Soul, or Subject, is competent, by being present to both of the ideas alike, to hold them together and at the same time to keep them distinct."

But if the plain facts be admitted that the pure idea of 'n' is never in the mind at all, when 'm' has once gone before; and that the feeling 'n-different-from-m' is itself an absolutely unique pulse of thought, the bottom of this precious quarrel drops out and neither party is left with anything to fight about. Surely such a consummation ought to be welcomed, especially when brought about, as here, by a formulation of the facts which offers itself so naturally and unsophistically.[14]

We may, then, conclude our examination of the manner in which simple involuntary discrimination comes about, by saying, 1) that its vehicle is a thought possessed of a knowledge of both terms compared and of their difference; 2) that the necessary and sufficient condition (as the human mind goes) for arousing this thought is that a thought or feeling of one of the terms discriminated should, as immediately as possible, precede that in which the other term is known; and 3) and that the thought which knows the second term will then also know the difference (or in more difficult cases will be continuously succeeded by one which does know the difference) and both of the terms between which it holds.

This last thought need, however, not be these terms with their difference, nor contain them. A man's thought can know and mean all sorts of things without those things getting bodily into it—the distant, for example, the future, and the past.[15] The vanishing term in the case which occupies us vanishes; but because it is the specific term it is and nothing else, it leaves a specific influence behind it when it vanishes, the effect of which is to determine the succeeding pulse of thought in a perfectly characteristic way. Whatever consciousness comes next must know the vanished term and call it different from the one now there.

Here we are at the end of our tether about involuntary discrimination of successively felt simple things; and must drop the subject, hopeless of seeing any deeper into it for the present, and turn to discriminations of a less simple sort.

The Process of Analysis.

And first, of the discrimination of simultaneously felt impressions! Our first way of looking at a reality is often to suppose it simple, but later we may learn to perceive it as compound. This new way of knowing the same reality may conveniently be called by the name of Analysis. It is manifestly one of the most incessantly performed of all our mental processes, so let us examine the conditions under which it occurs.

I think we may safely lay down at the outset this fundamental principle, that any total impression made on the mind must be unanalyzable, whose elements are never experienced apart. The components of an absolutely changeless group of not-elsewhere-occurring attributes could never be discriminated. If all cold things were wet and all wet things cold, if all hard things pricked our skin, and no other things did so; is it likely that we should discriminate between coldness and wetness, and hardness and pungency respectively? If all liquids were transparent and no non-liquid were transparent, it would be long before we had separate names for liquidity and transparency. If heat were a function of position above the earth's surface, so that the higher a thing was the hotter it became, one word would serve for hot and high. We have, in fact, a number of sensations whose concomitants are almost invariably the same, and we find it, accordingly, almost impossible to analyze them out from the totals in which they are found. The contraction of the diaphragm and the expansion of the lungs, the shortening of certain muscles and the rotation of certain joints, are examples. The converging of the eyeballs and the accommodation for near objects are, for each distance of the object (in the common use of the eyes) inseparably linked, and neither can (without a sort of artificial training which shall presently be mentioned) be felt by itself. We learn that the causes of such groups of feelings are multiple, and therefore we frame theories about the composition of the feelings themselves, by 'fusion,' 'integration,' 'synthesis,' or what not. But by direct introspection no analysis of them is ever made. A conspicuous case will come to view when we treat of the emotions. Every emotion has its 'expression,' of quick breathing, palpitating heart, flushed face, or the like. The expression gives rise to bodily feelings; and the emotion is thus necessarily and invariably accompanied by these bodily feelings. The consequence is that it is impossible to apprehend it as a spiritual state by itself, or to analyze it away from the lower feelings in question. It is in fact impossible to prove that it exists as a distinct psychic fact. The present writer strongly doubts that it does so exist. But those who are most firmly persuaded of its existence must wait, to prove their point, until they can quote some as yet unfound pathological case of an individual who shall have emotions in a body in which either complete paralysis will have prevented their expression, or complete anæsthesia will have made the latter unfelt.

In general, then, if an object affects us simultaneously in a number of ways, abcd, we get a peculiar integral impression, which thereafter characterizes to our mind the individuality of that object, and becomes the sign of its presence; and which is only resolved into a, b, c, d, respectively by the aid of farther experiences. These we now may turn to consider.

If any single quality or constituent, a, of such an object, have previously been known by us isolatedly, or have in any other manner already become an object of separate acquaintance on our part, so that we have an image of it, distinct or vague, in our mind, disconnected with bcd, then that constituent a may be analyzed out from the total impression. Analysis of a thing means separate attention to each of its parts. In Chapter XI we saw that one condition of attending to a thing was the formation from within of a separate image of that thing, which should, as it were, go out to meet the impression received. Attention being the condition of analysis, and separate imagination being the condition of attention, it follows also that separate imagination is the condition of analysis. Only such elements as we are acquainted with, and can imagine, separately, can be discriminated within a total sense-impression. The image seems to welcome its own mate from out of the compound, and to heighten the feeling thereof; whereas it dampens and opposes the feeling of the other constituents; and thus the compound becomes broken for our consciousness into parts.

All the facts cited in Chapter XI, to prove that attention involves inward reproduction, go to prove this point as well. In looking for any object in a room, for a book in a library, for example, we detect it the more readily if, in addition to merely knowing its name, etc., we carry in our mind a distinct image of its appearance. The assafœtida in 'Worcestershire sauce' is not obvious to anyone who has not tasted assafœtida per se. In a 'cold' color an artist would never be able to analyze out the pervasive presence of blue, unless he had previously made acquaintance with the color blue by itself. All the colors we actually experience are mixtures. Even the purest primaries always come to us with some white. Absolutely pure red or green or violet is never experienced, and so we can never be discerned in the so-called primaries with which we have to deal: the latter consequently pass for pure.—The reader will remember how an overtone can only be attended to in the midst of its consorts in the voice of a musical instrument, by sounding it previously alone. The imagination, being then full of it, hears the like of it in the compound tone. Helmholtz, whose account of this observation we formerly quoted, goes on to explain the difficulty of the case in a way which beautifully corroborates the point I now seek to prove. He says:

"The ultimate simple elements of the sensation of tone, simple tones themselves, are rarely heard alone. Even those instruments by which they can be produced (as tuning-forks before resonance-chambers), when strongly excited, give rise to weak harmonic upper partials, partly within and partly without the ear.... Hence the opportunities are very scanty for impressing on our memory an exact and sure image of these simple elementary tones. But if the constituents are only indefinitely and vaguely known, the analysis of their sum into them must be correspondingly uncertain. If we do not know with certainty how much of the musical tone under consideration is to be attributed to its prime, we cannot but be uncertain as to what belongs to the partials. Consequently we must begin by making the individual elements which have to be distinguished individually audible, so as to obtain an entirely fresh recollection of the corresponding sensation, and the whole business requires undisturbed and concentrated attention. We are even without the ease that can be obtained by frequent repetitions of the experiment, such as we possess in the analysis of musical chords into their individual notes. In that case we hear the individual notes sufficiently often by themselves, whereas we rarely hear simple tones, and may almost be said never to hear the building up of a compound from its simple tones."[16]

The Process of Abstraction.

Very few elements of reality are experienced by us in absolute isolation. The most that usually happens to a constituent a, of a compound phenomenon abcd, is that its strength relatively to bcd varies from a maximum to a minimum; or that it appears linked with other qualities, in other compounds, as aefg, or ahik. Either of these vicissitudes in the mode of our experiencing a may, under favorable circumstances, lead us to feel the difference between it and its concomitants, and to single it out—not absolutely, it is true, but approximately—and so to analyze the compound of which it is a part. The act of singling out is then called abstraction, and the element disengaged is an abstract.

Consider the case of fluctuations of relative strength or intensity first. Let there be three grades of the compound, as Abcd, abcd, and abcD. In passing between these compounds, the mind will feel shocks of difference. The differences, moreover, will serially increase, and their direction will be felt as of a distinct sort. The increase from abcd to Abcd is on the a side; that to abcD is on the d side. And these two differences of direction are differently felt. I do not say that this discernment of the a-direction from the d-direction will give us an actual intuition either of a or of d in the abstract. But it leads us to conceive or postulate each of these qualities, and to define it as the extreme of a certain direction. 'Dry' wines and 'sweet' wines, for example, differ, and form a series. It happens that we have an experience of sweetness pure and simple in the taste of sugar; and this we can analyze out of this wine-taste. But no one knows what 'dryness' tastes like, all by itself. It must, however, be something extreme in the dry direction; and we should probably not fail to recognize it as the original of our abstract conception, in case we ever did come across it. In some such way we get to form notions of the flavor of meats, apart from their feeling to the tongue, or of that of fruits apart from their acidity, etc., and we abstract the touch of bodies as distinct from their temperature. We may even apprehend the quality of muscle's contraction as distinguished from its extent, or one muscle's contraction from another's, as when, by practising with prismatic glasses, and varying our eyes' convergence whilst our accommodation remains the same, we learn the direction in which our feeling of the convergence differs from that of the accommodation.

But the fluctuation in a quality's intensity is a less efficient aid to our abstracting of it than the diversity of the other qualities in whose company it may appear. What is associated now with one thing and now with another tends to become dissociated from either, and to grow into an object of abstract contemplation by the mind. One might call this the law of dissociation by varying concomitants. The practical result of it will be to allow the mind which has thus dissociated and abstracted a character to analyze it out of a total, whenever it meets with it again. The law has been frequently recognized by psychologists, though I know of none who has given it the emphatic prominence in our mental history which it deserves. Mr. Spencer says:

"If the property A occurs here along with the properties B, C, D, there along with C, F, H, and again with E, G, B, . . . it must happen that by multiplication of experiences the impressions produced by these properties on the organism will be disconnected and rendered so far independent in the organism as the properties are in the environment, whence must eventually result a power to recognize attributes in themselves, apart from particular bodies."[17]

And still more to the point Dr. Martineau, in the passage I have already quoted, writes:

"When a red ivory ball, seen for the first time, has been withdrawn, it will leave a mental representation of itself, in which all that it simultaneously gave us will indistinguishably coexist. Let a white ball succeed to it; now, and not before, will an attribute detach itself, and the color, by force of contrast, be shaken out into the foreground. Let the white ball be replaced by an egg, and this new difference will bring the form into notice from its previous slumber, and thus that which began by being simply an object cut out from the surrounding scene becomes for us first a red object, then a red round object, and so on."

Why the repetition of the character in combination with different wholes will cause it thus to break up its adhesion with any one of them, and roll out, as it were, alone upon the table of consciousness, is a little of a mystery. One might suppose the nerve-processes of the various concomitants to neutralize or inhibit each other more or less and to leave the process of the common term alone distinctly active. Mr. Spencer appears to think that the mere fact that the common term is repeated more often than any one of its associates will, of itself, give it such a degree of intensity that its abstraction must needs ensue.

This has a plausible sound, but breaks down when examined closely. For it is not always the often-repeated character which is first noticed when its concomitants have varied a certain number of times; it is even more likely to be the most novel of all the concomitants, which will arrest the attention. If a boy has seen nothing all his life but sloops and schooners, he will probably never distinctly have singled out in his notion of 'sail' the character of being hung lengthwise. When for the first time he sees a square-rigged ship, the opportunity of extracting the lengthwise mode of hanging as a special accident, and of dissociating it from the general notion of sail, is offered. But there are twenty chances to one that that will not be the form of the boy's consciousness. What he notices will be the new and exceptional character of being hung crosswise. He will go home and speak of that, and perhaps never consciously formulate what the more familiar peculiarity consists in.

This mode of abstraction is realized on a very wide scale, because the elements of the world in which we find ourselves appear, as a matter of fact, here, there, and everywhere, and are changing their concomitants all the while. But on the other hand the abstraction is, so to speak, never complete, the analysis of a compound never perfect, because no element is ever given to us absolutely alone, and we can never therefore approach a compound with the image in our mind of any one of its components in a perfectly pure form. Colors, sounds, smells, are just as much entangled with other matter as are more formal elements of experience, such as extension, intensity, effort, pleasure, difference, likeness, harmony, badness, strength, and even consciousness itself. All are embedded in one world. But by the fluctuations and permutations of which we have spoken, we come to form a pretty good notion of the direction in which each element differs from the rest, and so we frame the notion of it as a terminus, and continue to mean it as an individual thing. In the case of many elements, the simple sensibles, like heat, cold, the colors, smells, etc., the extremes of the directions are almost touched, and in these instances we have a comparatively exact perception of what it is we mean to abstract. But even this is only an approximation; and in literal mathematical strictness all our abstracts must be confessed to be but imperfectly imaginable things. At bottom the process is one of conception, and is everywhere, even in the sphere of simple sensible qualities, the same as that by which we are usually understood to attain to the notions of abstract goodness, perfect felicity, absolute power, and the like; the direct perception of a difference between compounds, and the imaginary prolongation of the direction of the difference to an ideal terminus, the notion of which we fix and keep as one of our permanent subjects of discourse. This is all that I can say usefully about abstraction, or about analysis, to which it leads.

The Improvement of Discrimination by Practice.

In all the cases considered hitherto I have supposed the differences involved to be so large as to be flagrant, and the discrimination, where successive, was treated as involuntary. But, so far from being always involuntary, discriminations are often difficult in the extreme, and by most men never performed. Professor de Morgan, thinking, it is true, rather of conceptual than of perceptive discrimination, wrote, wittily enough:

"The great bulk of the illogical part of the educated community—whether majority or minority I know not; perhaps six of one and half a dozen of the other—have not power to make a distinction, and of course cannot be made to take a distinction, and of course never attempt to shake a distinction. With them all such things are evasions, subterfuges, come-offs, loop-holes, etc. They would hang a man for horse-stealing under a statute against sheep-stealing; and would laugh at you if you quibbled about the distinction between a horse and a sheep."[18]

Any personal or practical interest, however, in the results to be obtained by distinguishing, makes one's wits amazingly sharp to detect differences. The culprit himself is not likely to overlook the difference between a horse and a sheep. And long training and practice in distinguishing has the same effect as personal interest. Both of these agencies give to small amounts of objective difference the same effectiveness upon the mind that, under other circumstances, only large ones would have. Let us seek to penetrate the modus operandi of their influence— beginning with that of practice and habit.

That 'practice makes perfect' is notorious in the field of motor accomplishments. But motor accomplishments depend in part on sensory discrimination. Billiard-playing, rifle-shooting, tight-rope-dancing, demand the most delicate appreciation of minute disparities of sensation, as well as the power to make accurately graduated muscular response thereto. In the purely sensorial field we have the well-known virtuosity displayed by the professional buyers and testers of various kinds of goods. One man will distinguish by taste between the upper and the lower half of a bottle of old Madeira. Another will recognize, by feeling the flour in a barrel, whether the wheat was grown in Iowa or Tennessee. The blind deaf-mute, Laura Bridgman, has so improved her touch as to recognize, after a year's interval, the hand of a person who once has shaken hers; and her sister in misfortune, Julia Brace, is said to have been employed in the Hartford Asylum to sort the linen of its multitudinous inmates, after it came from the wash, by her wonderfully educated sense of smell.

The fact is so familiar that few, if any, psychologists have even recognized it as needing explanation. They have seemed to think that practice must, in the nature of things, improve the delicacy of discernment, and have let the matter rest. At most they have said: "Attention accounts for it; we attend more to habitual things, and what we attend to we perceive more minutely." This answer is true, but too general; it seems to me that we can be a little more precise.

There are at least two distinct causes which we can see at work whenever experience improves discrimination: First, the terms whose difference comes to be felt contract disparate associates and these help to drag them apart. Second, the difference reminds us of larger differences of the same sort, and these help us to notice it.

Let us study the first cause first, and begin by supposing two compounds, of ten elements apiece. Suppose no one element of either compound to differ from the corresponding element of the other compound enough to be distinguished from it if the two are compared alone, and let the amount of this imperceptible difference be called equal to 1. The compounds will differ from each other, however, in ten different ways; and, although each difference by itself might pass unperceived, the total difference, equal to 10, may very well be sufficient to strike the sense. In a word, increasing the number of 'points' involved in a difference may excite our discrimination as effectually as increasing the amount of difference at any one point. Two men whose mouth, nose, eyes, cheeks, chin, and hair, all differ slightly, will be as little confounded by us, as two appearances of the same man one with, and the other without, a false nose. The only contrast in the cases is that we can easily name the point of difference in the one, whilst in the other we cannot.

Two things, then, B and C, indistinguishable when compared together alone, may each contract adhesions with different associates, and the compounds thus formed may, as wholes, be judged very distinct. The effect of practice in increasing discrimination must then, in part, be due to the reinforcing effect, upon an original slight difference between the terms, of additional differences between the diverse associates which they severally affect. Let B and C be the terms: If A contract adhesions with B, and C with D, AB may appear very distinct from CD, though B and C per se might have been almost identical.

To illustrate, how does one learn to distinguish claret from burgundy? Probably they have been drunk on different occasions. When we first drank claret we heard it called by that name, we were eating such and such a dinner, etc. Next time we drink it, a dim reminder of all those things chimes through us as we get the taste of the wine. When we try burgundy our first impression is that it is a kind of claret; but something falls short of full identification, and presently we hear it called burgundy. During the next few experiences, the discrimination may still be uncertain—"which," we ask ourselves, "of the two wines is this present specimen?" But at last the claret-flavor recalls pretty distinctly its own name, 'claret,' "that wine I drank at So-and-so's table," etc.; and the burgundy-flavor recalls the name burgundy and some one else's table. And only when this different SETTING has come to each is our discrimination between the two flavors solid and stable. After a while the tables and other parts of the setting, besides the name, grow so multifarious as not to come up distinctly into consciousness; but pari passu with this, the adhesion of each wine with its own name becomes more and more inveterate, and at last each flavor suggests instantly and certainly its own name and nothing else. The names differ far more than the flavors, and help to stretch these latter farther apart. Some such process as this must go on in all our experience. Beef and mutton, strawberries and raspberries, odor of rose and odor of violet, contract different adhesions which reinforce the differences already felt in the terms.

The reader may say that this has nothing to do with making us feel the difference between the two terms. It is merely fixing, identifying, and so to speak substantializing, the terms. But what we feel as their difference, we should feel, even though we were unable to name or otherwise identify the terms.

To which I reply that I believe that the difference is always concreted and made to seem more substantial by recognizing the terms. I went out for instance the other day and found that the snow just fallen had a very odd look, different from the common appearance of snow. I presently called it a 'micaceous' look; and it seemed to me as if, the moment I did so, the difference grew more distinct and fixed than it was before. The other connotations of the word 'micaceous' dragged the snow farther away from ordinary snow and seemed even to aggravate the peculiar look in question. I think some such effect as this on our way of feeling a difference will be very generally admitted to follow from naming the terms between which it obtains; although I admit myself that it is difficult to show coercively that naming or otherwise identifying any given pair of hardly distinguishable terms is essential to their being felt as different at first.[19]

I offer the explanation only as a partial one: it certainly is not complete. Take the way in which practice refines our local discrimination on the skin, for example. Two compass-points touching the palm of the hand must be kept, say, half an inch asunder in order not to be mistaken for one point. But at the end of an hour or so of practice with them we can distinguish them as two, even when less than a quarter of an inch apart. If the same two regions of the skin were constantly touched, in this experience, the explanation we have been considering would perfectly apply. Suppose a line a b c d e f of points upon the skin. Suppose the local difference of feeling between a and f to be so strong as to be instantly recognized when the points are simultaneously touched, but suppose that between c and d to be at first too small for this purpose. If we began by putting the compasses on a and f and gradually contracted their opening, the strong doubleness recognized at first would still be suggested, as the compass-points approached the positions c and d; for the point e would be so near f, and so like it, as not to be aroused without f also coming to mind. Similarly d would recall e and, more remotely, f. In such wise c - d would no longer be bare c - d, but something more like abc - def, -- palpably differing impressions. But in actual experience the education can take place in a much less methodical way, and we learn at last to discriminate c and d without any constant adhesion being contracted between one of these spots and ab, and the other and ef. Volkmann's experiments show this. He and Fechner, prompted by Czermak's observation that the skin of the blind was twice as discriminative as that of seeing folks, sought by experiment to show the effects of practice upon themselves. They discovered that even within the limits of a single sitting the distances at which points were felt double might fall at the end to considerably less than half of their magnitude at the beginning; and that some, though not all, of this improved sensibility was retained next day. But they also found that exercising one part of the skin in this way improved the discrimination not only of the corresponding part of the opposite side of the body, but of the neighboring parts as well. Thus, at the beginning of an experimental sitting, the compass-points had to be a Paris line asunder, in order to be distinguished by the little-finger-tip. But after exercising the other fingers, it was found that the little-finger-tip could discriminate points only half a line apart.[20] The same relation existed betwixt divers points of the arm and hand.[21]

Here it is clear that the cause which I first suggested fails to apply, and that we must invoke another. What are the exact experimental phenomena? The spots, as such, are not distinctly located, and the difference, as such, between their feelings, is not distinctly felt, until the interval is greater than the minimum required for the mere perception of their doubleness. What we first feel is a bluntness, then a suspicion of doubleness, which presently becomes a distinct doubleness, and at last two different-feeling and differently placed spots with a definite tract of space between them. Some of the places we try give us this latest stage of the perception immediately; some only give us the earliest; and between them are intermediary places. But as soon as the image of the doubleness as it is felt in the more discriminative places gets lodged in our memory, it helps us to find its like in places where otherwise we might have missed it, much as the recent hearing of an 'overtone' helps us to detect the latter in a compound sound (supra, pp. 439-40). A dim doubleness grows clearer by being assimilated to the image of a distincter doubleness felt a moment before. It is interpreted by means of the latter. And so is any difference, like any other sort of impression, more easily perceived when we carry in our mind to meet it a distinct image of what sort of a thing we are to look for, of what its nature is likely to be.[22]

These two processes, the reinforcement of the terms by disparate associates, and the filling of the memory with past differences, of similar direction with the present one, but of more conspicuous amount, are the only explanations I can offer of the effects of education in this line. What is accomplished by both processes is essentially the same thing: they make small differences affect us as if they were large ones—that large differences should affect us as they do remains an inexplicable fact. In principle these two processes ought to be sufficient to account for all possible cases. Whether in fact they are sufficient, whether there be no residual factor which we have failed to detect and analyze out, I will not presume to decide.

Practical Interests Limit Discrimination.

It will be remembered that personal interest was named as a sharpener of discrimination alongside of practice. But personal interest probably acts through attention and not in any immediate or specific way. A distinction in which we have a practical stake in one which we concentrate our minds upon and which we are on the look-out for. We draw it frequently, and we get all the benefits of so doing, benefits which have just been explained. Where, on the other hand, a distinction has no practical interest, where we gain nothing by analyzing a feature from out of the compound total of which it forms a part, we contract a habit of leaving it unnoticed, and at last grow callous to its presence. Helmholtz was the first psychologist who dwelt on these facts as emphatically as they deserve, and I can do no better than quote his very words.

"We are accustomed," he says, "in a large number of cases where sensations of different kinds, or in different parts of the body, exist simultaneously, to recognize that they are distinct as soon as they are perceived, and to direct our attention at will to any one of them separately. Thus at any moment we can be separately conscious of what we see, of what we hear, of what we feel; and distinguish what we feel in a finger or in the great toe, whether pressure, gentle touch, or warmth. So also in the field of vision. Indeed, as I shall endeavor to show in what follows, we readily distinguish our sensations from one another when we have a precise knowledge that they are composite, as, for example, when we have become certain, by frequently repeated and invariable experience, that our present sensation arises from the simultaneous action of many independent stimuli, each of which usually excites an equally well-known individual sensation."

This, it will be observed, is only another statement of our law, that the only individual components which we can pick out of compounds are those of which we have independent knowledge in a separate form.

"This induces us to think that nothing can be easier, when a number of different sensations are simultaneously excited, than to distinguish them individually from each other, and that this is an innate faculty of our minds.

"Thus we find, among other things, that it is quite a matter of course to hear separately the different musical tones which come to our sense collectively; and we expect that in every case when two of them occur together, we shall be able to do the like.

"The matter becomes very different when we set to work to investigate the more unusual cases of perception, and seek more completely to understand the conditions under which the above-mentioned distinction can or cannot be made, as is the case in the physiology of the senses. We then become aware that two different kinds or grades must be distinguished in our becoming conscious of a sensation. The lower grade of this consciousness is that in which the influence of the sensation in question makes itself felt only in the conceptions we form of external things and processes, and assists in determining them. This can take place without our needing, or indeed being able, to ascertain to what particular part of our sensations we owe this or that circumstance in our perceptions. In this case we will say that the impression of the sensation in question is perceived synthetically. The second higher grade is when we immediately distinguish the sensation in question as an existing part of the sum of the sensations excited in us. We will say, then, that the sensation is perceived analytically. The two cases must be carefully distinguished from each other."[23]

By the sensation being perceived synthetically, Helmholtz means that it is not discriminated at all, but only felt in a mass with other simultaneous sensations. That it is felt there he thinks is proved by the fact that our judgment of the total will change if anything occurs to alter the outer cause of the sensation.[24] The following pages from an earlier edition show what the concrete cases of synthetic perception and what those of analytic perception are wont to be:

"In the use of our senses, practice and experience play a much larger part than we ordinarily suppose. Our sensations are in the first instance important only in so far as they enable us to judge rightly of the world about us; and our practice in discriminating between them usually goes only just far enough to meet this end. We are, however, too much disposed to think that we must be immediately conscious of every ingredient of our sensations. This natural prejudice is due to the fact that we are indeed conscious, immediately and without effort, of everything in our sensations which has a bearing upon those practical purposes, for the sake of which we wish to know the outer world. Daily and hourly, during our whole life, we keep our senses in training for this end exclusively, and for its sake our experiences are accumulated. But even within the sphere of these sensations, which do correspond to outer things, training and practice make themselves felt. It is well known how much finer and quicker the painter is in discriminating colors and illuminations than one whose eye is not trained in these matters; how the musician and the musical-instrument maker perceive with ease and certainty differences of pitch and tone which for the ear of the layman do not exist; and how even in the inferior realms of cookery and wine-judging it takes a long habit of comparing to make a master. But more strikingly still is seen the effect of practice when we pass to sensations which depend only on inner conditions of our organs, and which, not corresponding at all to outer things or to their effects upon us, are therefore of no value in giving us information about the outer world. The physiology of the sense-organs has, in recent times, made us acquainted with a number of such phenomena, discovered partly in consequence of theoretic speculations and questionings, partly by individuals, like Goethe and Purkinje, specially endowed by nature with talent for this sort of observation. These so-called subjective phenomena are extraordinarily hard to find; and when they are once found, special aids for the attention are almost always required to observe them. It is usually hard to notice the phenomenon again even when one knows already the description of the first observer. The reason is that we are not only unpractised in singling out these subjective sensations, but that we are, on the contrary, most thoroughly trained in abstracting our attention from them, because they would only hinder us in observing the outer world. Only when their intensity is so strong as actually to hinder us in observing the outer world do we begin to notice them; or they may sometimes, in dreaming and delirium, form the starting point of hallucinations.

"Let me give a few well-known cases, taken from physiological optics, as examples. Every eye probably contains muscœ volitantes, so called; these are fibres, granules, etc., floating in the vitreous humor, throwing their shadows on the retina, and appearing in the field of vision as little dark moving spots. They are most easily detected by looking attentively at a broad, bright, blank surface like the sky. Most persons who have not had their attention expressly called to the existence of these figures are apt to notice them for the first time when some ailment befalls their eyes and attracts their attention to the subjective state of these organs. The usual complaint then is that the muscœ volitantes came in with the malady; and this often makes the patients very anxious about these harmless things, and attentive to all their peculiarities. It is then hard work to make them believe that these figures have existed throughout all their previous life, and that all healthy eyes contain them. I knew an old gentleman who once had occasion to cover one of his eyes which had accidentally become diseased, and who was then in no small degree shocked at finding that his other eye was totally blind; with a sort of blindness, moreover, which must have lasted years, and yet he never was aware of it.

"Who, besides, would believe without performing the appropriate experiments, that when one of his eyes is closed there is a great gap, the so-called 'blind spot,' not far from the middle of the field of the open eye, in which he sees nothing at all, but which he fills out with his imagination? Mariotte, who was led by theoretic speculations to discover this phenomenon, awakened no small surprise when he showed it at the court of Charles II. of England. The experiment was at that time repeated with many variations, and became a fashionable amusement. The gap is, in fact, so large that seven full moons alongside of each other would not cover its diameter, and that a man's face 6 or 7 feet off disappears within it. In our ordinary use of vision this great hole in the field fails utterly to be noticed; because our eyes are constantly wandering, and the moment an object interests us we turn them full upon it. So it follows that the object which at any actual moment excites our attention never happens to fall upon this gap, and thus it is that we never grow conscious of the blind spot in the field. In order to notice it, we must first purposely rivet our gaze upon one object and then move about a second object in the neighborhood of the blind spot, striving meanwhile to attend to this latter without moving the direction of our gaze from the first object. This runs counter to all our habits, and is therefore a difficult thing to accomplish. With some people it is even an impossibility. But only when it is accomplished do we see the second object vanish and convince ourselves of the existence of this gap.

"Finally, let me refer to the double images of ordinary binocular vision. Whenever we look at a point with both eyes, all objects on this side of it or beyond appear double. It takes but a moderate effort of observation to ascertain this fact; and from this we may conclude that we have been seeing the far greater part of the external world double all our lives, although numbers of persons are unaware of it, and are in the highest degree astonished when it is brought to their attention. As a matter of fact, we never have seen in this double fashion any particular object upon which our attention was directed at the time; for upon such objects we always converge both eyes. In the habitual use of our eyes, our attention is always withdrawn from such objects as give us double images at the time; this is the reason why we so seldom learn that these images exist. In order to find them we must set our attention a new and unusual task; we must make it explore the lateral parts of the field of vision, not, as usual, to find what objects are there, but to analyze our sensations. Then only do we notice this phenomenon.[25]

"The same difficulty which is found in the observation of subjective sensations to which no external object corresponds is found also in the analysis of compound sensations which correspond to a single object. Of this sort are many of our sensations of sound. When the sound of a violin, no matter how often we hear it, excites over and over again in our ear the same sum of partial tones, the result is that our feeling of this sum of tones ends by becoming for our mind a mere sign for the voice of the violin. Another combination of partial tones becomes the sensible sign of the voice of a clarionet, etc. And the oftener any such combination is heard, the more accustomed we grow to perceiving it as an integral total, and the harder it becomes to analyze it by immediate observation. I believe that this is one of the principal reasons why the analysis of the notes of the human voice in singing is relatively so difficult. Such fusions of many sensations into what, to conscious perception, seems a simple whole, abound in all our senses.

"Physiological optics affords other interesting examples. The perception of the bodily form of a near object comes about through the combination of two diverse pictures which the eyes severally receive from it, and whose diversity is due to the different position of each eye, altering the perspective view of what is before it. Before the invention of the stereoscope this explanation could only be assumed hypothetically; but it can now be proved at any moment by the use of the instrument. Into the stereoscope we insert two flat drawings, representing the two perspective views of the two eyes, in such a manner that each eye sees its own view in the proper place; and we obtain, in consequence, the perception of a single extended solid, as complete and vivid as if we had the real object before us.

"Now we can, it is true, by shutting one eye after the other and attending to the point, recognize the difference in the pictures—at least when it is not too small. But, for the stereoscopic perception of solidity, pictures suffice whose difference is so extraordinarily slight as hardly to be recognized by the most careful comparison; and it is certain that, in our ordinary careless observing of bodily objects, we never dream that the perception is due to two perspective views fused into one, because it is an entirely different kind of perception from that of either flat perspective view by itself. It is certain, therefore, that two different sensations of our two eyes fuse into a third perception entirely different from either. Just as partial tones fuse into the perception of a certain instrument's voice; and just as we learn to separate the partial tones of a vibrating string by pinching a nodal point and letting them sound in isolation; so we learn to separate the images of the two eyes by opening and closing them alternately.

"There are other much more complex instances of the way in which many sensations may combine to serve as the basis of a quite simple perception. When, for example we perceive an object in a certain direction, we must somehow be impressed by the fact that certain of our optic nerve-fibres, and no others, are impressed by its light. Furthermore, we must rightly judge the position of our eyes in our head, and of our head upon our body, by means of feelings in our eye-muscles and our neck-muscles respectively. If any of these processes is disturbed we get a false perception of the object's position. The nerve-fibers can be changed by a prism before the eye; or the eyeball's position changed by pressing the organ towards one side; and such experiments show that, for the simple seeing of the position of an object, sensations of these two sorts must concur. But it would be quite impossible to gather this directly from the sensible impression which the object makes. Even when we have made experiments and convinced ourselves in every possible manner that such must be the fact, it still remains hidden from our immediate introspective observation.

"These examples" [of synthetic perception,' perception in which each contributory sensation is felt in the whole, and is a co-determinant of what the whole shall be, but does not attract the attention to its separate self] "may suffice to show the vital part which the direction of attention and practice in observing play in sense-perception. To apply this now to the ear. The ordinary task which our ear has to solve when many sounds assail it at once is to discern the voices of the several sounding bodies or instruments engaged; beyond this it has no objective interest in analyzing. We wish to know, when many men are speaking together, what each one says, when many instruments and voices combine, which melody is executed by each. Any deeper analysis, such as that of each separate note into its partial tones (although it might be performed by the same means and faculty of hearing as the first analysis) would tell us nothing new about the sources of sound actually present, but might lead us astray as to their number. For this reason we confine our attention in analyzing a mass of sound to the several instruments' voices, and expressly abstain, as it were, from discriminating the elementary components of the latter. In this last sort of discrimination we are as unpractised as we are, on the contrary, well trained in the former kind."[26]

After all we have said, no comment seems called for upon these interesting and important facts and reflections of Helmholtz.

Reaction-Time After Discrimination.

The time required for discrimination has been made a subject of experimental measurement. Wundt calls it Unterscheidungszeit. His subjects (whose simple reaction-time had previously been determined) were required to make a movement, always the same, the instant they discerned which of two or more signals they received. The exact time of the signal and that of the movement were automatically registered by a galvanic chronoscope. The particular signal to be received was unknown in advance, and the excess of time occupied by those reactions in which its character had first to be discerned, over the simple reaction-time, measured, according to Wundt, the time required for the act of discrimination. It was found longer when four different signals were irregularly used than when only two were used. In the former case it averaged, for three observers respectively (the signals being the sudden appearance of a black or of a white object),

0.050 sec.;
0.047 "
0.079 "

In the latter case, a red and a green signal being added to the former ones, it became, for the same observers,

0.157;
0.073;
0.132.[27]

Later, in Wundt's Laboratory, Herr Tischer made many careful experiments after the same method, where the facts to be discriminated were the different degrees of loudness in the sound which served as a signal. I subjoin Herr Tischer's table of results, explaining that each vertical column after the first gives the average results obtained from a distinct individual, and that the figure in the first column stands for the number of possible loudnesses that might be expected in the particular series of reactions made. The times are expressed in thousandths of a second.[28]

2	6	8.5	10.75	10.7	33	53
3	10	14.4	19.9	22.7	58.5	57.
4	16.7	20.8	29	29.1	75	84
5	25.6	31	....	40.1	95.5	138

The interesting points here are the great individual variations, and the rapid way in which the time for discrimination increases with the number of possible terms to discriminate. The individual variations are largely due to want of practice in the particular task set, but partly also to discrepancies in the psychic process. One gentleman said, for example, that in the experiments with three sounds, he kept the image of the middle one ready in his mind, and compared what he heard as either louder, lower, or the same. His discrimination among three possibilities became thus very similar to a discrimination between two.[29]

Mr. J. M. Cattell found he could get no results by this method,[30] and reverted to one used by observers previous to Wundt and which Wundt had rejected. This is the einfache Wahlmethode, as Wundt calls it. The reacter awaits the signal and reacts if it is of one sort, but omits to act if it is of another sort. The reaction thus occurs after discrimination; the motor impulse cannot be sent to the hand until the subject knows what the signal is. The nervous impulse, as Mr. Cattell says, must probably travel to the cortex and excite changes there, causing in consciousness the perception of the signal. These changes occupy the time of discrimination (or perception-time, as it is called by Mr. C.) But then a nervous impulse must descend from the cortex to the lower motor centre which stands primed and ready to discharge; and this, as Mr. C. says, gives a will-time as well. The total reaction-time thus includes both 'will-time' and 'discrimination-time.' But as the centrifugal and centripetal processes occupying these two times respectively are probably about the same, and the time used in the cortex is about equally divided between the perception of the signal and the preparation of the motor discharge, if we divide it equally between perception (discrimination) and volition, the error cannot be great.[31] We can moreover change the nature of the perception without altering the will-time, and thus investigate with considerable thoroughness the length of the perception-time.

Guided by these principles, Prof. Cattell found the time required for distinguishing a white signal from no signal to be, in two observers:

0.030 sec. and 0.050 sec.;
that for distinguishing one color from another was similarly:
0.100 and .110;
that for distinguishing a certain color from ten other colors:
0.105 and 0.117;
that for distinguishing the letter A in ordinary print from the letter Z:
0.142 and 0.137;
that for distinguishing a given letter from all the rest of the alphabet (not reacting until that letter appeared)
0.119 and 0.116;
that for distinguishing a word from any of twenty-five other words, from
0.118 sec. to 0.158 sec.
The difference depending on the length of the words and the familiarity of the language to which they belonged. Prof. Cattell calls attention to the fact that the time for distinguishing a word is often but little more than that for distinguishing a letter:
"We do not, therefore, distinguish separately the letters of which a word is composed, but the word as a whole. The application of this in teaching children to read is evident."
He also finds a great difference in the time with which various letters are distinguished, E being particularly bad.[32] I have, in describing these experiments, followed the example of previous writers and spoken as if the process by which the nature of the signal determines the reaction were identical with the ordinary conscious process of discriminative perception and volition. I am convinced, however, that this is not the case; and that although the results are the same, the form of consciousness is quite different. The reader will remember my contention (supra, p. 90 ff.) that the simple reaction-time (usually supposed to include a conscious process of perceiving) really measures nothing but a reflex act. Anyone who will perform reactions with discrimination will easily convince himself that the process here also is far more like a reflex, than like a deliberate, operation. I have made, with myself and students, a large number of measurements where the signal expected was in one series a touch somewhere on the skin of the back and head, and in another series a spark somewhere in the field of view. The hand had to move as quickly as possible towards the place of the touch or the spark. It did so infallibly, and sensibly instantly; whilst both place and movement seemed to be perceived only a moment later, in memory. These experiments were undertaken for the express purpose of ascertaining whether the movement at the sight of the spark was discharged immediately by the visual perception, or whether a 'motor-idea' had to intervene between the perception of the spark and the reaction.[33] The first thing that was manifest to introspection was that no perception or idea of any sort preceded the reaction. It jumped of itself, whenever the signal came; and perception was retrospective. We must suppose, then, that the state of eager expectancy of a certain definite range of possible discharges, innervates a whole set of paths in advance, so that when a particular sensation comes it is drafted into its appropriate motor outlet too quickly for the perspective process to be aroused. In the experiments I describe, the conditions were most favorable for rapidity, for the connection between the signals and their movements might almost be called innate. It is instinctive to move the hand towards a thing seen or a skin-spot touched. But where the movement is conventionally attached to the signal, there would be more chance for delay, and the amount of practice would then determine the speed. This is well shown in Tischer's results, quoted on p. 524, where the most practised observer, Tischer himself, reacted in one eighth of the time needed by one of the others.[34] But what all investigators have aimed to determine in these experiments is the minimum time. I trust I have said enough to convince the student that this minimum time by no means measures what we consciously know as discrimination. It only measures something which, under the experimental conditions, leads to a similar result. But it is the bane of psychology to suppose that where results are similar, processes must be the same. Psychologists are too apt to reason as geometers would, if the latter were to say that the diameter of a circle is the same thing as its semi-circumference, because, forsooth, they terminate in the same two points.[35]

The Perception of Likeness.

The perception of likeness is practically very much bound up with that of difference. That is to say, the only differences we note as differences, and estimate quantitatively, and arrange along a scale, are those comparatively limited differences which we find between members of a common genus. The force of gravity and the color of this ink are things it never occurred to me to compare until now that I am casting about for examples of the incomparable. Similarly the elastic quality of this india-rubber band, the comfort of last night's sleep, the good that can be done with a legacy, these are things too discrepant to have ever been compared ere now. Their relation to each other is less that of difference than of mere logical negativity. To be found different, things must as a rule have some commensurability, some aspect in common, which suggests the possibility of their being treated in the same way. This is of course not a theoretic necessity—for any distinction may be called a 'difference,' if one likes—but a practical and linguistic remark.

The same things, then, which arouse the perception of difference usually arouse that of resemblance also. And the analysis of them, so as to define wherein the difference and wherein the resemblance respectively consists, is called comparison. If we start to deal with the things as simply the same or alike, we are liable to be surprised by the difference. If we start to treat them as merely different, we are apt to discover how much they are alike. Difference, commonly so called, is thus between species of a genus. And the faculty by which we perceive the resemblance upon which the genus is based, is just as ultimate and inexplicable a mental endowment as that by which we perceive the differences upon which the species depend. There is a shock of likeness when we pass from one thing to another which in the first instance we merely discriminate numerically, but, at the moment of bringing our attention to bear, perceive to be similar to the first; just as there is a shock of difference when we pass between two dissimilars.[36] The objective extent of the likeness, just like that of the difference, determines the magnitude of the shock. The likeness may be so evanescent, or the basis of it so habitual and little liable to be attended to, that it will escape observation altogether. Where, however, we find it, there we make a genus of the things compared; and their discrepancies and incommensurabilities in other respects can then figure as the differentiæ of so many species. As 'thinkables' or 'existents' even the smoke of a cigarette and the worth of a dollar-bill are comparable—still more so as 'perishables,' or as 'enjoyables.'

Much, then, of what I have said of difference in the course of this chapter will apply, with a simple change of language, to resemblance as well. We go through the world, carrying on the two functions abreast, discovering differences in the like, and likenesses in the different. To abstract the ground of either difference or likeness (where it is not ultimate) demands and analysis of the given objects into their parts. So that all that was said of the dependence of analysis upon a preliminary separate acquaintance with the character to be abstracted, and upon its having varied concomitants, finds a place in the psychology of resemblance as well as in that of difference.

But when all is said and done about the conditions which favor our perception of resemblance and our abstraction of its ground, the crude fact remains, that some people are far more sensitive to resemblances, and far more ready to point out wherein they consist, than others are. They are the wits, the poets, the inventors, the scientific men, the practical geniuses. A native talent for perceiving analogies is reckoned by Prof. Bain, and by others before and after him, as the leading fact in genius of every order. But as this chapter is already long, and as the question of genius had better wait till Chapter XXII, where its practical consequences can be discussed at the same time, I will say nothing more at present either about it or about the faculty of noting resemblances. If the reader feels that this faculty is having small justice done it at my hands, and that it ought to be wondered at and made much more of than has been done in these last few pages, he will perhaps find some compensation when that later chapter is reached. I think I emphasize it enough when I call it one of the ultimate foundation-pillars of the intellectual life, the others being Discrimination, Retentiveness, and Association.

The Magnitude of Differences.

Earlier I spoke of differences being greater or less, and of certain groups of them being susceptible of a linear arrangement exhibiting serial increase. A series whose terms grow more and more different from the starting point is one whose terms grow less and less like it. They grow more and more like it if you read them the other way. So that likeness and unlikeness to the starting point are functions inverse to each other, of the position of any term in such a series.

Professor Stumpf introduces the word distance to denote the position of a term in any such series. The less like is the term, the more distant it is from the starting point. The ideally regular series of this sort would be one in which the distances—the steps of resemblance or difference—between all pairs of adjacent terms were equal. This would be an evenly gradated series. And it is an interesting fact in psychology that we are able, in many departments of our sensibility, to arrange the terms without difficulty in this evenly gradated way. Differences, in other words, between diverse pairs of terms, a and b, for example, on the one hand, and c and d on the other,[37] can be judged equal or diverse in amount. The distances from one term to another in the series are equal. Linear magnitudes and musical notes are perhaps the impressions which we easiest arrange in this way. Next come shades of light or color, which we have little difficulty in arranging by steps of difference of sensibly equal value. Messrs. Plateau and Delbœuf have found it fairly easy to determine what shade of gray will be judged by every one to hit the exact middle between a darker and a lighter shade.[38]

How now do we so readily recognize the equality of two differences between different pairs of terms? or, more briefly, how do we recognize the magnitude of a difference at all? Prof. Stumpf discusses this question in an interesting way;[39] and comes to the conclusion that our feeling for the size of a difference, and our perception that the terms of two diverse pairs are equally or unequally distant from each other, can be explained by no simpler mental process, but, like the shock of difference itself, must be regarded as for the present an unanalyzable endowment of the mind. This acute author rejects in particular the notion which would make our judgment of the distance between two sensations depend upon our mentally traversing the intermediary steps. We may of course do so, and may often find it useful to do so, as in musical intervals, or figured lines. But we need not do so; and nothing more is really required for a comparative judgment of the amount of a 'distance' than three or four impressions belonging to a common kind.

The vanishing of all perceptible difference between two numerically distinct things makes them qualitatively the same or equal. Equality, or qualitative (as distinguished from numerical) identity, is thus nothing but the extreme degree of likeness.[40]

We saw above that some persons consider that the difference between two objects is constituted of two things, viz., their absolute identity in certain respects, plus their absolute non-identity in others. We saw that this theory would not apply to all cases. So here any theory which would base likeness on identity, and not rather identity on likeness, must fail. It is supposed perhaps, by most people, that two resembling things owe their resemblance to their absolute identity in respect of some attribute or attributes, combined with the absolute non-identity of the rest of their being. This, which may be true of compound things, breaks down when we come to simple impressions. "When we compare a deep, middle, and a high note, e.g., C, f sharp, a'", we remark immediately that the first is less like the third than the second is. The same would be true of c d e in the same region of the scale. Our very calling one of the notes a 'middle' note is the expression of a judgment of this sort. But where here is the identical and where the non-identical part? We cannot think of the overtones; for the first-named three notes have none in common, at least not on musical instruments. Moreover, we might take simple tones, and still our judgment would be unhesitatingly the same, provided the tones were not chosen too close together.... Neither can it be said that the identity consists in their all being sounds, and not a sound, a smell, and a color, respectively. For this identical attribute comes to each of them in equal measure, whereas the first, being less like the third than the second is, ought, on the terms of the theory we are criticising, to have less of the identical quality.... It thus appears impracticable to define all possible cases of likeness as partial identity plus partial disparity; and it is vain to seek in all cases for identical elements."[41]

And as all compound resemblances are based on simple ones like these, it follows that likeness überhaupt must not be conceived as a special complication of identity, but rather that identity must be conceived as a special degree of likeness, according to the proposition expressed at the outset of the paragraph that precedes. Likeness and difference are ultimate relations perceived. As a matter of fact, no two sensations, no two objects of all those we know, are in scientific rigor identical. We call those of them identical whose difference is unperceived. Over and above this we have a conception of absolute sameness, it is true, but this, like so many of our conceptions (cf. p. 508), is an ideal construction got by following a certain direction of serial increase to its maximum supposable extreme. It plays an important part, among other permanent meanings possessed by us, in our ideal intellectual constructions. But it plays no part whatever in explaining psychologically how we perceive likenesses between simple things.

The Measure of Discriminative Sensibility.

In 1860, Professor G. T. Fechner of Leipzig, a man of great learning and subtlety of mind, published two volumes entitled 'Psychophysik,' devoted to establishing and explaining a law called by him the psychophysic law, which he considered to express the deepest and most elementary relation between the mental and the physical worlds. It is a formula for the connection between the amount of our sensations and the amount of their outward causes. Its simplest expression is, that when we pass from one sensation to a stronger one of the same kind, the sensations increase proportionally to the logarithms of their exciting causes. Fechner's book was the starting point of a new department of literature, which it would be perhaps impossible to match for the qualities of thoroughness and subtlety, but of which, in the humble opinion of the present writer, the proper psychological outcome is just nothing. The psychophysic law controversy has prompted a good many series of observations on sense-discrimination, and has made discussion of them very rigorous. It has also cleared up our ideas about the best methods for getting average results, when particular observations vary; and beyond this it has done nothing; but as it is a chapter in the history of our science, some account of it is here due to the reader.

Fechner's train of thought has been popularly expounded a great many times. As I have nothing new to add, it is but just that I should quote an existing account. I choose the one given by Wundt in his Vorlesungen über Menschen und Thierseele, 1863, omitting a good deal:

"How much stronger or weaker one sensation is than another, we are never able to say. Whether the sun be a hundred or a thousand times brighter than the moon, a cannon a hundred or a thousand times louder than a pistol, is beyond our power to estimate. The natural measure of sensation which we possess enables us to judge of the equality, of the 'more' and of the 'less,' but not of 'how many times more or less.' This natural measure is, therefore, as good as no measure at all, whenever it becomes a question of accurately ascertaining intensities in the sensational sphere. Even though it may teach us in a general way that with the strength of the outward physical stimulus the strength of the concomitant sensation waxes or wanes, still it leaves us without the slightest knowledge of whether the sensation varies in exactly the same proportion as the stimulus itself, or at a slower or a more rapid rate. In a word, we know by our natural sensibility nothing of the law that connects the sensation and its outward cause together. To find this law we must first find an exact measure for the sensation itself; we must be able to say: A stimulus of strength one begets a sensation of strength one; a stimulus of strength two begets a sensation of strength two, or three, or four, etc. But to do this we must first know what a sensation two, three, or four times greater than another, signifies. . . .

"Space magnitudes we soon learn to determine exactly, because we only measure one space against another. The measure of mental magnitudes is far more difficult. . . . But the problem of measuring the magnitude of sensations is the first step in the bold enterprise of making mental magnitudes altogether subject to exact measurement. . . . Were our whole knowledge limited to the fact that the sensation rises when the stimulus rises, and falls when the latter falls, much would not be gained. But even immediate unaided observation teaches us certain facts which, at least in a general way, suggest the law according to which the sensations vary with their outward cause.

"Every one knows that in the stilly night we hear things unnoticed in the noise of day. The gentle ticking of the clock, the air circulating through the chimney, the cracking of the chairs in the room, and a thousand other slight noises, impress themselves upon our ear. It is equally well known that in the confused hubbub of the streets, or the clamor of a railway, we may lose not only what our neighbor says to us, but even not hear the sound of our own voice. The stars which are brightest at night are invisible by day; and although we see the moon then, she is far paler than at night. Everyone who has had to deal with weights knows that if to a pound in the hand a second pound be added, the difference is immediately felt; whilst if it be added to a hundredweight, we are not aware of the differences at all. . . .

"The sound of the clock, the light of the stars, the pressure of the pound, these are all stimuli to our senses, and stimuli whose outward amount remains the same. What then do these experiences teach? Evidently nothing but this, that one and the same stimulus, according to the circumstances under which it operates, will be felt either more or less intensely, or not felt at all. Of what sort now is the alteration in the circumstances, upon which this alteration in the feeling may depend? On considering the matter closely we see that it is everywhere of one and the same kind. The tick of the clock is a feeble stimulus for our auditory nerve, which we hear plainly when it is alone, but not when it is added to the strong stimulus of the carriage-wheels and other noises of the day. The light of the stars is a stimulus to the eye. But if the stimulation which this light exerts be added to the strong stimulus of daylight, we feel nothing of it, although we feel it distinctly when it unites itself with the feebler stimulation of the twilight. The pound-weight is a stimulus to our skin, which we feel when it joins itself to a preceding stimulus of equal strength, but which vanishes when it is combined with a stimulus a thousand times greater in amount.

"We may therefore lay it down as a general rule that a stimulus, in order to be felt, may be so much the smaller if the already pre-existing stimulation of the organ is small, but must be so much the larger, the greater the pre-existing stimulation is. From this in a general way we can perceive the connection between the stimulus and the feeling it excites. At least thus much appears, that the law of dependence is not as simple a one as might have been expected beforehand. The simplest relation would obviously be that the sensation should increase in identically the same ratio as the stimulus, thus that if a stimulus of strength one occasioned a sensation one, a stimulus of two should occasion sensation two, stimulus three, sensation three, etc. But if this simplest of all relations prevailed, a stimulus added to a pre-existing strong stimulus ought to provoke as great an increase of feeling as if it were added to a pre-existing weak stimulus; the light of the stars e.g., ought to make as great an addition to the daylight as it does to the darkness of the nocturnal sky. This we know not to be the case: the stars are invisible by day, the addition they make to our sensation then is unnoticeable, whereas the same addition to our feeling of the twilight is very considerable indeed. So it is clear that the strength of the sensations does not increase in proportion to the amount of the stimuli, but more slowly. And now comes the question, in what proportion does the increase of the sensation grow less as the increase of the stimulus grows greater. To answer this question, every-day experiences do not suffice. We need exact measurements both of the amounts of the various stimuli, and of the intensity of the sensations themselves.

"How to execute these measurements, however, is something which daily experience suggests. To measure the strength of sensations is, as we saw, impossible; we can only measure the difference of sensations. Experience showed us what very unequal differences of sensation might come from equal differences of outward stimulus. But all these experiences expressed themselves in one kind of fact, that the same difference of stimulus could in one case be felt, and in another case not felt at all—a pound felt if added to another pound, but not if added to a hundred-weight. . . . We can quickest reach a result with our observations if we start with an arbitrary strength of stimulus, notice what sensation it gives us, and then see how much we can increase the stimulus without making the sensation seem to change. If we carry out such observations with stimuli of varying absolute amounts, we shall be forced to choose in an equally varying way the amounts of addition to the stimulus which are capable of giving us a just barely perceptible feeling of more. A light, to be just perceptible in the twilight need not be near as bright as the starlight; it must be far brighter to be just perceived during the day. If now we institute such observations for all possible strengths of the various stimuli, and note for each strength the amount of addition of the latter required to produce a barely perceptible alteration of sensation, we shall have a series of figures in which is immediately expressed the law according to which the sensation alters when the stimulation is increased...."

Observations according to this method are particularly easy to make in the spheres of light-, sound-, and pressure-sensation.... Beginning with the latter case,

"We find a surprisingly simple result. The barely sensible addition to the original weight must stand exactly in the same proportion to it, be the same fraction of it, no matter what the absolute value may be of the weights on which the experiment is made.... As the average of a number of experiments, this fraction is found to be about 1/3; that is, no matter what pressure there may already be made upon the skin, an increase or a diminution of the pressure will be felt, as soon as the added or subtracted weight amounts to one third of the weight originally there."

Wundt then describes how differences may be observed in the muscular feelings, in the feelings of heat, in those of light, and in those of sound; and he concludes his seventh lecture (from which our extracts have been made) thus:

"So we have found that all the senses whose stimuli we are enabled to measure accurately, obey a uniform law. However various may be their several delicacies of discrimination, this holds true of all, that the increase of the stimulus necessary to produce an increase of the sensation bears a constant ratio to the total stimulus. The figures which express this ratio in the several senses may be shown thus in tabular form:

$$
\begin{array}{ll}
\text{Sensation of light,} & \frac{1}{100} \\
\text{Muscular sensation,} & \frac{1}{17} \\
\left.\begin{array}{l}\text{Feeling of pressure,} \\ \text{`` `` warmth,} \\ \text{`` `` sound,}\end{array}\right\} & \frac{1}{3}
\end{array}
$$

"These figures are far from giving as accurate a measure as might be desired. But at least they are fit to convey a general notion of the relative discriminative susceptibility of the different senses.... The important law which gives in so simple a form the relation of the sensation to the stimulus that calls it forth was first discovered by the physiologist Ernst Heinrich Weber to obtain in special cases. Gustav Theodor Fechner first proved it to be a law for all departments of sensation. Psychology owes to him the first comprehensive investigation of sensations from a physical point of view, the first basis of an exact Theory of Sensibility."

So much for a general account of what Fechner calls Weber's law. The 'exactness' of the theory of sensibility to which it leads consists in the supposed fact that it gives the means of representing sensations by numbers. The unit of any kind of sensation will be that increment which, when the stimulus is increased, we can just barely perceive to be added. The total number of units which any given sensation contains will consist of the total number of such increments which may be perceived in passing from no sensation of the kind to a sensation of the present amount. We cannot get at this number directly, but we can, now that we know Weber's law, get at it by means of the physical stimulus of which it is a function. For if we know how much of the stimulus it will take to give a barely perceptible sensation, and then what percentage of addition to the stimulus will constantly give a barely perceptible increment to the sensation, it is at bottom only a question of compound interest to compute, out of the total amount of stimulus which we may be employing at any moment, the number of such increments, or, in other words, of sensational units to which it may give rise. This number bears the same relation to the total stimulus which the time elapsed bears to the capital plus the compound interest accrued.

To take an example: If stimulus A just falls short of producing a sensation, and if r be the percentage of itself which must be added to it to get a sensation which is barely perceptible—call this sensation 1 -- then we should have the series of sensation-numbers corresponding to their several stimuli as follows:

Sensation 0 = stimulus A;
    " 1 =   "   A (1 + r);
    " 2 =   "   A (1 + r)2;
    " 3 =   "   A (1 + r)3;
....
    " n =   "   A (1 + r)n.

The sensations here form an arithmetical series, and the stimuli a geometrical series, and the two series correspond term for term. Now, of two series corresponding in this way, the terms of the arithmetical one are called the logarithms of the terms corresponding in rank to them in the geometrical series. A conventional arithmetical series beginning with zero has been formed in the ordinary logarithmic tables, so that we may truly say (assuming our facts to be correct so far) that the sensations vary in the same proportion as the logarithms of their respective stimuli. And we can thereupon proceed to compute the number of units in any given sensation (considering the unit of sensation to be equal to the just perceptible increment above zero, and the unit of stimulus to be equal to the increment of stimulus r, which brings this about) by multiplying the logarithm of the stimulus by a constant factor which must vary with the particular kind of sensation in question. If we call the stimulus R, and the constant factor C, we get the formula:

$$S = C \log R,$$

which is what Fechner calls the psychophysischer Maasformel. This, in brief, is Fechner's reasoning, as I understand it.

The Maasformel admits of mathematical development in various directions, and has given rise to arduous discussions into which I am glad to be exempted from entering here, since their interest is mathematical and metaphysical and not primarily psychological at all.[42] I must say a word about them metaphysically a few pages later on. Meanwhile it should be understood that no human being, in any investigation into which sensations entered, has ever used the numbers computed in this or any other way in order to test a theory or to reach a new result. The whole notion of measuring sensations numerically, remains in short a mere mathematical speculation about possibilities, which has never been applied to practice. Incidentally to the discussion of it, however, a great many particular facts have been discovered about discrimination which merit a place in this chapter.

In the first place it is found, when the difference of two sensations approaches the limit of discernibility, that at one moment we discern it and at the next we do not. There are accidental fluctuations in our inner sensibility which make it impossible to tell just what the least discernable increment of the sensation is without taking the average of a large number of appreciations. These accidental errors are as likely to increase as to diminish our sensibility, and are eliminated in such an average, for those above and those below the line then neutralize each other in the sum, and the normal sensibility, if there be one (that is, the sensibility due to constant causes as distinguished from these accidental ones), stands revealed. The best way of getting at the average sensibility has been very minutely worked over. Fechner discussed three methods, as follows:

(1)   The Method of just-discernible Differences. Take a standard sensation S, and add to it until you distinctly feel the addition d; then subtract from S + d until you distinctly feel the effect of the subtraction;[43] call the difference here d'. The least discernible difference sought is d + d' / 2; and the ratio of this quantity to the original S (or rather to S + d - d') is what Fechner calls the difference-threshold. This difference-threshold should be a constant fraction (no matter what is the size of S) if Weber's law holds universally true. The difficulty in applying this method is that we are so often in doubt whether anything has been added to S or not. Furthermore, if we simply take the smallest d about which we are never in doubt or in error, we certainly get our least discernible difference larger than it ought theoretically to be.[44]

Of course the sensibility is small when the least discernible is large, and vice versâ; in other words, it and the difference-threshold are inversely related to each other.

(2)   The Method of True and False Cases. A sensation which is barely greater than another will, on account of accidental errors in a long series of experiments, sometimes be judged equal, and sometimes smaller; i.e., we shall make a certain number of false and a certain number of true judgments about the difference between the two sensations which we are comparing.

"But the larger this difference is, the more the number of the true judgments will increase at the expense of the false ones; or, otherwise expressed, the nearer to unity will be the fraction whose denominator represents the whole number of judgments, and whose numerator represents those which are true. If m is a ratio of this nature, obtained by comparison of two stimuli, A and B, we may seek another couple of stimuli, a and b, which when compared will give the same ratio of true to false cases."[45]

If this were done, and the ratio of a to b then proved to be equal to that of A to B, that would prove that pairs of small stimuli and pairs of large stimuli may affect our discriminative sensibility similarly so long as the ratio of the components to each other within each pair is the same. In other words, it would in so forth prove the Weberian law. Fechner made use of this method to ascertain his own power of discriminating differences of weight, recording no less than 24, 576 separate judgments, and computing as a result that his discrimination for the same relative increase of weight was less good in the neighborhood of 500 than of 300 grams, but that after 500 grams it improved up to 3000, which was the highest weight he experimented with.

(3)   The Method of Average Errors consists in taking a standard stimulus and then trying to make another one of the same sort exactly equal to it. There will in general be an error whose amount is large when the discriminative

sensibility called in play is small, and vice versâ. The sum of the errors, no matter whether they be positive or negative, divided by their number, gives the average error. This, when certain corrections are made, is assumed by Fechner to be the 'reciprocal' of the discriminative sensibility in question. It should bear a constant proportion to the stimulus, no matter what the absolute size of the latter may be, if Weber's law hold true.

These methods deal with just perceptible differences. Delboeuf and Wundt have experimented with larger differences by means of what Wundt calls the Methode der mittleren Abstufungen, and what we may call

(4) The Method of Equal-appearing Intervals. This consists in so arranging three stimuli in a series that the intervals between the first and the second shall appear equal to that between the second and the third. At first sight there seems to be no direct logical connection between this method and the preceding ones. By them we compare equally perceptible increments of stimulus in different regions of the latter's scale; but by the fourth method we compare increments which strike us as equally big. But what we can but just notice as an increment need not appear always of the same bigness after it is noticed. On the contrary, it will appear much bigger when we are dealing with stimuli that are already large.

(5) The method of doubling the stimulus has been employed by Wundt's collaborator, Merkel, who tried to make one stimulus seem just double the other, and then measured the objective relation of the two. The remarks just made apply also to this case.

So much for the methods. The results differ in the hands of different observers. I will add a few of them, and will take first the discriminative sensibility to light.

By the first method, Volkmann, Aubert, Masson, Helmholtz, and Kräpelin find figures varying from 1/3 or ¼ to 1/195 of the original stimulus. The smaller fractional increments are discriminated when the light is already fairly strong, the larger ones when it is weak or intense. That is, the discriminative sensibility is low when weak or overstrong lights are compared, and at its best with a certain medium illumination. It is thus a function of the light's intensity; but throughout a certain range of the latter it keeps constant, and in so far forth Weber's law is verified for light. Absolute figures cannot be given, but Merkel, by method 1, found that Weber's law held good for stimuli (measured by his arbitrary unit) between 96 and 4096, beyond which intensity no experiments were made.[46] König and Brodhun have given measurements by method 1 which cover the most extensive series, and moreover apply to six different colors of light. These experiments (performed in Helmholtz's laboratory, apparently,) ran from an intensity called 1 to one which was 100,000 times as great. From intensity 2000 to 20,000 Weber's law held good; below and above this range discriminative sensibility declined. The increment discriminated here was the same for all colors of light, and lay (according to the tables) between 1 and 2 per cent of the stimulus.[47] Delbœuf had verified Weber's law for a certain range of luminous intensities by method 4; that is, he had found that the objective intensity of a light which appeared midway between two others was really the geometrical mean of the latter's intensities. But A. Lehmann and afterwards Neiglick, in Wundt's laboratory, found that effects of contrast played so large a part in experiments performed in this way that Delbœuf's results could not be held conclusive. Merkel, repeating the experiments still later, found that the objective intensity of the light which we judge to stand midway between two others stands neither midway nor is a geometric mean. The discrepancy from both figures is enormous, but is least large from the midway figure or arithmetical mean of the two extreme intensities.[48] Finally, the stars have from time immemorial been arranged in 'magnitudes' supposed to differ by equal-seeming intervals. Lately their intensities have been gauged photometrically, and the comparison of the subjective with the objective series has been made. Prof. J. Jastrow is the latest worker in this field. He finds, taking Pickering's Harvard photometric tables as a basis, that the ratio of the average intensity of each 'magnitude' to that below it decreases as we pass from lower to higher magnitudes, showing a uniform departure from Weber's law, if the method of equal-appearing intervals be held to have any direct relevance to the latter.[49]

Sounds are less delicately discriminated in intensity than lights. A certain difficulty has come from disputes as to the measurement of the objective intensity of the stimulus. Earlier inquiries made the perceptible increase of the stimulus to be about 1/3 of the latter. Merkel's latest results of the method of just perceptible differences make it about 3/10 for that part of the scale of intensities during which Weber's law holds good, which is from 20 to 5000 of M.'s arbitrary unit.[50] Below this the fractional increment must be larger. Above it no measurements were made.

For pressure and muscular sense we have rather divergent results. Weber found by the method of just-perceptible differences that persons could distinguish an increase of weight of 1/40 when the two weights were successively lifted by the same hand. It took a much larger fraction to be discerned when the weights were laid on a hand which rested on the table. He seems to have verified his results for only two pairs of differing weights,[51] and on this founded his 'law.' Experiments in Hering's laboratory on lifting 11 weights, running from 250 to 2750 grams showed that the least perceptible increment varied from 1/21 for 250 grams to 1/114 for 2500. For 2750 it rose to 1/98 again. Merkel's recent and very careful experiments, in which the finger pressed down the beam of a balance counterweighted by from 25 to 8020 grams, showed that between 200 and 2000 grams a constant fractional increase of about 1/13 was felt when there was no movement of the finger, and of about 1/19 when there was movement. Above and below these limits the discriminative power grew less. It was greater when the pressure was upon one square millimeter of surface than when it was upon seven.[52]

Warmth and taste have been made the subject of similar investigations with the result of verifying something like Weber's law. The determination of the unit of stimulus is, however, so hard here that I will give no figures. The results may be found in Wundt's Physiologische Psychologie, 3d Ed. I. 370-2.

The discrimination of lengths by the eye has been found also to obey to a certain extent Weber's law. The figures will all be found in G. E. Müller, op. cit., part II, chap. X, to which the reader is referred. Professor Jastrow has published some experiments, made by what may be called a modification of the method of equal-appearing differences, on our estimation of the length of sticks, by which it would seem that the estimated intervals and the real ones are directly and not logarithmically proportionate to each other. This resembles Merkel's results by that method for weights, lights, and sounds, and differs from Jastrow's own finding about star-magnitudes.[53]

If we look back over these facts as a whole, we see that it is not any fixed amount added to an impression that makes us notice an increase in the latter, but that the amount depends on how large the impression already is. The amount is expressible as a certain fraction of the entire impression to which it is added; and it is found that the fraction is a well-nigh constant figure throughout an entire region of the scale of intensities of the impression in question. Above and below this region the fraction increases in value. This is Weber's law, which in so far forth expresses an empirical generalization of practical importance, without involving any theory whatever or seeking any absolute measure of the sensations themselves. It is in the...

Theoretic Interpretation of Weber's Law

...that Fechner's originality exclusively consists, in his assumptions, namely, 1) that the just-perceptible increment is the sensation-unit, and is in all parts of the scale the same (mathematically expressed, $Ds = const.$); 2) that all our sensations consist of sums of these units; and finally, 3) that the reason why it takes a constant fractional increase of the stimulus to awaken this unit lies in an ultimate law of the connection of mind with matter, whereby the quantities of our feelings are related logarithmically to the quantities of their objects. Fechner seems to find something inscrutably sublime in the existence of an ultimate 'psychophysic' law of this form.

These assumptions are all peculiarly fragile. To begin with, the mental fact which in the experiments corresponds to the increase of the stimulus is not an enlarged sensation, but a judgment that the sensation is enlarged. What Fechner calls the 'sensation' is what appears to the mind as the objective phenomenon of light, warmth, weight, sound, impressed part of the body, etc. Fechner tacitly if not openly assumes that such a judgment of increase consists in the simple fact that an increased number of sensation-units are present to the mind; and that the judgment is thus itself a quantitatively bigger mental thing when it judges large differences, or differences between large terms, than when it judges small ones. But these ideas are really absurd. The hardest sort of judgment, the judgment which strains the attention most (if that be any criterion of the judgment's 'size'), is that about the smallest things and differences. But really it has no meaning to talk about one judgment being bigger than another. And even if we leave out judgments and talk of sensations only, we have already found ourselves (in Chapter VI) quite unable to read any clear meaning into the notion that they are masses of units combined. To introspection, our feeling of pink is surely not a portion of our feeling of scarlet; nor does the light of an electric arc seem to contain that of a tallow-candle in itself. Compound things contain parts; and one such thing may have twice or three times as many parts as another. But when we take a simple sensible quality like light or sound, and say that there is now twice or thrice as much of it present as there was a moment ago, although we seem to mean the same thing as if we are talking of compound objects, we really mean something different. We mean that if we were to arrange the various possible degrees of the quality in a scale of serial increase, the distance, interval, or difference between the stronger and the weaker specimen before us would seem about as great as that between the weaker one and the beginning of the scale. It is these RELATIONS, these DISTANCES, which we are measuring and not the composition of the qualities themselves, as Fechner thinks. Whilst if we turn to objects which are divisible, surely a big object may be known in a little thought. Introspection shows moreover that in most sensations a new kind of feeling invariably accompanies our judgment of an increased impression; and that is a fact which Fechner's formula disregards.[54]

But apart from these a priori difficulties, and even supposing that sensations did consist of added units, Fechner's assumption that all equally perceptible additions are equally great additions is entirely arbitrary. Why might not a small addition to a small sensation be as perceptible as a large addition to a large one? In this case Weber's law would apply not to the additions themselves, but only to their perceptibility. Our noticing of a difference of units in two sensations would depend on the latter being in a fixed ratio. But the difference itself would depend directly on that between their respective stimuli. So many units added to the stimulus, so many added to the sensation, and if the stimulus grew in a certain ratio, in exactly the same ratio would the sensation also grow, though its perceptibility grew according to the logarithmic law.[55]

If D stand for the smallest difference which we perceive, then we should have, instead of the formula Ds = const., which is Fechner's, the formula Ds / s = const., a formula which interprets all the facts of Weber's law, in an entirely different theoretic way from that adopted by Fechner.[56]

The entire superstructure which Fechner rears upon the facts is thus not only seen to be arbitrary and subjective, but in the highest degree improbable as well. The departures from Weber's law in regions where it does not obtain, he explains by the compounding with it of other unknown laws which mask its effects. As if any law could not be found in any set of phenomena, provided one have the wit to invent enough other coexisting laws to overlap and neutralize it! The whole outcome of the discussion, so far as Fechner's theories are concerned, is indeed nil. Weber's law alone remains true as an empirical generalization of fair extent: What we add to a large stimulus we notice less than what we add to a small one, unless it happen relatively to the stimulus to be as great.

Weber's Law is probably purely physiological.

One can express this state of things otherwise by saying that the whole of the stimulus does not seem to be effective in giving us the perception of 'more,' and the simplest interpretation of such a state of things would be physical. The loss of effect would take place in the nervous system. If our feelings resulted from a condition of the nerve-molecules which it grew ever more difficult for the stimulus to increase, our feelings would naturally grow at a slower rate than the stimulus itself. An ever larger part of the latter's work would go to overcoming the resistances, and an ever smaller part to the realization of the feeling-bringing state. Weber's law would thus be a sort of law of friction in the neural machine.[57] Just how these inner resistances and frictions are to be conceived is a speculative question. Delbœuf has formulated them as fatigue; Bernstein and Ward, as irradiations. The latest, and probably the most 'real,' hypothesis is that of Ebbinghaus, who supposes that the intensity of sensation depends on the number of neural molecules which are disintegrated in the unit of time. There are only a certain number at any time which are capable of disintegrating; and whilst most of these are in an average condition of instability, some are almost stable and some already near to decomposition. The smallest stimuli affect these latter molecules only; and as they are but few, the sensational effect from adding a given quantity of stimulus at first is relatively small. Medium stimuli affect the majority of the molecules, but affect fewer and fewer in proportion as they have already diminished their number. The latest additions to the stimuli find all the medium molecules already disintegrated, and only affect the small relatively indecomposable remainder, thus giving rise to increments of feeling which are correspondingly small. (Pflüger's Archiv. 45, 113.)

It is surely in some such way as this that Weber's law is to be interpreted, if it ever is. The Fechnerian Maasformel and the conception of it as an ultimate 'psychophysic law' will remain an 'idol of the den,' if ever there was one. Fechner himself indeed was a German Gelehrter of the ideal type, at once simple and shrewd, a mystic and an experimentalist, homely and daring, and as loyal to facts as to his theories. But it would be terrible if even such a dear old man as this could saddle our Science forever with his patient whimsies, and, in a world so full of more nutritious objects of attention, compel all future students to plough through the difficulties, not only of his own works, but of the still drier ones written in his refutation. Those who desire this dreadful literature can find it; it has a 'disciplinary value;' but I will not even enumerate it in a footnote. The only amusing part of it is that Fechner's critics should always feel bound, after smiting his theories hip and thigh and leaving not a stick of them standing, to wind up by saying that nevertheless to him belongs the imperishable glory of the first formulating them and thereby turning psychology into an exact science (!).

"'And everybody praised the duke
Who this great fight did win.'
'But what good came of it at last?'
Quoth little Peterkin.
Why, that I cannot tell, said he,
'But 'twas a famous victory!'"

Notes

[1] Human Understanding, II. xi. 1, 2.
[2] Analysis, vol. I. p. 71.
[3] The Senses and the Intellect, page 411.
[4] Essays Philosophical and Theological: First Series, pp. 268-273.
[5] Montgomery in 'Mind,' x. 527. Cf. also Lipps: Grundtatsachen des Seelenlebens, p. 579 ff., and see below, Chapter XIX.

[6] *Stumpf (Tonpsychologie, I. 116 ff.) tries to prove that the theory that all differences are differences of composition leads necessarily to an infinite regression when we try to determine the unit. It seems to me that in his particular reasoning he forgets the ultimate units of the mind-stuff theory. I cannot find the completed infinite to be one of the obstacles to belief in this theory, although I fully accept Stumpf's general reasoning, and am only too happy to find myself on the same side with such an exceptionally clear thinker. The strictures by Wahle in the Vierteljsch. f. wiss. Phil. seem to me to have no force, since the writer does not discriminate between resemblance of things obviously compound and that of things sensibly simple.*

[7] *The belief that the causes of effects felt by us to differ qualitatively are facts which differ only in quantity (e.g. that blue is caused by so many ether-waves, and yellow by a smaller number) must not be confounded with the feeling that the effects differ quantitatively themselves.*

[8] *Herr G. H. Schneider, in his youthful pamphlet (Die Unterscheidung, 1877) has tried to show that there are no positively existent elements of sensibility, no substantive qualities between which differences obtain, but that the terms we call such, the sensations, are but sums of differences, loci or starting points whence many directions of difference proceed. 'Unterschiedsempfindüngs - Complexe' are what he calls them. This absurd carrying out of that 'principle of relativity' which we shall have to mention in Chapter XVII may serve as a counterpoise to the mind-stuff theory, which says that there are nothing but substantive sensations, and denies the existence of relations of difference between them at all.*

[9] *Cf. Stumpf, Tonpsychologie, I. 121, and James Ward, Mind, I. 464.*

[10] *The ordinary treatment of this is to call it the result of the fusion of a lot of sensations, in themselves separate. This is pure mythology, as the sequel will abundantly show.*

[11] *"We often begin to be dimly aware of a difference in a sensation or group of sensations, before we can assign any definite character to that which differs. Thus we detect a strange or foreign ingredient or flavor in a familiar dish, or of tone in a familiar tune, and yet are wholly unable for a while to say what the intruder is like. Hence perhaps discrimination may be regarded as the earliest and most primordial mode of intellectual activity." (Sully: Outlines of Psychology, p. 142. Cf. also G. H. Schneider: Die Unterscheidung, pp. 9-10.)*

[12] *In cases where the difference is slight, we may need, as previously remarked, to get the dying phase of n as well as of m before n-different-from-m is distinctly felt. In that case the inevitably successive feelings (as far as we can sever what is so continuous) would be four, m, difference, n, n-different-from-m. This slight additional complication alters not a whit the essential features of the case.*

[13] *Analysis, J. S. Mill's ed., II. 17. Cf. also pp. 12, 14.*

[14] *There is only one obstacle, and that is our inveterate tendency to believe that where two things or qualities are compared, it must be that exact duplicates of both have got into the mind and have matched themselves against each other there. To which the first reply is the empirical one of "Look into the mind and see." When I recognize a weight which I now lift as inferior to the one I just lifted; when, with my tooth now aching, I perceive the pain to be less intense than it was a minute ago; the two things in the mind which are compared would, by the authors I criticise, be admitted to be an actual sensation and an image in the memory. An image in the memory, by general consent of these same authors, is admitted to be a weaker thing than a sensation. Nevertheless it is in these instances judged stronger; that is, an object supposed to be known only in so far forth as this image represents it, is judged stronger. Ought not this to shake one's belief in the notion of separate representative 'ideas' weighing themselves, or being weighed by the Ego, against each other in the mind? And let it not be said that what makes us judge the felt pain to be weaker than the imagined one of a moment since is our recollection of the downward nature of the shock of difference which we felt as we passed to the present moment from the one before it. That shock does undoubtedly have a different character according as it comes between terms of which the second diminishes or increases; and it may be admitted that in cases where the past term is doubtfully remembered, the memory of the shock, as plus or minus, might sometimes enable us to establish a relation which otherwise we should not perceive. But one could hardly expect the memory of this shock to overpower our actual comparison of terms, both of which are present (as are the image and the sensation in the case supposed), and make us judge the weaker one to be the stronger.—And hereupon comes the second reply: Suppose the mind does compare two realities by comparing two ideas of its own which represent them—what is gained? The same mystery is still there. The ideas must still be known; and, as the attention in comparing oscillates from one to the other, past must be known with present just as before. If you must end by simply saying that your 'Ego,' whilst being neither the idea of m nor the idea of n, yet knows and compares both, why not allow your pulse of thought, which is neither the thing m nor the thing n, to know and compare both directly? 'Tis but a question of how to name the facts least artificially. The egoist explains them, by naming them as an Ego 'combining' or 'synthetizing' two ideas, no more than we do by naming them a pulse of thought knowing two facts.*

[15] *I fear that few will be converted by my words, so obstinately do thinkers of all schools refuse to admit the unmediated function of knowing a thing, and so incorrigibly do they substitute being the thing for it. E.g., in the latest utterance of the spiritualistic philosophy (Bowne's Introduction to Psychological Theory, 1887, published only three days before this writing) one of the first sentences which catch my eye is this: "What remembers? The spiritualistic says, the soul remembers; it abides across the years and the flow of the body, and gathering up its past, carries it with it" (p. 28). Why, for heaven's sake, O Bowne, can not you say 'knows it'? If there is anything our soul does not do to its past, it is to carry it with it.*

[16] *Sensations of Tone, 2d English Ed., p. 65.*

[17] *Psychology, I. 345.*

[18] *A Budget of Paradoxes, p. 380.*

[19] The explanation I offer presupposes that a difference too faint to have any direct effect in the way of making the mind notice it per se will nevertheless be strong enough to keep its 'terms' from calling up identical associates. It seems probable from many observations that this is the case. All the facts of 'unconscious' inference are proofs of it. We say a painting 'looks' like the work of a certain artist, though we cannot name the characteristic differentiæ. We see by a man's face that he is sincere, though we can give no definite reason for our faith. The facts of sense-perception quoted from Helmholtz a few pages below will be additional examples. Here is another good one, though it will perhaps be easier understood after reading the chapter on Space-perception than now. Take two stereoscopic slides and represent on each half-slide a pair of spots, a and b, but make their distances such that the a's are equidistant on both slides, whilst the b's are nearer together on slide 1 than on slide 2. Make moreover the distance ab = ab''' and the distance ab' = ab''.

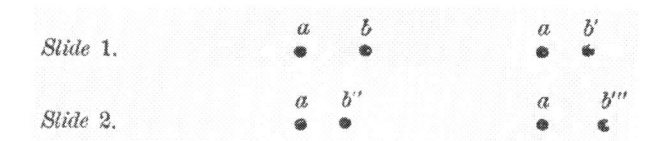

Slide 1.   a b   a b'

Slide 2.   a b''   a b'''

Then look successively at the two slides stereoscopically, so that the a's in both are directly fixated (that is, fall on the two foveæ, or centres of distinctest vision). The a's will then appear single, and so probably will the b's. But the now single-seeming b on slide 1 will look nearer, whilst that on slide 2 will look farther than the a. But, if the diagrams are rightly drawn, b and b''' must affect 'identical' spots, spots equally far to the right of the fovea, b in the left eye and b''' in the right eye. The same is true of b' and b''. Identical spots are spots whose sensations cannot possibly be discriminated as such. Since in these two observations, however, they give rise to such opposite perceptions of distance, and prompt such opposite tendencies to movement (since in slide 1 we converge in looking from a to b, whilst in slide 2 we diverge), it follows that two processes which occasion feelings quite indistinguishable to direct consciousness may nevertheless be each allied with disparate associates both of a sensorial and of a motor kind. Cf. Donders, Archiv f. Ophthalmologie, Bd. 13 (1867). The basis of his essay is that we cannot feel on which eye any particular element of a compound picture falls, but its effects on our total perception differ in the two eyes.
[20] A. W. Volkmann: Ueber den Einfluss der Uebung, etc., Leipzig Berichte, Math-phys. Classe, x, 1858, p. 67.
[21] Ibid., Tabelle I, p. 43.
[22] Professor Lipps accounts for the tactile discrimination of the blind in a way which (divested of its 'mythological' assumptions) seems to me essentially to agree with this. Stronger ideas are supposed to raise weaker ones over the threshold of consciousness by fusing with them, the tendency to fuse being proportional to the similarity of the ideas. Cf. Grundtatsachen, etc., pp. 232-3; also pp. 118, 492, 526-7.
[23] Sensations of Tone, 2d English Edition, p. 62.
[24] Compare as to this, however, what I said above, Chapter V.
[25] When a person squints, double images are formed in the centre of the field. As a matter of fact, most squinters are found blind of one eye, or almost so; and it has long been supposed amongst ophthalmologists that the blindness is a secondary affection superinduced by the voluntary suppression of one of the sets of double images, in other words by the positive and persistent refusal to use one of the eyes. This explanation of the blindness has, however, been called in question of late years. See, for a brief account of the matter, O. F. Wadsworth in Boston Med. and Surg. Journ., CXVI. 49 (Jan. 20, '87), and the replies by Derby and others a little later. - W. J.
[26] Tonempfindungen, Dritte Auflage, pp. 102-107.—The reader who has assimilated the contents of our Chapter V, above, will doubtless have remarked that the illustrious physiologist has fallen, in these paragraphs, into that sort of interpretation of the facts which we there tried to prove erroneous. Helmholtz, however, is no more careless than most psychologists in confounding together the object perceived. The organic conditions of the perception, and the sensations which would be excited by the several parts of the object, or by the several organic conditions, provided they came into action separately or were separately attended to, and in assuming that what is true of any one of these sorts of fact must be true of the other sorts also. If each organic condition or part of the object is there, its sensation, he thinks, must be there also, only in a 'synthetic'— which is indistinguishable from what the authors whom we formerly reviewed called an 'unconscious'—state. I will not repeat arguments sufficiently detailed in the earlier chapter but simply say that what he calls the 'fusion of many sensations into one' is really the production of one sensation by the co-operation of many organic conditions; and that what perception fails to discriminate (when it is synthetic') is not sensations already existent but not singled out, but new objective facts, judged truer than the facts already synthetically perceived—two views of the solid body, many harmonic tones, instead of one view and one tone, states of the eyeball-muscles thitherto unknown, and the like. These new facts, when first discovered, are known is states of consciousness never till that moment exactly realized before, states of consciousness which at the same time judge them to be determinations of the same matter of fact which was previously realized. All that Helmholtz says of the conditions which hinder and further analysis applies just as naturally to the analysis, through the advent of new feelings, of objects into their elements, as to the analysis of aggregate feelings into elementary feelings supposed to have been hidden in them all the while. The reader can himself apply this criticism to the following passages from Lotze and Stumpf respectively, which I quote because they are the ablest expressions of the view opposed to my own. Both authors, it seems to me, commit the

psychologist's fallacy, and allow their later knowledge of the things felt to be foisted into their account of the primitive way of feeling them.

Lotze says: "It is indubitable that the simultaneous assault of a variety of different stimuli on different senses, or even on the same sense, puts us into a state of confused general feeling in which we are certainly not conscious of clearly distinguishing the different impressions. Still it does not follow that in such a case we have a positive perception of an actual unity of the contents of our ideas, arising from their mixture; our state of mind seems rather to consist in (1) the consciousness of our inability to separate what really has remained diverse, and (2) in the general feeling of the disturbance produced in the economy of our body by the simultaneous assault of the stimuli.... Not that the sensations melt into one another, but simply that the act of distinguishing them is absent; and this again certainly not so far that the fact of the difference remains entirely unperceived, but only so far as to prevent us from determining the amount of the difference, and from apprehending other relations between the different impressions. Anyone who is annoyed at one and the same time by glowing heat, dazzling light, deafening noise, and an offensive smell, will certainly not fuse these disparate sensations into a single one with a single content which could be sensuously perceived; they remain for him in separation, and he merely finds it impossible to be conscious of one of them apart from the others. But, further, he will have a feeling of discomfort—what I mentioned above as the second constituent of his whole state. For every stimulus which produces in consciousness a definite content of sensation is also a definite degree of disturbance, and therefore makes a call upon the forces of the nerves; and the sum of these little changes, which in their character as disturbances are not so diverse as the contents of consciousness they give rise to, produce the general feeling which, added to the inability to distinguish, deludes us into the belief in an actual absence of diversity in our sensations. It is only in some such way as this, again, that I can imagine that state which is sometimes described as the beginning of our whole education, a state which in itself is supposed to be simple, and to be afterwards divided into different sensations by an activity of separation. No activity of separation in the world could establish differences where no real diversity existed; for it would have nothing to guide it to the places where it was to establish them, or to indicate the width it was to give them." *(Metaphysic, § 260, English translation.)*

Stumpf writes as follows: "Of coexistent sensations there are always a large number undiscriminated in consciousness, or (if one prefer to call what is undiscriminated unconscious) in the soul. They are, however, no fused into a simple quality. When, on entering a room, we receive sensations of odor and warmth together, without expressly attending to either, the two qualities of sensation are not, as it were, an entirely new simple quality, which first at the moment in which attention analytically steps in changes into smell and warmth.... In such cases we find ourselves in presence of an indefinable, unnamable total of feeling. And when, after successfully analyzing this total, we call it back to memory, as it was in its unanalyzed state, and compare it with the elements we have found, the latter (as it seems to me) may be recognized as real parts contained in the former, and the former seen to be their sum. So, for example, when we clearly perceive that the content of our sensation of oil of peppermint is partly a sensation of taste and partly one of temperature." *(Tonpsychologie, I. 107.)*

I should prefer to say that we perceive that objective fact, known to us as the peppermint taste, to contain those other objective facts known as aromatic or sapid quality, and coldness, respectively. No ground to suppose that the vehicle of this last very complex perception has any identity with the earlier psychosis—least of all is contained in it.

[27] *Physiol. Psych., II. 248.*
[28] *Wundt's Philos. Studien, I. 527.*
[29] *Ibid. p. 530.*
[30] *Mind, XI. 377 ff. He says:* "I apparently either distinguished the impression and made the motion simultaneously, or if I tried to avoid this by waiting until I had formed a distinct impression before I began to make the motion, I added to the simple reaction, not only a perception, but a volition."—*Which remark may well confirm our doubts as to the strict psychologic worth of any of these measurements.*
[31] *Mind, XI. 3.*
[32] *For other determinations of discrimination-time by this method cf. v. Kries and Auerbach, Archiv f. Physiologie, Bd. I. p. 297 ff. (these authors get much smaller figures); Friedrich, Psychologische Studien, I. 39. Chapter IX of Buccola's book, Le Legge del tempo, etc., gives a full account of the subject.*
[33] *If so, the reactions upon the spark would have to be slower than those upon the touch. The investigation was abandoned because it was found impossible to narrow down the difference between the conditions of the sight-series and those of the touch-series, to nothing more than the possible presence in the latter of the intervening motor-idea. Other disparities could not be excluded.*
[34] *Tischer gives figures from quite unpractised individuals, which I have not quoted. The discrimination-time of one of them is 22 times longer than Tischer's own! (Psychol. Studien, I. 527.)*
[35] *Compare Lipps's excellent passage to the same critical effect in his Grundtatsachen des Seelenlebens, pp. 390-393.—I leave my text just as it was written before the publication of Lange's and Münsterberg's results cited on pp. 92 and 432. Their 'shortened' or 'muscular' times, got when the expectant attention was addressed to the possible reactions rather than to the stimulus, constitute the minimal reaction-time of which I speak, and all that I say in the text falls beautifully into line with their results.*
[36] *Cf. Sully: Mind, X, 494-5; Bradley, ibid. XI. 83; Bosanquet: ibid. XI. 405.*
[37] *The judgment becomes easier if the two couples of terms have one member in common, if a - b and b - c, for example, are compared. This, as Stumpf says (Tonpsychologie, I. 131), is probably because the introduction of the fourth term brings*

involuntary cross-comparisons with it, a and b with d, b with c, etc., which confuses us by withdrawing our attention from the relations we ought alone to be estimating.

[38] J. Delbœuf: Éléments de Psychophysique (Paris, 1883), p. 64. Plateau in Stumpf, Tonpsych., I. 125. I have noticed a curious enlargement of certain 'distances' of difference under the influence of chloroform. The jingling of the bells on the horses of a horse-car passing the door, for example, and the rumbling of the vehicle itself, which to our ordinary hearing merge together very readily into a quasi-continuous body of sound, have seemed so far apart as to require a sort of mental facing in opposite directions to get from one to the other, as if they belonged in different worlds. I am inclined to suspect, from certain data, that the ultimate philosophy of difference and likeness will have to be built upon experiences of intoxication, especially by nitrous oxide gas, which lets us into intuitions the subtlety whereof is denied to the waking state. Cf. B. P. Blood: The Anæsthetic Revelation, and the Gist of Philosophy (Amsterdam, N.Y., 1874). Cf. also Mind, VII. 206.

[39] Op. cit. p. 126 ff.

[40] Stumpf, pp. 111-121.

[41] Stumpf, pp. 116-7. I have omitted , so as not to make my text too intricate, an extremely acute and conclusive paragraph, which I reproduce here: "We may generalize: Wherever a number of sensible impressions are apprehended as a series, there in the last instance must perceptions of simple likeness be found. Proof: Assume that all the terms of a series, e.g. the qualities of tone, c d e f g, have something in common, -- no matter what it is, call it X; then I say that the differing parts of each of these terms must not only be differently constituted in each, but must themselves form a series, whose existence is the ground for our apprehending the original terms in serial form. We thus get instead of the original series a b c d e f . . . the equivalent series Xa, Xb, Xg, . . . etc. What is gained? The question immediately arises: How is a b g known as a series? According to the theory, these elements must themselves be made up of a part common to all, and of parts differing in each, which latter parts form a new series, and so on ad infinitum, which is absurd."

[42] The most important ameliorations of Fechner's formula are Delbœuf's in his Recherches sur la Mesure des Sensations (1873), p. 35, and Elsas's in his pamphlet Über die Psychophysik (1886), p. 16.

[43] Reversing the order is for the sake of letting the opposite accidental errors due to 'contrast' neutralize each other.

[44] Theoretically, it would seem that it ought to be equal to the sum of all the additions which we judge to be increases divided by the total number of judgments made.

[45] J. Delbœuf Eléments de Psychophysique (1883), p. 9.

[46] Philos. Studien, IV. 588.

[47] Berlin Acad. Sitzungsberichte, 1888, p. 917. Other observers (Dobro. wolsky, Lamansky) found great differences in different colors.

[48] See Merkel's tables, loc. cit. p. 568.

[49] American Journal of Psychology, I. 125. The rate of decrease is small but steady, and I cannot well understand what Professor J. means by saying that his figures verify Weber's law.

[50] Philosophische Studien, V. 514-5.

[51] Cf. G. E. Müller: Zur Grandlegung der Psychophysik, §§ 68-70.

[52] Philosophische Studien, V. 287 ff.

[53] American J. of Psychology, III. 44-7.

[54] Cf. Stumpf, Tonpsychologie, pp. 397-9. "One sensation cannot be a multiple of another. If it could, we ought to be able to subtract the one from the other, and to feel the remainder by itself. Every sensation presents itself as an indivisible unit." Professor von Kries, in the Vierteljahrschrift für wiss. Philosophie, VI. 257 ff., shows very clearly the absurdity of supposing that our stronger sensations contain our weaker ones as parts. They differ as qualitative units. Compare also J. Tannery in Delbœuf's Eléments de Psychophysique (1883), p. 134 ff.; J. Ward in Mind, I. 464: Lotze, Metaphysik, § 258.

[55] F. Brentano, Psychologie, I. 9, 88 ff.—Merkel thinks that his results with the method of equal-appearing intervals show that we compare considerable intervals with each other by a different law from that by which we notice barely perceptible intervals. The stimuli form an arithmetical series (a pretty wild one according to his figures) in the former case, a geometrical one in the latter—at least so I understand this valiant experimenter but somewhat obscure if acute writer.

[56] This is the formula which Merkel thinks he has verified (if I understand him aright) by his experiments by method 4.

[57] Elsas: Ueber die Psychophysik (1886), p. 41. When the pans of a balance are already loaded, but in equilibrium, it takes a proportionally larger weight added to one of them to incline the beam.

Chapter XIV - Association[1]

After discrimination, association! Already in the last chapter I have had to invoke, in order to explain the improvement of certain discriminations by practice, the 'association' of the objects to be distinguished, with other more widely differing ones. It is obvious that the advance of our knowledge must consist of both operations; for objects at first appearing as wholes are analyzed into parts, and objects appearing separately are brought together and appear as new compound wholes to the mind. Analysis and synthesis are thus the incessantly alternating mental activities, a stroke of the one preparing the way for a stroke of the other, much as, in walking, a man's two legs are alternately brought into use, both being indispensable for any orderly advance.

The manner in which trains of imagery and consideration follow each other through our thinking, the restless flight of one idea before the next, the transitions our minds make between things wide as the poles asunder, transitions which at first sight startle us by their abruptness, but which, when scrutinized closely, often reveal intermediating links of perfect naturalness and propriety—all this magical, imponderable streaming has from time immemorial excited the admiration of all whose attention happened to be caught by its omnipresent mystery. And it has furthermore challenged the race of philosophers to banish something of the mystery by formulating the process in simpler terms. The problem which the philosophers have set themselves is that of ascertaining principles of connection between the thoughts which thus appear to sprout one out of the other, whereby their peculiar succession or coexistence may be explained.

But immediately an ambiguity arises: which sort of connection is meant? connection thought-of, or connection between thoughts? These are two entirely different things, and only in the case of one of them is there any hope of finding 'principles.' The jungle of connections thought of can never be formulated simply. Every conceivable connection may be thought of—of coexistence, succession, resemblance, contrast, contradiction, cause and effect, means and end, genus and species, part and whole, substance and property, early and late, large and small, landlord and tenant, master and servant, -- Heaven knows what, for the list is literally inexhaustible. The only simplification which could possibly be aimed at would be the reduction of the relations to a smaller number of types, like those which such authors as Kant and Renouvier call the 'categories' of the understanding.[2] According as we followed one category or another we should sweep, with our thought, through the world in this way or in that. And all the categories would be logical, would be relations of reason. They would fuse the items into a continuum. Were this the sort of connection sought between one moment of our thinking and another, our chapter might end here. For the only summary description of these infinite possibilities of transition, is that they are all acts of reason, and that the mind proceeds from one object to another by some rational path of connection. The trueness of this formula is only equalled by its sterility, for psychological purposes. Practically it amounts to simply referring the inquirer to the relations between facts or things, and to telling him that his thinking follows them.

But as a matter of fact, his thinking only sometimes follows them, and these so-called 'transitions of reason' are far from being all alike reasonable. If pure thought runs all our trains, why should she run some so fast and some so slow, some through dull flats and some through gorgeous scenery, some to mountain-heights and jewelled mines, others through dismal swamps and darkness? -- and run some off the track altogether, and into the wilderness of lunacy? Why do we spend years straining after a certain scientific or practical problem, but all in vain—thought refusing to evoke the solution we desire? And why, some day, walking in the street with our attention miles away from that quest, does the answer saunter into our minds as carelessly as if it had never been called for—suggested, possibly, by the flowers on the bonnet of the lady in front of us, or possibly by nothing that we can discover? If reason can give us relief then, why did she not do so earlier?

The truth must be admitted that thought works under conditions imposed ab extra. The great law of habit itself—that twenty experiences make us recall a thing better than one, that long indulgence in error makes right thinking almost impossible—seems to have no essential foundation in reason. The business of thought is with truth—the number of experiences ought to have nothing to do with her hold of it; and she ought by right to be able to hug it all the closer, after years wasted out of its presence. The contrary arrangements seem quite fantastic and arbitrary, but nevertheless are part of the very bone and marrow of our minds. Reason is only one out of a thousand possibilities in the thinking of each of us. Who can count all the silly fancies, the grotesque suppositions, the utterly irrelevant reflections he makes in the course of a day? Who can swear that his prejudices and irrational beliefs constitute a less bulky part of his mental furniture than his clarified opinions? It is true that a presiding arbiter seems to sit aloft in the mind, and emphasize the better suggestions into permanence, while it ends by droopping out and leaving unrecorded the confusion. But this is all the difference. The mode of genesis of the worthy and the worthless seems the same. The laws of our actual thinking, of the cogitatum, must account alike for the bad and the good materials on which the arbiter has to decide, for wisdom and for folly. The laws of the arbiter, of the cogitandum, of what we ought to think, are to the former as the laws of ethics are to those of history. Who but an hegelian historian ever pretended that reason in action was per se a sufficient explanation of the political changes in Europe?

There are, then, mechanical conditions on which thought depends, and which, to say the least, determine the order in which is presented the content or material for her comparisons, selections, and decisions. It is a suggestive fact that Locke, and many more recent Continental psychologists, have found themselves obliged to invoke a mechanical process to account for the aberrations of thought, the obstructive preprocessions, the frustrations of reason. This they found in the law of habit, or what we now call Association by Contiguity. But it never occurred to these writers that a process which could go the length of actually producing some ideas and sequences in the mind might safely be trusted to produce others too; and that those habitual associations which further thought may also come from the same mechanical source as those which hinder it. Hartley accordingly suggested habit as a sufficient explanation of all connections of our thoughts, and in so doing planted himself squarely upon the properly psychological aspect of the problem of connection, and sought to treat both rational and irrational connections from a single point of view. The problem which he essayed, however lamely, to answer, was that of the connection between our psychic states considered purely as such, regardless of the objective connections of which they might take cognizance. How does a man come, after thinking of A, to think of B the next moment? or how does he come to think A and B always together? These were the phenomena which Hartley undertook to explain by cerebral physiology. I believe that he was, in many essential respects, on the right track, and I propose simply to revise his conclusions by the aid of distinctions which he did not make.

But the whole historic doctrine of psychological association is tainted with one huge error—that of the construction of our thoughts out of the compounding of themselves together of immutable and incessantly recurring 'simple ideas.' It is the cohesion of these which the 'principles of association' are considered to account for. In Chapters VI and IX we saw abundant reasons for treating the doctrine of simple ideas or psychic atoms as mythological; and, in all that follows, our problem will be to keep whatever truths the associationist doctrine has caught sight of without weighing it down with the untenable incumbrance that the association is between 'ideas.'

Association, so far as the word stands for an effect, is between THINGS THOUGHT OF—it is THINGS, not ideas, which are associated in the mind. We ought to talk of the association of objects, not of the association of ideas. And so far as association stands for a cause, it is between processes in the brain—it is these which, by being associated in certain ways, determine what successive objects shall be thought. Let us proceed towards our final generalization by surveying first a few familiar facts.

The laws of motor habit in the lower centres of the nervous system are disputed by no one. A series of movements repeated in a certain order tend to unroll themselves with peculiar ease in that order for ever afterward. Number one awakens number two, and that awakens number three, and so on, till the last is produced. A habit of this kind once become inveterate may go on automatically. And so it is with the objects with which our thinking is concerned. With some persons each note of a melody, heard but once, will accurately revive in its proper sequence. Small boys at school learn the inflections of many a Greek noun, adjective, or verb, from the reiterated recitations of the upper classes falling on their ear as they sit at their desks. All this happens with no voluntary effort on their part and with no thought of the spelling of the words. The doggerel rhymes which children use in their games, such as the formula:

"Ana mana mona mike
Barcelona bona strike,"

used for 'counting out,' form another familiar example of things heard in sequence cohering in the same order in the memory.

In touch we have a smaller number of instances, though probably every one who bathes himself in a certain fixed manner is familiar with the fact that each part of his body over which the water is squeezed from the sponge awakens a premonitory tingling consciousness in that portion of skin which is habitually the next to be deluged. Tastes and smells form no very habitual series in our experience. But even if they did, it is doubtful whether habit would fix the order of their reproduction quite so well as it does that of other sensations. In vision, however, we have a sense in which the order of reproduced things is very nearly as much influenced by habit as is the order of remembered sounds. Rooms, landscapes, buildings, pictures, or persons with whose look we are very familiar, surge up before the mind's eye with all the details of their appearance complete, so soon as we think of any one of their component parts. Some persons, in reciting printed matter by heart, will seem to see each successive word, before they utter it, appear in its order on an imaginary page. A certain chess-player, one of those heroes who train themselves to play several games at once blindfold, is reported to say that in bed at night after a match the games are played all over again before his mental eye, each board being pictured as passing in turn through each of its successive stages. In this case, of course, the intense previous voluntary strain of the power of visual representation is what facilitated the fixed order of revival.

Association occurs as amply between impressions of different senses as between homogeneous sensations. Seen things and heard things cohere with each other, and with odors and tastes, in representation, in the same order in which they cohered as impressions of the outer world. Feelings of contact reproduce similarly the sights, sounds, and tastes with which experience has associated them. In fact, the 'objects' of our perception, as trees, men, houses, microscopes, of which the real world seems composed, are nothing but clusters of qualities which through simultaneous stimulation have so coalesced that the moment one is excited actually it serves as a sign or cue for the idea of the others to arise. Let a person enter his room in the dark and grope among the objects there. The touch of the matches will instantaneously recall their appearance. If his hand comes in contact with an orange on the table, the golden yellow of the fruit, its savor and perfume will forthwith shoot through his mind. In passing the hand over the sideboard or in jogging the coal-scuttle with the foot, the large glossy dark shape of the one and the irregular blackness of the other awaken like a flash and constitute what we call the recognition of the objects. The voice of the violin faintly echoes through the mind as the hand is laid upon it in the dark, and the feeling of the garments or draperies which may hang about the room is not understood till the look correlative to the feeling has in each case been resuscitated. Smells notoriously have the power of recalling the other experiences in whose company they were wont to be felt, perhaps long years ago; and the voluminous emotional character assumed by the images which suddenly pour into the mind at such a time forms one of the staple topics of popular psychologic wonder—

"Lost and gone and lost and gone!
   A breath, a whisper—some divine farewell—
   Desolate sweetness—far and far away."

We cannot hear the din of a railroad train or the yell of its whistle, without thinking of its long, jointed appearance and its headlong speed, nor catch a familiar voice in a crowd without recalling, with the name of the speaker, also his face. But the most notorious and important case of the mental combination of auditory with optical impressions originally experienced together is furnished by language. The child is offered a new and delicious fruit and is at the same time told that it is called a 'fig.' Or looking out of the window he exclaims, "What a funny horse!" and is told that it is a 'piebald' horse. When learning his letters, the sound of each is repeated to him whilst its shape is before his eye. Thenceforward, long as he may live, he will never see a fig, a piebald horse, or a letter of the alphabet without the name which he first heard in conjunction with each clinging to it in his mind; and inversely he will never hear the name without the faint arousal of the image of the object.[3]

The Rapidity of Association.

Reading exemplifies this kind of cohesion even more beautifully. It is an uninterrupted and protracted recall of sounds by sights which have always been coupled with them in the past. I find that I can name six hundred letters in two minutes on a printed page. Five distinct acts of association between sight and sound (not to speak of all the other processes concerned) must then have occurred in each second in my mind. In reading entire words the speed is much more rapid. Valentin relates in his Physiology that the reading of a single page of the proof, containing 2629 letters, took him 1 minute and 32 seconds. In this experiment each letter was understood in 1/28 of a second, but owing to the integration of letters into entire words, forming each a single aggregate impression directly associated with a single acoustic image, we need not suppose as many as 28 separate associations in a sound. The figures, however, suffice to show with what extreme rapidity an actual sensation recalls its customary associates. Both in fact seem to our ordinary attention to come into the mind at once.
The time-measuring psychologists of recent days have tried their hand at this problem by more elaborate methods. Galton, using a very simple apparatus, found that the sight of an unforeseen word would awaken an associated 'idea' in about 5/6 of a second.[4] Wundt next made determinations in which the 'cue' was given by single-syllabled words called out by an assistant. The person experimented on had to press a key as soon as the sound of the word awakened an associated idea. Both word and reaction were chronographically registered, and the total time-interval between the two amounted, in four observers, to 1.009, 0.896, 1.037, and 1.154 seconds respectively. From this the simple physiological reaction-time and the time of merely identifying the word's sound (the 'apperception-time,' as Wundt calls it) must be subtracted, to get the exact time required for the associated idea to arise. These times were separately determined and subtracted. The difference, called by Wundt the association-time, amounted, in the same four persons, to 706, 723, 752, and 874 thousandths of a second respectively.[5] The length of the last figure is due to the fact that the person reacting (President G. S. Hall) was an American, whose associations with German words would naturally be slower than those of natives. The shortest association-time noted was when the word 'Sturm' suggested to Prof. Wundt the word 'Wind' in 0.341 second.[6] -- Finally, Mr. Cattell made some interesting observations upon the association-time between the look of letters and their names. "I pasted letters," he says, "on a

revolving drum, and determined at what rate they could be read aloud as they passed by a slit in a screen." He found it to vary according as one, or more than one letter, was visible at a time through the slit, and gives half a second as about the time which it takes to see and name a single letter seen alone.

"When two or more letters are always in view, not only do the processes of seeing and naming overlap, but while the subject is seeing one letter he begins to see the ones next following, and so can read them more quickly. Of the nine persons experimented on, four could read the letters faster when five were in view at once, but were not helped by a sixth letter; three were not helped by a fifth, and two not by a fourth letter. This shows that while one idea is in the centre, two, three, or four additional ideas may be in the background of consciousness. The second letter in view shortens the time about 1/40, the third 1/60, the fourth 1/100, the fifth 1/200 sec.

"I find it takes about twice as long to read (aloud, as fast as possible) words which have no connection as words which make sentences, and letters which have no connection as letters which make words. When the words make sentences and the letters words, not only do the processes of seeing and naming overlap, but by one mental effort the subject can recognize a whole group of words or letters, and by one will-act choose the motions to be made in naming, so that the rate at which the words and letters are read is really only limited by the maximum rapidity at which the speech-organs can be moved. As the result of a large number of experiments, the writer found that he had read words not making sentences at the rate of ¼ sec., words making sentences (a passage from Swift) at the rate of 1/8 sec., per word.... The rate at which a person reads a foreign language is proportional to his familiarity with the language. For example, when reading as fast as possible the writer's rate was, English 138, French 167, German 250, Italian 327, Latin 434, and Greek 484; the figures giving the thousandths of a second taken to read each word. Experiments made on others strikingly confirm these results. The subject does not know that he is reading the foreign language more slowly than his own; this explains why foreigners seem to talk so fast. This simple method of determining a person's familiarity with a language might be used in school examinations.

"The time required to see and name colors and pictures of objects was determined in the same way. The time was found to be about the same (over ½ sec.) for colors as for pictures, and about twice as long as for words and letters. Other experiments I have made show that we can recognize a single color or picture in a slightly shorter time than a word or letter, but take longer to name it. This is because, in the case or words and letters, the association between the idea and name has taken place so often that the process has become automatic, whereas in the case of colors and pictures we must by a voluntary effort choose the name.[7]

In later experiments Mr. Cattell studied the time for various associations to be performed, the termini (i.e., cue and answer) being words. A word in one language was to call up its equivalent in another, the name of an author the tongue in which he wrote, that of a city the country in which it lay, that of a writer one of his works, etc. The mean variation from the average is very great in all these experiments; and the interesting feature which they show is the existence of certain constant differences between associations of different sorts. Thus:

From country to city, Mr. C.'s time was 0.340 sec.
" season " month " " " 0.399
" language " author, " " " 0.523
" author " work, " " " 0.596

The average time of two observers, experimenting on eight different types of association, was 0.420 and 0.436 sec. respectively.[8] The very wide range of variation is undoubtedly a consequence of the fact that the words used as cues, and the different types of association studied, differ much in their degree of familiarity.

"For example, B is a teacher of mathematics; C has busied himself more with literature. C knows quite as well as B that 7 + 5 = 12, yet he needs 1/10 of a second longer to call it to mind; B knows quite as well as C that Dante was a poet, but needs 1/20 of a second longer to think of it. Such experiments lay bare the mental life in a way that is startling and not always gratifying."[9]

The Law of Contiguity.

Time-determinations apart, the facts we have run over can all be summed up in the simple statement that objects once experienced together tend to become associated in the imagination, so that when any one of them is thought of, the others are likely to be thought of also, in the same order of sequence or coexistence as before. This statement we may name the law of mental association by contiguity.[10]

I preserve this name in order to depart as little as possible from tradition, although Mr. Ward's designation of the process as that of association by continuity[11] or Wundt's as that of external association (to distinguish it from the internal association which we shall presently learn to know under the name of association by similarity)[12] are perhaps better terms. Whatever we name the law, since it expresses merely a phenomenon of mental habit, the most natural way of accounting for it is to conceive it as a result of the laws of habit in the nervous system; in other words, it is to ascribe it to a physiological cause. If it be truly a law of those nerve-centres which co-ordinate sensory and motor processes together that paths once used for coupling any pair of them are thereby made more permeable, there appears no reason why the same law should not hold good of ideational centres and their coupling-paths as well.[13] Parts of these centres which have once been in action together will thus grow so linked that excitement at one point will irradiate through the system. The chances of complete irradiation will be strong in proportion as the previous excitements have been frequent, and as the present points excited afresh are numerous. If all points were originally excited together, the irradiation may be sensibly simultaneous throughout the system, when any single point or group of points is touched off. But where the original impressions were successive—the conjugation of a Greek verb, for example—awakening nerve-tracts in a definite order, they will now, when one of them awakens, discharge into each other in that definite order and in no other way.

The reader will recollect all that has been said of increased tension in nerve-tracts and of the summation of stimuli. We must therefore suppose that in these ideational tracts as well as elsewhere, activity may be awakened, in any particular locality, by the summation therein of a number of tensions, each incapable alone of provoking an actual discharge. Suppose for example the locality M to be in functional continuity with four other localities, K, L, N, and O. Suppose moreover that on four previous occasions it has been separately combined with each of these localities in a common activity. M may then be indirectly awakened by any cause which tends to awaken either K, L, N, or O. But if the cause which awakens K, for instance, be so slight as only to increase its tension without arousing it to full discharge, K will only succeed in slightly increasing the tension of M. But if at the same time the tensions of L, N, and O are similarly increased, the combined effects of all four upon M may be so great as to awaken an actual discharge in this latter locality. In like manner if the paths between M and the four other localities have been so slightly excavated by previous experience as to require a very intense excitement in either of the localities before M can be awakened, a less strong excitement than this in any one will fail to reach M. But if all four at once are mildly excited, their compound effect on M may be adequate to its full arousal.

The psychological law of association of objects thought of through their previous contiguity in thought or experience would thus be an effect, within the mind, of the physical fact that nerve-currents propagate themselves easiest through those tracts of conduction which have been already most in use. Descartes and Locke hit upon this explanation, which modern science has not yet succeeded in improving.

"Custom," says Locke, "settles habits of thinking in the understanding, as well as of determining in the will, and of motions in the body; all which seem to be but trains of motion in the animal spirits [by this Locke meant identically what we understand by neural processes] which, once set agoing, continue in the same steps they have been used to, which by often treading are worn into a smooth path, and the motion in it becomes easy and, as it were, natural."[14] Hartley was more thorough in his grasp of the principle. The sensorial nerve-currents, produced when objects are fully present, were for him 'vibrations,' and those which produce ideas of objects in their absence were 'miniature vibrations.' And he sums up the cause of mental association in a single formula by saying:

"Any vibrations, A, B, C, etc., by being associated together a sufficient Number of Times, get such a Power over a, b, c, etc., the corresponding Miniature Vibrations, that any of the Vibrations A, when impressed alone, shall be able to excite b, c, etc., the Miniatures of the rest."[15]

It is evident that if there be any law of neural habit similar to this, the contiguities, coexistences, and successions, met with in outer experience, must inevitably be copied more or less perfectly in our thought. If A B C D E be a sequence of outer impressions (they may be events or they may be successively experienced properties of an object) which once gave rise to the successive 'ideas,' a b c d e, then no sooner will A impress us again and awaken the a, than b c d e will arise as ideas even before B C D E have come in as impressions. In other words, the order of impressions will the next time be anticipated; and the mental order will so far forth copy the order of the outer world. Any object when met again will make us expect its former concomitants, through the overflowing of its brain-tract into the paths which lead to theirs. And all these suggestions will be effects of a material law.

Where the associations are, as here, of successively appearing things, the distinction I made at the outset of the chapter, between a connection thought of and a connection of thoughts, is unimportant. For the connection thought of is concomitance or succession; and the connection between the thoughts is just the same. The 'objects' and the 'ideas' fit into parallel schemes, and may be described in identical language, as contiguous things tending to be thought again together, or contiguous ideas tending to recur together.

Now were these cases fair samples of all association, the distinction I drew might well be termed a Spitzfindigkeit or piece of pedantic hair-splitting, and be dropped. But as a matter of fact we cannot treat the subject so simply. The same outer object may suggest either of many realities formerly associated with it—for in the vicissitudes of our outer experience we are constantly liable to meet the same thing in the midst of differing companions—and a philosophy of association that should merely say that it will suggest one of these, or even of that one of them which it has oftenest accompanied, would go but a very short way into the rationale of the subject. This, however, is about as far as most associationists have gone with their 'principle of contiguity.' Granted an object, A, they never tell us beforehand which of its associates it will suggest; their wisdom is limited to showing, after it has suggested a second object, that that object was once an associate. They have had to supplement their principle of Contiguity by other principles, such as those of Similarity and Contrast, before they could begin to do justice to the richness of the facts.

The Elementary Law of Association.

I shall try to show, in the pages which immediately follow, that there is no other elementary causal law of association than the law of neural habit. All the materials of our thought are due to the way in which one elementary process of the cerebral hemispheres tends to excite whatever other elementary process it may have excited at some former time. The number of elementary processes at work, however, and the nature of those which at any time are fully effective in rousing the others, determine the character of the total brain-action, and, as a consequence of this, they determine the object thought of at the time. According as this resultant object is one thing or another, we call it a product of association by contiguity or of association by similarity, or contrast, or whatever other sorts we may have recognized as ultimate. Its production, however, is, in each one of these cases, to be explained by a merely quantitative variation in the elementary brain-processes momentarily at work under the law of habit, so that psychic contiguity, similarity, etc., are derivatives of a single profounder kind of fact.

My thesis, stated thus briefly, will soon become more clear; and at the same time certain disturbing factors, which co-operate with the law of neural habit, will come to view.

Let us then assume as the basis of all our subsequent reasoning this law: When two elementary brain-processes have been active together or in immediate succession, one of them, on reoccurring, tends to propagate its excitement into the other.

But, as a matter of fact, every elementary process has found itself at different times excited in conjunction with many other processes, and this by unavoidable outward causes. Which of these others it shall awaken now becomes a problem. Shall b or c be aroused next by the present a? We must make a further postulate, based, however, on the fact of tension in nerve-tissue, and on the fact of summation of excitements, each incomplete or latent in itself, into an open resultant.[16] The process b, rather than c, will awake, if in addition to the vibrating tract a some other tract d is in a state of sub-excitement, and formerly was excited with b alone and not with a. In short, we may say:

The amount of activity at any given point in the brain-cortex is the sum of the tendencies of all other points to discharge into it, such tendencies being proportionate (1) to the number of times the excitement of each other point may have accompanied that of the point in question; (2) to the intensity of such excitements; and (3) to the absence of any rival point functionally disconnected with the first point, into which the discharges might be diverted.

Expressing the fundamental law in this most complicated way leads to the greatest ultimate simplification. Let us, for the present, only treat of spontaneous trains of thought and ideation, such as occur in revery or musing. The case of voluntary thinking toward a certain end shall come up later.

Take, to fix our ideas, the two verses from 'Locksley Hall':

"I, the heir of all the ages in the foremost files of time,"

and—

"For I doubt not through the ages one increasing purpose runs."

Why is it that when we recite from memory one of these lines, and get as far as the ages, that portion of the other lines which follows, and, so to speak, sprouts out of the ages, does not also sprout out of our memory, and confuse the sense of our words? Simply because the word that follows the ages has its brain-process awakened not simply by the brain-process of the ages alone, but by it plus the brain-processes of all the words preceding the ages. The word ages at its moment of strongest activity would, per se, indifferently discharge into either 'in' or 'one.' So would the previous words (whose tension is momentarily much less stronger than that of ages) each of them indifferently discharge into either of a large number of other words with which they have been at different times combined. But when the processes of 'I, the heir of all the ages,' simultaneously vibrate in the brain, the last one of them in a maximal, the others in a fading phase of excitement; then the strongest line of discharge will be that which they all alike tend to take. 'In' and not 'one' or any other word will be the next to awaken, for its brain-process has previously vibrated in unison not only with that of ages, but with that of all those other words whose activity is dying away. It is a good case of the effectiveness over thought of what we called on p. 258 a 'fringe.'

But if some one of these preceding words—'heir,' for example—had an intensely strong association with some brain-tracts entirely disjoined in experience from the poem of 'Locksley Hall'—if the reciter, for instance, were tremulously awaiting the opening of a will which might make him a millionaire—it is probable that the path of discharge through the words of the poem would be suddenly interrupted at the word 'heir.' His emotional interest in that word would be such that its own special associations would prevail over the combined ones of the other words.

He would, as we say, be abruptly reminded of his personal situation, and the poem would lapse altogether from his thoughts.

The writer of these pages has every year to learn the names of a large number of students who sit in alphabetical order in a lecture-room. He finally learns to call them by name, as they sit in their accustomed places. On meeting one in the street, however early in the year, the face hardly ever recalls the name, but it may recall the place of its owner in the lecture-room, his neighbors' faces, and consequently his general alphabetical position; and then, usually as the common associate of all these combined data, the student's name surges up in his mind.

A father wishes to show to some guests the progress of his rather dull child in Kindergarten instruction. Holding the knife upright on the table, he says, "What do you call that, my boy?" "I calls it a knife, I does," is the sturdy reply, from which the child cannot be induced to swerve by any alteration in the form of question, until the father recollecting that in the Kindergarten a pencil was used, and not a knife, draws a long one from his pocket, holds it in the same way, and then gets the wished-for answer, "I calls it vertical." All the concomitants of the Kindergarten experience had to recombine their effect before the word 'vertical' could be reawakened.

Professor Bain, in his chapters on 'Compound Association,' has treated in a minute and exhaustive way of this type of mental sequence, and what he has done so well need not be here repeated.[17]

Impartial Redintegration.

The ideal working of the law of compound association, were it unmodified by any extraneous influence, would be such as to keep the mind in a perpetual treadmill of concrete reminiscences from which no detail could be omitted. Suppose, for example, we begin by thinking of a certain dinner-party. The only thing which all the components of the dinner-party could combine to recall would be the first concrete occurrence which ensued upon it. All the details of this occurrence could in turn only combine to awaken the next following occurrence, and so on. If a, b, c, d, e, for instance, be the elementary nerve-tracts excited by the last act of the dinner-party, call this act A, and l, m, n, o, p be those of walking home through the frosty night, which we may call B, then the thought of A must awaken that of B, because a, b, c, d, e, will each and all discharge into l through the paths by which their original discharge took place. Similarly they will discharge into m, n, o, and p; and these latter tracts will also each reinforce the other's action because, in the experience B, they have already vibrated in unison. The lines in Fig. 40, p. 570, symbolize the summation of discharges into each of the components of B, and the consequent strength of the combination of influences by which B in its totality is awakened.

Hamilton first used the word 'redintegration' to designate all association. Such processes as we have just described might in an emphatic sense be termed redintegrations, for they would necessarily lead, if unobstructed, to the reinstatement in thought of the entire content of large trains of past experience. From this complete redintegration there could be no escape save through the irruption of some new and strong present impression of the senses, or through the excessive tendency of some one of the elementary brain-tracts to discharge independently into an aberrant quarter of the brain. Such was the tendency of the word 'heir' in the verse from 'Locksley Hall,' which was our first example.

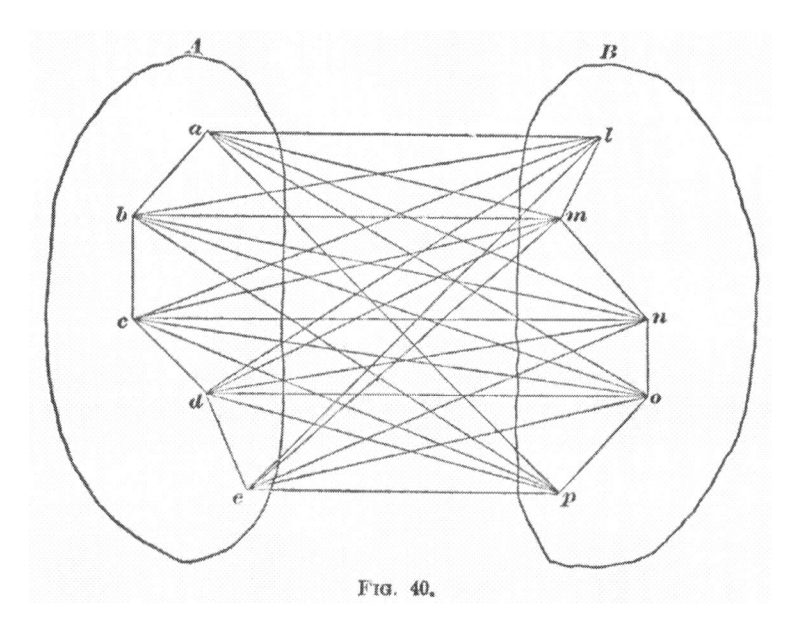

FIG. 40.

How such tendencies are constituted we shall have soon to inquire with some care. Unless they are present, the panorama of the past, once opened, must unroll itself with fatal literality to the end, unless some outward sound, sight, or touch divert the current of thought.

Let us call this process impartial redintegration. Whether it ever occurs in an absolutely complete form is doubtful. We all immediately recognize, however, that in some minds there is a much greater tendency than in others for the flow of thought to take this form. Those insufferably garrulous old women, those dry and fanciless beings who spare you no detail, however petty, of the facts they are recounting, and upon the thread of whose narrative all the irrelevant items cluster as pertinaciously as the essential ones,the slaves of literal fact, the stumblers over the smallest abrupt step in thought, are figures known to all of us. Comic literature has made her profit out of them. Juliet's nurse is a classical example. George Eliot's village characters and some of Dicken's minor personages supply excellent instances.

Perhaps as successful a rendering as any of this mental type is the character of Miss Bates in Miss Austen's 'Emma.' Hear how she redintegrates:

"'But where could you hear it?' cried Miss Bates. 'Where could you possibly hear it, Mr. Knightley? For it is not five minutes since I received Mrs. Cole's note—no, it cannot be more than five—or at least ten—for I had got my bonnet and spencer on, just ready to come out—I was only gone down to speak to Patty agian about the pork—Jane was standing in the passage—were not you, Jane? -- for my mother was so afraid that we had not any salting-pan large enough. So I said I would go down and see, and Jane said: "Shall I go down instead? for I think you have a little cold, and Patty has been washing the kitchen." "Oh, my dear," said I—well, and just then came the note. A Miss Hawkins—that's all I know—a Miss Hawkins, of Bath. But, Mr. Knightley, how could you possibly have heard it? for the very moment Mr. Cole told Mrs. Cole of it, she sat down and wrote to me. A Miss Hawkins—'"

But in every one of us there are moments when this complete reproduction of all the items of a past experience occurs. What are those moments? They are moments of emotional recall of the past as something which once was, but is gone for ever—moments, the interest of which consists in the feeling that our self was once other than it now is. When this is the case, any detail, however minute, which will make the past picture more complete, will also have its effect in swelling that total contrast between now and then which forms the central interest of our contemplation.

Ordinary or Mixed Association.

This case helps us to understand why it is that the ordinary spontaneous flow of our ideas does not follow the law of impartial redintegration. In no revival of a past experience are all the items of our thought equally operative in determining what the next thought shall be. Always some ingredient is prepotent over the rest. Its special suggestions or associations in this case will often be different from those which it has in common with the whole group of items; and its tendency to awaken these outlying associates will deflect the path of our revery. Just as in the original sensible experience our attention focalized itself upon a few of the impressions of the scene before us, so here in the reproduction of those impressions an equal partiality is shown, and some items are emphasized above the rest. What these items shall be is, in most cases of spontaneous revery, hard to determine beforehand. In subjective terms we say that the prepotent items are those which appeal most to our INTEREST.

Expressed in brain-terms, the law of interest will be: some one brain-process is always prepotent above its concomitants in arousing action elsewhere.

"Two processes," says Mr. Hodgson,[18] "are constantly going on in redintegration. The one a process of corrosion, melting, decay; the other a process of renewing, arising, becoming.... No object of representation remains long before consciousness in the same state, but fades, decays, and becomes indistinct. Those parts of the object, however, which possess an interest resist this tendency to gradual decay of the whole object.... This inequality in the object—some parts, the uninteresting, submitting to decay; others, the interesting parts, resisting it—when it has continued for a certain time, ends in becoming a new object."

Only where the interest is diffused equally over all the parts (as in the emotional memory just referred to, where, as all past, they all interest us alike) is this law departed from. It will be least obeyed by those minds which have the smallest variety and intensity of interests—those who, by the general flatness and poverty of their æsthetic nature, are kept for ever rotating among the literal sequences of their local an personal history.

Most of us, however, are better organized than this, and our musings pursue and erratic course, swerving continually into some new direction traced by the shifting play of interest as it ever falls on some partial item in each complex representation that is evoked. Thus it so often comes about that we find ourselves thinking at two nearly adjacent moments of things separated by the whole diameter of space and time. Not till we carefully recall each step of our cogitation do we see how naturally we came by Hodgson's law to pass from one to the other. Thus, for instance, after looking at my clock just now (1879), I found myself thinking of a recent resolution in the Senate about our legal-tender notes. The clock called up the image of the man who had repaired its gong. He suggested the jeweller's shop where I had last seen him; that shop, some shirt-studs which I had bought there; they, the value of gold and its recent decline; the latter, the equal value of greenbacks, and this, naturally, the question of how long they were to last, and of the Bayard proposition. Each of these images offered various points of interest. Those which formed the turning-points of my thought are easily assigned. The gong was momentarily the most interesting part of the clock, because, from having begun with a beautiful tone, it had become discordant and aroused disappointment. But for this the clock might have suggested the friend who gave it to me, or any one of a thousand circumstances connected with clocks. The jeweller's shop suggested the studs, because they alone of all its contents were tinged with the egoistic interest of possession. This interest in the studs, their value, made me single out the material as its chief source, etc., to the end. Every reader who will arrest himself at any moment and say, "How came I to be thinking of just this?" will be sure to trace a train of representations linked together by lines of contiguity and points of interest inextricably combined. This is the ordinary process of the association of ideas as it spontaneously goes on in average minds. We may call it ORDINARY, or MIXED, ASSOCIATION.

Another example of it is given by Hobbes in a passage which has been quoted so often as to be classical:

"In a discourse of our present civil war, what could seem more impertinent than to ask (as one did) what was the value of a Roman penny? Yet the coherence to me was manifest enough. For the thought of the war introduced the thought of the delivering up the King to his enemies; the thought of that brought in the thought of the delivering up of Christ; and that again the thought of the thirty pence, which was the price of that treason: and thence easily followed that malicious question; and all this in a moment of time; for thought is quick."[19]

Can we determine, now, when a certain portion of the going thought has, by dint of its interest, become so prepotent as to make its own exclusive associates the dominant features of the coming thought—can we, I say, determine which of its own associates shall be evoked? For they are many. As Hodgson says:

"The interesting parts of the decaying object are free to combine again with any objects or parts of objects with which at any time they have been combined before. All the former combinations of these parts may come back into consciousness; one must; but which will?"

Mr. Hodgson replies:

"There can be but one answer: that which has been most habitually combined with them before. This new object begins at once to form itself in consciousness, and to group its part round the part still remaining from the former object; part after part comes out and arranges itself in its old position; but scarcely has the process begun, when the original law of interest begins to operate on this new formation, seizes on the interesting parts and impresses them on the attention to the exclusion of the rest, and the whole process is repeated again with endless variety. I venture to propose this as a complete and true account of the whole process of redintegration."

In restricting the discharge from the interesting item into that channel which is simply most habitual in the sense of most frequent, Hodgson's account is assuredly imperfect. An image by no means always revives its most frequent associate, although frequency is certainly one of the most potent determinants of revival. If I abruptly utter the word swallow, the reader, if by habit an ornithologist, will think of a bird; if a physiologist or a medical specialist in throat diseases, he will think of deglutition. If I say date, he will, if a fruit-merchant or an Arabian traveller, think of the produce of the palm; if an habitual student of history, figures with A.D. or B.C. before them will rise in his mind. If I say bed, bath, morning, his own daily toilet will be invincibly suggested by the combined names of three of its habitual associates. But frequent lines of transition are often set at naught. The sight of C. Göring's 'System der kritischen Philosophie' has most frequently awakened in me thoughts of the opinions therein propounded. The idea of suicide has never been connected with the volumes. But a moment since, as my eye fell upon them, suicide was the thought that flashed into my mind. Why? Because but yesterday I received a letter from Leipzig informing me that this philosopher's recent death by drowning was an act of self-destruction. Thoughts tend, then, to awaken their most recent as well as their most habitual associates. This is a matter of notorious experience, too notorious, in fact, to need illustration. If we have seen our friend this morning, the mention of his name now recalls the circumstances of that interview, rather than any more remote details concerning him. If Shakespeare's plays are mentioned, and we were last night reading 'Richard II.,' vestiges of that play rather than of 'Hamlet' or 'Othello' float through our mind. Excitement of peculiar tracts, or peculiar modes of general excitement in the brain, leave a sort of tenderness or exalted sensibility behind them which takes days to die away. As long as it lasts, those tracts or those modes are liable to have their activities awakened by causes which at other times might leave them in repose. Hence, recency in experience is a prime factor in determining revival in thought.[20]

Vividness in an original experience may also have the same effect as habit or recency in bringing about likelihood of revival. If we have once witnessed an execution, any subsequent conversation or reading about capital punishment will almost certainly suggest images of that particular scene. Thus it is that events lived through only once, and in youth, may come in after-years, by reason of their exciting quality or emotional intensity, to serve as types or instances used by our mind to illustrate any and every occurring topic whose interest is most remotely pertinent to theirs. If a man in his boyhood once talked with Napoleon, any mention of great men or historical events, battles or thrones, or the whirligig of fortune, or islands in the ocean, will be apt to draw to his lips the incidents of that one memorable interview. If the word tooth now suddenly appears on the page before the reader's eye, there are fifty chances out of a hundred that, if he gives it time to awaken any image, it will be an image of some operation of dentistry in which he has been the sufferer. Daily he has touched his teeth and masticated with them; this very morning he brushed them, chewed his breakfast and picked them; but the rarer and remoter associations arise more promptly because they were so much more intense.[21]

A fourth factor in tracing the course of reproduction is congruity in emotional tone between the reproduced idea and our mood. The same objects do not recall the same associates when we are cheerful as when we are melancholy. Nothing, in fact, is more striking than our utter inability to keep up trains of joyous imagery when we are depressed in spirits. Storm, darkness, war, images of disease, poverty, and perishing afflict unremittingly the imaginations of melancholiacs. And those of sanguine temperament, when their spirits are high, find it impossible to give any permanence to evil forebodings or to gloomy thoughts. In an instant the train of association dances off to flowers and sunshine, and images of spring and hope. The records of Arctic or African travel perused in one mood awaken no thoughts but those of horror at the malignity of Nature; read at another time they suggest only enthusiastic reflections on the indomitable power and pluck of man. Few novels so overflow with joyous animal spirits as 'The Three Guardsmen' of Dumas. Yet it may awaken in the mind of a reader depressed with sea-sickness (as the writer can personally testify) a most dismal and woful consciousness of the cruelty and carnage of which heroes like Athos, Porthos, and Aramis make themselves guilty.

Habit, recency, vividness, and emotional congruity are, then, all reasons why one representation rather than another should be awakened by the interesting portion of a departing thought. We may say with truth that in the majority of cases the coming representation will have been either habitual, recent, or vivid, and will be congruous. If all these qualities unite in any one absent associate, we may predict almost infallibly that that associate of the going thought will form an important ingredient in the coming thought. In spite of the fact, however, that the succession of representations is thus redeemed from perfect indeterminism and limited to a few classes whose characteristic quality is fixed by the nature of our past experience, it must still be confessed that an immense number of terms in the linked chain of our representations fall outside of all assignable rule. To take the instance of the clock. Why did the jeweller's shop suggest the shirt-studs rather than a chain which I had brought there more recently, which had cost more, and whose sentimental associations were much more interesting? Both chain and studs had excited brain-tracts simultaneously with the shop. The only reason why the nerve-stream from the shop-tract switched off into the stud-tract rather than into the chain-tract must be that the stud-tract happened at that moment to lie more open, either because of some accidental alteration in its nutrition or because the incipient sub-conscious tensions of the brain as a whole had so distributed their equilibrium that it was more unstable here than in the chain-tract. Any reader's introspection will easily furnish similar instances. It thus remains true that to a certain extent, even in those forms of ordinary mixed association which lie nearest to impartial redintegration, which associate of the interesting item shall emerge must be called largely a matter of accident—accident, that is, for our intelligence. No doubt it is determined by cerebral causes, but they are too subtle and shifting for our analysis.

Association by Similarity.

In partial or mixed associations we have all along supposed the interesting portion of the disappearing thought to be of considerable extent, and to be sufficiently complex to constitute by itself a concrete object. Sir William Hamilton relates, for instance, that after thinking of Ben Lomond he found himself thinking of the Prussian system of education, and discovered that the links of association were a German gentleman whom he had met on Ben Lomond, Germany, etc. The interesting part of Ben Lomond, as he had experienced it, the part operative in determining the train of his ideas was the complex image of a particular man. But now let us suppose that that selective agency of interested attention, which may thus convert impartial redintegration into partial association—let us suppose that it refines itself still further and accentuates a portion of the passing thought, so small as to be no longer the image of a concrete thing, but only of an abstract quality or property. Let us moreover suppose that the part thus accentuated persists in consciousness (or, in cerebral terms, has its brain-process continue) after the other portions of the thought have faded. This small surviving portion will then surround itself with its own associates after the fashion we have already seen, and the relation between the new thought's object and the object of the faded thought will be a relation of similarity. The pair of thoughts will form an instance of what is called 'Association by Similarity.'[22]

The similars which are here associated, or of which the first is followed by the second in the mind, are seen to be compounds. Experience proves that this is always the case. There is no tendency on the part of SIMPLE 'ideas,' attributes, or qualities to remind us of their like. The thought of one shade of blue does not remind us of that of another shade of blue, etc., unless indeed we have in mind some general purpose like naming the tint, when we should naturally think of other blues of the scale, through 'mixed association' of purpose, names, and tints, together. But there is no elementary tendency of pure qualities to awaken their similars in the mind.

We saw in the chapter on Discrimination that two compound things are similar when some one quality or group of qualities is shared alike by both, although as regards their other qualities they may have nothing in common. The moon is similar to a gas-jet, it is also similar to a football; but a gas-jet and a foot-ball are not similar to each other. When we affirm the similarity of two compound things, we should always say in what respect it obtains. Moon and gas-jet are similar in respect of luminosity, and nothing else; moon and foot-ball in respect of rotundity, and nothing else. Foot-ball and gas-jet are in no respect similar—that is, they possess no common point, no identical attribute. Similarity, in compounds, is partial identity. When the same attribute appears in two phenomena, though it be their only common property, the two phenomena are similar is so far forth. To return now to our associated representations. If the thought of the moon is succeeded by the thought of a foot-ball, and that by the thought of one of Mr. X's railroads, it is because the attribute rotundity in the moon broke away from all the rest and surrounded itself with an entirely new set of companions—elasticity, leathery integument, swift mobility in obedience to human caprice, etc.; and because the last-named attribute in the foot-ball in turn broke away from its companions, and, itself persisting, surrounded itself with such new attributes as make up the notions of a 'railroad king,' of a rising and falling stock-market, and the like.

The gradual passage from impartial redintegration to similar association through what we have called ordinary mixed association may be symbolized by diagrams. Fig. 41 is impartial redintegration, Fig. 42 is mixed, and Fig. 43 similar association. A in each is the passing, B the coming thought. In 'impartial,' all parts of A are equally operative in calling up B.

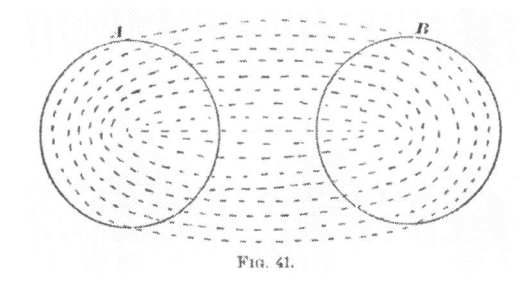

FIG. 41.

In 'mixed,' most parts of A are inert. The part M alone breaks out and awakens B.

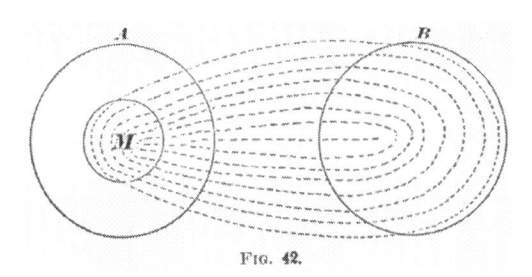

FIG. 42.

In 'similar,' the focalized part M is much smaller than in the previous case, and after awakening its new set of associates, instead of fading out itself, it continues persistently active along with them, forming an identical part in the two ideas, and making these, pro tanto, resemble each other.

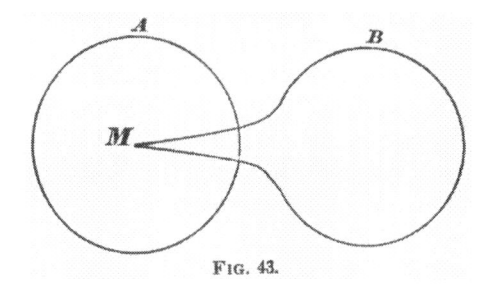

FIG. 43.

Why a single portion of the passing thought should break out from its concert with the rest and act, as we say, on its own hook, why the other parts should become inert, are mysteries which we can ascertain but not explain. Possibly a minuter insight into the laws of neural action will some day clear the matter up; possibly neural laws will not suffice, and we shall need to invoke a dynamic reaction of the form of consciousness upon its content. But into this we cannot enter now.

To sum up, then, we see that the difference between the three kinds of association reduces itself to a simple difference in the amount of that portion of the nerve-tract supporting the going thought which is operative in calling up the thought which comes. But the modus operandi of this active part is the same, be it large or be it small. The items constituting the coming object waken in every instance because their nerve-tracts once were excited continuously with those of the going object or its operative part. This ultimate physiological law of habit among the neural elements is what runs the train. The direction of its course and the form of its transitions, whether redintegrative, associative, or similar, are due to unknown regulative or determinative conditions which accomplish their effect by opening this switch and closing that, setting the engine sometimes at half-speed, and coupling or uncoupling cars.

This last figure of speech, into which I have glided unwittingly, affords itself an excellent instance of association by similarity. I was thinking of the deflections of the course of ideas. Now, from Hobbes's time downward, English writers have been fond of speaking of the train of our representations. This word happened to stand out in the midst of my complex thought with peculiarly sharp accentuation, and to surround itself with numerous details of railroad imagery. Only such details became clear, however, as had their nerve-tracts besieged by a double set of influences—those from train on the one hand, and those from the movement of thought on the other. It may possibly be that the prepotency of the suggestions of the word train at this moment were due to the recent excitation of the railroad brain-tract by the instance chosen a few pages back of a railroad king playing foot-ball with the stock-market.

It is apparent from such an example how inextricably complex are all the contributory factors whose resultant is the line of our reverie. It would be folly in most cases to attempt to trace them out. From an instance like the above, where the pivot of the Similar Association was formed by a definite concrete word, train, to those where it is so subtile as utterly to elude our analysis, the passage is unbroken. We can form a series of examples. When Mr. Bagehot says that the mind of the savage, so far from being in a state of nature, is tattooed all over with monstrous superstitions, the case is very like the one we have just been considering. When Sir James Stephen compares our belief in the uniformity of nature, the congruity of the future with the past, to a man rowing one way and looking another, and steering his boat by keeping her stern in a line with an object behind him, the operative link becomes harder to dissect out. It is subtler still in Dr. Holmes's phrase, that stories in passing from mouth to mouth make a great deal of lee-way in proportion to their headway; or in Mr. Lowell's description of German sentences, that they have a way of yawing and going stern-foremost and not minding the helm for several minutes after it has been put down. And finally, it is a real puzzle when the color pale-blue is said to have feminine and blood-red masculine affinities. And if I hear a friend describe a certain family as having blotting-paper voices, the image, though immediately felt to be apposite, baffles the utmost powers of analysis. The higher poets all use abrupt epithets, which are alike intimate and remote, and, as Emerson says, sweetly torment us with invitations to their inaccessible homes.

In these latter instances we must suppose that there is an identical portion in the similar objects, and that its brain-tract is energetically operative, without, however, being sufficiently isolable in its activity as to stand out per se, and form the condition of a distinctly discriminated 'abstract idea.' We cannot even by careful search see the bridge over which we passed from the heart of one representation of that of the next. In some brains, however, this mode of transition is extremely common. It would be one of the most important of physiological discoveries could we assign the mechanical or chemical difference which makes the thoughts of one brain cling close to impartial redintegration, while those of another shoot about in all the lawless revelry of similarity. Why, in these latter brains, action should tend to focalize itself in small spots, while in the others it fills patiently its broad bed, it seems impossible to guess. Whatever the difference may be, it is what separates the man of genius from the prosaic creature of habit and routine thinking. In Chapter XXII we shall need to recur again to this point.

Association in Voluntary Thought.

Hitherto we have assumed the process of suggestion of one object by another to be spontaneous. The train of imagery wanders at its own sweet will, now trudging in sober grooves of habit, now with a hop, skip, and jump darting across the whole field of time and space. This is revery, or musing; but great segments of the flux of our ideas consist of something very different from this. They are guided by a distinct purpose or conscious interest. As the Germans say, we nachdenken, or think towards a certain end. It is now necessary to examine what modification is made in the trains of our imagery by the having of an end in view. The course of our ideas is then called voluntary. Physiologically considered, we must suppose that a purpose means the persistent activity of certain rather definite brain-processes throughout the whole course of thought. Our most usual cogitations are not pure reveries, absolute driftings, but revolve about some central interest or topic to which most of the images are relevant, and towards which we return promptly after occasional digressions. This interest is subserved by the persistently active brain-tracts we have supposed. In the mixed associations which we have hitherto studied, the parts of each object which form the pivots on which our thoughts successively turn have their interest largely determined by their connection with some general interest which for the time has seized upon the mind. If we call Z the brain-tract of general interest, then, if the object abc turns up, and b has more associations with Z than have either a or c, b will become the object's interesting, pivotal portion, and will call up its own associates exclusively. For the energy of b's brain-tract will be augmented by Z's activity, -- an activity which, from lack of previous connection between Z and a or c, does not influence a or c. If, for instance, I think of Paris whilst I am hungry, I shall not improbably find that its restaurants have become the pivot of my thought, etc., etc.

But in the theoretic as well as in the practical life there are interests of a more acute sort, taking the form of definite images of some achievement, be it action or acquisition, which we desire to effect. The train of ideas arising under the influence of such an interest constitutes usually the thought of the means by which the end shall be attained. If the end by its simple presence does not instantaneously suggest the means, the search for the latter becomes an intellectual problem. The solution of problems is the most characteristic and peculiar sort of voluntary thinking. Where the end thought of is some outward deed or gain, the solution is largely composed of the actual motor processes, walking, speaking, writing, etc., which lead up to it. Where the end is in the first instance only ideal, as in laying out a place of operations, the steps are purely imaginary. In both of these cases the discovery of the means may form a new sort of end, of an entirely peculiar nature, an end, namely, which we intensely desire before we have attained it, but of the nature of which, even whilst most strongly craving it, we have no distinct imagination whatever. Such an end is a problem.

The same state of things occurs whenever we seek to recall something forgotten, or to state the reason for a judgment which we have made intuitively. The desire strains and presses in a direction which it feels to be right but towards a point which it is unable to see. In short, the absence of an item is a determinant of our representations quite as positive as its presence can ever be. The gap becomes no mere void, but what is called an aching void. If we try to explain in terms of brain-action how a thought which only potentially exists can yet be effective, we seem driven to believe that the brain-tract thereof must actually be excited, but only in a minimal and sub-conscious way. Try for instance, to symbolize what goes on in a man who is racking his brains to remember a thought which occurred to him last week. The associates of the thought are there, many of them at least, but they refuse to awaken the thought itself. We cannot suppose that they do not irradiate at all into its brain-tract, because his mind quivers on the very edge of its recovery. Its actual rhythm sounds in his ears; the words seem on the imminent point of following, but fail. What it is that blocks the discharge and keeps the brain-excitement here from passing beyond the nascent into the vivid state cannot be guessed. But we see in the philosophy of desire and pleasure, that such nascent excitements, spontaneously tending to a crescendo, but inhibited or checked by other causes, may become potent mental stimuli and determinants of desire. All questioning, wonder, emotion of curiosity, must be referred to cerebral causes of some such form as this. The great difference between the effort to recall things forgotten and the search after the means to a given end, is that the latter have not, whilst the former have, already formed a part of our experience. If we first study the mode of recalling a thing forgotten, we can take up with better understanding the voluntary quest of the unknown.

The forgotten thing is felt by us as a gap in the midst of certain other things. If it is a thought, we possess a dim idea of where we were and what we were about when it occurred to us. We recollect the general subject to which it relates. But all these details refuse to shoot together into a solid whole, for the lack of the vivid traits of this missing thought, the relation whereof to each detail forms now the main interest of the latter. We keep running over the details in our mind, dissatisfied, craving something more. From each detail there radiate lines of association forming so many tentative guesses. Many of these are immediately seen to be irrelevant, are therefore void of interest, and lapse immediately from consciousness. Others are associated with the other details present, and with the missing thought as well. When these surge up, we have a peculiar feeling that we are 'warm,' as the children say when they play hide and seek; and such associates as these we clutch at and keep before the attention. Thus we recollect successively that when we had the thought in question we were at the dinner-table; then that of our friend J. D. was there; then that the subject talked about was so and so; finally, that the thought came à propos of a certain anecdote, and then that it had something to do with a French quotation. Now all these added associations arise independently of the will, by the spontaneous process we know so well. All that the will does is to emphasize and linger over those which seem pertinent, and ignore the rest. Through this hovering of the attention in the neighborhood of the desired object, the accumulation of associates becomes so great that the combined tensions of their neural processes break through the bar, and the nervous wave pours into the tract which has so long been awaiting its advent. And as the expectant, sub-conscious itching there, bursts into the fulness of vivid feeling, the mind finds an inexpressible relief.

The whole process can be rudely symbolized in a diagram. Call the forgotten thing Z, the first facts with which we felt it was related, a, b, and c, and the details finally operative in calling it up, l, m, and n. Each circle will then stand for the brain-process underlying the thought of the object denoted by the letter contained within it.

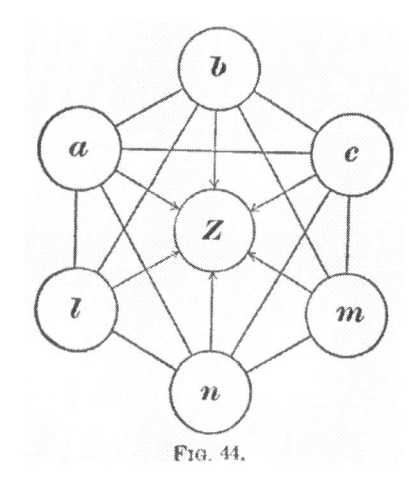

FIG. 44.

The activity in Z will at first be a mere tension; but as the activities in a, b, and c little by little irradiate into l, m, and n, and as all these processes are somehow connected with Z, their combined irradiations upon Z, represented by the centripetal arrows, succeed in helping the tension there to overcome the resistance, and in rousing Z also to full activity.

The tension present from the first in Z, even though it keep below the threshold of discharge, is probably to some degree co-operative with a, b, c in determining that l, m, n shall awake. Without Z's tension there might be a slower accumulation of objects connected with it. But, as aforesaid, the objects come before us through the brain's own laws, and the Ego of the thinker can only remain on hand, as it were, to recognize their relative values and brood over some of them, whilst others are let drop. As when we have lost a material object we cannot recover it by a direct effort, but only through moving about such neighborhoods wherein it is likely to lie, and trusting that it will then strike our eye; so here, by not letting our attention leave the neighborhood of what we seek, we trust that it will end by speaking to us of its own accord.[23]

Turn now to the case of finding the unknown means to a distinctly conceived end. The end here stands in the place of a, b, c, in the diagram. It is the starting-point of the irradiations of suggestion; and here, as in that case, what the voluntary attention does is only to dismiss some of the suggestions as irrelevant, and hold fast to others which are felt to be more pertinent—let these be symbolized by l, m, n. These latter at last accumulate sufficiently to discharge all together into Z, the excitement of which process is, in the mental sphere, equivalent to the solution of our problem. The only difference between this case and the last, is that in this one there need be no original sub-excitement in Z, co-operating from the very first. When we seek a forgotten name, we must suppose the name's centre to be in a state of active tension from the very outset, because of that peculiar feeling of recognition which we get at the moment of recall. The plenitude of the thought seems here but a maximum degree of something which our mind divined in advance. It instantaneously fills a socket completely moulded to its shape; and it seems most natural to ascribe the identity of quality in our feeling of the gaping socket and our feeling of what comes to fill it, to the sameness of a nerve-tract excited in different degrees. In the solving of a problem, on the contrary, the recognition that we have found the means is much less immediate. Here, what we are aware of in advance seems to be its relations with the items we already know. It must bear a causal relation, or it must be an effect, or it must contain an attribute common to two items, or it must be a uniform concomitant, or what not. We know, in short, a lot about it, whilst as yet we have no knowledge of acquaintance with it, or in Mr. Hodgson's language, "we know what we want to find beforehand, in a certain sense, in its second intention, and do not know it, in another sense, in its first intention."[24] Our intuition that one of the ideas which turn up is, at last, our quœsitum, is due to our recognition that its relations are identical with those we had in mind, and this may be a rather slow act of judgment. In fact, every one knows that an object may be for some time present to his mind before its relations to other matters are perceived. To quote Hodgson again:

"The mode of operation is common to voluntary memory and reason.... But reasoning adds to memory the function of comparing or judging the images which arise.... Memory aims at filling the gap with an image which has at some particular time filled it before, reasoning with one which bears certain time-and space-relations to the images before and after"—

or, to use perhaps clearer language, one which stands in determinate logical relations to those data round about the gap which filled our mind at the start. This feeling of the blank form of relationship before we get the material quality of the thing related will surprise no one who has read Chapter IX.

From the guessing of newspaper enigmas to the plotting of the policy of an empire there is no other process than this. We trust to the laws of cerebral nature to present us spontaneously with the appropriate idea:

"Our only command over it is by the effort we make to keep the painful unfilled gap in consciousness.[25] . . . Two circumstances are important to notice: the first is, that volition has no power of calling up images, but only of rejecting and selecting from those offered by spontaneous redintegration.[26] But the rapidity with which this selection is made, owing to the familiarity of the ways in which spontaneous redintegration runs, gives the process of reasoning the appearance of evoking images that are foreseen to be conformable to the purpose. There is no seeing them before they are offered; there is no summoning them before they are seen. The other circumstance is, that every kind of reasoning is nothing, in its simplest form, but attention."[27]

It is foreign to our purpose here to enter into any detailed analysis of the different classes of mental pursuit. In a scientific research we get perhaps as rich an example as can be found. The inquirer starts with a fact of which he seeks the reason, or with an hypothesis of which he seeks the proof. In either case he keeps turning the matter incessantly in his mind until, by the arousal of associate upon associate, some habitual, some similar, one arises which he recognizes to suit his need. This, however, may take years. No rules can be given by which the investigator may proceed straight to his result; but both here and in the case of reminiscence the accumulation of helps in the way of associations may advance more rapidly by the use of certain routine methods. In striving to recall a thought, for example, we may of set purpose run through the successive classes of circumstances with which it may possibly have been connected, trusting that when the right member of the class has turned up it will help the thought's revival. Thus we may run through all the places in which we may have had it. We may run through the persons whom we remember to have conversed with, or we may call up successively all the books we have lately been reading. If we are trying to remember a person we may run through a list of streets or of professions. Some item out of the lists thus methodically gone over will very likely be associated with the fact we are in need of, and may suggest it or help to do so. And yet the item might never have arisen without such systematic procedure. In scientific research this accumulation of associates has been methodized by Mill under the title of 'The Four Methods of Experimental Inquiry.' By the 'method of agreement,' by that of 'difference,' by those of 'residues' and 'concomitant variations' (which cannot here be more nearly defined), we make certain lists of cases; and by ruminating these lists in our minds the cause we seek will be more likely to emerge. But the final stroke of discovery is only prepared, not effected, by them. The brain-tracts must, of their own accord, shoot the right way at last, or we shall still grope in darkness. That in some brains the tracts do shoot the right way much oftener than in others, and that we cannot tell why, -- these are ultimate facts to which we must never close our eyes. Even in forming our lists of instances according to Mill's methods, we are at the mercy of the spontaneous workings of Similarity in our brain. How are a number of facts, resembling the one whose cause we seek, to be brought together in a list unless the one will rapidly suggest the other through association by similarity?

Similarity No Elementary Law.

Such is the analysis I propose, first of the three main types of spontaneous association, and then of voluntary association. It will be observed that the object called up may bear any logical relation whatever to the one which suggested it. The law requires only that one condition should be fulfilled. The fading object must be due to a brain-process some of whose elements awaken through habit some of the elements of the brain-process of the object which comes to view. This awakening is the operative machinery, the causal agency, throughout, quite as much so in the kind of association I have called by the name of Similarity, as in any other sort. The similarity between the objects, or between the thoughts (if similarity there be between these latter), has no causal agency in carrying us from one to the other. It is but a result—the effect of the usual causal agent when this happens to work in a certain particular and assignable way. But ordinary writers talk as if the similarity of the objects were itself an agent, co-ordinate with habit, and independent of it, and like it able to push objects before the mind. This is quite unintelligible. The similarity of two things does not exist till both things are there—it is meaningless to talk of it as an agent of production of anything, whether in the physical or the psychical realms.[28] It is a relation which the mind perceives after the fact, just as it may perceive the relations of superiority, of distance, of causality, of container and content, of substance and accident, or of contrast, between an object and some second object which the associative machinery calls up.[29]

There are, nevertheless, able writers who not only insist on preserving association by similarity as a distinct elementary law, but who make it the most elementary law, and seek to derive contiguous association from it. Their reasoning is as follows: When the present impression A awakens the idea b of its past contiguous associate B, how can this occur except through first reviving an image a of its own past occurrence. This is the term directly connected with b; so that the process instead of being simply A—b is A—a—b. Now A and a are similars; therefore no association by contiguity can occur except through a previous association by similarity. The most important supposition here made is that every impression on entering the mind must needs awaken an image of its past self, in the light of which it is 'apperceived' or understood, and through the intermediation of which it enters into relation with the mind's other objects. This assumption is almost universally made; and yet it is hard to find any good reason for it. It first came before us when we were reviewing the facts of aphasia and mental blindness. But we then saw no need of optical and auditory images to interpret optical and auditory sensations by. On the contrary, we agreed that auditory sensations were understood by us only so far as they awakened non-auditory images, and optical sensations only so far as they awakened non-optical images. In the chapters on Memory, on Reasoning, and on Perception the same assumption will meet us again, and again will have to be rejected as groundless. The sensational process A and the ideational process a probably occupy essentially the same tracts. When the outer stimulus comes and those tracts vibrate with the sensation A, they discharge as directly into the paths which lead to B as when there is no outer stimulus and they only vibrate with the idea a. To say that the process A can only reach these paths by the help of the weaker process a is like saying that we need a candle to see the sun by. A replaces a, does all that a does and more; and there is no intelligible meaning, to my mind, in saying that the weaker process coexists with the stronger. I therefore consider that these writers are altogether wrong. The only plausible proof they give of the coexistence of a with A is when A gives us a sense of familiarity but fails to awaken any distinct thought of past contiguous associates. In a later chapter I shall consider this case. Here I content myself with saying that it does not seem conclusive as to the point at issue; and that I still believe association of coexistent or sequent impressions to be the one elementary law.

CONTRAST has also been held to be an independent agent in association. But the reproduction of an object contrasting with one already in the mind is easily explained on our principles. Recent writers, in fact, all reduce it either to similarity or contiguity. Contrast always presupposes generic similarity; it is only the extremes of a class which are contrasted, black and white, not black and sour, or white and prickly. A machinery which reproduces a similar at all, may reproduce the opposite similar, as well as any intermediate term. Moreover, the greater number of contrasts are habitually coupled in speech, young and old, life and death, rich and poor, etc., and are, as Dr. Bain says, in everybody's memory.[30]

I trust that the student will now feel that the way to a deeper understanding of the order of our ideas lies in the direction of cerebral physiology. The elementary process of revival can be nothing but the law of habit. Truly the day is distant when physiologists shall actually trace from cell-group to cell-group the irradiations which we have hypothetically invoked. Probably it will never arrive. The schematism we have used is, moreover, taken immediately from the analysis of objects into their elementary parts, and only extended by analogy to the brain. And yet it is only as incorporated in the brain that such a schematism can represent anything causal. This is, to my mind, the conclusive reason for saying that the order of presentation of the mind's materials is due to cerebral physiology alone.

The law of accidental prepotency of certain processes over others falls also within the sphere of cerebral probabilities. Granting such instability as the brain-tissue requires, certain points must always discharge more quickly and strongly than others; and this prepotency would shift its place from moment to moment by accidental causes, giving us a perfect mechanical diagram of the capricious play of similar association in the most gifted mind. The study of dreams confirms this view. The usual abundance of paths of irradiation seems, in the dormant brain, reduced. A few only are pervious, and the most fantastic sequences occur because the currents run—'like sparks in burnt-up paper'—wherever the nutrition of the moment creates an opening, but nowhere else.

The effects of interested attention and volition remain. These activities seem to hold fast to certain elements, and by emphasizing them and dwelling on them, to make their associates the only ones which are evoked. This is the point at which an anti-mechanical psychology must, if anywhere, make it stand in dealing with association. Everything else is pretty certainly due to cerebral laws. My own opinion on the question of active attention and spiritual spontaneity is expressed elsewhere. But even though there be a mental spontaneity, it can certainly not create ideas or summon them ex abrupto. Its power is limited to selecting amongst those which the associative machinery has already introduced or tends to introduce. If it can emphasize, reinforce, or protract for a second either one of these, it can do all that the most eager advocate of free will need demand; for it then decides the direction of the next associations by making them hinge upon the emphasized term; and determining in this wise the course of the man's thinking, it also determines his acts.

The History of Opinion Concerning Association.

...may be briefly glanced at ere we end the chapter.[31] Aristotle seems to have caught both the facts and the principle of explanation; but he did not expand his views, and it was not till the time of Hobbes that the matter was again touched on in a definite way. Hobbes first formulated the problem of the succession of our thoughts. He writes in Leviathan, chapter III, as follows:

"By consequence, or train of thoughts, I understand that succession of one thought to another which is called, to distinguish it from discourse in words, mental discourse. When a man thinketh on anything whatsoever, his next thought after is not altogether so casual as it seems to be. Not every thought to every thought succeeds indifferently. But as we have no imagination, whereof we have not formerly had sense, in whole or in parts; so we have no transition from one imagination to another, whereof we never had the like before in our senses. The reason whereof is this. All fancies are motions within us, relics of those made in the sense: and those motions that immediately succeeded one another in the sense continue also together after sense: insomuch as the former coming again to take place, and be predominant, the latter followeth, by coherence of the matter moved, in such manner, as water upon a plane table is drawn which way any one part of it is guided by the finger. But because in sense, to one and the same thing perceived, sometimes one thing, sometimes another succeedeth, it comes to pass in time that, in the imagining of anything, there is no certainty what we shall imagine next; only this is certain, it shall be something that succeeded the same before, at one time or another. This train of thoughts, or mental discourse, is of two sorts. The first is unguided, without design, and inconstant; wherein there is no passionate thought, to govern and direct those that follow, to itself, as the end and scope of some desire, or other passion.... The second is more constant; as being regulated by some desire and design. For the impression made by such things as we desire, or fear, is strong and permanent, or, if it cease for a time, of quick return: so strong is it, sometimes, as to hinder and break our sleep. From desire ariseth the thought of some means we have seen produce the like of that which we aim at; and from the thought of that, the thought of means to that mean; and so continually, till we come to some beginning within our own power. And because the end, by the greatness of the impression, comes often to mind, in case our thoughts begin to wander, they are quickly again reduced into the way: which observed by one of the seven wise men, made him give men this precept, which is now worn out, Respice finem; that is to say, in all your actions, look often upon what you would have, as the thing that directs all your thoughts in the way to attain it.

"The train of regulated thoughts is of two kinds; one, when of an effect imagined we seek the causes, or means that produce it: and this is common to man and beast. The other is, when imagining anything whatsoever, we seek all the possible effects that can by it be produced; that is to say, we imagine what we can do with it, when we have it. Of which I have not at any time seen any sign, but in man only; for this is a curiosity hardly incident to the nature of any living creature that has no other passion but sensual, such as are hunger, thirst, lust, and anger. In sum, the discourse of the mind, when it is governed by design, is nothing but seeking, or the faculty of invention, which the Latins called sagacitas, and sollertia; a hunting out of the causes, of some effect, present or past; or of the effects, of some present or past cause."

The most important passage after this of Hobbes is Hume's:

"As all simple ideas may be separated by the imagination, and may be united again in what form it pleases, nothing would be more unaccountable than the operations of that faculty, were it not guided by some universal principles, which render it, in some measure, uniform with itself in all times and places. Were ideas entirely loose and unconnected, chance alone would join them; and 'tis impossible the same simple ideas should fall regularly into complex ones (as they commonly do) without some bond of union among them, some associating quality, by which one idea naturally introduces another. This uniting principle among ideas is not to be considered as an inseparable connection; for that has been already excluded from the imagination. Nor yet are we to conclude that without it the mind cannot join two ideas; for nothing is more free than that faculty: but we are only to regard it as a gentle force, which commonly prevails, and is the cause why, among other things, languages so nearly correspond to each other; nature in a manner pointing to every one those simple ideas which are most proper to be united in a complex one. The qualities from which this association arises, and by which the mind is after this manner conveyed from one idea to another, are three, viz., RESEMBLANCE, CONTIGUITY in time or place, and CAUSE and EFFECT.

"I believe it will not be very necessary to prove that these qualities produce an association among ideas, and upon the appearance of one idea naturally introduce another. 'Tis plain that in the course of our thinking, and in the constant revolution of our ideas, our imagination runs easily from one idea to any other that resembles it, and that this quality alone is to the fancy a sufficient bond and association. 'Tis likewise evident, that as the senses, in changing their objects, are necessitated to change them regularly, and take them as they lie contiguous to each other, the imagination must by long custom acquire the same method of thinking, and run along the parts of space and time in conceiving its objects. As to the connection that is made by the relation of cause and effect, we shall have occasion afterwards to examine it to the bottom, and therefore shall not at present insist upon it. 'Tis sufficient to observe that there is no relation which produces a stronger connection in the fancy, and makes one idea more readily recall another, that the relation of cause and effect betwixt their objects.... These are therefore the principles of union or cohesion among our simple ideas, and in the imagination supply the place of that inseparable connection by which they are united in our memory. Here is a kind of ATTRACTION, which in the mental world will be found to have as extraordinary effects as in the natural, and to show itself in as many and as various forms. Its effects are everywhere conspicuous; but as to its causes, they are mostly unknown, and must be resolved into original qualities of human nature, which I pretend not to explain."[32]

Hume did not, however, any more than Hobbes, follow out the effects of which he speaks, and the task of popularizing the notion of association and making an effective school based on association of ideas alone was reserved for Hartley[33] and James Mill.[34] These authors traced minutely the presence of association in all the cardinal notions and operations of the mind. The several 'faculties' of the Mind were dispossessed; the one principle of association between ideas did all their work. As Priestley says:

"Nothing is requisite to make any man whatever he is, but a sentient principle with this single law.... Not only all our intellectual pleasures and pains but all the phenomena of memory, imagination, volition, reasoning and every other mental affection and operation, are but different modes or cases of the association of ideas."[35]

An eminent French psychologist, M. Ribot, repeats Hume's comparison of the law of association with that of gravitation, and goes on to say:

"It is remarkable that this discovery was made so late. Nothing is simpler, apparently, than to notice that this law of association is the truly fundamental, irreducible phenomenon of our mental life; that it is at the bottom of all our acts; that is permits of no exception; that neither dream, revery, mystic ecstasy, nor the most abstract reasoning can exist without it; that its suppression would be equivalent to that of thought itself. Nevertheless no ancient author understood it, for one cannot seriously maintain that a few scattered lines in Aristotle and the Stoics constitute a theory and clear view of the subject. It is to Hobbes, Hume, and Hartley that we must attribute the origin of these studies on the connection of our ideas. The discovery of the ultimate law of our psychologic acts has this, then, in common with many other discoveries: it came late and seems so simple that it may justly astonish us.

"Perhaps it is not superfluous to ask in what this manner of explanation is superior to the current theory of Faculties.[36] The most extended usage consists, as we know, in dividing intellectual phenomena into classes, in separating those which differ, in grouping together those of the same nature and in giving to these a common name and in attributing them to the same cause; it is thus that we have come to distinguish those diverse aspects of intelligence which are called judgment, reasoning, abstraction, perception, etc. This method is precisely the one followed in Physics, where the words caloric, electricity, gravity, designate the unknown causes of certain groups of phenomena. If one thus never forgets that the diverse faculties are only the unknown causes of known phenomena, that they are simply a convenient means of classifying the facts and speaking of them, if one does not fall into the common fault of making out of them substantial entities, creations which now agree, now disagree, so forming in the intelligence a little republic; then, we can see nothing reprehensible in this distribution into faculties, conformable as it is to the rules of a sound method and of a good natural classification. In what then is Mr. Bain's procedure superior to the method of the faculties? It is that the latter is simply a classification while his is an explanation. Between the psychology which traces intellectual facts back to certain faculties, and that which reduces them to the single law of association, there is, according to our way of thinking, the same difference that we find in Physics between those who attribute its phenomena to five or six causes, and those who derive gravity caloric, light, etc., from motion. The system of the faculties explains nothing because each one of them is only a flatus vocis which is of value merely through the phenomena which it contains, and signifies nothing more than these phenomena. The new theory, on the contrary, shows that the different processes of intelligence are only diverse cases of a single law; that imagination, deduction, induction, perception, etc., are but so many determinate ways in which ideas may combine with each other; and that the differences of faculties are only differences of association. It explains all intellectual facts, certainly not after the manner of Metaphysics which demands the ultimate and absolute reason of things; but after the manner of Physics which seeks only their secondary and immediate cause."[37]

The inexperienced reader may be glad of a brief indication of the manner in which all the different mental operations may be conceived to consist of images of sensation associated together.

Memory is the association of a present image with others known to belong to the past. Expectation the same, with future substituted for past. Fancy, the association of images without temporal order.

Belief in anything not present to sense is the very lively, strong, and steadfast association of the image of that thing with some present sensation, so that as long as the sensation persists the image cannot be excluded from the mind. Judgment is 'transferring the idea of truth by association from one proposition to another that resembles it.'[38]

Reasoning is the perception that "whatever has any mark has that which it is a mark of"; in the concrete case the mark or middle term being always associated with each of the other terms and so serving as a link by which they are themselves indirectly associated together. This same kind of transfer of a sensible experience associated with another to a third also associated with that other, serves to explain emotional facts. When we are pleased or hurt we express it, and the expression associates itself with the feeling. Hearing the same expression from another revives the associated feeling, and we sympathize, i.e. grieve or are glad with him.

The other social affections, Benevolence, Conscientiousness, Ambition, etc., arise in like manner by the transfer of the bodily pleasure experienced as a reward for social service, and hence associated with it, to the act of service itself, the link of reward being dropped out. Just so Avarice when the miser transfers the bodily pleasures associated with the spending of money to the money itself, dropping the link of spending.

Fear is a transfer of the bodily hurt associated by experience with the thing feared, to the thought of the thing, with the precise features of the hurt left out. Thus we fear a dog without distinctly imagining his bite.

Love is the association of the agreeableness of certain sensible experiences with the idea of the object capable of affording them. The experiences themselves may cease to be distinctly imagined after the notion of their pleasure has been transferred to the object, constituting love there-for.

Volition is the association of ideas of muscular motion with the ideas of those pleasures which the motion produces. The motion at first occurs automatically and results in a pleasure unforeseen. The latter becomes so associated with the motion that whenever we think of it the idea of the motion arises; and the idea of the motion when vivid causes the motion to occur. This is an act of will.

Nothing is easier than for a philosopher of this school to explain from experience such a notion as that of infinitude. "He sees in it an ordinary manifestation of one of the laws of the association of ideas, -- the law that the idea of a thing irresistibly suggests the idea of any other thing which has been often experienced in close conjunction with it, and not otherwise. As we have never had experience of any point of space without other points beyond it, nor of any point of time without others following it, the law of indissoluble association makes it impossible for us to think of any point of space or time, however distant, without having the idea irresistibly realized, in imagination, of other points still more remote. And thus the supposed original and inherent property of these two ideas is completely explained and accounted for by the law of association; and we are enabled to see that if Space or Time were really susceptible of termination, we should be just as unable as we now are to conceive the idea."[39]

These examples of the Associationist Psychology are with the exception of the last, very crudely expressed, but they suffice for our temporary need. Hartley and James Mill[40] improved upon Hume so far as to employ but a single principle of association, that of contiguity or habit. Hartley ignores resemblance, James Mill expressly repudiates it in a passage which is assuredly one of the curiosities of literature:

"I believe it will be found that we are accustomed to see like things together. When we see a tree, we generally see more trees than one; a sheep, more sheep than one; a man, more men than one. From this observation, I think, we may refer resemblance to the law of frequency [i.e., contiguity], of which it seems to form only a particular case."

Mr. Herbert Spencer has still more recently tried to construct a Psychology which ignores Association by Similarity,[41] and in a chapter, which also is a curiosity, he tries to explain the association of two ideas by a conscious reference of the first to the point of time when its sensation was experienced, which point of time is no sooner thought of than its content, namely, the second idea, arises. Messrs. Bain and Mill, however, and the immense majority of contemporary psychologists retain both Resemblance and Contiguity as irreducible principles of Association.

Professor Bain's exposition of association is by common consent looked upon as the best expression of the English school. Perception of agreement and difference, retentiveness, and the two sorts of association, contiguity and similarity, are by him regarded as constituting all that is meant by intellect proper. His pages are painstaking and instructive from a descriptive point of view; though, after my own attempt to deal with the subject causally, I can hardly award to them any profound explanatory value. Association by Similarity, too much neglected by the British school before Bain, receives from him the most generous exemplification. As an instructive passage, the following, out of many equally good, may be chosen to quote:

"We may have similarity in form with diversity of use, and similarity of use with diversity of form. A rope suggests other ropes and cords, if we look to the appearance; but looking to the use, it may suggest an iron cable, a wooden prop, an iron girding, a leather band, or bevelled gear. In spite of diversity of appearance, the suggestion turns on what answers a common end. If we are very much attracted by sensible appearances, there will be the more difficulty in recalling things that agree only in the use; if, on the other hand, we are profoundly sensitive to the one point of practical efficiency as a tool, the peculiarities not essential to this will be little noticed, and we shall be ever ready to revive past objects corresponding in use to some one present, although diverse in all other circumstances. We become oblivious to the difference between a horse, a steam-engine, and a waterfall, when our minds are engrossed with the one circumstance of moving power. The diversity in these had no doubt for a long time the effect of keeping back their first identification; and to obtuse intellects, this identification might have been for ever impossible. A strong concentration of mind upon the single peculiarity of mechanical force, and a degree of indifference to the general aspect of the things themselves, must conspire with the intellectual energy of resuscitation by similars, in order to summon together in the view three structures so different. We can see, by an instance like this, how new adaptations of existing machinery might arise in the mind of a mechanical inventor. When it first occurred to a reflecting mind that moving water had a property identical with human or brute force, namely, the property of setting other masses in motion, overcoming inertia and resistance, -- when the sight of the stream suggested through this point of likeness the power of the animal, -- a new addition was made to the class of prime movers, and when circumstances permitted, this power could become a substitute for the others. It may seem to the modern understanding, familiar with water-wheels and drifting rafts, that the similarity here was an extremely obvious one. But if we put ourselves back into an early state of mind, when running water affected the mind by its brilliancy, its roar, and irregular devastation, we may easily suppose that to identify this with animal muscular energy was by no means an obvious effect. Doubtless when a mind arose, insensible by natural constitution to the superficial aspects of things, and having withal a great stretch of identifying intellect, such a comparison would then be possible. We may pursue the same example one stage further, and come to the discovery of steam power, or the identification of expanding vapor with the previously known sources of mechanical force. To the common eye, for ages, vapor presented itself as clouds in the sky; or as a hissing noise at the spout of a kettle, with the formation of a foggy curling cloud at a few inches' distance. The forcing up of the lid of a kettle may also have been occasionally observed. But how long was it ere any one was struck with the parallelism of this appearance with a blast of wind, a rush of water, or an exertion of animal muscle? The discordance was too great to be broken through by such a faint and limited amount of likeness. In one mind, however, the identification did take place, and was followed out into its consequences. The likeness had occurred to other minds previously, but not with the same results. Such minds must have been in some way or other distinguished above the millions of mankind; and we are now endeavoring to give the explanation of their superiority. The intellectual character of Watt contained all the elements preparatory to a great stroke of similarity in such a case; -- a high susceptibility, both by nature and by education, to the mechanical properties of bodies; ample previous knowledge or familiarity; and indifference to the superficial and sensational effects of things. It is not only possible, however, but exceedingly probable, that many men possessed all these accomplishments; they are of a kind not transcending common abilities. They would in some degree attach to a mechanical education almost as a matter of course. That the discovery was not sooner made supposes that something farther, and not of common occurrence, was necessary; and this additional endowment appears to be the identifying power of Similarity in general; the tendency to detect likeness in the midst of disparity and disguise. This supposition accounts for the fact, and is consistent with the known intellectual character of the inventor of the steam-engine."[42]

Dr. Hodgson's account of association is by all odds the best yet propounded in English.[43] All these writers hold more or less explicitly to the notion of atomistic 'ideas' which recur. In Germany, the same mythological supposition has been more radically grasped, and carried out to a still more logical, if more repulsive, extreme, by Herbart[44] and his followers, who until recently may be said to have reigned almost supreme in their native country.[45] For Herbart each idea is a permanently existing entity, the entrance whereof into consciousness is but an accidental determination of its being. So far as it succeeds in occupying the theatre of consciousness, it crowds out another idea previously there. This act of inhibition gives it, however, a sort of hold on the other representation which on all later occasions facilitates its following the other into the mind. The ingenuity with which most special cases of association are formulated in this mechanical language of struggle and inhibition, is great, and surpasses in analytic thoroughness anything that has been done by the British school. This, however, is a doubtful merit, in a case where the elements dealt with are artificial; and I must confess that to my mind there is something almost hideous in the glib Herbartian jargon about Vorstellungsmassen and their Hemmungen and Hemmungssummen, and sinken and erheben and schweben, and Verschmelzungen and Complexionen. Herr Lipps, the most recent systematic German Psychologist, has, I regret to say, carried out the theory of ideas in a way which the great originality, learning, and acuteness he shows make only the more regrettable.[46] Such elaborately artificial constructions are, it seems to me, only a burden and a hindrance, not a help, to our science.[47]

In French, M. Rabier in his chapter on Association,[48] handles the subject more vigorously and acutely than any one. His treatment of it, though short, seems to me for general soundness to rank second only to Hodgson's.

In the last chapter we already invoked association to account for the effect of use in improving discrimination. In later chapters we shall see abundant proof of the immense part which it plays in other processes, and shall then readily admit that few principles of analysis, in any science, have proved more fertile than this one, however vaguely formulated it often may have been. Our own attempt to formulate it more definitely, and to escape the usual confusion between causal agencies and relations merely known, must not blind us to the immense services of those by whom the confusion was unfelt. From this practical point of view it would be a true ignoratio elenchi to flatter one's self that one has dealt a heavy blow at the psychology of association, when one has exploded the theory of atomistic ideas, or shown that contiguity and similarity between ideas can only be there after association is done.[49] The whole body of the associationist psychology remains standing after you have translated 'ideas' into 'objects,' on the one hand, and 'brain-processes' on the other; and the analysis of faculties and operations is as conclusive in these terms as in those traditionally used.

Notes

[1] The theory propounded in this chapter, and a good many pages of the text, were originally published in the Popular Science Monthly for March, 1880.
[2] Compare Renouvier's criticism of associationism in his Essais de Critique générale, Logique, II. p. 493 foll.
[3] Unless the name belong to a rapidly uttered sentence, when no substantive image may have time to arise.
[4] In his observations he says that time was lost in mentally taking in the word which was the cue, "owing to the quiet unobtrusive way in which I found it necessary to bring it into view, so as not to distract the thoughts. Moreover, a substantive standing by itself is usually the equivalent of too abstract an idea for us to conceive properly without delay. Thus it is very difficult to get a quick conception of the word 'carriage,' because there are so many different kinds—two-wheeled, four-wheeled, open and closed, and in so many different possible positions, that the mind possibly hesitates amidst an obscure sense of many alterations that cannot blend together. But limit the idea to say a landau, and the mental association declares itself more quickly." (Inquiries, etc., p. 190.)
[5] Physiol. Psych., II. 280 fol.
[6] For interesting remarks on the sorts of things associated, in these experiments, with the prompting word, see Galton, op. cit. pp. 185-203, and Trautscholdt in Wundt's Psychologische Studien, I. 213.
[7] Mind, XI. 64-5.
[8] This value is much smaller than that got by Wundt as above. No reason for the difference is suggested by Mr. Cattell. Wundt calls attention to the fact that the figures found by him give an average, 0.720", exactly equal to the time interval which in his experiments (vide infra, chapter on Time) was reproduced without error either way, and to that required, according to the Webers, for the legs to swing in rapid locomotion. "It is not improbable," he adds, "that this psychic constant, of the mean association-time and of the most correct appreciation of a time-interval, may have been developed under the influence of the most usual bodily movements, which also have determined the manner in which we tend to subdivide rhythmically longer periods of time." (Physiol. Psch., II. 286). The rapprochement is of that tentative sort which it is no harm for psychologists to make, provided they recollect how very fictitious and incomparable mutually all these averages derived from different observers, working under different conditions, are. Mr. Cattell's figure throws Wundt's ingenious parallel entirely out of line.—The only measurements of association-time which so far seem likely to have much theoretic importance are a few made on insane patients by Von Tschisch (Mendel's Neurologisches Centralblatt, 15 Mai, 1885, 3 Jhrg., p. 217). The simple reaction time was found about normal in three patients, one with progressive paralysis, one with inveterate mania of persecution, one recovering from ordinary mania. In the convalescent maniac and the paralytic, however, the association-time was hardly half as much as Wundt's normal figure (0.28" and 0.23" instead of 0.7'—smaller also than Cattell's), whilst in the sufferer from delusions of persecution and hallucinations it was twice as great as normal (1.39" instead of 0.7"). This latter patient's time was six-fold that of the paralytic. Herr von Tschisch remarks on the connection of the short times with diminished power for clear and consistent processes of thought, and on that of the long times with the persistent fixation of the attention upon monotonous objects (delusions). Miss Marie Walitzky (Revue Philosophique, XXVIII. 583) has carried Von Tschisch's observations still farther, making 18,000 measurements in all. She found association-time increased in paralytic dementia and diminished in mania. Choice-time, on the contrary, is increased in mania.
[9] Mind, XII. 67-74.
[10] Compare Bain's law of Association by Contiguity: "Actions, Sensations, and States of Feeling, occurring together or in close succession, tend to grow together, or cohere, in such a way that, when any one of them is afterwards presented to the mind, the others are apt to be brought up in idea" (Senses and Intellect, p. 327). Compare also Hartley's formulation: "Any sensations A, B, C, etc., by being associated with one another a sufficient Number of Times, get such a power over the corresponding Ideas, a, b, c, etc., that any one of the sensations A, when impressed alone, shall be able to excite in the Mind b, c, etc., the ideas of the rest." (Observations on Man, part I. chap. I. § 2, Prop. X.) The statement in the text differs from these in holding fast to the objective point of view. It is things, and objective properties in things, which are associated in our thought.
[11] Encyclopædia Britannica, 9th Ed., article Psychology, p. 60, col. 2.
[12] Physiol. Psych., 2d ed. II. 300.
[13] The difficulty here as with habit überhaupt is in seeing how new paths come first to be formed. Experience shows that a new path is formed between centres for sensible impressions whenever these vibrate together or in rapid succession. A child sees a certain bottle and hears it called 'milk,' and thenceforward thinks the name when he again sees the bottle. But why the successive or simultaneous excitement of two centres independently stimulated from without, one by sight and the other by hearing, should result in a path between them, one does not immediately see. We can only make hypotheses. Any hypothesis of the specific mode of their formation which tallies well with the observed facts of association will be in so far forth credible, in spite of possible obscurity. Herr Münsterberg thinks (Beiträge zur exp. Psychologie, Heft 1, p. 132) that between centres

excited successively from without no path ought to be formed, and that consequently all contiguous association is between simultaneous experiences. Mr. Ward (loc. cit.) thinks on the contrary, that it can only be between successive experiences: "The association of objects simultaneously presented can be resolved into an association of objects successively attended to. . . . It seems hardly possible to mention a case in which attention to the associated objects could not have been successive. In fact, an aggregate of objects on which attention could be focused at once would be already associated." Between these extreme possibilities, I have refrained from deciding in the text, and have described contiguous association as holding between both successively and coexistently presented objects. The physiological question as to how we may conceive the paths to originate had better be postponed till it comes to us again in the chapter on the Will, where we can treat it in a broader way. It is enough here to have called attention to it as a serious problem.

[14] Essay, bk. II. chap. XXXIII. § 6. Compare Hume, who, like Locke, only uses the principle to account for unreasonable and obstructive mental associations:

"'Twould have been easy to have made an imaginary dissection of the brain, and have shown why, upon our conception of any idea, the animal spirits run into all the contiguous traces, and rouse up the other ideas that are related to it. But though I have neglected any advantage which I might have drawn from this topic in explaining the relations of ideas, I am afraid I must here have recourse to it, in order to account for the mistakes that arise from these relations. I shall therefore observe, that as the mind is endowed with a power of exciting any idea it pleases; whenever it dispatches the spirits into that region of the brain in which the idea is placed, these spirits always excite the idea, when they run precisely into the proper traces, and rummage that cell which belongs to the idea. But as their motion is seldom direct, and naturally turns a little to the one side or the other; for this reason the animal spirits, falling into the contiguous traces, present other related ideas in lieu of that which the mind desired at first to survey. This change we are not always sensible of; but continuing still the same train of thought, make use of the related idea which is presented to us, and employ it in our reasoning, as if it were the same with what we demanded. This is the cause of many mistakes and sophisms in philosophy; as will naturally be imagined, and as it would be easy to show, if there was occasion."

[15] Op. cit. prop. XI.
[16] See Chapter III, p. 82-5.
[17] I strongly advise the student to read his Senses and Intellect, pp. 544-556.
[18] Time and Space, p. 266. Compare Coleridge: "The true practical general law of association is this: that whatever makes certain parts of a total impression more vivid or distinct than the rest will determine the mind to recall these, in preference to others equally linked together by the common condition of contemporaeity or of contiguity. But the will itself, by confining and intensifying the attention, may arbitrarily give vividness or distinctness to any object whatsoever." (Biographia Litteraria, Chap. V.)
[19] Leviathan, pt. I. chap. III., init.
[20] I refer to a recency of a few hours. Mr. Galton found that experiences from boyhood and youth were more likely to be suggested by words seen at random than experiences of later years. See his highly interesting account of experiments in his Inquiries into Human Faculty, pp. 191-203.
[21] For other instances see Wahle, in Vierteljsch f. Wiss. Phil., IX. 144-417 (1885).
[22] I retain the title of association by similarity in order not to depart from common usage. The reader will observe, however, that my nomenclature is not based on the same principle throughout. Impartial redintegration connotes neural processes; similarity is an objective relation perceived by the mind; ordinary or mixed association is a merely denotative word. Total recall, partial recall, and focalized recall, of associates, would be better terms. But as the denotation of the latter word is almost identical with that of association by similarity, I think it better to sacrifice propriety to popularity, and to keep the latter well-worn phrase.
[23] No one has described this process better than Hobbes: "Sometimes a man seeks what he hath lost; and from that place and time wherein he misses it, his mind runs back from place to place and time to time to find where and when he had it; that is to say, to find some certain and limited time and place, in which to begin a method of seeking. Again, from thence his thoughts run over the same places and times to find what action or other occasion might make him lose it. This we call Remembrance, or calling to mind. Sometimes a man knows a place determinate, within the compass whereof he is to seek; and then his thoughts run over all the parts thereof, in the same manner as one would sweep a room to find a jewel, or as a spaniel ranges the field till he find a scent, or as a man should run over the alphabet to start a rhyme." (Leviathan, 165, p. 10.)
[24] Theory of Practice, vol. I. p. 394.
[25] Ibid. p. 394.
[26] All association is called redintegration by Hodgson.
[27] Ibid p. 400. Compare Bain, Emotions and Will, p. 377. "The outgoings of the mind are necessarily random; the end alone is the thing that is clear to the view, and with that there is a perception of the fitness of every passing suggestion. The volitional energy keeps up the attention on the active search: and the moment that anything in point rises before the mind, it springs upon that like a wild beast upon its prey."
[28] Compare what is said of the principle of Similarity by F. H. Bradley, Principles of Logic, pp. 294 ff.; E. Rabier, Psychologie, 187 ff.; Paulhan, Critique Philosophique, 2me Série, I. 458; Rabier, ibid. 460; Pillon, ibid. II. 55; B. P. Bowne, Introduction to Psych. Theory, 92; Ward, Encyclop. Britt. art. Psychology, p. 60; Wahle, Vierteljahrsch. f. wiss. Philos. IX. 426-431.

[29] Dr. McCosh is accordingly only logical when he sinks similarity in what he calls the "Law of Correlation, according to which, when we have discovered a relation between things, the idea of one tends to bring up the others" (Psychology, the Cognitive Powers, p. 130). The relations mentioned by this author are Identity, Whole and Parts, Resemblance, Space, Time, Quantity, Active Property, and Cause and Effect. If perceived relations among objects are to be treated as grounds for their appearance before the mind, similarity has of course no right to an exclusive, or even to a predominant, place.

[30] Cf. Bain, Senses and Intellect, 564 ff.; J. S. Mill, Note 39 to J. Mill's Analysis; Lipps, Grundtatsachen, 97.

[31] See, for farther details, Hamilton's Reid, Appendices D** and D***; and L. Ferri, La Psychologie de l'Association (Paris, 1883). Also Robertson, art. Association in Encyclop. Britannica.

[32] Treatise of Human Nature, part I. § IV.

[33] Observations on Man (London, 1749).

[34] Analysis of the Phenomena of the Human Mind (1829).

[35] Hartley's Theory, 2d ed. (1790) p. XXVII.

[36] [Current, that is, in France.—W. J.]

[37] La Psychologie Anglaise, p. 242.

[38] Priestley, op. cit. p. XXX.

[39] Review of Bain's Psychology, by J. S. Mill, in Edinb. Review, Oct. 1, 1859, p. 293.

[40] Analysis of the Phenomena of the Human Mind, J. S. Mill's edition, vol. I. p. 111.

[41] On the Associability of Relations between Feelings, in Principles of Psychology, vol. I. p. 259. It is impossible to regard the "cohering of each feeling with previously-experienced feelings of the same class, order, genus, species, and, so far as may be, the same variety," which Spencer calls (p. 257) 'the sole process of association of feelings.' as any equivalent for what is commonly known as Association by similarity.

[42] The Senses and the Intellect, pp. 491-3.

[43] See his Time and Space, chapter V, and his Theory of Practice, §§ 53 to 57.

[44] Psychologie als Wissenschaft (1824), 2.

[45] Prof. Ribot, in chapter I of his 'Contemporary German Psychology,' has given a good account of Herbart and his school, and of Beneke, his rival and partial analogue. See also two articles on the Herbartian Psychology, by G. F. Stout, in Mind for 1888. J. D. Morrell's Outlines of Mental Philosophy (2d ed., London, 1862) largely follows Herbart and Beneke. I know of no other English book which does so.

[46] See his Grundtatsachen des Bewusstseins (1883), chap. VI et passim, especially pp. 106 ff., 364.

[47] The most burdensome and utterly gratuitous of them are perhaps Steinthal's, in his Einleitung in die Psychologie, 2te Aufl. (1881). Cf. also G. Glogau: Steinthal's Psychologische Formeln (1886).

[48] Leçons de Philosophie, I. Psychologie, chap. XVI (1884).

[49] Mr. F. H. Bradley seems to me to have been guilty of something very like this ignoratio elenchi in the, of course, subtle and witty but decidedly long-winded critique of the association of ideas, contained in book II. part II. chap. I. of his Principles of Logic.

Chapter XV - The Perception of Time[1]

In the next two chapters I shall deal with what is sometimes called internal perception, or the perception of time, and of events as occupying a date therein, especially when the date is a past one, in which case the perception in question goes by the name of memory. To remember a thing as past, it is necessary that the notion of 'past' should be one of our 'ideas.' We shall see in the chapter on Memory that many things come to be thought by us as past, not because of any intrinsic quality of their own, but rather because they are associated with other things which for us signify pastness. But how do these things get their pastness? What is the original of our experience of pastness, from whence we get the meaning of the term? It is this question which the reader is invited to consider in the present chapter. We shall see that we have a constant feeling sui generis of pastness, to which every one of our experiences in turn falls a prey. To think a thing as past is to think it amongst the objects or in the direction of the objects which at the present moment appear affected by this quality. This is the original of our notion of past time, upon which memory and history build their systems. And in this chapter we shall consider this immediate sense of time alone. If the constitution of consciousness were that of a string of bead-like sensations and images, all separate,

"we never could have any knowledge except that of the present instant. The moment each of our sensations ceased it would be gone for ever; and we should be as if we had never been.... We should be wholly incapable of acquiring experience.... Even if our ideas were associated in trains, but only as they are in imagination, we should still be without the capacity of acquiring knowledge. One idea, upon this supposition, would follow another. But that would be all. Each of our successive states of consciousness, the moment it ceased, would be gone forever. Each of those momentary states would be our whole being."[2]

We might, nevertheless, under these circumstances, act in a rational way, provided the mechanism which produced our trains of images produced them in a rational order. We should make appropriate speeches, though unaware of any word except the one just on our lips; we should decide upon the right policy without ever a glimpse of the total grounds of our choice. Our consciousness would be like a glow-worm spark, illuminating the point it immediately covered, but leaving all beyond in total darkness. Whether a very highly developed practical life be possible under such conditions as these is more than doubtful; it is, however, conceivable.

I make the fanciful hypothesis merely to set off our real nature by the contrast. Our feelings are not thus contracted, and our consciousness never shrinks to the dimensions of a glow-worm spark. The knowledge of some other part of the stream, past or future, near or remote, is always mixed in with our knowledge of the present thing.

A simple sensation, as we shall hereafter see, is an abstraction, and all our concrete states of mind are representations of objects with some amount of complexity. Part of the complexity is the echo of the objects just past, and, in a less degree, perhaps, the foretaste of those just to arrive. Objects fade out of consciousness slowly. If the present thought is of A B C D E F G, the next one will be of B C D E F G H, and the one after that of C D E F G H I— the lingerings of the past dropping successively away, and the incomings of the future making up the loss. These lingerings of old objects, these incomings of new, are the germs of memory and expectation, the retrospective and the prospective sense of time. They give that continuity to consciousness without which it could not be called a stream.[3]

The Sensible Present Has Duration.

Let any one try, I will not say to arrest, but to notice or attend to, the present moment of time. One of the most baffling experiences occurs. Where is it, this present? It has melted in our grasp, fled ere we could touch it, gone in the instant of becoming. As a poet, quoted by Mr. Hodgson, says,

"Le moment où je parle est déjà loin de moi,"

and it is only as entering into the living and moving organization of a much wider tract of time that the strict present is apprehended at all. It is, in fact, an altogether ideal abstraction, not only never realized in sense, but probably never even conceived of by those unaccustomed to philosophic meditation. Reflection leads us to the conclusion that it must exist, but that it does exist can never be a fact of our immediate experience. The only fact of our immediate experience is what Mr. E. R. Clay has well called 'the specious present.' His words deserve to be quoted in full:[4]

"The relation of experience to time has not been profoundly studied. Its objects are given as being of the present, but the part of time referred to by the datum is a very different thing from the conterminous of the past and future which philosophy denotes by the name Present. The present to which the datum refers is really a part of the past—a recent past—delusively given as being a time that intervenes between the past and the future. Let it be named the specious present, and let the past, that is given as being the past, be known as the obvious past. All the notes of a bar of a song seem to the listener to be contained in the present. All the changes of place of a meteor seem to the

beholder to be contained in the present. At the instant of the termination of such series, no part of the time measured by them seems to be a past. Time, then, considered relatively to human apprehension, consists of four parts, viz., the obvious past, the specious present, the real present, and the future. Omitting the specious present, it consists of three . . . nonentities—the past, which does not exist, the future, which does not exist, and their conterminous, the present; the faculty from which it proceeds lies to us in the fiction of the specious present."
In short, the practically cognized present is no knife-edge, but a saddle-back, with a certain breadth of its own on which we sit perched, and from which we look in two directions into time. The unit of composition of our perception of time is a duration, with a bow and a stern, as it were—a rearward—and a forward-looking end.[5] It is only as parts of this duration-block that the relation of succession of one end to the other is perceived. We do not first feel one end and then feel the other after it, and from the perception of the succession infer an interval of time between, but we seem to feel the interval of time as a whole, with its two ends embedded in it. The experience is from the outset a synthetic datum, not a simple one; and to sensible perception its elements are inseparable, although attention looking back may easily decompose the experience, and distinguish its beginning from its end.
When we come to study the perception of Space, we shall find it quite analogous to time in this regard. Date in time corresponds to position in space; and although we now mentally construct large spaces by mentally imagining remoter and remoter positions, just as we now construct great durations by mentally prolonging a series of successive dates, yet the original experience of both space and time is always of something already given as a unit, inside of which attention afterward discriminates parts in relation to each other. Without the parts already given as in a time and in a space, subsequent discrimination of them could hardly do more than perceive them as different from each other; it would have no motive for calling the difference temporal order in this instance and spatial position in that.
And just as in certain experiences we may be conscious of an extensive space full of objects, without locating each of them distinctly therein; so, when many impressions follow in excessively rapid succession in time, although we may be distinctly aware that they occupy some duration, and are not simultaneous, we may be quite at a loss to tell which comes first and which last; or we may even invert their real order in our judgment. In complicated reaction-time experiments, where signals and motions, and clicks of the apparatus come in exceedingly rapid order, one is at first much perplexed in deciding what the order is, yet of the fact of its occupancy of time we are never in doubt.

Accuracy of Our Estimate of Short Durations.

We must now proceed to an account of the facts of time-perception in detail as preliminary to our speculative conclusion. Many of the facts are matters of patient experimentation, others of common experience.
First of all, we note a marked difference between the elementary sensations of duration and those of space. The former have a much narrower range; the time-sense may be called a myopic organ, in comparison with the eye, for example. The eye sees rods, acres, even miles, at a single glance, and these totals it can afterward subdivide into an almost infinite number of distinctly identified parts. The units of duration, on the other hand, which the time-sense is able to take in at a single stroke, are groups of a few seconds, and within these units very few subdivisions—perhaps forty at most, as we shall presently see—can be clearly discerned. The durations we have practically most to deal with—minutes, hours, and days—have to be symbolically conceived, and constructed by mental addition, after the fashion of those extents of hundreds of miles and upward, which in the field of space are beyond the range of most men's practical interests altogether. To 'realize' a quarter of a mile we need only look out of the window and feel its length by an act which, though it may in part result from organized associations, yet seems immediately performed. To realize an hour, we must count 'now! -- now! -- now! -- now! --' indefinitely. Each 'now' is the feeling of a separate bit of time, and the exact sum of the bits never makes a very clear impression on our mind.
How many bits can we clearly apprehend at once? Very few if they are long bits, more if they are extremely short, most if they come to us in compound groups, each including smaller bits of its own.
Hearing is the sense by which the subdivision of durations is most sharply made. Almost all the experimental work on the time-sense has been done by means of strokes of sound. How long a series of sounds, then, can we group in the mind so as not to confound it with a longer or a shorter series?
Our spontaneous tendency is to break up any monotonously given series of sounds into some sort of a rhythm. We involuntarily accentuate every second, or third, or fourth beat, or we break the series in still more intricate ways. Whenever we thus grasp the impressions in rhythmic form, we can identify a longer string of them without confusion.
Each variety of verse, for example, has its 'law'; and the recurrent stresses and sinkings make us feel with peculiar readiness the lack of a syllable or the presence of one too much. Divers verses may again be bound together in the form of a stanza, and we may then say of another stanza, "Its second verse differs by so much from that of the first stanza," when but for the felt stanza-form the two differing verses would have come to us too separately to be

compared at all. But these superposed systems of rhythm soon reach their limit. In music, as Wundt[6] says, "while the measure may easily contain 12 changes of intensity of sound (as in 12/8 time), the rhythmical group may embrace 6 measures, and the period consist of 4, exceptionally of 5 [8?] groups."

Wundt and his pupil Dietze have both tried to determine experimentally the maximal extent of our immediate distinct consciousness for successive impressions.

Wundt found[7] that twelve impressions could be distinguished clearly as a united cluster, provided they were caught in a certain rhythm by the mind, and succeeded each other at intervals not smaller than 0.3 and not larger than 0.5 of a second. This makes the total time distinctly apprehended to be equal to from 3.6 to 6 seconds. Dietze[8] gives larger figures. The most favorable intervals for clearly catching the strokes were when they came at from 0.3 second to 0.18 second apart. Forty strokes might then be remembered as a whole, and identified without error when repeated, provided the mind grasped them in five sub-groups of eight, or in eight sub-groups of five strokes each. When no grouping of the strokes beyond making couples of them by the attention was allowed—and practically it was found impossible not to group them in at least this simplest of all ways --16 was the largest number that could be clearly apprehended as a whole.[9] This would make 40 times 0.3 second, or 12 seconds, to be the maximum filled duration of which we can be both distinctly and immediately aware.

The maximum unfilled, or vacant duration, seems to lie within the same objective range. Estel and Mehner, also working in Wundt's laboratory, found it to vary from 5 or 6 to 12 seconds, and perhaps more. The differences seemed due to practice rather than to idiosyncrasy.[10]

These figures may be roughly taken to stand for the most important part of what, with Mr. Clay, we called, a few pages back, the specious present. The specious present has, in addition, a vaguely vanishing backward and forward fringe; but its nucleus is probably the dozen seconds or less that have just elapsed.

If these are the maximum, what, then, is the minimum amount of duration which we can distinctly feel?

The smallest figure experimentally ascertained was by Exner, who distinctly heard the doubleness of two successive clicks of a Savart's wheel, and of two successive snaps of an electric spark, when their interval was made as small as about 1/500 of a second.[11]

With the eye, perception is less delicate. Two sparks, made to fall beside each other in rapid succession on the centre of the retina, ceased to be recognized as successive by Exner when their interval fell below 0.044".[12]

Where, as here, the succeeding impressions are only two in number, we can easiest perceive the interval between them. President Hall, who experimented with a modified Savart's wheel, which gave clicks in varying number and at varying intervals, says:[13]

"In order that their discontinuity may be clearly perceived, four or even three clicks or beats must be farther apart than two need to be. When two are easily distinguished, three or four separated by the same interval . . . are often confidently pronounced to be two or three respectively. It would be well if observations were so directed as to ascertain, at least up to ten or twenty, the increase [of interval] required by each additional click in a series for the sense of discontinuity to remain constant throughout."[14]

Where the first impression falls on one sense, and the second on another, the perception of the intervening time tends to be less certain and delicate, and it makes a difference which impression comes first. Thus, Exner found[15] the smallest perceptible interval to be, in seconds:

From sight to touch 0.071
From touch to sight. 0.053
From sight to hearing 0.16
From hearing to sight 0.06
From one ear to another 0.064

To be conscious of a time interval at all is one thing; to tell whether it be shorter or longer than another interval is a different thing. A number of experimental data are on hand which give us a measure of the delicacy of this latter perception. The problem is that of the smallest difference between two times which we can perceive.

The difference is at its minimum when the times themselves are very short. Exner,[16] reacting as rapidly as possible with his foot, upon a signal seen by the eye (spark), noted all the reactions which seemed to him either slow or fast in the making. He thought thus that deviations of about 1/100 of a second either way from the average were correctly noticed by him at the time. The average was here 0.1840". Hall and Jastrow listened to the intervals between the clicks of their apparatus. Between two such equal intervals of 4.27" each, a middle interval was included, which might be made either shorter or longer than the extremes. "After the series had been heard two or even three times, no impression of the relative length of the middle interval would often exist, and only after hearing the fourth and last [repetition of the series] would the judgment incline to the plus or minus side. Inserting the variable between two invariable and like intervals greatly facilitated judgment, which between two unlike terms is far less accurate."[17] Three observers in these experiments made no error when the middle interval varied 1/60 from the extremes. When it varied 1/120, errors occurred, but were few, This would make the minimum absolute difference perceived as large as 0.355."

This minimum absolute difference, of course, increases as the times compared grow long. Attempts have been made to ascertain what ratio it bears to the times themselves. According to Fechner's 'Psychophysic Law' it ought always to bear the same ratio. Various observers, however, have found this not to be the case.[18] On the contrary, very interesting oscillations in the accuracy of judgment and in the direction of the error—oscillations dependent upon the absolute amount of the times compared—have been noticed by all who have experimented with the question. Of these a brief account may be given.

In the first place, in every list of intervals experimented with there will be found what Vierordt calls an 'INDIFFERENCE-POINT;' that is to say, an interval which we judge with maximum accuracy, a time which we tend to estimate as neither longer or shorter than it really is, and away from which, in both directions, errors increase their size.[19] This time varies from one observer to another, but its average is remarkably constant, as the following table shows.[20]

The times, noted by the ear, and the average indifference-points (given in seconds) were, for—

Wundt[21] 0.72
Kollert[22].. 0.75
Estel (probably)....................................... 0.75
Mehner... 0.71
Stevens[23].. 0.71
Mach[24]... 0.35
Buccola (about)[25].................................. 0.40

The odd thing about these figures is the recurrence they show in so many men of about three fourths of a second, as the interval of time most easy to catch and reproduce. Odder still, both Estel and Mehner found that multiples of this time were more accurately reproduced than the time-intervals of intermediary length;[26] and Glass found a certain periodicity, with the constant increment of 1.25 sec., in his observations. There would seem thus to exist something like a periodic or rhythmic sharpening of our time-sense, of which the period differs somewhat from one observer to the next.

Our sense of time, like other senses, seems subject to the law of contrast. It appeared pretty plainly in Estel's observations that an interval sounded shorter if a long one had immediately preceded it, and longer when the opposite was the case.

Like other senses, too, our sense of time is sharpened by practice. Mehner ascribes almost all the discrepancies between other observers and himself to this cause alone.[27]

Tracks of time filled (with clicks of sound) seem longer than vacant ones of the same duration, when the latter does not exceed a second or two.[28] This, which reminds one of what happens with spaces seen by the eye, becomes reversed when longer times are taken. It is, perhaps, in accordance with this law that a loud sound, limiting a short interval of time, makes it appear longer, a slight sound shorter. In comparing intervals marked out by sounds, we must take care to keep the sounds uniform.[29]

There is a certain emotional feeling accompanying the intervals of time, as is well known in music. The sense of haste goes with one measure of rapidity, that of delay with another; and these two feelings harmonize with different mental moods. Vierordt listened to series of strokes performed by a metronome at rates varying from 40 to 200 a minute, and found that they very naturally fell into seven categories, from 'very slow' to 'very fast.'[30] Each category of feeling included the intervals following each other within a certain range of speed, and no others. This is a qualitative, not a quantitative judgment—an æsthetic judgment, in fact. The middle category, of speed that was neutral, or, as he calls it, 'adequate,' contained intervals that were grouped about 0.62 second, and Vierordt says that this made what one might almost call an agreeable time.[31]

The feeling of time and accent in music, of rhythm, is quite independent of that of melody. Tunes with marked rhythm can be readily recognized when simply drummed on the table with the finger-tips.

We Have no Sense for Empty Time.

Although subdividing the time by beats of sensation aids our accurate knowledge of the amount of it that elapses, such subdivision does not seem at the first glance essential to our perception of its flow. Let one sit with closed eyes and, abstracting entirely from the outer world, attend exclusively to the passage of time, like one who wakes, as the poet says, "to hear time flowing in the middle of the night, and all things moving to a day of doom." There seems under such circumstances as these no variety in the material content of our thought, and what we notice appears, if anything, to be the pure series of durations budding, as it were, and growing beneath our indrawn gaze. Is this really so or not? The question is important, for, if the experience be what it roughly seems, we have a sort of special sense for pure time—a sense to which empty duration is an adequate stimulus; while if it be an illusion, it must be that our perception of time's flight, in the experiences quoted, is due to the filling of the time, and to our memory of a content which it had a moment previous, and which we feel to agree or disagree with its content now.

It takes but a small exertion of introspection to show that the latter alternative is the true one, and that we can no more intuit a duration than we can intuit an extension, devoid of all sensible content. Just as with closed eyes we perceive a dark visual field in which a curdling play of obscurest luminosity is always going on; so, be we never so abstracted from distinct outward impressions, we are always inwardly immersed in what Wundt has somewhere called the twilight of our general consciousness. Our heart-beats, our breathing, the pulses of our attention, fragments of words or sentences that pass through our imagination, are what people this dim habitat. Now, all these processes are rhythmical, and are apprehended by us, as they occur, in their totality; the breathing and pulses of attention, as coherent successions, each with its rise and fall; the heart-beats similarly, only relatively far more brief; the words not separately, but in connected groups. In short, empty our minds as we may, some form of changing process remains for us to feel, and cannot be expelled. And along with the sense of the process and its rhythm goes the sense of the length of time it lasts. Awareness of change is thus the condition on which our perception of time's flow depends; but there exists no reason to suppose that empty time's own changes are sufficient for the awareness of change to be aroused. The change must be of some concrete sort—an outward or inward sensible series, or a process of attention or volition.[32]

And here again we have an analogy with space. The earliest form of distinct space-perception is undoubtedly that of a movement over some one of our sensitive surfaces, and this movement is originally given as a simple whole of feeling, and is only decomposed into its elements—successive positions successively occupied by the moving body—when our education in discrimination is much advanced. But a movement is a change, a process; so we see that in the time-world and the space-world alike the first known things are not elements, but combinations, not separate units, but wholes already formed. The condition of being of the wholes may be the elements; but the condition of our knowing the elements is our having already felt the wholes as wholes.

In the experience of watching empty time flow—'empty' to be taken hereafter in the relative sense just set forth—we tell it off in pulses. We say 'now! now! now!' or we count 'more! more! more!' as we feel it bud. This composition out of units of duration is called the law of time's discrete flow. The discreteness is, however, merely due to the fact that our successive acts of recognition or apperception of what it is are discrete. The sensation is as continuous as any sensation can be. All continuous sensations are named in beats. We notice that a certain finite 'more' of them is passing or already past. To adopt Hodgson's image, the sensation is the measuring-tape, the perception the dividing-engine which stamps its length. As we listen to a steady sound, we take it in in discrete pulses of recognition, calling it successively 'the same! the same! the same!' The case stands no otherwise with time.

After a small number of beats our impression of the amount we have told off becomes quite vague. Our only way of knowing it accurately is by counting, or noticing the clock, or through some other symbolic conception.[33] When the times exceed hours or days, the conception is absolutely symbolic. We think of the amount we mean either solely as a name, or by running over a few salient dates therein, with no pretence of imagining the full durations that lie between them. No one has anything like a perception of the greater length of the time between now and the first century than of that between now and the tenth. To an historian, it is true, the longer interval will suggest a host of additional dates and events, and so appear a more multitudinous thing. And for the same reason most people will think they directly perceive the length of the past fortnight to exceed that of the past week. But there is properly no comparative time intuition in these cases at all. It is but dates and events, representing time; their abundance symbolizing its length. I am sure that this is so, even where the times compared are no more than an hour or so in length. It is the same with Spaces of many miles, which we always compare with each other by the numbers which measure them.[34]

From this we pass naturally to speak of certain familiar variations in our estimation of lengths of time. In general, a time filled with varied and interesting experiences seems short in passing, but long as we look back. On the other hand, a tract of time empty of experiences seems long in passing, but in retrospect short. A week of travel and sight-seeing may subtend an angle more like three weeks in the memory; and a month of sickness hardly yields more memories than a day. The length in retrospect depends obviously on the multitudinousness of the memories which the time affords. Many objects, events, changes, many subdivisions, immediately widen the view as we look back. Emptiness, monotony, familiarity, make it shrivel up. In Von Holtei's 'Vagabonds' one Anton is described as revisiting his native village.

"Seven years," he exclaims, "seven years since I ran away! More like seventy it seems, so much has happened. I cannot think of it all without becoming dizzy—at any rate not now. And yet again, when I look at the village, at the church-tower, it seems as if I could hardly have been seven days away."

Prof. Lazarus[35] (from whom I borrow this quotation), thus explains both of these contrasted illusions by our principle of the awakened memories being multitudinous or few:

"The circle of experiences, widely extended, rich in variety, which he had in view on the day of his leaving the village rises now in his mind as its image lies before him. And with it—in rapid succession and violent motion, not in chronologic order, or from chronologic motives, but suggesting each other by all sorts of connections—arise massive images of all his rich vagabondage and roving life. They roll and wave confusedly together, first perhaps one from the first year, then from the sixth, soon from the second, again from the fifth, the first, etc., until it seems as if seventy years must have been there, and he reels with the fulness of his vision. . . . Then the inner eye turns away from all this past. The outer one turns to the village, especially to the church-tower. The sight of it calls back the old sight of it, so that the consciousness is filled with that alone, or almost alone. The one vision compares itself with the other, and looks so near, so unchanged, that it seems as if only a week of time could have come between."

The same space of time seems shorter as we grow older—that is, the days, the months, and the years do so; whether the hours do so is doubtful, and the minutes and seconds to all appearance remain about the same.

"Whoever counts many lustra in his memory need only question himself to find that the last of these, the past five years, have sped much more quickly than the preceding periods of equal amount. Let any one remember his last eight or ten school years: it is the space of a century. Compare with them the last eight or ten years of life: it is the space of an hour."

So writes Prof. Paul Janet,[36] and gives a solution which can hardly be said to diminish the mystery. There is a law, he says, by which the apparent length of an interval at a given epoch of a man's life is proportional to the total length of the life itself. A child of 10 feels a year as 1/10 of his whole life—a man of 50 as 1/50, the whole life meanwhile apparently preserving a constant length. This formula roughly expresses the phenomena, it is true, but cannot possibly be an elementary psychic law; and it is certain that, in great part at least, the foreshortening of the years as we grow older is due to the monotony of memory's content, and the consequent simplification of the backward-glancing view. In youth we may have an absolutely new experience, subjective or objective, every hour of the day. Apprehension is vivid, retentiveness strong, and our recollections of that time, like those of a time spent in rapid and interesting travel, are of something intricate, multitudinous, and long-drawn-out. But as each passing year converts some of this experience into automatic routine which we hardly note at all, the days and the weeks smooth themselves out in recollection to contentless units, and the years grow hollow and collapse.

So much for the apparent shortening of tracts of time in retrospect. They shorten in passing whenever we are so fully occupied with their content as not to note the actual time itself. A day full of excitement, with no pause, is said to pass 'ere we know it.' On the contrary, a day full of waiting, of unsatisfied desire for change, will seem a small eternity. Tædium, ennui, Langweile, boredom, are words for which, probably, every language known to man has its equivalent. It comes about whenever, from the relative emptiness of content of a tract of time, we grow attentive to the passage of the time itself. Expecting, and being ready for, a new impression to succeed; when it fails to come, we get an empty time instead of it; and such experiences, ceaselessly renewed, make us most formidably aware of the extent of the mere time itself.[37] Close your eyes and simply wait to hear somebody tell you that a minute has elapsed. The full length of your leisure with it seems incredible. You engulf yourself into its bowels as into those of that interminable first week of an ocean voyage, and find yourself wondering that history can have overcome many such periods in its course. All because you attend so closely to the mere feeling of the time per se, and because your attention to that is susceptible of such fine-grained successive subdivision. The odiousness of the whole experience comes from its insipidity; for stimulation is the indispensable requisite for pleasure in an experience, and the feeling of bare time is the least stimulating experience we can have.[38] The sensation of tædium is a protest, says Volkmann, against the entire present.

Exactly parallel variations occur in our consciousness of space. A road we walk back over, hoping to find at each step an object we have dropped, seems to us longer than when we walked over it the other way. A space we measure by pacing appears longer than one we traverse with no thought of its length. And in general an amount of space attended to in itself leaves with us more impression of spaciousness than one of which we only note the content.[39] I do not say that everything in these fluctuations of estimate can be accounted for by the time's content being crowded and interesting, or simple and tame. Both in the shortening of time by old age and in its lengthening by ennui some deeper cause may be at work. This cause can only be ascertained, if it exist, by finding out why we perceive time at all. To this inquiry let us, though without much hope, proceed.

The Feeling of Past Time is a Present Feeling.

If asked why we perceive the light of the sun, or the sound of an explosion, we reply, "Because certain outer forces, ether-waves or air-waves, smite upon the brain, awakening therein changes, to which the conscious perceptions, light and sound, respond." But we hasten to add that neither light nor sound copy or mirror the ether- or air-waves; they represent them only symbolically. The only case, says Helmholtz, in which such copying occurs, and in which "our perceptions can truly correspond with outer reality, is that of the time-succession of phenomena. Simultaneity, succession, and the regular return of simultaneity or succession, can obtain as well in sensations as in outer events. Events, like our perceptions of them, take place in time, so that the time-relations of the latter can furnish a true copy of those of the former. The sensation of the thunder follows the sensation of the lightning just as the sonorous convulsing of the air by the electric discharge reaches the observer's place later than that of the luminiferous ether."[40]

One experiences an almost instinctive impulse, in pursuing such reflections as these, to follow them to a sort of crude speculative conclusion, and to think that he has at last got the mystery of cognition where, to use a vulgar phrase, 'the wool is short.' What more natural, we say, than that the sequences and durations of things should become known? The succession of the outer forces stamps itself as a like succession upon the brain. The brain's successive changes are copied exactly by correspondingly successive pulses of the mental stream. The mental stream, feeling itself, must feel the time-relations of its own states. But as these are copies of the outward time-relations, so must it know them too. That is to say, these latter time-relations arouse their own cognition; or, in other words, the mere existence of time in those changes out of the mind which affect the mind is a sufficient cause why time is perceived by the mind.

This philosophy is unfortunately too crude. Even though we were to conceive the outer successions as forces stamping their image on the brain, and the brain's successions as forces stamping their image on the mind,[41] still, between the mind's own changes being successive, and knowing their own succession, lies as broad a chasm as between the object and subject of any case of cognition in the world. A succession of feelings, in and of itself, is not a feeling of succession. And since, to our successive feelings, a feeling of their own succession is added, that must be treated as an additional fact requiring its own special elucidation, which this talk about outer time-relations stamping copies of themselves within, leaves all untouched.

I have shown, at the outset of the article, that what is past, to be known as past, must be known with what is present, and during the 'present' spot of time. As the clear understanding of this point has some importance, let me, at the risk of repetition, recur to it again. Volkmann has expressed the matter admirably, as follows:

"One might be tempted to answer the question of the origin of the time-idea by simply pointing to the train of ideas, whose various members, starting from the first, successively attain to full clearness. But against this it must be objected that the successive ideas are not yet the idea of succession, because succession in thought is not the thought of succession. If idea A follows idea B, consciousness simply exchanges one for another. That B comes after A is for our consciousness a non-existent fact; for this after is given neither in B nor in A; and no third idea has been supposed. The thinking of the sequence of B upon A is another kind of thinking from that which brought forth A and then brought forth B; and this first kind of thinking is absent so long as merely the thinking of A and the thinking of B are there. In short, when we look at the matter sharply, we come to this antithesis, that if A and B are to be represented as occurring in succession they must be simultaneously represented; if we are to think of them as one after the other, we must think them both at once."[42]

If we represent the actual time-stream of our thinking by an horizontal line, the thought of the stream or of any segment of its length, past, present, or to come, might be figured in a perpendicular raised upon the horizontal at a certain point. The length of this perpendicular stands for a certain object or content, which in this case is the time thought of, and all of which is thought of together at the actual moment of the stream upon which the perpendicular is raised. Mr. James Ward puts the matter very well in his masterly article 'Psychology' in the ninth edition of the Encyclopædia Britannica, page 64. He says:

"We may, if we represent succession as a line, represent simultaneity as a second line at right angles to the first; empty time—or time-length without time-breadth, we may say—is a mere abstraction. Now, it is with the former line that we have to do in treating of time as it is, and with the latter in treating of our intuition of time, where, just as in a perspective representation of distance, we are confined to lines in a plane at right angles to the actual line of depth. In a succession of events, say of sense-impressions, A B C D E . . . , the presence of B means the absence of A and C, but the presentation of this succession involves the simultaneous presence in some mode or other of two or more of the presentations A B C D. In reality, past, present, and future are differences in time, but in presentation all that corresponds to these differences is in consciousness simultaneously."

There is thus a sort of perspective projection of past objects upon present consciousness, similar to that of wide landscapes upon a camera-screen.

And since we saw a while ago that our maximum distinct intuition of duration hardly covers more than a dozen seconds (while our maximum vague intuition is probably not more than that of a minute or so), we must suppose that this amount of duration is pictured fairly steadily in each passing instant of consciousness by virtue of some fairly constant feature in the brain-process to which the consciousness is tied. This feature of the brain-process, whatever it be, must be the cause of our perceiving the fact of time at all.[43] The duration thus steadily perceived is hardly more than the 'specious present,' as it was called a few pages back. Its content is in a constant flux, events dawning into its forward end as fast as they fade out of its rearward one, and each of them changing its time-coefficient from 'not yet,' or 'not quite yet,' to 'just gone' or 'gone,' as it passes by. Meanwhile, the specious present, the intuited duration, stands permanent, like the rainbow on the waterfall, with its own quality unchanged by the events that stream through it. Each of these, as it slips out, retains the power of being reproduced; and when reproduced, is reproduced with the duration and neighbors which it originally had. Please observe, however, that the reproduction of an event, after it has once completely dropped out of the rearward end of the specious present, is an entirely different psychic fact from its direct perception in the specious present as a thing immediately past. A creature might be entirely devoid of reproductive memory, and yet have the time-sense; but the latter would be limited, in his case, to the few seconds immediately passing by. Time older than that he would never recall. I assume reproduction in the text, because I am speaking of human beings who notoriously possess it. Thus memory gets strewn with dated things—dated in the sense of being before or after each other.[44] The date of a thing is a mere relation of before or after the present thing or some past or future thing. Some things we date simply by mentally tossing them into the past or future direction. So in space we think of England as simply to the eastward, of Charleston as lying south. But, again, we may date an event exactly, by fitting it between two terms of a past or future series explicitly conceived, just as we may accurately think of England or Charleston being just so many miles away.[45]

The things and events thus vaguely or exactly dated become thenceforward those signs and symbols of longer time-spaces, of which we previously spoke. According as we think of a multitude of them, or of few, so we imagine the time they represent to be long or short. But the original paragon and prototype of all conceived times is the specious present, the short duration of which we are immediately and incessantly sensible.

To what Cerebral Process is the Sense of Time Due?

Now, to what element in the brain-process may this sensibility be due? It cannot, as we have seen, be due to the mere duration itself of the process; it must be due to an element present at every moment of the process, and this element must bear the same inscrutable sort of relation to its correlative feeling which all other elements of neural activity bear to their psychic products, be the latter what they may. Several suggestions have been made as to what the element is in the case of time. Treating of them in a note,[46] I will try to express briefly the only conclusion which seems to emerge from a study of them and of the facts—unripe though that conclusion be.

The phenomena of 'summation of stimuli' in the nervous system prove that each stimulus leaves some latent activity behind it which only gradually passes away. (See Chapter III) Psychological proof of the same fact is afforded by those 'after-images' which we perceive when a sensorial stimulus is gone. We may read off peculiarities in an after-image, left by an object on the eye, which we failed to note in the original. We may 'hark back' and take in the meaning of a sound several seconds after it has ceased. Delay for a minute, however, and the echo itself of the clock or the question is mute; present sensations have banished it beyond recall. With the feeling of the present thing there must at all times mingle the fading echo of all those other things which the previous few seconds have supplied. Or, to state it in neural terms, there is at every moment a cumulation of brain-processes overlapping each other, of which the fainter ones are the dying phases of processes which but shortly previous were active in a maximal degree. The AMOUNT OF THE OVERLAPPING determines the feeling of the DURATION OCCUPIED. WHAT EVENTS shall appear to occupy the duration depends on just WHAT PROCESSES the overlapping processes are. We know so little of the intimate nature of the brain's activity that even where a sensation monotonously endures, we cannot say that the earlier moments of it do not leave fading processes behind which coexist with those of the present moment. Duration and events together form our intuition of the specious present with its content.[47] Why such an intuition should result from such a combination of brain-processes I do not pretend to say. All I aim at is to state the most elemental form of the psycho-physical conjunction.

I have assumed that the brain-processes are sensational ones. Processes of active attention (see Mr. Ward's account in the long foot-note) will leave similar fading brain-processes behind. If the mental processes are conceptual, a complication is introduced of which I will in a moment speak. Meanwhile, still speaking of sensational processes, a remark of Wundt's will throw additional light on the account I give. As is known, Wundt and others have proved that every act of perception of a sensorial stimulus takes an appreciable time. When two different stimuli—e.g. a sight and a sound—are given at once or nearly at once, we have difficulty in attending to both, and may wrongly judge

their interval, or even invert their order. Now, as the result of his experiments on such stimuli, Wundt lays down this law:[48] that of the three possible determinations we may make of their order—
"namely, simultaneity, continuous transition, and discontinuous transition—only the first and last are realized, never the second. Invariably, when we fail to perceive the impressions as simultaneous, we notice a shorter or longer empty time between them, which seems to correspond to the sinking of one of the ideas and to the rise of the other.... For our attention may share itself equally between the two impressions, which will then compose one total percept [and be simultaneously felt]; or it may be so adapted to one event as to cause it to be perceived immediately, and then the second event can be perceived only after a certain time of latency, during which the attention reaches its effective maximum for it and diminishes for the first event. In this case the events are perceived as two, and in successive order—that is, as separated by a time-interval in which attention is not sufficiently accommodated to either to bring a distinct perception about.... While we are hurrying from one to the other, everything between them vanishes in the twilight of general consciousness."[49]

One might call this the law of discontinuous succession in time, of percepts to which we cannot easily attend at once. Each percept then requires a separate brain-process; and when one brain-process is at its maximum, the other would appear perforce to be in either a waning or a waxing phase. If our theory of the time-feeling be true, empty time must then subjectively appear to separate the two percepts, no matter how close together they may objectively be; for, according to that theory, the feeling of a time-duration is the immediate effect of such an overlapping of brain-processes of different phase—wherever and from whatever cause it may occur.

To pass, now, to conceptual processes: Suppose I think of the Creation, then of the Christian era, then of the battle of Waterloo, all within a few seconds. These matters have their dates far outside the specious present. The processes by which I think them, however, all overlap. What events, then, does the specious present seem to contain? Simply my successive acts of thinking these long-past things, not the long-past things themselves. As the instantly-present thought may be of a long-past thing, so the just-past thought may be of another long-past thing. When a long-past event is reproduced in memory and conceived with its date, the reproduction and conceiving traverse the specious present. The immediate content of the latter is thus all my direct experiences, whether subjective or objective. Some of these meanwhile may be representative of other experiences indefinitely remote.

The number of these direct experiences which the specious present and immediately-intuited past may embrace measures the extent of our 'primary,' as Exner calls it, or, as Richet calls it, of our 'elementary' memory.[50] The sensation resultant from the overlapping is that of the duration which the experiences seem to fill. As is the number of any larger set of events to that of these experiences, so we suppose is the length of that duration to this duration. But of the longer duration we have no direct 'realizing sense.' The variations in our appreciation of the same amount of real time may possibly be explained by alterations in the rate of fading in the images, producing changes in the complication of superposed processes, to which changes changed states of consciousness may correspond. But however long we may conceive a space of time to be, the objective amount of it which is directly perceived at any one moment by us can never exceed the scope of our 'primary memory' at the moment in question.[51]

We have every reason to think that creatures may possibly differ enormously in the amounts of duration which they intuitively feel, and in the fineness of the events that may fill it. Von Bær has indulged[52] in some interesting computations of the effect of such differences in changing the aspect of Nature. Suppose we were able, within the length of a second, to note 10,000 events distinctly, instead of barely 10, as now; if our life were then destined to hold the same number of impressions, it might be 1000 times as short. We should live less than a month, and personally know nothing of the change of seasons. If born in winter, we should believe in summer as we now believe in the heats of the Carboniferous era. The motions of organic beings would be so slow to our senses as to be inferred, not seen. The sun would stand still in the sky, the moon be almost free from change, and so on. But now reverse the hypothesis and suppose a being to get only one 1000th part of the sensations that we get in a given time, and consequently to live 1000 times as long. Winters and summers will be to him like quarters of an hour. Mushrooms and the swifter-growing plants will shoot into being so rapidly as to appear instantaneous creations; annual shrubs will rise and fall from the earth like restlessly boiling-water springs; the motions of animals will be as invisible as are to us the movements of bullets and cannon-balls; the sun will scour through the sky like a meteor, leaving a fiery trail behind him, etc. That such imaginary cases (barring the superhuman longevity) may be realized somewhere in the animal kingdom, it would be rash to deny.

"A gnat's wings," says Mr Spencer,[53] "make ten or fifteen thousand strokes a second. Each stroke implies a separate nervous action. Each such nervous action or change in a nervous centre is probably as appreciable by the gnat as is a quick movement of his arm by a man. And if this, or anything like this, is the fact, then the time occupied by a given external change, measured by many movements in the one case, must seem much longer than in the other case, when measured by one movement."

In hashish-intoxication there is a curious increase in the apparent time-perspective. We utter a sentence, and ere the end is reached the beginning seems already to date from indefinitely long ago. We enter a short street, and it is as if we should never get to the end of it. This alteration might conceivably result from an approach to the condition of Von Bær's and Spencer's short-lived beings. If our discrimination of successions became finer-grained, so that we noted ten stages in a process where previously we only noted one; and if at the same time the processes faded ten times as fast as before; we might have a specious present of the same subjective length as now, giving us the same time-feeling and containing as many distinguishable successive events, but out from the earlier end of it would have drooped nine tenths of the real events it now contains. They would have fallen into the general reservoir of merely dated memories, reproducible at will. The beginning of our sentences would have to be expressly recalled; each word would appear to pass through consciousness at a tenth of its usual speed. The condition would, in short, be exactly analogous to the enlargement of space by a microscope; fewer real things at once in the immediate field of view, but each of them taking up more than its normal room, and making the excluded ones seem unnaturally far away.

Under other conditions, processes seem to fade rapidly without the compensating increase in the subdivisibility of successions. Here the apparent length of the specious present contracts. Consciousness dwindles to a point, and loses all intuitive sense of the whence and whither of its path. Express acts of memory replace rapid bird's-eye views. In my own case, something like this occurs in extreme fatigue. Long illnesses produce it. Occasionally, it appears to accompany aphasia.[54] It would be vain to seek to imagine the exact brain-change in any of these cases. But we must admit the possibility that to some extent the variations of time-estimate between youth and age, and excitement and ennui, are due to such causes, more immediate than to the one we assigned some time ago.

But whether our feeling of the time which immediately-past[55] events have filled be of something long or of something short, it is not what it is because those events are past, but because they have left behind them processes which are present. To those processes, however caused, the mind would still respond by feeling a specious present, with one part of it just vanishing or vanished into the past. As the Creator is supposed to have made Adam with a navel—sign of a birth which never occurred—so He might instantaneously make a man with a brain in which were processes just like the 'fading' ones of an ordinary brain. The first real stimulus after creation would set up a process additional to these. The processes would overlap; and the new-created man would unquestionably have the feeling, at the very primal instant of his life, of having been in existence already some little space of time.

Let me sum up, now, by saying that we are constantly conscious of a certain duration—the specious present—varying in length from a few seconds to probably not more than a minute, and that this duration (with its content perceived as having one part earlier and the other part later) is the original intuition of time. Longer times are conceived by adding, shorter ones by dividing, portions of this vaguely bounded unit, and are habitually thought by us symbolically. Kant's notion of an intuition of objective time as an infinite necessary continuum has nothing to support it. The cause of the intuition which we really have cannot be the duration of our brain-processes or our mental changes. That duration is rather the object of the intuition which, being realized at every moment of such duration, must be due to a permanently present cause. This cause—probably the simultaneous presence of brain-processes of different phase-fluctuates; and hence a certain range of variation in the amount of the intuition, and in its subdivisibility, accrues.

Notes

[1] *This chapter is reprinted almost verbatim from the Journal of Speculative Philosophy, vol. XX. p. 374.*
[2] *James Mill, Analysis, vol. I. p. 319 (J. S. Mill's Edition).*
[3] *"What I find, when I look at consciousness at all, is, that what I cannot divest myself of, or not have in consciousness, if I have consciousness at all, is a sequence of different feelings. . . . The simultaneous perception of both sub-feelings, whether as parts of a coexistence or of a sequence, is the total feeling—the minimum of consciousness—and this minimum has duration. . . Time-duration, however, is inseparable from the minimum, notwithstanding that, in an isolated moment, we could not tell which part of it came first, which last. . . . We do not require to know that the sub-feelings come in sequence, first one, then the other; nor to know what coming in sequence means. But we have, in any artificially isolated minimum of consciousness, the rudiments of the perception of former and latter in time, in the sub-feeling that grows fainter, and the sub-feeling that grows stronger, and the change between them. . . .*

"In the next place, I remark that the rudiments of memory are involved in the minimum of consciousness. The first beginnings of it appear in that minimum, just as the first beginnings of perception do. As each member of the change or difference which goes to compose that minimum is the rudiment of a single perception, so the priority of one member to the other, although both are given to consciousness in one empirical present moment, is the rudiment of memory. The fact that the minimum of consciousness is difference or change in feelings, is the ultimate explanation of memory as well as of single perceptions. A former and a latter are included in the minimum of consciousness; and this is what is meant by saying that all consciousness is in the form of time, or that time is the form of feeling, the form of sensibility. Crudely and popularly we divide the course of time into past, present, and future; but, strictly speaking, there is no present; it is composed of past and future divided by an indivisible point or instant. That instant, or time-point, is the strict present. What we call, loosely, the present, is an empirical

portion of the course of time, containing at least a minimum of consciousness, in which the instant of change is the present time-point. . . . If we take this as the present time-point, it is clear that the minimum of feeling contains two portions—a sub-feeling that goes and a sub-feeling that comes. One is remembered, the other imagined. The limits of both are indefinite at beginning and end of the minimum, and ready to melt into other minima, proceeding from other stimuli.

"Time and consciousness do not come to us ready marked out into minima; we have to do that by reflection, asking ourselves, What is the least empirical moment of consciousness? That least empirical moment is what we usually call the present moment; and even this is too minute for ordinary use; the present moment is often extended practically to a few seconds, or even minutes, beyond which we specify what length of time we mean, as the present hour, or day, or year, or century.

"But this popular way of thinking imposes itself on great numbers even of philosophically-minded people, and they talk about the present as if it was a datum—as if time came to us marked into present periods like a measuring-tape." (S. H. Hodgson: Philosophy of Reflection, vol. I. pp. 248-254.)

"The representation of time agrees with that of space in that a certain amount of it must be presented together—included between its initial and terminal limit. A continuous ideation, flowing from one point to another, would indeed occupy time, but not represent it, for it would exchange one element of succession for another instead of grasping the whole succession at once. Both points—the beginning and the end—are equally essential to the conception of time, and must be present with equal clearness together." (Herbart: Psychol. als W., § 115.)

"Assume that . . . similar pendulum-strokes follow each other at regular intervals in a consciousness otherwise void. When the first one is over, an image of it remains in the fancy until the second succeeds. This, then, reproduces the first by virtue of the law of association by similarity, but at the same time meets with the aforesaid persisting image. . . . Thus does the simple repetition of the sound provide all the elements of time-perception. The first sound [as it is recalled by association] gives the beginning, the second the end, and the persistent image in the fancy represents the length of the interval. At the moment of the second impression, the entire time-perception exists at once, for then all its elements are presented together, the second sound and the image in the fancy immediately, and the first impression by reproduction. But, in the same act, we are aware of a state in which only the first sound existed, and of another in which only its image existed in the fancy. Such a consciousness as this is that of time. . . . In it no succession of ideas takes place." (Wundt: Physiol. Psych., 1st ed. pp. 681-2.) Note here the assumption that the persistence and the reproduction of an impression are two processes which may go on simultaneously. Also that Wundt's description is merely an attempt to analyze the 'deliverance' of a time-perception, and no explanation of the manner in which it comes about.

[4] The Alternative, p. 167.

[5] Locke, in his dim way, derived the sense of duration from reflection on the succession of our ideas (Essay, book II. chap. XIV. § 3; chap. XV. § 12). Reid justly remarks that if ten successive elements are to make duration, "then one must make duration, otherwise duration must be made up of parts that have no duration, which is impossible. . . . I conclude, therefore, that there must be duration in every single interval or element of which the whole duration is made up. Nothing, indeed, is more certain than that every elementary part of duration must have duration, as every elementary part of extension must have extension. Now, it must be observed that in these elements of duration, or single intervals of successive ideas, there is no succession of ideas, yet we must conceive them to have duration; whence we may conclude with certainty that there is a conception of duration where there is no succession of ideas in the mind." (Intellectual Powers. essay III. chap. V.) "Qu'on ne cherche point," says Royer Collard in the Fragments added to Jouffroy's Translation of Reid, "la durée dans la succession; on ne l'y trouvera jamais; la durée a précédé la succession; in notion de la durée a précédé la notion de la succession. Elle en est donc tout-à fait indépendante, dira-t-on? Oui, elle en est tout-à-fait indépendante."

[6] Physiol. Psych.," II. 54, 55.

[7] Ibid. II. 213.

[8] Philosophische Studien, II. 362.

[9] Counting was of course not permitted. It would have given a symbolic concept and no intuitive or immediate perception of the totality of the series. With counting we may of course compare together series of any length—series whose beginnings have faded from our mind, and of whose totality we retain no sensible impression at all. To count a series of clicks is an altogether different thing from merely perceiving them as discontinuous. In the latter case we need only be conscious of the bits of empty duration between them ; in the former we must perform rapid acts of association between them and as many names of numbers.

[10] Estel in Wundt's Philosophische Studien, II. 50. Mehner, ibid. II. 571. In Dietze's experiments even numbers of strokes were better caught than odd ones, by the ear. The rapidity of their sequence had a great influence on the result. At more than 4 seconds apart it was impossible to perceive series of them as units in all (cf. Wundt, Physiol. Psych., II. 214). They were simply counted as so many individual strokes. Below 0.21 to 0.11 second, according to the observer, judgment again became confused. It was found that the rate of succession most favorable for grasping long series was when the strokes were sounded at intervals of from 0.3" to 0.18" apart. Series of 4, 6, 8, 16 were more easily identified than series of 10, 12, 14, 18. The latter could hardly be clearly grasped at all. Among odd numbers, 3, 5, 7 were the series easiest caught ; next, 9, 15; hardest of all, 11 and 13; and 17 was impossible to apprehend.

[11] The exact interval of the sparks was 0.00205". The doubleness of their snap was usually replaced by a single-seeming sound when it fell to 0.00198", the sound becoming louder when the sparks seemed simultaneous. The difference between

these two intervals is only 7/100000 of a second; and, as Exner remarks, our ear and brain must be wonderfully efficient organs to get distinct feelings from so slight an objective difference as this. See Pflüger's Archiv, Bd. XI.

[12] Ibid. p. 407. When the sparks fell so close together that their irradiation-circles overlapped, they appeared like one spark moving from the position of the first to that of the second; and they might then follow each other as close as 0.015" without the direction of the movement ceasing to be clear. When one spark fell on the centre, the other on the margin, of the retina, the time-interval for successive apprehension had to be raised to 0.076".

[13] Hall and Jastrow: Studies of Rhythm. Mind, XI. 58.

[14] Nevertheless, multitudinous impressions may be felt as discontinuous, though separated by excessively minute intervals of time. Grünhagen says (Pflüger's Archiv, VI. 175) that 10,000 electric shocks a second are felt as interrupted, by the tongue (!). Von Wittich (ibid. II. 329), that between 1000 and 2000 strokes a second are felt as discrete by the finger. W. Preyer, on the other hand (Die Grenzen des Empfindungsvermögens, etc., 1868, p. 15), makes contacts appear continuous to the finger when 36.8 of them follow in a second. Similarly, Mach (Wiener Sitzgsb., LI. 2, 142) gives about 36. Lalanne (Comptes Rendus, LXXXII. p. 1314) found summation of finger-contacts after 22 repetitions in a second. Such discrepant figures are of doubtful worth. On the retina 20 to 30 impressions a second at the very utmost can be felt as discrete when they fall on the same spot. The ear, which begins to fuse stimuli together into a musical tone when they follow at the rate of a little over 30 a second, can still feel 132 of them a second as discontinuous when they take the shape of 'beats' (Helmholtz, Tonempfindungen, 3d ed. p. 270).

[15] Pflüger's Archiv, XI. 428. Also in Herrmann's Hdbh. d. Physiol., 2 Bd., I. Thl. pp. 260-262.

[16] Pflüger's Archiv, VII. 639. Tigerstedt (Bihang till Kongl. Svenska Vetenskaps-Akad. Handl., Bd. 8, Häfte 2, Stockholm, 1884) revises Exner's figures, and shows that his conclusions are exaggerated. According to Tigerstedt, two observers almost always rightly appreciated 0.05" or 0.06" of reaction-time difference. Half the time they did it rightly when the difference sank to 0.03", though from 0.03" and 0.06" differences were often not noticed at all. Buccola found (Le Legge del Tempo nei Fenomeni del Pensiero, Milano, 1883, p. 371) that, after much practice in making rapid reactions upon a signal, he estimated directly, in figures, his own reaction-time, in 10 experiments, with an error of from 0.010" to 0.018"; in 6, with one of 0.005" to 0.009"; in one, with one of 0.002"; and in 3, with one of 0.003".

[17] "Mind, XI. 61 (1886).

[18] Mach, Wiener Sitzungsb., LI. 2. 133 (1865); Estel, loc. cit. p. 65; Mehner, loc. cit. p. 586; Buccola, op. cit. p 378. Fechner labors to prove that his law is only overlaid by other interfering laws in the figures recorded by these experimenters; but his case seems to me to be one of desperate infatuation with a hobby. (See Wundt's Philosophische Studien, III. 1.)

[19] Curious discrepancies exist between the German and the American observers with respect to the direction of the error below and above the point of indifference—differences perhaps due to the fatigue involved in the American method. The Germans lengthened intervals below it and shortened those above. With seven Americans experimented on by Stevens this was exactly reversed. The German method was to passively listen to the intervals, then judge; the American was to reproduce them actively by movements of the hand. In Mehner's experiments there was found a second indifference-point at about 5 seconds, beyond which times were judged again too long. Glass, whose work on the subject is the latest (Philos. Studien, IV. 423), found (when corrections were allowed for) that all times except 0.8 sec. were estimated too short. He found a series of points of greatest relative accuracy (viz., at 1.5, 2.5, 3.75, 5, 6.25, etc., seconds respectively[)], and ([sic] thought that his observations roughly corroborated Weber's law. As 'maximum' and 'minimum' are printed interchangeably in Glass's article it is hard to follow.

[20] With Vierordt and his pupils the indifference point lay as high as from 1.5 sec. to 4.9 sec., according to the observer (cf. Der Zeitsinn, 1868, p. 112). In most of these experiments the time heard was actively reproduced, after a short pause, by movements of the hand, which were recorded. Wundt gives good reasons (Physiol. Psych., II. 289, 290) for rejecting Vierordt's figures as erroneous. Vierordt's book, it should be said, is full of important matter, nevertheless.

[21] Physiol. Psych., II. 286, 290.

[22] Philosophische Studien, I. 86.

[23] Mind, XI. 400.

[24] Loc. cit. p. 144.

[25] Op. cit. p. 376. Mach's and Buccola's figures, it will be observed, are about one half of the rest—sub-multiples, therefore. It ought to be observed, however, that Buccola's figure has little value, his observations not being well fitted to show this particular point.

[26] Estel's figures led him to think that all the multiples enjoyed this privilege; with Mehner, on the other hand, only the odd multiples showed diminution of the average error; thus, 0.71, 2.15, 3.55, 5, 6.4, 7.8, 9.3, and 10.65 second were respectively registered with the least error. Cf. Phil. Studien, II. pp. 57, 562-565.

[27] Cf. especially pp. 558-561.

[28] Wundt: Physiol. Psych., II. 287. Hall and Jastrow: Mind, XI. 62.

[29] Mehner: loc. cit. p. 553.

[30] "The number of distinguishable differences of speed between these limits is, as he takes care to remark, very much larger than 7 (Der Zeitsinn, p. 137).

[31] P. 19, § 18, 112.

[32] I leave the text just as it was printed in the Journal of Speculative Philosophy (for 'Oct. 1886') in 1887. Since then Münsterberg in his masterly Beiträge zur experimentellen Psychologie (Heft 2, 1889) seems to have made it clear what the

sensible changes are by which we measure the lapse of time. When the time which separates two sensible impressions is less than one third of a second, he thinks it is almost entirely the amount to which the memory-image of the first impression had faded when the second one overtakes it, which makes us feel how wide they are apart (p. 29). When the time is longer than this, we rely, he thinks, exclusively upon the feelings of muscular tension and relaxation, which we are constantly receiving although we give to them so little of our direct attention. These feelings are primarily in the muscles by which we adopt our sense-organs in attending to the signals used, some of the muscles being in the eye and ear themselves, some of them in the head, neck, etc. We here judge two time-intervals to be equal when between the beginning and end of each we feel exactly similar relaxations and subsequent expectant tensions of these muscles to have occurred. In reproducing intervals ourselves we try to make our feelings of this sort just what they were when we passively heard the interval. These feelings by themselves, however, can only be used when the intervals are very short, for the tension anticipatory of the terminal stimulus naturally reaches its maximum very soon. With longer intervals we take the feeling of our inspirations and expirations into account. With our expirations all the other muscular tensions in our body undergo a rhythmical decrease; with our inspirations the reverse takes place. When, therefore, we note a time-interval of several seconds with intent to reproduce it, what we seek is to make the earlier and later interval agree in the number and amount of these respiratory changes combined with sense-organ adjustments with which they are filled. Münsterberg has studied carefully in his own case the variations of the respiratory factor. They are many; but he sums up his experience by saying that whether he measured by inspirations that were divided by momentary pauses into six parts, or by inspirations that were continuous; whether with sensory tension during inspiration and relaxation during expiration, or by tension during both inspiration and expiration, separated by a sudden interpolated relaxation; whether with special notice taken of the cephalic tensions, or of those in the trunk and shoulders, in all cases alike and without exception he involuntarily endeavored, whenever he compared two times or tried to make one the same as the other, to get exactly the same respiratory conditions and conditions of tension, all the subjective conditions, in short, exactly the same during the second interval as they were during the first. Münsterberg corroborated his subjective observations by experiments. The observer of the time had to reproduce as exactly as possible an interval between two sharp sounds given him by an assistant. The only condition imposed upon him was that he should not modify his breathing for the purposes of measurement. It was then found that when the assistant broke in at random with his signals, the judgment of the observer was vastly less accurate than when the assistant carefully watched the observer's breathing and made both the beginning of the time given him and that of the time which he was to give coincide with identical phases thereof.—Finally, Münsterberg with great plausibility tries to explain the discrepancies between the results of Vierordt, Estel, Mehner, Glass, etc., as due to the fact that they did not all use the same measure. Some breathe a little faster, some a little slower. Some break their inspirations into two parts, some do not, etc. The coincidence of the objective times measured with definite natural phases of breathing would very easily give periodical maxima of facility in measuring accurately.

[33] "Any one wishing yet further examples of this mental substitution will find one on observing how habitually he thinks of the spaces on the clock-face instead of the periods they stand for; how, on discovering it to be half an hour later than he supposed, he does not represent the half hour in its duration, but scarcely passes beyond the sign of it marked by the finger." (H. Spencer: Psychology, § 336.)

[34] The only objections to this which I can think of are: (1) The accuracy with which some men judge of the hour of day or night without looking at the clock; (2) the faculty some have of waking at a preappointed hour; (3) the accuracy of time-perception reported to exist in certain trance-subjects. It might seem that in these persons some sort of a sub-conscious record was kept of the lapse of time per se. But this cannot be admitted until it is proved that there are no physiological processes, the feeling of whose course may serve as a sign of how much time has sped, and so lead us to infer the hour. That there are such processes it is hardly possible to doubt. An ingenious friend of mine was long puzzled to know why each day of the week had such a characteristic physiognomy to him. That of Sunday was soon noticed to be due to the cessation of the city's rumbling, and the sound of people's feet shuffling on the sidewalk; of Monday, to come from the clothes drying in the yard and casting a white reflection on the ceiling; of Tuesday, to a cause which I forget; and I think my friend did not get beyond Wednesday. Probably each hour in the day has for most of us some outer or inner sign associated with it as closely as these signs with the days of the week. It must be admitted, after all, however, that the great improvement of the time-perception during sleep and trance is a mystery not as yet cleared up. All my life I have been struck by the accuracy with which I will wake at the same exact minute night after night and morning after morning, if only the habit fortuitously begins. The organic registration in me is independent of sleep. After lying in bed a long time awake I suddenly rise without knowing the time, and for days and weeks together will do so at an identical minute by the clock, as if some inward physiological process caused the act by punctually running down.—Idiots are said sometimes to possess the time-measuring faculty in a marked degree. I have an interesting manuscript account of an idiot girl which says: "She was punctual almost to a minute in her demand for food and other regular attentions. Her dinner was generally furnished her at 12.30 P.M., and at that hour she would begin to scream if it were not forthcoming. If on Fast-day or Thanksgiving it were delayed, in accordance with the New England custom, she screamed from her usual dinner-hour until the food was carried to her. On the next day, however, she again made known her wants promptly at 12.30. Any slight attention shown her on one day was demanded on the next at the corresponding hour. If an orange were given her at 4 P.M. on Wednesday, at the same hour on Thursday she made known her expectation, and if the fruit were not given her she continued to call for it at intervals for two or three hours. At four on Friday the process would be repeated but would last less long; and so on for two or three days. If one of her sisters visited her

accidentally at a certain hour, the sharp piercing scream was sure to summon her at the same hour the next day," etc., etc.—For these obscure matters consult C. Du Prel: The Philosophy of Mysticism, chap. III. § 1.

[35] Ideale Fragen (1878). p. 219 (Essay, 'Zeit und Weile').

[36] Revue Philosophique, vol. III. p. 496.

[37] "Empty time is most strongly perceived when it comes as a pause in music or in speech. Suppose a preacher in the pulpit, a professor at his desk, to stick still in the midst of his discourse; or let a composer (as is sometimes purposely done) make all his instruments stop at once; we await every instant the resumption of the performance, and, in this awaiting, perceive, more than in any other possible way, the empty time. To change the example, let, in a piece of polyphonic music—a figure, for instance, in which a tangle of melodies are under way—suddenly a single voice be heard, which sustains a long note, while all else is hushed. . . . This one note will appear very protracted—why? Because we expect to hear accompanying it the notes of the other instruments, but they fail to come." (Herbart: Psychol. als W., §115.) -- Compare also Münsterberg, Beiträge, Heft 2, p. 41.

[38] A night of pain will seem terribly long; we keep looking forward to a moment which never comes—the moment when it shall cease. But the odiousness of this experience is not named ennui or Langweile, like the odiousness of time that seems long from its emptiness. The more positive odiousness of the pain, rather, is what tinges our memory of the night. What we feel, as Prof. Lazarus says (op cit. p. 202), is the long time of the suffering, not the suffering of the long time per se.

[39] On these variations of time-estimate, cf. Romanes, Consciousness of Time. in Mind, vol. III. p. 297; J. Sully, Illusions, pp. 245-261, 302-305; W. Wundt, Physiol. Psych., II. 287, 288; besides the essays quoted from Lazarus and Janet. In German, the successors of Herbart have treated of this subject: compare Volkmann's Lehrbuch d. Psych., § 89, and for references to other authors his note 3 to this section. Lindner (Lbh. d. empir. Psych.), as a parallel effect, instances Alexander the Great's life (thirty-three years), which seems to us as if it must be long, because it was so eventful. Similarly the English Commonwealth, etc.

[40] Physiol Optik, p. 445.

[41] Succession, time per se, is no force. Our talk about its devouring tooth, etc., is all elliptical. Its contents are what devour. The law of innertia is incompatible with time's being assumed as an efficient cause of anything.

[42] Lehrbuch d. Psych., § 87. Compare also H. Lotze, Metaphysik, § 154.

[43] The cause of the perceiving, not the object perceived!

[44] "'No more' and 'not yet' are the proper time-feelings, and we are aware of time in no other way than through these feelings," says Volkmann (Psychol., § 87). This, which is not strictly true of our feeling of time per se, as an elementary bit of duration, is true of our feeling of date in its events.

[45] We construct the miles just as we construct the years. Travelling in the cars makes a succession of different fields of view pass before our eyes. When those that have passed from present sight revive in memory, they maintain their mutual order because their contents overlap. We think them as having been before or behind each other; and, from the multitude of the views we can recall behind the one now presented, we compute the total space we have passed through.

It is often said that the perception of time develops later than that of space, because children have so vague an idea of all dates before yesterday and after to-morrow. But no vaguer than they have of extensions that exceed as greatly their unit of space-intuition. Recently I heard my child of four tell a visitor that he had been 'as much as one week' in the country. As he had been there three months, the visitor expressed surprise; whereupon the child corrected himself by saying he had been there 'twelve years.' But the child made exactly the same kind of mistake when he asked if Boston was not one hundred miles from Cambridge, the distance being three miles.

[46] Most of these explanations simply give the signs which, adhering to impressions, lead us to date them within a duration, or, in other words, to assign to them their order. Why it should be a time-order, however, is not explained. Herbart's would-be explanation is a simple description of time-perception. He says it comes when, with the last member of a series present to our consciousness, we also think of the first; and then the whole series revives in our thought at once, but with strength diminishing in the backward direction (Psychol. als Wiss., § 115; Lehrb. zur Psychol., §§ 171, 172, 175). Similarly Drobisch, who adds that the series must appear as one already elapsed (durchlaufene), a word which shows even more clearly the question-begging nature of this sort of account (Empirische Psychol., § 59). Th. Waitz is guilty of similar question-begging when he explains our time-consciousness to be engendered by a set of unsuccessful attempts to make our percepts agree with our expectations (Lehrb. d. Psychol., § 52). Volkmann's mythological account of past representations striving to drive present ones out of the seat of consciousness, being driven back by them, etc., suffers from the same fallacy (Psychol., § 87). But all such accounts agree in implying one fact—viz., that the brain-processes of various events must be active simultaneously, and in varying strength, for a time-perception to be possible. Later authors have made this idea more precise. Thus, Lipps:

"Sensations arise, occupy consciousness, fade into images, and vanish. According as two of them, a and b, go through this process simultaneously, or as one precedes or follows the other, the phases of their fading will agree or differ; and the difference will be proportional to the time-difference between their several moments of beginning. Thus there are differences of quality in the images, which the mind may translate into corresponding differences of their temporal order. There is no other possible middle term between the objective time-relations and those in the mind than these differences of phase." (Grundtatsachen des Seelenlebens, p. 588.) Lipps accordingly calls them 'temporal signs,' and hastens explicitly to add that the soul's translation of their order of strength into a time-order is entirely inexplicable (p. 591). M. Guyau's account (Revue

Philosophique, XIX. 353) hardly differs from that of his predecessors, except in picturesqueness of style. Every change leaves a series of trainées lumineuses in the mind like the passage of shooting stars. Each image is in a more fading phase, according as its original was more remote. This group of images gives duration, the mere time-form, the 'bed' of time. The distinction of past, present, and future within the bed comes from our active nature. The future (as with Waitz) is what I want, but have not yet got, and must wait for. All this is doubtless true, but is no explanation.

Mr. Ward gives, in his Encyclopædia Britannica article (Psychology. p. 65, col. 1), a still more refined attempt to specify the 'temporal sign.' The problem being, among a number of other things thought as successive, but simultaneously thought, to determine which is first and which last, he says: "After each distinct representation, a b c d, there may intervene the representation of that movement of attention of which we are aware in passing from one object to another. In our present reminiscence we have, it must be allowed, little direct proof of this intervention; though there is, I think, indirect evidence of it in the tendency of the flow of ideas to follow the order in which the presentations were at first attended to. With the movement itself when the direction of attention changes, we are familiar enough, though the residua of such movements are not ordinarily conspicuous. These residua, then, are our temporal signs.... But temporal signs alone will not furnish all the pictorial exactness of the time-perspective. These give us only fixed series; but the law of obliviscence, by insuring a progressive variation in intensity as we pass from one member of the series to the other, yields the effect which we call time-distance. By themselves such variations in intensity would leave us liable to confound more vivid representations in the distance with fainter ones nearer the present, but from this mistake the temporal signs save us; where the memory-continuum is imperfect such mistakes continually occur. On the other hand, where these variations are slight and imperceptible, though the memory-continuum preserves the order of events intact, we have still no such distinct appreciation of comparative distance in time as we have nearer to the present, where these perceptive effects are considerable.... Locke speaks of our ideas succeeding each other 'at certain distances not much unlike the images in the inside of a lantern turned round by the heat of a candle,' and 'guesses' that 'this appearance of theirs in train varies not very much in a waking man.' Now what is this 'distance' that separates a from b, b from c, and so on; and what means have we of knowing that it is tolerably constant in waking life? It is, probably, that, the residuum of which I have called a temporal sign; or, in other words, it is the movement of attention from a to b." Nevertheless, Mr. Ward does not call our feeling of this movement of attention the original of our feeling of time, or its brain-process the brain-process which directly causes us to perceive time. He says, a moment later, that " though the fixation of attention does of course really occupy rime, it is probably not in the first instance perceived as time— i.e. as continuous 'protensity,' to use a term of Hamilton's—but as intensity. Thus, if this supposition be true, there is an element in our concrete time-perceptions which has no place in our abstract conception of Time. In Time physically conceived there is no trace of intensity; in time psychically experienced, duration is primarily an intensive magnitude, and so far literally a perception." Its 'original' is, then, if I understand Mr. Ward, something like a feeling which accompanies, as pleasure and pain may accompany, the movements of attention. Its brain-process must, it would seem, be assimilated in general type to the brain-processes of pleasure and pain. Such would seem more or less consciously to be Mr. Ward's own view, for he says: "Everybody knows what it is to be distracted by a rapid succession of varied impressions, and equally what it is to be wearied by the slow and monotonous recurrence of the same impressions. Now these 'feelings' of distraction and tedium owe their characteristic qualities to movements of attention. In the first, attention is kept incessantly on the move; before it is accommodated to a, it is disturbed by the suddenness, intensity, and novelty of b; in the second, it is kept all but stationary by the repeated presentation of the same impression. Such excess and defect of surprises make one realize a fact which in ordinary life is so obscure as to escape notice. But recent experiments have set this fact in a more striking light, and made clear what Locke had dimly before his mind in talking of a certain distance between the presentations of a waking man. In estimating very short periods of time of a second or less, indicated, say, by the beats of a metronome, it is found that there is a certain period for which the mean of a number of estimates is correct, while shorter periods are on the whole over-, and longer periods under-estimated. I take this to be evidence of the time occupied in accommodating or fixing attention."
Alluding to the fact that a series of experiences, a b c d e, may seem short in retrospect, which seemed everlasting in passing, he says: "What tells in retrospect is the series a b c d e, etc.; what tells in the present is the intervening t1 t2 t3, etc., or rather the original accommodation of which these temporal signs are the residuum." And he concludes thus: "We seem to have proof that our perception of duration rests ultimately upon quasi-motor objects of varying intensity, the duration of which we do not directly experience as duration at all."

Wundt also thinks that the interval of about three-fourths of a second, which is estimated with the minimum of error, points to a connection between the time-feeling and the succession of distinctly 'apperceived' objects before the mind. The 'association-time' is also equal to about three fourths of a second. This association-time he regards as a sort of internal standard of duration to which we involuntarily assimilate all intervals which we try to reproduce, bringing shorter ones up to it and longer ones down. [In the Stevens result we should have to say contrast instead of assimilate, for the longer intervals there seem longer, and the shorter ones shorter still.] "Singularly enough," he adds (Physiol. Psych., II. 286), "this time is about that in which in rapid walking, according to the Webers, our legs perform their swing. It seems thus not unlikely that both psychical constants, that of the average speed of reproduction and that of the surest estimation of time, have formed themselves under the influence of those most habitual movements of the body which we also use when we try to subdivide rhythmically longer tracts of time."

Finally, Prof. Mach makes a suggestion more specific still. After saying very rightly that we have a real sensation of time—how otherwise should we identify two entirely different airs as being played in the same 'time'? how distinguish in memory the first stroke of the clock from the second, unless to each there clove its special time-sensation, which revived with it? -- he says "it is probable that this feeling is connected with that organic consumption which is necessarily linked with the production of consciousness, and that the time which we feel is probably due to the [mechanical?] work of [the process of?] attention. When attention is strained, time seems long; during easy occupation, short, etc.... The fatigue of the organ of consciousness, as long as we wake, continually increases, and the work of attention augments as continually. Those impressions which are conjoined with a greater amount of work of attention appear to us as the later." The apparent relative displacement of certain simultaneous events and certain anachronisms of dreams are held by Mach to be easily explicable as effects of a splitting of the attention between two objects, one of which consumes most of it (Beiträge zur Analyse der Empfindungen, p. 103 foll.). Mach's theory seems worthy of being better worked out. It is hard to say now whether he, Ward, and Wundt mean at bottom the same thing or not. The theory advanced in my own text, it will be remarked, does not pretend to be an explanation, but only an elementary statement of the 'law' which makes us aware of time. The Herbartian mythology purports to explain.

[47] It would be rash to say definitely just how many seconds long this specious present must needs be, for processes fade 'asymptotically,' and the distinctly intuited present merges into a penumbra of mere dim recency before it turns into the past which is simply reproduced and conceived. Many a thing which we do not distinctly date by intercalating it in a place between two other things will, nevertheless, come to us with this feeling of belonging to a near past. This sense of recency is a feeling sui generis, and may affect things that happened hours ago. It would seem to show that their brain-processes are still in a state modified by the foregoing excitement, still in a 'fading' phase, in a spite of the long interval.

[48] Physiol. Psych., II. 263.

[49] I leave my text as it was printed before Münsterberg's essay appeared. He denies that we measure any but minimal durations by the amount of fading in the ideational processes, and talks almost exclusively of our feelings of muscular tension in his account, whereas I have made no mention of such things in mine. I cannot, however, see that there is any conflict between what he and I suggest. I am mainly concerned with the consciousness of duration regarded as a specific sort of object, he is concerned with this object's measurement exclusively. Feelings of tension might be the means of the measurement, whilst overlapping processes of any and every kind gave the object to be measured. The accommodative and respiratory movements from which the feelings of tension come form regularly recurring sensations divided by their 'phases' into intervals as definite as those by which a yardstick is divided by the marks upon its length.

Let a_1, a_2, a_3, a_4, be homologous phases in four successive movements of this kind. If four outer stimuli 1, 2, 3, 4, coincide each with one of these successive phases, then their 'distances apart' are felt as equal, otherwise not. But there is no reason whatever to suppose that the mere overlapping of the brain-process of 2 by the fading process of 1, or that of 3 by that of 2, etc., does not give the characteristic quality of content which we call 'distance apart' in this experience, and which by aid of the muscular feelings gets judged to be equal. Doubtless the muscular feelings can give us the object 'time' as well as its measure, because their earlier phases leave fading sensations which constantly overlap the vivid sensation of the present phase. But it would be contrary to analogy to suppose that they should be the only experiences which give this object. I do not understand Herr Münsterberg to claim this for them. He takes our sense of time for granted, and only discusses its measurement.

[50] Exner in Hermann's Hdbch. d. Physiol., Bd. II. Thl. II. p. 281. Richet in Revue Philosophique, XXI. 568 (juin, 1886). See the next chapter, pp. 642-646.

[51] I have spoken of fading brain-processes alone, but only for simplicity's sake. Dawning processes probably play as important a part in giving the feeling of duration to the specious present.

[52] Reden (St. Petersburg, 1864), vol. I. pp. 255-268.

[53] Psychology, § 91.

[54] "The patient cannot retain the image of an object more than a moment. His memory is as short for sounds, letters, figures, and printed words. If we cover a written or printed word with a sheet of paper in which a little window has been cut, so that only the first letter is visible through the window, he pronounces this letter. If, then, the sheet is moved so as to cover the first letter and make the second one visible, he pronounces the second, but forgets the first, and cannot pronounce the first and second together." And so forth to the end. "If he closes his eyes and draws his finger exploringly over a well-known object like a knife or key, he cannot combine the separate impressions and recognize the object. But if it is put into his hand so that he can simultaneously touch it with several fingers, he names it without difficulty. This patient has thus lost the capacity for grouping successive... impressions... into a whole and perceiving them as a whole." (Grashey, in Archiv für Psychiatrie, Bd. XVI. pp. 672-673.) It is hard to believe that in such a patient the time intuited was not clipped off like the impressions it held, though perhaps not so much of it.

I have myself often noted a curious exaggeration of time-perspective at the moment of a falling asleep. A person will be moving or doing something in the room, and a certain stage of his act (whatever it may be) will be my last waking perception. Then a subsequent stage will wake me to a new perception. The two stages of the act will not be more than a few seconds apart; and yet it always seems to me as if, between the earlier and the later one, a long interval has passed away. I conjecturally account for the phenomenon thus, calling the two stages of the act a and b respectively: Were I awake, a would leave a fading process in my sensorium which would overlap the process of b when the latter came, and both would then appear in the same specious present, a belonging to its earlier end. But the sudden advent of the brain-change called sleep extinguishes a's fading process abruptly. When b then comes and wakes me, a comes back, it is true, but not as belonging to

the specious present. It has to be specially revoked in memory. This mode of revocation usually characterizes long-past things—whence the illusion.
[55] Again I omit the future, merely for simplicity's sake.

Chapter XVI - Memory

In the last chapter what concerned us was the direct intuition of time. We found it limited to intervals of considerably less than a minute. Beyond its borders extends the immense region of conceived time, past and future, into one direction or another of which we mentally project all the events which we think of as real, and form a systematic order of them by giving to each a date. The relation of conceived to intuited time is just like that of the fictitious space pictured on the flat back-scene of a theatre to the actual space of the stage. The objects painted on the latter (trees, columns, houses in a receding street, etc.) carry back the series of similar objects solidly placed upon the latter, and we think we see things in a continuous perspective, when we really see thus only a few of them and imagine that we see the rest. The chapter which lies before us deals with the way in which we paint the remote past, as it were, upon a canvas in our memory, and yet often imagine that we have direct vision of its depths.

The stream of thought flows on; but most of its segments fall into the bottomless abyss of oblivion. Of some, no memory survives the instant of their passage. Of others, it is confined to a few moments, hours, or days. Others, again, leave vestiges which are indestructible, and by means of which they may be recalled as long as life endures. Can we explain these differences?

Primary Memory.

The first point to be noticed is that for a state of mind to survive in memory it must have endured for a certain length of time. In other words, it must be what I call a substantive state. Prepositional and conjunctival states of mind are not remembered as independent facts—we cannot recall just how we felt when we said 'how' or 'notwithstanding.' Our consciousness of these transitive states is shut up to their own moment—hence one difficulty in introspective psychologizing.

Any state of mind which is shut up to its own moment and fails to become an object for succeeding states of mind, is as if it belonged to another stream of thought. Or rather, it belongs only physically, not intellectually, to its own stream, forming a bridge from one segment of it to another, but not being appropriated inwardly by later segments or appearing as part of the empirical self, in the manner explained in Chapter X. All the intellectual value for us of a state of mind depends on our after-memory of it. Only then is it combined in a system and knowingly made to contribute to a result. Only then does it count for us. So that the EFFECTIVE consciousness we have of our states is the after-consciousness; and the more of this there is, the more influence does the original state have, and the more permanent a factor is it of our world. An indelibly-imprinted pain may color a life; but, as Professor Richet says: "To suffer for only a hundredth of a second is not to suffer at all; and for my part I would readily agree to undergo a pain, however acute and intense it might be, provided it should last only a hundredth of a second, and leave after it neither reverberation nor recall."[1]

Not that a momentary state of consciousness need be practically resultless. Far from it: such a state, though absolutely unremembered, might at its own moment determine the transition of our thinking in a vital way, and decide our action irrevocably.[2] But the idea of it could not afterwards determine transition and action, its content could not be conceived as one of the mind's permanent meanings: that is all I mean by saying that its intellectual value lies in after-memory.

As a rule sensations outlast for some little time the objective stimulus which occasioned them. This phenomenon is the ground of those 'after-images' which are familiar in the physiology of the sense-organs. If we open our eyes instantaneously upon a scene, and then shroud them in complete darkness, it will be as if we saw the scene in ghostly light throught [sic] the dark screen. We can read off details in it which were unnoticed whilst the eyes were open.[3]

In every sphere of sense, an intermittent stimulus, often enough repeated, produces a continuous sensation. This is because the after-image of the impression just gone by blends with the new impression coming in. The effects of stimuli may thus be superposed upon each other many stages deep, the total result in consciousness being an increase in the feeling's intensity, and in all probability, as we saw in the last chapter, an elementary sense of the lapse of time.

Exner writes:

"Impressions to which we are inattentive leave so brief an image in the memory that it is usually overlooked. When deeply absorbed, we do not hear the clock strike. But our attention may awake after the striking has ceased, and we may then count off the strokes. Such examples are often found in daily life. We can also prove the existence of this primary memory-image, as it may be called, in another person, even when his attention is completely absorbed elsewhere. Ask someone, e.g., to count the lines of a printed page as fast as he can, and whilst this is going on walk a

few steps about the room. Then, when the person has done counting, ask him where you stood. He will always reply quite definitely that you have walked. Analogous experiments may be done with vision. This primary memory-image is, whether attention have been turned to the impression or not, an extremely lively one, but is subjectively quite distinct from every sort of after-image or hallucination.... It vanishes, if not caught by attention, in the course of a few seconds. Even when the original impression is attended to, the liveliness of its image in memory fades fast."[4] The physical condition in the nerve-tissue of this primary memory is called by Richet 'elementary memory.'[5] I much prefer to reserve the word memory for the conscious phenomenon. What happens in the nerve-tissue is but an example of that plasticity or of semi-inertness, yielding to change, but not yielding instantly or wholly, and never quite recovering the original form, which, in Chapter V, we saw to be the groundwork of habit. Elementary habit would be the better name for what Professor Richet means. Well, the first manifestation of elementary habit is the slow dying away of an impressed movement on the neural matter, and its first effect in consciousness is this so-called elementary memory. But what elementary memory makes us aware of is the just past. The objects we feel in this directly intuited past differ from properly recollected objects. An object which is recollected, in the proper sense of that term, is one which has been absent from consciousness altogether, and now revives anew. It is brought back, recalled, fished up, so to speak, from a reservoir in which, with countless other objects, it lay buried and lost from view. But an object of primary memory is not thus brought back; it never was lost; its date was never cut off in consciousness from that of the immediately present moment. In fact it comes to us as belonging to the rearward portion of the present space of time, and not to the genuine past. In the last chapter we saw that the portion of time which we directly intuit has a breadth of several seconds, a rearward and a forward end, and may be called the specious present. All stimuli whose first nerve-vibrations have not yet ceased seem to be conditions of our getting this feeling of the specious present. They give rise to objects which appear to the mind as events just past.[6]
When we have been exposed to an unusual stimulus for many minutes or hours, a nervous process is set up which results in the haunting of consciousness by the impression for a long time afterwards. The tactile and muscular feelings of a day of skating or riding, after long disuse of the exercise, will come back to us all through the night. Images of the field of view of the microscope will annoy the observer for hours after an unusually long sitting at the instrument. A thread tied around the finger, an unusual constriction in the clothing, will feel as if still there, long after they have been removed. These revivals (called phenomena of Sinnesgedächtniss by the Germans) have something periodical in their nature.[7] They show that profound rearrangements and slow settlings into a new equilibrium are going on in the neural substance, and they form the transition to that more peculiar and proper phenomenon of memory, of which the rest of this chapter must treat. The first condition which makes a thing susceptible of recall after it has been forgotten is that the original impression of it should have been prolonged enough to give rise to a recurrent image of it, as distinguished from one of those primary after-images which very fleeting impressions may leave behind, and which contain in themselves no guarantee that they will ever come back after having once faded away.[8] A certain length of stimulation seems demanded by the inertia of the nerve-substance. Exposed to a shorter influence, its modification fails to 'set,' and it retains no effective tendency to fall again into the same form of vibration at which the original feeling was due. This, as I said at the outset, may be the reason why only 'substantive' and not 'transitive' states of mind are as a rule recollected, at least as independent things. The transitive states pass by too quickly.

Analysis of the Phenomenon of Memory.

Memory proper, or secondary memory as it might be styled, is the knowledge of a former state of mind after it has already once dropped from consciousness; or rather it is the knowledge of an event, or fact, of which meantime we have not been thinking, with the additional consciousness that we have thought or experienced it before.
The first element which such a knowledge involves would seem to be the revival in the mind of an image or copy of the original event.[9] And it is an assumption made by many writers[10] that the revival of an image is all that is needed to constitute the memory of the original occurrence. But such a revival is obviously not a memory, whatever else it may be; it is simply a duplicate, a second event, having absolutely no connection with the first event except that it happens to resemble it. The clock strikes to-day; it struck yesterday; and may strike a million times ere it wears out. The rain pours through the gutter this week; it did so last week; and will do so in sœcula sœculorum. But does the present clock-stroke become aware of the past ones, or the present stream recollect the past stream, because they repeat and resemble them? Assuredly not. And let it not be said that this is because clock-strokes and gutters are physical and not psychical objects; for psychical objects (sensations for example) simply recurring in successive editions will remember each other on that account no more than clock-strokes do. No memory is involved in the mere fact of recurrence. The successive editions of a feeling are so many independent events, each snug in its own skin. Yesterday's feeling is dead and buried; and the presence of to-day's is no reason why it should resuscitate. A farther condition is required before the present image can be held to stand for a past original.

That condition is that the fact imaged be expressly referred to the past, thought as in the past. But how can we think a thing as in the past, except by thinking of the past together with the thing, and of the relation of the two? And how can we think of the past? In the chapter on Time-perception we have seen that our intuitive or immediate consciousness of pastness hardly carries us more than a few seconds backward of the present instant of time. Remoter dates are conceived, not perceived; known symbolically by names, such as 'last week,' '1850;' or thought of by events which happened in them, as the year in which we attended such a school, or met with such a loss.—So that if we wish to think of a particular past epoch, we must think of a name or other symbol, or else of certain concrete events, associated therewithal. Both must be thought of, to think the past epoch adequately. And to 'refer' any special fact to the past epoch is to think that fact with the names and events which characterize its date, to think it, in short, with a lot of contiguous associates.

But even this would not be memory. Memory requires more than mere dating of a fact in the past. It must be dated in my past. In other words, I must think that I directly experienced its occurrence. It must have that 'warmth and intimacy' which were so often spoken of in the chapter on the Self, as characterizing all experiences 'appropriated' by the thinker as his own.

A general feeling of the past direction in time, then, a particular date conceived as lying along that direction, and defined by its name or phenomenal contents, an event imagined as located therein, and owned as part of my experience, -- such are the elements of every act of memory.

It follows that what we began by calling the 'image,' or 'copy,' of the fact in the mind, is really not there at all in that simple shape, as a separate 'idea.' Or at least, if it be there as a separate idea, no memory will go with it. What memory goes with is, on the contrary, a very complex representation, that of the fact to be recalled plus its associates, the whole forming one 'object' (as explained in Chapter IX), known in one integral pulse of consciousness (as set forth on pp. 276 ff.) and demanding probably a vastly more intricate brain-process than that on which any simple sensorial image depends.

Most psychologists have given a perfectly clear analysis of the phenomenon we describe. Christian Wolff, for example, writes:

"Suppose you have seen Mevius in the temple, but now afresh in Titus' house. I say you recognize Mevius, that is, are conscious of having seen him before, because, although now you perceive him with your senses along with Titus' house, your imagination produces an image of him along with one of the temple, and of the acts of your own mind reflecting on Mevius in the temple. Hence the idea of Mevius which is reproduced in sense is contained in another series of perceptions than that which formerly contained it, and this difference is the reason why we are conscious of having had it before. . . . For whilst now you see Mevius in the house of Titus, your imagination places him in the temple, and renders you conscious of the state of mind which you found in yourself when you beheld him there. By this you know that you have seen him before, that is, you recognize him. But you recognize him because his idea is now contained in another series of perceptions from that in which you first saw him."[11]

Similarly James Mill writes:

"In my remembrance of George III., addressing the two houses of parliament, there is, first of all, the mere idea, or simple apprehension, the conception, as it is sometimes called, of the objects. There is combined with this, to make it memory, my idea of my having seen and heard those objects. And this combination is so close that it is not in my power to separate them. I cannot have the idea of George III.; his person and attitude, the paper he held in his hand, the sound of his voice while reading from it; without having the other idea along with it, that of my having been a witness of the scene. . . . If this explanation of the case in which we remember sensations is understood, the explanation of the case in which we remember ideas cannot occasion much of difficulty. I have a lively recollection of Polyphemus's cave, and the actions of Ulysses and the Cyclops, as described by Homer. In this recollection there is, first of all, the ideas, or simple conceptions of the objects and acts; and along with these ideas, and so closely combined as not to be separable, the idea of my having formerly had those same ideas. And this idea of my having formerly had those ideas is a very complicated idea; including the idea of myself of the present moment remembering, and that of myself of the past moment conceiving; and the whole series of the states of consciousness, which intervened between myself remembering, and myself conceiving."[12]

Memory is then the feeling of belief in a peculiar complex object; but all the elements of this object may be known to other states of belief; nor is there in the particular combination of them as they appear in memory anything so peculiar as to lead us to oppose the latter to other sorts of thought as something altogether sui generis, needing a special faculty to account for it. When later we come to our chapter on Belief we shall see that any represented object which is connected either mediately or immediately with our present sensations or emotional activities tends to be believed in as a reality. The sense of a peculiar active relation in it to ourselves is what gives to an object the characteristic quality of reality, and a merely imagined past event differs from a recollected one only in the absence of this peculiar feeling relation. The electric current, so to speak, between it and our present self does not close. But in their other determinations the re-recollected past and the imaginary past may be much the same. In other words, there is nothing unique in the object of memory, and no special faculty is needed to account for its formation. It is a synthesis of parts thought of as related together, perception, imagination, comparison and reasoning being analogous syntheses of parts into complex objects. The objects of any of these faculties may awaken belief or fail to awaken it; the object of memory is only an object imagined in the past (usually very completely imagined there) to which the emotion of belief adheres.

Memory's Causes.

Such being the phenomenon of memory, or the analysis of its object, can we see how it comes to pass? can we lay bare its causes?
Its complete exercise presupposes two things:

1) The retention of the remembered fact;
2) Its reminiscence, recollection, reproduction, or recall.

Now the cause both of retention and of recollection is the law of habit in the nervous system, working as it does in the 'association of ideas.'
Associationists have long explained recollection by association. James Mill gives an account of it which I am unable to improve upon, unless it might be by translating his word 'idea' into 'thing thought of,' or 'object,' as explained so often before.
"There is," he says, "a state of mind familiar to all men, in which we are said to remember. In this state it is certain we have not in the mind the idea which we are trying to have in it.[13] How is it, then, that we proceed in the course of our endeavor, to procure its introduction into the mind? If we have not the idea itself, we have certain ideas connected with it. We run over those ideas, one after another, in hopes that some one of them will suggest the idea we are in quest of; and if any one of them does, it is always one so connected with it as to call it up in the way of association. I meet an old acquaintance, whose name I do not remember, and wish to recollect. I run over a number of names, in hopes that some of them may be associated with the idea of the individual. I think of all the circumstances in which I have seen him engaged; the time when I knew him, the persons along with whom I knew him, the things he did, or the things he suffered; and, if I chance upon any idea with which the name is associated, then immediately I have the recollection; if not, my pursuit of it is vain.[14] There is another set of cases, very familiar, but affording very important evidence on the subject. It frequently happens that there are matters which we desire not to forget. What is the contrivance to which we have recourse for preserving the memory—that is, for making sure that it will be called into existence, when it is our wish that it should? All men invariably employ the same expedient. They endeavor to form an association between the idea of the thing to be remembered, and some sensation, or some idea, which they know beforehand will occur at or near the time when they wish the remembrance to be in their minds. If this association is formed, and the association or idea with which it has been formed occurs; the sensation, or idea, calls up the remembrance; and the object of him who formed the association is attained. To use a vulgar instance: a man receives a commission from his friend, and, that he may not forget it, ties a knot in his handkerchief. How is this fact to be explained? First of all, the idea of the commission is associated with the making of the knot. Next, the handkerchief is a thing which is known beforehand will be frequently seen, and of course at no great distance of time from the occasion on which the memory is desired. The handkerchief being seen, the knot is seen, and this sensation recalls the idea of the commission, between which and itself the association had been purposely formed."[15]
In short, we make search in our memory for a forgotten idea, just as we rummage our house for a lost object. In both cases we visit what seems to us the probable neighborhood of that which we miss. We turn over the things under which, or within which, or alongside of which, it may possibly be; and if it lies near them, it soon comes to view. But these matters, in the case of a mental object sought, are nothing but its associates. The machinery of recall is thus the same as the machinery of association, and the machinery of association, as we know, is nothing but the elementary law of habit in the nerve-centres.
And this same law of habit is the machinery of retention also. Retention means liability to recall, and it means nothing more than such liability. The only proof of there being retention is that recall actually takes place. The retention of an experience is, in short, but another name for the possibility of thinking it again, or the tendency to think it again, with its past surroundings. Whatever accidental cue may turn this tendency into an actuality, the permanent ground of the tendency itself lies in the organized neural paths by which the cue calls up the experience on the proper occasion, together with its past associates, the sense that the self was there, the belief that it really happened, etc., etc., just as previously described. When the recollection is of the 'ready' sort, the resuscitation takes place the instant the occasion arises; when it is slow, resuscitation comes after delay. But be the recall prompt or

slow, the condition which makes it possible at all (or in other words, the 'retention' of the experience) is neither more nor less then the brain-paths which associate the experience with the occasion and cue of the recall. When slumbering, these paths are the condition of retention; when active, they are the condition of recall.

A simple scheme will now make the whole cause of memory plain. Let n be a past event; o its 'setting' (concomitants, date, self present, warmth and intimacy, etc., etc., as already set forth); and m some present thought or fact which may appropriately become the occasion of its recall. Let the nerve-centres, active in the thought of m, n, and o, be represented by M, N, and O, respectively; then the existence of the paths M-N and N-O will be the fact indicated by the phrase 'retention of the event n in the memory,' and the excitement of the brain along these paths will be the condition of the event n's actual recall. The retention of n, it will be observed, is no mysterious storing up of an 'idea' in an unconscious state. It is not a fact of the mental order at all. It is a purely physical phenomenon, a morphological feature, the presence of these 'paths,' namely, in the finest recesses of the brain's tissue. The recall or recollection, on the other hand, is a psychophysical phenomenon, with both a bodily and a mental side. The bodily side is the functional excitement of the tracts and paths in question; the mental side is the conscious vision of the past occurrence, and the belief that we experienced it before.

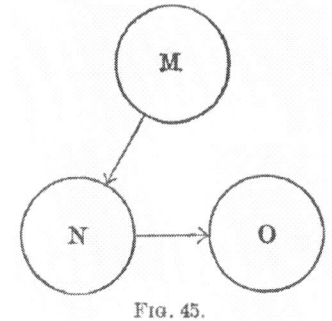

FIG. 45.

These habit-worn paths of association are a clear rendering of what authors mean by 'predispositions,' 'vestiges,' 'traces,' etc., left in the brain by past experience. Most writers leave the nature of these vestiges vague; few think of explicitly assimilating them to channels of association. Dr. Maudsley, for example, writes:

"When an idea which we have once had is excited again, there is a reproduction of the same nervous current, with the conscious addition that it is a reproduction—it is the same idea plus the consciousness that it is the same. The question then suggests itself, What is the physical condition of this consciousness? What is the modification of the anatomical substrata of fibres and cells, or of their physiological activity, which is the occasion of this plus element in the reproduced idea? It may be supposed that the first activity did leave behind it, when it subsided, some after-effect, some modification of the nerve-element, whereby the nerve-circuit was disposed to fall again readily into the same action; such disposition appearing in consciousness as recognition or memory. Memory is, in fact, the conscious phase of this physiological disposition when it becomes active or discharges its functions on the recurrence of the particular mental experience. To assist our conception of what may happen, let us suppose the individual nerve-elements to be endowed with their own consciousness, and let us assume them to be, as I have supposed, modified in a certain way by the first experience; it is hard to conceive that when they fall into the same action on another occasion they should not recognize or remember it; for the second action is a reproduction of the first, with the addition of what it contains from the after-effects of the first. As we have assumed the process to be conscious, this reproduction with its addition would be a memory or remembrance."[16]

In this passage Dr. Maudsley seems to mean by the 'nerve-element,' or 'anatomical substratum of fibres and cells,' something that corresponds to the N of our diagram. And the 'modification' he speaks of seems intended to be understood as an internal modification of this same particular group of elements. Now the slightest reflection will convince anyone that there is no conceivable ground for supposing that with the mere re-excitation of N there should arise the 'conscious addition' that it is a re-excitation. The two excitations are simply two excitations, their consciousnesses are two consciousnesses, they have nothing to do with each other. And a vague 'modification,' supposed to be left behind by the first excitation, helps us not a whit. For, according to all analogy, such a modification can only result in making the next excitation more smooth and rapid. This might make it less conscious, perhaps, but could not endow it with any reference to the past. The gutter is worn deeper by each successive shower, but not for that reason brought into contact with previous showers. Psychology (which Dr. Maudsley in his next sentence says "affords us not the least help in this matter") puts us on the track of an at least possible brain-explanation. As it is the setting o of the idea, when it recurs, which makes us conscious of it as past, so it can be no intrinsic modification of the 'nerve-element' N which is the organic condition of memory, but something extrinsic to it altogether, namely, its connections with those other nerve-elements which we called O—that letter standing in the scheme for the cerebral substratum of a great plexus of things other than the principal event remembered, dates, names, concrete surroundings, realized intervals, and what not. The 'modification' is the formation in the plastic nerve-substance of the system of associative paths between N and O.

The only hypothesis, in short, to which the facts of inward experience give countenance is that the brain-tracts excited by the event proper, and those excited in its recall, are in part different from each other. If we could revive the past event without any associates we should exclude the possibility of memory, and simply dream that we were undergoing the experience as if for the first time.[17] Wherever, in fact, the recalled event does appear without a definite setting, it is hard to distinguish it from a mere creation of fancy. But in proportion as its image lingers and recalls associates which gradually become more definite, it grows more and more distinctly into a remembered thing. For example, I enter a friend's room and see on the wall a painting. At first I have the strange, wondering consciousness, 'surely I have seen that before,' but when or how does not become clear. There only clings to the picture a sort of penumbra of familiarity, -- when suddenly I exclaim: "I have it, it is a copy of part of one of the Fra Angelicos in the Florentine Academy—I recollect it there!" But the motive to the recall does not lie in the fact that the brain-tract now excited by the painting was once before excited in a similar way; it lies simply and solely in the fact that with that brain-tract other tracts also are excited: those which sustain my friend's room with all its peculiarities, on the one hand; those which sustain the mental image of the Florence Academy, on the other hand, with the circumstances of my visit there; and finally those which make me (more dimly) think of the years I have lived through between these two times. The result of this total brain-disturbance is a thought with a peculiar object, namely, that I who now stand here with this picture before me, stood so many years ago in the Florentine Academy looking at its original.

M. Taine has described the gradual way in which a mental image develops into an object of memory, in his usual vivid fashion. He says:

"I meet casually in the street a person whose appearance I am acquainted with, and say to myself at once that I have seen him before. Instantly the figure recedes into the past, and wavers about there vaguely, without at once fixing itself in any spot. It persists in me for some time, and surrounds itself with new details. 'When I saw him he was bare-headed, with a working-jacket on, painting in a studio; he is so-and-so, of such-and-such a street. But when was it? It was not yesterday, nor this week, nor recently. I have it: he told me that he was waiting for the first leaves to come out to go into the country. It was before the spring. But at what exact date? I saw, the same day, people carrying branches in the streets and omnibuses: it was Palm Sunday!' Observe the travels of the internal figure, its various shiftings to front and rear along the line of the past; each of these mental sentences has been a swing of the balance. When confronted with the present sensation and with the latent swarm of indistinct images which repeat our recent life, the figure first recoiled suddenly to an indeterminate distance. Then, completed by precise details, and confronted with all the shortened images by which we sum up the proceedings of a day or a week, it again receded beyond the present day, beyond yesterday, the day before, the week, still farther, beyond the ill-defined mass constituted by our recent recollections. Then something said by the painter was recalled, and it at once receded again beyond an almost precise limit, which is marked by the image of the green leaves and denoted by the word spring. A moment afterwards, thanks to a new detail, the recollection of the branches, it has shifted again, but forward this time, not backward; and, by a reference to the calendar, is situated at a precise point, a week further back than Easter, and five weeks nearer than the carnival, by the double effect of the contrary impulsions, pushing it, one forward and the other backward, and which are, at a particular moment, annulled by one another."[18]

The Conditions of Goodness in Memory.

The remembered fact being n, then, the path N—O is what arouses for n its setting when it is recalled, and makes it other than a mere imagination. The path M—N, on the other hand, gives the cue or occasion of its being recalled at all. Memory being thus altogether conditioned on brain-paths, its excellence in a given individual will depend partly on the number and partly on the persistence of these paths.

The persistence or permanence of the paths is a physiological property of the brain-tissue of the individual, whilst their number is altogether due to the facts of his mental experience. Let the quality of permanence in the paths be called the native tenacity, or physiological retentiveness. This tenacity differs enormously from infancy to old age, and from one person to another. Some minds are like wax under a seal—no impression, however disconnected with others, is wiped out. Others, like a jelly, vibrate to every touch, but under usual conditions retain no permanent mark. These latter minds, before they can recollect a fact, must weave it into their permanent stores of knowledge. They have no desultory memory. Those persons, on the contrary, who retain names, dates and addresses, anecdotes, gossip, poetry, quotations, and all sorts of miscellaneous facts, without an effort, have desultory memory in a high degree, and certainly owe it to the unusual tenacity of their brain-substance for any path once formed therein. No one probably was ever effective on a voluminous scale without a high degree of this physiological retentiveness. In the practical as in the theoretic life, the man whose acquisitions stick is the man who is always achieving and advancing, whilst his neighbors, spending most of their time in relearning what they once knew but have forgotten, simply hold their own. A Charlemagne, a Luther, a Leibnitz, a Walter Scott, any example, in short, of your quarto or folio editions of mankind, must needs have amazing retentiveness of the purely physiological sort. Men without this retentiveness may excel in the quality of their work at this point or at that, but will never do such mighty sums of it, or be influential contemporaneously on such a scale.[19]

But there comes a time of life for all of us when we can do no more than hold our own in the way of acquisitions, when the old paths fade as fast as the new ones form in our brain, and when we forget in a week quite as much as we can learn in the same space of time. This equilibrium may last many, many years. In extreme old age it is upset in the reverse direction, and forgetting prevails over acquisition, or rather there is no acquisition. Brain-paths are so transient that in the course of a few minutes of conversation the same question is asked and its answer forgotten half a dozen times. Then the superior tenacity of the paths formed in childhood becomes manifest: the dotard will retrace the facts of his earlier years after he has lost all those of later date.

So much for the permanence of the paths. Now for their number.

It is obvious that the more there are of such paths as M—N in the brain, and the more of such possible cues or occasions for the recall of n in the mind, the prompter and surer, on the whole, the memory of n will be, the more frequently one will be reminded of it, the more avenues of approach to it one will possess. In mental terms, the more other facts a fact is associated with in the mind, the better possession of it our memory retains. Each of its associates becomes a hook to which it hangs, a means to fish it up by when sunk beneath the surface. Together, they form a network of attachments by which it is woven into the entire tissue of our thought. The 'secret of a good memory' is thus the secret of forming diverse and multiple associations with every fact we care to retain. But this forming of associations with a fact, what is it but thinking about the fact as much as possible? Briefly, then, of two men with the same outward experiences and the same amount of mere native tenacity, the one who THINKS over his experiences most, and weaves them into systematic relations with each other, will be the one with the best memory. We see examples of this on every hand. Most men have a good memory for facts connected with their own pursuits. The college athlete who remains a dunce at his books will astonish you by his knowledge of men's 'records' in various feats and games, and will be a walking dictionary of sporting statistics. The reason is that he is constantly going over these things in his mind, and comparing and making series of them. They form for him not so many odd facts, but a concept-system—so they stick. So the merchant remembers prices, the politician other politicians' speeches and votes, with a copiousness which amazes outsiders, but which the amount of thinking they bestow on these subjects easily explains. The great memory for facts which a Darwin and a Spencer reveal in their books is not incompatible with the possession on their part of a brain with only a middling degree of physiological retentiveness. Let a man early in life set himself the task of verifying such a theory as that of evolution, and facts will soon cluster and cling to him like grapes to their stem. Their relations to the theory will hold them fast; and the more of these the mind is able to discern, the greater the erudition will become. Meanwhile the theorist may have little, if any, desultory memory. Unutilizable facts may be unnoted by him and forgotten as soon as heard. An ignorance almost as encyclopædic as his erudition may coexist with the latter, and hide, as it were, in the interstices of its web. Those who have had much to do with scholars and savants will readily think of examples of the class of mind I mean.

In a system, every fact is connected with every other by some thought-relation. The consequence is that every fact is retained by the combined suggestive power of all the other facts in the system, and forgetfulness is well-nigh impossible.

The reason why cramming is such a bad mode of study is now made clear. I mean by cramming that way of preparing for examinations by committing 'points' to memory during a few hours or days of intense application immediately preceding the final ordeal, little or no work having been performed during the previous course of the term. Things learned thus in a few hours, on one occasion, for one purpose, cannot possibly have formed many associations with other things in the mind. Their brain-processes are led into by few paths, and are relatively little liable to be awakened again. Speedy oblivion is the almost inevitable fate of all that is committed to memory in this simple way. Whereas, on the contrary, the same materials taken in gradually, day after day, recurring in different contexts, considered in various relations, associated with other external incidents, and repeatedly reflected on, grow into such a system, form such connections with the rest of the mind's fabric, lie open to so many paths of approach, that they remain permanent possessions. This is the intellectual reason why habits of continuous application should be enforced in educational establishments. Of course there is no moral turpitude in cramming. If it led to the desired end of secure learning it would be infinitely the best method of study. But it does not; and students themselves should understand the reason why.

One's Native Retentiveness is Unchangeable.

It will now appear clear that all improvement of the memory lies in the line of ELABORATING THE ASSOCIATES of each of the several things to be remembered. No amount of culture would seem capable of modifying a man's GENERAL retentiveness. This is a physiological quality, given once for all with his organization, and which he can never hope to change. It differs no doubt in disease and health; and it is a fact of observation that it is better in fresh and vigorous hours than when we are fagged or ill. We may say, then, that a man's native tenacity will fluctuate somewhat with his hygiene, and that whatever is good for his tone of health will also be good for his memory. We may even say that whatever amount of intellectual exercise is bracing to the general tone and nutrition of the brain will also be profitable to the general retentiveness. But more than this we cannot say; and this, it is obvious, is far less than most people believe.

It is, in fact, commonly thought that certain exercises, systematically repeated, will strengthen, not only a man's remembrance of the particular facts used in the exercises, but his faculty for remembering facts at large. And a plausible case is always made out by saying that practice in learning words by heart makes it easier to learn new words in the same way.[20] If this be true, then what I have just said is false, and the whole doctrine of memory as due to 'paths' must be revised. But I am disposed to think the alleged fact untrue. I have carefully questioned several mature actors on the point, and all have denied that the practice of learning parts has made any such difference as is alleged. What it has done for them is to improve their power of studying a part systematically. Their mind is now full of precedents in the way of intonation, emphasis, gesticulation; the new words awaken distinct suggestions and decisions; are caught up, in fact, into a pre-existing net-work, like the merchant's prices, or the athlete's store of 'records,' and are recollected easier, although the mere native tenacity is not a whit improved, and is usually, in fact, impaired by age. It is a case of better remembering by better thinking. Similarly when schoolboys improve by practice in ease of learning by heart, the improvement will, I am sure, be always found to reside in the mode of study of the particular piece (due to the greater interest, the greater suggestiveness, the generic similarity with other pieces, the more sustained attention, etc., etc.), and not at all to any enhancement of the brute retentive power.

The error I speak of pervades an otherwise useful and judicious book, 'How to Strengthen the Memory,' by Dr. Holbrook of New York.[21] The author fails to distinguish between the general physiological retentiveness and the retention of particular things, and talks as if both must be benefited by the same means.

"I am now treating," he says, "a case of loss of memory in a person advanced in years, who did not know that his memory had failed most remarkably till I told him of it. He is making vigorous efforts to bring it back again, and with partial success. The method pursued is to spend two hours daily, one in the morning and one in the evening, in exercising this faculty. The patient is instructed to give the closest attention to all that he learns, so that it shall be impressed on his mind clearly. He is asked to recall every evening all the facts and experiences of the day, and again the next morning. Every name heard is written down and impressed on his mind clearly, and an effort made to recall it at intervals. Ten names from among public men are ordered to be committed to memory every week. A verse of poetry is to be learned, also a verse from the Bible, daily. He is asked to remember the number of the page in any book where any interesting fact is recorded. These and other methods are slowly resuscitating a failing memory."[22]

I find it very hard to believe that the memory of the poor old gentleman is a bit the better for all this torture except in respect of the particular facts thus wrought into it, the occurrences attended to and repeated on those days, the names of those politicians, those Bible verses, etc., etc. In another place Dr. Holbrook quotes the account given by the late Thurlow Weed, journalist and politician, of his method of strengthening his memory.

"My memory was a sieve. I could remember nothing. Dates, names, appointments, faces—everything escaped me. I said to my wife, 'Catherine, I shall never make a successful politician, for I cannot remember, and that is a prime necessity of politicians.' My wife told me I must train my memory. So when I came home that night, I sat down alone and spent fifteen minutes trying silently to recall with accuracy the principal events of the day. I could remember but little at first; now I remember that I could not then recall what I had for breakfast. After a few days' practice I found I could recall more. Events came back to me more minutely, more accurately, and more vividly than at first. After a fortnight or so of this, Catherine said, 'Why don't you relate to me the events of the day, instead of recalling them to yourself? It would be interesting, and my interest in it would be a stimulus to you.' Having great respect for my wife's opinion, I began a habit of oral confession, as it were, which was continued for almost fifty years. Every night, the last thing before retiring, I told her everything I could remember that had happened to me or about me during the day. I generally recalled the dishes I had had for breakfast, dinner, and tea; the people I had seen and what they had said; the editorials I had written for my paper, giving her a brief abstract of them. I mentioned all the letters I had sent and received, and the very language used, as nearly as possible; when I had walked or ridden—I told her everything that had come within my observation. I found I could say my lessons better and better every year, and instead of the practice growing irksome, it became a pleasure to go over again the events of the day. I am indebted to this discipline for a memory of somewhat unusual tenacity, and I recommend the practice to all who wish to store up facts, or expect to have much to do with influencing men."[23]

I do not doubt that Mr. Weed's practical command of his past experiences was much greeter after fifty years of this heroic drill than it would have been without it. Expecting to give his account in the evening, he attended better to each incident of the day, named and conceived it differently, set his mind upon it, and in the evening went over it again. He did more thinking about it, and it stayed with him in consequence. But I venture to affirm pretty confidently (although I know how foolish it often is to deny a fact on the strength of a theory) that the same matter, casually attended to and not thought about, would have stuck in his memory no better at the end than at the beginning of his years of heroic self-discipline. He had acquired a better method of noting and recording his experiences, but his physiological retentiveness was probably not a bit improved.[24]

All improvement of memory consists, then, in the improvement of one's habitual methods of recording facts. In the traditional terminology methods are divided into the mechanical, the ingenious, and the judicious.

The mechanical methods consist in the intensification, prolongation, and repetition of the impression to be remembered. The modern method of teaching children to read by blackboard work, in which each word is impressed by the four-fold channel of eye, ear, voice, and hand, is an example of an improved mechanical method of memorizing.

Judicious methods of remembering things are nothing but logical ways of conceiving them and working them into rational systems, classifying them, analyzing them into parts, etc., etc. All the sciences are such methods.

Of ingenious methods, many have been invented, under the name of technical memories. By means of these systems it is often possible to retain entirely disconnected facts, lists of names, numbers, and so forth, so multitudinous as to be entirely unrememberable in a natural way. The method consists usually in a framework learned mechanically, of which the mind is supposed to remain in secure and permanent possession. Then, whatever is to be remembered is deliberately associated by some fanciful analogy or connection with some part of this framework, and this connection thenceforward helps its recall. The best known and most used of these devices is the figure-alphabet. To remember numbers, e.g., a figure-alphabet is first formed, in which each numerical digit is represented by one or more letters. The number is then translated into such letters as will best make a word, if possible a word suggestive of the object to which the number belongs. The word will then be remembered when the numbers alone might be forgotten.

"The most common figure-alphabet is this:

```
1,  2,  3,  4,  5,   6,  7,  8,  9,  0.
t,  n,  m,  r,  l,  sh,  g,  f,  b,  s,
d,                   j,  k,  v,  p,  c,
                    ch,  c,          z,
                     g, qu.
```

"To briefly show its use, suppose it is desired to fix 1142 feet in a second as the velocity of sound: t, t, r, n, are the letters and order required. Fill up with vowels forming a phrase, like 'tight run' and connect it by some such flight of the imagination as that if a man tried to keep up with the velocity of sound, he would have a tight run. When you recall this a few days later great care must be taken not to get confused with the velocity of light, nor to think he had a hard run which would be 3000 feet too fast."[25]

Dr. Pick and others use a system which consists in linking together any two ideas to be remembered by means of an intermediate idea which will be suggested by the first and suggest the second, and so on through the list.

Thus,

"Let us suppose that we are to retain the following series of ideas: garden, hair, watchman, philosophy, copper, etc. . . . We can combine the ideas in this manner: garden, plant, hair of plant—hair; hair, bonnet, watchman; --watchman, wake, study, philosophy; philosophy, chemistry, copper; etc. etc." (Pick.)[26]

It is matter of popular knowledge that an impression is remembered the better in proportion as it is

1) More recent;
2) More attended to; and
3) More often repeated.

The effect of recency is all but absolutely constant. Of two events of equal significance the remoter one will be the one more likely to be forgotten. The memories of childhood which persist in old age can hardly be compared with the events of the day or hour which are forgotten, for these latter are trivial once-repeated things, whilst the childish reminiscences have been wrought into us during the retrospective hours of our entire intervening life. Other things equal, at all times of life recency promotes memory. The only exception I can think of is the unaccountable memory of certain moments of our childhood, apparently not fitted by their intrinsic interest to survive, but which are perhaps the only incidents we can remember out of the year in which they occurred. Everybody probably has isolated glimpses of certain hours of his nursery life, the position in which he stood or sat, the light of the room, what his father or mother said, etc. These moments so oddly selected for immunity from the tooth of time probably owe their good fortune to historical peculiarities which it is now impossible to trace. Very likely we were reminded of them again soon after they occurred; that became a reason why we should again recollect them, etc., so that at last they became ingrained.

The attention which we lend to an experience is proportional to its vivid or interesting character; and it is a notorious fact that what interests us most vividly at the time is, other things equal, what we remember best. An impression may be so exciting emotionally as almost to leave a scar upon the cerebral tissues; and thus originates a pathological delusion. "A woman attacked by robbers takes all the men whom she sees, even her own son, for brigands bent on killing her. Another woman sees her child run over by a horse; no amount of reasoning, not even the sight of the living child, will persuade her that he is not killed. A woman called 'thief' in a dispute remains convinced that every one accuses her of stealing (Esquirol). Another, attacked with mania at the sight of the fires in her street during the Commune, still after six months sees in her delirium flames on every side about her (Luys), etc., etc."[27]

On the general effectiveness of both attention and repetition I cannot do better than copy what M. Taine has written: "If we compare different sensations, images, or ideas, we find that their aptitudes for revival are not equal. A large number of them are obliterated, and never reappear through life; for instance, I drove through Paris a day or two ago, and though I saw plainly some sixty or eighty new faces, I cannot now recall any one of them; some extraordinary circumstance, a fit of delirium, or the excitement of haschish would be necessary to give them a chance of revival. On the other hand, there are sensations with a force of revival which nothing destroys or decreases. Though, as a rule, time weakens and impairs our strongest sensations, these reappear entire and intense, without having lost a particle of their detail, or any degree of their force. M. Brierre de Boismont, having suffered when a child from a disease of the scalp, asserts that 'after fifty-five years have elapsed he can still feel his hair pulled out under the treatment of the skull-cap.'—For my own part, after thirty years, I remember feature for feature the appearance of the theatre to which I was taken for the first time. From the third row of boxes, the body of the theatre appeared to me an immense well, red and flaming, swarming with heads; below, on the right, on a narrow floor, two men and a woman entered, went out, and re-entered, made gestures, and seemed to me like lively dwarfs: to my great surprise, one of these dwarfs fell on his knees, kissed the lady's hand, then hid behind a screen; the other, who was coming in, seemed angry, and raised his arm. I was then seven, I could understand nothing of what was going on; but the well of crimson velvet was so crowded, gilded, and bright, that after a quarter of an hour I was, as it were, intoxicated, and fell asleep.

"Every one of us may find similar recollections in his memory, and may distinguish in them a common character. The primitive impression has been accompanied by an extraordinary degree of attention, either as being horrible or delightful, or as being new, surprising, and out of proportion to the ordinary run of our life; this it is we express by saying that we have been strongly impressed; that we were absorbed, that we could not think of anything else; that our other sensations were effaced; that we were pursued all the next day by the resulting image; that it beset us, that we could not drive it away; that all distractions were feeble beside it. It is by force of this disproportion that impressions of childhood are so persistent; the mind being quite fresh, ordinary objects and events are surprising. At present, after seeing so many large halls and full theatres, it is impossible for me, when I enter one, to feel swallowed up, engulfed, and, as it were, lost in a huge dazzling well. The medical man of sixty, who has experienced much suffering, both personally and in imagination, would be less upset now by a surgical operation than when he was a child.

"Whatever may be the kind of attention, voluntary or involuntary, it always acts alike; the image of an object or event is capable of revival, and of complete revival, in proportion to the degree of attention with which we have considered the object or event. We put this rule in practice at every moment in ordinary life. If we are applying ourselves to a book or are in lively conversation, while an air is being sung in the adjoining room, we do not retain it; we know vaguely that there is singing going on, and that is all. We then stop our reading or conversation, we lay aside all internal preoccupations and external sensations which our mind or the outer world can throw in our way; we close our eyes, we cause a silence within and about us, and, if the air is repeated, we listen. We say then that we have listened with all our ears, that we have applied our whole minds. If the air is a fine one, and has touched us deeply, we add that we have been transported, uplifted, ravished, that we have forgotten the world and ourselves; that for some minutes our soul was dead to all but sounds. . . .

"This exclusive momentary ascendency of one of our states of mind explains the greater durability of its aptitude for revival and for more complete revival. As the sensation revives in the image, the image reappears with a force proportioned to that of the sensation. What we meet with in the first state is also to be met with in the second, since the second is but a revival of the first. So, in the struggle for life, in which all our images are constantly engaged, the one furnished at the outset with most force retains in each conflict, by the very law of repetition which gives it being, the capacity of treading down its adversaries; this is why it revives, incessantly at first, then frequently, until at last the laws of progressive decay, and the continual accession of new impressions bake away its preponderance, and its competitors, finding a clear field, are able to develop in their turn.

"A second cause of prolonged revivals is repetition itself. Every one knows that to learn a thing we must not only consider it attentively, but consider it repeatedly. We say as to this in ordinary language, that an impression many times renewed is imprinted more deeply and exactly on the memory. This is how we contrive to retain a language, airs of music, passages of verse or prose, the technical terms and propositions of a science, and still more so the ordinary facts by which our conduct is regulated. When, from the form and color of a currant-jelly, we think of its taste, or, when tasting it with our eyes shut, we magine [sic] its red tint and the brilliancy of a quivering slice, the images in our mind are brightened by repetition. Whenever we eat, or drink, or walk, or avail ourselves of any of our senses, or commence or continue any action whatever, the same thing happens. Every man and every animal thus possesses at every moment of life a certain stock of clear and easily reviving images, which had their source in the past in a confluence of numerous experiences, and are now fed by a flow of renewed experiences. When I want to go from the Tuileries to the Panthéon, or from my study to the dining-room, I foresee at every turn the colored forms which will present themselves to my sight; it is otherwise in the case of a house where I have spent two hours, or of a town where I have stayed three days; after ten years have elapsed the images will be vague, full of blanks, sometimes they will not exist, and I shall have to seek my way or shall lose myself.—This new property of images is also derived from the first. As every sensation tends to revive in its image, the sensation twice repeated will leave after it a double tendency, that is, provided the attention be as great the second time as the first; usually this is not the case, for, the novelty diminishing, the interest diminishes; but if other circumstances renew the interest, or if the will renovates the attention, the incessantly increasing tendency will incessantly increase the chances of the resurrection and integrity of the image."[28]

If a phenomenon is met with, however, too often, and with too great a variety of contexts, although its image is retained and reproduced with correspondingly great facility, it fails to come up with any one particular setting, and the projection of it backwards to a particular past date consequently does not come about. We recognize but do not remember it—its associates form too confused a cloud. No one is said to remember, says Mr. Spencer,

"that the object at which he looks has an opposite side; or that a certain modification of the visual impression implies a certain distance; or that the thing he sees moving about is a live animal. To ask a man whether he remembers that the sun shines, that fire burns, that iron is hard, would be a misuse of language. Even the almost fortuitous connections among our experiences cease to be classed as memories when they have become thoroughly familiar. Though, on hearing the voice of some unseen person slightly known to us, we say we recollect to whom the voice belongs, we do not use the same expression respecting the voices of those with whom we live. The meanings of words which in childhood have to be consciously recalled seem in adult life to be immediately present."[29]

These are cases where too many paths, leading to too diverse associates, block each other's way, and all that the mind gets along with its object is a fringe of felt familiarity or sense that there are associates. A similar result comes about when a definite setting is only nascently aroused. We then feel that we have seen the object already, but when or where we cannot say, though we may seem to ourselves to be on the brink of saying it. That nascent cerebral excitations can effect consciousness with a sort of sense of the imminence of that which stronger excitations would make us definitely feel, is obvious from what happens when we seek to remember a name. It tingles, it trembles on the verge, but does not come. Just such a tingling and trembling of unrecovered associates is the penumbra of recognition that may surround any experience and make it seem familiar, though we know not why.[30]

There is a curious experience which everyone seems to have had—the feeling that the present moment in its completeness has been experienced before—we were saying just this thing, in just this place, to just these people, etc. This 'sense of pre-existence' has been treated as a great mystery and occasioned much speculation. Dr. Wigan considered it due to a dissociation of the action of the two hemispheres, one of them becoming conscious a little later than the other, but both of the same fact.[31] I must confess that the quality of mystery seems to me a little strained. I have over and over again in my own case succeeded in resolving the phenomenon into a case of memory, so indistinct that whilst some past circumstances are presented again, the others are not. The dissimilar portions of the past do not arise completely enough at first for the date to be identified. All we get is the present scene with a general suggestion of pastness about it. That faithful observer, Prof. Lazarus, interprets the phenomenon the same way;[32] and it is noteworthy that just as soon as the past context grows complete and distinct the emotion of weirdness fades from the experience.

Exact Measurements of Memory

...have recently been made in Germany. Professor Ebbinghaus, in a really heroic series of daily observations of more than two years' duration, examined the powers of retention and reproduction. He learned lists of meaningless syllables by heart, and tested his recollection of them from day to day. He could not remember more than 7 after a single reading. It took, however, 16 readings to remember 12, 44 readings to remember 24, and 55 readings to remember 26 syllables, the moment of 'remembering' being here reckoned as the first moment when the list could be recited without a fault.[33] When a 16-syllable list was read over a certain number of times on one day, and then studied on the day following until remembered, it was found that the number of seconds saved in the study on the second day was proportional to the number of readings on the first—proportional, that is, within certain rather narrow limits, for which see the text.[34] No amount of repetition spent on nonsense-verses over a certain length enabled Dr. Ebbinghaus to retain them without error for 24 hours. In forgetting such things as these lists of syllables, the loss goes on very much more rapidly at first than later on. He measured the loss by the number of seconds required to relearn the list after it had been once learned. Roughly speaking, if it took a thousand seconds to learn the list, and five hundred to relearn it, the loss between the two learnings would have been one half. Measured in this way, full half of the forgetting seems to occur within the first half-hour, whilst only four fifths is forgotten at the end of a month. The nature of this result might have been anticipated, but hardly its numerical proportions. Dr. Ebbinghaus says:

"The initial rapidity, as well as the final slowness, as these were ascertained under certain experimental conditions and for a particular individual, . . . may well surprise us. An hour after the work of learning had ceased, forgetting was so far advanced that more than half of the original work had to be applied again before the series of syllables could once more be reproduced. Eight hours later two thirds of the original labor had to be applied. Gradually, however, the process of oblivion grew slower, so that even for considerable stretches of time the losses were but barely ascertainable. After 24 hours a third, after 6 days a fourth, and after a whole month a good fifth of the original labor remain in the shape of its after-effects, and made the relearning by so much the more speedy."[35]

But the most interesting result of all those reached by this author relates to the question whether ideas are recalled only by those that previously came immediately before them, or whether an idea can possibly recall another idea with which it was never in immediate contact, without passing through the intermediate mental links. The question is of theoretic importance with regard to the way in which the process of 'association of ideas' must be conceived; and Dr. Ebbinghaus's attempt is as successful as it is original, in bringing two views, which seem at first sight inaccessible to proof, to a direct practical test, and giving the victory to one of them. His experiments conclusively show that an idea is not only 'associated' directly with the one that follows it, and with the rest through that, but that it is directly associated with all that are near it, though in unequal degrees. He first measured the time needed to impress on the memory certain lists of syllables, and then the time needed to impress lists of the same syllables with gaps between them. Thus, representing the syllables by numbers, if the first list were 1, 2, 3, 4, . . . 13, 14, 15, 16, the second would be 1, 3, 5, . . .15, 2, 4, 6, . . .16, and so forth, with many variations.

Now, if 1 and 3 in the first list were learned in that order merely by 1 calling up 2, and by 2 calling up 3, leaving out the 2 ought to leave 1 and 3 with no tie in the mind; and the second list ought to take as much time in the learning as if the first list had never been heard of. If, on the other hand, 1 has a direct influence on 3 as well as on 2, that influence should be exerted even when 2 is dropped out; and a person familiar with the first list ought to learn the second one more rapidly than otherwise he could. This latter case is what actually occurs; and Dr. Ebbinghaus has found that syllables originally separated by as many as seven intermediaries still reveal, by the increased rapidity with which they are learned in order, the strength of the tie that the original learning established between them, over the heads, so to speak, of all the rest. These last results ought to make us careful, when we speak of nervous 'paths,' to use the word in no restricted sense. They add one more fact to the set of facts which prove that association is subtler than consciousness, and that a nerve-process may, without producing consciousness, be effective in the same way in which consciousness would have seemed to be effective if it had been there.[36] Evidently the path from 1 to 3 (omitting 2 from consciousness) is facilitated, broadened perhaps, by the old path from 1 to 3 through 2 -- only the component which shoots round through this latter way is too feeble to let 2 be thought as a distinct object. Mr. Wolfe, in his experiments on recognition, used vibrating metal tongues.

"These tongues gave tones differing by 2 vibrations only in the two lower octaves, and by 4 vibrations in the three higher octaves. In the first series of experiments a tone was selected, and, after sounding it for one second, a second tone was sounded, which was either the same as the first, or different from it by 4, 8, or 12 vibrations in different series. The person experimented upon was to answer whether the second tone was the same as the first, thus showing that he recognized it, or whether it was different, and, if so, whether it was higher or lower. Of course, the interval of time between the two tones was an important factor. The proportionate number of correct judgments, and the smallness of the difference of the vibration-rates of the two tones, would measure the accuracy of the tone-memory. It appeared that one could tell more readily when the two tones were alike than when they were different, although in both cases the accuracy of the memory was remarkably good. . . . The main point is the effect of the time-interval between the tone and its reproduction. This was varied from 1 second to 30 seconds, or even to 60 seconds or 120 seconds in some experiments. The general result is, that the longer the interval, the smaller are the chances that the tone will be recognized; and this process of forgetting takes place at first very rapidly, and then more slowly. . . . This law is subject to considerable variations, one of which seems to be constant and is peculiar; namely, there seems to be a rhythm in the memory itself, which, after falling, recovers slightly, and then fades out again."[37]

This periodical renewal of acoustic memory would seem to be an important element in the production of the agreeableness of certain rates of recurrence in sound.

Forgetting

In the practical use of our intellect, forgetting is as important a function as recollecting.

Locke says, in a memorable page of his dear old book:

"The memory of some men, it is true, is very tenacious, even to a miracle; but yet there seems to be a constant decay of all our ideas, even of those which are struck deepest, and in minds the most retentive; so that if they be not sometimes renewed by repeated exercise of the senses, or reflection on those kinds of objects which at first occasioned them, the print wears out, and at last there remains nothing to be seen. Thus the ideas, as well as children, of our youth, often die before us; and our minds represent to us those tombs to which we are fast approaching; where, though the brass and marble remain, yet the inscriptions are effaced by time, and the imagery moulders away. The pictures drawn in our minds are laid in fading colors; and, if not sometimes refreshed, vanish and disappear. How much the constitution of our bodies, and the make of our animal spirits, are concerned in this; and whether the temper of the brain makes this difference, that in some it retains the characters drawn on it like marble, in others like freestone, and in others little better than sand, I shall not here inquire, though it may seem probable that the constitution of the body does sometimes influence the memory; since we oftentimes find a disease quite strip the mind of all its ideas, and the flames of a fever in a few days calcine all those images to dust and confusion, which seemed to be as lasting as if graven in marble."[38]

This peculiar mixture of forgetting with our remembering is but one instance of our mind's selective activity. Selection is the very keel on which our mental ship is built. And in this case of memory its utility is obvious. If we remembered everything, we should on most occasions be as ill off as if we remembered nothing. It would take as long for us to recall a space of time as it took the original time to elapse, and we should never get ahead with our thinking. All recollected times undergo, accordingly, what M. Ribot calls foreshortening; and this foreshortening is due to the omission of an enormous number of the facts which filled them.

"As fast as the present enters into the past, our states of consciousness disappear and are obliterated. Passed in review at a few days' distance, nothing or little of them remains: most of them have made shipwreck in that great nonentity from which they never more will emerge, and they have carried with them the quantity of duration which was inherent in their being. This deficit of surviving conscious states is thus a deficit in the amount of represented time. The process of abridgment, of foreshortening, of which we have spoken, presupposes this deficit. If, in order to reach a distant reminiscence, we had to go through the entire series of terms which separate it from our present selves, memory would become impossible on account of the length of the operation. We thus reach the paradoxical result that one condition of remembering is that we should forget. Without totally forgetting a prodigious number of states of consciousness, and momentarily forgetting a large number, we could not remember at all. Oblivion, except in certain cases, is thus no malady of memory, but a condition of its health and its life."[39]

There are many irregularities in the process of forgetting which are as yet unaccounted for. A thing forgotten on one day will be remembered on the next. Something we have made the most strenuous efforts to recall, but all in vain, will, soon after we have given up the attempt, saunter into the mind, as Emerson somewhere says, as innocently as if it had never been sent for. Experiences of bygone date will revive after years of absolute oblivion, often as the result of some cerebral disease or accident which seems to develop latent paths of association, as the photographer's fluid develops the picture sleeping in the collodion film. The oftenest quoted of these cases is Coleridge's:

"In a Roman Catholic town in Germany, a young woman, who could neither read nor write, was seized with a fever, and was said by the priests to be possessed of a devil, because she was heard talking Latin, Greek, and Hebrew. Whole sheets of her ravings were written out, and found to consist of sentences intelligible in themselves, but having slight connection with each other. Of her Hebrew sayings, only a few could be traced to the Bible, and most seemed to be in the Rabbinical dialect. All trick was out of the question; the woman was a simple creature; there was no doubt as to the fever. It was long before any explanation, save that of demoniacal possession, could be obtained. At last the mystery was unveiled by a physician, who determined to trace back the girl's history, and who, after much trouble, discovered that at the age of nine she had been charitably taken by an old Protestant pastor, a great Hebrew scholar, in whose house she lived till his death. On further inquiry it appeared to have been the old man's custom for years to walk up and down a passage of his house into which the kitchen opened, and to read to himself with a loud voice out of his books. The books were ransacked, and among them were found several of the Greek and Latin Fathers, together with a collection of Rabbinical writings. In these works so many of the passages taken down at the young woman's bedside were identified that there could be no reasonable doubt as to their source."[40]

Hypnotic subjects as a rule forget all that has happened in their trance. But in a succeeding trance they will often remember the events of a past one. This is like what happens in those cases of 'double personality' in which no recollection of one of the lives is to be found in the other. We have already seen in an earlier chapter that the sensibility often differs from one of the alternate personalities to another, and we have heard M. Pierre Janet's theory that anæsthesias carry amnesias with them. In certain cases this is evidently so; the throwing of certain functional brain-tracts out of gear with others, so as to dissociate their consciousness from that of the remaining brain, throws them out for both sensorial and ideational service. M. Janet proved in various ways that what his patients forgot when anæsthetic they remembered when the sensibility returned. For instance, he restored their tactile sense temporarily by means of electric currents, passes, etc., and then made them handle various objects, such as keys and pencils, or make particular movements, like the sign of the cross. The moment the anæsthesia returned they found it impossible to recollect the objects or the acts. 'They had had nothing in their hands, they had done nothing,' etc. The next day, however, sensibility being again restored by similar processes, they remembered perfectly the circumstance, and told what they had handled or had done.

All these pathological facts are showing us that the sphere of possible recollection may be wider than we think, and that in certain matters apparent oblivion is no proof against possible recall under other conditions. They give no countenance, however, to the extravagant opinion that nothing we experience can be absolutely forgotten. In real life, in spite of occasional surprises, most of what happens actually is forgotten. The only reasons for supposing that if the conditions were forthcoming everything would revive are of a transcendental sort. Sir Wm. Hamilton quotes and adopts them from the German writer Schmid. Knowledge being a 'spontaneous self-energy' on the part of the mind,

"this energy being once determined, it is natural that it should persist, until again annihilated by other causes. This [annihilation] would be the case, were the mind merely passive.... But the mental activity, the act of knowledge, of which I now speak, is more than this; it is an energy of the self-active power of a subject one and indivisible: consequently a part of the ego must be detached or annihilated, if a cognition once existent be again extinguished. Hence it is that the problem most difficult of solution is not, how a mental activity endures, but how it ever vanishes."[41]

Those whom such an argument persuades may be left happy with their belief. Other positive argument there is none, none certainly of a physiological sort.[42]

When memory begins to decay, proper names are what go first, and at all times proper names are harder to recollect than those of general properties and classes of things.

This seems due to the fact that common qualities and names have contracted an infinitely greater number of associations in our mind than the names of most of the persons whom we know. Their memory is better organized. Proper names as well organized as those of our family and friends are recollected as well as those of any other objects.[43] 'Organization' means numerous associations; and the more numerous the associations, the greater the number of paths of recall. For the same reason adjectives, conjunctions, prepositions, and the cardinal verbs, those words, in short, which form the grammatical framework of all our speech, are the very last to decay. Kussmaul[44] makes the following acute remark on this subject:

"The concreter a conception is, the sooner is its name forgotten. This is because our ideas of persons and things are less strongly bound up with their names than with such abstractions as their business, their circumstances, their qualities. We easily can imagine persons and things without their names, the sensorial image of them being more important than that other symbolic image, their name. Abstract conceptions, on the other hand, are only acquired by means of the words which alone serve to confer stability upon them. This is why verbs, adjectives, pronouns, and still more adverbs, prepositions, and conjunctions are more intimately connected with our thinking than are substantives."

The disease called Aphasia, of which a little was said in Chapter II, has let in a flood of light on the phenomenon of Memory, by showing the number of ways in which the use of a given object, like a word, may be lost by the mind. We may lose our acoustic idea or our articulatory idea of it; neither without the other will give up proper command of the word. And if we have both, but have lost the paths of association between the brain-centres which support the two, we are in as bad a plight. 'Ataxic' and 'amnesic' aphasia, 'word-deafness,' and 'associative aphasia' are all practical losses of word-memory. We have thus, as M. Ribot says, not memory so much as memories.[45] The visual, the tactile, the muscular, the auditory memory may all vary independently of each other in the same individual; and different individuals may have them developed in different degrees. As a rule, a man's memory is good in the departments in which his interest is strong; but those departments are apt to be those in which his discriminative sensibility is high. A man with a bad ear is not likely to have practically a good musical memory, or a purblind person to remember visual appearance well. In a later chapter we shall see illustrations of the differences in men's imagining power.[46] It is obvious that the machinery of memory must be largely determined thereby.

Mr. Galton, in his work on English Men of Science,[47] has given a very interesting collation of cases showing individual variations in the type of memory, where it is strong. Some have it verbal. Others have it good for facts and figures, others for form. Most say that what is to be remembered must first be rationally conceived and assimilated.[48]

There is an interesting fact connected with remembering, which, so far as I know, Mr. R. Verdon was the first writer expressly to call attention to. We can set our memory as it were to retain things for a certain time, and then let them depart.

"Individuals often remember clearly and well up to the time when they have to use their knowledge, and then, when it is no longer required, there follows a rapid and extensive decay of the traces. Many schoolboys forgot their lessons after they have said them, many barristers forgot details got up for a particular case. Thus a boy learns thirty lines of Homer, says them perfectly, and then forgets them so that he could not say five consecutive lines the next morning, and a barrister may be one week learned in the mysteries of making cog-wheels, but in the next he may be well acquainted with the anatomy of the ribs instead."[49]

The rationale of this fact is obscure; and the existence of it ought to make us feel how truly subtle are the nervous processes which memory involves. Mr. Verdon adds that

"When the use of a record is withdrawn, and attention withdrawn from it, and we think no more about it, we know that we experience a feeling of relief, and we may thus conclude that energy is in some way liberated. If the . . . attention is not withdrawn, so that we keep the record in mind, we know that this feeling of relief does not take place. . . . Also we are well aware, not only that after this feeling of relief takes place, the record does not seem so well conserved as before, but that we have real difficulty in attempting to remember it."

This shows that we are not as entirely unconscious of a topic as we think, during the time in which we seem to be merely retaining it subject to recall.

"Practically," says Mr. Verdon, "we sometimes keep a matter in hand not exactly by attending to it, but by keeping our attention referred to something connected with it from time to time. Translating this into the language of physiology, we mean that by referring attention to a part within, or closely connected with, the system of traces [paths] required to be remembered, we keep it well fed, so that the traces are preserved with the utmost delicacy."

This is perhaps as near as we can get to an explanation. Setting the mind to remember a thing involves a continual minimal irradiation of excitement into paths which lead thereto, involves the continued presence of the thing in the 'fringe' of our consciousness. Letting the thing go involves withdrawal of the irradiation, unconsciousness of the thing, and, after a time, obliteration of the paths.

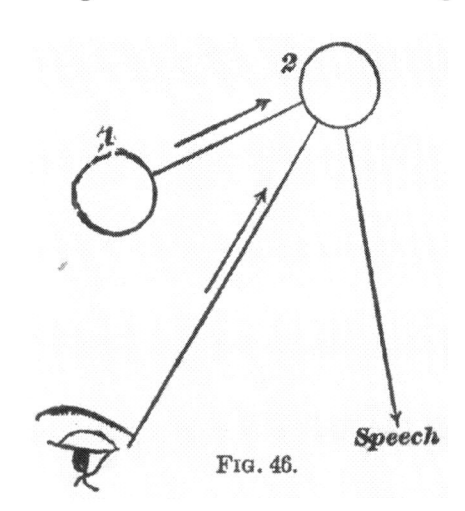

A curious peculiarity of our memory is that things are impressed better by active than by passive repetition. I mean that in learning by heart (for example), when we almost know the piece, it pays better to wait and recollect by an effort from within, then to look at the book again. If we recover the words in the former way, we shall probably know them the next time; if in the latter way, we shall very likely need the book once more. The learning by heart means the formation of paths from a former set to a later set of cerebral word-processes: call 1 and 2 in the diagram the processes in question; then when we remember by inward effort, the path is formed by discharge from 1 to 2, just as it will afterwards be used. But when we excite 2 by the eye, although the path 1 -- 2 doubtless is then shot through also, the phenomenon which we are discussing shows that the direct discharge from 1 into 2, unaided by the eyes, ploughs the deeper and more permanent groove. There is, moreover, a greater amount of tension accumulated in the brain before the discharge from 1 to 2, when the latter takes place unaided by the eye. This is proved by the general feeling of strain in the effort to remember 2; and this also ought to make the discharge more violent and the path more deep. A similar reason doubtless accounts for the familiar fact that we remember our own theories, our own discoveries, combinations, inventions, in short whatever 'ideas' originate in our own brain, a thousand times better than exactly similar things which are communicated to us from without.

FIG. 46.

A word, in closing, about the metaphysics involved in remembering. According to the assumptions of this book, thoughts accompany the brain's workings, and those thoughts are cognitive of realities. The whole relation is one which we can only write down empirically, confessing that no glimmer of explanation of it is yet in sight. That brains should give rise to a knowing consciousness at all, this is the one mystery which returns, no matter of what sort the consciousness and of what sort the knowledge may be. Sensations, aware of mere qualities, involve the mystery as much as thoughts, aware of complex systems, involve it. To the platonizing tradition in philosophy, however, this is not so. Sensational consciousness is something quasi-material, hardly cognitive, which one need not much wonder at. Relating consciousness is quite the reverse, and the mystery of it is unspeakable. Professor Ladd, for example, in his usually excellent book,[50] after well showing the matter-of-fact dependence of retention and reproduction on brain-paths, says:

"In the study of perception psycho-physics can do much towards a scientific explanation. It can tell what qualities of stimuli produce certain qualities of sensations; it can suggest a principle relating the quantity of the stimuli to the intensity of the sensation; it can investigate the laws under which, by combined action of various excitations, the sensations are combined [?] into presentations of sense; it can show how the time-relations of the sensations and percepts in consciousness correspond to the objective relations in time of the stimulations. But for that spiritual activity which actually puts together in consciousness the sensations, it cannot even suggest the beginning of a physical explanation. Moreover, no cerebral process can be conceived of, which—in case it were known to exist—could possibly be regarded as a fitting basis for this unifying actus of mind. Thus also, and even more emphatically, must we insist upon the complete inability of physiology to suggest an explanation for conscious memory, in so far as it is memory—that is, in so far as it most imperatively calls for explanation.... The very essence of the act of memory consists in the ability to say: This after-image is the image of a percept I had a moment since; or this image of memory is the image of the percept I had at a certain time—I do not remember precisely how long since. It would, then, be quite contrary to the facts to hold that, when an image of memory appears in consciousness, it is recognized as belonging to a particular original percept on account of its perceived resemblance to this percept. The original percept does not exist and will never be reproduced. Even more palpably false and absurd would it be to hold that any similarity of the impressions or processes in end organs or central organs explains the act of conscious memory. Consciousness knows nothing of such similarity; knows nothing even of the existence of nervous impressions and processes. Moreover, we could never know two impressions or processes that are separated in time to be similar, without involving the same inexplicable act of memory. It is a fact of consciousness on which all possibility of connected experience and of recorded and cumulative human knowledge is dependent that certain phases or products of consciousness appear with a claim to stand for (to represent)[51] past experiences to which they are regarded as in some respect similar. It is this peculiar claim in consciousness which constitutes the essence of an act of memory; it is this which makes the memory wholly inexplicable as a mere persistence or recurrence of similar impressions. It is this which makes conscious memory a spiritual phenomenon, the explanation of which, as arising out of nervous processes and conditions, is not simply undiscovered in fact, but utterly incapable of approach by the imagination. When, then, we speak of a physical basis of memory, recognition must be made of the complete inability of science to suggest any physical process which can be conceived of as correlated with that peculiar and mysterious actus of the mind, connecting its present and its past, which constitutes the essence of memory."

This passage seems to me characteristic of the reigning half-way modes of thought. It puts the difficulties in the wrong places. At one moment it seems to admit with the cruder sensationalists that the material of our thoughts is independent sensations reproduced, and that the 'putting together' of these sensations would be knowledge, if it could only be brought about, the only mystery being as to the what 'actus' can bring it about. At another moment it seems to contend that even this sort of 'combining' would not be knowledge, because certain of the elements connected must 'claim to represent or stand for' past originals, which is incompatible with their being mere images revived. The result is various confused and scattered mysteries and unsatisfied intellectual desires. But why not 'pool' our mysteries into one great mystery, the mystery that brain-processes occasion knowledge at all? It is surely no different mystery to feel myself by means of one brain-process writing at this table now, and by means of a different brain-process a year hence to remember myself writing. All that psychology can do is to seek to determine what the several brain-processes are; and this, in a wretchedly imperfect way, is what such writings as the present chapter have begun to do. But of 'images reproduced,' and 'claiming to represent,' and 'put together by a unifying actus,' I have been silent, because such expressions either signify nothing, or they are only roundabout ways of simply saying that the past is known when certain brain-conditions are fulfilled, and it seems to me that the straightest and shortest way of saying that is the best.

For a history of opinion about Memory, and other bibliographic references, I must refer to the admirable little monograph on the subject by Mr. W. H. Burnham in the American Journal of Psychology, vols. I and II. Useful books are: D. Kay's Memory, What It Is, and How to Improve It (1888); and F. Fauth's Das Gedächtniss, Studie zu einer Pädagogik, etc., 1888.

End of Vol. I.

Notes

[1] L'Homme et 1'Intelligence, p. 32.
[2] Professor Richet has therefore no right to say, as he does in another place (Revue Philosophique, XXI. 570): "Without memory no conscious sensation, without memory no consciousness." All he is entitled to say is: "Without memory no

consciousness known outside of itself." Of the sort of consciousness that is an object for later states, and becomes as it were permanent, he gives a good example: "Who of us, alas! has not experienced a bitter and profound grief, the immense laceration caused by the death of some cherished fellow-being? Well, in these great griefs the present endures neither for a minute, for an hour, nor for a day, but for weeks and months. The memory of the cruel moment will not efface itself from consciousness. It disappears not, but remains living, present, coexisting with the multitude of other sensations which are juxtaposed in consciousness alongside of this one persistent emotion which is felt always in the present tense. A long time is needed ere we can attain to forgetting it, ere we can make it enter into the past. Hæret lateri letalis arundo." (Ibid 583.)

[3] This is the primary positive after-image. According to Helmholtz, one third of a second is the most favorable length of exposure to the light for producing it. Longer exposure, complicated by subsequent admission of light to the eye, results in the ordinary negative and complementary after-images, with their changes, which may (if the original impression was brilliant and the fixation long) last for many minutes. Fechner gives the name of memory-after-images (Psychophysik, II 492) to the instantaneous positive effects, and distinguishes them from ordinary after images by the following characters: 1) Their originals must have been attended to only such parts of a compound original as have been attended to appearing. This is not the case in common visual after-images. 2) The strain of attention towards them is inward, as in ordinary remembering, not outward, as in observing a common after-image. 3) A short fixation of the original is better for the memory-after-image, a long one for the ordinary after-image. 4) The colors of the memory-after-image are never complementary of those of the original.

[4] Hermann's Hdbch., II. 2. 282.

[5] Rev. Philos., 562.

[6] Richet says: "The present has a certain duration, a variable duration, sometimes a rather long one, which comprehends all the time occupied by the after-reverberation [retentissement, after-image] of a sensation. For example, if the reverberation of an electric shock within our nerves lasts ten minutes, for that electric shock there is a present of ten minutes. On the other hand, a feebler sensation will have a shorter present. But in every case, for a conscious sensation [I should say for a remembered sensation] to occur, there must be a present of a certain duration, of a few seconds at least." We have seen in the last chapter that it is hard to trace the backward limits of this immediately intuited duration, or specious present. The figures which M. Richet supposes appear to be considerably too large.

[7] Cf. Fechner, Psychophysik, II. 499.

[8] The primary after-image itself cannot be utilized if the stimulus is too brief. Mr. Cattell found (Psychologische Studien, III. p. 93 ff.) that the color of a light must fall upon the eye for a period varying from 0.00275 to 0.006 of a second, in order to be recognized for what it is. Letters of the alphabet and familiar words require from 0.00075 to 0.00175 sec.—truly an interval extremely short. Some letters, E for example, are harder than others. In 1871 Helmholtz and Box had ascertained that when an impression was immediately followed by another, the latter quenched the former and prevented it from being known to later consciousness. The first stimulus was letters of the alphabet, the second a bright white disk. "With an interval of 0.0048 sec. between the two excitations [I copy here the abstract in Ladd's Physiological Psychology, p. 480], the disk appeared as scarcely a trace of a weak shimmer; with an interval of 0.0096 sec., letters appeared in the shimmer—one or two which could be partially recognized when the interval increased to 0.0144 sec. When the interval was made 0.0192 sec. the objects were a little more clearly discerned; at 0.0336 sec. four letters could be well recognized; at 0.0432 sec., five letters; and at 0.0528 sec. all the letters could be read." (Pflüger's Archiv, IV. 325 ff.)

[9] When the past is recalled symbolically, or conceptually only, it is true that no such copy need be there. In no sort of conceptual knowledge is it requisite that definitely resembling images be there (cf. pp. 471 ff.). But as all conceptual knowledge stands for intuitive knowledge, and terminates therein, I abstract from this complication, and confine myself to those memories in which the past is directly imaged in the mind, or, as we say, intuitively known.

[10] E.g. Spencer, Psychology, I. p. 448. How do the believers in the sufficiency of the 'image' formulate the cases where we remember that something did not happen—that we did not wind our watch, did not lock the door, etc.? It is very hard to account for these memories of omission. The image of winding the watch is just as present to my mind now when I remember that I did not wind it as if I remembered that I did. It must be a difference in the mode of feeling the image which leads me to such different conclusions in the two cases. When I remember that I did wind it, I feel it grown together with its associates of past date and place. When I remember that I did not, it keeps aloof; the associates fuse with each other, but not with it. This sense of fusion, of the belonging together of things, is a most subtle relation; the sense of non-fusion is an equally subtle one. Both relations demand most complex mental processes to know them, processes quite different from that mere presence or absence of an image which does such service in the cruder books.

[11] Psychologia Empirica, § 174.

[12] Analysis, I. 330-1. Mill believed that the various things remembered, the self included, enter consciousness in the form of separate ideas, but so rapidly that they are 'all clustered into one.' "Ideas called up in close conjunction . . . assume, even when there is the greatest complexity, the appearance, not of many ideas, but of one" (vol. I. p. 123). This mythology does not impair the accuracy of his description of memory's object.

[13] Compare, however, p. 251, Chapter IX.

[14] Professor Bain adds, in a note to this passage of Mill's: "This process seems best expressed by laying down a law of Compound or Composite Association, under which a plurality of feeble links of connection may be a substitute for one powerful and self-sufficing link."

[15] Analysis, chap. X.
[16] H. Maudsley, The Physiology of Mind (London, 1876), p. 513.
[17] The only fact which might plausibly be alleged against this view is the familiar one that we may feel the lapse of time in an experience so monotonous that its earlier portions can have no 'associates' different from its later ones. Sit with closed eyes, for example, and steadily pronounce some vowel-sound, thus, a—a—a—a—a-- . . . . thinking only of the sound. Nothing changes during the time occupied by the experiment, and yet at the end of it you know that its beginning was far away. I think, however, that a close attention to what happens during this experiment shows that it does not violate in the least the conditions of recall laid down in the text; and that if the moment to which we mentally hark back lie many seconds behind the present instant, it always has different associates by which we define its date. Thus it was when I had just breathed out, or in; or it was the 'first moment' of the performance, the one 'preceded by silence;' or it was 'one very close to that;' or it was 'one when we were looking forward instead of back, its now;' or it is simply represented by a number and conceived symbolically with no definite image of its date. It seems to me that I have no really intuitive discrimination of the different past moments after the experience has gone on some little time, but that back of the 'specious present' they all fuse into a single conception of the kind of thing that has been going on, with a more or less clear sense of the total time it has lasted, this latter being based on an automatic counting of the successive pulses of thought by which the process is from moment to moment recognized as being always the same. Within the few seconds which constitute the specious present there is an intuitive perception of the successive moments. But these moments, of which we have a primary memory-image, are not properly recalled from the past, our knowledge of them is in no way analogous to a memory properly so called. Cf. supra, p. 646.
[18] On Intelligence, I. 258-9.
[19] Not that mere native tenacity will make a man great. It must be coupled with great passions and great intellect besides. Imbeciles sometimes have extraordinary desultory memory. Drobisch describes (Empirische Psychol., p. 95) the case of a young man whom he examined. He had with difficulty been taught to read and speak. "But if two or three minutes were allowed him to peruse an octave page, he then could spell the single words out from his memory as well as if the book lay open before him. . . . That there was no deception I could test by means of a new Latin law-dissertation which had just come into my hands, which he never could have seen, and of which both subject and language were unknown to him. He read off [mentally] many lines, skipping about too, of the page which had been given him to see, no worse than if the experiment had been made with a child's story." Drobisch describes this case as if it were one of unusual persistence in the visual image ['primary memory,' vide supra, p. 643]. But he adds that the youth 'remembered his pages a long time.' In the Journal of Speculative Philosophy for Jan. 1871 (VI. 6) is an account by Mr. W. D Henkle (together with the stock classic examples of preternatural memory) of an almost blind Pennsylvania farmer who could remember the day of the week on which any date had fallen for forty-two years past, and also the kind of weather it was, and what he was doing on each of more than fifteen thousand days. Pity that such a magnificent faculty as this could not have found more worthy application!
What these cases show is that the mere organic retentiveness of a man need bear no definite relation to his other mental powers. Men of the highest general powers will often forget nothing, however insignificant. One of the most generally accomplished men I know has a memory of this sort. He never keeps written note of anything, yet is never at a loss for a fact which he has once heard. He remembers the old addresses of all his New York friends, living in numbered streets, addresses which they themselves have long since moved away from and forgotten. He says that he should probably recognize an individual fly, if he had seen him thirty years previous—he is, by the way, an entomologist. As an instance of his desultory memory, he was introduced to a certain colonel at a club. The conversation fell upon the signs of age in man. The colonel challenged him to estimate his age. He looked at him, and gave the exact day of his birth, to the wonder of all. But the secret of this accuracy was that, having picked up some days previously an army-register, he had idly turned over its list of names, with dates of birth, graduation, promotions, etc., attached, and when the colonel's name was mentioned to him at the club, these figures, on which he had not bestowed a moment's thought, involuntarily surged up in his mind. Such a memory is of course a priceless boon.
[20] Cf. Ebbinghaus: Ueber das Gedächtniss (1885), pp. 67, 45. One may hear a person say: "I have a very poor memory, because I was never systematically made to learn poetry at school."
[21] How to Strengthen the Memory; or, The Natural and Scientific Methods of Never Forgetting. By M. H. Holbrook, M.D. New York (no date).
[22] Page 39.
[23] Op. cit. p. 100.
[24] In order to test the opinion so confidently expressed in the text, I have tried to see whether a certain amount of daily training in learning poetry by heart will shorten the time it takes to learn an entirely different kind of poetry. During eight successive days I learned 158 lines of Victor Hugo's 'Satyr.' The total number of minutes required for this was 131 5/6 -- it should be said that I had learned nothing by heart for many years. I then, working for twenty-odd minutes daily, learned the entire first book of Paradise Lost, occupying 38 days in the process. After this training I went back to Victor Hugo's poem, and found that 158 additional lines (divided exactly as on the former occasion) took me 151 ½ minutes. In other words, I committed my Victor Hugo to memory before the training at the rate of a line in 50 seconds, after the training at the rate of a line in 57 seconds, just the opposite result from that which the popular view would lead one to expect. But as I was peceptibly tagged with other work at the time of the second batch of Victor Hugo, I thought that might explain the retardation; so I persuaded several other persons to repeat the test.

Dr. W. H. Burnham learned 16 lines of In Memoriam for 8 days; time, 14-17 minutes—daily average 14 ¾. He then trained himself on Schiller's translation of the second book of the Æneid into German, 16 lines daily for 26 consecutive days. On returning to the same quantity of In Memoriam again, he found his maximum time 20 minutes, minimum 10, average 14 27/48. As he feared the outer conditions might not have been as favorable this time as the first, he waited a few days and got conditions as near as possible identical. The result was maximum time 8 minutes; minimum 19 ½; average 14 3/48.

Mr. E. S. Drown tested himself on Virgil for 16 days, then again for 16 days, after training himself on Scott. Average time before training, 13 minutes 26 seconds; after training, 12 minutes 16 seconds. [Sixteen days is too long for the test, it gives time for training on the test-verse.]

Mr. C. H. Baldwin took 10 lines for l5 days as his test, trained himself on 450 lines 'of an entirely different verse,' and then took 15 days more of the former verse 10 lines a day. Average result: 3 minutes 41 seconds before, 3 minutes 2 seconds after, training. [Same criticism as before.]

Mr. E. A. Pease tested himself on Idyls of the King, and trained himself on Paradise Lost. Average result of 6 days each time: 14 minutes 34 seconds before, 14 minutes 55 seconds after, training. Mr. Burnham having suggested that to eliminate facilitating effect entirely from the training verses one ought to test one's self à là Ebbinghaus on series of nonsense-syllables, having no analogy whatever with any system of expressive verses. I induced two of my students to perform that experiment also. The record is unfortunately lost; but the result was a very considerable shortening of the average time of the second series of nonsense-syllables, learned after training. This seems to me, however, more to show the effects of rapid habituation to the nonsense-verses themselves than those of the poetry used between them. But I mean to prosecute the experiments farther, and will report in another place.

One of my students having quoted a clergyman of his acquaintance who had marvellously improved by practice his power of learning his sermons by heart, I wrote to the gentleman for corroboration. I append his reply, which shows that the increased facility is due rather to a change in his methods of learning than to his native retentiveness having grown by exercise: "As for memory, mine has improved year by year, except when in ill-health, like a gymnast's muscle. Before twenty it took three or four days to commit an hour-long sermon; after twenty, two days, one day, half a day, and now one slow analytic, very attentive or adhesive reading does it. But memory seems to me the most physical of intellectual powers. Bodily ease and freshness have much to do with it. Then there is a great difference of facility in method. I used to commit sentence by sentence. Now I take the idea of the whole, then its leading divisions, then its subdivisions, then its sentences."

[25] E. Pick: Memory and its Doctors (1888), p. 7.
[26] This system is carried out in great detail in a book called 'Memory Training,' by Wm. L. Evans (1889).
[27] Paulhan, L'Activité mental, et les Éléments de 1'Esprit (1889), p. 70.
[28] On Intelligence, I. 77-82.
[29] Psychology, § 201.
[30] Professor Höffding considers that the absence of contiguous associates distinctly thought-of is a proof that associative processes are not concerned in these cases of instantaneous recognition where we get a strong sense of familiarity with the object, but no recall of previous time or place. His theory of what happens is that the object before us, A, comes with a sense of familiarity whenever it awakens a slumbering image, a, of its own past self, whilst without this image it seems unfamiliar. The quality of familiarity is due to the coalescence of the two similar processes A + a in the brain (Psychologie, p. 188; Vierteljsch. f. wiss. Phil., XIII. 432 [1889]). This explanation is a very tempting one where the phenomenon of recognition is reduced to its simplest terms. Experiments have been performed in Wundt's laboratory (by Messrs. Wolfe, see below, p. 679, and Lehmann (Philosophische Studien,v. 96)), in which a person had to tell out of several closely resembling sensible impressions (sounds, tints of color) presented, which of them was the same with one presented a moment before. And it does seem here as if the fading process in the just-excited tract must combine with the process of the new impression to give to the latter a peculiar subjective tinge which should separate it from the impressions which the other objects give. But recognition of this immediate sort is beyond our power after a very short time has intervened. A couple of minutes' interval is generally fatal to it; so that it is impossible to conceive that our frequent instantaneous recognition of a face, e.g., as having been met before, takes place by any such simple process. Where we associate a head of classification with the object, the time-interval has much less effect. Dr. Lehmann could identify shades of gray much more successfully and permanently after mentally attaching names or numbers to them. Here it is the recall of the contiguous associate, the number or name, which brings about the recognition. Where an experience is complex, each element of the total object has had the other elements for its past contiguous associates. Each element thus tends to revive the other elements from within, at the same time that the outward object is making them revive from without. We have thus, whenever we meet a familiar object, that sense of expectation gratified which is so large a factor in our æsthetic emotions; and even were there no 'fringe of tendency' toward the arousal of extrinsic associates (which there certainly always is), still this intrinsic play of mutual association among the parts would give a character of ease to familiar percepts which would make of them a distinct subjective class. A process fills its old bed in a different way from that in which it makes a new bed. One can appeal to introspection for proof. When, for example, I go into a slaughter-house into which I once went years ago, and the horrid din of the screaming hogs strikes me with the overpowering sense of identification, when the blood-stained face of the 'sticker,' whom I had long ceased to think of, is immediately recognized as the face that struck me so before; when the dingy and reddened woodwork, the purple-flowing floor, the smell, the emotion of disgust, and all the details, in a word, forthwith re-establish themselves as familiar occupants of my mind; the extraneous associates of the past time are anything but prominent. Again, in trying to think of an engraving, say the portrait of Rajah Brooke prefixed to his

biography, I can do so only partially; but when I take down the book and, looking at the actual face, am smitten with the intimate sense of its sameness with the one I was striving to resuscitate, -- where in the experience is the element of extrinsic association? In both these cases it surely feels as if the moment when the sense of recall is most vivid were also the moment when all extraneous associates were most suppressed. The butcher's face recalls the former walls of the shambles; their thought recalls the groaning beasts, and they the face again, just as I now experience them, with no different past ingredient. In like manner the peculiar deepening of my consciousness of the Rajah's physiognomy at the moment when I open the book and say "Ah! that's the very face!" is so intense as to banish from my mind all collateral circumstances, whether of the present or of former experiences. But here it is the nose preparing tracts for the eye, the eye preparing them for the mouth, the mouth preparing them for the nose again, all these processes involving paths of contiguous association, as defended in the text. I cannot agree, therefore, with Prof. Höffding, in spite of my respect for him as a psychologist, that the phenomenon of instantaneous recognition is only explicable through the recall and comparison of the thing with its own past image. Nor can I see in the facts in question any additional ground for reinstating the general notion which we have already rejected (supra, p. 592) that a 'sensation' is ever received into the mind by an 'image' of its own past self. It is received by contiguous associates; or if they form too faint a fringe, its neural currents run into a bed which is still 'warm' from just-previous currents, and which consequently feel different from currents whose bed is cold. I agree, however, with Höffding that Dr. Lehmann's experiments (many of them) do not seem to prove the point which he seeks to establish. Lehmann, indeed, seems himself to believe that we recognize a sensation A by comparing it with its own past image a (loc. cit. p. 114), in which opinion I altogether fail to concur.

[31] *Duality of the Mind*, p. 84. The same thesis is defended by the late Mr. R. H. Proctor, who gives some cases rather hard to reconcile with my own proposed explanation, in 'Knowledge' for Nov. 8, 1884. See also Ribot, *Maladies de la Mémoire*, p. 149 ff.

[32] *Zeitschr. f. Völkerpsychologie u. s. w.*, Bd. v. p. 146.

[33] *Ueber das Gedächtniss, experimentelle Untersuchungen* (1885), p. 64.

[34] *Ibid.* § 23.

[35] *Op. cit.*, p. 103.

[36] All the inferences for which we can give no articulate reasons exemplify this law. In the chapter on Perception we shall have innumerable examples of it. A good pathological illustration of it is given in the curious observations of M. Binet on certain hysterical subjects, with anæsthetic hands, who saw what was done with their hands as an independent vision but did not feel it. The hand being hidden by a screen, the patient was ordered to look at another screen and to tell of any visual image which might project itself thereon. Numbers would then come, corresponding to the number of times the insensible member was raised, touched, etc. Colored lines and figures would come, corresponding to similar ones traced on the palm; the hand itself, or its fingers, would come when manipulated; and, finally, objects placed in it would come; but on the hand itself nothing could ever be felt. The whole phenomenon shows how an idea which remains itself below the threshold of a certain conscious self may occasion associative effects therein. The skin-sensations, unfelt by the patient's primary consciousness, awaken, nevertheless, their usual visual associates therein.

[37] I copy from the abstract of Wolfe's paper in 'Science' for Nov. 19, 1886. The original is in *Psychologische Studien*, III. 534 ff.

[38] *Essay conc. Human Understanding*, II. X. 5.

[39] Th. Ribot, *Les Maladies de la Mémoire*, p. 46.

[40] *Biographia Literaria*, ed. 1847, I. 117(quoted in Carpenter's *Mental Physiology*, chapter X, which see for a number of other cases, all unfortunately deficient, like this one, in the evidence of erect verification which 'psychical research 'demands). Compare also Th. Ribot, *Diseases of Memory*. chap. IV. The knowledge of foreign words, etc., reported in trance-mediums, etc., may perhaps often be explained by exaltation of memory. An hystero-epileptic girl, whose case I quoted in Proc. of Am. Soc. for Psychical Research, automatically writes an 'Ingoldsby Legend ' in several cantos, which her parents say she 'had never read.' Of course she must have read or heard it, but perhaps never learned it. Of some macaronic Latin-English verses about a sea-serpent which her hand also wrote unconsciously, I have vainly sought the original (see Proc., etc., p. 553).

[41] *Lectures on Metaph.*, II 212.

[42] Cf. on this point J. Delbœuf, *Le Sommeil et les Rêves* (1885), p 119 ff., R. Verdon, Forgetfulness, in *Mind*, II. 437.

[43] Cf. A. Maury, *Le Sommeil et les Rêves*, p. 442.

[44] *Störungen der Sprache*, quoted by Ribot, *Les Maladies de la M.*, p. 133.

[45] *Op. cit.* chap. III.

[46] "Those who have a good memory for figures are in general those who know best how to handle them, that is, those who are most familiar with their relations to each other and to things." (A. Maury, *Le Sommeil et les Rêves*, p. 443.)

[47] Pp. 107-121.

[48] For other examples see Hamilton's *Lectures*, II. 219, and A. Huber: *Das Gedächtniss*, p. 36 ff.

[49] *Mind*, II. 449.

[50] *Physiological Psychology*, pt. II. chap. X. § 23.

[51] Why not say 'know'? -- W. J.

imagination in a drowsy man's fancy by putting his hand into it, he may. perhaps, be awakened into a certainty greater than he could wish, that it is something more than bare imagination. So that the evidence is as great as we can desire, being as certain to us as our pleasure or pain, i.e. happiness or misery; beyond which we have no concernment, either of knowledge or being. Such an assurance of the existence of things without us is sufficient to direct us in the attaining the good and avoiding the evil which is caused by them, which is the important concernment we have of being made acquainted with them." (Ibid. bk. iv. chap. 11, § 8.)

[31] Bagehot, 'The Emotion of Conviction,' Literary Studies, I. 412-17.

[32] Psychologie Rationnelle, ch. 12.

[33] Two examples out of a thousand:

Reid, Inquiry, ch. ii § 9: "I remember, many years ago, a white ox was brought into the country, of so enormous size that people came many miles to see him. There happened, some months after, an uncommon fatality among women in child-bearing. Two such uncommon events, following one another, gave a suspicion of their connection, and occasioned a common opinion among the country people that the white ox was the cause of this fatality."

H. M. Stanley, Through the Dark Continent, ii. 388: "On the third day of our stay at Mowa feeling quite comfortable amongst the people, on account of their friendly bearing, I began to write in my note-book the terms for articles, in order to improve my already copious vocabulary of native words. I had proceeded only a few minutes when I observed a strange commotion amongst the people who had been flocking about me, and presently they ran sway. In a short time we heard war-cries ringing loudly and shrilly over the table-land. Two hours afterwards a long line of warriors were seen descending the table-land and advancing towards our camp. There may have been between five and six hundred of them. We, on the other hand, had made but few preparations except such as would justify us replying to them in the event of the actual commencement of hostilities. But I had made many firm friends among them and I hardly believed that I should be able to avert an open rupture. When they had assembled at about a hundred yards in front of our camp, Safeni and I walked up towards them and sat down midway. Some half-dozen of the Yowa people came near, and the shauri began.,'

" 'What is the matter, my friends?' I asked. 'Why do you come with guns in your hands, in such numbers, as though you were coming to fight? Fight? fight us, your friends! Tut! I this is some great mistake, surely.'

Mundelé' replied one of them. ... 'our people saw you yesterday make marks on some tara-tara [paper] [Classics editors note: James' Insertion]. This is very bad. Our country will waste, our goats will die, our bananas will rot, and our women will dry up. What have we done to you that you should wish to kill us? We have sold you food and we have brought you wine each day. Your people are allowed to wander where they please without trouble. Why is the Mundelé so wicked! We have gathered together to fight you if you do not burn that tara-tara now before our eyes. If you burn it we go away, and shall be your friends as heretofore.'

"I told them to rest there, and left Safeni in their hands as a pledge that I should return. My tent was not fifty yards from the spot, but while going towards it my brain was busy in devising some plan to foil this superstitious madness. My note-book contained a vast number of valuable notes. ... I could not sacrifice it to the childish caprice of savages.9s I was rummaging my book-box, I came across a volume of Shakespeare [Chandos edition] [Classics editors note: James' insertion] much worn and well thumbed, and which was of the same size as my field-book; its cover was similar also, and it might be passed for the field-book, provided that no one remembered its appearance too well. I took it to them. 'Is this the tara-tara, friends, that you wish burned?'

Yes, yes, that is it.'

Well, take it, and burn it. or keep it.'

"M-m. No, no, no. We will not touch it. It is fetish. You must burn it.'

" 'I! Well, let it be so. I will do anything to please my good friends of Mowa.'

"We walked to the nearest fire. I breathed a regretful farewell to my genial companion, which. during my many weary hours of night, had assisted to relieve my mind when oppressed by almost intolerable woes, and then gravely consigned the innocent Shakespeare to the flames, heaping the brush fuel over it with ceremonious care.

"Ah-h,' breathed the poor deluded natives sighing their relief. ...'There is no trouble now.'... End something approaching to a cheer was shouted among them, which terminated the episode of the burning of Shakespeare.

[34] 'Rationality, Activity, and Faith' (Princeton Review, July 1883, pp 64-9).

[35] J. Royce, The Religious Aspect of Philosophy (Boston, 1885). pp. 317-57.

[36] Chapter XXVII

[37] Prof. Royce puts this well in discussing idealism and the reality of an 'external world. " If the history of popular speculation on these topics could be written, how much of cowardice and shuffling would be found in the behavior of the natural mind before the question, 'How dost thou know of an external reality. Instead of simply and plainly answering: 'I mean by the external world in the first place something that I accept know of an external reality or demand, that I posit, postulate actively construct on the basis of sense-data,' the natural man gives us all kinds of vague compromise answers. ...Where shall these endless turnings and twistings have an end?..... All these lesser motives are appealed to, and the one ultimate motive is neglected. The ultimate motive with the man of every-day life is the will to have an external world. Whatever consciousness contains, reason will persist in spontaneously adding the thought: 'But there shall be something beyond this.'.. The popular assurance of an external world is the fixed determination to make one, now and henceforth." (Religious Aspect of philosophy, p. 304 -- the italics are my own.) This immixture of the will appears most flagrantly in the fact that although external matter

is doubted commonly enough, minds external to our own are never doubted. We need them too much, are too essentially social to dispense with them. Semblances of matter may suffice to react upon, but not semblances of communing souls. a psychic solipsism is too hideous a mockery of our wants, and, so far as I know, has never been seriously entertained.— Chapters ix and x of Prof. Royce's work are on the whole the dearest account of the psychology of belief with which I am acquainted.

[38] "The leading fact in Belief, according to my view of it, is our Primitive Credulity. We begin by believing everything; whatever is, is true.... The animal born in the morning of a summer day proceeds upon the fact of daylight; assumes the perpetuity of that fact. Whatever it is disposed to do. it does without misgivings. If in the morning it began around of operations continuing for hours, under the full benefit of day-light, it would unhesitatingly begin the same roll and in the evening. Its state of mind is practically one of unbounded confidence; but, as yet, it does not understand what confidence means.

"The pristine assurance is soon met by checks; a disagreeable experience leading to new insight. To be thwarted and opposed is one of our earliest and most frequent pains. It develops the sense of a distinction between free and obstructed impulses; the unconsciousness of an open way is exchanged for consciousness; we are now said properly to believe in what has never been contradicted, as we disbelieve in what has been contradicted. We believe that, after the dawn of day, there is before us a continuance of light; we do not believe that this light is to continue forever.

" Thus, the vital circumstance in belief is never to be contradicted—never to lose prestige. The number of repetitions counts for little in the process: we are as much convinced after ten as after fifty; we are more convinced by ten unbroken than by fifty for and one against." (Bain : The Emotions and the Will, pp. 511, 512.)

[39] Literature. D Hume : Treatise on Human Nature, part III. §§ vi-x A. Bain: Emotions and Will, chapter on Belief (also pp. 20 ff). J. Sully: Sensation and Intuition, essay iv J. Mill: Analysis of Human Mind Ch. Renouvier : Psychologie Rationnelle, vol. ii. pt. ii; and Esquisse d'une Classification systématique des Doctrines Mind, chapter xi Philosophiques, part vi. J. El. Newman: The Grammar of assent. J.Venn: Some Characteristics of Belief. V. Brochard: De l'Erreur, part ii chap. vi, ix; and Revue Philosophique, xxvii. 1. E· Habier: Psychologie, chap xxi, Appendix. Ollé Laprune: La Certitude Morale (1881). Cf. F. Stout: On Genesis of Cognition of Physical Reality, in 'Mind,' Jan. J Pikler: The Psychology of the Belief in Objective Existence(London, 1890).—Mill says that we believe present sensations; and makes our belief in all other things a matter of association with these. So far so good; but as he makes no mention of emotional or volitional reaction, Bain rightly charges him with treating belief as a purely intellectual state. For Bain belief is rather an incident of our active life. When a thing is such, to make us act on it, then we believe it, according to Bain. "But how about past things, or remote things, upon which no reaction of ours is possible? And how about belief in things which check action" says Sully; who considers that we believe s thing only when " the idea of it has an inherent tendency to approximate in character and intensity to a sensation." It is obvious that each of these authors emphasizes a true aspect of the question. My own account has sought to be more complete, sensation, association, and active reaction all being acknowledged to be concerned. The most compendious possible formula perhaps would be that out belief and attention are the same fact. For the moment, what we attend to is reality; Attention is a motor reaction; and we are so made that sensations force attention from us. On Belief and Conduct see an article by Leslie Stephen, Fortnightly Review, July 1888.

A set of facts have been recently brought to my attention which I hardly know how to treat, so I say a word about them in this footnote. Refer to a type of experience which has frequently found a place among the 'Yes' answers to the 'Census of Hallucinations,' and which is generally described by those who report it as an 'impression of the presence' of someone near them, although no sense lion either of sight, hearing, or touch is involved From the way in which this experience is spoken of by those who have had it, it would appear to be an extremely definite and positive state of mind, coupled with a belief in the reality of its object quite as strong as any direct sensation ever gives. And yet no sensation seems to be connected with it at all. Sometimes the person whose nearness is thus impressed is a known person, dead or living, sometimes an unknown one. His attitude and situation are often very definitely impressed, and so, sometimes (though not by way of hearing), are words which he wishes to say.

The phenomenon would seem to be due to a pure conception becoming saturated with the sort of stinging urgency which ordinarily only sensations bring. But I cannot yet persuade myself that the urgency in Question consists in concomitant emotional and motor impulses. The ' impression' may come quite suddenly and depart quickly; it may carry no emotional suggestions, and wake no motor consequences beyond those involved in attending to it. Altogether, the matter is somewhat paradoxical, and no conclusion can be come to until more definite data are obtained.

Perhaps the most curious case of the sort which I have received is the following. The subject of the observation, Mr. P., is an exceptionally intelligent witness, though the words of the narrative are his wife's.

"Mr. P. has all his life been the occasional subject of rather singular delusions or impressions of various kinds. If I had belief in the existence of latent or embryo faculties, other than the five senses, I should explain them on that ground. Being totally blind, his other perceptions are abnormally keen and developed, and given the existence of a rudimentary sixth sense, it would be only natural that this also should be more acute in him than in others. One of the most interesting of his experiences in this line was the frequent apparition of a corpse some years ago, which may be worth the attention of your Committee on that subject. At the lime Mr. P. had a music-room in Boston on Beacon Street, where he used to do severe and protracted practice with little interruption. Now, all one season it was a very familiar occurrence with him while in the midst of work to feel a cold draft of air suddenly upon his face, with a prickling sensation at the roots of his hair, when he would turn from the piano, and *a figure which he knew to be dead would come sliding under the crack of the door from without, flattening itself to squeeze through and rounding out again to the human form. It was of a middle-aged man, and drew itself along the carpet on hands and knees, but with head thrown back till it reached the sofa, upon which it stretched itself. It remained some moments, but vanished s if Mr. P. spoke or made a decided movement. The most singular point in the occurrence was its frequent repetition. Be might expect it on any day between two and four o'clock, and it came always heralded by the same sudden cold shiver, and was invariably the same figure which went through the same movements. He afterwards traced the whole experience to strong tea. He was in the habit of taking cold tea, which always stimulates him, for lunch, and on giving up this practice whenever saw this or any other apparition again. However, even allowing, as is doubtless true, that the event was a delusion of nerves first fatigued by over work and then excited by this stimulant, there is one point which is still wholly inexplicable and highly interesting to me. Mr. P. has no memory whatever of sight, nor conception of it. It is impossible for him to form any idea of what we mean by light or color, consequently he has no cognizance of any object which does not reach his sense of hearing or of touch, though these are so acute as to give a contrary impression some-times to other people. When he becomes aware of the presence of a person or an object, by means which seem mysterious to outsiders, he can always trace it naturally and legitimately to slight echoes, perceptible only to his keen ears, or to differences in atmospheric pressure, perceptible only to his acute nerves of touch; but with the apparition described, for the only time-in his experience, he was aware of presence, size, and appearance, without the use of either of these mediums. The figure never produced the least sound nor came within a number of feet of his person, yet he knew that it was a man, that it moved, and in what direction, even that it wore a full beard, which, like the thick curly heir, was partially gray; also that it war, dressed in the style of suit known as 'pepper and salt.' These points were all perfectly distinct and invariable each time. If asked how he perceived them, he will answer he cannot tell, he simply knew it. and so strongly and so distinctly that it is impossible to shake the opinion as to the exact details of the man's appearance. It would seem that in this delusion of the senses he really saw, as he has never done in the actual experiences of life, except in the first two years of childhood."*

On cross-examining Mr. P., I could not make out that there was anything like visual imagination involved, although he was quite unable to describe in just what terms the false perception was carried on. It seemed to be more like an intensely definite conception than anything else, a conception to which the feeling of present reality was attached, but in no such shape as easily to fail under the heads laid down in my text.

Made in the USA
Lexington, KY
12 July 2019